SEATTLE SURVIVAL GUIDE 3rd EDITION

THE ESSENTIAL HANDBOOK FOR SEATTLE AND EASTSIDE LIVING

SCHOOLS • ENVIRONMENT • CITY GOVERNMENT • VOLUNTEERING

CRIME • MEDIA

WEATHER

HEALTH

HOUSING PRICES

NEIGHBORHOODS • TRAFFIC • ARTS • PUBLIC TRANSPORTATION

SEATTLE SURVIVAL GUIDE 3rd EDITION

SOCIAL SERVICES • SPORTS • RECREATION • BUSINESS

THERESA MORROW

SASQUATCH BOOKS
SEATTLE

Printed in the United States of America.
Distributed in Canada by Raincoast Books Ltd.

00 99 98 97   4 3 2 1

Editors: Don Roberts and Sherri Schultz
Indexer: Sigrid Asmus
Design: Kris Morgan
Interior illustrations: Eldon Doty
Neighborhood illustrations: Spencer Johnson
Maps: Markus Frei, Millie Beard, and Mark LaPoint
Composition: Patrick Barber/Apraxia Design Laboratories,
    with Hyla Willis and Jerret Scot Cortese

Library of Congress Cataloging in Publication Data
Morrow, Theresa.
    Seattle survival guide, 3rd edition : the essential handbook for urban living /
Theresa Morrow.
        p. cm.
    Includes index.
    ISBN 1-57061-089-4
    1. Seattle (Wash.)-Handbooks, manuals, etc. 2. Seattle (Wash.)-Guidebooks.
I. Title.
    F899.S43M677   1996
979.7'772-dc20   96-19980

Sasquatch Books
615 Second Avenue
Seattle, Washington 98104
(206) 467-4300
books@sasquatchbooks.com
http://www.sasquatchbooks.com

Sasquatch Books publishes high-quality adult nonfiction and children's books
related to the Northwest (Alaska to San Francisco). For more information about
our titles, contact us at the above address or view our site on the World Wide Web.

CONTENTS

continued▶

INTRODUCTION

Cars snarled on 520. Contented cows changing places with computer chips. Woodstove smoke choking tykes. Web sites taking over. It's still a jungle out there!

And as we venture into the third edition of *Seattle Survival Guide,* it is evident that survival techniques are needed for an even larger geographic area. No longer does the term "Seattle" refer just to that hourglass with its waist squeezed by a lake and a Sound; now it also means that megalopolis to the east burgeoning and booming its way to citydom.

Seattleites have long tried to deny that the Eastside exists in its own right, but traffic isn't the only thing that flows between the two entities. Used to be that everybody's brother worked at Boeing; now everyone knows someone who works at Microsoft. We still love Discovery Park—but we might just sneak across to Marymoor to scale the climbing rock. And—let's admit it, Seattleites—all those who have never been to Molbak's, raise your hands. No hands? I rest my case.

With that in mind, we've added a chapter on the Eastside. Granted, it's just one chapter, and one that hits only the highlights. Our hope is that it will be useful to people everywhere in the "Greater Seattle area," as the planners like to call it. Whether we live on the Eastside or in Ballard, we all need to know how to avoid 405 at rush hour, how to find Aunt Martha's house in Kirkland, and how to get a peek at Bill Gates's new "house."

I confess that as a native Seattleite, my attitude toward the Eastside has through the years been a rather typical one. I turned up my nose at the word "cul-de-sac," panicking at the very thought of a road in a modern development from which there is no escape. I wondered how anyone could live in a place where your car is your best friend. (I asked a relative—yes, my relatives live on the Eastside—how anyone can walk on Main Street in Bellevue, and she said, "Walk? No one walks in Bellevue.") And I have done my share of bemoaning the loss of "country" over there, whining about how I used to go to Woodinville to ride horses and how I can't, absolutely can't, figure out how there could be a traffic jam in the Issaquah of my youth.

However, while researching the "Eastern Exposure" chapter, the proverbial scales fell from my eyes. I ate at Chace's Pancake Corral and realized that it's a neighborhood place too—not quite like the Still Life in Fremont, but neighborhood. In Marymoor Park I watched a spandexed guy put on his roller blades while he intently listened to a radio talk show about calcium supplements. I drank java in Kirkland and listened to a woman complain about her husband leaving her for a trophy wife. I watched people at Crossroads playing chess with giant pieces. I learned that the favorite Eastside gossip is about who tore down which house to build a mega-house-with-unattached-nanny's-quarters.

And you know what, Ballardites and Queen Anners? It was fun. The Eastside has its own culture, its own character—and it is not afraid to admit that fact. So the third edition of *Seattle Survival Guide* belatedly welcomes the Eastside as an integral part of our territory.

Whether you're looking for help in battling the floating bridges at rush hour, or just want to know how to get through downtown Seattle at any time, you'll find that in its third edition this book is still a guide to meeting the challenges of urban adventures. It's not a guidebook for tourists—it's for people who live in and around the city. It has, completely inadvertently, become a bible for newcomers: again and again while researching updates for this version, we heard from people who got to know the city with the *Survival Guide* in hand. (And often when we called the library to find out some fact or other, we'd get referred right back to this book—a nice feeling, that.)

It's been almost seven years since we put together the first *Seattle Survival Guide,* and things in Seattle have changed dramatically. Downtown has gone from a feared ghost town to a boomtown—with Niketown, Planet Hollywood, an almost-new waterfront, the promise of a new Nordstrom, and, just possibly, a new baseball stadium. The Mariners batted their way to a title; the Sonics leapt to one too. Starbucks has become a familiar word nationally, and there's hope—even excitement—in the Seattle School District with a military man at the helm.

So why the need for a survival guide? There are still homeless men and women living in the bushes and under freeway exits. There are still guns being toted, health care is still a question mark, and if your car hasn't been broken into, you are probably keeping it in your garage.

Then, too, there is a bothersome indication that the city's famed grassroots character is endangered: the Commons urban park proposal failed, the venerable co-op Group Health is holding hands with privately owned Virginia Mason, and pedestrian-only Pine Street is being given back to the cars. Dazzled by the glare of the neon from the trendy new stores, it's just possible we could forget what made Seattle so darned livable in the first place.

We talked to hundreds of savvy people in updating the *Seattle Survival Guide,* and we owe them a big "thank you" for the tips and wisdom herein. Special thanks to Skip Berger of *Eastsideweek* for his help with the Eastside chapter; ditto to John and Jane Kloeck of Bellevue,

who tirelessly answered such questions as "Did Junior really live on the Plateau?" and almost ended their marriage while trying to answer the question "If there was an accident on 405, and you had to get from Issaquah to Bothell..." Thanks to Randy Carmical at the Seattle School District and the folks at the Seattle Public Library Info Line, once again.

And thanks to our dedicated researchers, who scrambled to get police department statistics and corporate annual reports alike—an able Marilyn Giltner, who is happy that there are fewer gun permits being granted; Linda Fullerton, who turned out to be a sports fan(!); Frema Nadelson, whose telephone ear turned red from calling all the ethnic groups; Adam Morrow, who once again dogged the school and business sources and is probably out buying Starbucks stock right now; and Sarah Morrow, who diligently got to the bottom of the

rat complaints and forbade us from talking about grunge ever again. And thanks, of course, to Sasquatch Books publisher Chad Haight, who has incredible powers of persuasion and whose idea this book was in the first place, and to the editorial team of Don Roberts and Sherri Schultz.

As in the past, we've checked each and every phone number and address of the resources listed, but it's wise to call ahead to make sure a group is still functioning in the same location at the same number.

As Seattle increasingly leans its high-rises against the Cascades, it has begun to acknowledge that it is responsible as much for the bears on Tiger Mountain as for the Pike Place Market, as much for an I-90 spawning high-tech business parks as for the Mercer Mess. That's what this third *Seattle Survival Guide* is all about—how to make your way through the now even bigger urban maze that is Seattle.

Theresa Morrow

SEATTLE FROM A TO Z

Zoo-Doo? Boxers vs. briefs? Where to find old books? Some things just don't fit into categories, but they make Seattle what it is. Where would we be without Dave Niehaus's "My oh my" or the Bon Marché's Christmas star? Not in Seattle, that's for sure. So here they are, all those little things you didn't know you needed to know—an arbitrary list of factoids running the gamut from A to Z.

A

Number of clams in an **ACRE** of clams: 1,568,160

Number of clams sold annually by Ivar's, whose Pier 54 restaurant bills itself as "Ivar's Acres of Clams": 200,750

Number of years it takes for Ivar's to sell an acre of clams: 7.81

The most popular places to scatter your loved ones' **ASHES**: Puget Sound and Mt. Rainier.

OK, so it's not survival, but with Seattleites' outdoor bent, we don't necessarily want to end up encased in a coffin. In the case of Mt. Rainier, you need to get a (free) permit by calling (360) 569-2211, ext. 2303. To scatter ashes from a Washington State ferry, you pick a ride, and when the ferry is under way, ask for the mate. Tell him what you want and he'll ask the captain, who will most likely say it's OK. The captain will assign a member of the crew to escort you and the ashes to the stern, beyond the chain. Depending on the captain, the ferry might even stop while you scatter the ashes. This is a common request on the ferries, according to the Department of Transportation.

You can also scatter ashes from Seattle's bridges, with permission of the city—386-4251. (But never, not even for true urbanites, can you scatter them across the city from the Space Needle.)

B

BOBO'S BACK. Seattle's own gorilla—or at least what's left of him—has come home to the Museum of History and Industry (MOHAI). For the uninitiated, Bobo was a major attraction at the Woodland Park Zoo in the 1950s. Born in 1951 in Africa, where he was purchased by Bill Lohman, Bobo was sent to Anacortes as a gift to Bill's mom (thanks a lot, son!). After two years, Bobo went to the zoo to live. (Mrs. Lohman lived and slept in his cage the first week to help with the transition. Greater love than this. . .)

When he died at 16, Bobo weighed 521 pounds, was 6 foot 6 inches tall, and had a neck size of 48. His bones are at the Burke Museum, and his taxidermied body can be viewed at MOHAI. By the way, "bobo" means gorilla in Swahili.

C

COMIC CAPITAL. "Grunge is dead. Comics rule!"—Kim Thompson, Fantagraphics Books.

Thanks to such names as Lynda Barry and Gary Larsen, Seattle has a reputation for having a large concentration of alternative cartoonists. In fact, says Thompson, as the city of choice for cartoonists, "It's better than New York and Chicago, and close to or even with San Francisco." Fantagraphics is a draw itself—it's cartoonist Robert Crumb's publisher of choice. Its most popular comics? "Hate," "Eight Ball," and "Love and Rockets."

Two other local comics publishers: Mu Press and Starhead Comics.

Alternative comics outlets: There are about 37 comic book outlets in Seattle, but many congregate near the U District. Here are a few to get you started:

- The Comic Stand, 1311 NE 42nd
- Corner Comics II, 5226 University Way NE
- Rocket Comics, 8408 Greenwood Ave. N
- Zanadu, 1307 NE 45th St. and 1923 Third Ave.

D

There are about 1.2 **DOGS** per fire hydrant in Seattle.

Approximate number of fire hydrants in Seattle: 18,000

Approximate number of dogs licensed in the city: 22,000

According to *Fortune* magazine, Seattle is the No. 3 apparel **DESIGN** center in the country. We called *DNR* magazine in New York to verify this, and they merely sniffed. But what is true is that the city has seen a number of companies designing "young men's sportswear" come and go over the last decade. (This is different from the "outerwear" made by Seattle companies such as Pacific Trail, Eddie Bauer, and Helly–Hansen.) A number of ex-executives from the now defunct Britannia started their own apparel lines so they could stay in town. It's dangerous to list the companies (since some are under investigation, for example, by the IRS and since others are deeply into Chapter 11), but here are some of the well-known ones:

- Shah Safari (owns most of International News)
- Generra
- Union Bay Sportswear
- Fast (& Easy) Clothing

E

Woodland Park Zoo has an **ELEPHANT** yard filled with pachyderms. All the elephants there are females: three—Bamboo (weighing in at 8,500 pounds), Chai (7,000 pounds), and Sri (5,700 pounds)—are Asian, and one—Watoto (8,000 pounds)—is African. Watoto ("children" in Swahili) was so named because Seattle children raised the money for her purchase. She's the dominant matriarch. The Elephant Yard is 4.6 acres with an elephantine 11-foot-deep swimming pool that holds 40,000 gallons of water. There's room for an increase in population: Chai has been artificially inseminated with sperm from a Portland zoo male, but no results so far.

F

Just the **FACTS**. . . about Seattle:
Population: 516,259
Residents 18 years and over: 431,329
Residents under 18: 84,930
Square miles: 92
Land: 84 square miles
Water: 8 square miles
Parks: 5,000 acres
Location: 47°39' N, 122°17' W
City incorporation: Dec. 2, 1869
Housing units: 249,032
Housing units built before 1940: 90,162
Percent of residents with bachelor's degree or above: 37.9 percent
Stability: 213,602 residents lived in the same home for 5 years
Residents who speak a language other than English at home: 75,122
Source: U.S. census, City of Seattle

G

Shhhh. Don't tell anyone that we're talking about **GRUNGE** here. Seattleites hate the word and the idea, which they will tell you was invented by the national media. But as far away as Paris, if you mention Seattle, people say, "Oh, Seattle? Grunge."
But what's in a name anyway? Let's just talk about cool clubs—and we'll leave it under "G" for those who don't know that you should never say _____.

Clubs come and go in popularity, of course. Look in *The Stranger*, *The Rocket*, (*Seattle Times*) *Tempo*, or *Seattle Weekly*. Here are a few of the most famous:

Ballard Firehouse
Backstage (also in Ballard, what a rockin' town)
The Central*
China Club
Colourbox
Crocodile Cafe
Fenix/Fenix Underground
J&M Cafe*
Larry's*
Moe
New Orleans*
OK Hotel
Pioneer Square Saloon*
Showbox
Sit & Spin
Tropix Café and Beach Club

*clubs that usually stay within the blues/R&B genre

H

Number of **HEALTH CLUBS** in Seattle area: 80
Number of sports medical clinics: 60
Number of health club members who attend regularly: 40% during October and January, busiest months; 20–30% rest of the year

Seattle is full of **HISTORY**. The Museum of History and Industry, the city's preeminent historical museum, opened in 1951. It's at 2700 24th Avenue E and is open from 10am–5pm daily.

In addition, most neighborhoods have a **HISTORICAL SOCIETY**—check branch libraries for contacts.

The smell of the leather. The roar of the pipes. The feel of money. Stroll down 1st Avenue any Thursday night and you'll find one of Seattle's subcultures sprawled ostentatiously in front of the Central Tavern. Hundreds of shiny **HARLEY** Davidsons—and their also shiny yuppie owners—pose and primp at the Central as part of the Thursday night Harley parade. It begins at the Alki Tavern in West Seattle, progesses to the Central where Thursday is blues night and people in leather get in for free, and then a few diehards head for Fremont's "Buck-Buck-Buckaroo" (bikers never say just "Buckaroo").

I

The city, what with its rainy, rather damp atmosphere, is full of **IRRITANTS**. We called some allergy clinics to find out what makes Seattle sneeze: molds (especially in the fall); trees (February through April)—some say alders in particular; that Emerald City green grass (May through July), and some say that ever-present Scotch broom; and weeds (June through October).
The Northwest is one of the few regions in the country where pollen is present every month of the year, not just in the summer. But we don't have that much hay, you say? Mold and dust mites love our cool weather, and trees are just as much the enemy of the hay-fever sufferer as hay. About 80 percent of Northwest hay-fever victims have symptoms all year. Ah-choo!

Seattle, city of **INVENTIONS**. It's hard

to miss the Monorail and Boeing's airplanes, but here are a few lesser known Seattle creations, gleaned from Adam Woog's book *Sexless Oysters and Self-Tipping Hats: 100 Years of Invention in the Pacific Northwest*:

Gas station. Were it not for Standard Oil's John McLean, we might still be buying our gasoline in cans from the general store. A plaque at Waterfront Park (near the Aquarium) salutes this visionary, who opened the world's first gas station at Western Avenue and Holgate Street in 1907.

Happy Face. That round, yellow, giddily smiling critter is claimed to be the brainchild of ad man David Stern, hired to create a positive image for University Federal Savings & Loan (now University Savings Bank) in the turbulent 1960s. "Open a savings account and put on a happy face" was the slogan he dreamed up, and the happy-face buttons the bank produced to go with it were snapped up by the handfuls. The rest is pop-art history.

Electric guitar. Not only did Jimi Hendrix hail from the Seattle area, the electric guitar was invented here—or so it's claimed (not surprisingly, there are a few other competing claims). Music teacher Paul Tutmarc, experimenting with amplification methods, created an electric guitar in his north Seattle basement in 1931. Refused a patent because his technology was too similar to that of the telephone, Tutmarc went ahead and produced and sold his product, unpatented, for $39.50 and up.

Pictionary. Yes, the best-selling game that has embarrassed millions of nonartists was brought to us by a couple of Lake Union Cafe waiters. In 1984, waiter Rob Angel began developing Pictionary's word list while sitting in his backyard on nice days, then hooked up with an artist and a "money guy" and formed Pictionary Inc.

Since 1985, the game has sold more than 20 million copies worldwide.

J

Looking for a **JOB**? Linda Carlson's *How to Find a Good Job in Seattle* may be able to help you out, or at least save you some time: It lists hundreds of employers, joblines, and associations. Other recent books on the subject include *Seattle JobBank,* published annually, and *How to Get a Job in Seattle/Portland.* No money to spend, even on a job-hunting book? Pick up a free copy of the weekly *Employment Paper,* available on the street all over town.

K

John **KEISTER** of TV's "Almost Live" is Seattle's Komedy King. We took the liberty of asking him some questions:

Q: Are you not only president of the Hair Club but also a client?
A: Yes.

Q: Do you have to give the clothes back to Barneys?
A: Yes.

Q: What is your favorite Seattle neighborhood and why?
A: The U District, because I enjoy the constant variety of pierced body parts.

L

Number of times *Seattle Times* columnist Jean Godden used the word **LATTE** in her column in a year: 37
Number of times she used the word **LATTELAND** in her column in a year: 17

LATTE LINGO (believe it or not, this item is by special request from those too embarrassed to admit to espresso baristas that they don't know what they're ordering):

• Single latte—one shot espresso, steamed milk

- Double latte—two shots espresso, steamed milk
- Double tall—two shots espresso, double the milk
- Double tall skinny—ditto above, with 2% milk
- Double tall skinny with. . . —ditto above, with different flavors of Italian syrup thrown in
- Why bother—decaf latte with skim milk
- Cappuccino—espresso with foamed milk
- Americano—espresso watered down to accommodate U.S. tastes
- Mocha—latte with chocolate and whipped cream
- Granita—latte made with frozen milk, giving it the consistency of a Slurpee

M

Seattle-area **MICROBREWS** have not quite reached the latte stage in terms of addiction, but we do have a bunch. What's a microbrew? Ask the people who just learned what lattes are. It's handcrafted beer, and you can taste it in brewpubs. Here are just a few of the area's brewpubs and breweries:

Big Time Brewery & Alehouse
4133 University Way NE
545-4509
Classic brewpub, college crowd. Beers brewed on premises.

California & Alaska Street Brewery
4720 California Ave. SW
938-2476
West Seattle pub, view brewhouse in the bar. (They serve an ice cream float in stout beer. No comment.)

Hale's Ales #1
4301 Leary Way NW
782-0737
Sandwiches and meals accompanied by the smell of hops.

Hart Brewery & Pub
1201 First Ave. S
682-3377

Brew, burgers, and an old Seattle feel draws the crowds to this old warehouse turned brew-pub.

Maritime Pacific Brewing Co.
1514 NW Leary Way
782-6181
Located under the Ballard Bridge. Tours and tastings available.

Pacific Northwest Brewing Co.
322 Occidental Ave. S
621-7002
British-style ales served from traditional handpumps at restaurant.

Pike Place Brewery
1415 First Ave.
622-6044
In the Pike Place Historical District. Tours available. Recently expanded to include a 200-seat "interactive" pub and microbrew museum. Sells home-brewing supplies too.

Redhook Ale Brewery
3400 Phinney Ave. N
548-8000
The first craft brewery in Seattle, located in a historic building that once housed trolley cars. Tours daily; beers available in the Trolleyman Pub at the brewery.

N

There are approximately 800 **NUNS** in Seattle.

NUMBER of light bulbs in the Bon Marché Christmas star: 3,600

O

Number of times Dave Niehaus, Voice of the Mariners, says "My **OH** my" in a season: 200
Source: Kevin Cremin, Mariners statistician

OLD BOOKS: Every neighborhood, it seems, has a used bookstore, and lots of residents are addicted to them. Here's a sampling:

Beauty & the Books (Western Americana, science fiction, and more),

U District, 632-8510

Bibelots & Books, Inc. (children's, mysteries, classics), Eastlake, 329-6676

Book Affair (something of everything), Riverton Heights, 241-0629

Bowie & Co. (hardbacks only, rare and out-of-print, ephemera), Pioneer Square, 624-4100

Chameleon Books (African, African art), Capitol Hill, 323-0154

Cinema Books (film, television, theater), U District, 547-7667

The Couth Buzzard (science fiction, mysteries, awareness, etc.), Greenwood, 789-8965

David Ishii Bookseller (Asian Americana, fly-fishing, baseball), Pioneer Square, 622-4719

Gregor Books (literary first editions, Western Americana, out-of-print and unusual titles), West Seattle, 937-6223

Left Bank Books (politics, labor, philosophy, weird), Pike Place Market, 622-0195

Rainy Day Books (science fiction, romances, collectibles), Crown Hill, 783-3383

Titlewave Books (general stock and rare), Queen Anne, 282-7687

Twice Sold Tales (fiction and more; open till 2am most nights and all night Fridays), Capitol Hill, 324-2421; other branches in Wallingford and downtown Seattle.

P

What's hot and what's not? Absolutely nothing in their shops, say the city's **PAWNSHOPS**. Most commonly pawned: electronic equipment, cameras, jewelry. Percentage of people who get their stuff back: One shop says 90%, another says 20–40%, others around 80%. Who pawns: mostly middle-aged down-and-outers, though some shops say the clientele is younger these days. What about the rumor that pawnshops now offer lots of mountain bikes and roller blades? Not so. Those items go to the pawnshops without grating on the windows: sports consignment shops.

What does it take to be a Seafair **PIRATE**?

- You have to be sponsored by a member in good standing.
- You're on probation for a year and have to do things like polish the existing members' shoes, or get them drinks (it's no wonder women aren't members—they're too smart).
- You have to be loud and boisterous—just standing around looking big won't cut it.
- You are evaluated four times by the group, and you need to go to business meetings every other week (every week during the summer). Believe it or not, pirates go to pirate conventions around the world, and staunch members wear pirate rings.
- "If you can't hold your booze, you won't make it through the first year."
- You have to be interested in other people—the pirates entertain at nursing homes, hospitals, etc.
- You get two extra points if you're over 6 feet tall.

To join, or to enlist the pirates to entertain, write Seafair Pirates, P.O. Box 30674, Greenwood Station, Seattle, WA 98103.

Just to show they're up on the times (and to get insurance), the pirates do have a designated driver when they go out in their rig, the *Moby Duck*.

Their response to parents' complaints that they scare kids during parades? "Too bad you raised a sissy."

Oooh, those guys are mean.

Q

The city's full of **QUICK** people. Seattle runs:

February
- Duet Run, 5K; benefits First Aid Service Team (FAST)

March
- Big Climb for Leukemia, 69 flights (1,311 steps) up the Columbia Seafirst Center
- St. Patrick's Day Dash, 4 miles through downtown—many runners dress in "extremes of green"
- Sri Chinmoy, 10 miles; all-volunteer peace promotion

April
- Northwest Masters, 15K

May
- Top Run, 10K, 5K, Burke-Gilman Trail and I-5 express lanes
- Run for the Beach, 8K, Don Armeni Park, Alki; Puget Sound Alliance
- Beat the Bridge, 8K, begins in front of Hec Ed. Pavilion and runners have 27 minutes to get across Montlake Bridge before it opens, finish is inside Husky Stadium after a lap around the track; Juvenile Diabetes Fund
- Run UPC, 10K; Missions of University Presbyterian Church

June
- Sri Chinmoy, 10K
- Fremont Fun Run, 5K; Fremont Public Association
- Run with Pride, 10K, Seward Park, largest gay/lesbian-sponsored athletic event in the Northwest
- Shore Run & Walk, 6.7K; Fred Hutchinson Cancer Research Center

July
- Firecracker 5000, 5K, in and around Seattle Center
- Crown of Queen Anne, 3.3K, around the "crown" of the hill, prizes for wearing crowns or hats
- Starbucks Alki, 8K, skate,

walk, and run, Alki Beach; People for Puget Sound
- Sri Chinmoy Independence 5-miler
- Washington Mutual Tower Stairclimb, 56 flights; Cystic Fibrosis
- YMCA/Huling Family Fun Run, 5K, 1K
- College Inn Stampede, 4K
- Seafair Mazda Torchlight Run, 8K, costumes

August
- Seattle University Alumni 5K Fun Run & Walk, Seattle U to Volunteer Park and back

September
- Group Health Tunnel Run & Walk, 8K, 3K, Battery Street and Metro tunnels
- Emerald City Invitational, 8K, 5K, Woodland Park
- Sri Chinmoy half marathon, 13.1K
- Wheels and Heels of Fire, 10K, 5K bike ride; 15K wheelchair, kids' run, 3K walk, Greg Lemond mountain-bike race; start and finish near Kingdome; benefits Resource Center for the Handicapped
- WORK it, 5K, Walk or Run for Kids
- Rain City Classic, 5K, Green Lake

October
- Terry Fox Run, 10K
- Northwest Masters, 8K, 40 and over
- Sri Chinmoy Peace Race, 2K

November
- Dawg Dash, 6K, UW campus before game
- Toys for Tots Run, 10K; U.S. Marine Corps Reserve program
- Pratt & Chew Classic, 4K, Gas Works Park to Fremont Bridge to Brooklyn, to Pacific, Northlake and back to Gas Works (categories not by gender and age, but by gender and occupation); Emergency Feeding Program, prize for donating most canned goods

- Seattle Marathon/Half-Marathon: Marathon begins at Marymoor Park, Half-M. begins in Kenmore; also includes 8K Walk for Life and Breath to benefit American Lung Association

December
- Jingle Bell Run/Walk, 5K.

Source: *Northwest Runner* magazine

R

Always **READY**—that's the Seattle Fire Department. The 1,035 civilian and 988 uniformed employees work 24-hour shifts in 33 fire stations around the city.

- Number of calls in 1995: 14,728 fire calls, 50,533 medic aid calls
- Busiest time of the year: Fourth of July

What do they do while waiting for the alarm to ring? Well, the days of pinochle are over. Instead they clean the floor, eat at the beanery, read books, take showers, watch movies, drill, exercise, etc.

Why are there so many firefighters standing around at fires? Because the special fire suits they wear to withstand up to 1,000°F trap interior heat, so firefighting is limited to 10 minutes; firefighters have to rotate to prevent their bodies from overheating.

Biggest problem getting to a Seattle fire: Bridge openings and trains sometimes block the engines, so backup engines have to come from a different direction.

S

Most innocuous place to meet a **SAILOR**: The Queen Anne Maytag Laundry on Boston Street, just west of Queen Anne Avenue N. Whenever there's a ship in port, reliable sources tell us, at least a few clean-cut swabbies always find their way to this laundromat. Are its stellar washing facilities known in ports throughout the world, or is it just the closest laundromat to Elliott Bay? Check it out and see for yourself.

T

TATTOOS. Seattle's most common: roses and the sun tie for the honor. Could Seattle really be that boring? By way of contrast, we called several L.A. tattoo parlors, including Sunset Strip Tattoo ("Tattooers of the stars since 1971") and Tattoomania. They told us the most common L.A. tattoo is. . . roses.

Seattle's most unusual tattoos: a Scrabble board (on someone's back); a life-size Levi's pocket with a $100 bill sticking out of it (on somebody's rounded bottom) so they'd never be broke.

U

It's personal, but . . . what about your **UNDERWEAR**?

Do Seattle men wear briefs or boxers? Research for this short subject was difficult, at best. Both the Bon and Nordstrom men's departments said that they sold more briefs than boxers, but that it was very close and they had no numbers. Three physical therapists interviewed said they saw more briefs, but again boxers ran a close second. Some health-club types said young men wear briefs, older men boxers—except for the young prepsters, who wear boxers.

For the definitive answer, we sent the question through the electronic mail system at Adobe, the Pioneer Square software firm (where could you reach a more hip and representative Seattle sample?), with this result:

Totals: 50/50 exactly (excluding five obscene/nonresponsive replies)

Some survey comments:

"Briefs. Legal ones, of course. Boxing is no longer politically correct."

"Lacy women's underwear."

"Thongs."

"I'm willing to bet my 100% cotton boxers that most Adobe males are brief-wearers. Ever since my family moved to the Northwest, my brothers and I have noticed (from high school/college locker rooms and group living situations) that most Northwest males are brief-wearers. What gives?"

"Jockey shorts (otherwise known as 'marblebags') are something no grown man should wear."

"Women should be included in this question because a lot of gals like to wear boxers too, especially here in Seattle."

"I have seen many local bands play in their boxers—we may have started that fad (along with the one where guys wear women's leggings or fishnet stockings under mega-ripped jeans)."

"What about nothing at all? I demand equal representation (even though I'm a brief kinda guy)."

"What do male undergarment choices have to do with surviving in Seattle?" (Good question!)

"Briefs—but not the ones that come in packages of three. To be hip they should cost at least $8 a pair but not more than $25."

From a woman: "The only (young) guys I know who wear boxers are (1) from Southern California and (2) obnoxious. All the 'normal' ones (I get this info from their girlfriends) wear briefs."

V

The best (free) **VIEW** in town is from the Volunteer Park water tower. Number of steps in the water

tower: 106 on each staircase
(212 total).

Seattle's a great town for **VEGETAR-IANS** and organic-food junkies.
You can cook at home: the
natural-foods Puget Consumers'
Co-op has stores in eight neighborhoods. If you want to dine
out, the city offers nearly a dozen
exclusively vegetarian restaurants
to choose from. Or you can potluck it with like-minded folks:
Seattle boasts a sizeable chapter
of the vegetarian group EarthSave,
which holds monthly potluck
meetings (featuring guest speakers) and puts on an annual Thanksgiving potluck attended by hundreds. Call 781-6602 for info.

W

Ever wonder what those boats are
saying when they **WHISTLE** at
Seattle bridges? Generally, the
boats are asking the bridge to
open. They have to whistle dif-
ferently to indicate this, depending
on the bridge.
Seattle vessel whistle signals:
  ▮=Prolonged blast (4 seconds or
      more);
  I=Short blast (1 second);
  IIIII=Danger/no opening
      (5 or more short blasts)
Canal locks:
  Vessels with tows: ▮▮I
  Vessels needing half lock:
  ▮▮II,II
  Vessels needing full lock:
  ▮▮II,III
Here are the routines:
  Ballard Bridge: ▮I
  Fremont Bridge: ▮I
  University Bridge: ▮I
  Montlake Bridge: ▮I
  Evergreen Point Bridge: ▮I
  Spokane Street Bridge: ▮▮IIII
  First Avenue S Bridge: ▮▮▮
  16th Avenue S Bridge: ▮I▮
      (14th Avenue S)

X

Where do **X-PATRIATES** who've
moved to Seattle from other places
go to get a little bit of home?

- Philadelphians: Philadelphia
  Fevre Steak & Hoagie Shop,
  2332 E Madison—complete
  with Philadelphia newspapers.
- New Yorkers: Bagel Deli
  on 15th Avenue E ("They're
  even rude").
- New Mexicans: Santa Fe Cafe.
- Texans: Two Dagos from
  Texas; Rattlers Grill.
- Ex-cons: Armadillo Barbecue
  ("Prison-quality food").

Y

Yes, the mummies at **YE OLDE CURI-OSITY SHOP** on Pier 54 are real.
Sylvester was owned by a true
eccentric in California who kept
the mummy in a specially built
settee. He would often invite
guests over to his home and sit
them on the settee. When they
were ready to leave, he'd lift up
the lid of the settee and show
them what they'd been sitting on.
Anyway, Sylvester died of a gunshot
wound, still visible in the mummy's lower left side just above
the pelvic area. His body was
found in about 1895 by two cow-
boys riding in the Gila Bend
Desert in central Arizona, and
scientists say he was mummified
by natural dehydration caused by
the hot sands and dry air. If you
touch him, say the shop workers,
he feels just like leather.
Sylvester's partner for eternity
(or the life of Ye Olde Curiosity
Shop, which was founded in 1899)
is Sylvia, a Spanish emigrant
found in Central America. She's
assumed to have died of tuber-
culosis contracted during her
long sea voyage in the early part
of the 19th century. She was
found with her burial shoes on.

Ye Olde Curiosity Shop acquired
her from a man who was just
passing through town. He saw
Sylvester and asked if they wanted
a female to go along with him.
As for the names, owner Joe James
thought up both of them.

Z

Seattle uses 500 tons of **ZOO-DOO**
from the 1,215 animals who live
at Woodland Park Zoo. Call
625-POOP to hear the often
humorous Zoo-Doo Hotline
message. It costs $1–$2 for a bag
full, $3–$5 for a garbage can, $25
per small truckload, $30 per medi-
um truckload, and $45 per full-
size truckload. (By the way, the
zoo saves $40,000 a year by sell-
ing this stuff instead of sending it
to a landfill.) And in December,
you can get HoliDoo, vintage
screened doo packaged and
labeled for that hard-to-please
person on your list! Time to
get your name on fall sale list
is August 1.

CHAPTER

2

NEIGHBOR TO NEIGHBOR

PROFILES

HOUSING PRICES

MOVERS AND SHAKERS

CAUSES

CELEBRATIONS

SHOPPING

LEGENDS

HANGOUTS

There are over 100 neighborhoods in Seattle—and about 200 community organizations determined to protect them. Every neighborhood insists it is "one of Seattle's oldest." And most of them are: many were started by early-day developers who paid for streetcar lines to reach their plots of land.

Each of Seattle's little pockets of civilization has its own unique sense of identity, and the people who live there are prepared to fight to keep that neighborhood feeling—as city officials learned in the 1980s, when communities came under siege as apartment/condominium development raged. After those battles, the city created the Department of Neighborhoods.

The 1990s have brought increasing optimism to the city's poorest neighborhoods. Since housing there is far more affordable than elsewhere in the city, young families are discovering these areas and moving in. In Georgetown, Delridge, and Beacon Hill, old-timers will tell you over and over that things are changing for the better now that young families are choosing the city over the increasingly affluent suburbs.

WHERE'S THE LINE?

Why don't Seattle's neighborhoods have clear boundaries? Most of them started in Seattle's pioneer days as individual towns; only later were they annexed into the Seattle metropolis, attracted by such benefits as utilities and infrastructure.

As Seattle's population grew, neighborhoods became distinctive within themselves. What was once just Ballard, for instance, became Adams, Crown Hill, Sunset Hill, etc. West Seattle, like Ballard, became more of a geographic location, wherein were located the neighborhoods of Alki, Admiral, Delridge, and The Junction.

Only when residents began to organize politically did these small communities count themselves as part of a larger neighborhood, in order to gain more clout with City Hall. These boundaries were determined not by geographic landmarks, however, but by an area's particular "character"—which frustrated city planners seeking objective, mappable boundaries.

How to be effective on a community council:

- Be creative. Figure out what you want.
- Get educated on the issues.
- Get involved with the entire council; you can't carry issues by yourself. And considering different perspectives is healthy.
- Get plugged in with the people who make things move.
- Be open and willing to contact strangers. Be a networking person.
- Be willing to work your way around problem people you encounter. Don't be reluctant to hold people in government responsible. If you aren't getting the service you think is your due, ask to speak to a superior.
- Be willing to persevere.
- Be willing to step into the larger policy realm. Get laws changed and elect officials who will give you improved laws. If you don't get the laws changed, you'll just fight the same battles over and over.

Source: Various neighborhood council members

Even today, the Department of Neighborhoods has no neighborhood map, and in certain neighborhoods, there are disputes between residents about whether they live in, say, Fremont or Ballard. (And if a house is for sale, the boundaries really move. No one sells a house in "Rainier Valley," for instance; it suddenly becomes part of "Seward Park.")

FROM COW TOWNS TO COMMUNITY COUNCILS

Neighborhood organizations have arisen in various ways, most commonly in reaction to changing neighborhood conditions. Whether provoked by an influx of apartment building in single-family neighborhoods or by industrial pollution, neighbors have found ways of organizing to press city managers to preserve their communities.

The Seattle Neighborhood Coalition (SNC) is a classic example of an institution that has drawn together neighborhood activists from all over the city and from all walks of life: artists, poets, city employees, small-business owners, and other professionals. SNC's finest moment so far came in the '80s, in the midst of Seattle's neighborhood growing pains, when it took a stand against destruction of traditionally single-family neighborhoods throughout the city. The group got the ear of the city council and devised a scheme to bring development and neighborhood interests together and downzone many neighborhoods. Some SNC members helped form the political action group Vision Seattle.

City council members took heed, passing zoning legislation and encouraging individual neighborhood comprehensive plans that restricted new construction and encouraged growth where it could best be managed. The planning battle has yet to be won. Only one neighborhood plan has been adopted by the council. The other plans are on

SEATTLE'S NEIGHBORHOODS

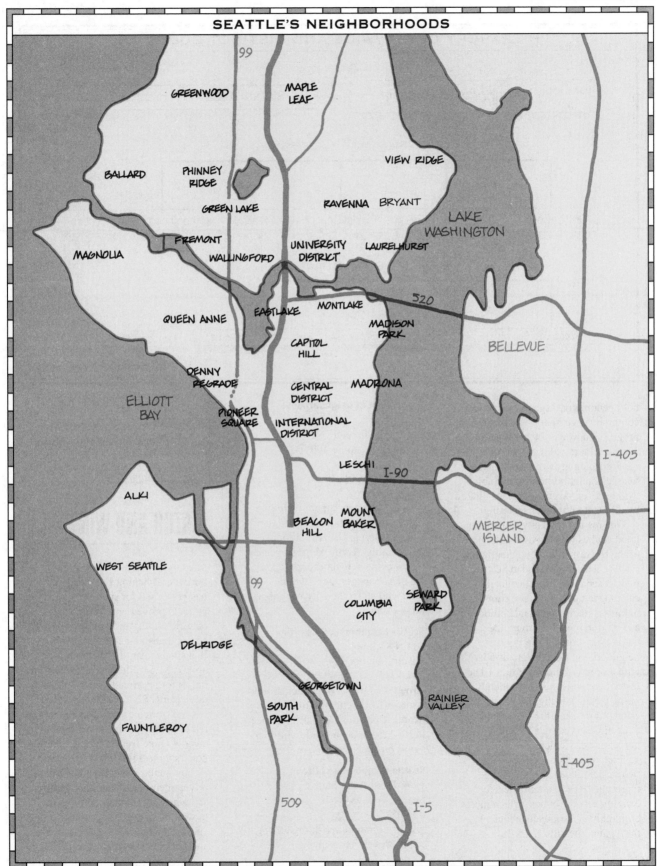

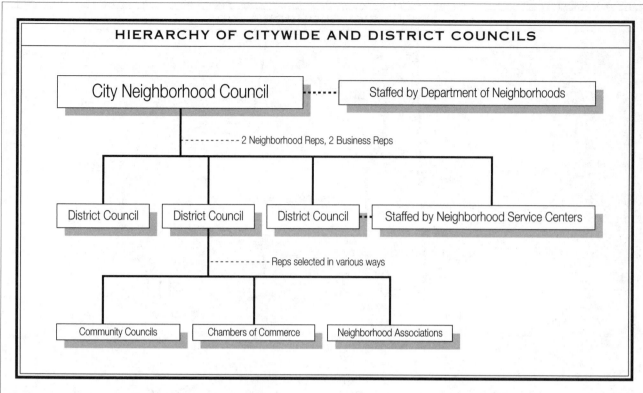

HIERARCHY OF CITYWIDE AND DISTRICT COUNCILS

City Neighborhood Council ┄┄ Staffed by Department of Neighborhoods

┄┄ 2 Neighborhood Reps, 2 Business Reps

District Council — District Council — District Council ┄┄ Staffed by Neighborhood Service Centers

┄┄ Reps selected in various ways

Community Councils — Chambers of Commerce — Neighborhood Associations

hold pending passage of a citywide comprehensive plan—and further progress on Mayor Norm Rice's "urban village" concept, a model for absorbing growth that envisions Seattle's neighborhoods as livable "villages" of varying densities, linked by efficient public transportation.

One result of the city's neighborhood studies was the establishment of the Department of Neighborhoods (DON). The DON divided Seattle into 13 separate district councils, each made up of business, community council, and neighborhood association representatives. (A community council is a type of neighborhood association, usually with a broad agenda of issues.) The district councils meet on a monthly basis, tackling such issues as growth, crime, traffic, and the like. Each council is served by a Neighborhood Service Center.

Each district council selects two residential and two business representatives to attend the City Neighborhood Council, which meets bimonthly at various locations throughout the city.

Department of Neighborhoods (DON)
Jim Diers, director
Arctic Bldg., Suite 400
700 Third Ave.
Seattle, WA 98104
684-0464
A 70-person department including historic preservation staff and the Citizens Service Bureau. Produces the monthly *Seattle Neighborhood News,* helps neighborhood organizations, manages the matching fund, and staffs the City Neighborhood Council.

Seattle Neighborhood Coalition
731 N 87th St.
Seattle, WA 98103
784-7217
Group of activists organized around issues affecting quality of life in Seattle. Sponsors regular town meetings where opposing sides air their views on such issues.

Seattle Neighborhood Group
1904 Third Ave., Suite 614
Seattle, WA 98101
624-0577
Assists communities in organizing crime prevention councils.

Vision Seattle
5031 University Way NE
Seattle, WA 98115
522-8835
Political action group involved with neighborhood issues.

MATCH AND WIN

The city's award-winning Neighborhood Matching Fund Program has been used for such projects as parks improvement, traffic studies, historic preservation plans, and comprehensive neighborhood plans. In a single year, the program gives around $1.5 million to neighborhoods for approved projects. The city awards $2 from the fund for every $1 of community match in either money, labor, or materials. The awards range from a couple thousand dollars up to $100,000.

For small projects (e.g., community gardens, tree plantings, public art) whose supporters don't want to wait as long as the larger projects take to get approved, there's a "Small and Simple" Neighborhood Matching

Fund Program. Neighborhood groups can apply six times a year to fund small projects costing up to $5,000 that can be completed within six months of the award.

The city's matching fund program was the first in the country, and the DON now gets requests for information from around the world. In 1991, it was cited by the Ford Foundation and Harvard University's Kennedy School of Government as one of the 10 most innovative government programs in the nation.

Neighborhood Matching Fund Program
684-0464

OF DESIGN MATTERS

On the horizon is an issue of great interest to Seattle's neighborhoods. The city is considering design review boards for five areas of the city. Roosevelt and a few other neighborhoods have developed their own building design criteria but, without the city nod, have no clout. If the city approves the design review boards, new projects would have to be built in character with the existing neighborhood structures. Whether the boards will allow neighborhoods to create their own design review criteria remains to be seen.

Urban Neighborhoods That Work

The city of Seattle presents a number of design awards each year, usually to notable buildings. In 1993 these awards were given to entire neighborhoods, based on criteria such as the presence of an identifiable neighborhood "center," pedestrian-friendly sidewalks, good public facilities, and a mix of housing types and densities. The winners:

- Admiral
- Ballard
- Capitol Hill/Broadway
- Fremont
- Green Lake
- International District

- Madison Park
- Madrona
- Wallingford

NEIGHBORHOOD SERVICE CENTERS (NSCs)

NSCs help link city government to local citizens. They help community groups network, assist neighborhood improvement efforts, and refer people to local social services. At the NSCs indicated with an asterisk (*) below, you can also purchase pet licenses and garbage stickers and pay City Light bills, combined utility bills, and parking tickets. Note: Several NSCs share office space with one another.

Ballard NSC*
Rob Mattson, coordinator
2305 NW Market St.
Seattle, WA 98107
684-4060

Capitol Hill NSC
Jose Cervantes, coordinator
501 19th Ave. E
Seattle, WA 98112
684-4574

Central NSC*
Ted Divina, coordinator
1825 S Jackson St.
Seattle, WA 98144
684-4767

Downtown NSC
Glenda Cassutt, coordinator
1825 S Jackson St.
Seattle, WA 98144
233-8560

Fremont NSC
Steve Louie, coordinator
708 N 34th St.
Seattle, WA 98103
684-4054

Greater Duwamish NSC
Stan Lock, coordinator
3801 Beacon Ave. S
Seattle, WA 98108
233-2044

Greenwood NSC
Beth Pflug, coordinator
8505 Greenwood Ave. N
Seattle, WA 98103
684-4096

Lake City NSC*
Yolanda Martinez, coordinator
12707 30th Ave. NE
Seattle, WA 98125
684-7526

Queen Anne/Magnolia NSC
Gary Johnson, coordinator
708 N 34th St.
Seattle, WA 98103
684-4812

Southeast NSC*
Ellen Broeske, coordinator
4859 Rainier Ave. S
Seattle, WA 98118
386-1931

Southwest NSC*
Ron Angeles, coordinator
4454 California Ave. SW
Seattle, WA 98116
684-7416

Southwest/White Center NSC*
Ron Angeles, coordinator
9407 16th Ave. SW
Seattle, WA 98106
684-7416

The Seattle Neighborhood Coalition meets the second Saturday of each month at 9am at the Greenhouse Cafe, 2205 Seventh Avenue. Neighborhood activists from around the city regularly attend these informal events, which are often standing room only. For info, call 784-7217.

University NSC*
Pamela Grea, coordinator
5214 University Way NE
Seattle, WA 98105
684-7542

West Seattle NSC*
Carla Cole, coordinator
4454 California Ave. SW
Seattle, WA 98116
684-7495

NEIGHBORHOOD PROFILES

Neighborhoods are like families. They all have their idiosyncrasies, secrets, and characters. It's risky, at best, to talk about them, much less write about them.

At the risk of offending thousands of people, we're profiling only some of the city's neighborhoods. The reason for this is that life is too short: even the simplest figure, the most common-knowledge hangout is the object of controversy when it comes to neighborhoods. (One north end resident merely said, "Bah," when asked if the Honey Bear Bakery is a hangout. Sigh.) So, it's with apologies to the good folk of Licton Springs, Pritchard Island, North Park, etc. that we either include them with a larger, adjacent neighborhood or save them for our next edition.

What follows is our clockwise tour of the neighborhoods, beginning in northwest Seattle with Ballard.

A few words about our sources

You'll probably notice that some neighborhoods, as described here, seem to overlap each other. That's because, as noted earlier, neighborhood **boundaries** are very rough; in some cases, the services within a neighborhood are actually found outside what most people consider its boundaries. In other cases, people disagree about the bound-

The Seattle Survival Guide Neighborhood Index

Most baby boomers	Green Lake, Wallingford
Where men outnumber women	Central District, Madrona
Where women outnumber men	Queen Anne
Most married	Magnolia
Least married	Downtown
Most divorced	Downtown, Queen Anne
Most kids under 5	Rainier Beach
Most kids under 18	Fauntleroy/Highland Park
Where kids are fleeing	Central District, Capitol Hill, Alki
Whitest community	University District/Ravenna, followed by Lake City
Most African Americans	Central District, followed by Beacon Hill
Most native Americans	Highland Park
Most Asians	Beacon Hill/Rainier Valley
Fastest growing neighborhood (1980–1990)	Rainier Beach (8.9% population increase)
Fastest shrinking neighborhood	Magnolia (−8.3% population decrease)
Highest housing unit increase (1980–1990)	Broadview (16%), followed by Lake City (14%)
Lowest housing unit increase	Downtown and Beacon Hill (0.7% each)

Source: U.S. census, Seattle Office for Long-Range Planning

aries, so we chose the most prevalent opinion.

Population, age, income, zoning, and **housing** information is from the 1990 census. **Median income** information is per household. If it seems low—and in some cases it does—that's simply the way median information works. Seattle's total median income per household is $29,353; per capita income is $18,308. Since this information is broken down by census tract, and neighborhood boundaries don't necessarily follow the tracts, it's approximate rather than definitive.

Rent averages were tough. The census figures were average rents per household or unit, and many seemed low—but weekly newspaper listings and local agents generally gave us similar figures (except for the trendy neighborhoods of the moment). Of course, rents fluctuate with supply and demand, view,

condition of apartment, etc. For example, Fremont's average rent is $455/month, but rents range from the rare $250 in older buildings up to $1,000.

House value averages were tough too; unless noted as census figures, these averages are from *Seattle Survival Guide* research. The market is no longer as hot as it was a few years back, but many census figures seemed too low. When things seemed out of whack, we called neighborhood realtors to ask for an average price, with mixed results. If a waterfront house worth a million sold recently, for example, the average got boosted pretty high. But in general, the values should be in the ballpark. (Remember, the census measures house value, not necessarily market value.) You might consult the Puget Sound Multiple Listing Association's table of house sales, available at real estate offices, to get a more complete picture.

Under **movers and shakers,** we've included only the names of neighborhood groups but not their phone numbers, which can change frequently. For the current contact name and phone number, call the appropriate Neighborhood Service Center (NSC), listed in this chapter, or the Department of Neighborhoods.

Crime is, of course, a concern for every neighborhood, so we've listed the appropriate **police precinct** and **crime watch groups** in each community. For crime maps indicating major offenses for each neighborhood area, see Chapter 17, "It's a Crime."

Public perks include parks, community centers, and schools. For a map showing the locations of all the athletic playfields in Seattle, see Chapter 11, "What Good Sports!"

We garnered much of the rest of our information by talking to people in the neighborhoods.

Hangouts are where the neighborhood residents meet, not necessarily destinations for the rest of the city (though, in some cases, they should be). But we couldn't resist adding some places that are "worth a detour" in hopes that, for example, a Ballardite might decide to drive to Rainier Beach to see Dead Horse Canyon.

NORTHWEST

The Northwest neighborhood is the vast expanse of Ballard.

BALLARD

Ballardites live in Ballard first, Seattle second. The area clearly stands apart, both to its residents and to the rest of Seattle. Our description includes as part of Ballard Crown Hill, Sunset Hill, Loyal Heights, Whittier Heights, North Beach, West Woodland, and Blue Ridge.

So how do the residents like being the butt of jokes by comics on "Almost Live" as well as countless other city jokers? They mind not at all. It's actually a source of pride and part of their identity.

There are those, however, who think this tolerance is damaging to the area's self-esteem, who wish the neighborhood would not see itself as a contrived, funny sort of place but instead as a serious community with its own set of values.

Ballard is very possibly coming to a crisis point. It has traditionally been a working-class neighborhood supported by the timber and fishing industries, but that's changing in a way the natives aren't so sure they like.

For example, Ballard cut its trees down for the nearby mills years ago and does not consider itself a tree-hugging community. "That's part of our heritage," says one native. "We like shrubs and flowers. Trees are a product and messy." It's true, there are few tree-lined streets, just well-kept yards with lots of flowers. But the newcomers, for the most part professional young families (called "carpetbaggers" by the old-timers), have started a group to "re-tree Ballard," creating an interesting conflict between old and new values. And, whereas the old community groups were considered tough and a bit rough, the new groups are run with, as one put it, "a velvet glove."

In the 1980s, developers discovered that a substantial amount of multi-family zoning existed in central Ballard and started taking advantage of it. The community rose up and got many areas down-zoned. But the issue hasn't gone away; Ballard is still vulnerable to multi-family clustering, since it is zoned for a much larger population than it has now.

Ballard comprises several areas. Old Ballard is centered at Market Street and Leary Way and is distinguished by lots of small bungalows

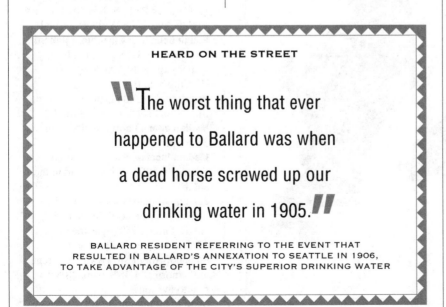

HEARD ON THE STREET

"The worst thing that ever happened to Ballard was when a dead horse screwed up our drinking water in 1905."

BALLARD RESIDENT REFERRING TO THE EVENT THAT RESULTED IN BALLARD'S ANNEXATION TO SEATTLE IN 1906, TO TAKE ADVANTAGE OF THE CITY'S SUPERIOR DRINKING WATER

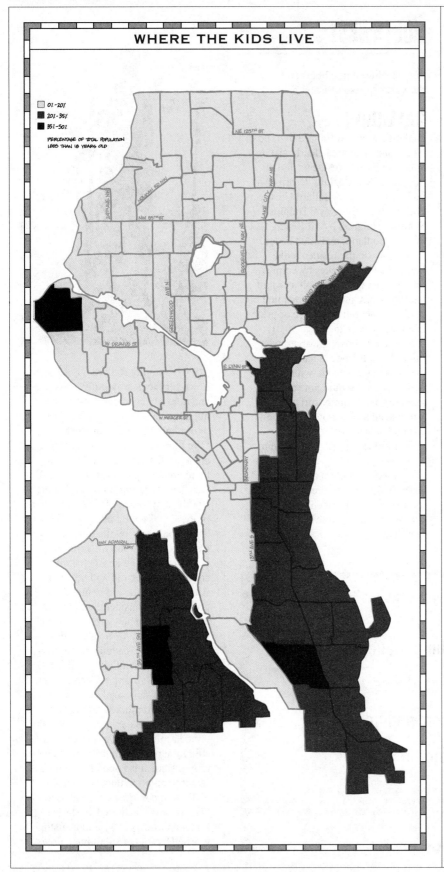

WHERE THE KIDS LIVE

0%–20%
20%–35%
35%–50%

PERCENTAGE OF TOTAL POPULATION
LESS THAN 18 YEARS OLD

and, increasingly, apartment buildings; Loyal Heights and Sunset Hill are more established single-family; Crown Hill, Blue Ridge, and North Beach feel more suburban.

History

Ballard was the first large-scale real estate development designed to attract Scandinavian immigrants. It worked. They came by the hundreds to work in the burgeoning pulp and cedar shingle mills along Salmon Bay. It was named after its developer, Captain William Ballard, who platted and incorporated the city of Ballard in 1888. Ballard was annexed to Seattle in 1906. The annexation decision is still a matter of debate; a regular topic in Ballard taverns is how to secede from the city.

Legends: Ballard is known for its high proportion of taverns/churches/ banks to its population. Old-timers say an ordinance dictated that at least one church be constructed for every three taverns in existence. But old Ballard City Hall was destroyed by an earthquake in the early 1960s and there's no record of the ordinance. Another (tall) story has it that the popular Denny's at 15th NW has a karaoke bar (Norwegian karaoke?!).

Stats

Rough boundaries (northern Ballard): N: Carkeek Park; S: NW 85th St.; E: Eighth Ave. NW; W: Puget Sound.

Rough boundaries (southern Ballard): N: NW 85th St.; S: Salmon Bay Waterway; E: Eighth Ave. NW; W: Shilshole Bay.

Population: 6,200 north of NW 85th St.; 27,982 south of NW 85th St.

Median age: 43 north of NW 85th St.; 37 south.

Median income: $36,000/household to the north; $29,477/household to the south.

Zoning: About 90% single-family detached to the north. About 65% single-family, 25% apartment, 10% commercial to the south.

Housing: About 80% own, 20% rent to the north; 51.48% own, 48.52% rent to the south.

Rent: $500/month

House value: $128,580 for a Ballard bungalow

Institutions

District Council: Ballard
NSC: Ballard
Movers and shakers: Sunset Hill Community Club (oldest continually operating community club of its kind in the city), Loyal Heights Community Council, North Beach Club, Olympic Manor Community Club, Blue Ridge Community Club, Ballard Chamber of Commerce, Ballard Merchants Association, Friends of Salmon Bay Park, Friends of Golden Gardens.
Local media: *Ballard News-Tribune, North Seattle Press*
Police precinct: North
Crime watch groups: Block watch
Causes: Apartment/condo construction displacing single-family homes, gentrification, Fred Meyer store proposed for Lake Washington Ship Canal, getting access to the proposed Burlington Northern commuter line from Seattle to Everett, monitoring Port of Seattle plans for Shilshole Marina, rehab of Ballard High School.
Public perks: Ballard Boys and Girls Club, Ballard and Loyal Heights community centers, Ballard Library, Leif Erikson Hall, Nordic Heritage Museum, Hiram Chittenden Government Locks, Shilshole Marina, Ballard and Gilman playgrounds; Carkeek, Golden Gardens, and Salmon Bay parks; Adams, Loyal Heights, North Beach, and Whittier elementary schools; Whitman Middle School, Ballard High School.
Neighborhood heroes: The late state senator Ted Peterson, who launched the campaign to rebuild Ballard's old city hall bell tower. The original tower came down in an earthquake—in fact, locals say much of Market Street is paved with its bricks. The new one now stands at Ballard Avenue and 22nd Avenue NW.

HEARD ON THE STREET

"The really great thing about Ballard is that a lot of people know each other. It has the feel of an earlier point in time. And a lot of people who grew up there still live there. It is the only area of Seattle that is a complete town unto itself. You could be born, go to school, live, die and be buried, and never have to leave."

BALLARD RESIDENT

Fun stuff

Beyond the malls: Ballard is unusual in that it has a distinct industrial area that supports its commercial area. Industry (fishing, commercial shipping) is along Salmon Bay Waterway. The Ballard Avenue Landmark District (south of Market Street) is Seattle's oldest still-working historical area. Market Street is a major shopping area and often a destination for the rest of the city. Loyal Heights has a shopping area at NW 80th and 24th NW, Crown Hill at NW 85th and 15th NW; business corners at 32nd NW and NW 65th and at Eighth NW and NW Market. Also, many stores (furniture refinishing, TV repair, hardware, etc.) along 15th NW; Larsen Bros. Bakery at Loyal Heights, on corner of 80th and 24th NW; Johnsen's Scandinavian Foods in central Ballard. The Bay movie theater has inexpensive film screenings.

Celebrations: Syttende Mai (May 17th, Norwegian Constitution Day) with parade and music; Seafoodfest in July; annual sidewalk sale; Tivoli and Yule Fest at Nordic Heritage Museum.

Hangouts: Ballard Smoke Shop, Denny's on 15th NW, Scandies, Sloop Tavern (sailing types), Hattie's Hat restaurant (with "Aunt Harriet's Room"), Vera's Coffee Shop, Traders Tavern (famous for the coldest beer in Seattle). The evening crowd, from Ballard as well as from the rest of the city, flocks to the many restaurants on Shilshole—Ray's Boathouse, Anthony's Home Port—and to the Backstage club for music.

Worth a detour: For romantics, try driving west on NW 85th Street at sunset to the top of the hill above Golden Gardens park. For curiosity seekers, the Locks are always worth a stop. To get close to boat traffic: head south on 24th Avenue NW all

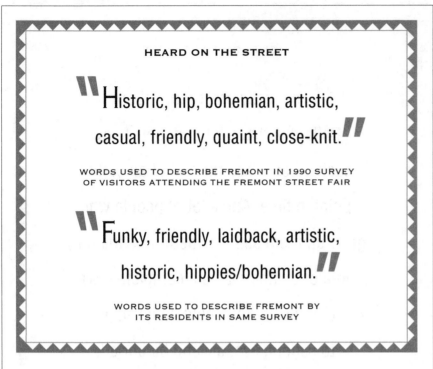

the way to the road end where there's a public dock you can walk out onto.

NORTH

North Seattle neighborhoods include Fremont, Green Lake, Greenwood, Phinney Ridge, and Wallingford.

FREMONT

Fremont is one of the city's eclectic close-in urban neighborhoods, a holdout of loyal Democratic residents who range from hippies turned capitalists to middle-class families struggling to hold onto that ol' Fremont neighborhood feeling. Ask a Fremont resident what L-3 means and he or she will immediately reel off the city zoning code as it applies to low-rise apartment buildings—and will usually add a snide comment about the city's shortsightedness in allowing the buildings to tower over existing bungalows. Fremont actually spawned the down-zones that saved some of Seattle's neighborhoods in the Royer years (the mid-'80s).

Fremont's a fighting neighborhood, and what is obvious is that its rage is caffeine-fueled—espresso machines have taken the place of old Harleys in this avant-garde neighborhood. Residents get all tanked up on lattes and hit Fremont's sacred soapbox of a statue, Richard Beyer's *People Waiting for the Interurban,* with a vengeance, draping trappings of the latest controversy on it. Radicals aren't the only ones who decorate the statue; anyone who wants to make a statement or announce an event gets a chance too. The telling thing is that people politely wait at least one week before redecorating.

Some say the apartment fight was actually lost; the average resident spends only a year and a half here (3½ years is the city average). That may be why Fremont's historic buildings are no longer held in such esteem. In a recent survey, 11% of those polled saw historic preservation as one of Fremont's best qualities, but 8% viewed the old buildings as one of the neighborhood's worst characteristics.

Whatever its politics, Fremont is a great place to be. It's filled with used clothing/goods shops, hidden art, granola-head hangouts, and brewery groupies.

History

Originally a mill town, during the Depression Fremont was where the down-and-outs settled. This proved irresistible in the '60s to hippies and bikers, and eventually the charm of Fremont spread to the middle-class, sweat-equity types.

Legends: People say there was a tunnel under N 35th Street and Fremont Avenue N to let speak-easy patrons escape police raids during Prohibition. A myth that needs to be laid to rest: Residents are not more likely to be artists or performers than elsewhere in the city. Only 16% say they are in the arts, whereas the city average is 17%.

Stats

Rough boundaries: N: N 50th St.; S: Lake Washington Ship Canal; E: Stone Way N; W: Eighth Ave. NW.

Population: 9,444

Median age: 34

Median income: $28,760/household

Zoning: Highly varied; single-family with older apartments and new high-density apartments, the latter especially in upper Fremont.

Housing: 36.25% own, 63.75% rent

Rent: $455/month

House value: $126,600 (census), $150,000–$500,000 on the ridge with views of Ballard.

Institutions

District Council: Lake Union

NSC: Fremont

Movers and shakers: Fremont Neighborhood Council, Fremont Chamber of Commerce, FremontWorks.

Local media: *Lake Union Review, North Seattle Press*

Police precinct: North

Crime watch groups: Some block watch

Causes: Integrating apartment dwellers into the community and appeasing the often-opposing points of view of the businesspeople and the residents. They alternately work together and then tear each other apart. Other issues: traffic, parking, the Quadrant Project development (which includes extending the Burke-Gilman Trail along the Ship Canal—very unpopular with industrial businesses).

Public perks: Fremont Library, Fremont Public Association (county-wide low-income assistance, food bank, etc.), *People Waiting for the Interurban,* Fremont Baptist Church, B.F. Day Elementary School.

Fun stuff

Beyond the malls: A little bit of everything, from offbeat shops to espresso bar/restaurants, mainly at the north end of the Fremont Bridge, on Fremont Avenue N between N 34th and N 36th streets. The Empty Space Theatre is located here. Fremont is the home of alternative retailers, with shops like Glamorama and Archie McPhee's (probably technically in Wallingford).

Celebrations: Fremont Fair and Solstice Parade in June (to which 90,000 people flock annually), Fremont Neighborhood Tour. On Sundays from May through December there's a craft and flea market, a smaller version of the Fremont Fair, near the Fremont Bridge.

Hangouts: Still Life in Fremont Coffeehouse, Red Door Alehouse, The Buckaroo tavern, Trolleyman Pub at the Red Hook Brewery, Triangle Tavern, Marketime Foods.

Worth a detour: Hall of Giants Park, with a huge troll forever crushing a (real) Volkswagen Beetle under the Aurora Bridge at N 35th Street and Aurora Avenue N.

GREEN LAKE

Mention swamps or alligators and residents in the Green Lake neighborhood will begin to sweat. Their nightmare is a lake turned swampland, and they fear that will happen if the weeds take over and the water quality isn't improved.

While most neighborhoods have a commercial area at their center, this one has a lake. And what a lake—it's so much a part of the city that if you haven't run (or biked, skated, or bladed) its 3 miles, you can't be called a Seattleite.

While many neighborhoods cringe in the shadow of new apartment buildings and condos, the Green Lake neighborhood has somehow avoided most of the impacts of regional growth, continuing to thrive as a strong single-family neighborhood. The apartments on the east side are for the most part older buildings with a mix of young people and senior citizens. There was a burst of newly constructed "skinny houses" a while back, but further such development was quickly squelched by city ordinance.

Crime has not increased considerably around the lake, with theft, residential burglary, and auto theft still the biggest concerns. On Aurora, prostitutes are the perennial problem, but the merchants have banded together to combat the world's oldest profession—successfully enough that they give advice to other neighborhoods (e.g., Georgetown) combating the same problem.

Around the lake, the word congestion takes on new meaning; it's best to just park on the outskirts and walk, especially if you're in a hurry. It doesn't help that Metro sewer overflow construction is adding to the melange of cars, buses, bikes, and sometimes tentative roller bladers.

Green Lakers vote mainly Democratic, with a more Republican vote closer to the lake.

History

Green Lake is a glacial lake that was turning into meadowland when Seattle's settlers decided to buy it. The area was annexed to the city in 1888, and before it was a true residential neighborhood it was a destination for people from Seattle; there was even an Auto Tourist Camp there in the 1920s. Under the Olmsted Park Plan, the lake was partially drained and filled, so as to produce the park which now surrounds the lake. Some houses that were originally built as lakefront still exist, but the lake has since moved away.

Legends: Green Lake John blazed the first trail to the lake in 1870 and lived as a hermit on the shore until, presumably, tourism ruined his hideout.

And then there's the story about the alligator (cayman, actually) found in the lake, apparently someone's pet let loose. When he was found in the mid-1980s, the Seattle media went wild, and he was on the front page more than the mayor.

Stats

Rough boundaries: N: N 85th St.; S: N 50th St.; E: I-5; W: Aurora Ave. N (Hwy. 99).

Two parks worth a detour:

• **Kubota Garden** is a contemplative 20-acre Japanese-American garden. Winding paths lead over curving bridges and through trees to streams, reflecting pools, and small waterfalls, all fed by natural springs. You'll find it in South Seattle at Renton Avenue S and 44th Avenue S.

• At **Walker Rock Garden** in West Seattle, it's tough to decide what's more amazing: Is it the nearly 20-foot, three-tiered semiprecious stone topped with a weather vane? Or the series of snowcapped mountains, miniature lakes, and winding roadways carved from red lava? Tours by appointment, May to September, 935-3036.

Population: 12,187
Median age: 35.4
Median income: $32,816/household
Zoning: 80% single-family homes, 20% multi-unit apartments, with six-plex apartments around the lake.
Housing: 54.9% own, 45.1% rent (east of the lake, 70% rent)
Rent: $503/month
House value: $149,400 (census)

Institutions

District Council: Northwest
NSC: Greenwood

Movers and shakers: Green Lake Community Council, Aurora Merchants Association, Green Lake Chamber of Commerce.
Local media: *North Seattle Press*
Police precinct: North
Crime watch groups: Block watch, Green Lake Community Council's Crime Watch Task Force, Aurora Merchants Association.
Causes: Metro's work on a huge combined sewer overflow system around the east side of the lake and down Ravenna Boulevard, water quality and preservation of Green Lake, remodel of Vitamilk plant, traffic safety around the lake and along bicycle/pedestrian pathways.
Public perks: Green Lake Community Center, Evans Pool, Green Lake and Woodland parks, Green Lake Library, Green Lake Golf Course, Queen City Lawn Bowling Club, Green Lake and Bagley elementary schools, Marshall Alternative School.

Fun stuff

Beyond the malls: Small shops and stores near the lake, including roller blade and bike rentals, numerous restaurants, aging strip malls along Aurora.
Celebrations: Daily betting by picnickers on whether the novice roller bladers will make it across the street from Gregg's; lots of events around the lake, including crew races, the Milk Carton Derby, and Christmastime lighting of luminaries (candles in paper bags).
Hangouts: This whole neighborhood is a hangout. But residents go to the Honey Bear Bakery (in Wallingford), The Little Red Hen, My Friends Cafe, The Urban Bakery, Duke's, Baskin-Robbins, Häagen-Dazs, Gregg's Greenlake Cycle (not a restaurant, but a hangout nonetheless). On Aurora, Twin Teepees (older set).
Worth a detour: Green Lake is a recreational paradise. You can walk, run, or skate on the 2.8-mile paved path around the lake. You can windsurf on the lake or swim in the indoor pool, and there are facilities for golf, tennis, soccer, baseball, and basket-

ball. If none of those suit your fancy, you can rent a kayak or canoe from Green Lake Boat Rentals. Want to learn how to use one first? Try the Green Lake Small Craft Center (684-4074) for classes.

GREENWOOD

Greenwood is one of those small spots where small lots and small homes attract young families, where mom-and-pop stores mingle with the large Fred Meyer, where kids and dogs play, if not in the streets, at least next to them.

Central to Greenwood is the corner of N 85th Street and Greenwood Avenue N, the old merchants' section, slowly taking on the aura of an antiques village. The neighborhood has seen the same influx of multi-family dwellings as other areas, but these have primarily businesses on the first level, housing above. Greenwood bungalows sell as soon as the sign goes up, if not before.

Quiet! Seattle likes quiet. You can be fined $190 for playing boom boxes, car stereos, or other portable audio equipment in a public place, loud enough to be heard 50 feet away. Check out the boom box–ordinance signs down by Seward Park. Speaking of quiet, the ambient daytime noise in Seattle is 55 decibels (the human voice at 3 feet is 60 decibels). At night, it's 10 decibels less. Shhhhh.

History

The corner of Greenwood and 85th was the end of the Phinney Line, a main route of the Seattle Municipal Railway. The trolleys turned around in the intersection until the line closed in 1941.

Stats

Rough boundaries: N: N 105th St.; S: N 70th St.; E: Aurora Ave. N; W: Eighth Ave. NW (overlaps Phinney Ridge, depending on the mood of the Greenwoodite you're talking to).
Population: 9,181
Median age: 35
Median income: $29,405/household
Zoning: Single-family detached units most common, followed by apartments of five or more units.
Housing: 58.6% own, 41.4% rent
Rent: $465/month (higher on the east side)
House value: $118,033 (census)

Institutions

District Council: Northwest
NSC: Greenwood
Movers and shakers: Greenwood Boys and Girls Club, Greenwood Senior Center, Greenwood Community Council, Greater Greenwood Chamber of Commerce.
Local media: *North Seattle Press, Phinney Ridge Review* (quarterly publication of Phinney Neighborhood Association that includes class schedules).
Police precinct: North
Crime watch groups: Block watch (set up and overseen by the community council's public safety committee).
Causes: Beautifying the environment, public safety, land use and growth.
Public perks: Greenwood Library, Boys and Girls Club, Phinney Neighborhood Center, Greenwood Food Bank, Greenwood Elementary School.

Fun stuff

Beyond the malls: Jumble of upscale stores at Greenwood Avenue N and N 72nd Street; at N 85th are antique shops, Thai and Indian restaurants,

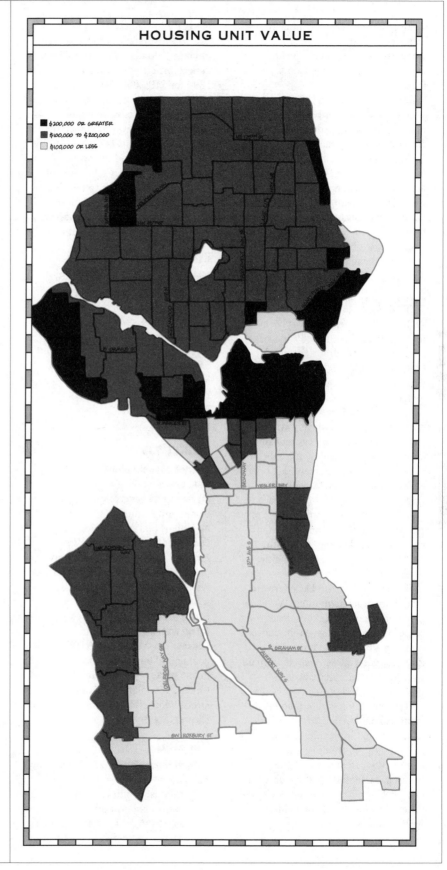

HOUSING UNIT VALUE

$200,000 OR GREATER
$100,000 TO $200,000
$100,000 OR LESS

small quaint stores, and Safeway and Fred Meyer.

Celebrations: Community picnic in July, Seafair Greenwood District Parade.

Hangouts: Greenwood Bakery, Woodland Park Pub, Home Espresso Repair (they serve espresso too).

Worth a detour: Actually in North Park, just north of Greenwood, Seattle City Light's Hoffman Substation features an amazing hidden park with whirligigs made of everything from old hiking boots to coffeepots, courtesy of Emil and Viva Gehrke. It was funded by the city's 1% for Art program and is at Fremont Avenue N and N 107th Street.

PHINNEY RIDGE

Phinney Ridge residents wryly say they are the overeducated and underpaid of Seattle. Public servants, government employees, teachers—this is their haunt. Consequently, Phinney Ridge residents are in the main extremely liberal and very political.

This neighborhood has graceful streets with older mid-size and small homes. It's obvious why it's called a ridge: it runs like a narrow backbone between Ballard and Woodland Park, and many of its homes are perched on the edges of the ridge. It's been discovered, and longtime residents fear that a more wealthy, upscale population is changing the diverse nature of the place.

This neighborhood has interesting neighbors of its own: in the Woodland Park Zoo. While this means an occasional monkey-on-the-loose, it also is a bittersweet amenity. Zoo programs attract visitors from all over the city, at times causing traffic headaches.

The Phinney Neighborhood Association should be the envy of every neighborhood in Seattle. It's not just a group griping about issues, it's a community center with programs for all ages, including after-school, child development, and senior citizen programs—even classes on home repair and a tool bank.

History

In a controversial transaction, Nellie Phinney sold the site of Woodland Park to the city of Seattle on Dec. 28, 1899 for $100,000. Many thought the Phinney estate was too far from the city center to ever have much use as a park; the mayor even vetoed the sale, but the veto was overridden by the city council and the property was bought. The Phinney Line, one of the city's early trolley-car routes, led to Phinney Ridge, prompting the development of the area. The line opened in 1907, reaching 85th Street in 1910.

Stats

Rough boundaries: N: N 75th St.; S: N 45th St.; E: Aurora Ave. N; W: Eighth Ave. NW.
Population: 14,773
Median age: 35.4
Median income: $32,924/household
Zoning: Single-family detached houses
Housing: 56% own, 44% rent
Rent: $460/month
House value: $134,475

Institutions

District Council: Northwest
NSC: Greenwood
Movers and shakers: Phinney Ridge Community Council, Phinney Neighborhood Association.
Local media: *North Seattle Press, Phinney Ridge Review* (quarterly publication of Phinney Neighborhood Association that includes class schedules).
Police precinct: North
Crime watch groups: Block watch
Causes: Growth issues, traffic, zoning and building, schools.
Public perks: Phinney Neighborhood Center, Woodland Park and the zoo, Greenwood Library, West Woodland Elementary School.

Fun stuff

Beyond the malls: Small shops along Phinney Avenue N
Celebrations: Monthly events at Phinney Neighborhood Center, such as a pancake breakfast in January, a dance in February, an auction

in March—you get the picture.
Hangouts: Mae's Phinney Ridge Cafe ("Graze at Mae's"), where tradition calls for Sunday morning gatherings over cinnamon rolls and coffee; Honey Bear Bakery (in Wallingford, but a big draw for the Ridge loungers), 74th Street Ale House.
Worth a detour: You'll find public art amid the animals and humans at the Woodland Park Zoo. A few examples: *Crocodile Mural,* made of stained glass and ceramic tiles, at the Tropical House; *Mesa,* a bronze picnic table near the zoo's north entry; a life-size, touchable bronze baby elephant in the Elephant Forest exhibit; ceramic-tile murals above the interior portals of the Elephant Barn; and lowland gorilla sculptures in the Tropical Rain Forest.

WALLINGFORD

Wallingford's proximity to the University of Washington is one reason for its sense of artsy excitement, but the UW's role in the community isn't all positive. Wallingford has long been a quiet, middle-class neighborhood, and residents fear that as the UW moves closer with its planned expansion, housing prices will rise and pressure for apartments will increase.

Nestled as it is by Green Lake, the University, and Fremont, Wallingford is one of the best close-in locations in the city. Residents know that and are especially proud of their area. Wallingford got a facelift during the 1980s with the development of Wallingford Center in an old school building, the establishment of the 45th Street Community Clinic, and the rehab of the Good Shepherd home.

Not everyone in the neighborhood is thrilled with what happened to the Good Shepherd Center, however. It's run by the Historic Seattle Preservation and Development Authority and is not so much a community center as a building for nonprofits. The Wallingford Senior Center, however, is in the building.

"**W**allingford is old folks,

it's young couples, it's young singles

in group-living situations, it's mixed-up

socially and economically."

WALLINGFORD RESIDENT

Wallingford houses are old Seattle bungalows, for the most part, and a few of the corner groceries that have always graced the neighborhood are still to be found. The population is primarily under-30s, with a high percentage of families.

History
Wallingford was one of the city's early residential neighborhoods for the middle class, with tracts of houses going up toward the end of the 1890s. When the gasworks plant was operating in the early part of the 1900s, Wallingford was industrial and plagued by air pollution, but after the plant closed, the air became clean again (well, as clean as anywhere in the city).

Stats
Rough boundaries: N: N 55th St. and McKinley Pl. N; S: Lake Union; E: I-5; W: Stone Way N or Aurora Ave. N.
Population: 12,203
Median age: 31
Median income: $29,070/household
Zoning: Primarily single-family residences, mixed with apartments.
Housing: 29.48% own, 70.52% rent
Rent: $471/month
House value: $153,650

Institutions
District Council: Lake Union
NSC: Fremont

Movers and shakers: Wallingford Community Council, Wallingford Chamber of Commerce.
Local media: *North Seattle Outlook/ University Herald, North Seattle Press*
Police precinct: North
Crime watch groups: Block watch
Causes: Traffic along N 45th Street, parking in residential neighborhoods, car prowls, protection of single-family areas from apartment development, the effect of the proposed Rapid Transit Project on the area, keeping the Wallingford-Wilmot Public Library operating, and the future of the closed Lincoln High School building.
Public perks: Gas Works Park, Wallingford Playground, Meridian Playground, Seattle Tilth, Wallingford-Wilmot Library, Latona Elementary School, Hamilton Middle School.

Fun stuff
Beyond the malls: Along N 45th, groceries, bakeries, taverns, ethnic restaurants, and the Guild 45th movie theater.
Celebrations: Seafair Wallingford Kiddies Parade, Wallingford Wurst Festival in September.
Hangouts: Julia's, Goldies, Jitterbug, Teahouse Kuan Yin, Wallingford Center, Honey Bear Bakery, Wide World Books & Maps, Dick's Drive-In, Stone Way Cafe, The Blue Star Cafe & Pub, Murphy's Pub.
Worth a detour: The Erotic Bakery on N 45th Street. Enough said.

NORTHEAST

Northeast Seattle neighborhoods include Laurelhurst, Maple Leaf, Ravenna, University District, and View Ridge.

LAURELHURST
Laurelhurst, which includes Windermere, has long been an upscale, wealthy neighborhood of manicured lawns and well-kept houses. The residents tend to be professionals; the streets are quiet during the afternoons, with only hired landscapers visible.

This is a tight-knit community, with its hub in the community center and school Parent Teacher Association. It's protective—one example of the residents' determination is their fight to prevent a health club facility from moving in.

Laurelhurst's biggest crime problem is residential burglaries. It had a land use controversy a while back with the 'copter pad at Children's Hospital and Medical Center, and now residents are keeping an eye out for any expansion plans by the hospital or Battelle Research Center.

History
The name "Laurelhurst" was coined by McLaughlin Realty, and indeed much of the neighborhood's history is a history of real estate development. There were characters, to be sure—"Uncle Joe" (William) Surber, Seattle's first police chief (and entire force!) homesteaded on 80 acres of Union Bay land, on what was to become the town of Yesler.

Henry Yesler funded the mill town until his two mills burned to the ground. It was a tightly knit place, and in 1900, 50 well-to-do men built the Seattle Golf Club there. Eventually, the club moved to Ballard, and three developers—Joseph McLaughlin, Frank Mead, and Paul Murphy—bought some of the golf course, some of the Surber property, and property belonging to Ellen Little Price, whose mansion, Colonsay, was a landmark.

The developers sold lots for as little as $1,000. Then the lake was lowered, and some lakeside homes were left with their docks high and dry—which later on made for some lawns sweeping down to the water. Sacred Heart Villa, then a children's home, moved there in 1918, to a site chosen by Mother Frances Cabrini. For some time prior to the development of University Village, the Laurelhurst shopping district was the main business area east of the U District. In 1920, the Laurelhurst Improvement Club was established to beautify and protect the area; it later became the Laurelhurst Community Council.

Stats

Rough boundaries: N: Sand Point Way N; S: Union Bay; E: Lake Washington; W: 37th Ave. NE.
Population: 7,433
Median age: 38
Median income: $52,137/household
Zoning: Single-family, few apartments
Housing: 73% own, 27% rent
Rent: $438 (census)
House value: $305,200 (613 houses valued at over $400,000)

Institutions

District Council: Northeast
NSC: University
Movers and shakers: Laurelhurst Community Club, Windermere Corporation.
Local media: *North Central Outlook/ University Herald, North Seattle Press*
Police precinct: North
Crime watch groups: Crime Watch, block watch
Causes: Expansion of surrounding facilities, opposition to new businesses in the residential area, UW growth.
Public perks: Laurelhurst Community

Center (which has programs for seniors and youth), Laurelhurst Elementary School.

Fun stuff

Beyond the malls: Main commercial strip is on Sand Point Way NE, centered at NE 45th Street; mostly retail with small upscale storefronts and some professional buildings.
Celebrations: Annual salmon bake first Thursday in August, home tour in the fall.
Hangouts: Mr. Peeper's Gifts, La Fleur restaurant, Great Harvest Bread Co., Sand Point Thriftway.
Worth a detour: The gardens at Children's Hospital, 4800 Sand Point Way NE. Across from Parking Lot 3, unusual border plants are arranged in delightful color combinations in an English country-garden style, running along the sidewalk and down a staggered flight of steps. Other landscaped areas include an extensive heather collection housed near Lot 6 at the southeast corner of the hospital.

MAPLE LEAF

Ask anyone in Maple Leaf about their neighborhood and they'll tell you that it won the national Neighborhood of the Year Award before neighborhood activism was an "in" thing. And they'll tell you about their logo, a maple leaf (of course) that is everywhere, including the water tower.

Maple Leaf evolved in the recent past from a middle-class, family community to a mostly retired community, and now it's swinging back toward the young people again. Lots of first-time home buyers are choosing small but affordable homes on the woodsy side streets. The elementary schools in the area are a big draw, as are two private schools.

Ironically enough, this neighborhood that was the driving force for Northgate and its malls in the first place is now feeling the impact from Northgate expansion, mostly in increased traffic.

Also spilling over from Maple

Leaf's northern neighbor is a problem with car prowls and car theft. Plans are to counter it by reinvigorating the block watch.

Maple Leaf residents have an intense interest in determining the area's future. They have quarterly neighborhood meetings, including one that's a sort of town-hall gathering to set the political agenda for the year.

Stats

Rough boundaries: N: NE 103rd St.; S: NE 75th St.; E: Lake City Way NE; W: I-5.
Population: 7,748
Median age: 36.3
Median income: $35,134/household
Zoning: Mostly single-family, with increasing number of apartment and condo units on the north edge.
Housing: 70.5% own, 29.5% rent
Rent: $480/month
House value: $130,150

Institutions

District Council: North
NSC: Lake City
Movers and shakers: Maple Leaf Community Council
Local media: Quarterly community council newsletter, *North Seattle Press*
Police precinct: North

Crime watch groups: Block watch, North Precinct Advisory Committee.
Causes: Traffic running through the neighborhood, land use, playground improvement. Community council has a Dollars for Scholars program to give scholarships to 4–5 students who need extra help.
Public perks: Maple Leaf Park and Playground, Sacajawea Playground, Sacajawea and Olympic View elementary schools.

Fun stuff

Beyond the malls: Business core NE 84th to NE 98th streets on Roosevelt; also some on Fifth Avenue NE near 85th. Some specialty shops such as metal manufacturing and plywood sales and model railroads.
Celebrations: Annual rummage sale in August at Olympic View

Elementary School to raise money for matching grants.

Hangouts: Maple Leaf Park for picnics, Reservoir Tavern, Maple Leaf Grill.

Worth a detour: The Camp Fire Boys and Girls Museum, in the basement of the Seattle-area council's headquarters at 8511 15th Avenue NE. Memorabilia on display include a 1913 Bluebird outfit, vintage cookbooks, and a shrine to various vintages of Camp Fire Mints, a prime fund-raising tool of the organization. It's free, but by appointment only: 461-8550.

RAVENNA-BRYANT

The standard saying about green Ravenna Park is "You feel like you're in the Cascades when you're actually in the middle of the city." The park is a critical part of this green neighborhood of lovely family houses and leafy trees.

Ravenna-Bryant is close to one of the city's largest employers (UW) and used to be filled with UW profs, a characteristic that's not so true these days. Residents are professionals for the most part, but, since the neighborhood is also close to I-5, they are not necessarily connected with the university.

It's a fairly self-contained community. With the University Village shopping center, a vibrant Puget Consumers' Co-op, bagels and espresso, schools and parks—what more could you need?

The community is working hard to make this the best neighborhood for families in the city. They've worked with the city to improve traffic flow—successfully, for the most part—and have succeeded in reducing crime in the area.

History

Ravenna's green character is due to the long wooded ravine through which flows the creek connecting Green Lake and Lake Washington. It was purchased in 1888 by the Rev. and Mrs. Beck and turned into Ravenna Park. Visitors—including

Got graffiti on your walls? Don't give up. To report graffiti, call 684-PKUP. If you want to paint it out, call the city's anti-graffiti coordinator, Sue Honaker, 684-5004. She organizes community groups to paint out graffiti and has a paint bank of 2,000 gallons in colors from purple to pukey green, and instructions for what treatment to use on any surface. The city tracks gang hot spots and hate graffiti, so be sure to record whatever is written before you do away with it. If a wall is repeatedly hit, the city will organize the painting of a mural there. Murals are generally free from vandalism, probably because would-be graffiti artists recognize them as belonging to somebody. To stop graffiti, says Honaker, all you have to do is pick up a paintbrush and continue to paint it out. "You can't let a vandal condition you to say, 'Why bother?' You have to condition the *vandal* to say that." Usually it takes only two attempts and they give up. The city spends $3 million annually to cover graffiti.

Theodore Roosevelt—paid a quarter to get in. In 1910 the city bought the park and diverted the waters of Green Lake into a sewer line, leaving the creek to be fed only through the many springs that are still to be seen along the paths there.

Stats

Rough boundaries:
N: NE 75th St.; S: Ravenna Park, University Village, and Calvary Cemetery; E: 35th Ave. NE; W: 15th Ave. NE.
Population: 6,887
Median age: 37.15
Median income: $32,468/household
Zoning: Predominantly single-family.
Housing: 65.3% own, 34.7% rent.
Rent: $500/month (census)
House value: $138,000 (census); $250,000+ (conventional wisdom)

Institutions

District Council: Northeast
NSC: University
Movers and shakers: Ravenna-Bryant Community Council, Ravenna Springs Community Council, Ravenna Creek Alliance, University Village Merchants Association.
Local media: *North Seattle Press*
Police precinct: North
Crime watch groups: Block watch
Causes: Making Ravenna Creek into a "greenway" through the neighborhood, restoring Ravenna Park, improving playfield.
Public perks: Ravenna Park and Playground, Ravenna-Eckstein Community Center, Bryant Elementary School, Eckstein Middle School, Roosevelt High School.

Fun stuff

Beyond the malls: NE 65th Street with eateries gathered near 21st Avenue NE, little corner stores like Puget Consumers' Co-op at 20th Avenue NE and Espresso Express at 15th Avenue NE.
Celebrations: At Christmastime, the houses on Park Road, south of Ravenna Park, turn their cul-de-sac into Candy Cane Lane. Residents set out luminaries so they can walk to

see the decorations instead of joining the throngs in traffic. Neighbors also join in park cleanups and ice cream socials.

Hangouts: Santa Fe Cafe, Bagel Oasis, Guido's Pizza, PCC.

Worth a detour: Ravenna Park is a truly spectacular city park. It is several degrees cooler down inside the ravine than up top, and there are plenty of places for picnics up top too. Residents say Calvary Cemetery is a good place to muse over gravestones of nuns and priests. No ghosts reported, though.

UNIVERSITY DISTRICT

The University District has about 22,000 residents, 10,000 of them students. That makes it a college town within the city, a stimulating, cultural experience for the rest of Seattle and a home away from home for students.

Central to the U District is the Ave, actually University Way, where the University Book Store serves as the anchor for a conglomeration of eclectic businesses—everything from used clothing stores to espresso spots to bong boutiques. Cheap and often good eating places dot the area; ethnic cafes abound.

The Ave evolved the last few years into a hangout for the city's stray and wanna-be stray kids. Most of those you see hanging around the street corners aren't UW students; they're high school or just-beyond kids who know where the drug action is. There are lots of panhandlers too; in fact, they hover around the Safeway store, making sure shoppers run the gauntlet of creative requests for spare change. This mix of characters has created a worrisome problem: People say they are scared to use cash machines at night, and crime is on the rise.

But in the midst of that activity is another kind. The neighborhood is vibrant: Couples flock to movie theaters, Meany Hall draws the cultural crowd, and the small stores attract shoppers from all over. The huge concentration of churches, given the dynamics of the rest of the place, is somewhat thought-provoking. The University Book Store is treated by its neighbors as a kind of personal library, the UW campus with its cherry trees and squirrels as a backyard.

But residents worry about the image of the Ave and about expansion under way currently at the UW. And they worry that developers will prevail in an ongoing fight over height limits.

History

Brooklyn was the first community to spring up in the U District and was annexed to Seattle in 1891. The UW moved from downtown to the present site in 1895. In 1909, the Alaska-Yukon Pacific Exposition put the U District on the map, as did the digging of the Montlake Cut linking Lake Washington and Lake Union.

Stats

Rough boundaries: N: Ravenna Blvd.; S: Portage Bay; E: 25th Ave. NE; W: I-5.

Population: 21,951

Median age: 24.05 (ages 18–21 dominate near the UW)

Median income: $16,497/household

Zoning: Much of the neighborhood is multi-unit apartments, many housing students. But as far as land area is concerned, about 60% is zoned single-family. Most of the multi-family units are south and west, closest to the UW; single-family houses are to the north.

Housing: 17.05% own, 82.95% rent

Rent: $384/month

House value: $157,625

Institutions

District Council: Northeast

NSC: University

Movers and shakers: University Park Community Club, University District Community Council, Greater University District Chamber of Commerce.

Local media: *North Central Outlook/ University Herald*, *North Seattle Press*, *The Daily* (UW's student paper). While not really locally oriented, KUOW radio (the UW's National Public Radio affiliate) and KCMU radio (a more counter-cultural UW station) do talk about events and issues in the area.

Police precinct: North

Crime watch groups: University District Crime Prevention Council

Causes: Traffic, especially during events at the UW—Montlake, University Way, NE 45th, and NE 50th streets are bottlenecks. Also drugs, UW campus expansion, graffiti, litter, parking, the fate of the University Heights school building.

Public perks: UW campus, University branch of the Seattle Public Library, Cowen and Ravenna parks, YMCA, YWCA, Talmadge Hamilton House (Senior Center), University Service League (operates University District Food Bank), University Adult Day Center (for the elderly and impaired), University Latch Key program, University District Youth Center.

Fun stuff

Beyond the malls: The Ave (which isn't an avenue at all, but University Way) is pedestrian-oriented, with shops and the University Book Store. University Village is more 'burboriented with parking and mall-like atmosphere. Roosevelt Way is auto-oriented, but with several neighborhood shops and hangouts up toward 65th. Moviegoers can choose from the Grand Illusion, Metro, Neptune, Seven Gables, and Varsity theaters.

Celebrations: University Street Fair in May, Greek Week in May (includes beer drinking, getting sick, water balloon contests, and other fine intellectual activities on Greek Row), opening day of boating season in May (includes beer and martini drinking—often by the parents of those who participated in Greek Week), crew races, Husky football in the fall.

Hangouts: By George in the UW undergrad library, the HUB (student union building), The Big Time Ale House, Giggles Comedy Nite Club, Allegro Espresso Bar, Espresso Roma.

Worth a detour: There's no more fabulous place to curl up with a book than the soft chairs in the vast, Gothic Graduate Reading Room in the UW's Suzzallo Library. Light streams through tall, arched stained-glass windows and from the room's two dozen chandeliers. At the south end, check out the living-room–like alcove with armchairs, floor lamps, and wood-paneled walls. To find the room, go through the library's main entrance and up the wide, curving stairs, and enter the room to your left.

VIEW RIDGE

If you went to the UW, you probably know someone who lives here. View Ridge is home to many UW profs and staff and has the distinction of cozying up to Magnuson Park. That has its advantages and, apparently, disadvantages: The community succeeded in closing down the Magnuson Park archery range after park neighbors had some close calls with stray arrows.

This is a pretty wealthy, upscale neighborhood—a sort of cousin to neighboring Windermere and Laurelhurst. Sand Point Country Club is here, for example.

Stats

Rough boundaries: N: NE 85th St., Inverness Dr.; S: Sand Point Way NE; E: Lake Washington; W: 35th Ave. NE.
Population: 13,290
Median age: 40.2 (about 20% are over 65)
Median income: $43,000/household (north); $35,932/household (south)
Zoning: Mostly single-family detached
Housing: 75.6% own, 24.4% rent
Rent: $545/month
House value: $188,875 (118 houses valued at over $400,000)

Institutions

District Council: Northeast

NSC: University
Movers and shakers: View Ridge Community Club
Local media: *North Central Outlook/ University Herald, North Seattle Press*
Police precinct: North
Crime watch groups: Crime Watch, block watch, Seattle Anti-Arson Foundation
Causes: Closure of Sand Point Naval Base and monitoring the future of the property, UW growth.
Public perks: Burke-Gilman Trail, North East Library, Magnuson Park, National Oceanic and Atmospheric Adminstration grounds, Bryant Playground, View Ridge Elementary School.

Property Tax Assessments

Typical residential property value and tax by school district. The levy rate is the number of dollars owed per $1,000 of assessed property value.

District	Average valuation 1995-96	Typical 1996 tax levy rate
Auburn	$121.100	$15.11
Bellevue	$251,800	$12.36
Enumclaw	$140,200	$14.17
Federal Way	$132,000	$15.52
Highline	$129,200	$13.64
Issaquah	$213,200	$14.49
Kent	$136,200	$15.91
Lake Washington	$189,600	$14.14
Mercer Island	$364,900	$11.72
Northshore	$186,300	$16.00
Renton	$128,800	$14.07
Riverview	$159,000	$15.03
Seattle	$169,850	$12.96
Shoreline	$167,800	$16.31
Skykomish	$63,000	$10.88
Snoqualmie Valley	$153,700	$14.88
South Central	$96,400	$15.13
Tahoma	$150,400	$14.95
Vashon Island	$180,500	$14.34

Source: King County Assessor's Office

Fun stuff

Beyond the malls: Albertson's, Puget Consumers' Co-op at NE 65th Street and 40th Avenue NE.

Community events: Community club annual meetings (called anniversaries) and monthly meetings, lots of events for Little League, Boy Scouts, etc.

Hangouts: The Sand Point Church is a hub, La Fleur restaurant, Salute (toward Ravenna), and nearby University Village.

Worth a detour: Near the National Oceanic and Atmospheric Administration buildings at Sand Point is Douglas Hollis's ingenious sculpture *A Sound Garden,* a collection of flutelike aluminum tubes that create eerie music as the wind blows. *A Sound Garden* is one of several pieces of public art along the beach, which adjoins Magnuson Park; look for a directory sign as you approach.

EAST

East Seattle includes Capitol Hill, the Central District, Eastlake, Leschi, Madison, Madrona, and Montlake.

CAPITOL HILL

Capitol Hill, which includes Stevens, Broadway, and Miller Park, has gone through gyrations of character, and part of its charm is that vestiges of each remain. Dick's Drive-In, for example, is a holdover from the groovy days and before; Holy Names Academy atop the hill marks the haven of large Catholic families that once lived in the huge classic box houses, many of which are now apartments or had been converted, first to apartments, then back to single-family homes again.

On Broadway, the scene is a mélange: gays walking hand-in-hand, grungers, upscale yuppies hitting the restaurants and movies, and senior citizens stopping in at the friendly QFC supermarket. Volunteer Park has a subculture of its own: nights a gay cruising place, days a

place to walk the dog and let the kids wade. The strip on 15th Avenue E is filled with would-be bohemians and doctor and nurse types from Group Health.

Gay groups say the population on the Hill is about 30–40% gay. Gay bashing has been a problem, mostly on the south hill.

Developers claim the areas in south Capitol Hill, along Pike and Pine streets and 10th to 12th avenues, are ripe for a wave of development. Once known as "Auto Row," it's now mostly office buildings and arts/entertainment facilities. Fifty-four percent of the buildings there are worth less than the land they sit on.

History

Capitol Hill was one of the city's prestigious early neighborhoods, with its fine big houses and its large park, first named City Park and then, after the Spanish-American War, Volunteer Park.

Stats

Rough boundaries: N: E Howe St.; S: E Madison; E: Interlaken Blvd.; W: I-5.

Population: 30,150

Median age: 33.5

Median income: $25,375/household (higher east of Broadway, lower west).

Zoning: Primarily 5+ unit structures, single-family homes, several group home facilities in Pike/Pine corridor.

Housing: 20% own, 80% rent (except east of 15th Ave. E near E Galer St., where 73% own).

Rent: $420/month

House value: $174,785 (census); $325,000 east of 15th Ave. E

Institutions

District Council: First Hill/Capitol Hill/Madison Park

NSC: Capitol Hill

Movers and shakers: Friends of Volunteer Park, Broadway Business Improvement Association, Capitol Park Council, Capitol Hill Community Council, Miller Park Neighborhood Association, Neighbors of

Holy Names, Pike-Union Corridor Steering Committee, First Hill Community Council, Capitol Hill Association for Parity (CHAP).

Local media: Capitol Hill Chamber newsletter, *Capitol Hill Times, Seattle Gay News*

Police precinct: East

Crime watch groups: Block watch, East Precinct Crime Prevention Coalition, The Q-Street Patrol.

Causes: Opposing siting of more congregate (group) housing in the neighborhood (the city can't regulate what's already there, residents say), the shape of development along Pine and Pike; on the north side of the hill, potential widening of Highway 520. Crime prevention is a big issue; in fact, the community council gave its Spirit Award to the East Precinct as a pat on the back. There's also an active (and successful) voucher program addressing panhandling.

Public perks: Henry Library, Miller Community Center, Community House; Boren, Interlaken, and Volunteer parks; Lowell and Stevens elementary schools, Meany Middle School, Cornish College of the Arts, Seattle Central Community College.

Neighborhood heroes: The late state representative Cal Anderson; city council member Jim Street.

Fun stuff

Beyond the malls: Small shops, myriad of restaurants, gourmet and gift shops, expensive boutiques, and large supermarkets—you name it. On Broadway, there are lots of places (e.g., Broadway Market) to pick up your attire of choice: Doc Martens and grunge, 1960s holdovers, and ethnic costumes all can be found. Theaters abound, both for movies (Broadway Market, Egyptian, Harvard Exit) and performing arts. On 15th Avenue E it's more homey and small town with little groceries, delis, and trinket shops scattered along a five-block strip.

Celebrations: Weekend street fair on 10th Avenue between Pike and Pine, gay pride parade in June.

Hangouts: Dilettante Chocolates,

B & O Espresso, Pacific Dessert Company, Deluxe Bar & Grill, La Cocina & Cantina, Charlie's, Neighbours, Ileen's Sports Bar, Surrogate Hostess, Espresso Roma, Gravity Bar.

Worth a detour: Lake View Cemetery, where the city's early elite—the Denny family, Doc Maynard, Chief Seattle's daughter Angeline—are buried; 15th Avenue E just north of Volunteer Park. Also, the General Petroleum Museum at Bellevue Avenue E and Pine Street, containing "petroleana" assembled by a retired Mobil Oil employee. You can't miss the neon Pegasus in the second-story window. It's free, but call first: 323-4789.

CENTRAL DISTRICT

Called the CD by almost everyone (and the Central Area by the rest), the Central District was settled by African Americans after World War II when Seattle's black population boomed. It's still a predominantly African American community today, with its roots in the churches, especially Mt. Zion Baptist Church, and its leadership in both the churches and the Seattle Urban League. Our description of the neighborhood includes Squire Park, Judkins Rejected, and Garfield.

Racial tension, crime, gangs, and economic depression have failed to daunt the spirit of the people. The Central Area Motivation Program (CAMP) is crucial to the neighborhood, with housing help, emergency services, jobs, home repair, rental space for meetings, and more. It also serves as a community hub.

The retail area of the CD is small, and that's one of the big pushes for the next few years. The mayor convened a citizens group, the Central Area Planning Committee, to attract developers. Black residents are being encouraged to support local black businesses and to open more businesses in keeping with the income level of the neighborhood.

History

William Grose bought land from Henry Yesler, and the Central District was born. Grose was the first CD landlord; his property ran along E Madison Street and included the hub of the new black community at 23rd Avenue and E Madison. The first community church was First African Methodist Episcopal. Later, another section of the CD, along Jackson Street, developed. You can read about it in *History of Seattle Central Area* by DeCharlene Williams, published by the Central Area Chamber of Commerce, 325-2864.

Legends: The old Mardi Gras Parade, which many in the CD claim was the forerunner to Seafair, was an elaborate affair in the '40s and '50s, with costumes, lots of music and food. It kicked off a week of dancing in the streets, right where the old Birdland nightclub, the hot spot for musicians from all over, used to be.

Stats

Rough boundaries: N: E Madison St.; S: I-90; E: Martin Luther King Jr. Way S; W: 12th Ave.
Population: 5,175 in CD proper; some say 36,000 in entire area, including Madrona, part of the ID, and part of Capitol Hill.
Median age: 37
Median income: $15,450/household
Zoning: About equal numbers of single-family and multi-family units
Housing: 30.95% own, 69.05% rent
Rent: $450/month (apartment); $550/month (small house)
House value: $100,000; some available for less as part of inner-city housing incentive program.

Institutions

District Council: Central
NSC: Central
Movers and shakers: Central Area Planning Committee, I Love Jackson Street Business Association, Central Area Neighborhood Association, Central Area Motivation Program, Seattle Urban League, Central Area Chamber of Commerce; Squire Park, Judkins Rejected, Plum Tree Park, Garfield, Harrison Denny, and Jackson Place South community councils.
Local media: *The Facts, The Medium*

Police precinct: East
Crime watch groups: East Precinct Crime Prevention Coalition, Central Area Neighbors Against Drugs (organizes marches against drug peddlers).
Causes: Crime and gangs, I-90 access ramps between I-5 and Lake Washington that have cut through the neighborhood, economic development, financing for small business, more retail businesses to service everybody, public safety.
Public perks: Judkins Park, Garfield Community Center, Langston Hughes Cultural Arts Center, Medgar Evers Pool, Douglass-Truth Library, Pratt Park and Arts Center; Colman, Minor, and Gatzert elementary schools, Washington Middle School, Garfield High School, Seattle University.
Neighborhood heroes: Lots of heroes, beginning with Rev. Dr. Samuel McKinney, pastor of Mt. Zion Baptist Church; Dr. Roz Woodhouse, Seattle Urban League; Marie Edwards, founder of Edwards Beauty School in the 1940s, which educated thousands of young blacks for careers in hair design; Rev. Robert Jeffrey, New Hope Baptist Church; DeCharlene Williams, Central Area Chamber of Commerce; Larry Gossett, CAMP.

Fun stuff

Beyond the malls: The commercial area is comb-shaped, with one "tooth" of the comb on E Madison Street from 12th to 15th avenues and further on down from 18th to 24th. Then there's a section on E Union Street from 15th down to 25th. The very brightly painted Cherry Street business area is from 23rd down to 30th. On Jackson Street, there is a strip of auto shops and small stores, the Central NSC, and at 23rd and Jackson, the Promenade 23 shopping center. Other centers are developing. On Rainier Avenue south of Dearborn Street (arguably in Beacon Hill, but used by CD residents) there are some eclectic places: Remo Borracchini's Italian Bakery and Mediterranean Market, Mutual Fish, and the Imperial Bowling Lanes.

Celebrations: Neighborhood "Bite"; May Day Fair; Kids Fair; Black Community Festival at Judkins Park; Kwanzaa (African Christmas); Juneteenth (June 17), a celebration of African American history with bands, picnic, exhibits, etc. at Gas Works Park.

Hangouts: Dill PickleOs, Catfish Corner, Ms. Helen's Soul Food restaurant, Philadelphia Fevre Steak & Hoagie Shop, Mama's Kitchen, Ezell's Fried Chicken.

Worth a detour: The African-American Reading Room in the Douglass-Truth branch of the Seattle Public Library, at 23rd Avenue and E Yesler Way. It contains over 7,000 volumes, including a collection of over 500 children's books that illustrate how African Americans have been portrayed in children's literature throughout the years.

EASTLAKE

Houses go down, luxury apartments go up. Industrial businesses fold, speculative office developers move in. That's Eastlake for you.

This little area around the eastern edge of Lake Union has long been known for its industrial/houseboat/residential mix, but the mix is rapidly changing. Office buildings (cheaper to build here than in downtown Seattle) are rapidly filling in any empty spaces, and the name Bruce Blume (a Seattle office building developer) has become a household phrase, not always used in a complimentary way.

Also here are some Fred Hutchinson Cancer Center facilities and the giant Marriott Residence Inn. The Center for Wooden Boats still holds court down at the southern tip of the lake, but further up toward the University Bridge, the office buildings are in control. (And the wooden boats are now watched by hundreds of diners at all those flashy new restaurants along South Lake Union.)

But all is not lost: there is still the occasional visit from a raccoon or beaver, and Canada geese should be the official Eastlake mascot. The houseboat community is still the country's largest and most picturesque, and Ward's Cove, on Fairview Avenue E, provides the Alaska fishing fleet with a home away from home.

Seaplane noise has been a big issue, especially for the houseboat owners. But the biggest issue of all is commercial development. As one activist says, "If the activists are successful, it will be a neighborhood. If not, it will be paved over for office buildings and human warehouses."

Those activists have not been complacent; they've put together the Eastlake Tomorrow project, which proposes such improvements as barriers to block noise from I-5, building design guidelines, a town center along Eastlake Avenue, and a redesign of Fairview Avenue to connect the shoreline parks with trails.

History

Before 1900, Eastlake was forested and threaded with Indian trails; then it was cleared for orchards and farms. By 1910, houseboats were being built for the working class, and by the '20s came a boom of apartment houses as Eastlake Avenue became the main north/south arterial.

In the 1960s, I-5 came through, carving up the neighborhood. In the early '70s, neighborhood activists began organizing to try to reunify the area. In fact, one of the most memorable events in Eastlake history was the Battle of Roanoke Reef. Developers proposed an over-water condo project and were met with a phalanx of activists with spears drawn. This cause célèbre resulted in environmental laws that protect public shoreline—and, of course, the condo idea was deep-sixed.

Stats

Rough boundaries: N: University Bridge; S: old City Light steam plant (now ZymoGenetics) on Eastlake Ave. E; E: I-5; W: Lake Union.
Population: 3,000
Median age: 33.5
Median income: $32,000/household
Zoning: Some single-family houses and houseboats, more low-rise apartments, commercial on Eastlake and Fairview avenues.
Housing: 23.7% own, 76.3% rent; the neighborhood is a mix of students, seniors, and in-home and downtown workers.
Rent: $471/month
House value: $275,000 (census)

Institutions

District Council: Lake Union
NSC: Fremont
Movers and shakers: Eastlake Community Council, Floating Homes Association.
Local media: *Lake Union Review, North Seattle Press*
Police precinct: East
Crime watch groups: East Precinct Crime Prevention Coalition
Causes: Overdevelopment, gentrification, destruction of single-family housing, loss of Seward School as a neighborhood elementary, parking, traffic, noise, no public meeting room, view blockage.
Public perks: Seward School (now housing an alternative school), Roanoke Park, street-end parks (Newton, Lynn, Hamlin), Fairview Bike Trail.
Neighborhood heroes: Bill Keasler, longtime Floating Homes Association president; Carol Eychaner and Chris Leman, former community council presidents; Jules James, proprietor of Lake Union Mail.

Fun stuff

Beyond the malls: Some funky places such as the original Red Robin restaurant, Lake Union Mail, Patrick's Fly Shop, small groceries and bars on Eastlake Avenue, marine uses on Fairview Avenue mixed in with new restaurants.
Hangouts: Tio's Bakery & Cafe, Lake Union Mail, Pete's Market (with an extensive wine selection), Pazzo's, 14 Carrot Cafe (for breakfast), Daly's (for burgers), The Zoo tavern (for beer).
Sidewalk chatter: "What happens in Eastlake this year will happen to your neighborhood next year."

LESCHI

Leschi is being discovered once again, much as it was when the streetcar ran from downtown Seattle to Lake Washington, bringing picnickers and residents. The slopes of Leschi are filling in with new buildings; summertime visitors are making parking impossible.

But what can you expect when you live in a beautiful place on the water? This is probably Seattle's hilliest neighborhood, with streets that wend their way up the hills in a series of dead ends and narrow lanes. The houses cling to the hillsides, all vying with each other for a peek at the lake.

The neighborhood was designated a recreation area by the Olmsted brothers in their 1903 plan for Seattle's parks and boulevards, and the residents are still attempting to preserve Leschi's portion of that plan. To see how, walk or drive the Olmsted Legacy Scenic Loop.

The neighborhood consists of loyal, liberal longtime residents mixed with newcomers.

Leschi gets lots of visitors. Trouble is, not everyone enjoying the area treats it with care: speeding along Lake Washington Boulevard is a huge problem. Combine pedestrians, bikes, and speeding cars and, well, you get the picture.

History

Leschi was named after Leschi, a Nisqually chief who refused to be shunted off to a reservation. Leschi was hung after an Indian attack left early settlers dead, but was later recognized as the scapegoat blamed for harm stemming from unfair treaties.

Stats

Rough boundaries: N: E Cherry St.; S: S Norman St.; E: Lake Washington; W: Martin Luther King Jr. Way S.
Population: 4,218
Median age: 33.7
Median income: $28,941/household
Zoning: Single-family detached and apartments
Housing: 48.9% own, 51.1% rent

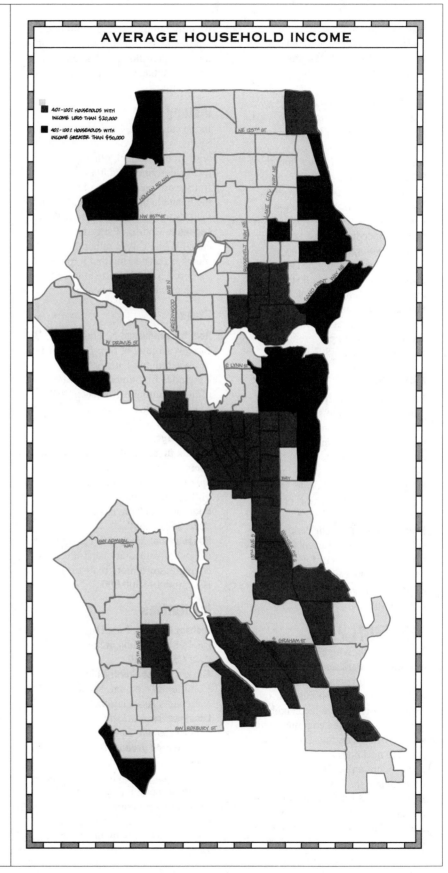

AVERAGE HOUSEHOLD INCOME

40%–100% HOUSEHOLDS WITH INCOME LESS THAN $20,000

40%–100% HOUSEHOLDS WITH INCOME GREATER THAN $50,000

Rent: $500/month
House value: $250,000–$350,000 with view; $180,000 without

Institutions

District Council: Central
NSC: Central
Movers and shakers: Leschi Improvement Council
Local media: *Leschi News* (monthly)
Police precinct: East
Crime watch groups: Block watch, East Precinct Crime Prevention Coalition.
Causes: Speeding traffic, crime, drugs, development and land use (e.g., overbuilding on the slopes), future of the vacant Shell station site on Lake Washington Boulevard.
Public perks: Frink and Leschi parks, public boat moorage, senior center, Barnett and Peppi playgrounds, Leschi Elementary School.

Fun stuff

Beyond the malls: Upscale shops along the lake, radio stations, restaurants, deli, bike shop. Steve, at the Leschi Market, makes great nitrate-free sausages.
Celebrations: Annual park cleanup
Hangouts: Leschi Lakecafe, BBQ concession stand in lakefront park, Pert's Deli.
Worth a detour: Leschi Park, at Lakeside Avenue S and Leschi Place, offers lovely views of Leschi Marina and the sailboats, as well as great swimming along the lake in the summer.

MADISON PARK

Madison Park, which includes Washington Park and Denny Blaine, prides itself on being a little village, self-sufficient to the point that some residents rarely leave the neighborhood. This oasislike community has some of the city's finest old houses, and fine new ones too. It is truly upscale, but unlike Broadmoor or Laurelhurst, the houses are mixed, from small wood-framed homes (and a couple of odd little Moorish stucco ones) to large colonials. The population isn't so mixed: mostly white,

wealthy families and professional types who are fiercely protective of their neighborhood and determined to keep the village atmosphere. They're succeeding.

History

In the early days, Madison Park was Seattle's version of Coney Island, with a Ferris wheel, other amusement rides, and even horse racing. In its more recent past, a ferry from the Eastside brought commuters and visitors to Madison Park until 1951.
Legends: Madison Park used to be called White City, a rather puzzling moniker considering that it referred to the proliferation of prostitutes offering their wares at the beach.

Stats

Rough boundaries: N: Union Bay; E: Lake Washington; S: E Denny Way; W: Washington Park Arboretum. (Excludes Broadmoor, a private, affluent community adjacent to Madison Park.)
Population: 6,458
Median age: 43
Median income: $47,000/household
Zoning: Single-family detached; apartments and condos north of the village toward the lake.
Housing: 58.1% own, 41.9% rent
Rent: $642/month
House value: $384,700 (census) (47% of houses valued at over $400,000); residents say a more realistic average is $250,000–$300,000.

Institutions

District Council: First Hill/ Capitol Hill/Madison Park
NSC: Capitol Hill
Movers and shakers: Madison Park Community Council, Madison Park Merchants Association.
Local media: *Madison Park Times*
Police precinct: East
Crime watch groups: Block watch
Causes: Expansion of Burke–Gilman Trail through Broadmoor and Madison Park (community is divided on the issue); monitoring possible zoning changes that would increase multifamily units; slowing down traffic;

filling hanging baskets for shops.
Public perks: Denny Blaine, Madison, and Viretta parks, Martin Luther King and McGilvra elementary schools.
Neighborhood heroes: Lola McKee, Madison Park Hardware owner— "Everybody knows Lola and Lola knows everybody."

Fun stuff

Beyond the malls: The villagelike commercial center is at the foot of E Madison Street. Varied upscale shops, restaurants, a jeweler, bakery, cheese store, children's clothing, hardware, bookstore, small grocery.
Celebrations: Picnic in the Park, Christmas Ship during the holidays.
Hangouts: The Attic (a destination at night, a lunchtime meeting place), Madison Park Bakery (early morning crowd), Madison Park Cafe, Tully's, Starbucks, The Red Onion.
Sidewalk chatter: "This is utopia if there is such a thing."

MADRONA

If you ask someone where they live in Madrona, they'll say, "Well, y'know where the Hi-Spot is? We're just two blocks down and one over . . ."

Typically, 34th Avenue has been the hub. It's the divider street too; wealthier and whiter to the east, black and lower/middle-income to the west. Some say as the neighborhood becomes more racially mixed, the line is finally blurring.

The crime divider is still 34th, however. Crime concerns on the east side of Madrona have to do with residential burglary, theft, and car theft. On the west side, things are rougher; rape, aggravated assault, robberies, and shootings are all on the list. The crime rate rises and falls with that of the Central District and is currently on the decrease.

From crime, however, can come renewed community spirit, as occurred after the 1985 murder of the Goldmark family in their Madrona home. The community pulled together in its fear and grief and discovered that the spirit existing before Madrona became a trendy place to live was still alive. There is still a small-town feeling.

From bungalows to lakeside mansions, Madrona is as varied architecturally as it is ethnically. Tree-lined streets have some of Seattle's most interesting houses, and the charm of it is that they don't all belong to the wealthy. The neighborhood is filled with artists and writers who thrive on the diversity of the surroundings.

History

Madrona's recent history is one of racial and economic diversity. The Madrona Playfield became known as the stomping ground of the Black Panthers during the late 1960s. They did military drills there, and had their headquarters in a storefront on 34th. At one point, a Madrona housewife decided she'd had it with the military bit and invited the Black Panthers over for tea. The idea was that the community mothers would meet with them and find a common ground for the good of the neighborhood. Three Black Panthers showed up in fatigues to face 20 perfectly coifed white matrons, who asked if the Panthers planned to hurt their children.

The Panthers said they wouldn't do anything to keep the children from being hurt, and that was it. "They had good manners," one mother remembers today.

Because of the tension that had existed, some residents cringed when Richard Beyer included a panther and a pig in the sculpture *Peaceable Kingdom* on the library grounds, but others thought it fitting, given Madrona's history.

Stats

Rough boundaries: N: E Denny Way; S: E Cherry St.; E: Lake Washington; W: 23rd Ave. or Martin Luther King Jr. Way S.
Population: 11,474
Median age: 34.4
Median income: $49,309/household on east, $25,000/household on west
Zoning: Primarily single-family and duplexes
Housing: On east side, 81.7% own, 18.3% rent; on west, 55% own, 45% rent.
Rent: $750/month on the east side (rentals are scarce); $500/month on the west.
House value: $201,854; low is $114,000 on west side, high is $720,000 on east.

Institutions

District Council: Central
NSC: Central
Movers and shakers: Madrona Community Council
Local media: Community council newsletter, *Madison Park Times, The Facts*
Police precinct: East
Crime watch groups: Block watch
Causes: Crime, safety on streets and in parks, promoting the local business area, "working to meet the needs of all and keep the neighborhood as healthy as we can."
Public perks: Larkins and Madrona parks, Madrona Elementary, Nova School, Madrona Dance Studio, Madrona–Sally Goldmark Library, Shelter House (recently renovated community center, available for meetings).

Neighborhood heroes: DeeDee Rainbow, who wears full rainbow garb, can be seen at most Seattle events, carrying a magic wand and handing out balloons to the kids; the late Nora Wood, known as "the mother of Madrona."

Fun stuff

Beyond the malls: 34th Avenue has several small businesses, including hairstylists, caterers, and restaurants.
Celebrations: Home Tour in April, May Fair (community party), neighborhood cleanup in the fall.
Hangouts: The Hi-Spot Cafe is Madrona's "community center"; people also hang out at Cool Hand Luke's.
Sidewalk chatter: "We live in a very unique neighborhood; it's been called 'peaceable kingdom' because we are so ethnically diverse."

MONTLAKE

To the rest of the residents of the city, Montlake is another name for gridlock, but to those who live tucked into the tree-lined streets between Washington Park Arboretum and the Museum of History and Industry (MOHAI), it's a peaceful paradise. Houses are expensive, and rightfully so, since many are old-style mini-mansions and gingerbreaded bungalows. Rumor has it lots of UW profs live in the neighborhood, giving it an intellectual bent (or at least reputation).

Montlake has always been a destination neighborhood, thanks to the always active playfield, MOHAI, and the Arboretum.

History

Before the Montlake Cut, people carried their boats between Lake Washington and Lake Union over a portage about three blocks wide. And back in the 1890s, what may have been Seattle's first bike path was developed along Interlaken Park. (By the way, the lush trees in Interlaken may look old, but they're second growth; the area was logged over like the rest of the city.)

Stats

Rough boundaries: N: Montlake Cut and Hwy. 520 bridge where it passes over Portage Bay; S and W: Interlaken Park; E: Arboretum.
Population: About 2,500
Median age: 37
Median income: $39,561/household (34% make over $50,000)
Zoning: Primarily single-family residential
Housing: 82.3% own, 17.7% rent
Rent: $750–$999/month
House value: $200,000–$400,000 (9% of houses valued at over $400,000)

Institutions

District Council: First Hill/ Capitol Hill/Madison Park
NSC: Capitol Hill
Movers and shakers: Montlake Community Club, Montlake Advisory Council
Local media: *Montlake Flyer*
Police precinct: East
Crime watch groups: Block watch
Causes: Proposed expansion of 520. This issue has raised the hackles of a neighborhood that's been hard-hit by traffic problems in the past. The city put in parking control to solve the problem of UW students cruising to find parking spaces, but there's still a problem with traffic jams during the annual fall festival at Saint Demetrios Church.
Public perks: MOHAI, Washington Park Arboretum, Montlake Library, McCurdy Park, Montlake Community Center, Montlake Elementary School.

Fun stuff

Beyond the malls: Small businesses at 24th Avenue E and E Lynn Street, with a few restaurants and Montlake Bicycle Shop.
Celebrations: Opening day of boating season in May, Saint Demetrios Church Fall Festival.
Hangouts: Grady's Pub and Eatery, The Daily Grind, Cafe Lago.
Worth a detour: Anytime's a good time to visit the Arboretum, but if you'd like a guided tour, show up

at the Visitors Center at 1pm any Sunday (543-8800). Highlights of this 200-acre public park include Azalea Way, the Foster Island nature trail (maps available at the Visitors Center), and the Japanese Garden and teahouse, which presents a tea ceremony every third Saturday afternoon (call 684-4725 for time and admission charge).

SOUTH

South Seattle includes the neighborhoods of Beacon Hill, Columbia City, Georgetown, Mt. Baker, Rainier Valley, Seward Park, and South Park.

BEACON HILL

Beacon Hill's diverse community is reflected in the many small businesses that dot the area. Services range from a full-scale Asian supermarket to small specialty markets. There are a dozen restaurants and delis offering everything from Southern-style barbecue to the Chinese version and, of course, the ubiquitous espresso.

Beacon Hill is as self-sufficient as it sounds. Things are so stable that the average homeowner has been here for 22 years. Seattle's early Asian community settled here, and in the 1980s, many Southeast Asians came to Beacon Hill. Today, that tradition of diversity continues: this is the home of choice for new immigrants from Hong Kong.

It's impossible to refer to just plain "Beacon Hill." North, mid-, and South Beacon Hill and Holly Park are four distinct areas within the neighborhood, a large, rectangular area that reaches lengthwise to the city's southern boundary. The further south you get, the more rural the neighborhood feels, until, in South Beacon Hill, you can still walk along streets that have paths instead of sidewalks.

Over the past few years, community activism on Beacon Hill has

been resurrected, thanks to the efforts of a number of citizen groups and community agencies. One of the most dynamic of the city's social services, El Centro de la Raza, is in North Beacon Hill.

Recently, residents say, some gang activity has moved into heretofore placid North Beacon Hill—and now crime prevention and public safety are the number one issues. The South Seattle Crime Prevention Council is making some headway.

The South Beacon Organizing Project and Holly Park Leaders are two efforts aimed at identifying and training leaders in the community to tackle the area's issues. South Beacon is also the home of the Holly Park Low-Income Housing Project, which has its own activist organizations, the Holly Park Community Council and Holly Park Neighborhood House.

Cultural diversity is Beacon Hill's greatest asset, but it's also the most formidable barrier to the establishment of community identity. Language and cultural barriers make it difficult to rally the community, even on issues that will have profound impacts on residents. But with the continued efforts of the committed groups, as one resident puts it, "Beacon Hill may yet lumber out of its sleep to play an integral role in its future."

History

The settlement of Beacon Hill began in the 1850s, when the first farm on South Beacon Hill was established by Dutch pioneer Henry Van Asselt. His 320-acre claim included the present Boeing Field. Others followed, farming and logging the heavily timbered land.

These early settlements were burned by Chief Leschi in the Indian Wars of 1855–56. Some people left, but Van Asselt stayed to rebuild. A number of years passed, understandably, before permanent residences were built. Two of the three mansions built on the hill are still standing: Judge E.A. Turner's house on 15th Avenue S, built in the 1890s, and Frank Black's home on Massachusetts Street. The third, Summerville Mansion at 28th Avenue S and Juneau, was destroyed in a fire.

Two of the hill's more infamous early buildings are no longer standing. The Pesthouse, built to accommodate those with contagious diseases, and the Lazy Husbands' Ranch, where fathers who neglected their families were sent to work (!), both burned down in 1915.

Beacon Hill was annexed to Seattle in bits and pieces. After World War II, the community experienced rapid growth and change. The predominantly white community was replaced with an integrated one of blacks, whites, Chinese, Japanese, Filipinos, and other ethnic groups. By 1980, Asians accounted for 39% of the population. There was racial tolerance at a time when Asian residential mobility was restricted elsewhere by prejudice. When the Chinese were being driven from Seattle, the Japanese (mostly families) moved away from the hostility and onto the hill.

At one point, Beacon Hill and First Hill were the only areas not strictly controlled as to racial diffusion by real estate covenants. During World War II the Chinese, employed in trades such as shipbuilding and aircraft manufacture, took the place of the interned Japanese in the area.

Stats

Rough boundaries: N: Dearborn St.; S: city limits; E: Rainier Ave. (north of S McClellan St.), then Martin Luther King Jr. Way S; W: I-5 and Airport Way S. (North Beacon Hill is between Dearborn to the north and Columbian Way to the south.)
Population: 30,805
Median age: 33
Median income: $26,274/household
Zoning: Multi-family and single-family housing in North Beacon Hill, single-family in south and central.
Housing: 54% own, 44% rent
Rent: $400/month (apartment), $650/month (2-3–bedroom house)
House value: Around $130,000,

higher on west side near 15th and Columbian Way, lower on east side of hill, as low as $80,000 in south end.

Institutions

District Council: Greater Duwamish
NSC: Greater Duwamish
Movers and shakers: Beacon Hill and Holly Park community councils, South Beacon Hill Steering Committee, North Beacon Hill Coalition, Sturgus Avenue Park Association, Beacon Hill Chamber of Commerce, Comet Lodge Cemetery Association.
Local media: *Beacon Hill News*
Police precinct: South
Crime watch groups: South Seattle Crime Prevention Council, Holly Park Crime Prevention Council, block watch
Causes: Crime prevention, greenbelt preservation, airplane noise, completion of Beacon Avenue median improvement, graffiti and litter, preserving the area's multicultural character. The Sturgus Avenue Park Association is addressing the impact of the I-90 project, and the Chamber is trying to invigorate the business districts.
Public perks: El Centro de la Raza, Pacific Medical Center, Jefferson Park Golf Course, Beacon Hill Library, Holly Park Neighborhood House, Jefferson and Van Asselt community centers, Beacon Hill and Van Asselt playgrounds; Dearborn, Lewis, Sturgus, 37th South, and Viewpoint parks; Beacon Hill, Dearborn Park, Kimball, Maple, Van Asselt, and Wing Luke elementary schools; Mercer Middle School, Cleveland High School.

Fun stuff

Beyond the malls: A print shop, antique store, dress shop, old-fashioned barbershop, full-scale hairstyling salon, fruit and vegetable stands, Asian bakery, and sporting goods store—they're all here. The main commercial areas are on top of the hill on Beacon Avenue S at McClellan St., and at Columbian Way.
Celebrations: Annual neighborhood

cleanup, International Food Fair in April, Halloween party for kids at Jefferson Park.
Hangouts: Jefferson Park Golf Course buzzes with activity (there's a restaurant and lawn bowling club too, along with a playground for the kids). Business groups meet at the South China Restaurant.
Sidewalk chatter: "We have a very diverse community here. I raised three kids and I'm still here. There's great education for all cultures in Beacon Hill."

COLUMBIA CITY

Charming little Columbia City exudes wholesome America, with its old storefronts and sparklingly pretty public library. The Columbia Funeral Home too deserves a place in the history books.

It's no wonder then that Columbia City looks upon itself as an old, established neighborhood; after all, it has more long-term residents than most places in Seattle. It's a single-family neighborhood, with lots of children and lots of trees. Early settlers began beautifying the neighborhood by planting trees when it was still a logging community, and today's residents are keeping up the tradition.

The neighbors in Columbia City and surrounding communities are active and vocal. Southeast Effective Development (SEED) developed a very complex neighborhood plan directed at a family atmosphere. It's the only neighborhood plan adopted before the city comprehensive plan, and the city is putting money into the community in increments. Among other programs, SEED runs a summer youth employment program; there's also a very active coaches' organization through the local recreation center.

History

Columbia City and the rest of Rainier Valley had one of the best stands of timber around, so developers plotted the land, set up a mill, and proceeded to build houses. The incentive to

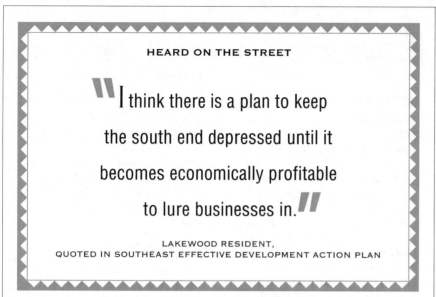

move there was the new streetcar line built by the land developer (a trick used by other neighborhood landholders of the day). He even added such amazing amenities as stores, a church, and a school. Because the route was pretty swampy, trestles had to be built and fill put in. But by 1892, the city petitioned King County to incorporate. It was named for the song "Columbia, the Gem of the Ocean."

Legends: Attorney H.H.A. Hastings was known for walking to his downtown Seattle office instead of using the newfangled streetcars. He went around the east side of Beacon Hill, where there were no real streets—about a 5-mile hike. Those who preferred walking may have been smart: Old-timers say people had to keep their umbrellas open inside the streetcars because they leaked so badly.

Another story has it that by 1896, streetcars ran all the way to Renton. The wife of one of the conductors ran the Columbia Hotel, and she kept a pigsty out back. Her helpful husband would pick up buckets of swill from the saloons in Renton, pile them on the streetcar, and bring them home. Lady passengers complained because they had to lift their skirts to avoid the swill that had slopped over onto the floor.

Stats

Rough boundaries: N: S Genesee St.; S: S Graham; E: 48th Ave S; W: Martin Luther King Jr. Way S.
Population: 5,363
Median age: 31.7
Median income: $19,783/household
Zoning: Single detached units most common, followed by 5+-unit apartments.
Housing: 44.7% own, 55.3% rent
Rent: $395/month (small house)
House value: About $90,000

Institutions

District Council: Southeast
NSC: Southeast
Movers and shakers: Columbia Merchants Association, Rainier Chamber of Commerce, Columbia City Neighbors, Southeast Effective Development, Pioneers of Columbia City and Vicinity.
Local media: Columbia City Neighbors newsletter, *South District Journal*
Police precinct: South
Crime watch groups: Block watch, South Seattle Crime Prevention Council.
Causes: Crime, traffic on 42nd Ave. S, health of business district, local beautification (trees, Genesee Park development to the north).
Public perks: Columbia Library, Rainier Community Center, Lakewood Playground, Genesee Park;

Graham Hill and Whitworth elementary schools.

Fun stuff

Beyond the malls: Retail core along 47th Avenue S. Nearby, on Rainier Avenue S, there's a boxing gym, a Japanese cinema, cafes, and small shops.
Celebrations: Historic Columbia City Festival and Kiddies' Parade during Seafair. The Columbia City pioneer group, restricted to neighborhood members who have been there for 50 years, meets once a year.
Hangouts: El Palacio, Puget Consumers' Co-op's Seward Park store, Bob's Quality Meats; for breakfast and lunch it's Betty's Grill, famous for its hamburgers (the old-timers call it "The Hole in the Wall"); for drinks, it's the Elbow Room.
Worth a detour: Columbia City's business district is 100 years old, and most of the medical and law offices, banks, stores, bars, and restaurants are in historic buildings that look like a movie set.

GEORGETOWN

Georgetown positively defines the term "mixed-use." Small, neat houses nestle up to industry; numerous old and new warehouses sell everything from fasteners and hinges to wine grapes. And tucked here and there behind the container rigs are clapboard houses, some painted up in keeping with their turn-of-the-century history, some merely longtime blue-collar homes.

Drop into the Koffee Kup on Albro Place and you might hear the story of warehouses and industrial buildings increasingly attempting to knock out single-family housing. It's not that Georgetown doesn't *want* to be industrial—that's been its role, after all, for decades. And, because of its location in the fertile Duwamish River Valley, Georgetown was also one of Seattle's early farming villages. There are some vestiges of that left: Julius Rosso has a wholesale nursery (though he's trying to turn it into warehouse space) and there's an aquatic nursery too.

The uniqueness of this neighborhood lies in its odd—and oddly charming—mix of uses, and young families are beginning to recognize that. The low house prices don't hurt either and, in the past few years, there have come to be children playing in the side streets once again. The residents hope the new families will help the neighborhood keep a balance in this highly industrial area.

The Georgetown Crime Prevention Council has worked hard at keeping a lid on crime, and has solicited the help of the north end's Aurora merchants, who are experts in getting the world's oldest profession out of a neighborhood. It seems to be working, except for the occasional bust when the police round up a vanload of prostitutes working the area along E Marginal Way.

As part of its pride in its industrial character, residents want to renovate Rainier Brewery's old plant—as well as the steam plant at Boeing Field.

History

Georgetown was an open party town in the early years, with 26 all-night saloons. This was where the Seattle Brewing & Malting Co., forerunner of Rainier Brewery, produced its sudsy stuff and spurred growth of the little town from 1892 until Prohibition. (The Brewing & Malting Co. building later became Rainier Cold Storage & Ice, which burned in 1988.)

Stats

Rough boundaries: N: S Dawson/ Brandon streets; S: city limits; E: Airport Way S and I-5; W: Duwamish Waterway.
Population: 1,238
Median age: 34.9
Median income: $21,023/household
Zoning: Single-family houses and two-bedroom rentals are most common. Nearly 60% of the houses were built before 1940.
Housing: 30.1% own, 69.9% rent
Rent: $289/month
House value: $58,200 (census) (eight houses valued at over $100,000)

Institutions

District Council: Greater Duwamish
NSC: Greater Duwamish
Movers and shakers: Concerned Citizens of Georgetown
Local media: *Beacon Hill News*
Police precinct: South
Crime watch groups: Georgetown Crime Prevention Council
Causes: Airplane noise, both from Boeing Field and the Sea-Tac flight path; protecting single-family houses (the community succeeded in getting some protection, but continues to petition to prevent the loss of housing to industry). Also fought siting of a prison on Hudson Street and is keeping an eye on a new motel going up.
Public perks: Georgetown Playground; Georgetown City Hall, which is on the National Register of Historic Places; the old Hat & Boots gas station on Corson Way S, which should be.

Fun stuff

Beyond the malls: Small shopping district with florist, drugstore, food bank. Carleton Avenue Grocery is local corner store. Many restaurants on Fourth Avenue S.
Celebrations: Neighborhood clean-up in April
Hangouts: Koffee Kup Cafe (been there 30 years), Andy's Diner, Randy's Restaurant (below Boeing), Jules Maes Saloon and Eatery.
Sidewalk chatter: "I'd say Georgetown is holding its own and is more stable than most places."

MT. BAKER

Mt. Baker is an anomaly: there are ritzy homes on the ridge overlooking Lake Washington; then an imaginary line is drawn at the crest of the hill, and more modest homes face Rainier Valley to the west. On one side you see a fruit truck delivering to the mansions; on the other you might find a ramshackle fruit stand serving the shopping-bag set.

The neighborhood once had the reputation of being rundown; during the 1960s, in fact, many houses were "redlined," threatened with condemnation. With the help of federal subsidies, the area was spruced up, and today it attracts many professionals—doctors, lawyers, and politicos, especially on top of the ridge. It's characterized by the wide boulevard along Hunter, a lovely tree-lined main street, and the winding Mt. Baker Boulevard.

Mt. Baker is primarily a family neighborhood with a strong community club—so strong, in fact, that when the community clubhouse burned down in 1992, it was rebuilt in just 10 months. Volunteers raised more than $200,000, coupled it with insurance money and volunteer labor, and the clubhouse rose from the ashes.

Stats

Rough boundaries: N: I-90; S: S Genesee St.; E: Lake Washington; W: Rainier Ave. S.
Population: 11,139
Median age: 35.4
Median income: $28,528/household
Zoning: Single-family detached most common, followed by small (five-unit) apartments.
Housing: 64.45% own, 35.55% rent
Rent: $300/month rent (west side); rentals are scarce on east side
House value: $400,000–$500,000 along the ridge (192 houses valued at over $400,000); $250,000 east of 31st Ave. S, $125,000 west of 31st.

Institutions

District Council: Southeast
NSC: Southeast
Movers and shakers: Mt. Baker Community Club, Mt. Baker Preschool Co-op, Southeast Effective Development (SEED), Parent Teacher Student Association, Mt. Baker Housing Association.
Local media: *Mt. Baker View* (community club newsletter)
Police precinct: South
Crime watch groups: Block watch, South Seattle Crime Prevention Council.
Causes: Playground in Mt. Baker Park, tracking Seattle comprehensive plan, future of Colman School build-

ing, supporting cooperative housing projects, speeding traffic in the neighborhood, rapid transit, crime prevention, and the impact of the Seafair Races on the neighborhood.

Public perks: Mt. Baker Park swimming beach, Lake Washington Boulevard, Colman Park, Mt. Baker Rowing and Sailing Center, Colman Playground, Hawthorne and John Muir elementary schools, Franklin High School.

Neighborhood heroes: Mayor Norm Rice, once president of the community club; city council member Jane Noland; county council member Ron Sims; former city attorney Doug Jewett. "A politician on every corner."

Fun stuff

Beyond the malls: Rainier Avenue and Martin Luther King Jr. Way are main shopping areas; some small shops on S McClellan Street.

Celebrations: Newcomer potluck in the fall, Christmas Ship program, Martin Luther King Jr. scholarship program, Day in the Park (May or early June).

Hangouts: Mt. Baker Park, Baker's Beach Cafe.

Worth a detour: On summertime Bicycle Saturdays and Sundays (announced in local papers), bicyclists can pedal down scenic Lake Washington Boulevard, unimpeded by cars. The route between Mt. Baker's Colman Park and Seward Park is closed to auto traffic and open to bikes during those days.

RAINIER VALLEY

You can easily see why this area is called Rainier Valley: it's a flat plain squeezed in between a ridge along Lake Washington to the east and Beacon Hill to the west. If you head south on grittily lively Rainier Avenue S, you seem to be headed directly toward the ice-cream-cone peak of Mount Rainier. Our description includes as part of Rainier Valley the areas called Brighton, Dunlap, Rainier Beach, and Rainier View.

To the south, Rainier Valley is topiary trees, little houses with big views and people working on cars in their driveways. It's ridged by ravines—a geologist's heaven.

Central Rainier Valley is a bit tougher, especially bordering Rainier Avenue. This, however, is the location of the Rainier Beach Community Center, a beehive of activity where on a Saturday morning you might find kids playing pool, adults swimming *in* a pool, a drill team marching to a not-so-different drummer, and kids, kids, kids. (South Shore Middle School is actually in the center.) Further north, big willows dot the parks, and Vietnamese signs begin to appear on the shops and churches.

The neighborhood is primarily Southeast Asian and African American, but there are a good many white faces too, both in the central valley and along the lake. "This is the greatest cultural mix in Seattle," says one community activist.

Houses can be found for about $20,000 less than in the rest of the city, even those with a view. Rainier Beach residents feel one reason the Valley hasn't experienced the growth occurring elsewhere is that they've been shortchanged by the city. "They try to put things out here that won't be accepted anywhere else," one resident grumbled. And the amenities other neighborhoods have just haven't materialized; for example, the community has been trying to get an auditorium—even has passed levies for it—to no avail. Until a few years ago, there were no anchor store draws in the valley to help the local economy and encourage young families to move in, residents say. But with Safeway upgrading at nearby Genesee and Rainier, and Olson's Food Store moving into the same area, things are on the upswing.

Of course, residents admit that crime has long been a major issue for Rainier Valley, presenting a challenge that the neighborhood has responded to by forming a Neighbors Against Drugs committee that is increasingly successful. Residents also have refused to give in to graf-

fiti, responding with paint-out parties and perseverance. A paint van holds cans of paint matching every building in the business area. In fact, the neighborhood has much less graffiti than downtown Seattle.

Houses in Brighton have large yards overlooking the lake; Dunlap has good beaches, the area's schools, and the community center; and Rainier Beach and Rainier View have, appropriately enough, beach and view homes mixed with modest housing.

Several very active churches are at the hub of the community, swaying more opinion than any individual. Rainier Beach Presbyterian and Rainier Beach United Methodist have large congregations, as do St. Paul's Catholic Church and Dunlap Baptist. And there are a slew of small congregations with dynamic names like "Macedonian Church of God in Christ" and the "Greater Victorious Church."

History

Rainier Beach was once called "Boeing Engineer Hill" because of all the Boeing workers living there. The valley has a history of farms, farms, and more farms. Many of the houses were postwar welcomes for the men returning home. And remember when Martin Luther King Jr. Way was Empire Way? The folks at the Empire Way Tavern at MLK Way S and Orcas Street do; they even have the old street signs on the outside walls to prove it.

Stats

Rough boundaries: N: S Graham St.; S: city limits; E: Lake Washington; W: Martin Luther King Jr. Way S. (Brighton is roughly from S Graham to Othello or Kenyon streets; Dunlap is Othello south to Rainier Beach.)

Population: 23,413

Median age: 33

Median income: $29,000/household

Zoning: Single-family detached units most common; some 5+ unit apartment houses in Dunlap.

Housing: 63.7% own, 36.3% rent

Rent: $399/month, less near valley floor

House value: $85,000–$90,000 in Dunlap ($110,000 for small house with view, of which there are many); slightly higher in Brighton; about $150,000 for house with view in Rainier Beach.

Institutions

District Council: Southeast
NSC: Southeast
Movers and shakers: Rainier Beach Community Club, Rainier Beach United, Rainier Beach Chamber of Commerce, Rainier View Community Club, Neighbors Against Drugs, Brighton Dunlap Community Council.
Local media: Community club newsletter, *Beacon Hill News, South District Journal.*
Police precinct: South
Crime watch groups: Neighbors Against Drugs, South Seattle Crime Prevention Council.
Causes: The Brighton Dunlap Community Council, which has its own office and paid staff, coordinates a long list of community efforts. Project CARE aims to improve the status of senior citizens living independently in the neighborhood with such programs as Bus Watch, in which businesses adopt a bus stop and keep it clean and safe. At the other end of the spectrum, the council has been involved in outreach to improve the high neighborhood infant mortality rate and has raised money for a Rainier Valley Youth Chorus. And there's a jobs campaign and a resource center, open to all community groups, that provides a rare commodity in the south end: a copying place complete with computer and printer. Crime prevention is also an issue, as is the cultural development and preservation of Kubota Gardens. In Rainier Beach, the community is involved in upgrading the appearance of Waters Avenue, a rather scenic main route, and in protecting single-family zoning.
Public perks: Hutchinson and Rainier Beach community centers, Rainier Beach Library, Kubota Garden, Lakeridge Park and Playground, Hutchinson and Othello playgrounds,

Pritchard Island swimming beach, public boat ramp and swimming beach on Lake Washington in Atlantic City Park; Brighton, Dunlap, Emerson, and Rainier View elementary schools, South Shore Middle School, Rainier Beach High School, Sharples Alternative School.
Neighborhood heroes: Norm Chamberlain of the Chamber of Commerce, champion of the anti-graffiti movement; Louisa Saemmer, the activist credited with saving Sturtevant Ravine; the late baseball player Fred Hutchinson, the cancer research center's namesake.

Fun stuff

Beyond the malls: Large commercial area with groceries, restaurants, and many small shops and services along Rainier Avenue S. The stores range from a Harley-Davidson dealership to a Thai video store.
Celebrations: Community cleanup (sponsored by community club)
Hangouts: Rainier Beach Community Center is a focal point for the neighborhood, but people also meet in the Stock Market Foods deli, at the Colonial Pancake House, and at the Lakeside Tavern ("Pool, darts, and games"), in Rainier Beach at Rainier and 68th.
Worth a detour: In the southernmost reaches of the city is an area residents call Dead Horse Canyon. They surmise the name came from what was found there years ago.

Today, *sans* dead horses, it's a beautifully deep canyon, a good example of Seattle's ridge-filled topography. To get there, follow Waters Avenue south to Lakeridge Park and wind east through the canyon to the lake.

SEWARD PARK

The Seward Park neighborhood, which includes Lakewood, is a slice of urban evolution, with its old renovated estates sitting cheek by jowl with 1950s ramblers. The residents have what's possibly the most attractive amenity in Seattle: Lake Washington Boulevard, where seniors walk, dogs pee, and in the summer teenagers jolt the neighbors awake with boom boxes (the city passed a noise ordinance just to stop those boom boxes).

And there's the park itself, that green peninsula filled with cherry trees and other established plantings (there's even a sign that says, "Danger: Poison Oak").

The large Jewish community is evidenced by the Park Deli (722-NOSH) and the large Ezra Bessaroth congregation.

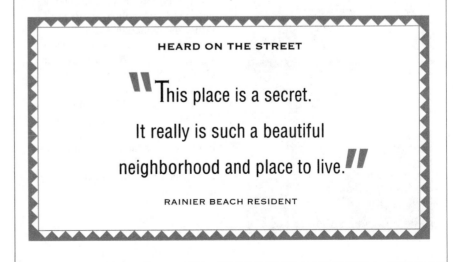

HEARD ON THE STREET

"This place is a secret. It really is such a beautiful neighborhood and place to live."

RAINIER BEACH RESIDENT

History

Seward Park was originally called Bailey Peninsula. The city acquired it in 1911, and it was the beginning of the Olmsted winding parkway through the south end, including Jefferson Park on Beacon Hill.

Legends: As late as 1916, someone claimed to have seen a cougar at the park. Men readied their shotguns and wanted to organize a hunting party, but the city officials claimed they could protect the public and asked the men to put down their arms, which they did, presumably reluctantly. No one quite believed in the cougar until a year later when a streetcar conductor had the unenviable job of cleaning a dead one off the front of a streetcar. Whether it was the same one or not is debatable, but it was a cougar, according to the unhappy conductor.

Stats

Rough boundaries: N: S Genesee St.; S: S. Willow St.; E: Lake Washington; W: 48th Ave. S.
Population: 4,676
Median age: 37.6
Median income: $38,490/household
Zoning: Single-family detached

Housing: 79.5% own, 20.5% rent
Rent: $500/month
House value: $180,000–$190,000; $1 million and up for lakefront houses

Institutions

District Council: Southeast
NSC: Southeast
Movers and shakers: Lakewood/Seward Park Community Club, Rainier Chamber of Commerce.
Local media: Lakewood/Seward Park Community Club newsletter, *South District Journal*.
Police precinct: South
Crime watch groups: Block watch, Southeast Crime Prevention Council
Causes: Restoring Seward Park's family-oriented atmosphere; reducing loud noise.
Public perks: Seward Park with pottery studio and beach, Lake Washington Boulevard, Lakewood Marina, Martha Washington Park, Lakewood Playground.

Fun stuff

Beyond the malls: Business area at 51st and Dawson and along Wilson has small shops, a large grocery, a drugstore, video store, law firm, restaurants.
Celebrations: Summertime jazz concerts and pow-wow in Seward Park; during Seafair, there's a one-day celebration at Seward Park, with hot dog roast, footrace, and fireworks. The community club is the site of a huge yard sale, holiday crafts fair, raffle, and numerous social events.
Hangouts: Seward Park, Boulevard Espresso, Puget Consumers' Co-op.
Worth a detour: Seward Park is a spectacular 277-acre wilderness that juts out into Lake Washington. A 2½-mile waterfront trail encircling the park makes a pleasant walk; or head right into the old-growth Douglas fir forest. There's also a bathhouse, an art studio, and an outdoor amphitheater.

SOUTH PARK

Wanted: Young people—and their kids. South Park, like many other old Seattle neighborhoods, would like to see young people move in and take an interest in the issues of the day. Gradually the neighborhood has been taken over by industrial uses, and in an effort to get families back, the community is sponsoring such programs as jobs for teenagers. Residents, most of whom live in small houses, hope to see a resurgence in residential uses, and think that may happen given the affordable houses here compared to elsewhere in the city.

History

Located as it is on the Duwamish River, South Park had some of the best farmland around in the early days. It was the center of truck farming; a large Italian population tended the fertile soil. Joe Desimone of Pike Place Market fame came from this area. But the river that provided the good soil also contributed to its disappearance. The Duwamish became more and more an industrial waterway and soon all the "beautiful ground" was covered over for industry, grumble longtime residents.

Stats

Rough boundaries: N and E: Duwamish River; S: city limits; W: Hwy. 509.
Population: 2,809
Median age: 30.9
Median income: $20,612/household
Zoning: Industrial along the Duwamish; 61% single-family houses, the rest multi-family.
Housing: 41.9% own, 58.1% rent
Rent: $339/month
House value: $65,200 (census)

Institutions

District Council: Greater Duwamish
NSC: Greater Duwamish
Movers and shakers: South Park Area Redevelopment Committee, South Park Community Club, Greater South Park Business Association, Historic Duwamish.

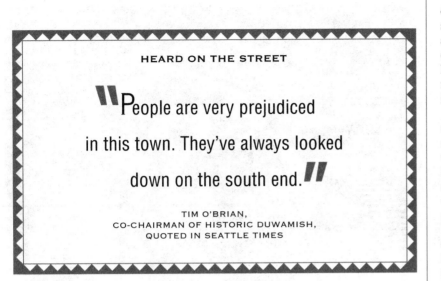

Police precinct: West

Crime watch groups: Block watch

Causes: Proximity of industry and residences, opposing proposed correctional facility, South Transfer Station pollution, schools, improving drainage system.

Public perks: South Park Community Center, Concord Elementary School, South Park Playground.

Fun stuff

Beyond the malls: Restaurants, taverns, grocery, health clinic, mail service, antiques, dental office, very small commercial strip at the end of the bridge on 14th Avenue S.

Community events: August's "Big Deal Day" is a 60-year-old neighborhood picnic with booths, bands, food, and games.

Hangouts: County Line Restaurant, Rascals.

Worth a detour: The South Park Community Center at SW Thistle Street and Eighth Avenue S is graced with a number of creations by Seattle artist Ginny Ruffner, courtesy of the city's 1% for Art program. Artworks in the sidewalk include inlays depicting each day of the year, with special holidays highlighted, and a treatment of the alphabet, with each letter and its symbol in Braille, Morse code, and hand signs. All of the artwork has been incorporated into a game devised by Ruffner that children of all ages can play.

SOUTHWEST

Southwest Seattle includes Alki, Delridge, Fauntleroy, and West Seattle.

ALKI

Think Alki and you think sand, volleyball, roller blades, teenagers, and cruisin'.

Alki's young population (largest age group is 25–34 years) has recently become entangled in a bitter battle over multi-family units that are rapidly swallowing up the older beachfront apartments and homes. The high-rises are winning; hurry if you want to see the little beach houses huddled together with old floats and seashells hanging off their decks. Apartments are literally being built around and over them, and their front yards are increasingly littered with multi-use permit (MUP) signs.

Alki has always been a close community, but increasing rents have changed the profile of the residents, and old-timers say it's less sociable than in the past.

However, the attempt a few years back to reduce noise and cruising along the beach has succeeded. You can see the police van parked there on weekends; residents say the police sit inside with a laptop computer and type in license numbers. If someone goes by too many times in four hours—voilà, they're cited. At community meetings, any cops present invariably get a pat on the back.

The Admiral area is above Alki, on top of Duwamish Head, with its own shopping district and a fairly well-off bunch of residents, some living in houses with an incomparable easterly view of downtown, others with a westerly view out toward the Olympic Mountains.

History

Seattle's founders arrived in 1851 and anchored the schooner *Exact* off Alki Point. A monument in Alki Beach Park honors such well-known pioneers as the Dennys, the Borens, the Terrys, and the Bells. It was a sign of their optimism that the white settlers named this point "New York Alki," "alki" being a Chinook Indian term meaning "by-and-by." The beach became the city's playground, and people flocked to an elaborate natatorium of baths and swimming pools built in 1905.

Stats

Rough boundaries: For Alki, N: Duwamish Head; S: SW Jacobson Rd.; E: top of the ridge; W: Puget Sound. For Admiral, N: Duwamish Head; S: Charlestown St.; E: SW Admiral Way; W: the Alki neighborhood.

Population: 18,008

Median age: 39

Median income: $37,200/household

Zoning: Single-family detached units most common, followed by structures of five or more units.

Housing: 62.5% own, 37.5% rent in Alki; 58.7% own, 41.3% rent in Admiral.

Rent: $700–$1,000/month

House value: Alki lots go for $100,000, with non-view houses $170,000–$180,000 and still appreciating as anti-cruising ordinance proves itself. N Admiral houses average $200,000. With view, prices rise into the $260,000 range.

Institutions

District Council: Southwest
NSC: Southwest/West Seattle
Movers and shakers: Alki Recreation Center Advisory Board, Alki Elementary PTA, Alki Congregational Church, Greater Harbor 2000; Alki, Admiral, and Duwamish Peninsula community councils.
Local media: *Alki News* (community council newletter), *West Seattle Herald, Admiral's Bridge* (monthly)
Police precinct: South
Crime watch groups: Block watch, West Seattle Anti-Crime Council
Causes: Multi-family zoning, plan remapping, traffic and parking; in Admiral, retaining open space, monitoring the increasing multi-family housing. Community activists solved the problem of Metro's treatment plant; it will soon be a storm water–only plant when Alki sewage goes via tunnel to West Point. Now they're watchdogging the impact of this work and that of other agencies affecting the SW Harbor Avenue Corridor.
Public perks: Alki Beach (with artists' studio in the old bathhouse), Alki and Hiawatha community centers; Don Armeni, Me-Kwa-Mooks, Schmitz, and Weather Watch parks; Alki, Lafayette, and Schmitz Park elementary schools, Madison Middle School, West Seattle High School.
Neighborhood heroes: City council member Tom Weeks, former council member Delores Sibonga.

Fun stuff

Beyond the malls: Alki is very beach-oriented; mostly restaurants, some T-shirt stands, and espresso places. In Admiral, the Admiral Junction is the most active commercial area, with small shops, a Puget Consumers' Co-op, and the historic Admiral Twin Theater.
Celebrations: Sand castle contest on Alki Beach, pirates' landing at beginning of Seafair, volleyball any sunny day.
Hangouts: On Alki Beach, Spud Fish and Chips, Alki Bakery, Pegasus Pizza, The Point Grill, Alki Home-

stead ("best fried chicken after Ezell's and wonderful martinis" in an original log home).
In Admiral, the Peace Cafe.
Worth a detour: Kids like climbing the circular staircase at the old Alki Point and Light Station, at 3201 Alki Avenue SW. The Coast Guard gives free tours noon–4pm on weekends and holidays. For info, call 286-5423.

DELRIDGE

For a long time, Delridge has been the Rodney Dangerfield of West Seattle. The residents finally got tired of getting no respect, so they broke away from the Southwest District Council to form their own district council. They wanted to heighten the image of Delridge in the eyes of other residents as well as city officials. The breakup has created some hard feelings, but Delridge at least feels more powerful because of it.

This is one of those neighborhoods made up of several small ones, including Youngstown, Pigeon Point, Puget Ridge, Cottage Grove, Riverview, Highland Park, and High Point. Delridge has more undeveloped land than nearly anyplace in the city; as a consequence, development pressure is pretty fierce, and things have been transformed in the past five or so years. The influx of huge apartment complexes is changing the crowd,

forcing out old-timers and low-income residents. To bring people together and involve new residents, community activists are giving tours of the neighborhood.

History

Delridge was named for the dell that sits between two ridges west of the Duwamish Waterway. The people on the hill (Pigeon Point) were shipbuilders and sailors; down the hill were fishermen and steelworkers. And at one time, primarily Italians settled around Bethlehem Steel (now Salmon Bay Steel).

Stats

Rough boundaries: N: SW Spokane St; S: city limits; E: SW Marginal Way; W: 35th Ave. SW.
Population: 24,853
Median age: 30.5
Median income: $28,000/household
Zoning: Industrial along the river, otherwise single-family with multi-family west of Delridge Way SW and near city limits.
Housing: 49.9% own, 50.1% rent in upper Delridge (north of SW Brandon St.); 52% own, 48% rent in the rest of the valley.
Rent: $384/month
House value: $84,000–$100,000; $100,900 for upper Delridge (census)

Institutions

District Council: Delridge
NSC: Southwest/White Center
Movers and shakers: Highland Park Action Committee, Myrtle Street Neighborhood Group; Cottage Grove, High Point, Pigeon Point, Puget Ridge, Riverview, and Youngstown community councils.
Local media: Community association newsletter, *West Seattle Herald/ White Center News*
Police precinct: South
Crime watch groups: Block watch
Causes: Improving the infrastructure (the roads, sewage system, and transportation), resisting development pressure, preserving greenbelts, building new community centers next to Delridge Community Center; in Pigeon Point, getting UW to let the neighborhood have some of its defunct West Seattle Research Lab grounds for a park, battling Services Group of America's "helistop"; in Highland Park, the First Avenue S Bridge and the neighborhood's accessibility to the rest of the city. Reclaiming the closed West Seattle Hospital buildings and grounds for multiple community uses has gathered a coalition of activists and human service agencies. The community has stopped businesses from dumping sewage into Longfellow Creek.
Public perks: West Seattle Golf Course, Camp Long, High Point Library, Southwest Youth and Family Services, Hughes Playground; Puget, Roxhill, and Westcrest parks; Delridge, High Point, and Southwest community centers; Cooper, High Point, Highland Park, Hughes, Roxhill, and Sanislo elementary schools; Denny Middle School, Chief Sealth High School, South Seattle Community College (which includes an arboretum and is planning an extensive Chinese garden to be designed by a team from Chongqing, China).
Neighborhood heroes: The late poet Richard Hugo, who immortalized his neighborhood in *The Real West Marginal Way*.

Fun stuff

Beyond the malls: No real neighborhood commercial center, but residents shop at Westwood Village at SW Barton Street between 25th and 29th avenues SW, and at Kmart and Food Giant on Delridge Way SW.
Celebrations: Christmas Party, annual summer picnic.
Worth a detour: You can practice rock climbing on Schurman Rock in forested Camp Long, at SW Dawson Street and 35th Avenue SW, or explore the Animal Tracks Nature Trail. There are also guided nature walks and programs for kids.

FAUNTLEROY

Fauntleroy is gradually becoming a wealthy neighborhood of large homes overlooking the Sound, and not everyone is happy about that. Residents say their small town is disappearing. Used to be that there was a mix of low- and middle-income families as well as one or two wealthy families like the Colmans, owners of the Wyckoff Co., which for years has coated pilings with creosote at the mouth of the Duwamish River.

But as the view property was discovered, the small beach homes have been demolished and large ones are taking their place. Inland, though, staid brick houses with impeccable yards still have that distinctly Scottish feeling, indicative of the early settlers.

Fauntleroy includes what some residents think of as a blight and others as charming: a Washington State Ferry terminal for the Vashon Island/Southworth car ferries.

History

Fauntleroy was named by Navy Lt. George Davidson in 1857 when he was charting Puget Sound south of Elliott Bay. He named it after his sweetheart, Ellinor Fauntleroy. (He also named Mt. Ellinor in the Olympics after her and Mt. Constance after her sister.) Early Scottish settlers came in by boat around the turn of the century and settled here,

forming one of the first West Seattle communities. Those Scotsmen and -women had clear priorities; they started Fauntleroy Community Church and the Fauntleroy YMCA first thing off the boat.

Stats

Rough boundaries: N: SW Fontanelle St. with a jog south along California Ave. SW, then SW Thistle St.; S: Marine View Dr.; E: 35th Ave. SW; W: Puget Sound.
Population: 8,462
Median age: 40
Median income: $39,000/household
Zoning: Single detached units most common, followed by apartments of five or more units.
Housing: 79.8% own, 20.2% rent
Rent: $500/month (census)
House value: $155,000 (census); waterfront/view property is anywhere from $200,000 to over $795,000.

Institutions

District Council: Delridge
NSC: Southwest/White Center
Movers and shakers: Fauntleroy Community Council, Fauntleroy Community Church, Fauntleroy YMCA, Friends of Lincoln Park.
Local media: Community council newsletter, *West Seattle Herald/White Center News*.
Police precinct: South
Crime watch groups: Block watch
Causes: Fighting substance abuse in Lincoln Park, ferry issues (traffic, parking, sewage dumping), cleaning up Fauntleroy Creek.
Public perks: Fauntleroy and Lincoln parks, Southwest Library, Arbor Heights Elementary School.
Neighborhood heroes: Gypsy Rose Lee hailed from Fauntleroy, as do the mountain-climbing twins Jim and Lou Whittaker.

Fun stuff

Beyond the malls: Small strip of shops, beauty parlor, dentists, lawyers, Greek restaurant, bakery, mainly near 45th Ave. SW and SW Wildwood.
Celebrations: Annual beach walk

that's also a progressive salmon dinner, the main community fundraiser.

Hangouts: Fauntleroy YMCA, Georgie Cafe.

Worth a detour: Lincoln Park, one of the city's prettiest parks, and its Colman Pool, an outdoor saltwater pool open summers only.

WEST SEATTLE

West Seattle is many things to many people—none of them dull. It's the old Rexall Drug sign, it's the street clock in the Junction. It's wide California Avenue SW with views east to the Cascades and west to the Olympics, it's friendly people being immortalized in larger-than-life murals.

It incorporates some little communities: Fairmount, Gatewood, Genesee Hill, The Junction, Seaview; many West Seattleites consider Alki, Fauntleroy, and even Delridge all part of West Seattle. The purer than purists refer to the whole area as Duwamish Peninsula instead of West Seattle.

The murals are the first thing you'll hear about—the residents, young and old, are bursting their buttons over them. Most are located around California Avenue SW and SW Alaska Street; one features a horse galloping off the wall. The murals are a good sign of what the neighborhood is about, a mix of history and renewed community spirit.

The second thing you'll hear about is a book called *West Side Story,* giving the history of the peninsula. The third thing is—well, it depends. You might hear about The Junction no longer having any anchor stores, or about ArtsWest, the arts organization operating a storefront gallery and producing chamber music concerts in area churches.

History

Trolleys from Admiral Way, Fauntleroy and downtown met at The Junction, of course, in the old days. The 11 historic murals painted on the buildings commemorate the old town, which originally was only the trolley station and residences. The south end of West Seattle, down by Fauntleroy Cove and Arroyo Beach, was originally summer cottages only, and the ferry from downtown brought vacationers to SW Carroll Street south of Alki Point and to Harbor Avenue SW, near where Salty's restaurant is now.

Stats

Rough boundaries: N: SW Charlestown St.; S: SW Othello or Webster streets (since we're including Gatewood, though some say it's part of Fauntleroy); E: 35th Ave. SW and Avalon Way SW; W: Puget Sound. Perimeter areas include north to Duwamish Head, east to the Duwamish Waterway, and south to the city limits—in other words, the Duwamish Peninsula.

Population: 16,053

Median age: 35

Median income: $32,150/household

Zoning: At the top of the hill, there are primarily single-family homes, with multi-family buildings of five or more units increasing along the California Avenue SW corridor as far south as Morgan Street Junction.

Housing: 63.8% own, 36.2% rent

Rent: $440/month

House value: "Go west, go west," a realtor says—west of 35th, that is. Houses on top of the hill run $200,000–$300,000; prices increase as you get closer to the bluff, with Genesee Hill highest—up to $795,000. $140,000 for house without view.

Institutions

District Council: Southwest

NSC: Southwest/West Seattle

Movers and shakers: West Seattle Chamber of Commerce, Junction Business Improvement Association, Morgan Street Junction Association, Southwest Seattle Historical Society, ArtsWest, Greater Harbor 2000.

Local media: *West Seattle Herald*

Police precinct: South

Crime watch groups: South Seattle Crime Prevention Council

Causes: Impact of the Port of Seattle's proposed expansion of its container terminal from the mouth of the Duwamish River west to Harbor Avenue SW, affecting all of the Duwamish Peninsula. In The Junction, traffic and graffiti; in Morgan Street Junction, monitoring high-rises and traffic.

Public perks: West Seattle YMCA, Lowman Beach Park, Fairmount Playground, the closed Genesee Hill elementary school, Fairmount Park and Gatewood elementary schools.

Neighborhood heroes: The late Ivar Haglund, whose family lived on the hill over Alki; actresses Dyan Cannon and the late Frances Farmer, former West Seattleites.

Fun stuff

Beyond the malls: Alaska Street Junction on California Avenue SW is the hub, with lots of little shops and cafes—and murals. Morgan Street Junction is at Morgan Street, California Avenue, and Fauntleroy Avenue; it's a shopping area for Gatewood, part of Fauntleroy, and much of High Point.

Celebrations: West Seattle Sidewalk Sale (July street fair), West Seattle Hi-Yu Community parade and picnic,

and other events connected with Seafair.

Hangouts: Husky Deli ("an institution—been there 40 years"), Snubby's, Blake's Bakery, Capers, the California and Alaska Street Brewery.

Worth a detour: The Walker Rock Garden would, in England, be considered a "folly." Milton Walker created it between 1959 and 1980. It's a series of towers, walls, miniature mountains, lakes, paths, fountains, a patio, and a fireplace—all built with thousands of semiprecious stones, rocks, crystals, geodes, and chunks of glass from all over the world. Milton's gone, but his legacy lives on—and you can tour the garden by appointment from Easter through Labor Day. It's at 5407 37th Avenue SW, 935-3036.

WEST

West Seattle neighborhoods include Magnolia and Queen Anne.

MAGNOLIA

Magnolia, which for our purposes includes Lawton, part of Interbay, and Carleton Park, is stuck out on a manmade peninsula, and the isolation suits it just fine. In fact, residents don't even have their tongues in cheek when they call it "Camelot." There are, after all, only three ways in and out: over the Magnolia Bridge, by way of W Dravus Street, or sneaking in the back way through the Salmon Bay interchange at Fishermen's Terminal.

This is a very small town, with professionals and young families, not much crime (even residential burglars who prey on wealthy neighborhoods leave Magnolia alone), and a mix of very expensive glass-fronted houses on the bluff and tiny, charming (if expensive) bungalows.

Magnolia loves Discovery Park and hates the West Point Metro Sewage Plant. It's not too crazy about the Port of Seattle either;

everyone's a little suspicious about the port's future plans for piers 90 and 91. Most recently, the tidelands by Perkins Lane were threatened by development, but the threat seems to have disappeared for the time being.

History

If it's true that some nearsighted explorer mistook madronas for magnolias, it seems that the residents weren't perturbed. In response to a suggestion that the neighborhood be named Madrona Bluff, the women of the local Garden Club campaigned to get everyone in the neighborhood to plant magnolias. Starting in 1948, the Buena Vista Garden Club planted one tree a year to make it truly Magnolia Bluff.

Actually, Magnolia began life as Smith's Cove, named for Dr. Henry Smith, who staked a claim near the deep cove in 1852. From there, things boomed: Interbay became a rail hub, and by 1900, Magnolia itself was a dairyland from which milk was hauled to Queen Anne Hill and Denny Hill. Truck farmers moved in too, and at Pier 91, Englishman's Boathouse rented boats so residents could go out and tend their crab pots. The Merchants Exhibition—a kind of farmers' market—at Smith Cove was a red-letter day when people came from all around to buy goods. Fort Lawton was established on the bluff in 1898, during the Spanish-American War, and battleships became as much a part of the neighborhood culture as dairy cows.

Stats

Rough boundaries: N: Lake Washington Ship Canal; S and W: Puget Sound; E: 15th Ave. W.
Population: 11,920
Median age: 39
Median income: From $58,470/household on southwest side to $32,000/household elsewhere.
Zoning: Single detached units, a few apartments of 5 or more units
Housing: 58.5% own (nearly all on the southwest side), 41.5% rent (most on the east side).

Rent: $535–$757/month (small apartment); $1,100/month (small house)
House value: From $157,300 on the east side to $173,000 on top of the hill to an overall average of $312,500 (640 houses on the southwest side and top of hill valued at over $400,000).

Institutions

District Council: Queen Anne/Magnolia
NSC: Queen Anne/Magnolia
Movers and shakers: Magnolia Community Club, Friends of Discovery Park, Magnolia Chamber of Commerce. The community has a Helpline service, through which people can get groceries, furniture, help with rent money, or a ride to a job interview.
Local media: *Magnolia News*
Police precinct: West
Crime watch groups: Block watch
Causes: West Point Secondary Sewage plant, noise from Port of Seattle terminals and connecting rail yards, FAA flight paths (Magnolia is at odds with Laurelhurst and View Ridge over who should get the jet noise), concerns about proposed expansion of the native American cultural center at Discovery Park.
Public perks: Magnolia Library, Bay View Playground, Magnolia Community Center; Discovery, Lawton, and Magnolia parks; Lawton and Blaine elementary schools, African American Academy (housed in Magnolia Elementary School).

Fun stuff

Beyond the malls: Small restaurants with a lot of take-out food for families, gourmet shops, large and small groceries, pub, centered around 32nd Ave. W and McGraw St.
Celebrations: Seafair's Magnolia Summer Festival in August features juried art show, live stage entertainment, food vendors, and sidewalk sale. And there's a kids' parade and main parade the same weekend.
Hangouts: Village Pub, The Great Scoop, Cafe Appassionato, The Upper Crust Bakery, Magnolia Espresso, Starbucks (there are seven

latte shops in Magnolia). In family-oriented Magnolia, families hang out at the community center, where there's always something going on, from aerobics to fencing.

Worth a detour: Discovery Park, where you can follow self-guided nature trails through thick forests along dramatic sea cliffs, or take a guided nature walk on Saturday afternoons (386-4236). What else? Jog the 2.1-mile trail along Magnolia Bluff, or take in a native American art exhibit at the Daybreak Star Arts Center.

QUEEN ANNE

Queen Anne Hill rises 456 feet, towering above downtown and the Denny Regrade. It is larger than many Washington State cities, population-wise. Queen Anne is really several different neighborhoods. Those who live on top of the hill look down their noses, almost literally, at "lower Queen Anne" by the Seattle Center, where the population is younger. Those on north Queen Anne live with the active Seattle Pacific University contingent of students among student-type housing. To the east is the old Queen Anne High School (now plush condominiums). To the west is McClure Middle School, the Queen Anne Community Center, and Kinnear Park. And central to it all is the Counterbalance, the nickname for Queen Anne Avenue N from Roy to Galer streets. A counterbalance was actually used in the 1890s to get old trolleys up the steep southern slope of the hill.

Residents are admirably loyal to the neighborhood; on average people have lived here 16.99 years. Queen Anne's draft neighborhood plan includes a few other interesting stats: over half the residents have two or more cars, and over half the residents park one or more car on the street. One in five keep two or more cars on the street.

History

The big question is, why is the hill named Queen Anne? Why do we care about the ill-fated queen anyhow? Queen Anne historian Emory

Gustafson says it's because the early bigwigs (lumber barons) liked the Queen Anne style of architecture, built the turreted, wrapped porch houses, and named the hill after them.

Queen Anne is putting together a history book and trying to find a place to put David Denny's original real estate office, a log cabin. The cabin was moved from Queen Anne to Federal Way, and historians want to move it back. Denny's house—a mansion in the style of the times—is gone, though his horse barn is still there, near the Queen Anne post office. Queen Anne's oldest building still standing is in the 1600 block of Fourth Avenue N, built in 1889.

Denny settled the lower hill, where Seattle Center now is. Doc Smith, an old Seattle settler, developed the west slope of the hill near Interbay, and it housed a sort of League of Nations neighborhood. Finnish houses there are on the historical register, and the Finnish Brotherhood Hall is still standing. As Queen Anne developed, the rich built on the periphery of the hill (where the view was), the blue-collar workers on the flats.

Legends: In 1979, members of the Love Israel family caused a stir when they built a very ugly addition to a church located at Sixth Avenue W and W Halladay Street. Their reasoning? "God wants it there."

Stats

Rough boundaries: N: Lake Washington Ship Canal; S: Denny Way; E: Lake Union; W: 15th Ave. W.
Population: About 30,000
Median age: 36
Median income: $32,853/household
Zoning: Multi-family units are booming along the west side of the hill (near Interbay and Kinnear Park) and will continue to do so. Elsewhere there are old, single-family neighborhoods-within-the-neighborhood. Established condominiums and apartments along the Counterbalance are favorites for both the young and seniors.
Housing: 43.5% own, 56.5% rent (more renters are on lower Queen

Anne than at the top of the hill).
Rent: $625/month
House value: $249,000 (363 houses valued at over $400,000)

Institutions

District Council: Queen Anne/Magnolia
NSC: Queen Anne/Magnolia
Movers and shakers: Queen Anne Community Council, Queen Anne Historical Society, Queen Anne Chamber of Commerce, Queen Anne Neighborhood Salon Association (as in intellectual salons, organized through the *Utne Reader*), Citizens Against Tower Expansion.
Local media: *Queen Anne News*
Police precinct: West
Crime watch groups: West Precinct Advisory Council
Causes: Maintaining residential character, discouraging rezoning of residential areas, traffic, parking, monitoring port and Metro activity. Residents are also asking that the TV towers not be extended. On the south side, view blockage is an issue; on the east side, noise.
Public perks: Seattle Center, Queen Anne Community Center, Parsons Gardens, Betty Bowen Viewpoint, East Queen Anne Playground, Queen Anne Lawn Bowling Club, Queen Anne Library; Elliott Bay, Kerry, Kinnear, "Bhy" Kracke, Myrtle Edwards, and Rodgers parks; Coe and John Hay elementary schools, McClure Middle School, Seattle Pacific University.
Neighborhood heroes: Paige Miller, Port of Seattle commissioner.

Fun stuff

Beyond the malls: There are about 2,000 businesses. The main shopping area of small stores and supermarkets is on top of the hill. The Queen Anne Thriftway brings in the throngs. There's another strip along lower Queen Anne, including the Uptown Cinema.
Celebrations: Queen Anne Fun Run.
Hangouts: Up top, joggers hang out on Bigelow Avenue N, which has been nicknamed Jog Avenue because

of the hundreds of half-naked, sweating bodies seen there; Thriftway (the wine department is rumored to be the best place to pick up young established women, not to mention men); Olympic Pizza House, Starbucks, The 5 Spot, McGraw Street Bakery, Tea Cup, Standard Bakery, Queen Anne Avenue Books, Video Isle, Ken's Market, Paragon. Down below: Mountaineers Club, Tower Books (especially the espresso cart), Pizzeria Pagliacci.

Sidewalk chatter: "There are lots of working-class families on the hill. I think there are misconceptions that it's all upper-middle-class. . . fairly well off. . . and that's not the case."

DOWNTOWN

Downtown neighborhoods include Denny Regrade, the International District, and Pioneer Square.

DENNY REGRADE

The Regrade (which includes Belltown) is home to a wide range of social classes: transients, the "working poor" in low-income apartments, and middle- and upper-middle-class residents, many of whom are flocking to the new high-rises. Currently, most households are occupied by one resident.

A hangout for theater types and artists (many of whom have studio/lofts in the area), the Regrade is home to numerous offbeat restaurants, art galleries, and nightclubs as well as the Belltown Theatre Center and the Annex and AHA! theaters.

The *P-I* once rightly described the Regrade's buildings as "like a Seattle history text." They range from old corner brick buildings to new glassy high-rises. Residents have been trying to steer the tide of development toward multi-family residences instead of the commercial buildings that pop up like toadstools in the fall.

Crime is a persistent concern in the Regrade, but as the population is expected to double quickly due

to the number of apartments and condominium projects in the pipeline, residents hope the criminal element will move on.

History

Once upon a time the city fathers said, "Enough." The city just plain had too many hills. So they flattened one, and the result was Denny Regrade.

Denny Hill disappeared by increments. First, it was cut away for a regrade of First Avenue between Pike Street and Denny Way. Then the west side was dumped into Elliott Bay, and piece by piece it continued to be leveled until by about 1912 it was completely flattened. According to Roger Sale's *Seattle, Past to Present,* 20 million gallons of water a day were pumped from Lake Union to the top of the hill to force boulders, clay, and rocks down into a central tunnel.

Why did the city fathers do away with the hill? They perceived it was in the way of downtown Seattle's growth—but it's only now that the city seems at all interested in developing that area.

Stats

Rough boundaries: N: Denny Way; S: Stewart St.; E: Sixth Ave.; W: Elliott Ave.
Population: 3,666 (47% growth since 1980)
Median age: 44.2
Median income: $15,211/household
Zoning: Commercial, multi-family
Housing: 17.9% own, 82.1% rent
Rent: $299+/month (low-income apartment), on up to $600+ (luxury high-rise).
House value: $212,500 (condos)

Institutions

District Council: Downtown
NSC: Downtown
Movers and shakers: Denny Regrade Business Association, Denny Regrade Community Council, Denny Hill Association, Denny Regrade Property Owners Association, Team Regrade.
Local media: *Seattle Downtown News, Regrade Dispatch*
Police precinct: West
Crime watch groups: Denny Regrade Crime Prevention Council; neighborhood has hired private security firms to patrol blocks.
Causes: Public safety, security, housing, a cleanup program for Regrade Park at Third and Bell, public toilets, social services.
Public perks: "Not many"—Regrade Park, P-Patch at Elliott Avenue and Vine, Bell Street Pier.

Fun stuff

Beyond the malls: Hip fashion boutiques along First Avenue between Union and Bell streets, Wall of Sound music, antique/kitsch/thrift shops galore, numerous tiny corner groceries as well as the slightly larger Ralph's Grocery and Dan & Rey's Market. Pike Place Market is a short walk down the street. Two movie theaters: the United Artists Cinema, where all movies are $2, and the Cinerama.
Celebrations: Annual cleanup program; Belltown Inside Out festival, featuring home tours and events in Regrade Park, sometimes occurs dur-

HEARD ON THE STREET

"It's the week of Chinese New Year. The previous day, the Lion danced throughout the International District. You walk up King Street and the sidewalk is littered with the red paper and charred labels from exploding packs of firecrackers. At midnight the previous evening, the waiters came out of the restaurants, lighting firecrackers and tossing them into the air. That to me is community character."

DEAN WONG,
PHOTOGRAPHER AND WRITER,
INTERNATIONAL EXAMINER

ing summer or fall.

Hangouts: Crocodile Cafe, Cyclops, Two Bells Tavern, Mama's Mexican Kitchen, Virginia Inn, Penny University, Palmers, Belltown Pub, Speakeasy, Sit & Spin.

Worth a detour: The Subterranean Cooperative of Urban Dreamers (SCUD) building at Western and Wall, next to the Cyclops cafe, that's covered in 392 Jell-O molds. The most unusual are alligators, zodiac signs, a 1976 penny mold, and the head of Scooby Doo. (There's also a Barbie cake pan spray-painted to look like a Jell-O mold pan.) So why did Diane Szukovathy decorate the building thus? It's a work of art, she says. It took her four months of shop-

ping from Belltown to Tacoma to come up with them all.

INTERNATIONAL DISTRICT

The ID, as it's casually called, began as a bachelor community in the 19th century when Chinese men were recruited to work on the railroads. By the 1920s, when most had earned enough to send for their families, the ID had become a truly Asian American community of Japanese, Chinese, and Filipinos. It is said to be the only place in the U.S. where the three immigrant groups settled together. In the 1960s, Southeast Asians entered the mix, settling pri-

marily in what's sometimes called "Little Vietnam," centered at 12th Avenue and Jackson Street.

The majority of ID residents today live at poverty level, and their main concerns are housing and public safety. Flats above shops in the low-rise brick buildings that characterize the area have been adequate in the past, but there aren't enough of them any longer. Families settling in the ID compound the problem, and the community is trying to find more land for low- and middle-income family housing. Few property owners live in the district and most own the buildings free and clear, provoking fears they may sell out to developers of more lucrative upscale housing.

Sitting on the edge of Seattle's busy downtown, the ID is facing the challenge of holding back the bulldozers that herald high-rise development. But if the federal government gets its way, residents won't have to worry about going upscale: the feds want to put a $50 million jail here.

History

The ID has such a rich past that it is recording it all in an oral history project. The district began with the first Chinese man, Chin Chun Hock, who started Wa Chong Co., labor contractors, near the waterfront. Chun Hock did quite a business, in more ways than one—he had 13 wives. His business thrived and he and other contractors brought in workers for lumber, rail, and fishing jobs.

But in 1886, anti-Chinese riots drove out many of the Chinese. In 1907, labor contractors filled in the tideflats to develop what is now the International District, and the Chinese who braved the riots to stay in Seattle settled there. The Chong Wa Benevolent Association was formed to mediate problems; today it operates a school of Chinese culture and language. There are 27 tongs, Chinese fraternal organizations formed for security, still in existence, each with its own facilities.

The Japanese first settled in 1879,

and soon became Seattle's largest minority population. The Toyo Club, now Bush Garden, was formed in 1920 and was the second-largest gambling club on the West Coast. The Japanese American Citizens League formed in 1930, and remained active through the internment years of World War II.

Housing conditions had begun to deteriorate in the 1950s, and by 1970 came to a head when the Ozark Hotel fire claimed 20 lives, pointing out the deadly consequences of substandard conditions. In its aftermath the Ozark ordinance was added to Seattle's building code, requiring that apartment buildings with four or more stories had to meet current minimum fire standards. That, coupled with I-5 roaring through the neighborhood, demolishing housing in its path, prompted activists to work on housing issues through the 1970s.

The ID was known as Chinatown until 1964, when then-mayor Wes Uhlman proclaimed it the International District.

Stats

Rough boundaries: N: Yesler Way; S: S Dearborn St.; E: 12th Ave. S; W: Fourth Ave. S.
Population: Approximately 2,500; 48% Asian/Pacific Islanders (primarily Chinese and Filipino), 37% white, 10% African American, 3% American Indian, 3% other races.
Median age: 45
Median income: $7,254/household
Zoning: Residential/commercial/hotel is most common building type; 30 of the original hotel buildings remain.
Housing: 1.3% own, 98.7% rent
Rent: Under $199/month
House value: $87,500

Institutions

District Council: Downtown
NSC: Downtown
Movers and shakers: ID Economic Association, ID Housing Alliance; ID Improvement Association, ID Emergency Center, Chinatown ID Preservation and Development Authority, InterIm Community

Development Association, ID Drop-In Center.
Local media: *International Examiner, Northwest Asian Weekly, Seattle Chinese Post.*
Police precinct: West
Crime watch groups: All the community groups are involved in crime prevention. The ID has its own Emergency Center in the person of Donnie Chinn who, with his bank of volunteers, is on call day and night. The ID Housing Alliance educates residents on concerns relating to crime.
Causes: Public safety, development impact from Kingdome and Union Station redevelopment, housing, parking, drug crimes near 12th and Jackson.
Public perks: Hing Hay Park and Chinese Pavilion, ID Community Garden, Wing Luke Museum, Nippon Kan Theatre, Yesler Community Center.
Neighborhood heroes: "Uncle Bob" Santos, longtime activist and director of the Chinatown ID Preservation and Development Authority; the late Seattle city council member Wing Luke, the first Chinese person elected to political office in the continental U.S.

Fun stuff

Beyond the malls: "You can get anything done you need to get done within five blocks." Small shops—groceries, herbalists, specialty stores, restaurants—on the first story of old low-rise brick apartment buildings, and the granddaddy of them all, the expansive Asian supermarket Uwajimaya. Check the alleys too; they're full of interesting shops. Vietnamese businesses cluster up toward 12th and Jackson; try the Viet Wah Market, Eng Suey Plaza, and Asian Plaza.
Celebrations: July's ID Summer Festival and Street Fair, with lion dancers, taiko drummers, and other cultural happenings; Chinese New Year, Harvest Moon Festival, Vietnamese New Year.
Hangouts: Any of the little restaurants, especially House of Hong

and the Four Seas, and the ID Drop-In Center.
Worth a detour: Just below Yesler Way, on the hill leading to the ID proper, are terraced gardens filled with exotic plants and planting methods. In the 1970s, each of the community's low-income elderly residents received a plot of earth here. A path winds through the gardens, which are oddly quiet despite their proximity to major thoroughfares.

Interested in touring the whole district? Chinatown Discovery conducts various walking tours, some including dinner or a dim sum lunch at a Chinese restaurant. They prefer groups; call for rates, 236-0657.

PIONEER SQUARE

Pioneer Square is the city's most venerable downtown neighborhood, with its mix of street people, nightclubs, social service centers, art studios, and penthouse residents. It's noisy, vibrant, and somewhat European in feeling, with its squares, cafes, and galleries.

As a neighborhood, Pioneer Square is complicated. It's governed by a preservation board that bands together—usually—with a strong community council and merchants' group. The big issue? Maintaining the wonderful balance that gives the Square its character. As myriad office/residential projects get approval, gentrification threatens to smooth the charmingly rough edges of the city's oldest neighborhood.

Crime has been a serious concern in Pioneer Square, resulting in a strong movement to limit work-release prisoners in the area, increase police patrols, and tighten security in office buildings. Residents fight over whether the benches in Occidental Park attract too many homeless people; the homeless people say this is their neighborhood, too.

The roughest part of the area is at Second and Yesler; safest—usually—is down by the jazz clubs on First, unless the crowd gets *too* jazzed.

History

Pioneer Square's history goes back to the settlement of the city, when Doc Maynard donated a plot of land to Henry Yesler to start a lumber mill. The "Skid Road" to that mill became Yesler Way, once the heart of Pioneer Square. Hotels, taverns, and shops—all wood-framed—sprang up around the new industry.

On June 6, 1889, a furniture maker left a pot of glue on the stove and it caught fire, burning the entire city to the ground. The residents rebuilt the neighborhood in brick, with most of Pioneer Square's new buildings designed by architect Elmer Fisher. But there was still a problem: the tide from Elliott Bay backed up plumbing and flooded streets, so then sidewalks and streets were raised one story. Shopkeepers were faced with creating entire new storefronts on their *second* stories. Passageways below ground were sealed; you can see them by taking Pioneer Square's Underground Tour (682-4646).

Pioneer Square was pretty much abandoned when the city's center shifted north, and it became home for the city's derelicts until the 1960s, when it was threatened with becoming a parking lot. Following the destruction of the ornate Hotel Seattle, city activists forced the formation of one of the nation's first historic preservation districts and saved the remaining vintage buildings.

Legends: There are so many that you could fill a book with them. In fact, Murray Morgan did: *Skid Road,* the best account of the area's history. After the fire, Pioneer Square became populated with "box-houses"—combination variety music halls, brothels, and taverns. Wine ran in rivers through the basements of these establishments, and Morgan's book tells all about them.

Stats

Rough boundaries: N: Cherry St.; S: Dearborn St.; E: I-5; W: Elliott Bay.
Population: 1,675 (the area grew by 32% in the decade between 1980 and 1990).
Median age: 43.6
Median income: $6,599/household (53.6% live in poverty)
Zoning: Historic, renovated office buildings with rooftop condominiums and ground-floor retail businesses. Little middle-income housing; mostly low-income and upscale.
Housing: 1.7% own, 98.3% rent
Rent: From $149/month (single-room occupancy) to $700+/month (older apartment).
House value: $150,000–$350,000 (condo)

Institutions

District Council: Downtown
NSC: Downtown
Movers and shakers: Pioneer Square Community Council, Pioneer Square Historic Preservation Board, Pioneer Square Business Improvement Area.
Local media: *Seattle Downtown News*
Police precinct: West
Crime watch groups: West Precinct Advisory Council, committees of Pioneer Square Community Council, Friends of Diane (named for Diane Ballasiotes, killed by a work-release prisoner in this neighborhood).
Causes: Social services for the street people and homeless, crime, historic preservation, Occidental Park use, conflict between new upscale residents and low- (or no-) income types.
Public perks: Occidental and Waterfall parks, Klondike Gold Rush National Park, Kingdome.
Neighborhood heroes: Ralph Anderson, credited with starting the preservation movement; Walter Carr, owner of Elliott Bay Books; Casey Carmody, crime watch activist; Tina Bueche, neighborhood activist; Alan Black, property manager for much of the Square; the late Bill Speidel, author of tongue-in-cheek books about Seattle history.

Fun stuff

Beyond the malls: Pioneer Square is a cafe society, with a bookstore (Elliott Bay Books) at its center and galleries and espresso bars throughout. Restaurants, nightclubs, and rise-and-fall theater groups provide nightlife, and the many Asian rug shops *always* have a sale. Most businesses are located on First Avenue between Cherry and King streets. And there's some commercial activity underground: Underground Tours parade tourists—for a fee—through the city's main streets of yore.
Celebrations: Fire Festival in June, Mardi Gras/Fat Tuesday (complete with Spam Carving Contest), First Thursday evening gallery openings.
Hangouts: Torrefazione Italia (espresso), New Orleans Cafe (jazz), Grand Central Bakery, Elliott Bay Books, Sneakers Bar & Restaurant, OK Hotel, Ruby Montana's, and dozens more.
Worth a detour: The Klondike Gold Rush National Historic Park (117 S Main Street, 553-7220) may be the second-smallest national park in America—and indoors at that—but it's full of interesting artifacts and information about the event that transformed Seattle into the commercial center of the Northwest. On summer Sundays, the rangers lead an interesting walking tour of Pioneer Square. One block east is Waterfall Park, the Seattle-born United Parcel Service's gift to the city and a lovely spot for lunch on a warm day.

EASTERN EXPOSURE

TECHIES

CUL-DE-SACS

GREENBELTS

BEACHES

CHATEAUS

MALLS

SCHOOLS

PARKS

T*he Eastside is a whole clump of erstwhile Seattle bedroom communities that have suddenly grown into boomtowns. The communities are relatively young, wealthy, and sprawling. They ought to emit the odor of lake algae, centered as they*

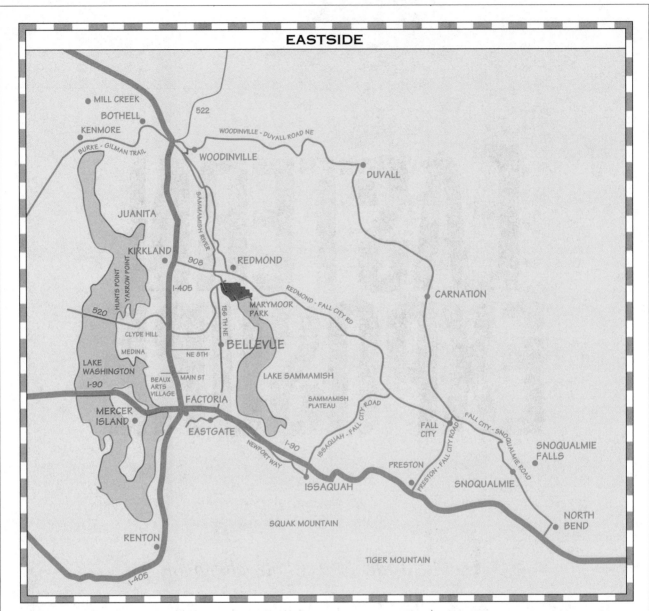

EASTSIDE

Eastside Population

Community	1980	1990	1995	% change '80–'95
Bellevue	73,903	86,872	102,000	38%
Issaquah	5,536	7,786	9,025	39%
Kirkland	18,785	40,059	42,350	126%
Mercer Island	21,522	20,816	21,290	-1%
Redmond	23,318	35,800	40,030	72%
Seattle	493,846	516,259	532,900	8%

Source: 1995 Population Trends for Washington State, Office of Financial Management

are on, around, and between two lakes, Lake Washington and Lake Sammamish. But they actually smell of chips—computer chips, that is, not the old-fashioned Northwest timber kind. This is software country, where young geniuses flock to work in high-tech cubicles and play in clean suburban parks. This is where a giant corporation, Microsoft, spawned development in a wilderness with burbling brooks, a waterfall of monumental proportions, a backdrop of mountains, and—the area's most prized possession—open space.

Whether you're a newcomer to the

region or an old-time Seattleite who's afraid to go across those bridges, here's a primer of the 20 key things you should know about the Eastside.

1. WHAT IS IT? WHERE IS IT?

See those mountains to the east? Between Lake Washington and that impressive range lie a couple of rivers, another lake, a valley or two, and a maze of freeways, swirling exits, and intersections. There are more shopping centers than you can count on both your hands—and a panhandler in Bellevue Square? Forget it. Not only that, while Seattle lobbies desperately for support for its schools, Eastside citizens almost unfailingly pass school levies. And there are more and more of those Eastsiders every day; Redmond, for example, anticipates adding 15,600 residents by the year 2012.

Where the East Stands

How Eastside cities fit in with Washington's 20 most populous cities.

Median Family Income, 1995

Hunts Point	$115,233
Beaux Arts	$88,237
Medina	$87,942
Yarrow Point	$82,578
Woodinville	$61,324
Bellevue	$54,261
Redmond	$50,396
Mercer Island	$46,367
Kirkland	$44,649
Seattle	$39,860

Source: Puget Sound Regional Council

1. Seattle
2. Spokane
3. Tacoma
4. Bellevue
5. Everett
13. Kirkland
14. Redmond

Eastside Boundaries

North: Bothell/Kenmore (at the northern end of Lake Washington) stretching east to Woodinville (or, more specifically, the Woodinville-Duvall Road).
South: Renton's northern city limits. (Note: Some in Renton may consider their city to be part of the Eastside, but ask an Eastsider if it is and you'll get either a laugh or a resounding "no.")
West: The eastern shore of Lake Washington. Includes Mercer Island.
East: Snoqualmie Pass, for purists, but for most, North Bend.

2. WHO ARE THEY?

Eastsiders all wear Seahawks T-shirts, roller blades, Ray-Bans, and Lycra. And they all drive Mercedes. At least, that's what a Seattleite will tell you.

Eastsiders spend much of their time apologizing for being, well, more clean-cut and all-American than people who live in Seattle. The reality is that the average Eastsider's income is about twice that of a Seattleite, according to the U.S. Census. Most Eastsiders are newcomers: the population has grown four times faster in the recent past than has Seattle's. That's mostly because of jobs in the high-tech corridor, but it's also because of the Eastside's open parks, highly ranked schools, and relatively crime-free subdivisions.

3. COMMUNITY CULTURE

The Eastside is a jumble of communities, each with its own personality, quirks, and Starbucks. With an apolo-

While the west side of the Eastside is bristling with business parks and malls, there is a movement in what is sometimes called the "redneck" Eastside to hold back the cement. Some folks in the little, still-rural communities of the Snoqualmie Valley (Duvall, Carnation, Snoqualmie, Fall City, Preston) want to secede from King County. They even have a potential name: Cedar County.

gy to those neglected, here are a few.
Bellevue: Time was when this was just a crossroads with a gas station and a grocery store, surrounded by strawberry fields. And that time was not so long ago. Bellevue was incorporated in 1953; its first high-rise, built way back in 1969, towered above its low-rise neighbors at 13 stories high.
Most common description: Metropolitan.
Bothell: Bothell and the surrounding Northshore area stretches along the Sammamish River; its communities (Kenmore in King County, Mill Creek in Snohomish County) have their share of little creeks and lakes. This is becoming a preferred place to live for households in which Mom works in Seattle and Dad in Redmond. But it is best known for its location between two highways: I-405 and SR 522. It's ultra-convenient for corporate car-culture, and Bothell accommodates that with a plethora of master-planned corporate campuses.
Most common description: Technology corridor.

Issaquah: "Issaquah traffic jam" used to be an oxymoron. No more. This little village is now a booming suburb, with chateau-style houses going up on the surrounding hills faster than the candy makers at Boehm's can churn out truffles. These days Issaquah's streets are filled with a combination of hotshot attorneys and busloads of tourists.
Most common description: Quaint (but that stands to be replaced by the phrase "What a jam on Front Street!").
Kirkland: Four miles of waterfront, a ringing bell tower, and the Seahawks headquarters. That's Kirkland, once a sleepy village with its face blinking out onto the lake. Today, this is a yacht-y sort of place, where boaters mingle with upland java drinkers in quaint espresso haunts and where public art and galleries run rampant. It still feels a bit older than many of the other Eastside communities—and somehow more similar to Seattle's neighborhoods, perhaps because some of its homes date to the 1880s—but it boasts a very upscale populace.

Carillon Point, aptly named for the tall carillons that ring every half hour, is a complex of shops, sailboats, and restaurants. (Horsey types hang out at Bridle Trails State Park; see "Horse Heaven.")
Most common description: Waterfront.

Mercer Island: The I-90 floating bridges bring you to the doorstep of this little, semirural, very protected urban island. Pundits call it "Mercedes Island" for its upscale housing and wealthy residents, but residents don't care—much. The parks are nice, kids play in the streets, the view of Seattle is the best, and the street grates have poetry inscribed on them—but you can't afford to buy there, so forget it.
Most common description: Residential community.
Redmond: Redmond has two claims to fame, both beginning with "M": Microsoft and Marymoor. As Microsoft's home base, Redmond is making sure its favorite company is not lonely. It's opening its arms to more and more high-tech companies, including biotech enterprises, sports-medicine equipment firms, and every software entrepreneur you can think of. Marymoor Park gets the techies out in the open, with a Velodrome, a climbing wall, and lots of trails.
Most common description: Microsoft.
Runner-up: Congestion.
Sammamish Plateau: High above Issaquah and to the east of Lake Sammamish is this relatively new settlement of sports stars, mega-houses, and cul-de-sacs. The most settled of the developments is Klahanie, a secluded and sought-after escape from the realities of life below. The area is increasingly becoming its own "city," with malls creeping up the hillside so the residents never have to leave.
Most common description: The Plateau.
Woodinville: Wines, horses, and Molbak's Greenhouse. Houses with decks, big green backyards, and perfect gardens. Chateau Ste. Michelle and Redhook Ale Brewery. Need we say more? (Well, okay. There's a car auction yard too.)
Most common description: Country.

4. EASTSIDE LEXICON

Cross a bridge and you may encounter some local dialect that requires translation.

The Compound: The modest, 18,000-square-foot Mercer Island pad of billionaire, former Microsoft founder, and entrepreneur Paul Allen (he lives there with his mother).
Bill's house: Not to outdo Allen, but Bill Gates's place will be about 50,000 square feet, if it ever gets completed. It's being built in Medina (from Highway 520, look south—it's the gash in the hillside that's full of construction equipment).
Chateaus: Houses, mostly on the Sammamish Plateau, with three-car garages, mammoth master bedrooms, many-turreted or peaked roofs, beauty-barked yards—and visible security systems.
Tear-downs: What was there before the mega-houses in Bellevue and Mercer Island. Also, anything existing along the lakefront that's more than 10 years old, as in "He bought a little tear-down for $1 million and built himself a mega-house-with-view in its place."
New Orange County: What Eastsiders fear the most, as in "We're becoming the new Orange County."
Eastside Time Zone: This refers to a proposal, launched by the newspaper *Eastsideweek*, to set Eastside clocks back two hours every day at noon, thereby creating a longer workday—an Eastsider's idea of heaven. Then, at 10 p.m., clocks would advance two hours, and everyone would be well rested by morning.

Horse lovers have lots of company in the vicinity of Woodinville. There are so many horses—more per capita than in any other community in the state—that just outside of town, in unincorporated King County, some "Walk" buttons at intersections are placed at saddle height, so riders can easily push the button to change the light without dismounting.

Non-mall: Crossroads Shopping Center. Eastsiders really hate it if you call this place a mall. Crossroads goes out of its way to make you feel at home, with ethnic cafes, a giant chess set, and a children's play center (and a great used bookstore too).

"Are you vested?": Question asked of Microsoft employees at almost every party. (Those who would answer yes have most likely already moved to their villa in Switzerland.)

Near Campus: Near Microsoft's Redmond headquarters, which resembles nothing so much as a college campus with playfields and campus "greens."

Gold Coast: The Lake Washington communities, from Beaux Arts to Hunts Point.

The Points: Yarrow, Hunts, and Evergreen Points.

The Silicon Forest: Eastside's high-tech concentration.

Some Seattle jargon for that land beyond the moat:

Blah-vue: Bellevue.

Swell-vue: Ditto.

Yuppieville: Anywhere "over there."

Token Lake: Totem Lake (well, have you ever seen the lake?).

Eastside jargon when referring to Seattle:
"Where's that?"

5. IN THE SWIM

Little beaches and big ones. Beaches where you can flex your pecs and show off your tan, as well as those where the tykes are most welcome. Whatever sort of beach you're looking for, you'll find that Eastside swimming beaches are tops. (Even diehard Seattleites sneak over to the ones we've listed below!)

Lake Washington

Meydenbauer Beach Park
419 98th Ave. NE
From Lake Washington Boulevard, just follow the signs. Children's play area, disabled access, lifeguards 11 a.m.-7 p.m.

Chism Park
1175 96th Ave. SE
From Main Street, head south on 101st Avenue SE. You'll intersect 97th SE. Picnic sites.

Wander through the parking lot of the Mercer Island QFC sometime and look carefully at the numerous four-wheel-drive vehicles parked there. Can you find any that have mud on them or show any other sign they've ever been taken anywhere rougher than the Bellevue Square parking garage?

Newcastle Beach Park
4400 Lake Washington Blvd. SE
On 405, take the 112th Avenue SE exit, turn right, and follow the signs.

Kirkland

Waverly Beach Park
Waverly Way and Sixth Ave. W

Juanita Beach Park
9703 Juanita Dr.
From 405, take the NE 116th Street exit, and head west on 116th to Juanita Drive. Sandy beach, boat pier.

Mercer Island

Luther Burbank Park
North of I-90 on N Mercer Way. Look for signs. Tennis courts, picnic area, summer concerts, docks.

Groveland Beach Park
Take W Mercer Way to SE 58th, and turn west to 80th Avenue SE. Little and pretty.

Lake Sammamish

Lake Sammamish State Park
20606 SE 56th St.
Follow I-90 to the Issaquah exit and follow signs into the park. Big and very popular picnic area.

Idylwood Park
3650 W Lake Sammamish Pkwy.

6. WORTH CROSSING THE WATER

Seems as if something's always happening on the Eastside, from concerts at a winery to horse shows. But worth crossing the 520 bridge? This is.

Pacific Northwest Arts and Crafts Fair
Bellevue Square
454-4900
Nationally acclaimed juried show, held on the fourth weekend in July. Arts and food booths. This megaevent has been around for more than 50 years, and never once rained out.

Renters' World

Apartments are a way of life on the Eastside, but vacancy rates are dwindling as the number of jobs outstrips the housing supply.

	Average rent (1-bdrm apt.)	Vacancy rate
Bellevue East	$571	2.1%
Bellevue West	727	1.9%
Bothell/Northshore	542	4.9%
Issaquah	641	0%
Kirkland	673	5%
Mercer Island	639	1.4%
Redmond	655	3.3%
Seattle (Downtown)	756	4%
Seattle (Capitol Hill)	599	1.7%
Woodinville/Totem Lake	591	6.2%

Source: Seattle-Everett Real Estate Research Report, 1996

7. HORSE HEAVEN

You can see some prize-winning (and *veeery* valuable) horseflesh in Horse Country East.

Evergreen Classic Benefit Horse Show
Redmond
667-5096 or 823-2802
Marymoor Park's horse ring gets gussied up to host a very competitive horse-jumping competition in August. Weekday events are free; there's a small charge on weekends.

Evergreen Fairgrounds
Monroe
Each year, the fairgrounds in Monroe hosts four horse shows:
Spring Benefit Horse Show (April)
Spring National Horse Show (April)
Pacific Northwest Horse Show (May)
Northwest Autumn Finals Horse
   Show (September)

Do It Yourself
If you want to ride instead of watch, rent a horse at Tiger Mountain Outfitters in Issaquah (392-5090) or at Kelly's Riding and Boarding Ranch, also in Issaquah (392-6979).
   Or use your own horse and head

for the hills of Kirkland's Bridle Trails State Park: 481 acres and 28 miles of riding trails.
   To learn how to ride, visit the Eastside Riding Academy, where you can even be part of a medieval theme party (827-2992).

8. CULTURAL ICONS

Sure, lattes are the drink of choice on the Eastside, and newer is for the most part considered better, but there are a few touchstone gathering places that have served as Eastside social centers since long before The Campus was ever conceived.

Bellevue Barber Shop, Main Street, Bellevue. Began life around 1930 as Wright's Barber Shop and still cutting, right there next to Toys Cafe, another near-icon.

Chace's Pancake Corral, Bellevue Way SE, Bellevue. Coffee like it used to be, a wagon-wheel lamp, syrup in a keg; everybody there knows everybody else there.

Gilbert's Main St. Bagel Deli, Main

Street, Bellevue. Well, okay, so it's not an icon, but the Harley riders hang out there every Sunday morning.

Winters House, Bellevue Way SE, Bellevue. Pink "Spanish"-style house is the only Bellevue site listed on the National Register of Historic Places.

Triple X Drive-In, between Gilman Boulevard and I-90, Issaquah. Last remaining Triple X; vintage-car owners gather here, especially on Saturday nights. But you may be too late to use the actual drive-in part: this cultural icon is threatened, and may be replaced by an office building.

Roanoke Inn, north of I-90 on Mercer Island. An old roadhouse turned tavern.

Mar-T Cafe, North Bend. Diner of "Twin Peaks" TV fame. Yes, they serve cherry pie.

Carnation Dairy Farm, Carnation Road, Carnation. Home of contented cows, just like those on the milk cartons. Tours available.

9. HOUSE TO HOUSE

Bellevue: Apartments to luxury homes on lakefront. Average price: Bellevue East, $205,786; Bellevue West, $391,543.

Kirkland: Condos to houses on acre-size lots (Bridle Trails) to old, established-neighborhood houses. Average price: $256,786.

Issaquah: New development houses and relatively new (e.g., Klahanie) Sammamish Plateau mega-houses. Average price: $260,268.

Redmond: Subdivision houses to custom-designed homes. Average price: $211,648.

Woodinville: Upscale houses with decks on large lots. Average price: $226,565.

Bothell/Northshore: Mixed bag: everything from upscale to small fixer-uppers. Average price: $182,553.

Mercer Island: Contemporary architecture, mega-houses. Average price: $468,666.

See also the Property Tax Assessment table in Chapter 2, "Neighbor to Neighbor."

Source: Northwest Multiple Listing Services, 1996

10. HIT THE TRAIL

The Eastside is full of trails, but the 27-mile Sammamish River Trail is the king of them all. (And for those who like connecting trails, the Lake to Lake Trail is worth a try on some sunny Saturday—call 296-4169 for info.) The Burke-Gilman Trail, beginning at Seattle's Gas Works Park, connects to the Sammamish River Trail at Kenmore's Log Boom Park. The River Trail runs past Chateau Ste. Michelle winery and the Velodrome, the bicycle racetrack at Marymoor Park. Take your blades.

11. EASTSIDE ROADSIDE ATTRACTIONS

Snoqualmie Falls
Snoqualmie
It falls 270 feet, and at the bottom you can stand with your mouth open and taste the mist from the cascade. From the top, you can hear and watch the whole thing against the backdrop of the Salish Lodge, a stylish redo of the old Snoqualmie Lodge with great views of the falls and pretty great food to boot. The falls can get crowded on weekends, but it's an interesting international crowd.

To get there: From Seattle, take I-90 east to Snoqualmie Falls exit (Exit 27). Follow signs through Snoqualmie to the falls.

Bellevue Botanical Garden
12001 Main St.
Bellevue
462-2749
Thirty-six acres of gardens, with a perennial bed guaranteed to make you rush home and redesign your own garden. Open daily, dawn to dusk.

To get there: Take I-405 to NE Eighth St., then east to 120th.

Chateau Ste. Michelle Winery
14111 NE 145th
Woodinville
488-1133
Music and art in the amphitheater in the summer (call for a schedule), wine in the tasting rooms all year round. The chateau is on 87 acres of an old estate that has maintained its stately character. The landscaping was designed by New York's Olmsted family. Open daily.

To get there: Take Exit 23 east from I-405. Follow SR 522 to the Woodinville exit. At stop sign, turn right and continue to NE 175th St. Turn right again, and go over railroad tracks to stop sign. Turn left onto Hwy. 202. Proceed 2 miles to the winery.

Redhook Brewery
14300 NE 145th St.
Woodinville
483-3232
Across the street from Chateau Ste. Michelle, the beer drinkers get their turn. Tours, pub, and, of course, a beer garden. Ask them what *Reinheitsgebot* means.

To get there: Take Exit 23 east from I-405. Follow SR 522 to the Woodinville exit. At stop sign, turn right and continue to NE 175th St. Turn right again, and go over railroad tracks to stop sign. Turn left onto Hwy. 202. Redhook is opposite the winery.

The Herbfarm
32804 Issaquah-Fall City Rd.
Fall City
784-2222
From lavender lemonade to sleep-inducing herbs, you'll find it here at the legendary Herbfarm. You can take a class, eat dinner (but reserve *waaaay* ahead and set aside plenty of money), or just wander the theme gardens.

To get there: Take I-90 to Fall City exit.

Boehm's Edelweiss Chalet
255 NE Gilman Blvd.
Issaquah
392-6652
For 40 years, this landmark chalet has been a sort of "Julian and the Chocolate Factory" of the Eastside. When Issaquah was still a sleepy village known only to skiers who wanted hot chocolate on their way down from Snoqualmie Pass, Julian Boehm built this tribute to his Austrian home. You can take a tour of the chocolate factory and his former apartment, or get married on the grounds in the High Alpine Chapel. (Unfortunately, just plain candy customers often have to wait for busloads of tourists to get their turns at the candy counter.)

To get there: From eastbound I-90, take Exit 17. Turn right off the exit, then left onto Gilman Blvd.

Rosalie Whyel Museum of Doll Art
1116 108th Ave. NE

Bellevue
455-1116
Honest, it's not an homage to Barbie. This is probably the most extensive doll museum you'll ever see. We know, we know—you never wanted to see one at all. But this one is so professionally curated that it may well convince you to begin thinking of dolls as an art form.

To get there: Exit I-405 at NE Eighth westbound.

Carnation Dairy Farm
28901 NE Carnation Rd.
Carnation
788-1511
See those contented cows up close. Free self-guided tours on Saturdays in the summer. Dairy farm, barns, gardens, gift shop.

12. HIGH-ACHIEVING SCHOOLS

Ask anyone with kids why they live on the Eastside and the answer is likely to be "the schools." Eastside schools have reputations for excellence, especially those in the Mercer Island district, which consistently tops the list in terms of test scores. There are seven school districts, two of which are very small (Snoqualmie

Eastside Graduation Percentage, by District

Bellevue	76.96%
Issaquah	92.53%
Lake Washington	88.19%
Mercer Island	96.11%
Northshore	89.62%
Riverview	100%
Snoqualmie	85.75%

Source: Superintendent of Public Instruction

and Riverview, which serves Carnation).

Bellevue School District
12111 NE First St.
Bellevue
455-6015
Twenty-eight schools; approximately 15,000 students. Serves Clyde Hill, Medina, Hunts Point, Yarrow Point, and Beaux Arts, as well as portions of Renton, Issaquah, Redmond, and unincorporated King County.

Issaquah School District
565 NW Holly St.
Issaquah
557-7000
Approximately 11,000 students. Serves Issaquah, Preston, and portions of the rest of the Eastside and unincorporated King County. Ask about the district and everyone will tell you about its technology focus; its students actually learn to install a computer network. The district is also adding schools as the population burgeons.

Lake Washington School District
10903 NE 53rd
Kirkland
828-3200
Thirty-four schools; approximately 24,000 students. Serves Juanita, Kirkland, and Redmond. The district is adding new schools almost daily.

Mercer Island School District
4160 86th Ave. SE
Mercer Island
236-3330
Serves the island only, with five schools. Always comes out on top in state tests, and always passes school levies.

Northshore School District
18315 Bothell Way NE
Bothell
489-6000
Serves approximately 19,000 students in Bothell, Woodinville, Kenmore, and surrounding areas. And that number is growing: enrollment increases about 1.5% annually.

Riverview School District
32240 NE 50th St.

Carnation
(206) 333-4115
Approximately 3,000 students, who do in fact have a view of a river—the Snoqualmie River, to be specific—from their homes in Duvall and Carnation. The district also encompasses the treed acres up to Snoqualmie Pass.

Snoqualmie School District
P.O. Box 400
Snoqualmie
(206) 888-2334
Serves just over 4,000 students in Fall City, North Bend, Snoqualmie, and the pastoral acres in between and up to the top of the Pass.

13. INFO SOURCES

To find out more about the Eastside, try (a) sitting down at a Starbucks and striking up a conversation, or (b) calling the best general Eastside resource, the visitors bureau.

East King County Convention and Visitors Bureau
520 112th Ave. NE, Suite 101
Bellevue, WA 98004
455-1926
(800) 252-1926
The bureau distributes a relocation package; it contains mostly realtors' brochures, but does include a resource pamphlet that has great information. The bureau also has informational brochures galore and bike maps. The friendly people there can direct you to the community resource of your choice.

City Halls

City of Bellevue
11511 Main St.
Bellevue, WA 98009
455-6800

Bothell City Hall
18305 101st Ave. NE
Bothell, WA 98011
486-3256

City of Issaquah
135 Sunset Way
Issaquah, WA 98027
391-1000

Don't get excited. "Poo Poo Point" does not refer to a baby's diaper. It is said to have been named after the sound made by a steam train that used to circle the mountain with loads of timber. "Sammamish," on the other hand, combines two Native American words: "samma," meaning the sound of the blue crane, and "mish," meaning river.

High-Tech Company Locations

Seattle	27.87%
Bellevue	14.25%
Redmond	9%
Kirkland	4.54%
Bothell	4.38%
Kent	4.22%

Source: Seattle-Everett Real Estate Research Report

City of Kirkland
123 Fifth Ave.
Kirkland, WA 98033
828-1111

City of Redmond
15670 NE 85th St.
Redmond, WA 98052
556-2190

Woodinville City Hall
13209 NE 175th
Woodinville, WA 98072
489-2700

Crime Anyone?
King County provides crime maps for unincorporated King County (that means the city crime rates are not included) at its Web site: (http://marge.metrokc.gov/crimemap/) The site has some pretty cool charts, and it sorts crimes by zip code or countywide, either monthly or quarterly. (It also philosophizes: "The first part of stopping crime is knowing where to look for it…")

Other Resources
Eastsideweek: Cheeky and weekly, with great events listings. Free; available in every Starbucks and 700 other places around the Eastside.

Journal-American: Daily and local.

Seattle Times: Daily Seattle paper with an East Bureau that covers local news.

14. WANNA JOB?

Is the Eastside really the high-tech corridor? Well, a total of 547 technology firms are located on the 405 corridor—and that number is increasing. And there's an emerging corridor along I-90, from 405 to Issaquah, in the so-called Eastgate area.

Whether you have a great idea brewing in your basement or just plain want those big-bucks stock options, here are a few of the better-known Eastside high-tech businesses.

Attachmate Corporation
Bellevue
644-4010
Connectivity; software to automate routine tasks.

The Eastside is a bit difficult to gather information about, because it includes so many small communities. But the granddaddy of all Eastside cities is the venerable Bellevue, and, true to its high-tech character, it has a nifty computerized information network called Bellevue Online. The network gives you access to 300 listings, from phone numbers to "how to" information. For tips on downloading the software, call 455-6835; for direct access to the online bulletin board, dial in 688-2850.

You're lost. There's not a gas station in sight. Where to ask for directions in the asphalt desert of the Eastside? Starbucks, of course. Pull into the parking lot, take your map inside, and while your latte is being made, at least five people will tell you where you need to go. (Of course, they'll use malls as landmarks, so be prepared. "It's just past Crossroads. . .")

Edmark Corporation
Redmond
556-8400
Educational software.

Microsoft
Redmond, Bellevue, Bothell, World
882-8080
Just about every kind of computer software.

Nintendo
Redmond
882-2040
Lotsa games. About 875 employees in Redmond.

Sierra On-Line
Bellevue
649-9800
Games.

Wall Data
Kirkland
814-9255
Connectivity; software.

15. PICK OF THE PARKS

"Greenbelt" is synonymous with the Eastside, and its abundant parks do a lot to counter the "greybelt" of freeways that squiggle like snakes through the area. Each community boasts parks ranging from road-end docks to huge mountain preserves. Here are a few of the most boasted-about.

Mercer Slough Nature Park
1625 118th Ave. SE
Bellevue
450-0207
A full 320 acres of wetland in the heart of Bellevue. Boardwalk and other trails, or take your canoe.

Kelsey Creek Park
13204 SE Eighth Pl.
Bellevue
455-7688
Barns and a farmyard; cute little calves, lambs, and piglets; trails; pioneer log cabin.

Kirkland Waterfront
Lake Washington Blvd.
Kirkland
Word has it that the best-muscled guys (and gals!) on the Eastside can be seen, if not had, at Houghton Beach. And many other parks line the shores of Kirkland too.

Marymoor Park
6046 W Lake Sammamish Pkwy. NE
Redmond
296-2966
You (and their wives) might think those guys who fly remote-control airplanes need to get a life, but there they are at Marymoor painting, gluing, and puttering over the fleet. And the climbers? They're out on the climbing rock, while the bike racers are zooming around the only Velodrome in the Northwest (you can watch them on Fridays at 7:30 p.m., April to November, $3).

Park on the Lid
Mercer Island
This park covers I-90 at Mercer Island with playfields, paths, and picnic areas. You won't believe you're over the action.

Cougar Mountain Regional Park
Issaquah
296-4232
About 2,800 acres of trails, wildlife, and wetlands. You can see black bear, virgin forests, and the abandoned site of Newcastle, where coal was once king. Call to get a map of trails (many open to horses as well as walkers). From I-90, take Exit 13, then go west on Newport Way, and south at 164th Ave. SE to Lakemont Blvd.

Lake Sammamish State Park
20606 SE 56th St.
Issaquah
455-7010
People line up overnight to reserve the group picnic areas here, but you don't have to do that to enjoy the playfields, barbecues, etc. See "In the Swim."

Tiger Mountain State Forest
Issaquah
The largest of the three "Issaquah Alps" (the others are Squak and Cougar), this mountain is threaded with trails. Paragliders leap from Poo Poo Point, and horses canter on the horse paths. And oh yes—nudists do what they do at a 40-acre family nudist park on the mountain (the Bare Buns Fun Run?). There are caves and a lake, too.

16. THE EASTSIDE DOWNSIDE: TRAFFIC

"Longer than a red light in Redmond." Local real estate pundit Tom Kelly coined this phrase appropriately: drivers have been known to go through puberty and middle age all while sitting at one Eastside stoplight. Downtown Redmond is impossible, Issaquah's Front Street is often jammed, and I-405 can be stopped up end to end on a rainy Friday night; I-90 is almost always the bridge of choice.

There are only four routes to the Eastside from Seattle: via Renton (gruesome at rush hour), via Bothell (ugly at rush hour), Highway 520 (doubly ugly), and I-90 (okay in the HOV lane). The best way might be by ferry, but there isn't one.

Think of the main freeways as a rectangle: I-90 is the bottom leg, running east-west; 520 is the top leg, running east-west; 405 is the right side, running north-south; and I-5 is the left side, running north-south through Seattle. While one problem is getting over the bridges, many people think the tougher challenge is getting across the Eastside from, say, Renton to Woodinville.

The Eastside Quiz

Try this question on your Eastside friends:

Q: There's an accident on 405 and you need to get from Issaquah to Bothell. How do you do it?

A: It's virtually impossible.

Well, okay. It might not be impossible. Try this one. Take I-90 west to the Newport Way. exit and go north on W Sammamish Parkway to Willows Road. Turn left on 124th, then right on 132nd. Go past the Redhook Brewery and Chateau Ste. Michelle, then left on 522. Take E Riverside to Bothell.

Got Your Compass?

The other problem with getting around on the Eastside is figuring out where the heck you're going. With new subdivisions popping up where cow pastures used to be, and with winding roads the norm, there's no obvious logic in street names and addresses. (Forget about using a map—they're always outdated.)

Steve Johnston, who has been fielding questions about the Eastside for years in his "Hey Johnston" Seattle Times column, gets asked repeatedly how you're supposed to figure out the Eastside street system. Actually, Johnston explains, there is some logic. There's a dividing line, for example: Main Street in Bellevue. Streets north of Main are generally designated "Northeast," and those to the south are "Southeast." But there

Ken Griffey, Jr., and his pals can sometimes be seen on the streets of Issaquah (they reside close by, on the Sammamish Plateau). There's a close-knit jock community at Canter Grove, where they presumably toss around a baseball now and then. Griffey, Jay Buhner, and Chris Bosio of the Mariners all live there (as does Ken Easley of Seahawks fame). Musician Kenny G, on the other hand, is a lowlander. He's a Hunts Point resident.

are so many exceptions to the rule, and quirky things like pieces of the same road appearing all over the place, that confusion is still rampant.

Johnston's Rule: "The Eastside rule for telling people where you live should be: 'Stay where you are. I'll come get you.'"

One other point of potential confusion: The Fall City Road, a famed country drive, is actually several roads. The Redmond-Fall City Road (Highway 202) becomes the Fall City-Snoqualmie Road; then there are the Issaquah-Fall City Road, the Preston-Fall City Road, and the Fall City-Carnation Road.

17. SHOPPING & MORE SHOPPING

Says one Eastsider: "Everything I need is within five minutes of my place." Well, the five minutes might be debated (see the section on Eastside traffic), but the point is taken. There's literally more shopping east of the lake than in Seattle.

Annual Retail Sales

Greater Bellevue core: $1.5 billion

Greater Downtown Seattle $921 million

Source: Seattle-Everett Real Estate Research Report

Shopping Spots

Where to shop? Lots of places, but here are a few places to go when the going gets tough.

Bellevue Square

Bellevue Way and NE Eighth

Bellevue

454-2431

More than 200 stores and restaurants. Bellevue Art Museum on the third level. A social center for those giggly preteens, and a shopping center for all.

Crossroads Shopping Center

156th NE and NE Eighth

Bellevue

644-1111

A full 40 acres of shopping. A public market, international food, live music, giant chess set, day care, Bellevue mini-city hall, specialty stores. Don't call it a mall or you'll have your bar code invalidated. Preferred term: "old-fashioned friendly neighborhood."

Factoria Square

128th SE and SE 38th

Bellevue

747-7344

More than 80 shops. "Less expensive than other malls," says one Eastside shopper.

To get there: It's south of I-90. From I-90 eastbound, take the Richard's Road/Factoria exit. Turn

Bellevue was once home to a whaling fleet that used to pass through the Ballard Locks and winter at Meydenbauer Bay. The fleet left for good in 1946. That same year, Kemper Freeman, Sr., founded a newfangled shopping center called Bel-Square. Bellevueites stopped missing the ships once they discovered the cash registers of Bel-Square, which today houses more than 200 stores.

right onto 128th SE and go just past SE 38th Street.

Factory Stores of America

Outside of North Bend
(206) 888-4505
Can't miss these outlet stores, 50 of them to be exact.

To get there: Take Exit 31 from I-90.

Gilman Village

Issaquah
392-6802
A collection of old buildings that are now home to antique shops and specialty stores.

To get there: Take Exit 17 off I-90. Go south one block on Front Street to reach Gilman Boulevard, then take a right and continue across the railroad tracks. You'll see the village on your right.

18. WHAT'S IN A NAME?

What are people looking for when they move to the Eastside? Many are hoping to find it at the end of a cul–de–sac. Check out these Eastside subdivision names and you may have the answer:
Beaver Lake
Audubon Park
Autumn Wind
Swiftwater
Sierra Klahanie
Highland Creek Chaparral
Rainbow Lake Ranch
Summer Meadows
The Park at Pine Lake
Cimarron
Green Acres
The Villages
Pacific Estates
Summer Ridge
Sahalee
Timberline
Swan Crest
Hunterswood Knoll
Daniel's Ranch
English Cove
Hidden Ridge
Creekside

Get the point?

19. A CULTURED PLACE

Performing arts, public art, and music can be had in virtually every Eastside community, but here are two particularly notable cultural landmarks.

Bellevue Art Museum

Bellevue Square
454-6021
Admission: $3 admission; Tues. free

An art museum in a mall? Well, where better to attract the common man and woman? The Bellevue Art Museum, on the third level of Bellevue Square, has grown into an institution that focuses on reflecting its immediate community. Thus, more art and technology are in BAM's future (and the museum may move out of that mall soon).

Village Theatre

303 Front N
Issaquah
392-2202
Issaquah's acclaimed theater mixes fringe acts and musicals-and bills itself as a family theater, true to the nature of the town. Actually, there are two Village Theatres: the new one offers large-scale performances, and the old Village Theatre, 120 Front St. N, presents new, intimate works on a smaller stage.

20. CONSCIENCE OF THE EASTSIDE

Is there any name that brings as many accolades—or angry roars—as that of Harvey Manning? If you don't know him from his work to save trees, you probably know him as the author of many Mountaineers guidebooks. Manning actually named the Issaquah Alps, and he almost singlehandedly saved his home territory, Cougar Mountain.

LOCAL STREET SMARTS

*Y*ou can see I-5, you can almost feel its roar, but you followed the green signs and arrows and suddenly you're stranded in the middle of downtown, with everybody honking, jaywalkers flipping you the finger, and those cops on bikes frowning your way. And no more green signs. On your radio, copter jockeys are talking about such obscurities as the eastern high-rise and the bus barn, and all you want to do is abandon the old heap, hike to wherever the state signmakers are yukking it up over the fate of saps like you, and begin some serious torture.

Relax. It could be worse—you could be on I-5, snarled in the ever-present bottleneck near the Convention Center.

Seattle has the dubious distinction of being the sixth-worst city in the nation when it comes to traffic congestion. Sometimes the problems are generated by the one-way streets and lack of direction signs, but mostly it's because there are a heck of a lot of cars out there.

Five hundred thousand cars zoom in and out of Seattle each day. Actually, they don't zoom—they crawl. Average speed during rush hour is 22 mph (9 mph on some stretches). And rush hour is actually rush *hours:* from 6 to 9 in the morning and from 3:30 to 6:30 in the afternoon. What's more, people are rushing from

farther away than in the past. Consider these facts:

- In 1980 the average trip length in the region was 6.5 miles and took 14 minutes.
- In the year 2000 the average trip will be 7.9 miles and take 20 minutes.
- In 2020 the average trip will be 8.3 miles and take 26 minutes.

Source: Puget Sound Regional Council

WHAT WE LIKE TO DRIVE

Seattleites buy 1.81 cars per household. In the 1990s, what are we buying?

- First-choice car: Honda Civic
- Second-choice: Ford Taurus
- Third-choice: Almost any 4WD pickup truck—especially those with expanded cabs

Favorite makes by type:
- Compact pickup: Toyota
- Big truck: Ford, F-series
- Sport/utility vehicle: Ford Explorer

- Minivan: Chrysler Plymouth Voyager
- Small specialty: All Mazdas: RX7 (first), MX6 (second), Miata (third)
- Sedan: Honda Accord
- Mid-size specialty: Thunderbird

Overall comment about Seattle car purchases: "Seattle seems to have more of a taste for Japanese cars than does the rest of the country."
Source: Cole & Weber

UNLOCKING THE GRID

All those new cars—and new people—are making gridlock a way of life. But don't worry, you can find ways to survive the traffic crunch. Consider chucking the car and biking it, busing it, or walking it. Or learn a basic premise: the fastest route between points A and B is often a full-ish circle. To put it another way, Seattle shortcutting is an art not to be taken lightly.

The best shortcutters understand Seattle's logical street layout. With all those hills in the way, the streets might not seem to follow any pattern, but they do. Here are some favorite tricks of locals:

J-C-M-S-U-P. When downtown, first of all, rely on the old reliable: Jesus Christ Made Seattle Under Protest. For the uninitiated, this saying, ingrained in natives since birth, holds the key to city-center navigation. The first letter of each word represents

There are two basic street classifications: arterials and non-arterials. Arterials are protected from cross traffic; that is, intersecting side streets have at least a yield sign and usually a stop sign. And commercial vehicles in excess of 10,000 pounds gross vehicle weight cannot travel on an arterial except when that's the only way to get to a destination. Unless otherwise posted, the speed limit is 30 mph on arterials and 25 mph on non-arterials. Arterials have a yellow centerline on the pavement.

a downtown street or two streets of the same letter in sequence from south to north: J is for James, C for Cherry and Columbia, M for Marion and Madison, S for Spring and Seneca, U for University and Union, P for Pike and Pine.

Tic-tac-toe. Citywide, here's the method used by one street-smart individual:

"Draw the lines of the old tic-tac-toe game; then we can name the 'boxes' made by those lines with compass directions. The box at 12:00 high is north, the box at 1:30 is northeast, 3 o'clock is east, and so on. Of course, the box in the middle would have no compass direction, and that's exactly as it is in the center of Seattle where the streets are without compass directions. All other streets in the city will have a direction, either before or after the street's name or number, depending on

whether they are technically a street or an avenue.

"Streets run east to west and, unless in the downtown area, will have a compass direction before the name or number. For example: 1502 NE 65th Street or 4101 SW Manning Street. And, as you might expect, the avenues run north to south and the compass directions come after the name or number. For example: 4775 Brooklyn Avenue NE, or 5707 47th Avenue S. The not-so-common diagonal thoroughfares are often called 'ways' (like Denny Way or Yesler Way), but they may just as often be called roads or drives.

"Now for the good news: There is an easy way to keep all this straight. Remember Brooklyn Avenue NE? First of all, no one ever says 'Avenue Brooklyn.' Avenue always comes after the name or number and so do the compass directions. If you need another mnemonic, then look at this way of spelling 'aveNuE.' It has an NE in it, so if I hear Brooklyn NE or 35th NE, I think of Brooklyn aveNuE, or 35th aveNuE."

Source: *Seattle Homes,* by Jim Stacey

THE ART OF SHORTCUTTING

Look at it as a challenge. It's rush hour, you have to get to the waterfront, and you're up on Broadway. You know it'll take an hour to get through all the lights on Madison. Tootle north on Broadway to Harvard. Zip down Harvard to the Eastlake overpass, cut down Denny to just before Fifth Avenue with the monorail in sight. Turn left on a little zag to Fifth, then quickly dodge cars and pilings under the monorail to get over to Wall. Turn right (quick, get in the right-hand lane so you don't get in the Highway 99 entrance crunch), and zip down to Alaskan Way. It's clear sailing from here. And don't you feel smug?

Feeling vain? Vanity plates are replacing bumper stickers as the way to make a statement en route.

- Cost of vanity plates: $45 for Mount Rainier plate; renewal is $30/year plus excise tax.
- The state license-plate people can—and do—turn down vanity name requests if they consider them offensive.
- Number of vanity licenses in Washington State in 1996: 79,918
- Words that have been used up for vanity plates: Anything to do with sports—anything with the words ski, golf, or Huskies.

Source: Washington State Dept. of Licensing

With effort and initiative, you can achieve a sublime level of navigating skill. Creatively chain together smaller throughways that will run at least 10 blocks in any single direction. Success depends on the degree to which you are willing to cut U-turns where permissible, negotiate speed islands, and do some sharp heel-and-toe work. If you have to go through a neighborhood, go slow—you'll still beat the freeway traffic.

Consider the "forgotten roads" that the wise drive to avoid the no-man's-land of the I-5 corridor. Dexter is one—broad, fast, and usually empty. Another "highway of choice" is Aurora, traffic lights and all.

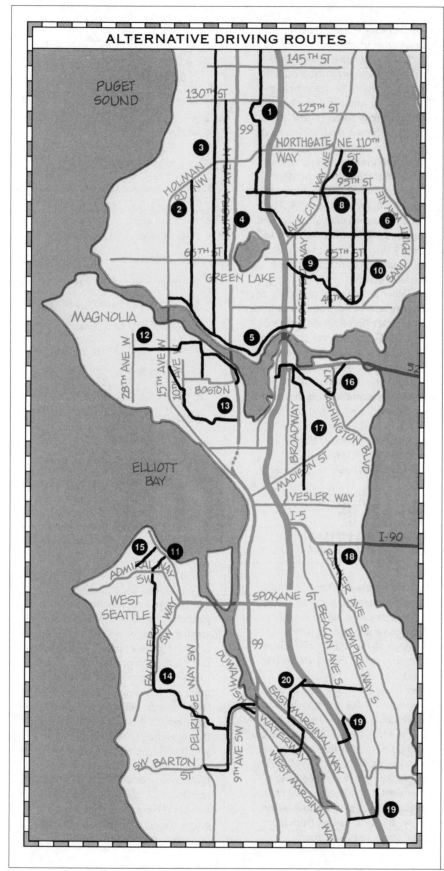

ALTERNATIVE DRIVING ROUTES

CUTTING IT SHORT

Northwest Seattle

Areas to avoid: Intersections at N 85th Street and Aurora Avenue N, NW 85th Street and 15th Avenue NW.

Best north/south access: Third Avenue NW, Dayton Avenue N, also Eighth Avenue NW from Leary Way to Holman Road.

Open east/west access: N 130th Street, NW 80th Street, NW 75th Street.

1. North Green Lake to city limits, avoiding I-5: To stay out of the freeway crawl around Northgate, get off I-5 at N 85th Street and go west to Meridian. Head north to 205th and beyond (with slight detours around North Seattle Community College and Haller Lake).

2. Eighth Avenue NW: Good access north/south from Leary Way to Holman Road.

3. Alternative to Aurora: Greenwood Avenue N from N 36th Street to N 145th Street. Speed islands, residential—go slow.

4. Alternative to Greenwood or Aurora: Fremont Avenue N from 65th Street NW to 130th Street NW, but can be slow because it becomes heavily residential as it progresses north.

5. U District to Ballard, avoiding 45th: From the U District, take Brooklyn Avenue NE or 15th Avenue NE south to N Pacific Street. Then head west on Pacific until it becomes N 34th Street. At the Fremont Bridge, turn right on Fremont Avenue N, which blends into Fremont Place, which then turns into N 36th and becomes Leary Way NW to access Ballard from the south. Better yet, turn right before Fremont—Stone Way to Bridge Way N to Fremont Way and onto Leary is a good alternative route.

Northeast Seattle

Areas to avoid: University Way and NE 45th (or almost anywhere and 45th), NE Northgate Way, Lake City Way NE.

Best north/south access: Sand Point Way NE; 35th, 25th, and 15th avenues.

Best east/west access: NE 65th and 75th streets.

6. Magnuson Park to Shilshole: NE 75th west to Banner Place N is a quick way to get from far northeast to far northwest. This shortcut works in reverse from west to east if you take 80th instead of 75th.

7. U District to Lake City, avoiding Lake City Way: 25th Avenue NE to Ravenna Avenue NE makes a great scenic route moving from north U District area to Lake City. Ravenna begins curving parallel to Lake City Way after crossing 85th Street.

8. 35th Avenue NE north or south to 92nd Street and west to north Green Lake or Aurora: 92nd is a vital throughway to the west side, though you may have to detour around a number of speed islands.

9. Traveling east to west from View Ridge, avoiding 65th: Take 40th Avenue NE to NE 52nd Place, turn right, and this merges into 39th Avenue NE, then to NE Blakely

Sage drivers at Yellow Cab depend for their livelihood on the more esoteric shortcuts. Military Road off Airport Way next to Boeing Field is a great "sneak" under the freeway, says one. Ditto that for Albro Place, the Boeing Access Road, and SW 129th Street. An experienced driver calls the Aloha jog west across lower Queen Anne Hill vital to his success.

Street. (This winds around, a little narrow.) Go up 25th Avenue NE to the Ravenna Park area, by taking a left onto 55th NE and then an immediate right onto Ravenna Avenue NE, to get up to a left turn onto NE Ravenna Boulevard and into the U District or Ravenna.

10. Traveling north or south, avoiding Sand Point Way or 35th: 40th Avenue NE has good access between 88th Street on its north end and Sand Point Way on the south end; good alternative to Sand Point or the congested area of 35th NE.

Southwest/Central Seattle

Areas to avoid: California Avenue SW as well as Fauntleroy Way.

Good north/south access: Airport Way S, 35th Avenue SW, 49th Avenue SW.

Best east/west access: SW Thistle Street, in West Seattle.

11. From Admiral district to Harbor Avenue SW: Get off the hill onto Harbor SW in West Seattle on Fairmount Avenue SW.

12. Shortcuts to Nickerson Street (north side of Queen Anne Hill): From Magnolia on the west side, take W Dravus Street east to 11th Avenue W; go left to Bertona Street and right to Nickerson. You can go right on Third Avenue W prior to Nickerson to access the top of Queen Anne Hill. (But go slow—residents have complained and Big Brother is watching.) When coming from the east and using Dexter Avenue N as a parallel alternative to Westlake Avenue N, cut a corner to the Third Avenue hill from Florentia Street, just past the Fremont Bridge.

13. Avoiding the Mercer Mess: Go around the south side of Queen Anne Hill by taking Aloha off Queen Anne or Highway 99. Go west to First Avenue W, then go left one block to W Olympic Place, which merges into Olympic Way W. This goes to 10th Avenue W, then take a left one block on Howe Street to 11th Avenue W, which turns into Gilman Drive, leading to 15th Avenue W.

Or stay away from Mercer Street

entirely by backtracking to another freeway entrance. For I-5 going north, use the Olive Way entrance. Get onto Olive eastbound from Boren, cross over the freeway, stay in the left lane, and you'll merge with cars coming down Olive to enter the freeway northbound. To go south on I-5, follow Boren north to Howell, turn right, and follow the signs to I-5 south. It's worth the foray into

For those of you who don't relish the idea of shortcutters using your neighborhood for their backroad driving, here's a tip. The City of Seattle Engineering Department runs a Neighborhood Speed Watch Program that lends out a radar unit free to one person in the neighborhood and trains him or her to use it. Information on speeding vehicles is recorded on a form— make, model, license number, and color. And the residents can clock speeds. Once the Engineering Department receives the forms, it tracks down the culprits via license plate numbers and sends a letter saying the residents are concerned. What does the Department find? That most speeders live in the neighborhood. For information on the Speed Watch Program, call 684-0815.

Ever noticed that most people in Seattle drive in the left lane of the freeway (the "passing" lane) and just plain stay there? Some people say, if you are in a hurry, try driving in the right lane. Because of the propensity of Northwesterners to stay in the left lane, the "slow" lane actually can be faster because it's less congested.

downtown even if you have to go as far as University Street to approach the dreaded I-5.

If you're going from downtown to Highway 520 and want to avoid I-5, go east on Denny to Olive Way. When Olive becomes E John Street, follow it until you see 15th Avenue E, where you take a little jog to the left. Take this to E Thomas and continue east until you reach 23rd Avenue E, which will take you to 520 via Montlake. Better yet, dip into the Arboretum from 23rd and take the less crowded Arboretum on-ramp.

14. Highland Park Way: Take Highland Park Way exit from First Avenue S bridge on Duwamish Waterway. Follow it to Holden Street, then turn right to 16th Avenue SW, and take a right and immediate left on Austin Street. This merges into Dumar Way SW, which becomes Sylvan Way hill. Merge into SW Morgan Street. From here, 40th Avenue SW is better than 38th for northern access because it eventually merges into Fairmount Avenue SW. That goes down a scenic route to Harbor Avenue SW. Slight right-hand

jog at SW Hanford Street to stay on 40th. (W Marginal Way SW is a much quicker alternative to this northern access if you don't want to cut through any neighborhoods.)

15. Ferry Avenue SW: Ferry also cuts down from top of hill to Harbor Avenue SW, joining at area of Salty's restaurant.

For a shortcut to the airport, see Chapter 5, "Carless in Seattle."

16. Roanoke Street: To access Roanoke Street on the way to Montlake, take Eastlake Avenue E north, then go right on E Louisa or E Lynn streets, and take a left on Boylston Avenue E, then turn left to Roanoke. An alternative to the 24th Avenue E paralysis when getting onto 520 is to take Roanoke to Delmar Drive E to Boyer Avenue E to Lake Washington Boulevard in the Arboretum, then go left up to the more isolated eastbound 520 on-ramp.

17. Avoiding Broadway: 15th Avenue E is a good, if crowded, parallel to Broadway on Capitol Hill. Follow it north until it turns into Boston, then turn right on 11th (or Federal) and wind down to Roanoke, where you can either head down to Montlake

If you can't beat the traffic jam, try a little Moby Dick or War and Peace. The Seattle Public Library lends books on tape. Or if it's missed business you're fretting about, you can get a Mitsubishi car fax at Car Toys for about $1,200. The folks at Car Toys recommend you pull over before actually faxing those documents, though.

or up to the U District. Try 12th Avenue E, too.

Southeast Seattle

Best north/south access: 23rd Avenue E and Jackson Street; Beacon Avenue S, Martin Luther King Jr. Way, and Wilson/Seward Park Avenue S.

Best east/west access: Graham, Orcas, and Othello streets.

18. Around Jefferson Park: Cheasty Boulevard to Beacon Avenue S or Columbian Way and 15th Avenue S helps dodge broken streets around the Jefferson Park golf course. To access Cheasty Boulevard shortcut, turn right off Martin Luther King Jr. Way onto S Winthrop Street, which merges into Cheasty Boulevard S. No signals, a great scenic shortcut.

19. Crossing I-5: Military Road south of Beacon Hill is a good I-5 under-crossing. Also the Boeing Access Road (south of Boeing Field); eastbound it intersects with Martin Luther King Jr. Way for open access all the way north through Madrona.

20. From SE to SW: Graham Street west to Swift Avenue S, then north to Albro Place, over I-5, west to Ellis Avenue to E Marginal Way, south on 16th Avenue S, and across the 14th Avenue S bridge to Cloverdale Street. This route carries you almost from Seward Park on the far southeast side almost to Lincoln Park on the far southwest side.

AND MORE...

That takes care of the four sides and the center of the city. But here are a few general tips:

In the fast lane. Express lanes are always the fastest. Commuter High-Occupancy-Vehicle (HOV) lanes, marked with a diamond on the pavement, are another good alternative (north and south on I-5, westbound on 520). Most HOV lanes are now for two-or-more persons, but some are still three-or-more, so watch the signs.

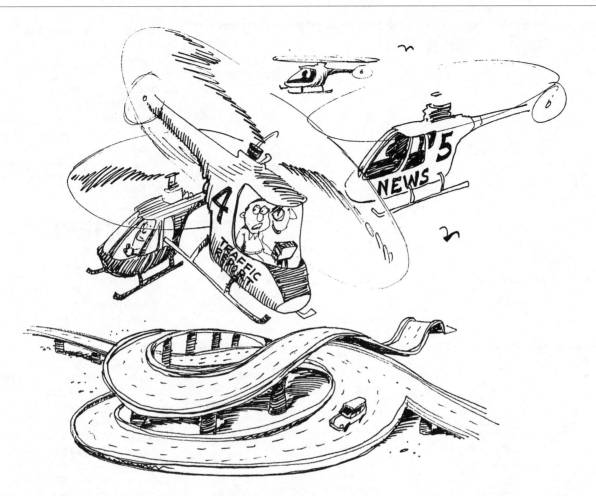

Lid watch. A tip to the daring: Police usually hang out just on the west side of the Mercer Island Lid (tunnel).

Alaskan Way Viaduct. It may be ugly and it's definitely not the safest place during a major earthquake, but the Alaskan Way Viaduct section of Highway 99 is a route you can count on to be virtually stopless. Even with the 50 mph speed limit (40 mph on 99 at the viaduct's north and south ends), it's a good alternative to I-5 at rush hour. However, accessing it can be tricky. Beware of making a U-turn when heading south on First to get to the Royal Brougham Way ramp, the best access to 99 from Pioneer Square—police watch from a nearby parking lot.

East/westbound. During the half hour between 5:30 and 6pm there just isn't any good path across Lake Washington. In general, I-90 is less crowded than SR 520.

North/southbound I-405. At rush hour, try to avoid this entirely. Best alternative is, believe it or not, I-5 to I-90. Some desperate souls do anything to avoid I-405. They choose to go around the lake, up to Mountlake Terrace, and then east, but that's only if I-405 is really congested. On the east side, Bellevue Way, which parallels I-405 from I-90 to 520, can often save some time.

North on Lake City Way. If you're heading to the north end of Lake Washington, 522 (Lake City Way) can be a decent alternative on some days.

Redmond bottleneck. The stoplight at the end of 520 often causes congestion. If you're going into Redmond, the best way to avoid this stoppage is to exit at NE 51st Street. Turn right at the ramp to Lake Sammamish Parkway, then north on Redmond Way. This will take you right into town.

Downtown exits. Heading from the north into downtown on I-5, avoid the Union Street exit, which drops you into the middle of one of the most congested spots in Seattle (partly due to the Convention Center).

Convention Center bottleneck. If you're heading north on I-5, you can avoid the mess around the Convention Center by taking the Madison Street exit to Ninth. It eventually becomes an entrance and you're back on I-5—ahead of all those trucks stuck under Freeway Park.

Fastest route to ferry. Used to be that to reach the ferry you had to endanger your life to out-race the trains, so the city jury-rigged a solution that has you praying there won't be an

High-accident intersections

Intersection	Accidents/year	Average daily traffic
Ninth and Mercer	42	39,500
Fifth and Blanchard	24	14,400
Fifth and Mercer	20	40,600
Martin Luther King Way S and S Graham	17	36,200
Renton Avenue S and S Henderson	16	19,400
Mercer and Westlake	15	45,300
Rainier S and S Orcas	15	23,300
Fifth and Union	14	36,400
Broadway E and E Olive	14	32,900
Delridge Way SW and SW Orchard	14	21,800
15th Avenue NE and NE 50th	13	21,500

Source: City of Seattle Engineering Department

INSIDE EDGE

Ever wondered how you are supposed to drive through those intersections with traffic islands in the neighborhoods? You're probably doing it wrong: According to Seattle police, you can make a left-hand turn at the island by just cutting left—that's right, you don't have to go all the way around it. The police say the reason for this leniency is that large trucks and fire engines can't circle the islands to make left turns. Of course, you need to make sure no one is coming at you from the left.

earthquake while you're stuck beneath the viaduct. No matter which direction you're coming from as you approach Colman Dock—where you catch the Bainbridge Island and Bremerton car ferries or the passenger ferries for Vashon Island and Bremerton—you have to get into the line for the ferry from the south. Coming from I-5, take the Fourth Avenue S exit onto Fourth; then turn right (west) on Royal Brougham, cross the train tracks, and zoom across First Avenue. Just past First, the signs direct you into a strange, dark road under the viaduct, heading north. That tunnel-like path leads you past the active train tracks and eventually onto Alaskan Way, where you simply get in the left-hand lane and turn into the terminal entrance. (If you try to sneak into the terminal entrance off Alaskan Way from the north, if not ticketed by the police, you may be throttled by annoyed commuters who follow the rules.)

Pike Place Market to Pioneer Square. First and Second avenues can be abysmal in the late afternoon. Duck down to Western Avenue and miss them both.

Pioneer Square to Lake Union. Get onto Western as soon as you can, and follow it north to the entrance to the Battery Street tunnel. Take your life in your hands merging with Highway 99 traffic and, once out of the tunnel, turn off at the first right, or the next right if you miss it; then zip up to Westlake.

Sources: Metro traffic reporters, Seattle Survival Guide research, assorted traffic survivors, and shortcut sleuths

TRAFFIC LINGO

Copter jockeys, those rush-hour referees, almost never talk about street locations. They speak a language of their own. Here's a translation:

The brewery (as in, "There's a slowdown by the brewery"): Rainier Brewery, the big building with the red "R" beside I-5 just south of downtown near Spokane Street.

The eastern high-rise (as in, "There's a complete stall at the 520 eastern high-rise"): This, and its related "western high-rise," refers to the ramps on each end of the floating bridges, where the roadway begins to rise as it approaches land.

The bus barn (as in, "a car fire in the road near the bus barn is causing slowdown as drivers turn to gawk"): It's the exit for buses only off I-5 at N 175th Street.

Mercer Street exit (as in, "traffic is at a complete stop at the Mercer Street exit"): This isn't, of course, an exit onto Mercer Street at all. Mercer runs one way eastbound. You're really exiting onto Fairview.

The viaduct (as in, "the viaduct is the best bet southbound"): the Alaskan Way Viaduct, part of Highway 99, that runs from south of downtown into Aurora Avenue on those pillars above Alaskan Way.

Mercer Island Lid (as in, "complete standstill at the Mercer Island Lid"): The tunnel that cuts through Mercer Island.

Top 20 accident locations in King County

State Hwy	Location	Accidents in a year	Accident rate*	Accident rate (4-yr. avg.)
900	SR 515 to I-405	104	11.1	12.1
900	Between Mill Ave & Rainier S	57	10.8	9.0
900	Hardie Ave to SR 515	40	10.6	7.3
515	Between SR 516 & SE 235th	118	10.5	9.3
519	Route from Fourth S I-5 exit to Colman Dock	36	9.8	12.4**
99	Hwy 18 to S 320th (Federal Way)	141	9.3	8.5
202	Between NE 164th & NE 180th	114	8.6	7.7***
99	Between S 320th & SR 509	130	8.0	8.0
NE 145th St	Between I-5 & SR 522	117	7.8	6.4
99	Between N 85th & N 145th	281	7.6	8.0
99	Between N 145th & N 175th	162	7.2	7.3**
900	132nd SE to 164th SE	60	7.0	6.1
NE 145th St	Between SR 99 & I-5	64	6.9	5.4**
99	N 175th St to county line	134	6.9	6.1
99	Between SR 518 & SR 599	140	6.6	5.6
515	Between SE 208th & SE 126th	116	6.3	5.7
99	S 170th St to SR 518	67	6.3	5.7
164	Hwy 18 to M St (Auburn)	64	6.3	6.2
99	Northbound, between Elliott Ave & Broad	121	6.2	4.4
167	Between I-405 and SR 900 (Renton)	84	6.0	6.2

* Accident rate is based on the number of accidents per million vehicle miles (1995 figures)
** 3-year Average
*** 2-year Average
Source: Department of Transportation

WHERE THE CARS MEET

Hear the word "congestion" and what comes to mind? Not something you treat with nasal spray but those horrible intersections where one car sneaks through at a time. Sometimes that's because of stoplights, sometimes because of a bottleneck (as in the case of the Montlake Bridge, where 58,900 cars every 24 hours squeeze into a street that has arterial sclerosis).

- **Most congested intersections:** First prize goes to First Avenue S bridge and E Marginal Way S.

Runners-up: Fairview and Mercer, Aurora Avenue N and Denny Way, Lake City Way NE and NE 145th, 15th W and W Dravus.
- **Longest lights:** We award first prize to Greenwood Avenue N and N 145th Street. The light is set at a 150-second cycle length in the afternoon in heavy traffic. Second prize: California Avenue SW and SW Alaska Street, where the light is set at a 120-second cycle from 11am to 7:30pm.

Actuated or progressed?

If some signals seem slower than others, it's not just your imagination.

Signals are operated by three different methods. Some—especially those at large or major intersections, such as Greenwood N and N 145th—are *actuated*. This means that the presence of a car or pedestrian directly activates the signal cycle. Pressure-sensitive sensors beneath the asphalt detect a car's weight on the road. Pedestrians, of course, activate the signal by hitting the "walk" button.

Signals at intersections along a straight-shot thoroughfare—such as NE 45th and NE 50th streets—are *progressed*. This means that each light's cycle is timed "progressively" and varied throughout the day to cycle in keeping with the flow of the traffic, thus eliminating as much stop-and-go movement as possible.

Taking advantage of progressed lights is a great way to cut travel time. For instance, say there is no traffic on NE 45th heading east. You could travel from the freeway to 15th Avenue NE (UW) through a half-dozen lights without stopping if you were doing the speed limit. That's because each light is timed progressively; each light cycles to "green"

We can't surmise that it's because of frustration over a crowded 99, but the Aurora Bridge has long been known as the suicide bridge. An average of three people jump from the bridge per year. The toll in recent years? 1991: none. 1992: three. 1993: one. 1994: none. 1995: nine. Source: Seattle/King County Medical Examiner's Office

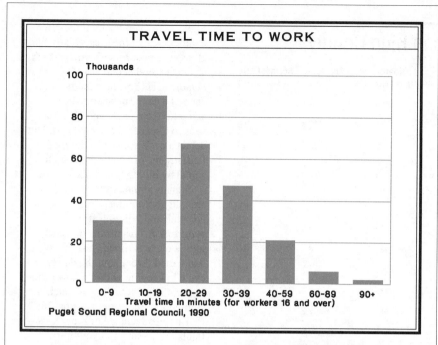

TRAVEL TIME TO WORK

Thousands

Travel time in minutes (for workers 16 and over)

0-9 · 10-19 · 20-29 · 30-39 · 40-59 · 60-89 · 90+

Puget Sound Regional Council, 1990

just as you get to it.

A third signal method pre-times lights at all-way–walk intersections with the emphasis on pedestrian safety rather than optimum traffic flow (such as near schools, by the Market, etc.).

At non-signaled intersections, there must be five or more accidents in a year before the intersection will be considered for signal installment.
Source: Seattle Engineering Department

WHEN IN A RUSH...

So it seems as if rush hour starts at 2pm on Fridays? Projections show that by the year 2000, peak-period hours of delay on the freeway/expressways will double. Twenty years after that, they'll triple. That doesn't even take into account the clogged arterials.

One other thing about rush hour multiplication: Between 1988 and 2000, roughly $500 million worth of gasoline will be wasted by vehicles sitting on congested roadways in the Central Puget Sound region, according to a study by the Puget Sound Regional Council.

THOSE DAMNABLE (BUT LOVELY) BRIDGES

Seattle's horrendous traffic funnels both north/south and east/west onto 161 narrow bridges. And, as if that's not enough, many are drawbridges that go up to let boat traffic through, thus blocking auto traffic. Drawbridges are a frustrating part of Seattle's character, and almost everyone has a love-hate relationship with them. You love them from afar at sunset but hate them when they spring up in front of you like a brick wall.

The Montlake Bridge opens on demand every half hour from 12:30pm until 3:30pm, and again at 6:00pm and 6:30pm. It's closed during rush hours, 6:30am–9am and 3:30–6pm. Outside of those hours, it opens on demand except 6:30am–11pm, when boats must contact the bridge an hour beforehand to schedule an opening.

HOV TATTLERS

Ever wonder if anyone actually reports violators in the HOV lanes?

Well, they do—in droves. In 1995, 21,500 people called in to report that a car just whizzed by them in the diamond lane with fewer than three (or in some cases two) riders. In the same year, 28,143 violation reports were processed (in other words, many of those 21,500 callers reported violations more than once). These tattlers are called HEROs, because they report the violations on the 24-hour hotline, 764-HERO.

The program is run by Metro, the state's Department of Transportation, and the State Patrol. The state Department of Licensing uses the license-plate number to furnish the name and address of the vehicle owner. This info is then entered into the

Where bridges are concerned, weight and revenue take precedence. The ship canal bridges will open anytime for ships of 1,000 gross tons or more, and those on the Duwamish River will open for ships of 5,000 gross tons or more. A tug going out to pick up one of the large vessels is also allowed immediate clearance, presumably because it is contributing to Seattle's economy and status as a Pacific Rim port. So when you see a little tug stopping traffic to go through the bridge, it means it's going to pick up one of the large ships (although it may be days before the tug and ship in tow reappear).

It seems a lot longer, but the truth is that when a bridge goes up, it's open for only 3 to 3½ minutes on average. Remember that the next time you're stuck at the University Bridge staring at the car in front of you and wishing you were on the other side.

HERO personal computer, which tracks how many times that vehicle has been reported. The first time, the violator gets an HOV-lane brochure in the mail. The second time triggers a personal letter from the Department of Transportation with another brochure. The third time prompts a letter from the Washington State Patrol, and the fourth time an "action memo" is sent to the State Patrol and you're in trouble.

FREE PARKING

If surviving in traffic takes certain skills, sleuthing out Seattle's free or cheap parking spaces takes even more. Free parking spaces in Seattle are an endangered species. The ones listed were free the last time we saw them.

In general, you're going to find most free parking on the rim of what's normally considered downtown—before 8am. Many times if you get there at 7:55 you'll find a spot, and by 8:05 you may be plumb out of luck. (P.S. If you have a good stereo system in your car, don't bother reading any further: Just pay for a safe spot.)

For those willing to play parking roulette, the general rule of thumb is that if it doesn't say "No Parking" (in one way or another), you *can* park there without being ticketed. And if you are ticketed, contest it: Legally you're safe. Read signs carefully— many are free for an hour or four, and others say no parking north of sign (which implies that it's free south of sign).

The "no parking 30 feet from corner" signs can often be stretched to, say, 15 feet without a meter maid noticing. No guarantees for that tip, though.

If you really like to live dangerously, try parking in an alley and putting a note in the window that says, "Just loading" or "My car broke— I'll move it as soon as I can." (No guarantees for that one either—but it has been known to work for brief periods of time.)

South end/waterfront
1. On the west side of First Avenue (between Dearborn and Royal

Seattle's bridges open on demand for boats—except during weekday rush hours, when they are closed to small-boat traffic. Most ship canal bridges are closed to boats Monday-Friday 7–9am, 4–6pm; the Montlake Bridge is closed 6:30–9am, 3:30–6pm. And on the Duwamish, the First Avenue S Bridge is closed 6–9am and 3–6pm. Large oceangoing vessels still get an open bridge, though, even during those hours.

Average one-way commute times, nationwide

	Minutes
New York	30.6
Washington, D.C.	29.5
Chicago	28.1
Los Angeles	26.4
Houston	26.1
Atlanta	26
Baltimore	26
San Francisco	25.6
Seattle	**24.3**
Boston	24.2
Dallas	24.1
Philadelphia	24.1
Miami	24.1
Detroit	23.4
U.S. average	23.2

Source: U.S. Census Bureau

Brougham north of Gerry Sportswear Building) there's unlimited free parking. (The east side is one free hour only; south of the Gerry Building on the west side is two hours only.)
2. The east side of a little strip along Railroad Way just off First Avenue S (just behind Franglor's Creole Cafe).
3. South of S Jackson Street underneath the Alaskan Way Viaduct and along Alaskan Way: The largest free parking area in Seattle is filled at night with the cars of ferry commuters (who usually move their cars by 8am each morning) and during the day with Adobe employees' cars. Still, there always seems to be a way to squeeze your car in—especially if you drive far enough south. Careful, though: It's not paved in parts, mammoth potholes and puddles abound, and you may have to chance it over the ruts of the unused railroad tracks.

Lincoln Towing, which has a contract with the city, tows 15 to 20

The city turns its ticket collections over to Continental Credit and SCA. If you don't pay, they send stops on vehicle registrations and tab renewals even to other states, so they'll get you no matter what. Continental sends out 3,000 delinquent notices per week. Here's how outrageous a ticket can become:

Ticket for no proof of insurance: $475

Ticket for not carrying driver's license: $47

Delinquent charge (after 15 days): $47

Collection fees: $256.05

Interest (12% per annum per month): $39.56

Total: $864.61

ticketed cars per day from under the viaduct south of Jackson Street. Reasons for the tickets vary: parking at an angle in parallel parking zone, parking too close to the railroad tracks, parking over 24 hours, and parking in "no parking east of here" zones. It is poorly signed. But if you're lucky, you'll find a good, free spot here.

4. South Lane Street (much of the street, with some exceptions, a small one a few blocks south of Jackson in the International District).

5. Maynard Avenue south of S Lane.

6. Occidental Avenue south of King Street: there are few angle-in parking spots. Watch for loading docks, but as long as you stay clear

of ramps, you should be OK. These fill up early.

7. Yesler Way, where it crosses I-5: Free parking abounds on both sides of the street as well as carpool-only spaces 7–10am.

North end/Pike Place Market

1. Heading north, it's a bit tougher to scam a free space. With the new developments along the waterfront and in Belltown, most of the free parking is disappearing. But it's still worth a try.

2. Elliott Avenue (one-way southbound) is virtually a free-for-all, though it fills early (before 8:30am) with the cars of students from the Art Institute of Seattle.

3. A half-dozen of the cross streets between Elliott Avenue, Western Avenue, and First Avenue allow unlimited parking (north from Battery Street). A bit of Bell Street (between Western and Elliott) is approachable only from Elliott— but is the closest place to Pike Place Market to scam a space. These spots fill before 8am almost every day.

PARKING FACTOIDS

- Parking per hour downtown: $1. In less popular areas it can go down to 60 cents. Lowest is 25 cents in the Roosevelt neighborhood.
- Number of parking meters in Seattle: 9,000
- How many meters are looted in a year: None. The city installed new parking meters made of iron that are nearly impossible to loot. About 20 to 30 are vandalized per year, though.

AND IF YOU GET CAUGHT

To pay a parking ticket, go to the cashier's window on the first floor of the Public Safety Building, Third

Hourly parking meter rates

San Francisco	$1.50
Seattle	**$1**
Denver	$1
Los Angeles	$1
San Diego	$1
Portland	75 cents
Sacramento	50 cents
Vancouver, B.C.	50 cents (Cdn.)

Avenue and James Street. Hours are 8am–5pm. Or mail your check to P.O. Box 34108, Seattle, WA 98124-1108. Include your license plate number on the check.

However, consider talking to the magistrate before forking over the fine. The city won't say how many parking fines are lessened or forgiven altogether if a case is contested, but if you're really strapped, it's a good idea to throw yourself on the magistrate's mercy. He or she will almost always give you a break—and will allow you to pay over time.

TICKET FACTOIDS

- Parking tickets issued annually: approximately 900,000
- Cost of overtime parking ticket: $20
- Cost of ticket for parking in loading zone: $23
- Cost of ticket for parking in commercial truck loading zone: $39
- Most expensive parking ticket: $175 for parking in a space reserved for the handicapped
- What happens if you don't pay in 15 days: It doubles.
- Unpaid parking tickets in 1995: 128,180
- Uncollected parking ticket amount owed to Seattle: $25 million

Source: Seattle Survival Guide research and Washington State Dept. of Licensing

WHEN THERE'S NO CHOICE BUT TO PAY...

When in doubt, use a privately owned lot. The rationalization here is that if the time runs out, a city parking ticket will cost you at least $20 and go on your record (and if you don't pay it'll go up—and after only three unpaid tickets the City of Seattle will issue a warrant). Privately owned parking lots (Diamond, Central, United Parking) run anywhere from $2.75 to $10.50 a day. Usually prepayment is required; however, if you forget to prepay and find a notice on your windshield, it will run you the equivalent of the lot's daily charge. Lots charging any more than $10 a day should be boycotted.

WHAT IT COSTS

In commercial lots, unless you're willing to park on the outskirts of downtown and walk a ways, you'll pay, on average, $7.45 per day ($93.34/month) downtown; $5.54 ($46.86/month) on First Hill; and $3.54 ($35.79/month) on Lower Queen Anne. In the Denny Regrade area, lots run about $4/day if you get there before 9:30am.

Lots charging less than $5 a day are becoming as rare as logging trucks. A couple of under-$4 spaces still exist downtown, and there are plenty in the $6–$8 range and many in the $9–$10 range. Here are the last of the species:

- Queen Anne Avenue north of Thomas Street: $2
- First Avenue N north of Denny Way: $3.50
- First Avenue S south of King: $3.75/day
- Virginia and Terry: $4/day
- Fourth and Jackson: $5/day

TROUBLE CALLS

When you see anything wrong with traffic signs or signals in Seattle, call the City of Seattle Engineering Department at 386-1206 or, after business hours, 386-1218.

DOWNTOWN GAS PUMPS

The concrete jungle has few gas stations and fewer garages where you can get anything repaired. But here are some gas stations close in:
Seattle Center area: Denny and Broad; Queen Anne and Denny Way; also one at Westlake and Mercer
Midtown: 1001 Fourth Avenue, in parking garage; Fourth and Columbia Parking, at entrance of parking garage
Kingdome: 511 S Dearborn

SEEING PINK ELEPHANTS

There's also a gas station at the downtown Elephant Car Wash, at 616 Battery. You can't miss the revolving pink neon sign. The original car wash, started in 1951 at 2763 Fourth Avenue S, was not called Elephant Car Wash, but when the enterprising owners held a contest for a new sign and logo in 1956, the winner was the distinctive neon elephant that can now be seen at both Seattle locations and in Tacoma, Federal Way, and Puyallup (these last are called Li'l Elephants). Wouldn't you know—there are also two in California.

The signs have attained cult status. They've been featured on the cover of *Car Wash* magazine (oh, did you miss that issue?). And Elephant Car Washes were mentioned in *Cosmopolitan* as a place the '90s woman

Instead of turning their pockets inside out when stuck at the parking meters in downtown Seattle, some people just give up and get $10 worth of quarters every payday to feed the parking meters.

can still go to meet a nice guy (mostly referring to the young urban professional males that frequent the place for their weekly car washes, although the guys who work at Elephant say it was referring to them).

As if that wasn't enough, a New York ad agency wanted to use the name and logo on a New York phone book. Ah, the price of fame.

As for local recognition, you can find a miniature elephant logo on the ceiling of Von's, a downtown restaurant on Pine Street. Tourist mementos include stickers, key chains, postcards, and the like.

The Elephant signs are some of the last remaining big flashing neon signs around. Why, even historical preservation types were on their side when talk started a few years ago about reducing the number of large signs around Seattle. One thing's sure: The elephants will never forget their support.

The two Seattle car washes are now owned by Bob Haney.

THE TOE TRUCK

Contrary to popular belief, the little pink "toe truck" at Lincoln Towing is just a teenager. Though it's not a Seattle old-timer, the truck (along

Move into a neighborhood and can't find a legit place to park? If there is an existing permit system in the neighborhood (ask around) and you want a permit, call 684-5086. If you want to establish a permit system in the neighborhood, call 684-7570. It'll cost you about $80 per month.

with the Elephant Car Wash sign) has found a place in Seattle lore. In 1980, the punsters at Lincoln Towing got the idea for the truck and asked Seattle body shop expert Ed Ellison to build it. He made it out of a Volkswagen bus, reconstructing the body with fiberglass. A Seattle sculptor molded the five toes on top and the Lincolns put a light inside so the toes would light up.

In 1996 the Lincolns commissioned Ed Ellison and son Steve to create a second "Toe Truck," which now resides at Lincoln Towing's Aurora Avenue location. This one sports a set of right toes (the original is a leftie) atop a customized Chevy van. The toes are longer, wider, and "more curved over," but they're just as pink as the original and just as attention-grabbing. On its maiden voyage, Toe Truck Too—gussied up with a huge garter around its big toe—transported a Lincoln Towing employee and his bride to their wedding.

While the original Toe Truck is retired and sits in state at the I-5 Mercer exit, its sibling stands in at Seafair parades, promotions, and auto safety talks at local schools. Lincoln Towing tells us it's open to Tow Truck appearances at all kinds of

special events, so if you have a burning desiire for huge pink toes, call them up.

CARPOOLS— ONE SOLUTION

Everybody's pushing carpools, and with good reason. They're not only good for you, they're good for society as well. And they save money. Seattle Commuter Services (a city group) offers low-cost carpool parking throughout downtown Seattle and surrounding areas.

The parking costs $75/quarter per carpool. Most carpool lots serve only cars carrying three or more people, but a couple of lots are open to two-person carpools. There's competition for the spots: there are 4,000 to 6,000 participants.

Carpool resources

Metro Carpool ride-matching
625-4500

Metro Vanpools
625-4500

Seattle Commuter Services, carpool parking
684-0816

TRAFFIC RESOURCES

City of Seattle Engineering Department
600 Fourth Ave.
Seattle, WA 98101
684-5349
City department responsible for roadways.

Puget Sound Regional Council
1011 Western, #500
Seattle, WA 98104
464-7090
Working on regional transportation plan.

Regional Transit Authority
821 Second Ave.
Seattle, WA 98104
684-6776
Working on regional transit plan.

Seattle Police Traffic Section
610 Third Ave.
Seattle, WA 98104
684-8762

Traffic violations
684-5600

Illegal parking on public property/abandoned vehicles
684-8763

Impounded vehicles on public property
684-5444

Complaints about vehicle impounds and tows
386-1297

To report trucks over legal requirements
684-5086

Residential parking permits
684-5-86
684-7570

Washington State Department of Transportation Information
440-4000

Driver licensing locations

1200 Third Ave. (renewals only)
464-6846

464 12th Ave.
720-3025

320 N 85th St.
545-6755

907 N 135th St.
368-7261

8830 25th Ave. SW
933-3420

CARLESS IN SEATTLE

Light rail, commuter trains, Regional Transit Plans — all the billion-dollar dreams are still just that. Although our grandchildren may someday have to deal with subway graffiti, currently our alternatives to driving consist solely of busing it, hoofing it, biking it, or jumping on a ferry. But plenty of Seattleites refuse to join ranks with the drivers stuck on overpasses: more than 10,000 workers pedal their way to city offices daily, while another bunch of pencil pushers carpool, zooming down those diamond-studded lanes. About 120,000 trips to and from work are made on Metro buses every day. And each day 15,000–18,000 commuters float to their jobs aboard ferries.

RIDING THE BUS

Metro buses 75 million passengers from stop to stop annually (those aren't all different passengers—this figure counts how many trips people make and includes free-zone riders). It's easy and cheap. Each bus route has a published timetable with a route map, a schedule of times, and fare information. The schedule tells when the bus will arrive at major bus stops along the route.

You can pick up timetables on the buses and at many locations around the city (libraries, shopping

Don't bother swearing at the bus driver for not letting you get on in the middle of the block. And don't bang on the doors of the bus either. Drivers are allowed to pick up passengers only in bus zones—that's why they won't stop for you even if you sprint to catch that bus that's only half a block away from the stop.

Metro fares

	1 Zone	2 Zone
Adults	$1.10/peak $0.85/off-peak	$1.60/peak $1.10/off-peak
Youth/student (5–17 yrs.)	$0.75	$0.75
Seniors/disabled (with permit)	$0.25	$0.25

Source: Metro

centers, and community colleges). Or you can call Metro's 24-hour number: 553-3000. They'll send you a timetable or tell you when to appear at the bus stop. New schedules are published three times a year: in February, June, and September.

You can get a free color map of the entire transit system by stopping by Metro's office in the Exchange Building (Second and Marion) or the customer service center on the mezzanine level of the Westlake bus tunnel station (several entrances around Fourth and Pine). Metro has a Web site too: http://transit.metrokc.gov.

CLINKING COINS

Hmmm—what's wrong with this picture? There's a big push to get people out of their cars and onto public transportation. Everyone's talking light rail, express buses, neighborhood shuttles, gas tax, getting employers to force employees to carpool. So Metro raises its fares—twice between 1991 and 1993.

You now have to come up with a greenback plus one shiny dime for a one-zone ride at rush hour. If you cross the city limits during peak commuting hours, you need a two-zone fare—a crisp bill, two big quarters, and a shiny dime. Unless you start your ride in the downtown free zone, pay when you get on the bus if you're coming into town. Going out of town, pay when you get off. And Metro drivers don't carry change,

so have the right coins—or folded bill and coins—in hand.

The free zone is just that—a ride-free area that is one of the best things about Seattle's public transportation system. The free-zone borders are in downtown Seattle—Jackson Street on the south, Sixth Avenue on the east, Battery Street on the north, and the waterfront on the west; hours for riding free are between 6am and 7pm.

Ticket books and passes

You can save a little money by buying bus tickets in books of 10 or 20. If you use the bus a lot, invest in a monthly, three-month, or annual pass. (Check with your boss first: some local employers subsidize bus passes.) The charges for peak-hour passes are listed below; off-peak monthly and annual passes are available too.

Monthly pass: $39.50 one-zone/peak, $57.50 two-zone/peak.

Three-month pass: $109 one-zone/peak, $159 two-zone/peak.

Annual pass: $435 one-zone/peak, $633 two-zone/peak.

You can buy a pass by mail or at:

- Metro's 821 Second Avenue office
- Westlake bus tunnel station, mezzanine level
- Bartell's drugstores
- Albertson's supermarkets
- Selected Seafirst Versateller machines (call Seafirst at 461-0800 to find out which ones).

Or call 624-PASS. Ticket books are also available from all the above locations except Seafirst bank machines.

WHERE AM I?

You catch the bus and you know where you want to get off, but soon you are reading or daydreaming, and before you know it you're in West Seattle. Metro bus drivers are not required to call out stops; in fact, they don't have to say anything unless they've been asked a question. To be fair, many of them do call out the stops—in fact, there's one who rattles off all the buses you can transfer to at a given stop. He's a marvel—although you sure can't daydream with him yelling out a long list of memorized route numbers.

To make sure you get the word, when you board the bus, ask the driver to call out your stop. When you hear the call, pull the signal cord above the window. And say thanks.

DOGS, BIKES, AND BUSES

Yes, you can take Fido on the bus, but he or she "may not occupy a seat." So says Metro's drivers' bible, "The Book." The dog has to be leashed or on your lap, and if he turns out to be a troublemaker, the driver can kick him off. For anything bigger than a lap dog, you pay the same fare for the dog as you pay for yourself. Other pets are allowed only if they're in a container or the driver decides they look safe.

As for your bike, it's not allowed inside the bus. However, all buses have bike racks. You can pick up a free brochure from Metro on how to use the racks.

Not all buses can accommodate wheelchairs. But 81% of Metro's fleet and 79% of the routes are wheelchair accessible. Schedules are marked with an "L" sign (meaning lift-equipped) to indicate accessibility.

Metro safety statistics

Operator assaults	1993	1994	1995
Driver-injury assaults	39	15	11
Driver–non-injury assaults	89	83	71
Total	128	98	82

Source: Metro

BUT IS IT SAFE?

In 1987 a driver lost his job because he was carrying a gun on the bus. He took the case to the judge, and the state supreme court ruled it was Metro's prerogative to say drivers can't carry weapons.

Metro is quick to say that it's the safest bus system in the nation. Here's how it stacks up:

- Total 1995 ridership: 73.4 million
- Total miles traveled: about 38 million
- About one security incident every two days
- About 21 passenger accidents per month, or 255 for the year, or about one accident annually per 288,000 passenger trips.

Between 9pm and 5am only, you may ask the driver to stop the bus at a location along its route other than a regular stop. The driver will determine whether safety allows for that stop, however.

Metro's bicycle team—transit security agents who belong to the Seattle Police Department's bicycle squad—can move easily through traffic jams, using alleys, sidewalks, or even stairways to respond to calls for assistance from driver and passengers. Metro also has a youth team that works with school-age children, a gang team that focuses on gang members, and a boarding team that can be assigned to ride troubled routes, or to be visible in problem zones or at bus shelters.

PARK IT AND RIDE

Metro provides a number of Park & Ride lots where you can leave your car for free and catch a bus or carpool. The lots fill up, so get there early. (Not in a carpool, but want to be? Metro offers a ride-matching service; call 625-4500.)

In-city sites are at North Jackson Park (Fifth Avenue NE and NE 133rd Street), Northgate (Fifth Avenue NE and NE 112th Street), North Seattle (First Avenue NE and NE 100th Street), Roosevelt (NE 75th Street & 11th Avenue NE), Green Lake (two lots: I-5 and NE 65th Street). There are 138 other locations throughout the region. Call 553-3000 to get a map.

Six thousand to 10,000 umbrellas are left on Metro buses annually. If you lose something on the bus, call 553-3090. Maybe someone turned it in. Most unusual thing turned in to Metro's lost and found? A human heart.

THE BUS TUNNEL

At last, Seattle has an underground public transportation system—the bus tunnel. Beneath the downtown area, buses wind through subterranean passages, serving destinations such as the U District, Southcenter, Sea-Tac Airport, Bellevue, and Northgate. Unfortunately, buses still rumble down Seattle's surface streets, notably on Third Avenue (where, consequently, no parking is allowed).

The advantages of the tunnel can be expressed in mere minutes:

- Time it takes a bus to travel through downtown Seattle on surface streets during rush hour: 20 to 25 minutes.
- Time it takes a bus in the tunnel: 8 minutes.

The bus tunnel operates between 5am and 7pm Monday through Friday and between 10am and 6pm Saturday. There are five tunnel stations. In each station, the bus stops in an area called a bay—a specific space at the loading platform. The bays are labeled with letters of the alphabet—A–B are northbound, C–D bays are southbound. Signs list the routes that stop at each bay. In an average hour, 38 buses are making trips through the tunnel—19 each way—so if you're just going from station to station downtown, you shouldn't have to wait long.

Each of the five stations is enhanced with art designed to reflect the area the station serves. You can get a free guide to the art in the bus tunnel from Metro's customer service outlet in the Westlake bus tunnel station.

TUNNEL FACTS

- Amount of dirt taken out of tunnel: 900,000 cubic yards, or six stories high if piled across a football field.
- Where it went: Various landfills (e.g., Federal Way, Paine Field).
- Cost of tunnel: $450 million.
- Length of tunnel: 1.3 miles.
- Depth of tunnel: 60 feet below street level.
- Number of elevators in the tunnel: 28.
- Number of escalators: 46.
- Record-setter: The longest and steepest escalator west of the Mississippi is in the Pioneer Square tunnel station.
- Breda Costruzioni Ferroviarie: No, it's not an espresso bar. It's the Italian company that built the bus shells for the tunnel buses. There were a few snags in the buses—in the gear systems, for example—but angst and expenses have been forgotten now that all the buses are rolling. These special Italian buses run on electricity in the tunnel and switch to diesel when they come up for air.

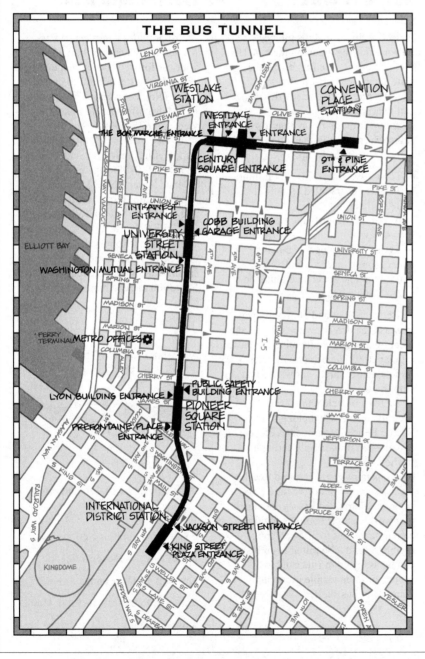

THE BUS TUNNEL

THE STREETCAR

Metro operates the Waterfront Streetcar, which came from Australia. It serves a real transportation purpose as it travels from the waterfront up Main Street and into the International District. You can jump on at any one of the nine stations along the route.

Caution: Unlike Metro buses, the streetcar isn't free downtown; it costs $1.10 during peak hours and 85 cents at other times. And it takes forever to get from the International District to Pier 70. (In the summer you can get crushed by gawking tourists.)

Want to make a career out of avoiding gridlock? Try the Metro jobline, 684-1313, or the Port of Seattle, 728-3290.

TALKING TO METRO

King County Metro Transit (Metro)
821 Second Ave.
Seattle, WA 98104
Bus info: 553-3000 (24 hours) or
684-1739 (TTY/TDD users)
Driver commendations and
complaints: 553-3060 or 684-2029
(TTY/TDD users)
Lost and found: 553-3090
Pass information and sales: 624-PASS
Ride-match/vanpool info: 625-4500
Traffic update (recording): 684-1420
Transit director's office: 684-1441

OTHER BUS SERVICES

Leaving town? These buses may be able to help you get away.

Community Transit
778-2185
Trips in Snohomish County.

Pierce Transit
(800) 562-8109
Trips in Pierce County.

Gray Line of Seattle
720 S Forest St.
624-5077
Scheduled sight-seeing tours, airport service, and charter buses.

Greyhound
811 Stewart St.
(800) 231-2222
Greatest number of scheduled bus routes connecting Seattle with other cities. For package service, call 628-5555.

TRAIN TO NOWHERE

Although not a very practical transportation option for most folks (it travels between Westlake Center and Seattle Center, a distance of 12 blocks), the Monorail still wows the tourists. So wait till friends come to visit if you can't justify spending a dollar on a 90-second thrill just for yourself (75 cents for kids; free for children under 5). Trains leave every 15 minutes from 9am to 11pm. There's a move afoot to extend the Monorail's route, but don't hold your breath.

Seattle Center/Monorail
441-6038

HEY, CABBIE!

Seattle's not much of a taxi town. The fares are expensive and cabs can be hard to find. Downtown, cabs often congregate near Westlake Center, on Pine Street between Third and Fourth avenues.

STREET WALKERS

Walking instead of driving affords you some of the same advantages as kayaking instead of power boating.

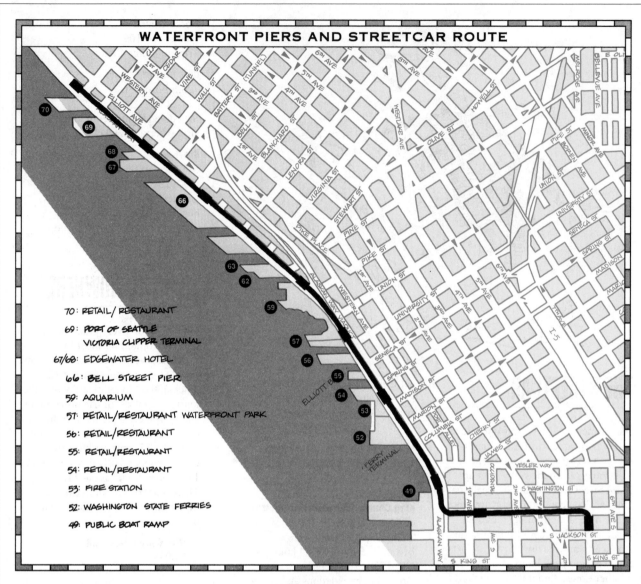

WATERFRONT PIERS AND STREETCAR ROUTE

70: RETAIL/RESTAURANT
69: PORT OF SEATTLE
    VICTORIA CLIPPER TERMINAL
67/68: EDGEWATER HOTEL
66: BELL STREET PIER
59: AQUARIUM
57: RETAIL/RESTAURANT WATERFRONT PARK
56: RETAIL/RESTAURANT
55: RETAIL/RESTAURANT
54: RETAIL/RESTAURANT
53: FIRE STATION
52: WASHINGTON STATE FERRIES
49: PUBLIC BOAT RAMP

You can slip down narrow passages, weave unorthodox routes around obstacles, and actually take in the scenery.

Especially in downtown Seattle, where one-way streets and massive structures block the way for autos, feet can save the day. That's not to say there aren't hazards: Seattle doesn't have the reputation of being the Jaywalking Ticket Capital for nothing (more about that later).

PEDESTRIAN SHORTCUTS

City planners and developers have finally begun to consider the plight of pedestrians in a city where it frequently rains. Almost all of the newer high-rises have a tunnel or inside path where you can cut corners and avoid traffic. With escalators and elevators inside the buildings, you need never climb a hill again. The trick is to look for high-rises that take up a complete block. They usually have access on both sides of the building

and an internal route that does not depend on stairs. (See the map on page 84.)

1. From the waterfront uphill to Sixth Avenue: Walk up the Marion Street overpass from the ferry terminal to First Avenue; enter the lobby of the Federal Building on First between Madison and Marion. Then take the elevator to the fourth floor to get out at Second Avenue. Cross the street and take the covered escalator up the First Interstate Plaza. Walk through the bank to Third Avenue. (Use the revolving doors or you might get yelled at for letting the wind into the lobby.) Then cross the street to the 1001 Fourth Avenue Building, and take the escalators up to Fourth Avenue.

From there you can either head uptown via the pedestrian bridge that runs across Spring, or cross the street and take the escalator (or elevator) in the Seattle Public Library from Fourth up to Fifth Avenue. If you don't mind passing through a metal detector, you can then go one more block uphill by crossing Fifth to the U.S. Courthouse and taking the elevator there up to Sixth.

2. From Second Avenue and University uptown: Thank goodness for the Washington Mutual Tower. It not only offers a route up the hill, but it is pretty inside as well. Enter it from Second, and take an escalator or elevator to the main lobby on Third, taking a peek at the peregrine falcon video on the way. Cross the street to Seattle Tower and take an elevator to the fifth floor. There is a covered outdoor walkway and a bridge to the Four Seasons Olympic mezzanine.

Leave the hotel by the main entrance (where the doorman is, on University) and cross the street to Rainier Square. Take the underground walkway there past Eddie Bauer and on to One or Two Union Square on Sixth Avenue. (You can also exit on Fifth.)

3. From First Avenue uphill to Fifth at Marion: On First enter the Norton Building between Marion and Columbia streets. Take the escalator up to Second. Cross Second and Columbia to the second-floor lobby of the Dexter Horton Building and take the elevator up one floor to Third. At Third, cross at Cherry and go to the Public Safety Building. Take the elevator up to Fourth Avenue (on the fourth floor of the building). Cross Fourth and Cherry to the Columbia Seafirst Center and take the escalator up to the second-floor atrium.

There's a great pedestrian tunnel here—but you have to ask people where because it's somewhat hidden. Follow it to the Seafirst Fifth Avenue Plaza building, where an elevator

Experiencing wanderlust, but don't have a car? Take a ride on a historic bus or trolley instead. The Metro Employees Historic Vehicle Association sponsors low-cost Saturday and Sunday excursions throughout the year, around Seattle and beyond. Past destinations have included Snohomish; Vashon Island; Tacoma's Point Defiance Park; fall foliage in the Cascade foothills; and Seattle's best Christmas lights. Fares vary, but are generally $3–$6 for adults, less for seniors and children. For upcoming trips, call the recorded message hotline, 633-4590.

will take you up to the lobby. You'll find yourself on Fifth and Marion.

4. Northbound from Cherry to Spring, beginning on Fourth: Enter the Columbia Seafirst Center on Fourth and Cherry, take the escalator up to the atrium's second floor. Take the tunnel to the Seafirst Fifth Avenue Plaza Building (see above) and go up to the Fifth Avenue level. Cross Fifth and Marion to the fifth-floor lobby of the Bank of California Building and take the elevator down to the first-floor lobby on Fourth. Cross Fourth and Madison to the fifth-floor lobby of the 1001 Fourth Avenue Building. Take the escalator or elevator to the Third Avenue lobby and entrance near Spring Street.

5. The underground concourse between department stores and Westlake Center: Definitely not a lengthy shortcut, but the bus tunnel station does provide a dry way to get from the Bon Marché to Nordstrom or Westlake Center. You can go into Nordstrom, head to the bottom floor, and walk across the tunnel under Pine and get to Westlake Center, or past Westlake Center to the Bon, where you can take an escalator up and exit on Third Avenue.

6. Waterfront to Pike Place Market: Go into the parking garage across from the Seattle Aquarium below the Pike Place Market. Take the elevator up to the skybridge that crosses over to the Market.

7. International District to Kingdome, avoiding traffic (not shown on map): From the International District, you can see the big Dome, but between you and it are the tunnel and a maze of traffic. Try crossing Fifth Avenue S on Jackson, then cross the Amtrak parking lot, duck into the King Street Station, go down the stairs through the dingy hallway and out the taxi entrance. Voilà! You're at the Kingdome parking lot.

Source: Seattle Survival Guide research

LOOK BOTH WAYS

Cars, for the most part, watch out for other cars, not for pedestrians walking or crossing the streets. Painted crosswalks and even traffic signals cannot always be depended on to stop those 3,000-pounders. It's best to do what your mom told you and look both ways carefully (and over your shoulder for turning traffic) before stepping off a curb.

According to the Harborview Injury Prevention and Research Center, 80% to 90% of the drivers who see you in a crosswalk won't stop. They're subject to a $47 ticket for that infraction, and the police have gotten pretty vigilant about giving tickets. In 1995, 849 drivers were given tickets.

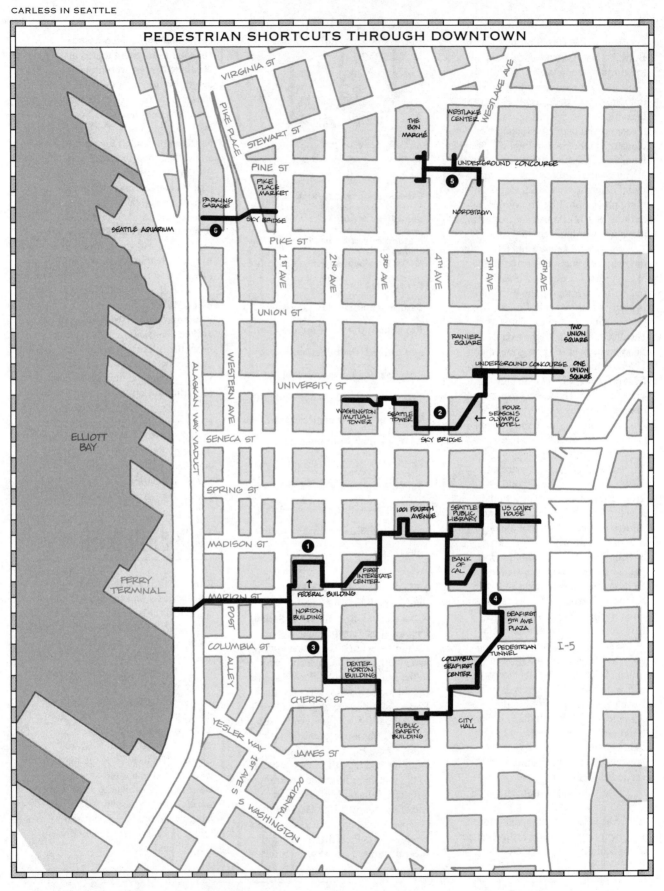

PEDESTRIAN SHORTCUTS THROUGH DOWNTOWN

Jaywalkers get tickets too, although the city has not been as aggressive about this in recent years. But if you are a blatant violator or cause a traffic problem, don't be surprised if you're ticketed. Jaywalking tickets cost $38. (If you don't pay, the city won't come after you unless you rack up several of them—they're considered mere infractions. And there are no figures on how many contested jaywalking tickets are thrown out, but those who've tried arguing their case say they either get a lesser fine or none at all.) Some 1,026 jaywalkers were issued tickets in 1995.

Though jaywalking is common, the risks are considerable, and we don't mean the fine. In fact, when you're surrounded by moving hunks of steel, any kind of walking can be hazardous to your health. In 1994, 460 pedestrians were injured by motor vehicles in Seattle; 10 died as a result. Of the fatalities:

- 3 occurred at intersections with a traffic signal
- 4 occurred in the middle of the block (read: jaywalkers)
- 3 occurred at intersections without a signal

As you'd expect, pedestrian-car accidents are concentrated in the downtown area and along busy arterials.
Source: Seattle Engineering Department

Where injuries are concerned, kids, in particular, take the brunt of it. Kids ages 5 to 9 have the highest rate of pedestrian injuries, often from darting out from between parked cars. Here's a stat to curl any parent's hair: For young school-age children, pedestrian injuries are the leading cause of death from trauma and are second only to cancer as the leading cause of death overall. Harborview and Children's hospitals treat about 80 kids involved in pedestrian-car accidents per year.

EXERCISE ALTERNATIVE

Feel like getting your exercise by walking but aren't crazy about gas fumes? Try mall walking, the latest fad (especially for senior citizens) at the sprawling shopping centers. At Northgate Mall, for example, walkers pace up and down from 7:30am until the shops open around 9:30am. The mall is ¼ mile from one end to the other. Every Wednesday morning from 7am to 9pm, there are two nurses and an exercise physiologist on hand to do free blood-pressure testing and health checks, and to give out information on walking. For info, contact Northwest Hospital, 365-7587.

Bellevue Square also has a walking program, sponsored by Overlake Hospital. Sea-Tac Mall in Federal Way has a program sponsored by St. Francis Hospital.

ALL ABOUT STAIRS

Since Seattle has so many hills, it's only natural that we have so many stairs. One Seattle man has taken this to the extreme: Don Glickstein, urban staircase scholar extraordinaire. He pawed through card files at the city Engineering Department to compile a database of all of Seattle's outdoor stairways, when they were built, where they are, and of what they're made.

He says if you put the city's stairs together, you'd have a staircase of 24,002 steps and 1,245 landings, rising 2.7 miles—and those are just the ones maintained by the Engineering Department, not those belonging to the Parks Department or the UW.

A few notable stairways from Don's list:

Oldest: In Queen Anne, at Second Avenue N and Ward Street, 34 steps of monolith concrete with pipe railings, built in 1906. And on Second Avenue N between Prospect and Ward, monolith concrete, 75 steps, pipe railings, also 1906.

Longest: Pigeon Hill, from SW Charlestown to Marginal Place SW, 228 steps, five landings, made with prefabricated concrete slabs and wooden hand railings. (The slabs are from Seattle's defunct trolley system.)

Most landings: On S Lucile Street, connecting 18th Avenue S to 20th S, 28 landings, 169 steps.

Joggers' favorite: In Eastlake, on E Blaine, from Lakeview to Broadway, 211 steps, 9 landings, pipe rails.

Wooden staircase: The longest of Seattle's seven all-wood staircases is on 20th NE, between NE 100th and NE 98th, 37 steps.

Shortest: On Queen Anne's W Garfield between Ninth Avenue W upper and Ninth W lower, 2 steps.

WITH WHEELS AND HELMETS

Two percent of the city's commuters ride bikes to get to work. That makes Seattle one of the highest cycling commuter communities of comparable size nationwide.

The most common bike route destination is the U District. If you're going there from downtown, it's best to go up Broad, then head north on Dexter. Follow it to the Fremont Bridge, cross it, get onto N Pacific Street and then onto the Burke-Gilman Trail, which leads you straight to the University.

Main cause of accidents for adult cyclists: riding against traffic. Main causes of accidents for kids on bikes: ages 4–5, riding out of driveways without looking; ages 6–7, intersection crossings; ages 8–9, running stop signs.

On the brighter side, more kids in Seattle wear bicycle helmets than in other cities—but that's still only 5%. (In Portland the rate is 1%; in San Francisco it's 0.5%.) Every summer Bartell's Drugs offers discount coupons for kids' and adults' bike helmets.

BICYCLING Q & A

Q: What traffic laws apply to bicyclists?
A: All.

Q: What position in the lane should a bicyclist use?
A: If you're going at the speed of traffic, use the middle of the lane. If you're slower, ride as near to the right side of the right through-lane as is safe except when preparing to turn, when passing another bicycle or vehicle, or on a one-way street (where it's legal to ride on the left). If the right through-lane is too narrow to permit sharing with cars, and when drain grates or the like prevent riding on the shoulder, bicyclists should ride in the middle of the right lane. You are required to ride on the shoulder only on limited-access highways. When five or more vehicles are lined up behind you, you must pull off the road and let them by.

Q: What lane position should a bicyclist use through an intersection?
A: The same as a car, but where the intersection is particularly scary, it's a good idea just to dismount and use the crosswalk. (Sometimes it's faster too.)

Q: Is it illegal to ride side by side?
A: No, the law allows bicyclists to ride two abreast.

Q: Can I put my bike on a bus?
A: Yep—if you're going to the right place. All Metro buses have bike racks, and using them is free. (You still have to pay your passenger fare.)

City bike riding is a serious thing; one false move and you lose your life or a limb. There are one or two bicycle fatalities per year. Although 250 bicycle-car accidents are reported each year, most bike accidents don't involve cars. Ninety percent of all bike accidents are caused by rider error. Where do they happen? At intersections and on suburban streets and—to an overwhelming extent—in the U District.

The city gives out free bicycling maps that specify several urban, scenic bike loops. Call the Engineering Department at 684-7583. King County puts out a map too, in conjunction with REI. The county map is $4 at REI or Metsker Maps. And then there's a book called *Touring Seattle by Bicycle* by Peter Powers and Renee Travis. It has 3-D foldout maps with contours, points of interest, route profiles, and even a calorie counter. Plus, there are usually two routes for the same area, one challenging and one easier.

BIKE FACTS

- The Burke-Gilman Trail has over one million users per year: 70% are on wheels (bikes or skates), and 30% are pedestrians.
- Over 45% of Americans do some bicycling. It's estimated that well over 50% of Seattleites use a bike to some degree.
- Since 1973 more bikes than cars have been sold in the United States.
- Seven to eight percent of UW students and faculty commute by bicycle.
- The new I-90 bike system is in place; the bike route is on the north side of the tunnel.

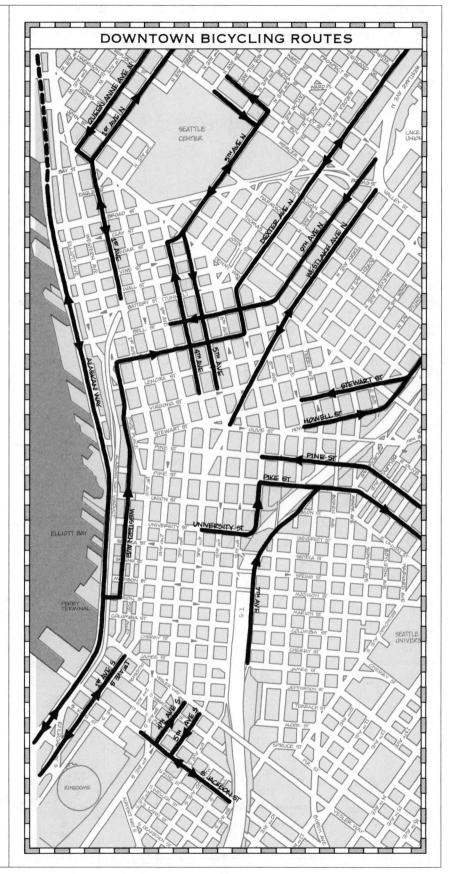

DOWNTOWN BICYCLING ROUTES

SEATTLE BICYCLING ROUTES

EXISTING

PROPOSED

Bikers' resources

Cascade Bicycle Club

P.O. Box 31299
Seattle, WA 98103
522-3222

Over 2,500 members belong to
this club. Membership is $17 a year.
A ride line (522-BIKE and press #1)
lists local rides, mileage, type of
people going (singles, unemployed,
married, etc.), and contact number.
The group meets monthly and
has several committees, including
BATS (Bicycles as Alternative
Transportation).

Seattle Engineering Dept.
Bicycle Program

684-7583

An advocacy office within the city
giving out information and taking
complaints and concerns. Has a
safety program too.

Sports, etc.

P.O. Box 9272
Seattle, WA 98109
286-8566

Free paper with ride calendar,
club listings, tours, maps, news,
and features. Nine issues per year.
Available at bike shops and REI.

AT SEA LEVEL

Twenty-five ferries ply the Sound on
10 routes. From Seattle, you can go
to Bainbridge Island, Vashon Island,
and the Kitsap Peninsula (Bremerton,
Kingston, and Southworth). The trip
to Bainbridge is the fastest: 35 minutes. Fares are $3.50 round-trip for
passengers, $5.90 one-way for car
and driver. Most ferries leave from
Colman Dock, but ferries for Vashon
Island and Southworth also leaves
from the Fauntleroy terminal in West
Seattle.

Unfortunately, ferries and waiting
go together, like rain and slugs. But
if you're in a carpool of at least three
or a vanpool of at least five, you may
be able to get a free Ferry Fast Lane
permit that will guarantee you a spot

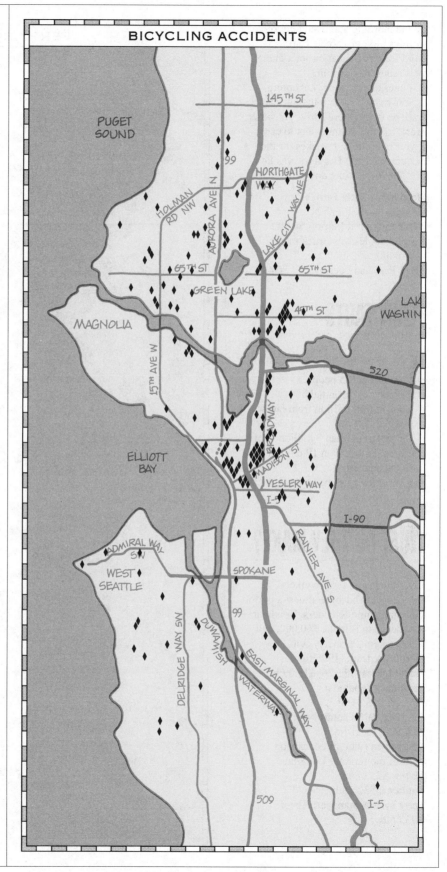

BICYCLING ACCIDENTS

on the morning and evening ferry sailings of your choice. Call 515-3495 for an application for a one-year renewable permit.

Other than car- or vanpooling, the only way to avoid the lines is to walk on or get there early. The other secret to ferry riding is not to care if you're on time. It makes for the perfect excuse: "The ferry was late," or "The ferry broke down."

Washington State Ferries
Colman Dock, Pier 52
Alaskan Way at Marion Street
Info/schedules/tolls/truck rates:
464-6400
Ferry Fast Lane permits: 515-3495

FERRY FACTS

The Washington State Ferry system:

- Employs 1,575 people.
- Operates 20 terminals.
- Took in $68 million from fares in 1992.
- Carries more than 8 million vehicles and more than 19 million riders annually.
- Consumes 12.8 million gallons of fuel per year.

WHAT DO THEY MAKE?

Over the years, ferry workers' salaries have become almost a parlor guessing game for riders. You hear that deckhands make $60,000, and ticket takers a princely sum. Here's the truth (1996 figures):
Ticket takers: $11.26–$16.09/hr.
Terminal attendants: $10.58–$15.11/hr.
On-dock traffic controllers: $10.58–$15.11/hr.
AB seamen (who direct cars on and off the ferry): $18.08/hr.
Mates: $25.08/hr.
Captains: $32.76/hr.
Ferry system manager: About $93,660/yr.

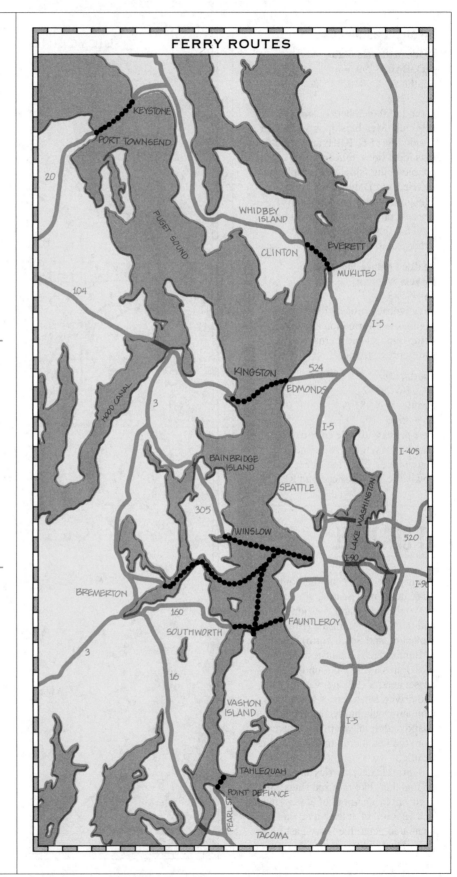

FERRY ROUTES

CRAZY ABOUT FERRIES?

If you just adore the green-and-white double-enders, take a free ride across Lake Roosevelt between Wilbur and Republic in eastern Washington. The *Martha S.* holds 12 cars and runs between 6am and 11pm.

A bit of ferry trivia: Back in the 1950s one of the hottest ferry controversies concerned the landing signal used by ferries as they approached the dock. The landing signal was described as "a groan and a grunt." After seven years of debate, the issue was resolved when the ferry system reinstated "a warp and two woofs," or what's better known as "one long and two short" blasts. It's a familiar and listened-for signal to regular ferry users; when they hear it from a few blocks away, they know they'd better run for the boat.

AMTRAK

The train is a lovely way to travel, if a bit slow and often late, and Amtrak *has* been working on getting real china back in the dining car à la the Orient Express.

The main thing about train travel is that it's relaxed and friendly—Amtrak's employee-training program seems to really work. You just need to have enough time to enjoy the trip. You can go on the cheap in the coach car, but if you can, spring for the sleeper rooms; you'll be a lot more comfortable.

Amtrak leaves Seattle for two end destinations: Los Angeles and Chicago. But it does have several routes. The Coast Starlight, a nighttime trip down the coast to L.A., is probably

the most popular, and the Empire Builder, through Idaho, Montana, and on across the North Central states to Chicago, is a beautiful ride through unspoiled mountain country. The Pioneer route goes to Chicago too, but first drops down to Portland and then runs through mid-America. The Mount Rainier route is a commuter-type run to Portland with stops at Tacoma, Olympia, and the like. For the first time in 14 years, there's a passenger-train link to Vancouver, B.C., from Seattle. The new Mount Baker International run leaves Seattle's Amtrak station daily at 7:45am, arriving in Vancouver at 11:40am. You can stay all day, then leave for Seattle at 6pm, arriving at 9:55pm. Cost: $42–$58, depending on type of seating. Reservations are required. (There's a diner, if you feel like traveling in style.)

Amtrak
King Street Station
Third and Jackson
Reservations or information:
(800) 872-7245
Baggage, lost and found, package express: 382-4128

GRIDLOCKED SKIES

Seattle-Tacoma International Airport officials freely admit they're in trouble because of the threefold increase in landings and takeoffs since 1959. Capacity at the airport is 400,000 flights per year, and the Port of Seattle (which runs the airport) says that will be reached in about seven years. A proposed third runway has many citizens up in arms over the threatened potential increase in volume in an already very noisy city sky.

The first key to getting in and out of the airport hassle-free is to leave the car behind. Some alternatives:

Airporters
431-5906, 431-5904
Serves communities from as far away as Bellingham. Call for information, departure times, etc.

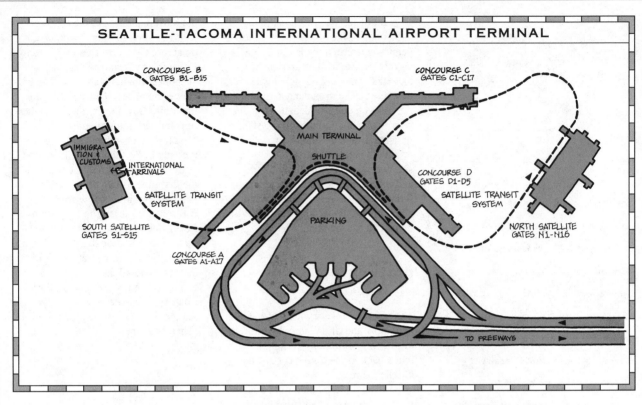

SEATTLE-TACOMA INTERNATIONAL AIRPORT TERMINAL

Sea-Tac's Express Parking means you pull onto the third floor of the parking garage and park, paying at a machine near the elevators in the garage. You have to estimate the time you'll be parked. The temptation is to just pay for the hour, then figure no one will know how much longer you're there. But the truth is, the lot is monitored by a person at a TV screen who watches how long the cars are parked, so get back there ASAP.

Gray Line Airport Express
626-6088
Drops off and picks up passengers at hotels throughout downtown. $13 round-trip, $7.50 one-way.

Greyhound
(800) 231-2222
Makes several daily trips to the airport from downtown Seattle and vice versa. $6 one-way, $11 round-trip weekends; $5 one-way, $10 round-trip weekdays.

Metro
553-3000
Has three routes serving the airport.

Seattle-Tacoma International Taxi Association (STITA)
246-9999
STITA is a cooperative cab company that gets choice spots at the airport cab stands. The drivers have to wear clean uniforms and have reliable, clean cars. The cars are painted white with a green-and-white logo on the side. Taking a taxi from within the city limits costs $28–$30—and can cost as much as $40 if the traffic is bad.

SuperShuttle
622-1424
You may have to be ready quite a bit ahead of time, but this service offers 24-hour door-to-door service. Fares start at $16 first person, $5 second, $3 each passenger after that.

Trying to find your car in the Sea-Tac Airport parking garage can take longer than your flight did. Try always parking on the eighth (top) floor; that way you'll always remember where your car is—and because that floor is uncovered, it usually has available spaces.

A few more options

Limousine services run from $25 up and can take eight to nine people at the flat rate. And many hotels provide **courtesy car service** to and from the airport.

ROUTE OF CHOICE

If you absolutely must drive to the airport, it's best to avoid I-5. From downtown take Alaskan Way or the viaduct south. That puts you on E Marginal Way. Turn off onto the First Avenue S bridge and follow Highway 509, which is usually fairly uncongested, to the airport. You can also take Highway 99 all the way south to 170th S. Turn right there and right again after going under the overpass. This route has lots of stoplights—509 really is best.

AIRPORT SERVICES

The airport has a foreign exchange center, run by Mutual of Omaha, which is open 6am–9:30pm daily. (Travel insurance is available here in case you get that if-God-had-wanted-people-to-fly-(s)he-would-have-given-them-wings feeling.) You can also pick up tickets from a travel agent at this desk.

Other services include:

- Cash machines. At least four machines, open 24 hours.
- Two US West communication centers, one in the main terminal and one at the north terminal. You can use the copy machines, fax (outgoing only), and booths with phones and desks. There's a small conference room available on a first-come, first-served basis.
- VIP room that includes a large conference room, kitchen, large lounge, two offices, and two smaller studios for small meetings. But it isn't for riff-raff; it's for Port of Seattle trade or business customers.

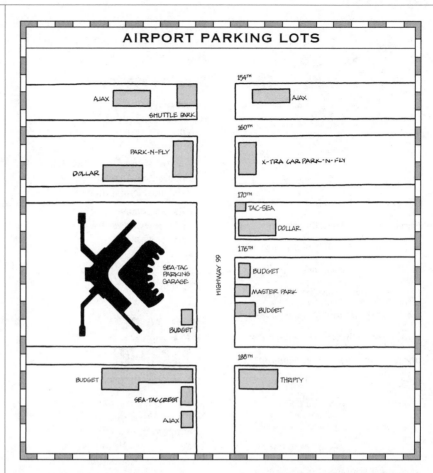

AIRPORT PARKING LOTS

- Large rooms that rent out for wedding receptions (quick getaway variety). Call 433-5605 for catering reservations.
- An auditorium for 250 people.
- Tours. If you've always been fascinated with airport workings, this is the ticket. Groups can get a free tour (for kids, the youngest age is kindergartener). In a recent six-month period 4,500 people took airport tours. Call three weeks in advance, 433-5386.
- Meditation room. For those *lonnng* waits.
- Barbershop, shower, and shoeshine shop. All in main terminal (a second shoeshine shop is located in the north satellite).
- An extensive art collection, including works by Louise Nevelson, Robert Rauschenberg, Alden Mason, and Frank Stella. Call the Aviation Communications Office at 433-4645 for a brochure and map.

Airport parking rates

Agency	Daily	Weekly
Ajax	$8.95	(third day free)
Budget (2 valet lots)	$9.95	$64.00
Budget (self-park)	$7.00	$46.00
Dollar Park–N–Fly	$7.00	$42.00
Doug Fox	$8.75	$52.00
Master Park (valet)	$8.75	
Sea-Tac Crest	$5.00	$35.00
Shuttle Park	$6.75	$40.50
Tac-Sea	$7.00	$4.75/day
Thrifty	$9.95	$64.95
Valet	$9.50	$66.50
Xtra Car Park–N–Fly	$6.50	$39.00

Source: Individual parking services. For more info, call Sea-Tac's Skyline information number, 431-4444, or toll-free (800) 544-1965.

The absolutely best-kept secret at the airport is Ken's Baggage and Frozen Food Storage. Its name doesn't say enough: this little gem of a shop will do almost anything for you. It's down on the baggage claim level just under the escalators. Ken's will notarize your letter, unlock your car, lend you jumper cables, make you copies, store everything from skis to computers while you're away, and even sell or store dog kennels. They'll package your bike for shipping, deliver stuff, rent you a baby stroller, and take care of your UPS and Federal Express business. Ken's is privately run. 433-5333.

Seattle-Tacoma International Airport
17205 International Blvd.
Seattle, WA 98158
433-5217
Airport information: 431-4444

King County Airport
Boeing Field
7233 Perimeter Rd. S
Seattle, WA 98108
296-7380
Reliever airport for Sea-Tac, with smaller planes and no scheduled passenger traffic. Boeing Field is the 11th busiest airport in the nation in terms of landings and takeoffs. It has many corporate and private planes (Burlington Northern and Nordstrom, for example), private pilots, and flying clubs.

Seaplane service

Kenmore Air
6321 NE 19375th St.
Seattle, WA 98155
486-8400
Flights to British Columbia, Kitsap Peninsula, San Juan and Whidbey islands, and Semiahmoo.

Seattle Seaplanes
1325 Fairview Ave. E
Seattle, WA 98102
329-9638
Flights to Canada, the San Juans—"anywhere there's water."

HOW TO GET A PASSPORT

If you're planning to get out of North America, you need a passport. It's important to apply for it right away—it takes 2½ to 3 weeks to get a new passport, although they'll put a rush on it if you sound desperate. Go to the Seattle Passport Agency with evidence of U.S. citizenship and proof of identification, plus two passport photos. (There are plenty of passport-photo places near the Federal Building, and they know the required dimensions of the shot.) And take $65 (adults) or $40 (minors). Thirteen-year-olds and up need to apply in person.

In 1974, there were 202 daily flights out of Sea-Tac. The number rose to 900 in 1992 and is predicted to reach 1,100 per day in the year 2000.

If you need to renew your passport and have had one within the last 12 years, you can renew by mail—provided you submit your old passport with the new application.

The office is open Monday through Friday, 8am–3pm. If you call, they'll send you a booklet answering questions about visas and passports.

Seattle Passport Agency
Federal Bldg., Room 992
915 Second Ave.
Seattle, WA 98174
Information: 220-7777, 220-7788

THE CONCRETE JUNGLE

The phrase "bright lights, big city" never did apply to Seattle, especially not in recent years, when the downtown area seemed to be heading for ghost town status. But suddenly downtown is booming: Nordstrom is moving to the old Frederick's building, new theaters and a new symphony hall are on the way, Harbor Steps gives us an entrance to the area from the water, the waterfront boasts a new marina and conference center with access to the Pike Place Market, new hotels are popping up—even Niketown has joined the march to make this a vibrant place.

Was it only yesterday that threats of a gutted city center made politicians quake in their boots? Just imagine: Five years from now Seattle may boast a new baseball stadium, a cleaned-up waterfront, shiny department and specialty stores downtown, and, most of all, the status of a true city center.

WHERE IS DOWNTOWN ANYWAY?

The absolute center of downtown is at Fourth and University—the University of Washington–owned tract where the Four Seasons Olympic Hotel and Security Pacific Tower are. From there downtown fans out, south to the Kingdome and International District, and north through the Denny Regrade to Seattle Center and Mercer Street. It's bounded on the west by Elliott Bay and the central waterfront, and on the east by I-5, though most maps show downtown as including Pill Hill, up to Broadway.

Downtown has:

A financial district. Well, sort of. The banks do tend to cluster in one area. Several securities companies are near the First Interstate Building at Third and Marion, but others are scattered throughout the city. So you might say the financial district lies roughly between Second and Fifth avenues, from Columbia to Union.

A shopping district. The cluster of Westlake Center, Nordstrom, and the Bon Marché along Pine Street used to be *the* shopping district. No more.

THE place to stay in Seattle for that really special night is the penthouse suite at the Sorrento Hotel. Amenities? Baby grand piano, library, fireplace, deck with hot tub, kitchen, canopy bed in master suite, sitting room. All for only $1,200 per night.

It's now just part of the district that runs to University Street to the south and into Belltown at the north, extends to Seventh Avenue, and easily includes the stretch to the waterfront. New furniture stores abound down on Western Avenue, thanks partially to the Harbor Steps, an urban stairway with waterfalls and open space. And Belltown, that erstwhile down-at-heels neighborhood, has some of the city's best restaurants.

The central business district shopping area encompasses 4 million of the 7.7 million square feet that constitute all of downtown—more space than in any of the suburban malls on the outskirts.

- Downtown office space: 24.6 million square feet
- Downtown office vacancies: 13.66%
- Downtown retail space: 5 to 8 million square feet

A theater district. Well, this is a matter of debate, though it's difficult to see how anyone could say there is a theater district, since both performing and movie houses are spread all over town.

Downtown parks
- Waterfront Park on Alaskan Way
- Freeway Park between University and Seneca streets over I-5
- Westlake Plaza next to Nordstrom on Pine Street and Fourth Avenue
- Occidental Park on First and Washington
- Waterfall Gardens on Main and Second
- Victor Steinbrueck Park at the Pike Place Market
- Pioneer Square Park at Pioneer Square
- Denny Park on Denny and Eighth
- Myrtle Edwards Park and adjacent Elliott Bay Park, along waterfront north of Pier 70

Downtown Seattle's largest hotels

Seattle Sheraton Hotel and Towers	880 rooms
The Westin Hotel	865 rooms
Stouffer Madison	554 rooms
Four Seasons Olympic Hotel	450 rooms
Crowne Plaza	415 rooms
Edgewater Inn	240 rooms
Seattle Downtown Hilton	237 rooms
The Warwick Hotel	230 rooms
Mayflower Park Hotel	187 rooms
Sixth Avenue Inn	166 rooms

Hotels. Seattle has 7,230 guest rooms in 43 hotels and motels, including the venerable Four Seasons Olympic Hotel as the leader in luxury, and such boutique hotels as the Sorrento, Alexis, and Inn at the Market. These command similar rates: average daily rate is $200 a night. Other "first tier" hotels bring in $65 less per night on average.

A waterfront. The Bell Street Pier at Pier 66 is rejuvenating the waterfront, inviting tourists and locals alike to see the workings of the Port of Seattle, while at the same time offering typical waterfront amenities such as the new Anthony's restaurant. There's a new marina, the Odyssey maritime museum (to open in 1997), fish markets, a seafood processor, and an international conference center. A hotel and condos are planned for across the street. The pier and the Pike Place Market are connected by a pedestrian bridge at Bell Street. The port's headquarters at Pier 69 adds some class to the north end of the waterfront (go inside and ask to see the "stream" that runs through the first-floor hallway).

Conventions. With more than 200 conventions held in the city each year, you shouldn't be surprised at all those people sporting name tags, especially if you're anywhere near the Washington Convention and Trade Center between Pike and Union.

Neighborhoods

- Pioneer Square: 20 blocks of historic mixed use.
- Denny Regrade/Belltown: Mixed use, commercial and residential.
- International District: Center of Asian cultures, businesses, and housing.

URBAN POCKETS

The Seattle Design Commission presents annual awards for "Urban Designs That Work." The criteria are whether the space is used and people feel comfortable there. Past downtown winners:

- First Interstate Plaza
- Nordstrom Espresso Bar, Fifth Avenue
- The Norton Building, Second Avenue entrance
- Post Alley from Seneca to Madison

To gain a more in-depth appreciation of Seattle's architecture and urban design, take one of the "Viewpoints" walking tours offered by the Seattle Architectural Foundation every year. Areas explored by past tours include First Avenue, the warehouses-turned-design-studios on Western Avenue, and the bus tunnel.

(Other tours cover areas outside downtown, such as the UW campus and Capitol Hill's historic Harvard/Belmont neighborhood.) Contact the foundation for a free brochure listing tours and prices.

Seattle Architectural Foundation
1333 Fifth Ave.
Seattle, WA 98101
667-9184

THOSE SKYSCRAPERS, HIGH-RISES, AND TOWERS

What constitutes, exactly, a high-rise? Everyone knows that the Columbia Seafirst Center scrapes the sky, no matter what its height. But what about the Dexter Horton Building? And the Norton Building? Those can seem pretty high, especially when the fire alarm rings and you have to descend numerous flights of stairs to reach the bottom.

But true high-rises, we've decided, are those that are taller than the Smith Tower, which, at about 500 feet, was for 48 years the tallest building west of the Mississippi. (It took the 605-foot Space Needle to break the record—if you consider the Space Needle a building. Most say the record was officially broken by the old Seafirst Building, now the 1001 Fourth Avenue Building, which opened in 1969.) Seattle now has a number of skyscrapers that look down on Ivar's salmon flag waving atop the Smith Tower. Their height varies depending on where you measure from.

- Columbia Seafirst Center, 76 stories, 954 feet
- Two Union Square, 56 stories, 886 feet
- Washington Mutual Tower, 55 stories, 730 feet (above Third Avenue)

The best way to see the city in style is from the top of the Smith Tower, once the tallest building west of the Mississippi. Pay $2 for adults and $1 for seniors and children in the main floor hallway and ride the elevator, still with a human operator, up to the 35th floor. Once there you can wander outside on the balconies and look down on office workers having lunch, or you can examine the Chinese Room, decorated in imported blackwood furniture.

You won't be on the very top; that's saved for the salmon flag that once in a while, in a high wind, rips off its "bubble" and tumbles down Third Avenue. The bubble was once a light directing ships into the harbor.

The triangular peak of the tower just above the Chinese Room is the private residence of a tower employee—now that's a home with a view!

- Security Pacific Tower, 40 stories, 667 feet
- One Union Square, 36 stories, 631 feet
- AT&T Gateway Tower, 62 stories, 620 feet
- First Interstate Center, 48 stories, 605 feet
- City Centre, 44 stories, 584 feet

- Bank of California, 41 stories, 570 feet
- Seafirst Fifth Avenue Plaza, 42 stories, 543 feet
- 1001 Fourth Avenue Building, 50 stories, 500+ feet
- 1000 Second Avenue Building, 40 stories, 500 feet

Two that qualify for high-rise status but are under 500 feet in elevation: Fourth and Blanchard Building at 440 feet and Century Square, 354.71 feet.

HIGH-RISE ROLLERS

Who's behind Seattle's high-rises? Martin Selig, a very short man with a penchant for very tall buildings. But he's not the only high-rise developer in town. The big names, high-rise-wise (they all develop shorter buildings too) are:

Prescott: City Centre, Century Square

Martin Selig: Columbia Center (later sold to Seafirst), Key Tower (now 1000 Second Avenue Building), Metropolitan Park Building, Fourth and Blanchard Building, and Fourth and Battery Building.

Unico: Security Pacific Tower, Two Union Square, One Union Square.

Wright Runstad & Co.: First Interstate Center, Washington Mutual Tower.

And the Smith Tower? It's run by the Smith Tower Limited Partnership, a San Francisco investment partnership formed after Ivar Haglund tried to sell it to the city for $1. The city said a polite "No thanks."

THE CAP FLAP

You can't have a conversation about high-rises without having a conversation about CAP (Citizen Alternative Plan). So FYI, here's an explanation: In May 1989, citizens passed the

There are 25 walruses lining the top of the Arctic Building on Third and Cherry—a legacy from the men's Arctic Club, who built the building in 1916. The building was designed by A. Warren Gould. The original walrus tusks were terra-cotta, and people feared they'd fall onto pedestrians below ("Marvin was speared by a falling tusk"). So in the 1950s the tusks were removed, leaving some sad-looking tuskless walruses. When Stickney-Murphy architects renovated the building in 1981–82, they replaced the tusks with specially cast epoxy ones. Also worth checking out: the plaster cornices of fruits and vegetables in the Dome Room off Cherry Street. Originally a ballroom, the room is now used for city events.

CAP initiative, which changed the city Land Use Code to set an annual limit on the square footage of usable new office space for which permits can be issued downtown. The annual limit under CAP is 500,000 square feet through 1994, and 1 million square feet for 1995 through 1999. Projects with less than 50,000 square feet of office space are exempt from CAP. And 85,000 square feet of the yearly limit is set aside per year for projects

between 50,000 and 85,000 square feet in size. For projects larger than 85,000 square feet, a design review panel decides which ones receive the CAP allocation.

HIGH-RISE NICKNAMES

- Washington Mutual Tower: The Phillips-head screwdriver building
- Fourth and Blanchard Building: The Darth Vader building
- First Interstate Center: Vacuum cleaner–tube building
- 1001 Fourth Avenue Building: Box for the Space Needle
- Security Pacific Tower (let's see. . . it was the Rainier Tower until Security Pacific bought Rainier Bank, but now that Security Pacific is no more. . .): Golf tee
- Century Square: Electric razor building (formerly the Ban Roll-On building)
- Second and Seneca Building: The real Ban Roll-On building
- Federal Building: Thermal underwear building
- AT&T Gateway Tower: Hmmmm—well, consider it from the waterfront and you won't let your kids look until they're of age.

HIGH-RISE FAVORITES AND NOT-SO

Columnist Jean Godden once asked *Seattle Times* readers about their favorite and least favorite buildings. Here's what she learned:

- Favorite building: Washington Mutual Tower
- Runner-up: Second and Seneca Building
- Third choice: The Space Needle (believe it or not)

Try counting the 42 stories of the Smith Tower. Even including the basement, you won't find them all. For some reason, the builders fudged on how many stories high the building was. But everyone still says the Smith Tower is 42 stories.

- Worst building: Kingdome
- Runner-up: The Blob on lower Queen Anne
- Third worst: The Safeco Building

WHERE TO GO WHEN YOU HAVE TO GO

Some call it the toilet-tissue issue. Others the burning issue of public restrooms. When it comes to glamor, the restroom-with-a-view in the Columbia Seafirst Center wins pants down, so to speak. But it's hardly public, and we're talking survival here. A person could wander up and down Spring, Marion, and beyond in search of a place to go. The issue is so critical that a UW architecture student did his master's thesis on public restrooms in Seattle.

Truly public restrooms in downtown Seattle
- The main fire station in Pioneer Square on Main Street
- Two in the Pike Place Market. But if you don't want to use them (and a lot of people don't), ask a merchant for a key to one of the merchants' restrooms. PPM merchants are incredibly accommodating.

- The public library, on basement level A and the third and fourth floors
- The King County Administration Building, Fourth and James, all floors
- The King County Courthouse, Third and James, all floors, near the interior stairwells
- Seattle Municipal Building, Fourth and James
- Public Safety Building, Fourth and Cherry
- Federal Building, Second and Marion
- The ferry terminal (Colman Dock), both at street level and upstairs
- The Aquarium

Quasi-public restrooms
- Greyhound bus depot
- Amtrak's King Street Station
- Pier 70
- The Bon Marché parking garage
- Westlake Center, on the second floor back in the corner, with little signage until you're on top of it. (Undoubtedly designed, says one merchant, by someone without kids.)

Other quasi-public restrooms can be found in high-rises; just wander through the lobby areas and look for out-of-the-way doors, sometimes not even marked. Some department stores have not only restrooms but comfortable lounges as well. And hotels are great resources; they almost always have a restroom off the lobby.

LITTLE-KNOWN RESTROOM FACTOIDS

- The bus tunnel stations have no restrooms.
- The health department gets two complaints per day regarding public urination or defecation downtown.

Based on a survey of businesses in the downtown core, Denny Regrade, International District, and Pioneer Square:

- 32% allow people to use their restrooms
- 60% have problems with public urination
- 58% clean up urine or feces on the sidewalk in front of their doors daily
- Percentage willing to let a public restroom be located within a distance of three blocks: 68% yes, 21% maybe
- Percentage willing to let a public restroom be located within a distance of one block: 55% yes, 21% maybe

Source: Downtown Human Services Council

THE GREAT PISSING MATCH

Underneath Pioneer Square, right smack under the pergola, is a hidden secret: an expansive marble room, Seattle's first public restroom. Built in 1908 and opened in 1909 by the

In King County, restaurants, theaters, auditoriums, and meeting halls are required by county code to have public restrooms—"public" meaning customers. But the truth is, customer or not, if you ask, they'll let you use them; if they don't, look pained. Or put on your customer look and march to the restroom without saying a word. Fast-food places, like McDonald's, are easiest.

parks department, the bathroom extends underground throughout the entire (triangular) square. Original access to it was at each end of the pergola; today the only access is through a manhole.

When it opened, it was something to be proud of—the only restroom on the West Coast built in an open area, not hidden away in some municipal building.

It was beautiful: The stalls were made of 1⅛-inch–thick Alaskan marble dividers; there was a shoeshine and concession area where you could buy newspapers, a stand for wet towels, and a lobby area with benches. The little square-block skylights that still exist in much of Pioneer Square provided light, and the square's totems and trees were there specifically to dress up the bathroom entrance.

But beautiful or not, the restroom was a questionable amenity from the beginning. Its construction was the obsession of one politician who, amidst the grumbles of his city cohorts, twisted the arms of the park board until they took on the project. The city later grudgingly bought the site. But there were plumbing problems—high tide, for example, created some drainage difficulties—and the bathroom closed down in 1939.

In the 1970s, there was a move to get the city to open the bathrooms again. The city met the outcry with a shake of the bureaucratic head and the announcement that the walls were weak. Engineers set about constructing crude braces down there. "It's just an excuse," screamed bathroom proponents, who figured the city simply didn't want to deal with the dark side of public restrooms.

Some say the city sneaked around and dumped sand down there. In fact, rumor has it that one man took some work-study students down there to try to take the mess of sand away bucket by bucket.

The bathrooms are still there, though they're ankle-deep in slimy dirt and other debris. The toilets are there, the urinals on the floor, the marble intact. The city has flushed

any idea of opening the restrooms for the time being.

Source: Son Voung, UW architecture student who authored the thesis "Public Restrooms for Seattle"

DOWNTOWN STUFF TO DO

The Downtown Seattle Association (DSA) sponsors events downtown, obviously to attract you and your pocketbook. The events are fun—and mostly free.

Easy Streets: A parking program by DSA, Easy Streets works like this: Spend $20 at a downtown store displaying a special decal and you get a token for a parking discount or a free bus ride.

Maritime Festival: Music, tours, and events on the waterfront in May.

Take a Market Classroom Tour, an introduction to the Market's food resources. You learn the difference between farm tables and highstalls and how to pump vendors for information about their products. The course is offered in January, March, June, and September. Other classes focus on spring blooms or holiday traditions. All are held on most Saturdays from 9am to 10:30am (and Wednesdays in summer) and cost $5 per person. 682-7453.

Out to Lunch: Free lunchtime concerts all summer in parks and plazas throughout downtown. Pick up location brochures at the public library and downtown buildings.

Holidays in the Heart of the City: DSA brings an antique carousel to Westlake Park, has horse-drawn carriages going up and down the streets, and sponsors caroling contests during the winter holiday season.

Downtown Seattle Association
500 Union St., Suite 325
Seattle, WA 98101
623-0340
Business and activities.

THE PIKE PLACE MARKET

Despite the outrage and hoopla about New York interlopers laying claim to the Pike Place Market, ask anyone who the owner of the Market is and they'll tell you it belongs to everyone in Seattle. Those are our floor tiles and our clock, after all, and we're proud of almost everything that happens in the Market. Just let someone try to take it away and—well, the lawsuits and tempers fly and flare.

The Market works almost like any other business. In 1973, the Pike Place Market Preservation and Development Authority (PDA) was formed to act as landlord and manager for 80% of the buildings in the Market Historic District. The PDA does promotion and manages parking lots and low-income housing, including distributing discount coupons to the Market's low-income residents.

The Market is as exciting for merchants as for customers. For example, every morning at 9am the craftspeople assemble at the north end of the Market for roll call. The Market Master (Millie Padua has been doing this for years) calls out names in order of seniority and each vendor chooses the table he or she will sell on that day. Artists must sell

Who's really who at Pike Place Market: Careful Market watchers may see celebrities lying on the floor—in floor tiles, that is. The sale of more than 45,000 name-imprinted tiles in the Main and North arcades helped fund the Market's new floor in the 1980s. Look for Ronald and Nancy Reagan in rows 351 and 352, near Pike Place Fish. Row 38 contains the prime numbers from one to 100, given by a woman in honor of her mathematician husband. There's also a tile bearing L. Ron Hubbard's name.

two days a week to stay on the seniority list and must sell on two weekdays to sell on a Saturday. A long waiting list of artisans—as many as 400—await space at the Market tables.

As for the farmers, they have first pick of the stalls. But as Seattle grows, the distance farmers have to come grows too. And the number of farmers drops. Because of increased promotion, the number of farmers with selling permits seems to have stabilized at around 100. On any given day, there will be about 60 of them at the Market.

How many farmers?
- 1907: Market opens with 6 farmers
- 1937: More than 600 farmers
- 1942: Japanese internment cuts farmer-sellers by half: 300 farmers
- 1960: 60 farmers

- 1976: 40 farmers
- 1987: 99 farmers
- 1990: 100 farmers
- 1992: 100 farmers
- 1995: 129 farmers

Source: Pike Place Market PDA

Know those stallers
Market terms revolve around selling-stalls. Lowstalls (sometimes called wet tables) are the daystalls rented to Market farmers, those who grow their own. Most of those are on the west side of Pike Place. Highstalls are rented to agents of farmers, those who buy wholesale.

Market facts
- 223 daystalls are on the Market's Main and North arcades.
- 36 farmers travel more than 100 miles each way to sell at the Market.
- 400 different products are sold by Market farmers in a year.
- 220 craftspeople sell at the Market. More than half have been there five years or more.
- 2,000 daffodil bulbs are planted in rooftop flower boxes in the Market each year.
- 300,000 pounds of cardboard and 36,000 pounds of newsprint are recycled in the Market each year.

Source: Pike Place Market PDA annual reports

Market tips
Best time to shop at the Market de-

Want to hang out with the Market merchants or stallers? You can usually find some on the second floor of Lowell's (Main Arcade) or at Seattle's Best Coffee (Post Alley).

Instead of heading down First Avenue when you need to get someplace south on foot, duck through the Market. How to avoid the crowds in the Main Arcade? Go downstairs to the second level, where it's relatively calm, or stay in the center of Pike Place (the street) and ignore the yells from drivers.

pends on what you're there for. For ambience, best time is about 7am, when the farmers are setting up and the dew is still on the sweet peas. For fresh goods, best time is 8–11am, before the lunch crowds get there. For bargains, best time is late afternoon. If the farmers have had a good day, they sometimes drop prices. If they've closed out their till, you can sometimes get things gratis.

If you become a regular at certain Market stands, the merchants will save things for you. And the merchants are experts. Tell them whether you want peaches to eat now or save for later. And ask how to cook that fish.

Be assertive with Market merchants. Go ahead and pick the vegetable you want from the display—never allow the farmer to pick one out for you, no matter how much you get yelled at.

Craftspeople get into the Market based on seniority, so those with the longest ties choose the best days, namely weekends. If you want to see the regulars, shop weekends; if you want to see the newest crafts, come Monday. According to the rules, everything has to be made by the craftspeople themselves.

If you park in the Market parking garage, Market merchants will validate your parking ticket and you can park free. A list of the 32 participating merchants is available in the garage.

Market resources

Pike Place Market Preservation and Development Authority
85 Pike St., Room 500
Seattle, WA 98101
682-7453

Pike Place Merchants Association
85 Pike St., Suite 312
Seattle, WA 98101
587-0351
Publishes the monthly *Pike Place Market News,* the "community rag you can't live without," full of news about the Market.

MARKET MUSIC

Musicians play in 13 different spots in the Pike Place Market (marked with a musical note on the sidewalk) for $10 a year, or $3 a quarter. They can play in one spot, but if another performer is waiting, they have to yield after one hour. The Market issued about 150 performer permits in 1995, and there are some who play but aren't registered. The best say they can make up to $100 per day; many don't cover the price of a beer. The two favorite spots are under the clock and at the foot of Pine Street. Larger groups go down to the entrance to the Hillclimb in front of the musicians mural.

Musical names to know

Market musicians often go on to fame: Artis the Spoonman, for example, has been on David Letterman's show. Others still around include: Johnny Hahn, everybody's favorite, who wheels his piano in and plays his own compositions; Jeanne Towne, the blind lady with the guitar; Eagle Park Slim, blues guitarist, who says he's played with Chuck Berry and B.B. King; Howlin' Hobbit, acoustic blues; Whamdiddle, hammer dulcimer players; Pike Place Trio, classical music; Lee Dehin, acoustic guitar, old-time folk tunes, in front of Starbucks; Gumbo Jazz, vaudeville tunes in 1920s costumes, tap dances too; Robert Crowley, recorder, baroque pieces; and Willie Herbert Williams and Roosevelt Franklin, a cappella performers, blues, gospel, and soul.

Here's a tip: If you're at the waterfront and want to go to the Market without going up all the Hillclimb stairs, duck into the parking garage and use its elevator.

THE BUCK STOPS HERE

What? Can't find the Wall Street Journal *on every corner? And stock-brokers wear Rockports to work? Not to worry. After all, America's richest software entrepreneur has turned the Eastside into a high-tech megalopolis, there are little Mario Bros. jogging all*

over the Kingdome, and just what does Immunex do in those biotech offices? (Not to mention that we do at least have a Wall Street.)

And what of Boeing, that paragonic patriarch? It's still the nation's biggest exporter, even if it's no longer alone at the top. (That means that when Boeing threatens to lay off people, no one even thinks of turning off the city's lights anymore.)

Worldwide we're no slouches either. International trade—especially with the Pacific Rim—is spawning expanded port facilities and pushing Seattle-Tacoma International Airport to its limits.

Could it be that when our forefathers named Seattle "Alki," which every latte-drinker worth his or her salt knows means "New York by-and-by," they knew someday we'd beat out the Big Apple at its own game?

The ins and outs of Seattle Big Biz are hidden in annual reports, boards of directors, and stock profiles. At least, they are hidden until you look at the names and companies and find that they are, for the most part, incestuous. Most big-business board members serve on many boards—in fact, looking at the following list, it's hard to imagine that some do anything but go to board meetings.

So here it is, a primer of Seattle's Bigtimers. Companies are ranked by annual revenue. For CEOs, we give a rundown of the *total* salary (what they made in compensation, stock options, and benefits); for other top execs there are just straight salary figures, which in some cases include bonuses or incentive pay.

The "stock" category for CEOs under "1995 Take-Home Pay" includes the value, in shares or cash, derived from the execution of stock options (or stock appreciation rights, as they are sometimes called) during the year.

The "benefits" category includes payments made by the company for things such as profit sharing, matching funds for investment plans, supplemental benefit plans, company-paid insurance, company cars, etc. Also note: Most companies have a policy of not paying company executives on the board a director's stipend or expenses.

The sources for this information, including the ages given for board members, are 1995 annual reports and proxies. Names of stock analysts are from the 1996 *Nelson's Directory of Investment Research.*

THE TOP FIVE

1. The Boeing Company

7755 E Marginal Way
Seattle, WA 98108
655-2121

The Big Daddy of the Northwest. When Boeing catches cold, the entire city sneezes. Boeing's orders are down, layoffs are under way, and the only bright spot is the 777 production. The company employs 105,000 workers in the Puget Sound area, give or take several thousand depending on those orders. Boeing doesn't dominate as it once did (1 in 5 regional jobs were connected to Boeing in 1969; now it's 1 in 10), but still has no peer in the Northwest.

Stats

Employees: 105,000
1995 Revenue: $19.5 billion
1995 Profit: $393 million
NYSE symbol: BA

Who's the boss

Frank Shrontz, Chairman. In May 1996, Shrontz stepped down as CEO of Boeing. His successor is Philip M. Condit. Shrontz will retain his chairmanship for a few years. This Boise native nabbed a law degree from University of Idaho (1954) before studying 'neath the ivy at Harvard (MBA, 1958). Employed by Boeing since 1958, except for stints in government (1973–76 as Asst. Secretary of Air Force and Asst. Secretary of Defense). Took over reins in 1986 from legendary CEO T. A. Wilson, who ran Boeing for 17 years.

Philip M. Condit, President and CEO.

Ronald B. Woodard, President of

Boeing Commercial Airplane Group and Sr. Vice President of Boeing.

C. Gerald King, President of Boeing Defense and Space Group and Sr. Vice President of Boeing.

Boyd E. Givan (pronounced Guy-van), Chief Financial Officer and Sr. Vice President. Succeeded longtime CFO and board member Harold W. Haynes in April 1990.

Lawrence W. Clarkson, Sr. Vice President, Planning and International Development.

D. P. Beighle, Sr. Vice President.

John Schmit, Sr. Vice President, Operations.

Robert Davis, Sr. Vice President, Engineering and Technology.

1995 take-home pay

Frank Shrontz: $1.656 million salary plus bonus, $287,122 stock, $85,289 benefits, $2,028,411 total.

Philip M. Condit: $932,422 salary plus bonus.

Boyd E. Givan: $607,470 salary plus bonus.

C. Gerald King: $581,130 salary plus bonus.

The board of directors

Annual stipend: $26,000 plus $2,000/meeting plus expenses.

Frank Shrontz, 64, Chairman of the Board. Other boards: Citicorp, Boise Cascade, 3M.

Philip M. Condit, 54. Other boards: John Fluke Manufacturing Co.

Robert A. Beck, 70. Connection: The Prudential Insurance Co. (Chairman Emeritus). Other boards: Texaco, Xerox, Campbell Soup Co.

John E. Bryson, 52. Other boards: First Interstate Bancorp, The Times Mirror Company, Edison International.

John B. Fery, 66. Connection: Boise Cascade. Other boards: Hewlett-Packard, Albertson's, U.S. Bancorp.

Paul E. Gray, 64. Connection: Massachusetts Institute of Technology (Chairman). Other boards: Arthur D. Little Inc., Eastman Kodak Co., New England Mutual

Life Insurance Co.

Harold J. Haynes, 70. Connection: Bechtel Group, Inc. (Senior Counselor), Chevron (retired Chairman and CEO). Other boards: Paccar, Citicorp, Saudi Arabian Oil Co.

Stanley Hiller, Jr., 71. Connection: Hiller Investment Co. (Senior Partner), a private investment firm, and KeyTronic Corp. (CEO).

Charles M. Pigott, 66. Connection: Paccar (Chairman and CEO). Other boards: Chevron, *The Seattle Times*.

Franklin D. Raines, 47. Connection: Federal National Mortgage Association (Fannie Mae) (Vice Chairman), Pfizer, Inc.

Rozanne L. Ridgway, 60. Connection: The Atlantic Council of the

The Corporate Bigtimers still hang out at the Metropolitan Grill, where the Guess the Dow contest continues. But to run into the bosses of the boss, try Union Square Grill under Two Union Square, the Rainier Club (if you can get in), the Washington Athletic Club, and the Columbia Tower Club. Power lunches continue—but the big change is that the prevailing smell is not necessarily that of the three martinis. Cigars have emerged within the suspenders crowd; humidors abound in Seattle's upscale lunch spots. Hold your nose.

United States (Co-chairperson). Other boards: Bell Atlantic Corp., Citicorp, RJR Nabisco, 3M, The Sara Lee Corp., Union Carbide Corp.

George H. Weyerhaeuser, 69. Connection: Weyerhaeuser (Chairman). Other boards: Safeco, Chevron.

Stock analysts: Peter Jacobs at Ragen MacKenzie; Jack Modzelewski at PaineWebber.

2. PriceCostco, Inc. Wholesale Corporation

10809 120th Ave. NE
Kirkland, WA 98083
828-8100

Jeff Brotman and Jim Sinegal founded Costco in 1983, jumping into the cut-rate warehouse retailing business just as the industry was taking off. Last year they saw $17.9 billion in revenue come in from 250 stores, which are football-field large, charge a slight cut (about 10%, compared to retail's 25%) above wholesale, and exact an annual fee from 6.7 million members. Costco is growing at a ferocious pace in the '90s, as it did in the mid-'80s. It has hit Canada (52 stores) and the U.K. (five stores) and it continues worldwide expansion. Costco's not a bad place to work, either: store workers are among the highest paid in the industry. In 1993, the company merged with Price Co., which operates the Price Club warehouses. Note: 19% of the company's stock is owned by Carrefour Nederland B.V., an international retailing concern.

Stats

Employees: 40,000 companywide
1995 Revenue: $18.2 billion
1995 Profit: $133 million
NASDAQ symbol: PCCW

Who's the boss

James D. Sinegal, President, CEO. Worked in retail for decades (Fed-Mart, Builders Emporium, The Price Co.) before teaming up with Brotman.

Richard D. DiCerchio, Exec. Vice President, COO

SHARING BOARD MEMBERS: THE CROSS-POLLINATION OF CORPORATIONS

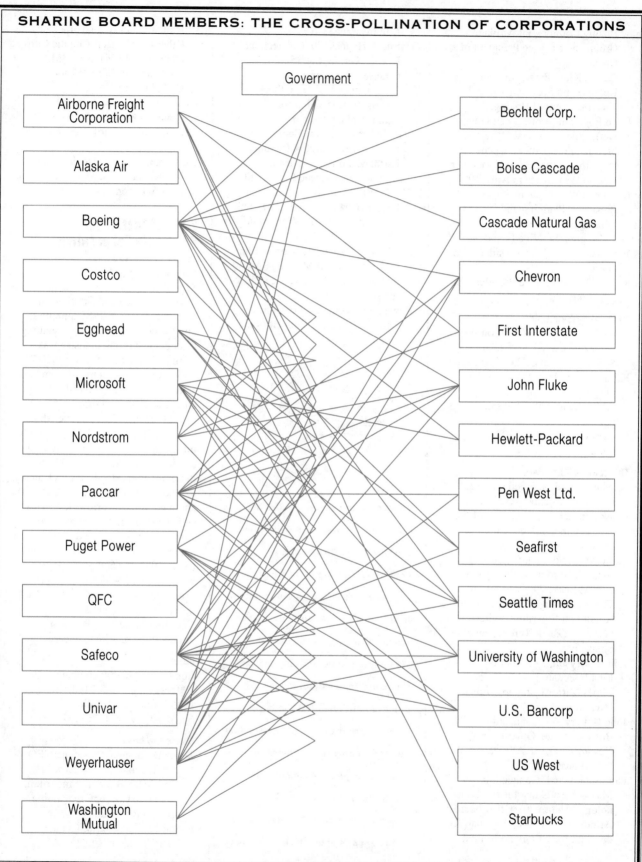

Merchandising.

Franz E. Lazarus, Exec. Vice President, COO International Operations.

Robert E. Craves, Sr. Vice President, Marketing and Administration.

Richard A. Galanti, Sr. Vice President, CFO.

Edward B. Maron, Jr., Exec. Vice President, Canadian Division COO.

Thomas K. Walker, Sr. Vice President, Construction and Purchasing.

1995 take-home pay
Jeff Brotman: $305,769 salary.
James Sinegal: $305,769 salary.
Edward Maron, Jr.: $297,710.
Richard DiCerchio: $265,000.

The board of directors
Annual stipend: None. ($1,000/ meeting plus expenses.)

Jeffrey H. Brotman, 53, Chairman of the Board. UW grad ('64), also attended law school there ('67). Before creating Costco, worked for an oil exploration company. Also co-founded The Brotman Group, which operates a chain of 30 men's and women's apparel shops. Ran Costco until 1988, when he let Sinegal take over the CEO's chair. Connection: Starbucks Coffee, Seafirst. Other boards: Sweet Factory, Garden Botanika.

James Sinegal, 59. Connection: Price Enterprise.

Daniel Bernard. Connection: Carrefour S.A. (CEO).

Richard DiCerchio, 52. Other boards: Price Co., Fed-Mart Corp.

Richard A. Galanti. Connection: former associate with DLJ.

Hamilton E. James, 44. Connection: Donaldson, Lufkin and Jenrette Securities (Managing Director— James oversees DLJ's mergers and acquisitions and merchant banking activities. DLJ, along with Merrill Lynch, took Costco public in 1985). Other boards: County Seat Stores Inc.

Richard Libenson. Connection: Price Co. (merger).

John W. Meisenbach, 59. Connection: Meisenbach, Cashman and Martin Inc. (a financial services company he founded and currently presides over). Other boards: Expeditors International.

Frederick O. Paulsell, Jr., 56. Connection: Foster Paulsell & Baker, an investment banking firm (President). Former Exec. Vice President of Foster and Marshall and American Express.

Stock analyst: Mary Fleckenstein at Ragen MacKenzie.

3. Weyerhaeuser Company
33663 Weyerhaeuser Way S
Federal Way, WA 98477
682-6640

Though not technically a Seattle company, Weyerhaeuser wields prodigious influence in the city. It owns 11% of the land in King County, and 2.7 million acres of timberland in the Northwest alone; that's about 3.5 billion cubic feet of wood. It is the largest private owner of softwood timber in the world and one of North America's largest producers of forest products. It's a mammoth company that has managed to stay somewhat within the family.

After 25 years, George Weyerhaeuser stepped down as CEO in 1991, though he remains chairman of the board. He's also one of the most powerful men in the city. A member of the national Business Roundtable, he helped create the Washington Roundtable and King County 2000.

George's two sons are in the business: George Jr. is a VP in the paper company, and David is in the hardwood division. The Weyerhaeuser family still holds family reunions, and it's a safe bet they aren't munching beans and wienies: 250 members share a fortune worth over $900 million and control 12% of the company's stock.

Like all forest product companies, Weyerhaeuser took its lumps during the recession of 1991, largely because of housing-start declines in Japan. In fact, the company recorded a net loss for that year, spawning a massive reorganization and a new modest goal: "to be the Best Forest Products Company in the World."

Stats
Employees: 39,400 worldwide
1995 Revenue: $11.8 billion
1995 Profit: $799 million
NYSE symbol: WY

Who's the boss
John W. "Jack" Creighton, Jr., President and CEO, took over from George Weyerhaeuser in 1991.

William R. Corbin, Exec. Vice President, Timberlands and Distribution.

Richard C. Gozon, Exec. Vice President, Pulp, Paper, and Packaging.

Steven R. Hill, Sr. Vice President, Human Resources.

Norman E. Johnson, Sr. Vice President, Technology.

Thomas M. Luthy, Sr. Vice President, Wood Products.

William C. Stivers, Sr. Vice President and CFO.

1995 take-home pay
Jack Creighton: $806,480 salary, $750,000 bonus, $111,093 benefits, $1.668 million total.

R. C. Gozon: $723,580 salary plus bonus.

W. R. Corbin: $721,845 salary plus bonus.

W. C. Stivers: $610,206 salary plus bonus.

N. E. Johnson: $517,303 salary plus bonus.

The board of directors
Annual stipend: $35,000 plus $1,500/ meeting plus expenses.

George Weyerhaeuser, 69, Chairman of the Board. Other boards: Boeing, Safeco, Chevron.

Jack Creighton, 63. Other boards: QFC, Portland General Corp., Washington Energy Co.

William Clapp, 54. Connection: Matthew G. Norton Co. (Chairman and President). Other boards: Alaska Air Group.

W. John Driscoll, 66. Other boards: Comshare Inc., Northern States Power, The St. Paul Cos., John Nuveen & Co.

Don Frisbee, 72. Connection: Pacifi-Corp, formerly Pacific Power and Light (Chairman). Other boards: First Interstate Bancorp, Reed College, Standard Insurance.

Phillip Hawley, 70. Connection: Carter Hawley Hale Stores (Chairman, CEO, and middle-name-sake). Other boards: AT&T, ARCO, BankAmerica, Johnson and Johnson.

Martha R. Ingram, 60. Connection: Ingram Industries Inc. Other boards: Vanderbilt University.

John Kieckhefer, 51. Connection: Took over for father, Robert, who retired from the board at age 71 in 1989. President of Kieckhefer Associates Inc. (investment and trust management) of Prescott, Arizona, and involved in commercial cattle operations.

William Ruckelshaus, 63. Connection: Browning-Ferris Industries (Chairman), William D. Ruckelshaus Associates, and government background. Ruckelshaus was head of the Environmental Protection Agency under Reagan and served in the Nixon administration before being axed in the Watergate "Saturday Night Massacre." An attorney to be reckoned with: Local top-drawer law firm Perkins Coie turns to him for legal advice. Was Sr. Vice President of Weyerhaeuser, 1976–83. Other boards: Nordstrom, Monsanto, Cummins Engine.

Richard H. Sinkfield, 53. Connection: Rogers and Hardin law firm (Senior Partner). Other boards: Vanderbilt University, Atlanta Urban League, Inc.

Stock analysts: Daniel F. Nelson at Ragen MacKenzie; Richard Schneider at PaineWebber.

4. Microsoft Corporation

One Microsoft Way
Redmond, WA 98052-6399
936-8080

Bill Gates has himself become a household word—and object of curiosity, as evidenced by the surge of books about the wunderkind.

Gates dropped out of Harvard at 19 and teamed up with high school buddy Paul Allen in 1975 to create what would become the dominant software company in the computer industry and spawn a high-tech culture in the Northwest. In the process Gates and Allen became very rich—Gates is the youngest self-made billionaire in history. Allen left some years ago to start another business (Asymetrix Corp. in Bellevue), but still retains a chunk of Microsoft's stock, worth billions, and rejoined the board of directors in 1990. Gates himself doesn't see his big money in annual salary—he controls enough stock to pay the heat bill and then some.

Microsoft has been described as a velvet sweatshop, a great place to work if high-tech is your life. In theory there are no clocks, you wear what you want, and you set your own hours—but they are expected to be long. Gates himself is often in the office late into the night and on weekends. It's an intensely creative atmosphere and has few corporate trappings; the Redmond headquarters is referred to as a "campus."

Want to get a job with one of Seattle's major employers? Here are a few of their joblines:

Boeing: 965-3111

First Interstate Bank: 292-3551

Safeco: 545-3233

Seafirst: 358-7523

Starbucks: 447-4123

University of Washington: 543-6969

Stats

Employees: 17,800 worldwide
1995 Revenue: $5.94 billion
(fiscal 1995 ended June 30)
1995 Profit: $1.45 billion
NASDAQ symbol: MSFT

Who's the boss

William H. Gates, Chairman and CEO. Variously described as technological wunderkind and billionaire workaholic. Scored perfect 800 on math SAT.

Steven A. Ballmer, Exec. Vice President, Sales and Support.

Robert J. Herbold, Exec. Vice President, COO.

Bernard P. Vergnes, Sr. Vice President Microsoft, President of Microsoft Europe.

1995 take-home pay

William Gates: $415,580 total (salary plus bonus).

Steven Ballmer: $411,974 (salary plus bonus).

Robert J. Herbold: $740,133 (salary plus bonus).

Bernard P. Vergnes: $526,445 (salary plus bonus).

The board of directors

Annual stipend: $8,000/year plus $1,000/meeting for all directors except Gates and Allen.

William H. Gates, 40. Chairman of the Board, CEO.

Paul G. Allen, 42. Connection: Founder with Gates. Other boards: Asymetrix Corp. (Chairman), Portland Trail Blazers (owner), Egghead Software.

Richard A. Hackborn, 58. Connection: Hewlett-Packard.

David F. Marquardt, 46. Connection: TVI Management (General Partner), a venture-capital limited partnership. Other boards: Auspex Systems Inc.

Robert D. O'Brien, 81. Connection: Paccar (Chairman, 1965–78) and Univar (Chairman 1974–83).

William G. Reed, Jr., 57. Connection: Simpson Investment Co. (Chairman), parent of Simpson Timber. Other boards: Safeco, Washington Mutual Savings Bank, *The Seattle Times.*

Jon Shirley, 57. Shirley retired as COO in 1990, but is still on the board. Other boards: Mentor Graphics Corp.

Stock analyst: Scott W. McAdams at Ragen MacKenzie.

5. Paccar Inc.

777 106th Ave. NE
Bellevue, WA 98004
455-7400

The largest producer of class-8 heavy trucks in North America, Paccar builds the 18-wheelers that log the long miles in the U.S. (under the Kenworth and Peterbilt brands) and U.K. (under the Foden brand). Paccar passed Navistar in 1989 as the nation's leading truck manufacturer and now holds nearly one-quarter of the market. Over 500 Paccar dealers sell the trucks in the U.S., Canada, U.K., and Australia. The company also owns Al's Auto Supply, Grand Auto, and an oil equipment subsidiary.

Stats

Employees: 14,000 nationwide
1995 Revenue: $4.57 billion
1995 Profit: $252.8 million
NASDAQ symbol: PCAR

Who's the boss

Charles M. Pigott, Chairman and CEO. The Seattle-born, Stanford-educated grandson of Paccar's founder, Chuck Pigott (pronounced with a hard "g," as in "spigot") has been CEO since 1967—longer than some of his employees have been alive. His influence in Seattle doesn't live up to the size of his company, but that doesn't necessarily apply to his influence in business—he's on the boards of Boeing, Chevron, and *The Seattle Times;* a few years ago the *Times* described him as being "notably absent from the councils of power," noting that his favorite philanthropy was the Boy Scouts.
David J. Hovind, President, took over from retiring president Joseph Dunn in 1991.
Michael A. Tembreull, Exec. Vice President.
Gary S. Moore, Sr. Vice President.

Mark C. Pigott, Sr. Vice President.

1995 take-home pay

Charles Pigott: $980,000 salary plus undetermined bonus, $434,813 stock, $1.415 million plus bonus total.
D. J. Hovind: $520,000.
M. A. Tembreull: $399,039.
M. C. Pigott: $398,558.
G. S. Moore: $244,616.

The board of directors

Annual stipend: $35,000 plus $5,000/meeting.
Charles Pigott, 66, Chairman of the Board. Other boards: Boeing, Chevron, *The Seattle Times.*
David J. Hovind, 55, President. Came up through the ranks.
Richard P. Cooley, 72. Connection: Seafirst. Other boards: Egghead Inc., Ackerley Communications.
John M. Fluke, 53. Connection: John Fluke Manufacturing. Other boards: U.S. Bank of Washington.
Dr. Carl H. Hahn, 69. Connection: Volkswagen AG (retired Chairman of Board of Management). Other boards: British Petroleum, AGIV. (Note: Elected to serve remainder of T. A. Wilson's term as Paccar director.)
Harold J. Haynes, 70. Connection: Bechtel Group, Inc. (Senior Counselor), Chevron (retired Chairman and CEO). Other boards: Boeing, Citicorp, Saudi Arabian Oil Co.
James C. Pigott, 59. Connection: Familial (brother of Charles). James has been President of Pigott Enterprises Inc., a private investment firm, since 1983. Also President of Management Reports and Services, a business reports franchising firm. Other boards: Americold Corp.
Mark C. Pigott, 42. Vice chairman of Paccar, son of Charles.
John W. Pitts, 69. Connection: MacDonald, Dettwiler and Associates Ltd. (President and CEO), a high-tech manufacturing company. Other boards: British Columbia Sugar Refinery Ltd., British Columbia Telephone Co.
Michael A. Tembreull, 49. Vice chairman of Paccar, Inc.

James H. Wiborg, 71. Connection: Univar Corp. and VWR Corp. (Chairman and Chief Strategist for both). Other boards: Penwest Ltd., PrimeSource Corp.

Stock analyst: Paul Latta at Ragen MacKenzie.

THE NEXT FIVE

6. Nordstrom Inc.

1501 Fifth Ave.
Seattle, WA 98101
628-2111

The area's top retailer, if not in volume then certainly in prestige and polish, Nordstrom prides itself on the best service and highest-quality merchandise. The secret's been getting out in the last few years: The company has been opening stores nationwide, and now has 77.

The company continues to be plagued by labor problems, despite a vote by employees in the Seattle stores to terminate their longstanding union contract. African Americans have complained about discrimination too. But through it all, the shoppers have remained fiercely loyal: the company reaps millions in free advertising with the license plate frames proclaiming "I'd rather be shopping at Nordstrom" that are pasted on nearly every BMW in Bellevue.

Stats

Employees: 42,945 nationwide
1995 Revenue: $4.11 billion
1995 Profit: $27.7 million
NASDAQ symbol: NOBE

Who's the boss

Blake W. Nordstrom, Co-president.
Erik B. Nordstrom, Co-president.
J. Daniel Nordstrom, Co-president.
James A. Nordstrom, Co-president.
Peter E. Nordstrom, Co-president.
William E. Nordstrom, Co-president.
Raymond A. Johnson, Executive.
John J. Whitacre, Executive.
John A. Goesling, Exec. Vice President and Treasurer.
Jack Irving, Exec. Vice President.
Cynthia C. Paur, Exec. Vice President.

1995 take-home pay

Raymond A. Johnson: $344,167
salary.
John J. Whitacre: $344,167 salary.
John A. Goesling: $322,083 salary.
Jack Irving: $290,000 salary.
Cynthia C. Paur: $267,500 salary.

The board of directors

Annual stipend: $15,000 plus
$1,000/meeting.
Bruce Nordstrom, 62. Retired (Former co-chairman).
James Nordstrom, 56. Retired (Former co-chairman).

Microsoft Culture has not permeated
the rest of big business, for some
reason. But the flex (if long) hours,
the sweatshirt uniform, and the
high-tech "campus" home away from
home all seem to work for the nerdy
types. And food? Here's what
Microsoft's cafeteria dishes out
for some 7,000 employees:

- Meals served: 2,400 a day

- Slices of pizza served: 600 a day

- Drinks served (free): 7,500 a day

- Pounds of pasta cooked: 10,000
  a month

- Pounds of chicken (white meat)
  cooked: 25,000 a month

- Pounds of fish cooked: up to
  5,000 a month

- Thanksgiving turkeys cooked: 52

Source: Microsoft Corp.

John Nordstrom, 59. Retired (Former co-chairman).
John McMillan, 64. Retired (Former co-chairman).
Philip M. Condit, 54. Connection: President and CEO of Boeing.
D. Wayne Gittinger, 63. Connection: Law firm of Lane Powell Spears Lubersky (Partner). The Seattle firm handles legal matters for Nordstrom.
John F. Harrigan, 70. Connection: Union Bank (retired Chairman).
Raymond Johnson, 54. Co-chairman of the Board.
Charles A. Lynch, 68. Connection: Fresh Choice, Inc. of Santa Clara, California.
Ann D. McLaughlin, 54. Connection: New American Schools Development Corp. (President and CEO). Former U.S. Secretary of Labor under President Reagan.
Alfred E. Osborne, Jr., 51. Connection: Director and Associate Professor of Business Economics at the UCLA Graduate School of Management.
William Ruckelshaus, 63. Connection: Browning-Ferris Industries (Chairman) and government. Other boards: Weyerhaeuser, Monsanto, Cummins Engine.
Elizabeth C. Vaughan, 67. Connection: Salar Enterprises, Portland (President).
John J. Whitacre, 43. Co-chairman of the Board.
Stock analyst: Lesa Stroufe at Ragen MacKenzie.

7. Safeco Corporation

Safeco Plaza
Seattle, WA 98185
545-5000

A financial company that operates a number of insurance/finance arms, Safeco trades mostly in business, property, and life and health insurance. It also has credit, investment, and property subsidiaries (the Winmar Co., an arm of Safeco Properties, is developing malls in the burbs all around Seattle). Catastrophes and weather-related claims plagued the insurance giant a couple of years ago,

---

so much so that it dropped its Canadian business. Safeco is optimistic, however, about its Suretylink computer processing and communications network, which streamlines the issuing and reporting of bonds.

Stats

Employees: 7,000 nationwide
1995 Revenue: $3.87 billion
1995 Profit: $399 million
NASDAQ symbol: SAFC

Who's the boss

Roger H. Eigsti, President and CEO, following Bruce Maines, who passed the torch in 1991.
Boh A. Dickey, Exec. Vice President, CFO.
Eddie L. Hendrickson, President, Safeco Properties.
Dan D. McLean, President of Property and Casualty Insurance Cos. (took over from James Cannon, who retired in 1992).
Richard Zunker, President, Life and Health Insurance.
William F. Meany, President, Safeco Credit.

1995 take-home pay

Roger Eigsti: $650,000 salary, $65,000 bonus, $310,300 stock, $93,265 benefits, total $1,118,565.
Boh Dickey: $390,000 salary.
D. D. McLean: $277,500 salary.
R. E. Zunker: $250,000 salary.

The board of directors

Annual stipend: $24,000 plus $1,500/ meeting plus expenses.
Roger H. Eigsti, 53, President and CEO. Other boards: Washington Mutual Savings Bank.
Phyllis J. Campbell, 44. Connection: President and CEO of U.S. Bank of Washington. Other boards: Puget Sound Power and Light.
Robert S. Cline, 58. Connection: Airborne Freight Corp. (Chairman and CEO). Other boards: Seafirst.
Boh A. Dickey, 51. Exec. Vice President.
John Ellis, 67. Connection: Puget Sound Power and Light. Other boards: Washington Mutual Savings Bank, Associated Electric and Gas Insurance Services Inc., Baseball Club of Seattle, UTILX Corp.

William P. Gerberding, 66. Connection: University of Washington (President Emeritus). Other boards: Washington Mutual Savings Bank.

Joshua (Jay) Green III, 59. Connection: Joshua Green Corp., U.S. Bancorp. Grandson of People's Bank founder, and chairman of same until it was taken over by U.S. Bank.

William W. Krippaehne, Jr., 45. Connection: President and CEO of Fisher Cos. (KOMO).

William G. Reed, Jr., 57. Connection: Simpson Investment Co., formerly Simpson Timber (Chairman and CEO). Other boards: Washington Mutual Savings Bank, Microsoft Corp, *The Seattle Times*.

Judith M. Runstad, 51. Connection: Foster, Pepper and Shefelman (Co-managing Partner in the Seattle law firm retained by Safeco). Other boards: Seattle Branch of Federal Reserve Bank of San Francisco.

Paul W. Skinner, 48. Connection: Skinner Corp. (President of the Seattle investment company). Skinner took over this Safeco director's seat when his father, legendary Seattle businessman and philanthropist David E. "Ned" Skinner, died in 1988. Other boards: Seafirst.

George H. Weyerhaeuser, 69. Connection: Weyerhaeuser (Chairman and retired CEO). Other boards: Boeing, Chevron.

William R. Wiley, 64. Connection: Sr. Vice President for Science and Technology at Battelle Memorial Institute. Other boards: Northwest Natural Gas, Federal Reserve Bank of San Francisco (Seattle Branch).

Stock analyst: Daniel Nelson at Ragen MacKenzie.

8. Airborne Freight Corporation

3101 Western Ave.
Seattle, WA 98111
285-4600

Airborne Express (the company differentiates between the service, Express, and the parent company, Freight) delivered 225 million documents in the U.S. in 1995, 4.6 million overseas, via a fleet of 105 airplanes. Impressive numbers—and numbers that manage to compete with Federal Express, the giant of the industry. Airborne's headquarters are in Seattle, but its heart is in the Midwest. Like Federal, Airborne operates a centralized hub (in Wilmington, Ohio) through which all packages must pass before delivery.

Stats
Employees: over 18,000 company-wide
1995 Revenue: $2.239 billion
1995 Profit: $23.8 million ($23.5 million available to shareholders)
NYSE symbol: ABF

Who's the boss
Robert S. Cline, Chairman and CEO. Took over in 1984 from Holt Webster after serving as CFO since 1978.
Robert G. Brazier, President and COO.
Roy C. Liljebeck, Exec. Vice President and CFO.
John J. Cella, Exec. Vice President, International Division.
Kent W. Freudenberger, Exec. Vice President, Marketing.
Raymond T. Van Bruwaene, Exec. Vice President, Field Services.

1995 take-home pay
Robert Cline: $486,538 salary, $15,400 stock, $4,800 benefits, $506,738 total.
Robert G. Brazier: $420,615.
Roy C. Liljebeck: $266,000.
John J. Cella: $266,000.
Kent Freudenberger: $266,000.
Ray Van Bruwaene: $266,000.

The board of directors
Annual stipend: $22,000 plus $1,000/meeting.
Robert Cline, 58, Chairman of the Board and CEO. Other boards: Seafirst, Safeco, Metricom.
Robert Brazier, 58, President. Connection: Former Vice President of Pacific Air Freight, Inc.
Andrew F. Brimmer, 69. Connection: Brimmer and Company consulting firm (President). Other boards:

BankAmerica, Gannett Company, Navistar International Corporation.

James H. Carey, 63. Connection: Briarcliff Financial Associates of New York (Principal). Other boards: Midland Co., Cowen Fund, Inc.

Andrew B. Kim, 59. Connections: Sit/Kim International Investment Associates (President). Other boards: Vertical Group, Hyundai Dragon Fund (Dublin, Ireland).

Harold M. Messmer, Jr., 50. Connection: Robert Half International Inc. (Chairman, CEO, and President), a temporary personnel company. Other boards: Health Care Property Investors Inc., Pacific Enterprise.

Richard M. Rosenberg, 65. Connection: Bank of America (Chairman and CEO). Former (1986–87) President and COO of Seafirst. Other boards: Northrop Corp., Potlatch Corp.

Andrew V. Smith, 71. Connection: US West Communications (retired President); was President of Pacific Northwest Bell before PNB was swallowed by US West). Other boards: Univar, Cascade Natural Gas, PrimeSource.

William Swindells, 65. Connection: Willamette Industries, Inc. (chairman). Other boards: Standard Insurance Co., Oregon Steel Mills.

Stock analyst: Mary Fleckenstein at Ragen MacKenzie.

9. Univar Corporation

6100 Carillon Point
Kirkland, WA 98033
889-3400

Univar is an industrial chemical distributor that operates through two subsidiaries, Van Waters & Rogers Inc. (United States) and Van Waters & Rogers Ltd. (Canada). Their business includes everything from domestic distribution of pest-control chemicals to training firemen in Phoenix how to deal with chlorine spills. In 1992 the company began to expand into global markets. Univar Europe was formed from the acquisition of four chemical distribution

companies; the catch was that the European investment was funded through the sale of 1.9 million newly issued shares to the Dow Chemical Co. Even with that, the company reported a loss in '95.

Univar's board is sprinkled with representatives of Pakhoed Holding N.V., a shipping concern based in the Netherlands, with which it entered a stock exchange agreement in 1986. Univar is also well represented on the board of VWR Corp., a distribution company formerly based in Bellevue. VWR was once a subsidiary of Univar; the company broke itself up into two new entities, VWR and Momentum Distribution, in early 1990. VWR is now based in the eastern U.S., and Momentum is still in Bellevue.

Stats

Employees: 3,124 in U.S.
1995 Revenue: $1.91 billion
1995 Loss: $23.7 million
NYSE symbol: UVX

Who's the boss

James H. Wiborg, Chairman and Chief Strategist. Was CEO of Univar 1983–86.

James W. Bernard, President and CEO.

James P. Alampi, Sr. Vice President, President Van Waters & Rogers Inc.

James L. Fletcher, Sr. Vice President.

Paul H. Hough, Sr. Vice President, President Van Waters & Rogers Ltd.

1995 take-home pay

James Bernard: $482,308 salary.
James Alampi: $279,734.
Paul H. Hough: $229,730 salary plus bonus.
James Fletcher: $196,810.

The board of directors

Annual stipend: $10,000 plus $1,500–$4,500/meeting.

James Wiborg, 70, Chairman. Other boards: VWR Corp., Paccar, Penwest Ltd.

James Bernard, 58. Other boards: VWR Corp., U.S. Bank of Washington.

Sjoerd D. Eikelboom, 59. Connec-

tion: Royal Pakoed N.V. (Sr. Vice President).

Richard E. Engebrecht, 68. Connection: Momentum Distribution, Inc. (ex-President and ex-CEO). Other boards: Penwest Ltd., VWR.

Roger L. Kesseler, 58. Connection: Dow Chemical Co.

Curtis P. Lindley, 70. Connection: Penwest Ltd. (retired Chairman), Univar (former Exec. Vice President). Other boards: VWR Corp.

N. Stewart Rogers, 65. Connection: Penwest Ltd. (Chairman).

Robert S. Rogers, 71. Connection: Familial. Brother of N. Stewart Rogers (former Univar Sr. Vice President), brother-in-law of James Wiborg (Chairman). President of Lands-West Inc. Other boards: VWR Corp.

John G. Scriven, 52. Connection: Dow Chemical Company (Vice President).

Andrew V. Smith, 71. Connection: US West Communications (ex-President). Other boards: VWR Corp., Airborne Freight Corporation, Cascade Natural Gas, PrimeSource.

Roy E. Wansik, 51. Connection: Pakhoed Corp. (President)

Nicolaas J. Westdijk, 54. Connection: Royal Pakhoed N.V.

Stock analysts: Paul Latta at Ragen MacKenzie; William Whitlow, Jr. at Pacific Crest Securities.

10. Alaska Air Group Inc.

19300 Pacific Highway S
Seattle, WA 98188
431-7040

That face on the tail of Alaska Airlines' planes is smiling again. After reporting its first-ever loss in 1992, in '95 Alaska had a good year again. The Air Group includes Alaska Airlines and Horizon Air, a small regional carrier the company bought in 1986.

Stats

Employees: 10,467 companywide
1995 Revenue: $1.417 billion
1995 Profit: $17.3 million
NYSE symbol: ALK

Who's the boss

John F. Kelly, Chairman, President, and CEO.

George D. Bagley, President and CEO, Horizon Air.

John R. Fowler, Vice President, Maintenance and Engineering.

Harry G. Lehr, Sr. Vice President, Finance.

Michel A. Swanigan, Vice President, Flight Operations.

1995 take-home pay

John F. Kelly: $317,154 salary, $47,678 bonus, $10,170 benefits, $375,002 total.

Harry G. Lehr: $222,577.

John R. Fowler: $178,654.

Michel A. Swanigan: $177,981.

George D. Bagley: $170,813.

The board of directors

Annual stipend: $15,000 plus $1,000/meeting.

John F. Kelly, 51. Chairman. Connection: Former President and CEO of Horizon Air Industries Inc.

William H. Clapp, 54. Connection: Matthew G. Norton Co. (President), an investment/holding company. Other boards: Horizon Air, Weyerhaeuser.

Ronald F. Cosgrave, 64, Chairman Emeritus. Connection: Alaska Northwest Properties (Chairman). Retired Chairman and CEO of Alaska Airlines Inc.

Mary Jane Fate, 62. Connection: Baan o yeel kon Corp. (President and Exec. Director, 1981–89), an Alaska Native village corporation. Also general manager of family dental business.

Bruce Kennedy, 57. Chairman Emeritus.

R. Marc Langland, 54. Connection: Northrim Bank (President), Norcap Ltd., an investment firm (President).

Byron I. Mallott, 52. Connection: Sealaska Corp. (retired CEO), a regional Alaska Native corporation.

Robert L. Parker Jr., 47. Connection: Parker Drilling Co. (President and CEO), a Tulsa, Oklahoma, oil and gas drilling contractor.

Richard A. Wien, 60. Connection: Florcraft Inc. (Chairman and CEO), an Alaskan retail flooring company. Other boards: National Bank of Alaska.

Stock analysts: Thomas Longman at Lehman Bros.; William Whitlow at Pacific Crest Securities.

FIVE MORE BIG ONES

11. Puget Sound Power and Light

Puget Power Bldg.
10608 NE Fourth
Bellevue, WA 98004
454-6363

Puget Power is the state's largest private utility and, mainly because of the civic activity of Chairman John Ellis, is also one of the companies that make things happen—for better or worse—in Seattle. John Ellis, a 67-year-old businessman, activist, and musician (he's been known to jam with a pick-up band now and then), is one-half of the most powerful pair of brothers in the city. The other 50% is 74-year-old Jim, who was responsible for the creation of Metro, led the fight for Forward Thrust (a bond issue that led, among other things, to the building of the Kingdome), bridged I-5 with Freeway Park, and headed up the committee that built the convention center. John is no slouch himself, having led campaigns for causes ranging from nuclear power to Bellevue parks to keeping the Mariners in Seattle.

Puget Power serves 1.9 million people within a 4,500-square-mile service area that includes most of the Puget Sound area and part of Kittitas County. But apparently that's not enough: the power company is now looking north to British Columbia for expansion.

Stats

Employees: 2,150 companywide
1995 Revenue: $1.179 billion
1995 Profit: $135.7 million
NYSE symbol: PSD

Who's the boss

Richard R. Sonstelie, President and CEO, following in the dauntingly famous footsteps of John Ellis, who stepped down as CEO in 1992.

William S. Weaver, Exec. Vice President and CFO.

Gary B. Swofford, Sr. Vice President, Operations.

Sheila M. Vortman, Sr. Vice President, Corporate Relations.

1995 take-home pay

Richard Sonstelie: $388,817 salary, $140,000 bonus, $15,736 benefits, $544,553 total.

W. S. Weaver: $256,275 salary.

Gary B. Swofford: $163,138.

Sheila M. Vortman: $133,138.

The board of directors

Annual stipend: $14,000 plus $800/meeting.

John Ellis, 67, Chairman of the Board, 27 years with Puget Power, 17 as CEO (retired end of '92). Other boards: Safeco, Washington Mutual Savings Bank, Associated Electric and Gas Insurance Services.

Richard R. Sonstelie, 50, CEO. Other boards: Utech Venture Capital.

Douglas P. Beighle, 63. Connection: Boeing (Sr. Vice President and Secretary). Other boards: Washington Mutual Savings Bank.

Charles W. Bingham, 62. Connection: Weyerhaeuser (retired Exec. Vice President).

Phyllis J. Campbell, 44. Connection: U.S. Bank of Washington (President and CEO). Other boards: U.S. Bancorp, Regent of WSU, government (Seattle Chamber of Commerce).

John D. Durbin, 60. Connection: Hostar Inc., a hotel equipment company (retired President and CEO). Also General Partner of John Durbin and Associates, an industrial real estate concern. Other boards: John Fluke Manufacturing Co., Inc.

Daniel J. (Dan) Evans, 70. Connection: politics. U.S. Senator (1983–89), Washington State

Governor (1965–77), and President of the Evergreen State College (1977–83). Retired from Senate in 1989 (Slade Gorton won his seat); now mainly visible as commentator for KIRO. Other boards: Washington Mutual Savings Bank, Tera Computer Co., Burlington Northern.

Nancy L. Jacob, 53. Connection: Academia and investing. Finance and business professor at UW (served as dean of UW graduate business school 1981–88); managing director of Capital Trust Co.

William S. Weaver, 52. Connection: Previously held partnership in Perkins Coie law firm.

R. Kirk Wilson, 57. Connection: Thrifty Foods Inc. (President and CEO).

Stock analyst: Bert F. Kramer at PaineWebber.

12. Egghead Software

22705 E Mission
Liberty Lake, WA 99019
(509) 922-7031

Egghead is still considered a home-grown Seattle business, though it recently moved even farther east than its previous Issaquah address. Now a Spokanite, the software retailer is pulling itself up by its boot straps. Seattle biz notables Paul Allen and Sam Stroum have long been involved in the company and appear to be there for the duration. Egghead has 168 retail stores.

Stats

Employees: 2,700 companywide
1995 Revenue: $862.6 million
1995 Profit: $2.7 million
NASDAQ symbol: EGGS

Who's the boss

Terence Strom, President and CEO.
Elmer N. Baldwin, Vice President, Corporate, Government, and Education Sales.
Diane E. Cousineau, Vice President, Store Operations.
Peter A. Janssen, Vice President, Merchandising and Advertising.
Ronald J. Smith, Vice President, Distribution and Real Estate.

1995 take-home pay

Terence M. Strom: $600,000 total cash compensation.
Peter A. Janssen: $200,000.
Elmer N. Baldwin: $198,564.
Ronald J. Smith: $147,308.

The board of directors

Annual stipend: $25,000 plus $1,000/meeting.

Terence M. Strom, 51. Connection: Best Buy Co., Inc. (consumer electronics retail chain).

Paul G. Allen, 42. Connection: Microsoft, Asymetrix Corp. (Chairman). Other boards: Vulcan Ventures (President and sole shareholder), a private investment company; Portland Trail Blazers (Chairman).

Richard P. Cooley, 72. Connection: Seafirst. Other boards: Paccar Inc., Ackerley Communications.

Steven E. Lebow, 41. Connection: Donaldson, Lufkin & Jenrette Securities Corp. (Managing Director of the Investment Banking Division).

Linda Fayne Levinson, 53. Connection: Fayne Levinson Associates, Inc., a management consulting firm. Other boards: Genentech, Inc.

George P. Orban, 49. Connection: Orban Partners (General Partner), a private investment company. Other boards: Ross Stores, Inc. (Founder and Director).

Samuel N. Stroum, 74. Connection: Samuel Stroum Enterprises (Principal), a private investment company; UW Board of Regents. Other boards: Seafirst.

Stock analyst: Scott McAdams at Ragen MacKenzie.

13. Quality Food Centers (QFC)

10112 NE 10th St.
Bellevue, WA 98004
455-3761

The largest independent supermarket chain in the state, QFC operates 62 stores in the Seattle/King County area. The 41-year-old business has a reputation for great service in the grocery game. Lately it's been going after the upscale shopper, upgrading its departments to compete with markets such as the yuppified Larry's.

QFC was founded in 1955 by L. H. (Vern) Fortin and remained in the Fortin family until 1986, when a private investment firm (Sloan Adkins and Co.), headed by now-Chairman Stuart Sloan, bought the company.

Stats

Employees: 4,200
1995 Revenue: $729.8 million
1995 Profit: $21.6 million
NASDAQ symbol: QFCI

Who's the boss

Stuart M. Sloan, Chairman and CEO. Half of the Sloan Adkins and Co. that bought QFC in 1986. He currently owns 45.5% of QFC's stock. Prior to that, he served as President of Schuck's Auto Supply.

Dan Kourkoumelis, President and COO.

Marc W. Evanger, Vice President, CFO, and Secretary-Treasurer.

1995 take-home pay

Stuart Sloan: $0 (Sloan receives no salary; however, Sloan Capital Co., controlled by Sloan, receives a management fee of not greater than 0.2% of QFC's revenues. That equaled $981,000 in 1995.)

Dan Kourkoumelis: $275,000.
Marc Evanger: $150,000.

The board of directors

Annual stipend: $5,000 plus $500/meeting.

Stuart Sloan, 52, Chairman of the Board. Connection: Egghead Software (former President and CEO). Other boards: Anixter International Inc., Cucina! Cucina! Inc.

Dan Kourkoumelis, 45, President. Other boards: Western Association of Food Chains, Expeditors International.

Jack W. Creighton, Jr., 63. Connection: Weyerhaeuser (President). Other boards: Washington Energy Co., Portland General Corp., Unocal.

Fred B. McLaren, 61. Connection: Hughes Markets Inc. (President), a Los Angeles-based supermarket chain. Other boards: Western Association of Food Chains, Food Marketing Institute.

Maurice F. Olson, 52. Connection: Olson's Food Stores (former Chairman and CEO). Other boards: Associated Grocers Inc.

Sheli Z. Rosenberg, 54. Connection: Equity Group Investments (President and CEO). Other boards: Anixter International, Sealy Corporation, CFI Industries Inc.

Ronald A. Weinstein, 55. Connection: Sloan Capital Cos. (a former Principal with the firm). Also Chairman of B&B Auto Parts. Other boards: Molbak's Inc., Coinstar Inc.

Samuel Zell, 54. Connection: Equity Group Investment (Chairman of the Board). Other boards: Anixter International, Sealy Corporation.

Stock analysts: Lesa Stroufe at Ragen MacKenzie; Gary Giblen at Smith Barney.

14. Eagle Hardware and Garden, Inc.

981 Powell Ave. SW
Renton, WA 98055
227-5740

Eagle Hardware began life in 1990—and now where else would you go to be dwarfed by 20-high shelves of wrenches and hammers? Eagle now has 24 stores in the Pacific Northwest, Utah, Montana, and Hawaii. And who's hawking the Eagle wares? The likes of Jay Buhner, Edgar Martinez, and Randy Johnson. The connection between being a Mariner and working on your house eludes some, but . . . hey, this is marketing! Eagle's executive officers DO have experience in the world of hardware, however. Seven of the nine were previously with Pay 'N Pak. Eagle's main competition is Home Depot.

Stats

Employees: 2,600
1995 Revenue: $615.7 million
1995 Profit: $11.3 million
NASDAQ symbol: EAGL

Who's the boss

David J. Heerensperger, Chairman and CEO.
Richard T. Takata, President and COO.

Ronald P. Maccarone, Exec. Vice President and CFO.
Dale W. Craker, Exec. Vice President, Store Operations.
John P. Foucrier, Exec. Vice President, Administration and Human Resources.

Seattle is Co-op Capital, what with the likes of the homegrown REI (Recreational Equipment Inc.) and Group Health Cooperative of Puget Sound. REI is the nation's largest co-op, and thereby also Seattle's largest, followed by Group Health, then Puget Consumers' Co-op and the People's Memorial Association. There are hundreds of smaller co-ops, not to mention agricultural co-ops and credit unions. Why is Seattle such a co-op–happy city? People surmise it's because of the strong Scandinavian community here (co-ops have long been a part of Scandinavian culture) and the pioneering spirit that's always interested in alternative ways of getting things accomplished. Want to start your own co-op? Call Northwest Cooperative Federation, 4201 Roosevelt Way NE, Seattle, WA 98105, 632-4559. Leslie Fritchman is the director.

1995 take-home pay

David J. Heerensperger: $330,354 salary, plus $51,177 bonus, $3,500 benefits, $385,031 total.
Richard T. Takata: $206,118 salary.
John P. Foucrier: $127,408 salary.
Dale W. Craker: $95,097 salary.

The board of directors

Annual Stipend: $12,000.
David J. Heerensperger, 59. Chairman of the Board. Connection: Pay 'N Pak (former chairman and CEO).
Richard T. Takata, 46. Connection: Pay 'N Pak, Worldwide Consumer Products, Ltd.
Ronald D. Crockett, 56. Connection: Emerald Downs (President and General Partner), B.F.G. Corporation (Chairman and CEO until 1995).
Harlan D. Douglass, 59. Connection: Real estate developer in Spokane. Other boards: Inland Northwest Bank.
Herman Sarkowsky, 70. Connection: Sarkowsky Investment Corp. (private investment firm), Egghead. Other boards: Synetic, Inc., Seattle First National Bank.
Theodore M. Wight, 53. Connection: Walden Investors (General Partner). Other boards: RehabCare Corp., Interling Software Corp.

Stock analysts: Alan Rifkin at Dain Bosworth; Mary Fleckenstein at Ragen MacKenzie.

15. Plum Creek Timber Company, Limited Partnership

999 Third Ave., Suite 2300
Seattle, WA 98104
467-3600

Plum Creek proudly says it's the largest private timberland owner in the Pacific Northwest and the nation too. It once was a part of Burlington Resources, but went public as Plum Creek in 1989. With over two million acres of timberland and 10 manufacturing facilities, for it's success the company depends largely on housing starts countrywide and in Japan, as well as on the price of Canadian lumber.

Plum Creek has added wood chips

as a new source of revenue, as well as land acquisition to offset poor world housing markets.

Stats
Employees: 1,850
1995 Revenue: $585.1 million
1995 Profit: $110.7 million
NYSE Symbol: PCL

Who's the boss
Rick R. Holley, President and CEO.
Charles P. Grenier, Exec. Vice President.
William R. Brown, Vice President, Resource Management.
Diane M. Irvine, Vice President and CFO.
James A. Kraft, Vice President, Law.

1995 take-home pay
Not available.

The board of directors
Annual stipend: No annual meeting.
David D. Leland, Chairman of the Board.
Rick R. Holley, President and CEO.
Ian B. Davidson. Connection: Chairman and CEO of D. A. Davison & Co.
George M. Dennison. Connection: President, University of Montana.
Charles P. Grenier. Exec. Vice President, Plum Creek.
William E. Oberndorf. Connection: SPO Partners & Co. (Managing Director).
William J. Patterson. Connection: SPO Partners & Co. (Managing Director).
John H. Scully. Connection: SPO Partners & Co. (Managing Director).

Stock analysts: William Whitlow at Pacific Crest Securities; Mary Fleckenstein at Ragen MacKenzie.

SEATTLE'S OWN

Starbucks Coffee
2203 Airport Way S
Seattle, WA 98134
447-1575

For all you latte lovers, Starbucks Coffee went public in July 1992 selling at 17 cents a share. By November of that year, the shares went for 34 cents. The company's ambition is soaring too: Starbucks planned to open 200 new stores in 1995 but instead opened over 250. The goal for the year 2000 is 2,000 stores.

Stats
Employees: 11,500
1995 Revenue: $465.2 million
1995 Profit: $26.1 million
NASDAQ symbol: SBUX

Who's the boss
Howard Schultz, Chairman and CEO.
Orin Smith, President and COO.
Howard Behar, President, Starbucks International.
Scott Bedbury, Sr. Vice President, Marketing.
Dave Olsen, Sr. Vice President, Coffee.
John Rodgers, Sr. Vice President, New Business Development.
Arthur Rubinfeld, Sr. Vice President, Real Estate.
Deidra Wager, Sr. Vice President, Retail Operations.

1995 take-home pay
Howard Schultz: $333,269 salary, $201,000 bonus, $534,269 total.
Orin C. Smith: $250,000 salary, $125,000 bonus, $375,000 total.
Howard P. Behar: $199,001 salary, $100,000 bonus, $299,001 total.
Deidra Wager: $153,846 salary, $75,000 bonus, $228,846 total.
Dave Olsen: $154,491 salary, $67,000 bonus, $221,491 total.

The board of directors
Stipend: $1000/meeting.
Howard Schultz, 42, Chairman. Connection: Before buying Starbucks, Schultz was with Hammarpact USA, a Swedish housewares company.
Barbara Bass, 44. Connection: I. Magnin, Emporium Weinstock. Other boards: DFS Group Limited, The Bombay Company Inc.
Adrian Bellamy, 53. Connection: Airport Group International Holdings, DFS Group Limited. Other boards: Compass Ltd., The Gap Inc., Gucci Group N.V.
Jeffrey H. Brotman, 53. Connection: Costco. Other boards: Seafirst, Sweet Factory, Garden Botanika, Seattle Foundation.
Craig J. Foley, 51. Connection: Chancellor Capital Management Inc. Other boards: Gadzooks, EuroEnterprise.
Arlen I. Prentice, 58. Connection: Kibble & Prentice, a financial services firm. Other boards: Western Drug Distributors (Drug Emporium), Northland Telecommunications Corp., Percon, Inc.
James G. Shennan, Jr., 54. Connection: S&O Consultants and Addison Consultants, management consulting firms. Other boards: Trinity Ventures, Souplantation, Medical Self Care, Smith Sport Optics, Sweet Factory.

Stock analyst: Mary Fleckenstein at Ragen MacKenzie.

RESOURCE LIST

Periodicals

Daily Journal of Commerce
Box 11050
Seattle, WA 98111
622-8272

Marple's Business Newsletter
911 Western Ave., Suite 509
Seattle, WA 98104
622-0155
Michael Parks does a great job with this insiders' look at biz.

Puget Sound Business Journal
101 Yesler Way
Seattle, WA 98104
583-0701
This business weekly puts out an annual *Book of Lists,* ranking the "biggest, richest, fastest-growing players on the local business scene."

Washington CEO
2505 Second Ave., Suite 602
Seattle, WA 98121-1426
441-8325
Business magazine for CEOs.

Research

Seattle Public Library

Securities and Company Information
    Desk
Downtown Library, Second Floor
1000 Fourth Ave.
Seattle, WA 98104
386-4650
Mon.–Thurs., 9am–9pm.
Fri., 9am–6pm.
The Seattle Public Library has a
special Securities and Company
Information Desk where you can
get stock and bond quotations, find
out about government securities,
get info on particular companies,
see annual reports, get the latest
foreign exchange rate, and more.
(Don't expect everything to be
up-to-date though.)

So how do you get on those
boards that pay at least 10 grand
plus another thou for showing up
for a meeting? You've gotta be
born into it—or know somebody
in high places. And who better
to get to know than the top dog.
Here are 10 of the top-paid execs
in Seattle.

- Frank A. Shrontz, Boeing

- Jack Creighton, Jr., Weyerhaeuser

- Stuart Sloan, QFC

- Charles M. Pigott, Paccar

- Philip M. Condit, Boeing

- Robert J. Herbold, Microsoft

- Charles E. Robinson, Pacific
  Telecom

- Wendell P. Hurlbut, Esterline
  Corporation

- Raymond J. Vecci, Alaska Air
  Group

- Barry A. Ackerley, Ackerley
  Communications

Source: *Puget Sound Business
Journal*'s *1996 Book of Lists*.

THE POWERS THAT BE

The big house in Olympia seems to draw from local politics, as evidenced by the 1996 race, when it seemed like every Seattle-area politician was scrambling to change places with Governor Mike Lowry. But through it all, life at city hall goes on as usual.

There are still dogs-in-parks issues to be resolved and a few dogs-in-Kingdome (as in who gets to cook them) issues too. There are boards to be appointed and citizens to appease. There are stadiums to be built and a downtown to refurbish. And there is the ill-fated Seattle Commons urban park plan to mourn.

HIZZONER AND FRIENDS

Seattle mayor Norm Rice began his first $109,164-a-year, four-year term at the beginning of 1990. Like all city officials, the mayor is elected at-large in a nonpartisan election. His duties include preparing the city budget; giving an annual "State of the City" address in June to the city council; vetoing legislation (the mayor can veto an ordinance passed by the council, but the council can override the veto by a two-thirds vote of all members); appointing heads of city departments, including chief of police, fire chief, director of community development, and others.

The mayor's office is on the 12th floor of city hall, but to reach him you have to go through staff people and squeeze into a tight schedule of meetings, speeches, and hand-shaking events. The best way to get in touch with the mayor is through someone on his staff.

Local executive salaries
- Norm Rice, mayor (elected): $109,164
- Gary Locke, King County executive (elected): $119,406
- Mic Dinsmore, Port of Seattle executive director (appointed): $168,588

Source: Seattle Survival Guide research

CITY HALL

Seattle Mayor's Office
600 Fourth Ave., 12th floor
Mayor Norm Rice: 684-4000

24-hour answering service:
524-2707

Deputy Mayor
684-4000

Deputy Chiefs of Staff
684-4000

Legal Counsel
684-4000

Communications Director
684-8126

Office Manager
684-4000

Executive departments
Citizens Service Bureau
684-8811

Department of Neighborhoods
684-0464

Housing and Human Services
684-8057

Office of Intergovernmental Relations
684-8055

Office of Management and Budget
684-8080

Office for Women's Rights
684-0390

Planning Department
684-8056

Purchasing
684-0444

CITY COUNCIL

Every Monday at 2pm, nine city council members sit down and hammer out city policies and/or ordinances. They pass laws on zoning codes, traffic regulations, housing codes, and crime. Their posts are sought after and fought for on an at-large basis—meaning that everyone in the city votes for all council members. Council members serve for four years, in staggered terms so that campaign signs don't simply take over the city at any one time.

Seattle City Council
1106 Municipal Bldg.
600 Fourth Ave.
Seattle, WA 98104
Information: 684-8888

Executive Director
Nancy Glaser, 684-8888

City Council Clerk
Theresa Dunbar, 684-8888

Council Members
Jan Drago, president
684-8801
e-mail: jan.drago@ci.seattle.wa.us
Term ends 1997

Martha Choe
684-8802
e-mail: martha.choe@ci.seattle.wa.us
Term ends 1999

Cheryl Chow
684-8804
e-mail: cheryl.chow@ci.seattle.wa.us
Term ends 1997

Sue Donaldson
684-8806
e-mail: sue.donaldson@ci.seattle.wa.us
Term ends 1999

You can fairly easily navigate city government if you are on the Internet. Just don't expect entertainment on the site; it's fairly dry stuff, with lots of phone numbers. The city has a home page on the Web at http://www.ci.seattle.wa.us and all the council members now have e-mail. They can be reached at council@ci.seattle.wa.us.

Paul Kraabel
684-8805
e-mail: paul.kraabel@ci.seattle.wa.us
Term ends 1997

John Manning
684-8800
e-mail: john.manning@ci.seattle.wa.us
Term ends 1999

Jane Noland
684-8803
e-mail: jane.noland@ci.seattle.wa.us
Term ends 1997

Margaret Pageler
684-8807
e-mail:
margaret.pageler@ci.seattle.wa.us
Term ends 1999

Tina Podlodowski
684-8808
e-mail:
tina.podlodowski@ci.seattle.wa.us
Term ends 1999

FROM IDEA TO BILL

If you have an idea for a bill you'd like the city council to pass, you have to convince a council member to sponsor your proposal. You can work with any of the members, since they're elected at large, but it's best to go to the chair of the committee under which your idea falls.

Once you have a sponsor, you can be confident your idea will go before the committee, so now's the time to lobby all of the members. Set up appointments with them by calling the committee director (684-8888).

When the committee begins considering your proposal, you'll probably be asked to come and talk about it. A public hearing may be arranged before the committee, but this often depends on the level of interest—citizen activity, letters received, calls, and so forth—surrounding the proposal.

If the committee recommends the proposal, it goes before the full city council for consideration. If there is enough support, another public hear-ing may be called before the council. (The chairs of the committees call all hearings, so winning their support helps move the process along to passage by the full council.)

Don't forget the mayor. You need to make sure he's on your side so he doesn't veto the whole thing even if the council approves it.

Full city council meetings are held each Monday at 2pm in Room 1101, Seattle Municipal Building, 600 Fourth Avenue. And they have committee meetings daily at 9:30am and 2pm. A hearings calendar listing all meetings is published weekly. To get on the mailing list, call 684-8888.

WHO'S ON WHAT COMMITTEE

Because most of the council work is done in committee, it's important to know who's who and when the committees meet. Call 684-8888 for current committee information.

Business, Economic, and Community Development
Jan Drago (chair), Margaret Pageler (vice chair), Tina Podlodowski (member), Cheryl Chow (alternate). Meets first and third Tuesdays at 9:30am. Economic development, downtown and neighborhood business issues, revenue and consumer affairs, intergovernmental relations, land-use and design issues, etc.

Finance and Budget
Martha Choe (chair), Paul Kraabel (vice chair), Jane Noland and Cheryl Chow (members),Tina Podlodowski (alternate). Meets first and third Wednesdays at 9:30am. Budget, capital plan taxes, fees, personnel, audits, economic development, human rights, etc.

Health, Housing, Human Services, Education, and Libraries
Cheryl Chow (chair), Tina Podlodowski (vice chair), Paul Kraabel (member), John Manning (alternate). Meets second and fourth Wednesdays at 9:30am.Public health, housing and human service needs of families and older citizens, block grants, domestic violence, education, library system, etc.

Neighborhoods and Neighborhood Planning
Tina Podlodowski (chair), Cheryl Chow (vice chair), Jane Noland (member), Sue Donaldson (alternate). Meets second and fourth Tuesdays at 2pm. Neighborhood planning, outreach and projects, capital funding, Neighborhood Matching Funds and assistance programs, industrial centers planning, etc.

Parks, Public Grounds, and Recreation
Sue Donaldson (chair), John Manning (vice chair), Martha Choe (member), Paul Kraabel (alternate). Meets second and fourth Wednesdays at 2pm. Parks, public grounds, recreation, community centers, zoo and aquarium, Seattle Center, property management, open space, urban renewal, etc.

Personnel and Labor Policy
Paul Kraabel (chair), Jan Drago (vice chair), John Manning (member), Jane Noland and Tina Podlodowski (members for labor policy matters only); Margaret Pageler (alternate for labor policy matters only). Meets first and third Wednesdays at 2pm. Quality work force, labor issues, collective bargaining; oversees major institution policies and master plans.

Public Safety

Jane Noland (chair),Sue Donaldson (vice chair),Margaret Pageler (member), Jan Drago (alternate). Meets second and fourth Tuesdays at 9:30am. Crime and fire prevention, law enforcement, justice, corrections and emergency services,coordinates with other government agencies.

It always helps to know someone, even if it's the person holding down the front desk. Begin by asking friendly questions, but don't waste their time. There's a reason why some lobbyists in Olympia used to spend thousands of dollars on presents for the legislative secretaries. Their knowledge and powers are too often underestimated. If you really want to be an effective influence on city government, take a staff member to lunch. Develop a solid working relationship with a couple of the council members, and don't forget their underlings. If you're non-confrontational, secretaries and staff people will go out of their way to help you. (Among city council members themselves, there's an element of "who-might-run-against-me" paranoia that sometimes gets in the way, perhaps because the terms are fairly short and that campaign is always on their minds.)

Technology and Telecommunications

Tina Podlodowski (chair), Jane Noland (vice chair), Martha Choe, Cheryl Chow, Sue Donaldson, Jan Drago, John Manning (members). Meets second Thursdays at 2pm. New committee on city information technology planning and implementation, cable telecommunications and telecommunications planning, Public Access Network, and citizen technology literacy and access issues.

Transportation

John Manning (chair), Martha Choe (vice chair), Jan Drago (member), Jane Noland (alternate). Meets first and third Tuesdays at 2pm. City and regional transportation policies, street and sidewalk construction, traffic control and parking; coordinates with other governments and neighborhoods in Seattle.

Utilities and Environmental Management

Margaret Pageler (chair), Jane Noland (vice chair), Sue Donaldson and Paul Kraabel (members), Martha Choe (alternate). Meets every Thursday at 9:30am. Seattle City Light, Seattle Water Department, Solid Waste Utility, Drainage and Wastewater Utility, environmental priorities, utility rates, environmental stewardship, water and energy resources, etc.

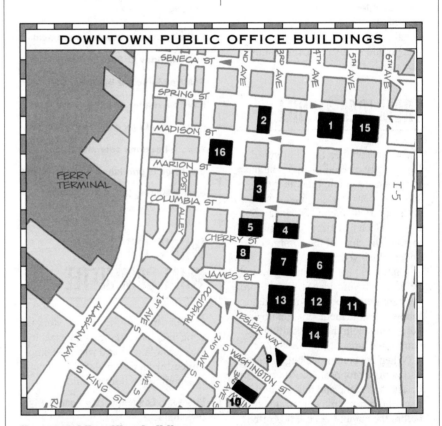

DOWNTOWN PUBLIC OFFICE BUILDINGS

Key to public office buildings

1. Library
2. City Light Building
3. City Credit Union Building
4. Arctic Building
5. Dexter Horton Building
6. Municipal Building
7. Public Safety Building
8. Alaska Building
9. Prefontaine Building
10. Third and Main Building
11. King County Jail
12. King County Administration Building
13. King County Courthouse
14. King County Garage
15. Federal Courthouse
16. Federal Building

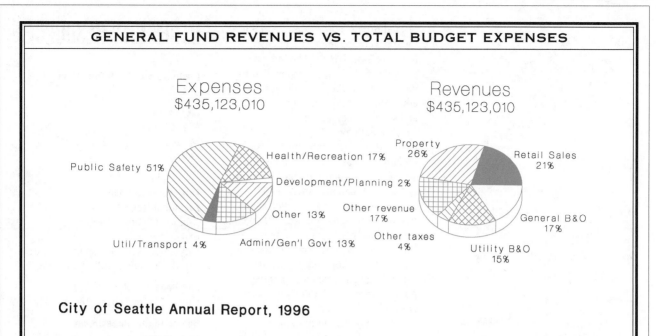

GENERAL FUND REVENUES VS. TOTAL BUDGET EXPENSES

Expenses
$435,123,010

Revenues
$435,123,010

Public Safety 51%
Health/Recreation 17%
Development/Planning 2%
Other 13%
Util/Transport 4%
Admin/Gen'l Govt 13%

Property 26%
Retail Sales 21%
Other revenue 17%
General B&O 17%
Other taxes 4%
Utility B&O 15%

City of Seattle Annual Report, 1996

YOUR TAX DOLLARS

Each October the city budget goes from the mayor to the council in draft form. The city's fiscal year follows the calendar year, so the annual budget goes into effect in January.

For the year 1996 the city budget revenues equaled $1.7 billion. About $405 million of that came from taxes; the rest comes from grants, fines, and fees. Where the money gets spent is something else again.

1996 expenditures:

- Utilities and transportation: $977 million.
- Public safety (fire, police, municipal court): $232 million.
- Health and human services (including parks): $220 million.
- General government (executive, law, etc.): $137 million.
- Development (construction and land use, neighborhoods, hearing examiner): $26 million.
- Other (neighborhood matching fund, bonds debt service, etc.): $86 million.

The city's official newspaper — the one in which all legal notices can be found — is the Daily Journal of Commerce. If you're hoping to bid for consulting jobs or public works projects, keep one eye on the DJC.

OTHER CITY FACTS

- The city has 11,443 employees.
- Seattle's average property tax is $2,202.
- Average monthly City Light bill: $38.34

VOTING INFORMATION

The city's elections are the responsibility of the King County Superintendent of Elections. For registration information, call 296-1600 or 296-1565.

VITAL STATS

Many people don't darken the door of city hall unless they need copies of birth or death certificates. To get a copy of a birth certificate, you need to write or visit Vital Records Department, King County Administration Building, 500 Fourth Avenue, Room 214, Seattle, 98104, 296-4769. You need to know the person's name, birthdate, parents' names (including mother's maiden name), and the city in Washington State where the birth occurred. Cost: $11. For a death certificate, go to the same place, giving the name, date of death, and city in King County where the death occurred. And hand over $11. This office has birth certificates for all people born after 1954 in Wash-

Want to be a street vendor and sell espresso or popcorn from a cart? A city permit will cost you $60 a year. But that's not the tricky part; you have to get permission from the business adjacent to your chosen sidewalk spot before you can acquire a permit. And you must have a $1 million insurance policy (so the city isn't liable). Carts cost between $10,000 and $20,000. You can vend food, nonalcoholic beverages, and flowers — but not T-shirts (that's what most permit requests are for, though). For information on a permit, call 684-5267.

ington State. To get a pre-1954 birth certificate or a death certificate from outside King County, call the state's Center for Health Statistics section in Olympia at (360) 753-5936. They'll tell you where to write.

COMPLAINTS, COMPLAINTS

You can't always get what you want, as the song says, but the way to get satisfaction from the city is to call the Citizens Service Bureau, 684-8811. This office has consumer books, a city directory, and hotline numbers. It takes complaints about everything except the police department and

elected officials. For example, a hot topic for complainers is seaplane noise on Lake Union. The bureau compiles Lake Union seaplane complaints and passes them along to a committee of residents of the area and seaplane companies.

About 500 people per week call to sound off about one thing or another to six staffers. They'll answer your questions about garbage pickup and other practical matters, and they'll also explain the mayor's position on an issue to you. They'll take your comments on an issue as well. They send a weekly report to the mayor stating how many people call on a given issue and what their positions are—including whatever colorful quotes seem appropriate.

Other numbers to remember:

City Department Information
386-1234
The switchboard will get you to the department you're after.

Seattle Parks and Recreation Department
Compliments and concerns.
684-4837

There's a copy center in Room 608, Municipal Building, where you may copy public records and documents. The convenience is nice, but it ain't cheap. It costs 25 cents for the first page of each document or book and 10 cents for each additional page or copies, plus tax.

OTHER CITY RESOURCES

Business and Tax Information
684-8484

City Attorney
Mark Sidran
Municipal Bldg., 12th floor
684-8200
Elected position.

Finance Department
Elizabeth Reveal
Municipal Bldg., Room 101
684-8383
City's bookkeeper, comptroller, treasurer, and auditor rolled into one.

Fire Department
Chief: Claude Harris, 386-1401

Human Rights Department
684-4500

Licenses and Consumer Affairs
684-8484

Marriage Licenses
403 King County
   Administration Bldg.
296-3933

Parks and Recreation
684-4075

Police Department
Chief: 684-5577
Police, internal investigations:
684-8797

Senior Citizens
Mayor's Office: 684-0500

Senior Support
Division on Aging: 684-0660

Job Lines
City jobs: 684-7999
County jobs: 296-5209
Federal jobs: 553-0888
Post Office jobs: 442-6240
State jobs: (360) 753-5368

KING COUNTY

King County is undergoing major changes, thanks to a merger with Metro effective January 1, 1994. Until that date, the county has nine

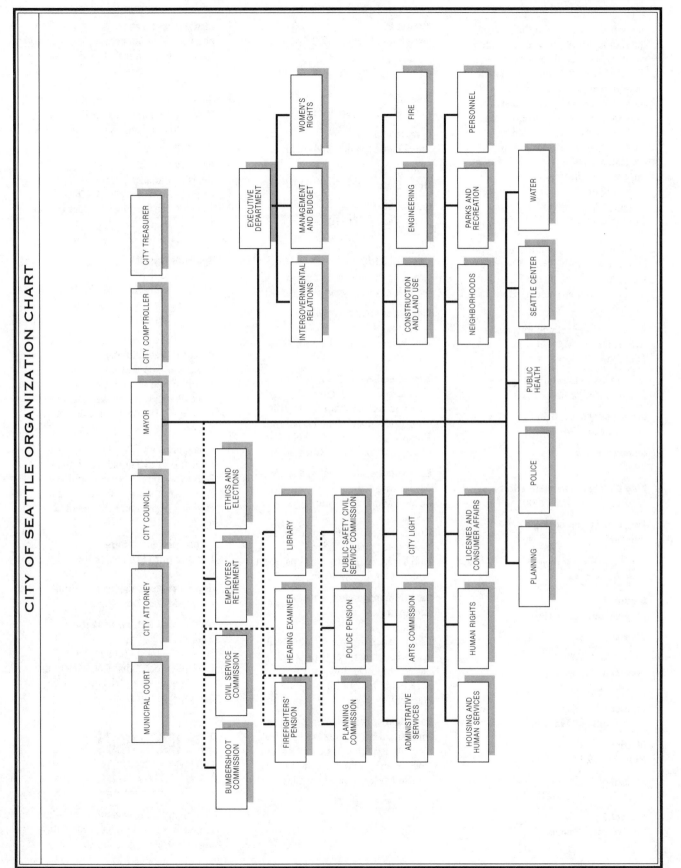

CITY OF SEATTLE ORGANIZATION CHART

council members; with the merger, that number will grow to 13, with members elected from new county districts. How the county will then be organized is anybody's guess. It's probable there will be a transit section, though the other Metro departments (hazardous and industrial waste, sewers, transit, water pollution control, etc.) will be melded into one big happy county family.

The King County Council meets Mondays at 1:30pm at 402 King County Courthouse, Third and James.

Like the city council, county council members are elected to four-year terms, with elections held in odd-numbered years. The executive is elected too.

General county council information
296-1000
Fax: 296-0198

Council administrator:
Gerald Peterson, 296-1020

King County executive:
Gary Locke, 296-4040

County Auditor:
296-1655

King County prosecuting attorney:
Norm Maleng, 296-9000

King County ombudsman:
296-3453

King County Council and Districts

District 1
Maggi Fimia: 296-1001

District 2
Cynthia Sullivan: 296-1002

District 3
Louise Miller: 296-1003

District 4
Larry Phillips: 296-1004

District 5
Ron Sims: 296-1005

District 6
Rob Mckenna: 296-3457

District 7
Pete von Reichbauer: 296-7777

District 8
Greg Nickels: 296-1008

District 9
Kent Pullen: 296-1009

District 10
Larry Gossett: 296-1010

District 11
Jane Hague (chair): 296-1011

District 12
Brian Derdowski: 296-1012

District 13
Chris Vance: 296-1013

Committees

County committees change around the first of every year.

Committee-of-the-Whole
Mondays, 9:30am.
Jane Hague (chair), Louise Miller (vice chair), full council.

Budget and Fiscal Management
Wednesdays, 1:30pm.
Pete von Reichbauer (chair); Ron Sims (vice chair); Brian Derdowski, Rob McKenna, Greg Nickels, Larry Phillips, Chris Vance (members).

Economic Development and Regional Governance
Second and fourth Thursdays, 9:30am.
Ron Sims (chair); Pete von Reichbauer (vice chair); Brian Derdowski, Rob McKenna, Larry Phillips, Kent Pullen, Cynthia Sullivan.

Growth Management, Housing, and Environment
Wednesdays, 9:30am.
Chris Vance (chair); Cynthia Sullivan (vice chair); Pete von Reichbauer, Brian Derdowski, Rob McKenna, Larry Phillips, Jane Hague.

Law, Justice, and Human Services
First and third Tuesdays, 9:30am.
Kent Pullen (chair); Larry Gossett (vice chair), Brian Derdowski, Louise Miller, Ron Sims, Chris Vance.

Management, Labor, and Customer Services
Second, third, fourth Tuesdays at 2pm.
Larry Gossett (chair); Brian Derdowski (vice chair); Maggi Fimia, Rob McKenna, Louise Miller, Cynthia Sullivan, Chris Vance, Pete von Reichbauer.

Regional Policy
Fourth Thursdays, 3pm.
Cynthia Sullivan (chair); Chris Vance (vice chair); Brian Derdowski, Larry Gossett, Jane Hague, Pete von Reichbauer.

Regional Transit
First Thursdays, 3pm.
Maggi Fimia (chair); Rob McKenna (vice chair); Greg Nickels, Kent Pullen, Chris Vance, Pete von Reichbauer.

Regional Water Quality
Third Thursdays, 3pm.
Maggi Fimia (chair); Rob McKenna (vice chair); Greg Nickels, Kent Pullen, Chris Vance, Pete von Reichbauer.

Transportation
First and third Thursdays, 9:30am.
Rob McKenna (chair); Maggi Fimia (vice chair); Larry Gossett, Jane Hague, Greg Nickels, Pete von Reichbauer.

Unincorporated Affairs
Fist and third Fridays, 9:30am.
Greg Nickels (chair); Brian Derdowski (vice chair); Maggi Fimia, Louise Miller, Kent Pullen.

Utilities and Natural Resources
Thursdays, 1:30pm.
Brian Derdowski (chair); Larry Phillips (vice chair); Rob McKenna, Jane Hague, Greg Nickels, Louise Miller, Ron Sims.

THE INEVITABLE PROPERTY TAX

Jog on up to the seventh floor of the King County Administration Building, 500 Fourth Avenue, and sit down at the computer terminals in the Public Information Unit. You can call up a bunch of information on houses and property (yours or someone else's) including: property characteristics; property assessed value history; property folio number and map location; taxpayers' names and addresses; and a history of local and state appeals since 1984.

It's a great service provided by the King County Assessor's Office, although it may not offset your property tax payments.

About those payments: Just how does a property's value get set? The assessor determines the value of your property by one or more of three methods:

Market. This is based on the sales of similar properties—it's the primary method used for residences.

Replacement cost. This determines cost to replace existing structure. Usually used for new construction.

Income. This is used only for business property valuation, and measures the income expected from a managed property.

Legally, you don't have to let the assessor into your house when he or she comes around. But psychologically, it's probably a good idea. If you refuse, you might be suspected of hiding an expensive remodeling project, and the inspector's imagination could get carried away. It's to your advantage to let the assessor look around, say those in the department.

How to find out what's really happening inside the Port: Call Portwatch, a watchdog group that monitors every meeting (283-0555). Its members are outraged at the way the Port spends public money.

Every two years the assessor comes calling to revalue your house. He or she looks at other houses in the area and recent sales to get the "true and fair value" of your property. (See also Chapter 2, "Neighbor to Neighbor," for average tax assessments.)

APPEALING THE INEVITABLE

Out of the 600,000 pieces of property in King County that are assessed every other year, tax assessments on roughly 20,000 are appealed. Reductions are granted in about two out of three cases. Here's how to appeal:

Review your property data at the Public Information Unit, seventh floor of King County Administration Building. If you still aren't satisfied, get forms from the Board of Appeals/ Equalization: 296-3496. You must appeal within 30 days of your valuation notice or July 1, whichever is later. You need a comparative value estimate from realtors or publications. And you can look at every home in the county in the computer databank at the assessor's office, if you like.

The board will then hold a hearing on your case, though you might have to wait 6 to 12 months for it.

If the board decides you're right, the members will recommend a new assessment.

If they say you're wrong, you can appeal the decision to the State Board of Appeals.

You don't need an attorney to appeal, but you'd better be prepared to put in some time proving you couldn't sell your house for the amount it's assessed. The state pays most attention to other sales in the area.

King County Assessor's Office
296-7300
Assessor: Scott Noble, 296-5195

Office of Tax Advisor
296-5202

County Board of Appeals/Equalization
296-3496

State Board of Appeals
(360) 753-5446

GOING BACK . . .

If you want to see your house's early tax history, try the Washington State Regional Archives, which has records going back to 1860. The oldest information is limited to name, legal description, assessed value, and taxes, but most of the time there is a photo attached and it's fun to see what the house looked like when it was new. Call the archives, (206) 764-4276.

METRO

Metro has in recent years merged with King County, which has made a difference to its employees. But its most important function to those of us racing for that departing bus is still the running of the transit system.

Metro names
Executive director:
Rick Walsh, 684-1983
Clerk of the council (agendas, meetings, committees): 684-1014

Best time to check court records?

First thing in the morning. Hours are

8:30am–4:30pm.

Metro Staff Offices
Exchange Bldg.
821 Second Ave.
Seattle, WA 98104-1598
General administration: 684-2100
Customer assistance (transit):
553-3000

PORT OF SEATTLE

The Port of Seattle keeps those terminals on the waterfront open and operates the Seattle-Tacoma International Airport. The Port operates on a $149 million annual budget and collects $32.6 million in taxes, garnering the rest of its money from leases, moorage fees, etc.

If the Port has had its troubled waters, as headline writers like to say, it's also had some stormy skies. The Issue of the Decade is the expansion of Sea-Tac International Airport. The Port is going ahead with a third runway, despite opposition from a whole bunch of citizens living under the flight paths or around Sea-Tac.

The Port also runs the container terminals on the waterfront, Shilshole Marina, and Fishermen's Terminal. It's constructed the new Bell Street Harbor project, on Pier 66, which includes a short-stay marina and some open space. And the Port's headquarters at Pier 69 boasts art and interpretive exhibits and a cafeteria, among other services open to the public.

The Port Commission has five members who serve four-year terms. They meet the second and fourth Tuesdays at noon (they meet in executive session first—no public allowed—and then the regular public meeting gets going at 1pm). The meetings on the second Tuesdays are at Pier 69 at the north end of Alaskan Way, and those on the fourth Tuesdays are at the Sea-Tac airport auditorium. To get onto the commission agenda, call 728-3210.

Port Commission
Gary Grant (term ends Dec. 31, 1999)
Jack Block (Dec. 31, 1997)
Patricia Davis (Dec. 31, 1997)
Paige Miller (Dec. 31, 1997)
Paul Schell (Dec. 31, 1999)

Port Commissioners office
728-3034
Executive Director:
Mic Dinsmore, 728-3201
Deputy Director:
Andrea Riniker, 728-3263
Secretary: 728-3199

MISCELLANEOUS GOVERNMENT RESOURCES

Federal Aviation Administration
227-1913

Federal Communications Commission
821-9037

Federal Emergency Management Agency
487-4600

Health and Human Services
FDA: 486-8788
Family Administration: 553-2775
Health Care Financing: 553-0425

Puget Sound Regional Council
464-7090
PSRC includes representatives of the region's county, city, and port governments. It makes recommendations on such things as regional transportation.

Washington State Department of Transportation
District Office: 440-4000

SEATTLE'S COURTS

"Tell it to the judge" takes on a whole new meaning when *you* are the one who's doing the telling. The first thing you need to know is *which* judge to tell it to.

King County District Court
King County Courthouse
Third and James
Seattle, WA 98104
296-3617
Traffic cases: 296-3565; Civil Department: 296-3550; Small Claims Court: 296-3558.

King County Superior Court
Third and James
Seattle, WA 98104
Clerk: 296-9300; Info: 296-9100;
Juvenile Court Clerk: 296-1413.
Civil and criminal cases.

State Court of Appeals
Clerk: 464-7750
Cases appealed from superior court decisions, both civil and criminal. Takes two years, with approximately 2,000 cases pending now.

U.S. Bankruptcy Court
315 Park Place Bldg., Suite 315
1200 Sixth Ave.
Seattle, WA 98101
553-7545
Only bankruptcy cases.

U.S. District Court
1010 Fifth Ave.
Seattle, WA 98104
553-5598
Federal civil cases and criminal felonies.

U.S. Court of Appeals
553-2937
Handles appeals from U.S. District Court, Bankruptcy Court, etc. Second-highest court, under U.S. Supreme Court. The Ninth Circuit Court of Appeals has a branch office in Seattle; headquarters are in San Francisco.

The city's municipal court hears all misdemeanors (crimes carrying a maximum sentence of one year in jail and a $5,000 fine) and civil disputes under $10,000. Every week 120 jury trials are scheduled for a court system that was designed to handle 12. Prosecutors have to prioritize their caseload—the more violent and flagrant cases rise above the petty.

If the defendant chooses to disappear—many do—the judge issues a bench warrant (usually $1,000) for the defendant's arrest. Municipal court judges issue, on average, 110 warrants per day. In an early Monday session in Department One, bench warrants are passed out like morning coffee.

Things have improved somewhat from 1985, when six judges sat on municipal court benches with 6,386 trials requested. Since 1989, there've been nine judges on municipal court benches; 6,479 trials were scheduled in 1995.

Seattle's municipal judges, elected to four-year terms, are Fred Bonner, Helen L. Halpert, Judith M. Hightower, George W. Holifield, Ronald Kessler, C. Kimi Kondo, Ron A. Mamiya, Stephen R. Schaefer, and Michael F. Hurtado.

A typical week works like this: On Friday, a list is made of all the cases set to go to trial the following week; a certain number are set for Monday, some for Tuesday, and so forth. If you are involved in a case coming to trial and you're not sure when or where it will be heard, call the Calendar and Trial Coor-

MUNI COURTS

It's known as "The Zoo," "a pit," and "Court of the Rocket Docket." If you're unfamiliar with how it works, Seattle Municipal Court can seem like the judicial equivalent of the proverbial Chinese fire drill. Expect to be confused, expect an interminable wait, and you will not be disappointed. The municipal court system is one of the hottest potatoes in Seattle politics. It is overheated and overcrowded, and most people involved agree that the system has broken down.

The problem, grossly simplified, is this: If you are accused of a misdemeanor, you are entitled to a jury trial. You can demand a jury trial for a charge of swiping a six-pack from 7-Eleven. If you are no fool, you realize that if you demand a jury trial your case will be delayed and delayed, prosecutors will have trouble contacting witnesses, and your case may ultimately be dismissed.

dinator (684-5679); calling that number after 3:30pm on Friday will connect you to a recording with the next week's schedule.

Municipal Court General Information
Public Safety Bldg. (PSB)
610 Third Ave.
684-5600

Calendar and Trial Coordinator
684-5679

Warrants
Room 105: 684-5690

Court Administrator
Esther Bauman
Room 1100: 684-8707

Judges' Chambers
Room 1100: 684-8709

Courtrooms
The judges rotate from courtroom to courtroom (known as "Departments"), but you can reach them by calling 684-8709; the clerk will tell you where they are that day.

TRAFFIC COURT

For serious offenses, such as driving while intoxicated (DWI) or reckless driving, you have to appear in municipal court. But for other citations, such as parking violations and traffic violations, you tell it to a traffic court magistrate.

Traffic court is a division of municipal court, but it's not just traffic court: the six magistrates—attorneys who have been appointed judges pro tempore—aren't limited to traffic disputes, although that area does make up 65% of their caseload.

To contest a traffic citation, fill out the back of the ticket and the court will send you a hearing date, which will be about four to six weeks in the future. Your hearing will take place in a magistrate's office on the first floor of the Public Safety Building. Expect to wait 10 to 30 minutes; the actual hearing will take about 5 minutes. The magistrate will have a copy of the citation (the officer who gave it

to you won't be there) and will talk with you about it.

If you've got a good excuse and a good driving record, chances are the magistrate will knock down the fine or toss out the violation altogether. If the magistrate is not willing to do that, you can appeal his or her decision to a municipal court judge.

Magistrate Hearing Dept.
Public Safety Bldg., Room 106
Continuances and hearing dates:
684-5600

Recorded Parking Citation Information
684-5600

Recorded Info on All Other Citations
684-5600

LEGAL REFERRALS AND RESOURCES

American Civil Liberties Union of Washington
642-2180
General information and referrals.

Better Business Bureau
431-2222
Answers consumers' inquiries about reliability and performance of companies and organizations. Alerts consumers to fraud and misrepresentation; helps clear up misunderstandings. BBB has free booklets on many subjects (after the first free one, they cost 50 cents each).

King County Bar Association Lawyer Referral & Information Service
623-2551
Hours 8am–5pm (closed 12:30–1:30pm). Half-hour talk with a $20 fee if referral is made.

State Attorney General
464-6684 or (800) 551-4636
Legal complaints and inquiries.

FROM GAVEL TO MICROFICHE

Very often, valuable information is hidden away in the courts, and accessing court files is not difficult, although it is time consuming. With a few exceptions, court documents are public records. All you need are the names of the parties involved.

At King County Superior Court you can access criminal, civil, probate, and domestic case records for the last 10 years. Go to the clerk's office, file department, on the sixth floor of the courthouse. Look up the name of the parties involved on microfiche to find a case number. Take the case number to the clerks and wait until they bring you the records. (For older cases, you can find the records on microfiche filed by name.) It's usually busy and you'll have to wait about 10 minutes. Great spot for attorney watching.

YOUR CIVIC DUTY

When that call comes, raise your right hand and swear.... Some people just stop there; others begin then and there to pray that their number will be called so they can do their civic duty by serving on a jury.

A Seattle resident can serve on a variety of juries, including Municipal Court, King County Superior Court, and the Federal Grand Jury. All of these juries are chosen from names on the voter registration list. The Muni Court sends out approximately 150 summons a week and uses only about 70 of those people a week. King County Superior Court uses a pool of 100,000 people and chooses 800 people a week. Approximately one-third of those actually serve. The pay is a pittance: $10 per day plus reimbursement for any mileage or bus pass the juror uses. The average time a juror serves is two weeks.

The Grand Jury draws every 30 days from a pool of candidates from all of Western Washington. It is updated every two years. Jurors serve on either a trial jury or a grand jury, and there are two courthouses, one in Seattle and one in Tacoma. The pay is better: $40 per day plus transportation costs and sometimes hotels and meals.

EXCUSES, EXCUSES

You are required by law to serve on a jury when called, and most people step up to the jury box without a problem. But some would-be jurors dream up creative excuses, some more valid than others. In a one-month period, here's why people were excused:

1. Doctor's recommendation.
2. Person not located.
3. No response.
4. Job-related reasons.
5. Financial reasons.
6. Person had moved out of area.
7. School-related reasons.
8. Child-care reasons.
9. Vacation.
10. Person deceased.

But jurors don't always get off when they give an excuse; in fact, very often they'll be told to come in anyway or will be called at a later date.

CHAPTER

9

FILM AT ELEVEN

NEWS

DAILIES

MAGAZINES

PUBLICATIONS

TELEVISION

REPORTERS

INTERVIEWS

WEEKLIES

RADIO

MEDIA

It should come as no surprise that the local news scene is heading for cyberspace even as we speak. After all, there are times when it seems the Seattle headlines and sound bites trip over each other gushing about Gates, Microsoft, and Starwave, all homegrown communications household names. The Speakeasy Cafe in Belltown has crowds of info-hungry folk mixing their latte-drinking with Net-surfing, and you do have your own Web site by now, don't you?

The newest kid on the block is MSN News, part of the Microsoft News Network online service begun in 1995. MSN is, at old-fashioned press time, still to be proven, but it does have the local news sources—*The Seattle Times* and the *P-I* as well as the TV stations—looking carefully over their shoulders. The *Times* and the *P-I* have dipped tentatively into the Internet, as have many other publications. Since Web sites come and go like partly cloudy days, we are not even attempting to list all of them here; maybe someday we will on the so-far nonexistent *Survival Guide* site.

Even with all these news toes testing the Internet waters, there are still a plethora of upstart 'zines and special-interest publications to keep the interest of the noncyberized Seattleite. Those not listed here can be found lying on the counters at any espresso bar in town.

Nothing gets people as upset as a change in their favorite section: the comics. Gripe about it by calling the *Times*, 464-2440, or the *P-I*, 448-8051. Or actually, maybe we do get upset about other things. Top complaints at the *Times*: delivery problems, grammar/spelling.

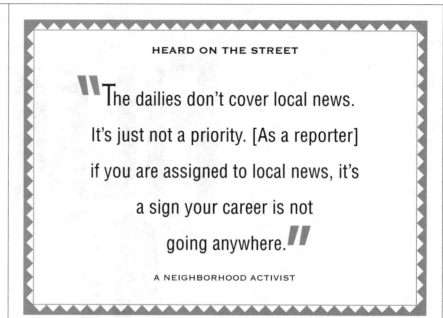

WHERE WE GET OUR NEWS

Seattle boasts two main daily newspapers, *The Seattle Times* (aka Fairview Fanny) and the *Seattle Post-Intelligencer* (aka the Pig-I). The city has seven primary TV stations, with the three major network affiliates (KING, KOMO, KIRO) vying for the lead. A slew of radio stations capture the listening public, partly because of the phenomenon of road congestion and its captive audience of disgruntled commuters.

News of Choice

- Denis Hayes, Bullitt Foundation: *New York Times, Newsweek, P-I,* and "thousands of environmental books."
- Speight Jenkins, General Director, Seattle Opera: *New York Times* for most news; looks at the *P-I, Seattle Times,* and *Seattle Weekly*—mostly for music reviews.
- Liz Stroup, City Librarian: *Seattle Times, P-I, Seattle Weekly,* and the *New York Times*. Always looks forward to Channel 9's Friday night lineup of "Washington Week in Review," and "Wall Street Week." Also listens to KUOW and NPR and reads every library journal the library gets.

Source: Seattle Survival Guide research

RULES OF THE REPORTORIAL ROAD

There are ways to talk to reporters, whether they're from newspapers, radio, or TV, and it pays not to be naive. The first rule is to remember that reporters are people, not sharks. But they are people whose job is to question anyone about anything—and their bosses buy their ink in a barrel (or their broadcast tape by the yard).

Don't talk about "managing the news." Any reporter worth half a day's paycheck will bristle at those words, and the news will end up managing you.

Call a reporter with a tip only if it's really a story. Ask yourself, "Who cares about what I'm about to spill? Is it important? Is it new?"

If you do give a reporter a story, obey the unwritten rule of news etiquette: Don't immediately call the reporter's competitor and give him or her the same story. Everybody wants a scoop, and it's to your advantage to be the source of that Big Story.

The media learn who quotable sources are and call on them for comments on breaking news all the time. Good quotes are short, especially for TV and radio. They can be a little longer for print media, but if you want to be quoted accurately, keep it brief.

If you want someone's head to roll, call these reporters. If they call you, say "no comment." At the *Times*: Peter Lewis, Eric Nalder, Duff Wilson. At the *P-I*: James Wallace.

Anytime you speak with a reporter, it's on the record (can be printed). If a conversation is being taped, the reporter has to tell you and get your consent.

If you agree to talk "off the record" (cannot be used for publication or broadcast), get that agreement from the reporter before you speak. And be clear about what's off the record and what's on. Beware of reporters who go back and forth between off the record and on—they (and you) might have trouble later distinguishing what was on and what was off.

If you tell a reporter something off the record, he or she will most likely call you back and try to get you to say it on the record, hoping you'll change your mind. (That's one reason reporters let you talk off the record in the first place— that and the hope they can get the information confirmed elsewhere.)

If you give background information, it can be attributed to "a spokesperson" or "an informed source" but not to you; expect the people close to you to know who that obscure source is.

At the end of the interview, with the tape recorder or camera off and the notebook closed, remember you are still on the record. Reporters often get their best quotes when their subject is relaxed.

If a story is wrong, don't hesitate to call the reporter. You're likely to get a better response that way than by going over his or her head to the editor. After all, alienating a reporter doesn't get you far. But if all else fails, call an editor.

Good reporters don't read a story to a source before it's published; don't bother to ask.

FAIRVIEW FANNY, THE PIG-I, AND BEYOND

Seattle's print media have the reputation of being like the Northwest itself: laid-back and relaxed.

The *Seattle Times* and the *Post-Intelligencer* are both dailies, but the resemblance ends there, or so the folks at each will tell you, despite their 1983 Joint Operating Agreement. JOAs are decried as part of a pernicious national trend to concentrate newspaper ownership in fewer and fewer hands. (Nationally, fewer than 30 corporations control over 50% of all news media.)

Under the JOA, ads, circulation, and production are done for both papers by the *Times*. In exchange, the *P-I* remains the morning paper, the *Times* the afternoon one, at least for the time being. Nationally, morning papers are the most successful as far as circulation goes. One result of the JOA that makes folks at the *P-I* sad is that the *P-I* has basically lost its presence in the Sunday paper, a joint publication. There is a *P-I* section, and it usually features an analytical piece that's worth looking for, but

that's just it: You have to look. There truly is competition between news staffs (despite the fact that reporters at one paper are often married to or living with someone from the other paper). "The competition," says former *Times* ombudsman Frank Wetzel, "is a matter of ego." The *P-I* does a good job of breaking news stories and is much more the "newspaper of record" than the larger *Times*. For years, the sentiment in the city was that if you wanted to find out what was happening locally, you

How you can tell when one newspaper is "chasing" another on a story: In the case of the *Times*, if the *P-I* breaks a story, the *Times'* early morning reporters scramble to get it in their second or third editions. So if a *P-I* story doesn't appear in the *Times'* first edition and does in the second or third, it's been chased. (Another way to tell is if you are a news source and you get calls from the *Times* at 6:30am. That means you should run right out and buy a *P-I*.) If the *P-I* is chasing a *Times* story, it has all the time in the world, from noon, when the *Times'* last edition is out, to about 9pm. Both papers will usually bury a story in back sections if the other paper has broken it—sometimes to an absurd degree.

had to read the *P-I*. But in recent years the *Times* has made an effort to cover more local news with metro and suburban zoned pages.

The *P-I* is still the fast read, and is, after all, there in the morning. But it has trouble holding on to reporters. The *Times* is more inbred, with decisions made by committee, and a little slower off the mark. But the *Times* is strong in investigative reporting and big on full-blown features illustrated by lots of graphics. The *Times* won a Pulitzer for its 1989 *Exxon Valdez* oil spill coverage and has won awards— and some criticism—for its exposé on Brock Adams, then a U.S. senator from Washington state. In 1995, the *Times* almost single-handedly brought in alleged arsonist Martin Pang after a warehouse fire that ended with several Seattle firemen dead.

If you want to stage an event in the morning and have it appear the same day in the *Times,* hold it before 11am. Even at that you'll miss the first couple of editions. But if you want an event to be covered first in the *P-I,* wait until 2pm.

The *Times* is at an advantage when it comes to national news that happens on the East Coast because of the time difference; but it's at a disadvantage when it comes to final stock market readings. You can get the final stock quotes from the *Times* if you get the night final, which you can only buy at newsstands. The stock quote hotline on the *Times* Infoline, 464-2000, is category 9800; for instructions on how to use it, call category 9801.

DEADLINES

At the Times: First edition: 8am. Second edition: 11:15am. Night final: 1:35pm. Final Sunday edition deadline: 8pm Saturday. Most Sunday editions are on the streets by Friday, though; the deadline for that edition is noon Friday.

At the P-I: First edition: 9pm. Second edition: 11pm–midnight (a second-edition *P-I* can be recognized by a little star under the name—remakes of the second edition have an additional star). The *P-I* is basically closed on Saturday, since it all but disappears from the Sunday paper.

THEY GET LETTERS...

The *Seattle Times* publishes about 20% of the letters to the editor it receives, choosing brief, well-written responses to news, editorials, or columns. The *Times* gets 30 to 75 letters in a day—the number of letters dwindles when the weather is good or during the holidays. If your letter has been chosen, the *Times* will call to verify your name, address, and phone number.

If you're moved to write, pull out the typewriter and hammer away immediately. Letters about stale news are considered stale themselves. It's OK to respond to someone else's letter to the editor; dialogues between letter writers are sometimes the most interesting part of the paper. Oh,

and out-of-town letters don't stand much chance.

The *P-I* publishes about 13% of its letters, or about 5 of the 30 or 40 it receives in a day. Those that get published have legible signatures, phone numbers, and addresses, and are well written and succinct — the shorter the better.

Some people write letters to the editor every day or every week—this drives editors crazy. If you ever want to get published, save your letter for that one irresistible issue, and don't keep calling about when it will be published.

At the *P-I*, the letters editor will verify a letter for possible publication within about a week. If you don't hear by then, your letter has probably been round-filed. Getting a call saying your letter is being considered doesn't guarantee publication. Something better may come in and bump yours, but at least you've gotten to first base.

Perennial letter-writing subjects
These subjects draw the most letters:
- Abortion
- Capital punishment
- Forest management
- Global warming
- Ozone layer

Seattle Post-Intelligencer
Letters to the Editor
P.O. Box 1909
Seattle, WA 98111-1909
Online: http://www.seattle-pi.com

The Seattle Times
Letters Editor
P.O. Box 70
Seattle, WA 98111
Online: http://www.seattletimes.com

SEATTLE DAILY FACTS

Circulation figures given below
are from the 1996 edition of *Gales
Directory of Publications and
Broadcast Media.*

Seattle Post-Intelligencer
101 Elliott Ave. W
Seattle, WA 98119
Mailing: P.O. Box 1909
Seattle, WA 98111-1909
448-8000
Newsroom: 448-8350
Circulation: 204,905 Mon.–Fri.,
180,548 Sat., 507,171 Sun.
(with *Seattle Times*)

Publisher: Virgil Fassio
Executive editor: J.D. Alexander
Owner: The Hearst Corporation
Editorial page editor: Charles
Dunsire, 448-8387
Reader representative: 448-8051
Notable columnists: Susan Paynter
has taken over from Jean Godden,
who moved to the *Times,* as the
Seattle lifestyle columnist. John
Hahn does people features, Carol
Smith-Monkman is the local general
business columnist, Art Thiel has a
large following in sports.
North and South bureaus: 448-8033

The Seattle Times
1120 John St.
(Fairview Ave. N and John St.)
Seattle, WA 98109
Mailing: P.O. Box 70
Seattle, WA 98111
464-2111
Newsroom: 464-2200
Circulation: 231,446 Mon.–Fri.,
225,831 Sat., 507,171 Sun. (with *P-I*)
Publisher: Frank Blethen
Executive editor: Michael Fancher
Owner: The Blethen family, with a
minority interest held by Knight-
Ridder Corporation

Editorial page editor: Mindy
Cameron, 464-2773
Notable columnists: Emmett Watson
(native son stuff), Eric Lacitis (news-
based, cynical comments). John
Hinterberger (food) has a column in
Pacific Magazine, the Sunday supplement; Jean Godden was stolen away
from the *P-I* for her pithy comments
on "Latteland"; Blaine Newnham and
Steve Kelley, the columnists sports
people love to hate and hate to love,
continue to track sports.

The *Times* has three zoned editions, a ploy to attract waning reader-
ship. It's working, at least to the
degree that local news is finally
being given its due.
North News Bureau: 745-7800
South News Bureau: 464-2475
East News Bureau: 453-2130
West News Bureau: Oops—still no
news from across the water.

When the *Times* redesigned the
entire paper in the summer of 1993, it
divvied things up to make it more
readable. So now there are lots and
lots of things like digests, focus sections, and newsletter-y columns.
Here are a few.

InfoLine: Free service with variety of topics from health to local deaths, pass conditions to mortgage rates. Call 464-2000.

News in a hurry: Summarizing of the major stories in the paper, this is always on page A2.

For the Record: Formerly called "Sports at a Glance," this is a roundup of the news briefs in the sports world, 464-2275.

TV columnist: Reviews shows and points you in the right direction for your viewing pleasure, 464-2313.

Community calendar: 464-2296.

Gardening: Every Friday, the paper runs a "Practical Gardener" column, with calendar of gardening-related events, 464-2354.

Business Monday: Weekly biz section with main feature, profiles, and strategy pieces, sprinkled with inside "memos" about local companies, 464-2266.

Food section: One of the paper's most popular sections (the *Times* still has a test kitchen, a phenomenon among modern papers), 464-2300.

AND THE REST OF THE FIELD

The *Times* and the *P-I* aren't the only two dailies in the race for readers. Running on their heels are *The News Tribune* (formerly *The Tacoma News Tribune*) and the *Journal-American*. Up north *The Herald* and to the west *The Sun* (Bremerton) hold forth; south in Olympia, *The Olympian* publishes daily, and the *Valley Daily News* publishes in Kent, Auburn, and Renton. The *Daily Journal of Commerce* comes out daily except Sunday.

These smaller dailies often do a great job in local news (*The News Tribune* is touted by many newsies as the best paper around, though it has the reputation of being difficult to work for). They jab the big guys and needle them with turf wars, especially over the south Seattle/north Tacoma area.

Daily Journal of Commerce
P.O. Box 11050
Seattle, WA 98111
622-8272
Circulation: 6,445 (statewide)
Publishers: M.E. and D.O. Brown

The Herald
P.O. Box 930
Everett, WA 98206
(206) 339-3000
Circulation: 52,000 daily; 62,000 Sunday.
Owner: *The Washington Post*

Journal-American
1705 132nd Ave. NE
Bellevue, WA 98005
455-2222
City desk: 453-4230
Circulation: 30,000
Owner: Northwest Media, Inc., a wholly owned subsidiary of Persis Corp., which recently made a sweep through the Northwest and now owns the *Peninsula Daily News* in Port Angeles and the Mercer Island, Bothell, and Woodinville weeklies. Also picked up the *Valley Daily News* in south Seattle. The *J-A* is a bible to Eastsiders; good local sports coverage.

The News Tribune
1950 S State St.
Tacoma, WA 98405
City desk: (206) 597-8511
Editorial page: (206) 597-8638
Seattle bureau: 467-9836
Circulation: 131,000
Owner: McClatchy Newspapers

The Olympian
P.O. Box 407
Olympia, WA 98507
City editor: (360) 754-5420
Owner: Gannett Corporation

The Sun
545 Fifth St.
Bremerton, WA 98310
(360) 377-3711
Circulation: 41,630
Owner: John Scripps, Scripps-Howard

Valley Daily News
P.O. Box 130
Kent, WA 98035
872-6660

Circulation: 33,000
Owner: Northwest Media, Horvitz Family

ONCE A WEEK

Eastsideweek
1008 Western Ave., Suite 300
Seattle, WA 98104
623-0500
Online: http://www.speakeasy.org/eastsideweek
Sister paper to *Seattle Weekly*, urbanely covering Lake Washington's eastside communities.

Puget Sound Business Journal
720 Third Ave., Suite 800
Seattle, WA 98104
583-0701
Circulation: 18,000
Publisher: Mike Flynn
The *Puget Sound Business Journal* gets its fair share of stories that the bigger papers miss. This lively weekly has a biz bent and puts out excellent annual supplement sections on such things as leasing rates and the top companies and executives in the area. Its "Book of Lists" is a must-have for local businesses.

Seattle Weekly
1008 Western Ave., Suite 300
Seattle, WA 98104
623-0500
Circulation: 70,000
Publisher: David Brewster
The *Weekly* is Seattle's answer to the *Village Voice*—a sophisticated alternative weekly that's been variously described as scrappy, liberal, conservative, a social calendar, an iconoclast, and a gossip sheet. "Weekly Wash" features pithy comments from publisher Brewster and his minions; the "Goings On" calendar is the only way to find out everything happening in the city; and the Arts and Leisure section has the best arts coverage hands down. In late 1995, the *Weekly* went free, a move that paid off with a huge, almost overnight jump in circulation, from 31,000 to 70,000. You can find it all over town.

The Stranger

1202 E Pike St., Suite 1225
Seattle, WA 98122
323-7101

The Stranger is the brash upstart newspaper *Seattle Weekly* used to be. It's also easily Seattle's edgiest, most outspoken, and maybe even most creative newspaper—not afraid to take on anyone or anything, frequently very funny, and never dull. Look for its Advertisement of the Week, and lots of original comics. Personals ads are not for the narrow-minded and/or timid. *Stranger* writer Lewis Kamb recently won a first-place award from the Society of Professional Journalists, Western Washington Chapter, for an exposé about financial problems at a local AIDS charity.

NEIGHBORHOOD PAPERS

As the city grows, local papers have become more important than ever. They're the only place you can find out well in advance what kind of apartment building is planned for your block, or when the old hardware store owner on the corner retires.

Unfortunately, most community papers are run on a shoestring and some are much better run than others. Those that have been basically gutted and turned into shoppers with a few press-release promo pieces on the front page aren't even worth picking up, but the rest can be invaluable.

The last few years have seen lots of consolidation among the city's local papers. The only independently run ones are the *North Seattle Press* (which also puts out the *Lake Union Review*), the *West Seattle Herald/White Center News,* the *NW Asian Weekly,* and the *Pike Place Market News.* The Pacific Media Group puts out the rest, sometimes just changing the front page or the flag.

North of Seattle, *The Enterprise* covers Shoreline, The Highlands, Lake City, and Lake Forest Park. *The Seattle Times* recently bought three papers covering south King County:

the *Federal Way News,* the *Highline Times,* and the *Des Moines News.*

Newspapers and publications addressing the city's ethnic groups are listed in Chapter 12, "Ethnicity: Diversity at Work."

COLLEGE PAPERS

For a better grasp of contemporary culture, as lived by 20-year-olds, pick up a college paper where they're left thrown around campus.

City Collegian

Seattle Central Community College
1701 Broadway
Seattle, WA 98122
587-6959

The Daily

University of Washington
144 Communications Bldg., DS-20
Seattle, WA 98195
543-2670

UW newspaper published daily except weekends; weekly in summer. *The Daily* is not only a darned good paper, but fun to read as well.

Ebbtide

Shoreline Community College
16101 Greenwood Ave. N
Seattle, WA 98133
546-4101

Spectator

Seattle University
Broadway and Madison
Seattle, WA 98122
296-6470

SPU Falcon

Seattle Pacific University
3215 Third Ave. W
Seattle, WA 98119
281-2104

TRADE PUBLICATIONS

Aero Mechanic

9125 15th Pl. S
Seattle, WA 98108
763-1300

A trade journal for aero mechanics.

Auto and Flat Glass Journal

P.O. Box 12099
Seattle, WA 98102
322-5120

National magazine for auto glass replacement industry.

Computing Resources for the Professional

Computing Information Center
University of Washington
ACC, HG-45
Seattle, WA 98195
543-5970

Established 1981; bimonthly.

Diversity News

1800 112th Ave. NE, Suite 100W
Bellevue, WA 98004
455-0185

Business magazine for women- and minority-owned businesses.

Grange News

Mailing: P.O. Box 1186
Olympia, WA 98507
(360) 943-9911

Tabloid for farm organizations and cooperatives; established 1912.

The Guide

1720 E. Olive Way
Seattle, WA 98102
323-3769

Commercial construction.

Insurance Week

1001 Fourth Ave., Suite 3029
Seattle, WA 98154
624-6965

Marine Digest

1201 First Ave. S, Suite 200
Seattle, WA 98134
682-3607

Magazine established in 1922 for maritime industry.

Marine Response Bulletin

1201 First Ave. S, Suite 200
Seattle, WA 98134
682-3607

Weekly newsletter for those involved in oil spill response on the West Coast; legislation, regulation, industry activity.

Marple's Business Newsletter
117 W Mercer St., Suite 200
Seattle, WA 98119
281-9609
Michael Parks does a great job with
this insiders' look at biz.

Stocks & Commodities
Technical Analysis, Inc.
3517 SW Alaska St.
Seattle, WA 98126-2791
938-0570
Monthly magazine covering computerized investing, charting, broker-
age, and advising services. Purpose
is to explain methods of trading
publicly held stocks and bonds,
mutuals, etc.

Vernon Publications, Inc.
3000 Northup Way
Bellevue, WA 98004
827-9900
Produces *Milepost, Nurse Practitioner Journal,* and *Pacific Builder
and Engineer,* a semimonthly
construction magazine.

Washington CEO
2505 Second Ave., Suite 602
Seattle, WA 98121

441-8415
Business magazine for CEOs.

Washington Teamster
553 John St.
Seattle, WA 98109
441-7470
Quarterly union publication.

RELIGIOUS PUBLICATIONS

Episcopal Voice
1551 10th Ave. E
Seattle, WA 98102
325-4200
Monthly publication of the Episcopal
Diocese of Olympia; lots of news
about goings-on at Capitol Hill landmark St. Mark's Cathedral.

Jewish Transcript
2031 Third Ave., Suite 200
Seattle, WA 98121
441-4553
Published twice a month by the
Jewish Federation of Greater Seattle.

The Progress
910 Marion St.
Seattle, WA 98104
382-4850
Weekly Catholic paper established
in 1897. Publisher is Archbishop
Murphy.

NEWSPRINT PUBLICATIONS

Active Singles Life
3450 Sixth Ave. S
Seattle, WA 98134
223-5537
Monthly.

The Bicycle Paper
4710 University Way NE, Suite 214
Seattle, WA 98105
322-8393
Covers Northwest cycling; published nine times a year by
Northwest Classics.

Common Ground
3631 Interlake Ave. N
Seattle, WA 98103
632-8528
Monthly covering issues of community, spirituality, and holistic health.

Downtown Source
1100 Denny Way
Seattle, WA 98109
464-8789
Information about downtown Seattle, published by *The Seattle Times*.

Issue Watch
Municipal League of Seattle
604 Central Bldg.
810 Third Ave.
Seattle, WA 98104-1651
622-8333
Ten times/year; nonpartisan tabloid on city/county/state government. Established in 1911.

mirror
1100 Denny Way
Seattle, WA 98109
464-8495
Paper for and by teenagers, published by *The Seattle Times*.

The New Times
Silver Owl Publications
P.O. Box 51186
Seattle, WA 98115
524-9071
New Age monthly.

PCC Sound Consumer
4201 Roosevelt Way NE
Seattle, WA 98105
547-1222
Monthly news on nutrition, health, and the environment, published by Puget Consumers' Co-op. Sent to members and free at all stores. The circulation's nothing to sneeze at: 42,000.

Seattle Downtown News
1201 Third Ave.
Securities Bldg.
Seattle, WA 98101
623-8296
Weekly newspaper about life in the city's core.

Seattle Gay News
1605 12th Ave., Suite 31
Seattle, WA 98122
324-4297
Weekly gay and lesbian news magazine; circulation about 20,000.

Seattle's Child Newspaper
2107 Elliott Ave., Suite 303
Seattle, WA 98121
441-0191
Monthly news for parents; includes calendar essential to the Seattle child.

TWIST Weekly
600 First Ave., Suite 227A
Seattle, WA 98104
443-7661
Gay newspaper covering Washington and Oregon.

LOCALLY PRODUCED MAGAZINES

Seattle's reputation as a magazine graveyard is dwindling slightly. *Seattle* magazine has risen from the dead—and so far seems to be thriving. Adams Publishing, which used to produce *Pacific Northwest*, has turned its attention to *Seattle* and dropped the regional rag.

The other new magazine is not really Seattle's, but it's produced here: *Slate*, the online publication put out by Microsoft with Michael Kinsley of "Crossfire" fame at the helm. Kinsley has been on the cover of *Newsweek* and written about in *The New Yorker*—the East Coast just may have realized Seattle exists, thanks to the bachelor editor.

Alaska Airlines Magazine
2701 First Ave., Suite 250
Seattle, WA 98121
441-5871
In-flight magazine from Paradigm Press, which also publishes *Horizon Air* and *Midwest Express* in-flights.

Always Jukin'
221 Yesler Way
Seattle, WA 98104
233-9460
Monthly for jukebox owners and collectors.

Back Nine
1826 NE Serpentine Pl.
P.O. Box 55427
Seattle, WA 98155
672-3598
Northwest golfing; six issues a year (during summer only).

Canoe Magazine
10526 NE 68th St., Suite 3
Kirkland, WA 98033
827-6363
Bimonthly publication on canoeing. Also publishes *Complete Guide to Whitewater Paddling* and related titles.

Fishermen's News
West Wall Bldg., Suite 110
Fishermen's Terminal
4005 20th Ave. W
Seattle, WA 98199
282-7545
A monthly established in 1945 reporting on Pacific Coast commercial fishing. Also publishes *RV Today*.

Fishing & Hunting News
Outdoor Empire
511 Eastlake Ave. E
Seattle, WA 98109
624-3845
Has a gigantic circulation of 109,000, including editions for other states.

Freedom Socialist
Freedom Socialist Party
5018 Rainier Ave. S
Seattle, WA 98118
722-2453
Socialist/feminist quarterly, established in 1966. Circulation of about 10,000.

Inside the Seahawks
5729 Lakeview Dr. NE
Kirkland, WA 98033
781-3291
Weekly during the football season, monthly otherwise.

Landmarks
835 Securities Bldg.
Seattle, WA 98101
622-3538
Quarterly on Northwest history.

Northwest Health
521 Wall St.
Seattle, WA 98121
448-5999
Bimonthly about fitness, health, and more, for members of Group Health Cooperative. Circulation about 200,000.

Northwest Yachting
5206 Ballard Ave. NW
Seattle, WA 98107
789-8116
Monthly with boating news and features.

Nor'Westing Magazine
1066 Seaview Ave. NW
Seattle, WA 98109
783-8939
Monthly about pleasure boating.

Pacific Northwest Quarterly
4045 Brooklyn Ave. NE, JA-15
Seattle, WA 98105
543-2992
University of Washington history journal on the Pacific Northwest, Western Canada, and Alaska. Established in 1906.

Seattle
701 Dexter N, Suite 101
Seattle, WA 98109
284-1750
Published monthly by Adams Publishing.

Signpost
Washington Trails Association
1305 Fourth Ave., Suite 518
Seattle, WA 98101
625-1367
Monthly on backpacking, hiking, and the outdoors, established in 1966.

Slate
On the World Wide Web at http://www.slate.com
Microsoft's venture into the political magazine world. The online publication seeks to put "high-caliber journalism on the Internet, providing thoughtful commentary on public policy and culture."

OTHER PRESS CONTACTS

Associated Press
201 Boren Ave. N
Seattle, WA 98109
682-1812

The New York Times
P.O. Box 18375
Seattle, WA 98118
723-2626
Seattle correspondent: Timothy Egan

United Press International
110 Cherry, Suite 200
Seattle, WA 98104
233-9155

NEWSSTANDS

Bulldog News
401 Broadway E
322-6397
4208 University Way NE
632-NEWS
More than 1,800 titles in stock.

Read All About It International Newsstand
93 Pike St. (in the Market)
624-0140
More than 1,500 magazine and newspaper titles to choose from.

Steve's Broadway News
204 Broadway E
324-READ
International newspapers and magazines; over 2,000 titles.

Ynot Magazines and News
2016 S 320th St. (Federal Way)
941-8171
1117 First Ave. (Seattle)
464-0377

For arts and ethnic publications, see Chapter 10, "Canvases and Curtain Calls," and Chapter 12, "Ethnicity: Diversity at Work," respectively.

BROADCAST MEDIA

If you want to reach an audience, don't forget radio. Many people listen all day long, and those who aren't glued to their radios are sometimes glued to the driver's seat of the car, where they're most likely punching the dial in complete boredom.

If you tune in to the AM band, you're likely to meet the most profitable programming around: religious or inspirational programs.

Radio stations come and go, but there are some that hang in there, such as KING, KIRO, KOMO, and KVI. Seattleites listen to whatever is their pleasure—music, sports, or talk—but informal polls show KIRO-AM coming in first for on-the-spot news coverage (it's on day and night at any newsroom city desk worth its salt). KIRO is so successful that it has been one of the top-rated stations for almost 10 years. Its average cost for commercials ranks up there nationally.

The other favorite in this city of newshounds is National Public Radio (NPR). KUOW (94.9-FM), the UW-affiliated station, is based in Seattle, and KPLU (88.5-FM), one of the nation's top jazz stations, comes out of Pacific Lutheran University in Tacoma. They are in a head-to-head battle for listeners in this relatively limited area, with KPLU making an aggressive move to capture Seattle out from under KUOW's nose. Both stations carry the NPR shows "Morning Edition," "All Things Considered" "Car Talk," and "Fresh Air"; KUOW also airs "Prairie Home Companion" and BBC news.

KUOW has dropped much of its classical music programming in favor of more talk shows, such as the successful "Talk of the Nation." It's not alone in leaping into the talk show format; this seems to be the trend of the '90s. KVI has a full slate of rabble-rousing talk show hosts, from Rush Limbaugh to Michael Reagan;

KJR is all sports talk, with Nancy Donnellan, the "No. 1 female sports talk-show host in America," who's now a syndicated star hailing from New York. The Sports Babe, as Donnellan lets herself be called, discusses everything from the NFL draft to the Boston Red Sox. And over on KIRO, there's talk on both AM and FM. In fact, depending on the day of the week, you can learn how to buy a house, where to travel, and how to grow rhodies, all via the air waves.

HEARD IT ON THE RADIO

Rock

KISW (100-FM): album-oriented rock.
KNDD (107.7-FM): "The End," alternative rock.
KXRX (96.5-FM): adult album-oriented rock.
KZOK (102.5-FM): classic rock.

Pop and Top 40, old and new

KBSG (1210-AM, 97.3-FM): oldies, '50s/'60s/'70s pop.
KIXI (880-AM, 107.7-FM): AM is '40s/'50s/'60s hits; FM is '80s adult contemporary.
KOMO (1000-AM): news, adult contemporary.
KZOK (1590-AM): metal.
KMTT-FM (103.7): "The Mountain," easy-listening rock.
KLTX (95.7-FM): "K-Lite," adult contemporary.
KNHC (89.5-FM): contemporary hit radio run by Seattle School District.
KPLZ (101.5-FM): contemporary hit radio.
KUBE (93.3-FM): contemporary hit music.

News/talk

KEZX (1150-AM): business talk/news.
KING (1090-AM): talk radio.
KIRO (710-AM): adult programming, news, information, sports, special events—the Mariners' station. Jim French, Gary Christianson, Dave

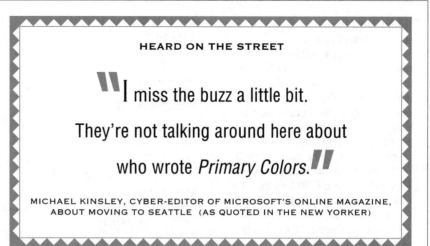

Ross, "KIRO Sportsline" with Wayne Cody.
KIRO (100.7-FM): news and talk; real estate with Tom Kelly, travel with Rick Steves, gardening with George Pinyuh, etc.
KJR (950-AM): all sports.
KUOW (94.9-FM): public radio with news-based format. Morning "Weekday" talk show features local issues/personalities.
KVI (570-AM): news talk, Rush Limbaugh, and even Michael Reagan hold forth. (And, the epitome of bad taste, there's even a "Best of Rush Limbaugh" show from midnight to 1am.)

Jazz, rhythm & blues

KBCS (91.3-FM): Jazz, folk, blues, world music. Pacifica News daily at 3pm. Public radio.
KEZX (98.9-FM): soft rock, jazz, folk and easy listening.
KPLU (88.5-FM): jazz and NPR news. Public radio.

African-American/soul

KRIZ (1420-AM): urban, contemporary music; rhythm & blues; jazz; gospel. Community Potpourri, Mon.–Fri., 7–8am.

Classical

KING (98.1-FM): 24-hour classical music.

Religious

KBLE (1050-AM): religious-oriented

news and inspiration.
KCIS (630-AM): religious music, information; some interviews and counseling.
KCMS (105.3-AM): contemporary Christian.
KGNW (820-AM): Christian.

Other

KCMU (90.3-FM): new/alternative music from UW. There's been a big rebellion at KCMU as volunteer staff object to management's policies and programming changes. The jury is out as to what KCMU will grow up to be.
KKDZ (1250-AM): just for kids, with a phone line and related *KidStar 1250* magazine.
KMPS (1300-AM, 94.1-FM): country.

TV TOWN

Seattle is unusual in that there isn't strong viewer loyalty to one station or another. As far as news shows go, though, KING and KOMO take turns being the front-runners, while KIRO continues to lag. KIRO thought its big-money solution, taking the news "out of the box," would do the trick, but it has just resulted in cries to put the news back in the box—and add substance. Maybe that's why KIRO lost its affiliation with CBS, to the surprise of many viewers. KSTW is now the CBS affiliate, with KIRO getting its network programming from United Paramount Network and its news from CNN.

Jean Enersen at KING is still TV-news queen, reigning as she has for 23 years through ownership changes and all. (When the *Providence Journal* of Rhode Island bought the station, long owned by the venerable Seattleite Dorothy Bullitt, it did a pretty clean sweep of staff.) KOMO is still owned by the Fisher family of Fisher flour fame; KIRO, by the Mormon-owned Bonneville International Corporation. All three stations organize a considerable number of public service projects.

National network affiliates

KOMO-TV, Channel 4 (ABC)
100 Fourth Ave. N
Seattle, WA 98109
Assignment desk: 443-4141
Public service director: 443-4157

KING-TV, Channel 5 (NBC)
333 Dexter Ave. N
Seattle, WA 98109
Assignment desk: 448-3850
Public service director: 448-3693
Public service announcements: 448-3790

KIRO-TV, Channel 7 (UPN; CNN News)
2807 Third Ave.
Seattle, WA 98121
Assignment desk: 728-8307
Public service director: 728-8202
KIRO-TV Eastside Bureau
13010 Northup Way, Suite 2 C-3
Bellevue, WA 98005

KCTS-TV, Channel 9 (PBS)
401 Mercer St.
Seattle, WA 98109
Assignment editor: 728-6463
Program information: 443-6677

KSTW-TV, Channel 11 (CBS)
2036 Sixth Ave.
Seattle, WA 98121
682-7763
News is now at 11pm, not 10pm.

Independents

KCPQ-TV, Channel 13
P.O. Box 98828
Tacoma, WA 98498
Public service director: 625-1313

KTZZ-TV, Channel 22
945 Dexter Ave. N
Seattle, WA 98109
282-2202

Say you try a recipe and it flops. You can call the *Seattle Times* test kitchen and they'll help you figure out what went wrong. 464-2300.

LOCAL TV TALK

Tired of watching everyone else be interviewed? Get yourself on a local talk show—or get some tickets and applaud on command as part of the audience.

KING has the Emmy-winning "Almost Live," hosted by John Keister. "Almost Live" pokes fun at Seattle's sacred cows and, appropriately enough, airs just before "Saturday Night Live" at 11:30pm Saturdays. For tickets, call 421-5555. KOMO takes care of the afternoon with "Northwest Afternoon," 3–4pm weekdays, a panel show with audience. For tickets, call 443-8333.

"Town Meeting," also on KOMO, likes to get the crowd stirred up and arguing. This show tackles current, controversial issues and presents both sides. It's a bit contrived and sensational, but does hit good topics. It airs 6–7pm Sundays. For tickets, call 443-4186.

CANVASES AND CURTAIN CALLS

Interesting—*if there's one word to describe the local arts scene, that's it. Sometimes as in, "Uh. . .interesting," as spoken by a person viewing* Hammering Man *in front of the Seattle Art Museum. Or, "Interesting?" as queried by an eyebrow-raising patron at the*

Cyclops as she contemplated a lawn-mower tire turning on a rotisserie over a backyard barbecue. Or better yet, "Inter. . .," as attempted by a would-be conversationalist at a Pearl Jam concert.

A Seattle arts scene that caught the national eye in the early 1990s was grunge, and the resulting popularity of Doc Martens and flannel shirts made many original grungers wish they lived in Cleveland. But the rest of Seattle's arts community is as lively as ever. In fact, among the plethora of groups in the city, the arts groups are undoubtedly the most alive, most contentious, and probably the most hungry.

For some reason, we buy tickets, but we don't support the arts with our wallets in other ways. In fact, per capita support of the arts in Seattle is below the national average.

Most Seattle arts organizations are in the black—"just barely," according to one arts watcher. Ticket sales account for 50% to 75% of arts organizations' incomes. For the rest, the organizations have to compete for the public's interest not only with one another, but also with the Great Outdoors. In this town, when it's a choice between becoming a patron of SAM and buying new skis, well, the skis too often win.

MAJOR ARTS ORGANIZATIONS

Total approximate operating budgets:

Seattle Opera: $12 million
Pacific Northwest Ballet:
    $10 million
Seattle Symphony: $9.6 million
Seattle Art Museum: $8.3 million
Seattle Repertory Theatre:
    $6 million
Intiman Theatre: $3.4 million
A Contemporary Theatre (ACT):
    $3.1 million
Seattle Children's Theatre:
    $4 million
Seattle Group Theatre: $1.1 million
Bathhouse Theatre: $862,422
Empty Space Theatre: $715,000
On the Boards: $600,000
Northwest Chamber Orchestra:
    $520,000

ART, EVEN UNDERFOOT

Almost everywhere you go in Seattle, you'll stumble upon a piece of public art (sometimes literally, as in the case of manhole covers designed by artists or the duck footprints on Western Avenue). High art to whimsy, the artwork you see may have been funded by a city ordinance, unique when it was passed in 1973.

City law says 1% of certain capital improvement program funds must go to the purchase and installation of artworks on city property. To date the results of the 1% ruling include bronze dance steps imbedded in the

sidewalks on Broadway, spinning whirligigs at a City Light electrical substation, that *Hammering Man,* and a variety of other art treasures dotting the city.

Seattle City Light funds approximately 50% to 60% of this "1% for art" program. In 1993, two major bond issues contributed funds to the program, one for Seattle Center and one for redevelopment of five community centers.

ART BY COMMITTEE

Guidelines for the 1% program, administered by the Seattle Arts Commission, stipulate that at least half the money expended over a five-year period goes to artists residing in the Pacific Northwest. The majority of the 1% projects are awarded based on an open call for applications; however, in some cases, a limited number of artists are invited to apply, and in other cases, artists or completed works are chosen directly by an evaluation panel.

SAC's Public Art Committee appoints an evaluation panel for each project. Panels of three or more include at least one artist; remaining members may be museum professionals, arts educators, critics, or patrons. A majority vote determines the project selection, and if no artist, work, or proposal can be agreed upon, the panel can decline selection altogether.

Panel selection is finalized by formal vote of the full Arts Commission.

HOW TO GET SOME OF THAT 1%

Want public funding for your artwork? Prepare for a highly competitive undertaking. Artists compete with other artists, minority artists complain they don't get their fair share, and the Medusa of arts politics raises its head. Until recently, the Seattle Arts Commission was under heavy attack for being an insiders' circle, "a closed loop," as one artist put it, with the same artists and their friends getting all the projects. But that circle seems to be widening—local artists think the process has been more fair than in recent years.

SAC announces a public art project by placing an ad in the "1%" column of its newsletter, *Seattle Arts*, and an-

How to really get public arts money: Getting funding (as well as getting into a gallery) depends on whom you know. "The term 'networking,'" says one arts administrator, "was invented in Seattle." Grab onto the coattails of successful artists, use them for references, or have them put in a good word for you. Get to know arts administrators and curators. Opportunities mysteriously come up when you know somebody. Of course, your work has to be good too.

nouncements in other media. Artists can then request a prospectus on the project from the Arts Commission.

WHO'S ON THE ARTS COMMISSION, ANYWAY?

The Seattle Arts Commission began in 1971 and consists of 15 policy-making volunteers appointed by the mayor. The commission oversees grants funding of artists and organizations in all disciplines, including visual arts, theater, music, dance, and the literary arts. At least half the commissioners are active in the arts or arts administration. The paid staff is housed at Seattle Center. Members of the commission come and go, but as of 1996 they are:

Roger Bass
Kevin Carl
Donna Gogerty
Carissa Smith Hunt
Bea Kiyohara
James Leong
Jack Mackie
Merlee Markishtum
Tom Pechar
Vivian Phillips-Scott
Julie Speidel
J.T. Stewart
C. Jairus Stratton
Ron Thomas
H.S. Wright, III

Seattle Arts Commission
312 First Ave. N
Seattle, WA 98109
684-7171
Director: Wendy Ceccherelli

A PEEK INTO THE CORPORATE WORLD

Somewhere between publicly funded art and private or commercial collections lie corporate art collections. Though some corporate collections, such as Microsoft's, are ordinarily displayed in work spaces inaccessible to the public, several collections—or at least portions of them—are on public view. Some of the notable ones:
University of Washington Medical Center, UW campus: An entire program that includes not only artworks (about 120 pieces) but also perform-

Allied Arts of Seattle lobbies against destruction of low-cost housing for artists and also has a list of what housing is available to artists in the city. Call 624-0432.

ing arts and artists in residence. For information, call 548-6308.

Safeco Insurance Company, 45th at Brooklyn in the U District: A collection of more than 600 works by Northwest artists (including 50 pieces of Pilchuck glass), exhibited in the mezzanine, lobby, and other locations in the building. The main exhibition changes six times a year. For information and tours, call 545-6100.

The Prescott Collection of Pilchuck Glass, City Centre, 1420 Fifth Avenue: A permanent collection of works by 36 artists from the international glassmaking community, all formerly or currently affiliated with the Stanwood glass school. For information, call 623-7385.

Sheraton Hotel and Towers, 1400 Sixth Avenue: More than 2,000 pieces of art, some of which are always on display in the hotel's public

areas, others in the rooms themselves. For information, call 621-9000 and ask for the concierge.

Unico Properties, One Union Square, 600 University Street: Exhibitions change quarterly; on display in the main lobby. Exhibits are both corporate-owned and gathered from local artists.

VISUAL ARTS VENUE

A well-established Seattle arts (and social) tradition is First Thursday in Pioneer Square. The art galleries have simultaneous openings the first Thursday evening of every month, with wine and nibbles at some galleries. The idea was born about 1982 when several gallery owners downtown, noting that something

along the same lines was taking place in the University District, decided that combined openings would attract the largest crowds.

They were right; the crowds pour in. As at most openings, the point is much more to see and be seen than to examine the art, especially because crowding is not conducive to art appreciation anyway. But folks do buy. Gallery owners love First Thursday; so do the aficionados. First Thursday maps are available at most Pioneer Square galleries.

SECRETS OF GALLERY SURVIVAL

New galleries in Seattle come and go with the seasons; no one wants to guess at the average lifespan of a gallery, but all agree that new ones are up against it in this city. The reason? The same reason music groups have an uphill battle. People primarily come to Seattle not for art but for the great outdoors; the pull of the mountains and Puget Sound is greater than that of the galleries. Another problem is that artists tend to move from gallery to gallery without sticking with one long enough to get themselves—or the gallery—established.

The secret, according to successful gallery owners, is to find a niche where you have a following, or to diversify to the point of having something for everyone.

PLAY IT AGAIN, SAM

Limestone, pink arches, terra-cotta, grand sweeping staircase—the Seattle Art Museum downtown at First and University is pure Robert Venturi, and some people love it, some hate it. But whatever your architectural bent, you have to admit the place is exciting.

SAM facts:

- The museum is 155,000 square feet.
- It cost $60.1 million.
- Three galleries are devoted to Katherine White's African art collection: one to garments and household items, a second to masks and costumed characters, and a third to sculpture.
- The museum's collection includes more than 20,000 objects.
- The old Volunteer Park museum, now called the Seattle Asian Art Museum (SAAM), has been completely refurbished and houses the extensive Asian art collection.

SAM names to know

- Mary Gardner Neill, director
- Trevor Fairbrother, deputy director of art, curator of modern art
- Bill Rathbun, curator of Asian Art
- John Stevenson, associate curator of Asian Art

- Steve Brown, curator of native American art

SAM director Mary Gardner Neill followed in the substantial footsteps of Jay Gates, who stepped down in late 1993. The position is endowed by a member of the Nordstrom family, so its official title is the Illsley Ball Nordstrom Director.

FREE FOR ALL

Bellevue Art Museum
Bellevue Square
454-3322
Tuesdays free. Open every day.
Free parking.

Frye Art Museum
704 Terry Ave.
622-9250
Always free. Undergoing major renovation.

Henry Art Gallery
UW campus
543-2280
Always free to UW students and faculty. Free for all on Thursdays.

The Center on Contemporary Art (COCA) is a mecca for artists new to Seattle's visual arts scene. It is, undiscovered artists say, truly open to new people, unlike the many galleries that have their own stables of artists. COCA's Northwest Annual Competition is open to every city artist. COCA, 65 Cedar Street, 728-1980.

The days when artists could bring their work in off the streets and be discovered by a gallery owner have gone the way of the Lana Turner/soda fountain story. Artists say it helps to have a middleman—a socialite, patron, or arts consultant—take your work in for you.

Closed Mondays. Renovation in progress; reopens March 1997.

Museum of History and Industry
2700 24th Ave. E
324-1125
Open every day. No one will be turned away due to inability to pay.

Nordic Heritage Museum
3014 NW 67th
789-5707
Free first Tuesday of the month.

Seattle Art Museum
100 University St.
654-3100
Free first Thursday of the month.
Closed Mondays.

Seattle Asian Art Museum
Volunteer Park
654-3100
Free first Thursday of the month.
Closed Mondays.

Wing Luke Asian Museum
417 Seventh Ave. S
623-5124
Thursdays free. Closed Mondays.

You can rent a work of art from SAM's Rental/Sales Gallery for three months for 7.5% of the purchase price. The work is from Northwest artists only (you can buy it after you live with it for up to six months). Stop by the Rental/Sales Gallery next to SAM on the first floor of the Arcade Plaza Building from 11am to 5pm Monday through Friday, or 11am to 3pm on Saturday (use Second Avenue entrance on Saturday). Or call 625-8997.

ALL THE CITY'S A STAGE

It's always being bantered about that Seattle has the largest theater-going population of any city outside New York. True? Possibly—you'll certainly find enough actors to supply the casts for several plays a night. In recent years, actors and actresses have flocked to Seattle, and as the available jobs became glutted, they created their own. Seattle now has a booming fringe theater scene: Over 35 off-Broadway–type groups present cutting-edge drama.

The Actors Equity Guild here has about 430 members, up from 350 in 1990. Another 500 or more non-union actors and actresses are out there too.

FRINGE THEATERS

One group that was a mere fledgling a few years ago is now where it's at: the League of Fringe Theaters (LOFT), a coalition of many small local companies. The great thing about LOFT is that tickets to its stages are cheap—often as little as $5. LOFT also puts on the popular Fringe Theater Festival every spring, featuring dozens of different plays performed in theaters around Capitol Hill. And LOFT's evening hotline, 637-7373, provides info on performances, auditions, and workshops.

AND FOR THE KIDS

Seattle Children's Theatre (SCT) is a big boon to parents looking for something to do with their kids. It's also a boon to kids who hope their future is on the screen or stage.

The SCT faculty teaches acting classes for kids ages 3 to 19 from fall through spring. (Your child can learn how to be a clown instead of just improvising.) Classes include mime, makeup, comedy, dramatic scenes, playwriting, and more. Cost per quarter runs from $35 to $185, depending on the subject.

Festival fare: Check out the Fringe Theater Festival (325-5446) or the Seattle International Film Festival (324-9996), both held in the spring around Capitol Hill. Or go to the Seattle Shakespeare Festival, 467-6283.

How to break into Seattle's acting scene: Phone local theaters to see what auditions are coming up (all the theaters have open call at least once a year). Attend a League of Fringe Theaters (LOFT) meeting; pick up a copy of *The Actor's Handbook: Seattle & the Pacific Northwest.* And any evening, Equity actors can use the Actors Equity Guild Hotline, 637-7332 (updated regularly), to find out about everything from auditions to possible ushering/cleanup jobs and cheap temporary housing. Other hotlines: LOFT, 637-7373; the Washington State Film Board, 464-6074; and the *Seattle Times* Infoline, 464-2000 press 2787. *Seattle Weekly* and the Friday *P-I* list auditions too. And The Play's the Thing, Seattle's drama bookstore, has an audition board that's updated weekly; for info, call 322-PLAY.

SCT produces six professional performances a year. In 1993, it moved to the new 480-seat Charlotte Martin Theatre at the Seattle Center (at Second Avenue N and Thomas Street).

The performances are usually smash hits—with adults as well as kids—and tickets sell out quickly. After each performance the actors and actresses return to the stage to answer questions from kids in the audience.

Seattle Children's Theatre
P.O. Box 9640
Seattle, WA 98109
Box office: 441-3322
Drama classes: 443-0807

MUSICALLY SPEAKING

Seattle's music scene isn't all grunge. A plethora of clubs offer folk, jazz, blues, world beat, "alternative rock," and more. The Paramount and Moore theaters host concerts by better-known artists. The summer Concerts on the Pier feature performers such as Lyle Lovett and the Neville Brothers in an open-air waterfront setting. And the venerable Folklife (May) and Bumbershoot (September) festivals draw thousands of appreciative fans every year from around the Northwest—attendance at Folklife in 1995 was 200,000.

On the classical scene, a number

Folks with some musical talent (but not a Juilliard degree) could join one of the numerous choral groups in town: Seattle Men's Chorus, Seattle Peace Chorus, Seattle Women's Ensemble, City Cantabile Choir, and more. Call the Seattle Arts Commission for numbers and info.

Most-sought-after acting jobs: the Seattle Repertory Theatre, which pays the most and has the most visibility nationally, and the 5th Avenue Theatre road shows.

of organizations offer concert series throughout the year. Most series run from fall through spring, taking a break in the summer.

Music series

Ladies Musical Club
International Artists Series
Tickets: 622-6882
The Ladies have been offering music to Seattle since the turn of the century. Concerts, held at Meany Theater, present artists such as pianist Joseph Kalichstein and guitarist Christopher Parkening.

Northwest Chamber Orchestra
343-0445
The NCO presents concerts at the Seattle Art Museum and UW's Kane Hall throughout the year.

Seattle International Music Festival
233-0993
Formerly the Santa Fe Chamber Music Festival, SIMF presents concerts every day during its June run. Held at the UW, Seattle Art Museum, Meydenbauer Center in Bellevue, Orcas Island, San Juan Island, and Vancouver, B.C.

Seattle Opera
389-7676
Under the direction of Speight Jenkins, five to six operas take the stage each year. But popular as it is, don't look for the return of those interna-

tionally acclaimed stagings of Wagner's *Ring* cycle anytime soon—it won't happen again until the next millennium. The *Ring* returns, with costumes and staging for all four operas lavishly revamped, in the summer of 2001.

Seattle Symphony
443-4747
The symphony is clashing its cymbals over the new concert hall, Benaroya Hall, being built downtown at Second and University. While the building is in the rubble stage (Benaroya is scheduled to

Where to hear jazz? Of course, there's Jazz Alley (beware the hefty cover charge for the first show—the second show costs less). But you can also catch some fine student performances by watching the bulletin boards at Cornish— renowned for its jazz program. Some of the local high school jazz bands have also made a name for themselves. Otherwise, try Salute in Citta, New Orleans Creole Restaurant in Pioneer Square, or Serafina. If you can't get out, listen to KPLU-FM, or to some CDs from Bud's Jazz Records in Pioneer Square. For connections, join Earshot, a group that stages concerts and festivals locally; 547-6763.

TicketMaster fees are not included in tickets' advertised prices. And sometimes superior seats are held for purchasers of expensive package tickets that include dinner, parking, and other extras. But there's virtually no alternative source for many tickets, so concertgoers have to play by TicketMaster's rules.

open in Fall of 1998), the group will continue to perform several concerts a month at the Seattle Opera House.

AND ABOUT THAT HANDLING FEE

A large percentage of Seattle concert tickets are sold almost exclusively through TicketMaster. In exchange for the convenience of computerized access to every ticket on sale, customers can expect to pay a service charge (called a "telephone handling fee" or a "convenience charge" or an "outlet fee") of anywhere from $1 to almost $5. (When you buy in person, the charge is usually less.) Because of differences in sales agreements, the proportion of service charge to ticket price varies.

TicketMaster

In-person purchases at the Wherehouse (all locations), Blockbuster Music, PayLess Drug Stores, and Tower Records/Video (4321 University Way NE or 500 Mercer St.); also

at several locations where cash-only purchases are handled. For telephone purchases and information about fine-arts events, 292-ARTS; for other events, 628-0888.

FAVORITE OPERAS

For the 1995–96 season, Seattle's favorite operas (based on number of tickets sold) were *Carmen* and Wagner's *Ring* cycle extravaganza, complete with live fire and live horses on stage. Nineteen ninety-five was the last chance ever to see the current staging of the *Ring*, so the entire 35,000 tickets sold out fast. And as for everybody's favorite opera, *Carmen*—well, is there anyone on the planet who doesn't have the urge to hum along *sotto voce* during the "Toreador Song"?

DANCING UP A STORM

Seattle has spawned nationally known dancer-choreographers Mark Morris and Trisha Brown, among others, and our city still boasts a wide range of dance. The University of Washington's popular World Dance series brings in acclaimed companies from around the U.S. and abroad. The avant-garde On the Boards performance series often includes a dance concert or two by artists such as Seattle's Pat Graney. Cornish College and the UW present annual shows by dance faculty and students; local studios such as Dance on Capitol Hill, Co-Motion, and the city-operated Madrona Dance Studio also offer occasional concerts. And of course, there's the stellar Pacific Northwest Ballet (don't forget to get those *Nutcracker* tickets early).

Dance series

Most series run from fall through spring, taking a break in the summer.

Want to get a taste of a Concert on the Pier without paying the substantial admission price? Join fellow economizers at Victor Steinbrueck Park, which overlooks Pier 62/63. It's NOT just like being there—the performers are far away and the sound can be marred by the freeway between you and the music—but it's hard to beat the price.

On the Boards
325-7901
Most concerts at Washington Hall Performance Gallery, but at press time planning to move to the former ACT space at 100 W. Roy. Call for location.

Pacific Northwest Ballet
Ballet tickets: 441-2424
Performs at Seattle Opera House. PNB's *Nutcracker*, with costumes designed by famed author/illustrator Maurice Sendak, is a spectacular holiday tradition for people who may never go to another ballet all year. Tickets for the December performances go on sale in October—buy them early, as most performances do sell out.

UW World Dance Series
543-4880
Concerts at Meany Theater.

ENTERTAINMENT ON THE CHEAP

Ticket prices for Seattle arts events are nowhere near the ransoms paid for Broadway shows, but unless you have a personal trust fund, going out can get pricey in a hurry. Try buying day-of-show tickets, ushering, or attending preview performances.

Day of show

Try Ticket/Ticket, a half-price ticket agency with booths at Broadway Market and Pike Place Market. Ticket/Ticket handles nearly all theaters in town (from the Rep to fringe productions) and also sells cut-rate entry to dance and musical events on the day of show. Unless a play is the talk of the town, chances are they'll have tickets for that night's performance at half price (plus a service charge). There's validated 30-minute parking in the garage below the Pike Place Market location and at the Broadway Market, too. Don't bother calling—they won't tell you over the phone what they've got.

Ticket/Ticket
Broadway Market, Second Level
401 Broadway E
324-2744
Open Tues–Sun 10am–7pm.
Cash only.

Ticket/Ticket
Pike Place Market
First and Pike
324-2744
Open Tues–Sun, noon–6pm.
Cash only.

If that's not enough, try Ticket-Master's discount ticket booth at Westlake Center, or call their hotline for daily discounted ticket info. They're particularly likely to have discount tickets for shows at comedy clubs.

TicketMaster Discount Ticket Booth
Westlake Center
Speeding Tickets Hotline: 233-1111
Mon–Fri 10am–9pm; Sat 10am–7pm;
Sun 11am–6pm.
Cash only.

Cheap-seat guide to theaters

Most theaters welcome **volunteer ushers** with open arms. Pass out programs for half an hour, see the show for free. The bigger theaters have regular lists of ushers who sign up to work one performance for every show in a season, as well as a list of emergency ushers they can call in a pinch. Theaters especially need volunteers during the winter holidays, when big annual productions (ACT's *A Christmas Carol*, The Group's *Voices of Christmas*) stretch the regular usher roster.

All the large theaters hold **preview performances** the week before a show opens that carry a cheaper ticket price than the regular-run seats. Check on these early, though; preview seats go mighty fast. Also note: Double-dipping on the cheap tickets is legal—Ticket/Ticket sells half-price preview tickets on the day of show.

Rush tickets (last-minute sales) and **discounts** for students, seniors, and actors are available at some theaters—but don't leave home without your ID.

A Contemporary Theatre (ACT)
Ushering: ACT has a regular roster of volunteer ushers who are scheduled to work one performance of all shows during the season. Over 300 ushers now crowd the list, but the ushering coordinator says they need emergency ushers who can be called on short notice. Call ACT, 292-7660, and leave a message for the ushering coordinator.
Rush/Previews/Discounts: ACT schedules three preview performances prior to the Tuesday-night opening of a show: Friday, Saturday, and Monday. Tickets are $15.50. Half-price tickets for seniors on the day of show; half-price tickets for anyone a half hour before showtime.

The Bathhouse Theatre
Ushering: The Bathhouse has a regular list of ushers, but has room for more. Leave a message for the volunteer usher coordinator, at the Bathhouse box office, 524-9108.
Rush/Previews/Discounts: The theater stages preview performances on the Saturday, Sunday, and Tuesday before the Wednesday-night opening.

Subscribers get first crack at the previews (and sometimes snap up most of the tickets), but everyone else gets a shot at $15 a pop. Rush tickets are $7.50 for any performance ten minutes before showtime, depending on availability; they are available to all patrons on Tuesdays through Thursdays, but to students and seniors only on Fridays through Sundays. And ask about pay-what-you-will shows.

Empty Space Theatre
Ushering: Ushers work one performance of every production, ushering, stuffing programs, and helping clean up after the show. There's also a list of emergency ushers who can be called on short notice. Call 547-7633 and ask for the house manager.
Rush/Previews/Discounts: The theater usually runs four preview performances the week of opening night, which sell out fast. A preview ticket is $14, compared with $16 to $22 during the regular run. There's always a pay-what-you-will performance too. Empty Space offers half-price tickets on the day of show for students, actors, and senior citizens. Half-price rush tickets are available 15 minutes before showtime for anyone.

Intiman Theatre
Ushering: Intiman keeps a roster of people who pay $5 for the season and usher once per show, as well as a list of emergency ushers who'll show up on a moment's notice. Usually the entire season is taken care of with the first list. Call 269-1901 and ask for the volunteer coordinator.
Rush/Previews/Discounts: Intiman has four preview performances before opening night; tickets are $19. Anyone may purchase seats ten minutes before showtime for half price. Students and seniors can purchase half-price tickets at the box office on the day of show. There's a pay-what-you-will performance the Thursday after opening night; tickets go on sale two weeks before the show, and sell quickly.

Seattle Group Theatre
Ushering: Call 441-9480 to sign up

for the season. You'll be sent a volunteer packet and be expected to usher once during each production of the season, and to find a replacement for yourself if you can't show up for an assigned performance.

Rush/Previews/Discounts: Students and seniors can get advance tickets for $3 off and can purchase tickets on the day of show for half price. Open rush tickets are sold 10 minutes before showtime for half price. Two preview performances run before opening night; tickets are $12. And of course, the Group has discounts for groups of 10 or more. There's always a pay-what-you-will performance too.

Seattle Repertory Theatre
Ushering: The Rep doesn't use volunteer ushers, but does offer discounts for preview shows and rush tickets.

Rush/Previews/Discounts: Three previews run before the Wednesday opening night; tickets range from $10 to $23. Any day except Saturday, student rush tickets at $10 are available 10 minutes before the show if there are empty seats, and open rush tickets go on sale a half hour before curtain at half price.

Other cheap seats

- The Seattle Opera has half-price tickets for seniors and students 15 minutes before curtain.

Space Finder **is a guide to local performing-arts venues, published by the Seattle and King County arts commissions. They didn't print enough to sell. Have a look at the downtown or most branch libraries.**

- Seattle Symphony has half-price tickets for students and seniors one hour before performance, and tickets are $8 for students on Sunday afternoons.
- Village Theatre (Issaquah) discounts some tickets for seniors and students.
- Northwest Chamber Orchestra performances are $2.50 off for seniors and students.

SAVED: THE MUSIC HALL'S LEGACY

Seattle lost the Music Hall, formerly at Seventh Street and Olive Way, to a wrecking ball, but soon after the dust settled, theater preservationists got a city ordinance passed to protect the few remaining historic theaters. The legislation allows theater owners to sell the unused development potential of their buildings to other developers. It also creates a mechanism for the city to provide interim financial aid for theater renovation.

What's been saved? Check out the Paramount, the 5th Avenue, and the Moore. The Eagles Auditorium has a landmark designation and now houses A Contemporary Theatre. The exterior of the Coliseum, a former movie theater at Fifth and Pike, has landmark designation as well, though the only drama you'll find inside is that of Banana Republic, the trendy clothing store.

A LESSON IN THEATER DESIGN

For those who think a rake is what you use for leaves in the yard, and for those of you ready to buy that "best seat" front center, here's a cursory lesson about Seattle's theaters.

Most theaters in Seattle have what is known as a "proscenium arch" that forms the opening to the

stage. The Opera House stage is a classic example.

You'll also find thrust stages ("theater in the semi-circle," as at ACT). These stages extend out into the audience, with seating arranged on three sides of the stage. The thrust stage is designed to create a sense of intimacy between actors and audience. You may feel a performance is transformed into a tactile, dynamic experience, or you may find your viewing concentration broken by the more obvious presence of the audience surrounding the stage.

Then there's the arena stage, also known as "theater in the round." Seattle has two, at UW's Penthouse Theater and at ACT. Seating completely surrounds the stage and presents the greatest challenge for designers, choreographers, and directors, who must plan performances with a view from the audience's every angle.

Seattle's older theaters usually have a large middle section of seats separated from smaller seating areas by aisles in the orchestra and balconies. In newer theaters seats tend to be arranged fanlike, spreading back from the stage, broken only by aisles on the far sides. Visibility is usually improved with greater "rake" or slope of the seats.

Keep in mind that good acoustics depend on both the design of the theater and the quality of the amplification/sound system used (if any). Some theaters, such as Meany Theater, have been designed for both musical and theatrical performances, and provide very good viewing and acoustics. Other theaters, such as Intiman, are designed for theatrical performances, and do not provide the best acoustics for the most exquisite chamber music concert. In performance spaces you'll find theater design does not lend itself to "mixing"; listeners mainly hear the instruments directly in front of them.

Some theaters designed as vaudeville houses (such as the Moore) are generally long and deep and not equipped to hold sound in the same way as those designed for the symphony.

Theater design includes the work of acousticians, who work with the architects to make the most of space and sound. Have you ever gazed in awe at the thousands of lavish sculpted figures adorning the house of the Pantages Theatre in Tacoma? More than a monument to the Goddess of Theater, these ornate interiors break up or absorb sound, resulting in better listening quality.

The best acoustics can be found in the most unexpected places. Check out the rows beneath the lip of balconies, at the back of the house, and theaters where sound is not lost in high, open spaces.

Sources: SSG research; Mac Perkins of Pacific Northwest Theater Association

THE BEST AND WORST SEATS

A Contemporary Theatre (ACT)
700 Union Street
Seattle, WA 98101
Box office: 292-7676
In September 1996, ACT moved into its new location in the remodeled Eagles Auditorium, called Kreielsheimer Place, a historic building near the Convention Center. With two completely new 390-seat theaters—one with a thrust stage, one with an arena stage—ACT almost doubles its seating capacity and claims there are "no bad seats." More music to your ears: During performances, subscribers can park for $2.50 at the Convention Center garage close by—a vast improvement over the parking squeeze at the old lower Queen Anne venue.

ACT will continue to present *A Chirstmas Carol* every year, and the Flying Karamazov Brothers every other year—look for the Brothers to return in 1998.

Bagley Wright Theatre
155 Mercer St.
Seattle, WA 98109
Box office: 443-2222

The newest and most modern of the Seattle theaters, the Bagley Wright is home to the Seattle Repertory Theatre (SRT) and the PONCHO Forum, a small theater that houses SRT's Stage 2 season and New Play Workshop Series. The main house has a proscenium stage with a wide hall and a balcony. This large 850-seat house was designed mainly for spoken voice, so musical performances need a boost from acousticians.

The mezzanine seats can be difficult for tall patrons—the rows are pretty close together. And for short people, the front row of the balcony is a problem because the railing is right at eye level. Occasionally, sightlines aren't as good from the far side seats, though sets are usually designed with that flaw in mind. The balcony can seem steep to older playgoers, who might want to stick with the main-floor seats.

The PONCHO Forum is a 133-seat intimate theater.

The Rep pulls in 250,000 ticketholders a year and in 1990 won a Tony award for regional theater.

Bathhouse Theatre
7312 W Greenlake Dr. N
Seattle, WA 98103
Box office: 524-9108

Originally built in 1927 as (what else?) a bathhouse, the building served as a dressing room for swimmers at Green Lake before its transformation into a theater in 1969.

The Bathhouse is small (174 seats) and, like the ACT theater, has a three-quarter thrust stage. Visually, there are no bad seats. They're pretty close together, though, so you do get to know your neighbors. Anyway, you don't get much choice; the Bathhouse has no assigned seats and no seating chart.

Broadway Performance Hall
1625 Broadway
Seattle, WA 98122
Box office: 325-3113
The Broadway Performance Hall, or BPH, has excellent sightlines from its 295 seats, which are in steeply raked rows facing back from a proscenium stage. The stage is all that remains of the old Broadway High School auditorium after Seattle Central Community College built on the site in 1979. This is a very versatile theater, with half of all its performances dance, one-fourth music, and one-fourth lectures. BPH has very good acoustics for music and speaking voice.

5th Avenue Theatre

1308 Fifth Ave.
Seattle, WA 98101
Box office: 625-1900

The 5th Avenue is probably the most beautiful theater in Seattle. Its lavish, elegant interior, with its hand-sculpted suspended ceiling and gilded motifs, was patterned after the Imperial Chinese throne room, located in Beijing's Forbidden City. This proscenium-stage theater, built in 1926, has 2,130 seats and a balcony that stretches 200-plus feet up from the stage (a moderate size by musical standards).

Try to get seats up front on the first level or in the first few rows of the balcony; if you can't, take binoculars.

Although the 5th Avenue has a very good house system, achieving quality sound is always challenging, especially when road or touring shows perform. However, the theater does have a state-of-the-art sound system and a Sennheiser Infrared Listening System for the hearing impaired, which is available at no charge.

Intiman Playhouse

201 Mercer St.
Seattle, WA 98109
Box office: 269-1900

Visibility and acoustics are excellent in this pleasantly raked 424-seat, proscenium-thrust theater. Performances focus on the spoken word. The Intiman is also pretty good for chamber music, though not for anything larger.

Jane Addams Auditorium/Civic Light Opera Company

11051 34th Ave. NE
Seattle, WA 98125
Box office: 363-2809

One of the few theaters in Seattle to do large musicals with large orchestras, the Civic Light Opera has an unusual mix of local talent in its professional, semiprofessional, and volunteer company.

CLO is housed in the Jane Addams Auditorium at the Summit School, a large, nicely graduated house with proscenium-arched stage. Most of the theater's seats provide good viewing, with the exception of the first few rows. Here performers on stage may be obstructed from view by the waving arms of the orchestra director or the heads of musicians. (Without an orchestra pit, musicians are arranged at the base of the stage.)

Beware of rows K forward. At the Jane Addams, these rows don't afford a broad view of productions and they fall within a "cone of silence," a triangular area beginning at front rows A and B, seats 5 and 6, and projecting back through rows C through H, terminating middle center at about row H. Within this area, sound is "muddy" because of the position of speakers at the stairs on either side of the stage.

Best acoustics are just under the lip of the balcony in rows L through S. There, words and music sound clearer after bouncing off the balcony overhang. You'll find lots of legroom in row L because of the separating aisle. Acoustics are also quite good at the rear of the hall beneath the balcony, but only if your eagle-eyes can make up for the distance from the stage. Would be nice if they had padded seats.

Kane Hall

University of Washington
Seattle, WA 98195
543-2985

Acoustic quality of performances at Kane Hall varies, although the original intention of the place was for academic lectures. The auditorium has 708 seats, a stage that's really a lecture platform, and a balcony. Music mixes less here, which means you will tend to hear only the instruments directly in front of you.

KeyArena

First Ave. N and Thomas St.
Customer service: 684-7200

The KeyArena is a large performance, sports, and exhibition arena with 17,000 seats. The Arena features touring rock music performers who bring their own sound systems. It is difficult to achieve high-quality sound in such an enormous space, and success depends on each show's equipment. Stay away or be prepared.

Meany Theater

University of Washington
George Washington Lane at
NE 40th St.
Seattle, WA 98195
Box office: 543-4880

An excellent place to see dance and hear opera, Meany Theater has a wide proscenium stage with a shallow 1,206-seat house. This space was designed more for singing voice, music, and dance performances than for drama and spoken voice.

Meany's proscenium opening is the widest in Seattle, giving the hall good sightlines for dance performances. Audience members used to be able to see into the wings, but proper masking has solved that problem. Sit in the first two rows of the balcony only if you are tall enough to see over the edge of the balcony partition. All seats in Meany Theater cost the same.

The Moore Theater

1932 Second Ave.
Seattle, WA 98101
Box office: 443-1744

Originally a vaudeville venue, the Moore seats about 1,400 and has a long, deep, and ornate house, proscenium stage, and two balconies, the second of which is closed. Acoustics here vary from good to poor. Deep under the balcony are dead zones, but up to about 15 rows under the lip of the balcony the seats are OK.

Sightlines tend to be very good, but avoid the steeply raked balcony if you are susceptible to vertigo or nosebleeds.

New City Theatre

1634 11th Ave.
Seattle, WA 98122
323-6800

Avant-garde and new material from local artists and directors is the specialty in the small, 100-seat "multiple configuration" theater. Seating arrangements vary depending on the type of performance. Sightlines and acoustics are excellent; theater is intimate.

Nippon Kan Theater

628 S Washington St.
Seattle, WA 98104
224-0181
Built in 1910, this 400-seat theater is small and intimate—an ideal setting for solo performances. All kinds of musical offerings here.

Paramount Theatre

901 Pine St.
Seattle, WA 98101
Box office: 682-1414
This proscenium-stage theater has 2,832 seats divided between the main floor and two balconies. The Paramount has a new state-of-the-art sound system that is usually augmented or changed depending on the show—concert sounds are as individual as the performers; lectures and plays are all different as well. But for the best musical experience no matter what the equipment, try sitting just under the lip of the balcony. The Paramount has been remodeled to its original 1928 grandeur—the whole place was gutted, and everything (including the gold leaf) was cleaned or repainted; the effort included removing, cleaning, and rehanging the 3,000,000 beads on the original chandeliers. The three-tiered Grand Lobby sports original 1920s furniture. All the seats in the theater are new, the stage was enlarged by 20 feet each way, and (perhaps best of all) the women's restrooms have been expanded to 17 stalls.

The Penthouse Theatre

University of Washington
45th and 17th NE
Seattle, WA 98195
543-4880
The first "theater in the round" in the United States, the Penthouse has 160 seats in its oval-shaped house. Its small size affords clear acoustics and unusual perspectives. Sightlines are very good. The historic landmark has been renovated and moved from south campus to north campus to be closer to the drama teaching facilities.

Seattle Opera House

Seattle Center
351 Mercer St.
Seattle, WA 98109
Opera tickets: 389-7676
Ballet tickets: 441-2424
Symphony tickets: 443-4747
The Opera House has 3,017 pleasantly raked, comfortable seats, but watch out for the back rows under the balcony—you'll want your money back when you can't hear.

Box seats are best if you can afford them. They cost between $75 and $85 a night for center seats, $65 to $71 for side seats. No surprise—best ones are center first balcony.

Short people shouldn't sit mid-center main floor at the Opera House, where it flattens out, or they'll be dodging the head of the tall guy in front all night. The two balconies offer greater visibility than does the main floor.

The Opera House gang is made up of the Seattle Opera, Pacific Northwest Ballet, and the Seattle Symphony. They're all crowding in there until the new symphony hall is completed.

Studio Theater

Meany Theater (see above)
The "Mini Meany," as it is sometimes called, has 224-plus seats. It's a black-box theater that plays as an endstage. Both acoustics and sightlines are very good. The Studio Theater is used by the UW's School of Drama, as is the Playhouse Theatre on University Way and 41st.

Washington Hall Performance Gallery

153 14th Ave.
Seattle, WA 98122
325-7901
As long as the On the Boards series continues to play here (they were planning to move at press time), plan ahead if you want a good seat. Shows at this 220-seat theater nearly always sell out, and with no reserved seating you'll need to arrive early. Seats in the balcony give the best view for dance performances. Originally built as a ballroom, the theater has fabulous acoustics, say touring groups.

AND ON THE SILVER SCREEN

Seattle is full of movie theaters, including some spectacular movie palaces whose decor adds an extra dimension to the moviegoing experience. If you're seeking bargain films, there are several discount theaters to choose from. Some show pretty lightweight films; others are close to first-run (e.g., the Crest).

- Admiral Theater: All shows $2
- Bay: All shows $2
- Crest: All shows $2
- Roxy: All shows $2
- Seven Gables Theaters: For $22 you can buy a discount pass good for five Monday–Thursday admissions to Seven Gables Theaters (Broadway Market, Egyptian, Guild 45th, Harvard Exit, Metro, Neptune, Seven Gables, and Varsity).
- United Artists Seattle Center: All shows $2

Come spring, Broadway fills with moviegoers hurrying from theater to theater for the three-week Seattle International Film Festival (SIFF), which presents dozens of films from all over the world. Program schedules appear around town several weeks prior to the beginning of the festival; you can buy single tickets or choose from several kinds of multi-film passes, which reduce your admission price somewhat. Buy early: some films do sell out, particularly toward the end of the festival as word gets out about the good ones.

Seattle International Film Festival
324-9996

PLUGGING IN

Since the city's art scene is spread around, plugging into your scene of choice can be problematic. What if you're tired of Jazz Alley and want

Seattle magazine tracks the city in a section called "Seattle Index." The latest on the Seattle International Film Festival (but no figures for quarts of popcorn consumed):

Number of films shown at the first Seattle film festival in 1974: 20 films viewed by 20,000 people.

Number of films shown in 1995: 200-plus, watched by 110,000 people.

Most heavily attended premiere in festival history: In 1995, 2,115 people turned up when Mel Gibson introduced his film *Braveheart* (he later won that year's Academy Award for best director).

Quirkiest world premiere: A past-midnight screening of *Total Recall*.

Most demanding (and popular) festival section: Secret Film Festival attendees must sign an oath of silence before being seated.

Award given to the best film in each of six categories: The Golden Space Needle Award.

Approximate number of reels of film used each year: 1,500.

something a bit more underground? And what if all you know about rock concerts is what's advertised at the Moore? To find out about the underbelly of Seattle's art world, you have to hang out, watch coffeehouse windows, and do some investigating.

Flyers and posters are the medium of choice for most arts groups. Here are a few places to look for the latest flyers from some of the more avant-garde groups:

- Allegro Espresso Bar (U District)
- B&O Espresso (Broadway)
- Cyclops (Belltown)
- Elliott Bay Cafe, First and Main (Pioneer Square)
- Espresso Roma (Broadway and U District)
- OK Hotel (under the viaduct between Main and Washington)
- Still Life in Fremont Coffeehouse (Fremont)
- Virginia Inn, art bar (downtown)

Seattle's arts community is no longer centered on Capitol Hill, where generations of Cornish College art students have frequented the taverns and coffee shops. The artists—as much as they gather anywhere—have moved downtown. You'll find groups of them at Crocodile Cafe, Wall of Sound, the Frontier Room, and the Two Bells Tavern in Belltown; the Virginia Inn on First Avenue; Re-bar in the Cascade neighborhood; Torrefazione Italia in Pioneer Square; and the OK Hotel under the viaduct.

General info sources

- *Seattle Best Places,* Sasquatch Books: galleries and their specialties, theater, opera, dance, and music organizations.
- Seattle Center Hotline: what's happening at the Center. Call 684-8582 and press 4 for arts info.
- *Seattle Post-Intelligencer:* daily (Fridays—"What's Happening" section).
- *Seattle Times:* daily (Thursdays—"Tempo" section).
- *Seattle Weekly:* Wednesdays (extensive "Goings On" calendar).

- *The Stranger:* Thursdays (visual arts and performance calendars).

Area arts publications

Blues To-Do's
P.O. Box 22950
Seattle, WA 98122
328-0662
Comprehensive news of the blues in Seattle and the Pacific Northwest. See "Blue Stars"—sun-sign forecasts in the blues idiom. Free personals. Published monthly.

Earshot Jazz
3429 Fremont Pl. N, Suite 303
Seattle, WA 98103
547-6763
Local jazz scene.

Encore Publishing
87 Wall St., Suite 315
Seattle, WA 98121
443-0445
Programs for individual groups (ACT, Pacific Northwest Ballet, Seattle Chamber Music Festival, Seattle International Music Festival, Seattle Opera, Seattle Repertory Theatre, Seattle Symphony).

The Rocket
2028 Fifth Ave.
Seattle, WA 98121
728-7625
Best source of info about alternative-rock scene.

Seattle Arts
312 First Ave. N
Seattle, WA 98109
684-7171
Monthly arts newsletter published by the Seattle Arts Commission.

Victory Music Review
P.O. Box 7517
Bonney Lake, WA 98390
(206) 863-6617
Folk and ethnic music.

HELP FROM ALLIED ARTS

Allied Arts of Seattle has been around since 1954. In the early days it advocated for (and won) a city arts commission and worked on such things as billboard removal, street tree plantings, and public funding for art. Currently, it is involved with downtown architecture, historic preservation, and issues affecting small arts organizations and individual artists.

Allied Arts members can serve on the following committees: Arts Education, Metropolitan Arts, Urban Environment, Historic Preservation, Architecture and Education, and Housing. The well-respected organization also publishes *Access, A Guide to the Visual Arts in Washington State.*

Its sister organization, the Allied Arts Foundation, provides direct project support grants for a wide variety of individual artists, arts organizations, and coalitions of arts groups. They can also act as an umbrella organization for groups without nonprofit status that are applying for government or foundation grants.

Allied Arts of Seattle/Allied Arts Foundation
105 S Main St., Suite 201
Seattle, WA 98104
624-0432

MORE ARTS RESOURCES

Artech Inc.
728-8822
Fine arts handling, including exhibition design and installation, packing and crating, shipping, custom fabrication of sculpture stands, art collections management, rental of temporary display walls, storage, restoration, and repair of damaged artworks.

Artist Trust
1402 Third Ave., Suite 415
Seattle, WA 98101
467-8734
Information, services, and fellowships for artists in the state. Quarterly newsletter.

Bumbershoot
1725 Westlake Ave. N Suite 202
Seattle, WA 98121

281-7788
September arts festival at the Seattle Center.

Business Volunteers for the Arts
600 University St., Suite 1200
Seattle, WA 98101
389-7272
Places volunteers from businesses with nonprofit arts and cultural organizations.

Centrum
P.O. Box 1158
Port Townsend, WA 98368
(206) 385-3102
Offers performances, workshops, jazz and other festivals, and short-term writers' residences.

Fabrication Specialties
527 S Portland St.
Seattle, WA 98108
763-8292
Collaborates with artists on both public and private pieces fabricated in metal, concrete, glass, or stone.

Fremont Fine Arts Foundry
154 N 35th St.
Seattle, WA 98103
632-4880
Visual arts facility that includes 10 artist studio-residences, a day studio for classes, workshops, or individual projects, a stone-carving yard, a hot-glass shop, a darkroom, the Fremont Fine Arts Gallery, and a foundry equipped for casting nonferrous metals, mostly bronze and aluminum.

911 Media Arts Center
117 Yale Ave. N
Seattle, WA 98109
682-6552
Contemporary arts resource center. Performances, exhibitions, newsletter, and video editing facility.

Pacific Northwest Arts & Crafts Fair
301 Bellevue Square
Bellevue, WA 98004
454-4900
July arts fair.

PONCHO (Patrons of Northwest Civic, Cultural and Charitable Organizations)
Lloyd Bldg., Suite 717
Sixth and Stewart
Seattle, WA 98101

623-6233
Nonprofit organization that raises money for the arts through its annual wine auction and other gala events. Groups funded include the Seattle Opera, the UW's Henry Gallery, and A Contemporary Theatre.

Washington Alliance for Arts Education (WAAE)
158 Thomas St.
Seattle, WA 98109
441-4501
Promotes arts education programs.

Washington Lawyers for the Arts
219 First Ave. S, Suite 315-A
Seattle, WA 98104
292-9171
Offers low-cost legal referrals for artists and arts organizations.

Washington State Arts Alliance
P.O. Box 21867
Seattle, WA 98101
448-1909
Advocacy for arts at the state, county, and city level.

SEATTLE'S LITERARY SCENE

Seattle is one of the readingest towns around. There's at least one bookstore in every neighborhood, everyone reads on the bus (to their own personal thresholds of nausea), and everyone, it seems, is working on a novel. . .or would like to be.

Seattle's major independent bookstore is the phenomenal Elliott Bay Book Company, which stocks more than 150,000 titles (the all-time best seller? Brenda Ueland's *If You Want to Write,* a small paperback of essays about creativity). But some think the real soul of the Seattle book scene is in the small specialty stores—The Play's the Thing (for drama), Beyond the Closet (for gay and lesbian issues and literature), Wide World Books (for one of the best travel book selections in the country), and any number of mystery, cookbook, and kids'-bookstores. The existence of such

stores may be threatened by the arrival of superstores such as Barnes & Noble—with discounts and selection going for them—but Seattle readers, it seems, are a loyal bunch.

Now there is even a place where all the city's book lovers can see and be seen. The Northwest Bookfest, an annual literary celebration, is free (with suggested donation) and happens in October at Pier 48 on the waterfront. In 1995 the festival drew over 23,000 "bookies." Authors participate in discussions, readings, workshops, etc., and there's bookmaking, art books, a performance stage, characters in costume—just about anything book-related that you can imagine. The festival raises money for regional literary organizations and is presented by *The Seattle Times*. For info, call 789-9868. (On the Internet: http://www.speakeasy. org/nwbookfest.)

There aren't a lot of outlets for book reviews besides the daily papers, which is surprising considering the size of the reading public. *Seattle Weekly*'s Books Quarterly is published in March, June, September, and December, and the *Elliott Bay Booknotes* is another good source.

Seattle's literary ghosts hang out at the Blue Moon, a comfortably run-down tavern on 45th Street in the University District. It was a favorite haunt of Pulitzer Prize–winning poet Theodore Roethke, for one, and it is said that Jack Kerouac and Dylan Thomas dropped by when visiting Seattle. Whether the graffiti on the walls is literature is debatable, but it's certainly inspiring. The current literati who frequent the place will tell you not only what's going on but what should be going on—and more.

LITERARY MAGAZINES

Local magazines come and go with the frequency of spring rains. At press time, these seemed to be the keepers.

Bellowing Ark
P.O. Box 45637
Seattle, WA 98145
545-8302
Bellowing Ark is one of Seattle's long-standing publications, around now for some 10 years. Bucking some of the more prevalent current themes, the *Ark* publishes anything, literary or not, that proves in some way that "life is worth living."

Fine Madness
P.O. Box 31138
Seattle, WA 98103-1138

Primarily poetry, some fiction and nonfiction. Published twice a year.

Poetry Northwest
Administration Building, Room 201
University of Washington
Seattle, WA 98195
Quarterly poetry journal with a strong reputation.

Raven Chronicles
P.O. Box 95918, University Station
Seattle, WA 98145
Multicultural fiction, poetry, art. Published three times per year.

Seattle Review
Department of English GN-30
University of Washington
Seattle, WA 98195
543-9865
The *Review,* published two times a year since the mid-1970s, features poetry, fiction, interviews with Northwest writers, and a series called "Writers and their Craft," which addresses problems and solutions in writing.

Spindrift
Shoreline Community College
16101 Greenwood Ave. N
Seattle, WA 98133
546-4789
Published once a year, includes work by Shoreline students, faculty, staff, and other local writers.

PUBLISHERS

Seattle isn't exactly New York, but there are publishers here, and some of them are thriving. Most publish for quite specific niches, from North-westiana to cleaning services, and several have received some attention from the rest of the country.

Farther afield, several Port Townsend presses garner attention: Copper Canyon Press published a National Book Critics Circle Award-winning volume of poetry, and Loompanics has an underground following for their incendiary, system-circumventing how-to books. And Microsoft Press, in Redmond, publishes (what else?) computer books.

Trade book publishers

Alaska Northwest Books
2208 NW Market St., Suite 300
Seattle, WA 98107
784-5071
Nonfiction related to Alaska, western Canada, and Northwest U.S.; history, biography, geography, reference, arts, culture, crafts, cooking, field guides, travel, sports, posters, maps, and children's books.

Bay Press
115 W Denny Way
Seattle, WA 98119
284-5913
A notable list of books on culture, criticism, gay issues and culture, and other social issues.

Black Heron Press
P.O. Box 95676
Seattle, WA 98145
363-5210
Quality fiction and books on book publishing.

Broken Moon Press
Box 24585
Seattle, WA 98124-0585
548-1340
International poetry, fiction, and non-fiction.

Cloudcap
P.O. Box 27344
Seattle, WA 98125
365-9192
Mountaineering books, outdoor guides.

Epicenter Press
Box 82368
Kenmore, WA 98028
485-6822
Art, photography, Northern nonfiction (Alaska and western Canada); Umbrella Books imprint publishes Alaska and West Coast destination guides.

Fantagraphics Books
7563 Lake City Way NE
Seattle, WA 98115
524-1967
The country's leading publisher of underground and alternative comics.

Fjord Press
Box 16349
Seattle, WA 98116-0349
935-7376
Ethnic American fiction; translations of European literature.

Left Bank Books
92 Pike St.
Seattle, WA 98105
622-0195
Anarchist titles.

Mountaineers Books
1001 SW Klickitat Way, Suite 201
Seattle, WA 98134
223-6303
Mountaineering, backpacking, hiking, cross-country skiing, bicycling, canoeing, kayaking, nature and conservation, outdoor how-to, guidebooks and maps, nonfiction adventure travel accounts, biographies of outdoors people, reprint editions of mountaineering classics.

Open Hand Publishing Inc.
Box 22048
Seattle, WA 98122
323-2187
Multicultural books promoting social change.

Owl Creek Press
1620 N 45th St
Seattle, WA 98103
633-5929
Runs an annual poetry contest that results in one full-length book and one chapbook; also publishes some fiction and two Northwest anthologies.

Parenting Press Inc.
11065 Fifth Ave. NE
Seattle, WA 98125
364-2900
Child care and development, children's books.

Peanut Butter Publishing
226 Second Ave. W
Seattle, WA 98119
281-5965
Cookbooks, fiction, trade, law, and medical books. Subsidy press.

Sasquatch Books
615 Second Ave., Suite 260
Seattle, WA 98104
467-4300
Pacific Northwest books: gardening, cooking, travel (the *Best Places* series), general nonfiction, and children's books.

Seal Press
3131 Western Ave., Suite 410
Seattle, WA 98121-1028
283-7844
Fiction, poetry, nonfiction by women.

University of Washington Press
P.O. Box 50096
Seattle, WA 98145
543-4050
Scholarly nonfiction, reprints, imports, films and filmstrips, and videos.

LITERARY EVENTS ABOUT TOWN

Many bookstores around town schedule readings by local and visiting authors. Check the "Readings and Lectures" section of *Seattle Weekly* to see what's current.

Bumbershoot
Seattle Center
281-7788
Seattle's blowout arts fair carries a full four days of literary events, from

an independent (read: small) press fair to a slew of local, regional, national, and international readers and panel discussions. There are children's events, including readings by young writers. The festival publishes *Ergo!,* a literary journal featuring the festival's writers. Over Labor Day weekend.

Elliott Bay Book Company

101 S Main St.
624-6600
Elliott Bay, the hub of Seattle's literary scene, brings authors on tour (and sometimes between tours) for intimate readings in its downstairs room near the cafe (sometimes impeded by the clatter-ing of the espresso machine). Most readings (there's at least one almost every day) are free, and their monthly calendar notes related readings at other venues around the city ($4 for a year's subscription).

Red Sky Poetry Theater

324-8815
Meeting weekly since 1981, Red Sky is one of Seattle's most established open mikes—poetry and performance art of all kinds on Sunday evenings (7:30pm) at the Globe Cafe, 1531 14th Street (Capitol Hill). Some weeks there are featured readers and special events. Red Sky puts out a poetry journal, *Open Sound,* one or two times a year, in the same spirit: submitters are responsible for their own poetry; there's no editing—or typesetting, for that matter. A $2-per-person donation is just that—if you can't afford it, go anyway.

Rendezvous at New City

New City Theatre
1634 11th St.
323-6801
This series pairs national and local writers for a cabaret-style evening. The atmosphere is festive (aided and abetted by the bar and DJ), and the focus is on risk-taking, innovative new works. Rendezvous runs from September through June, on the second Tuesday of the month. $4 admission.

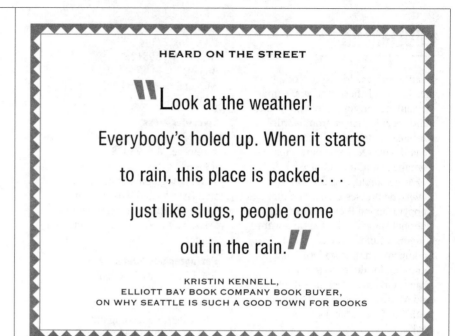

Seattle Arts and Lectures

621-2230
This highly touted lecture series has been bringing such luminaries as Toni Morrison, Robert Hughes, and V. S. Naipaul to Seattle since 1987. Authors are asked to lecture, not to read, and to expand on ideas begun in their books instead of hawking a new volume. Season tickets, once in short supply and high demand, are much easier to obtain these days. Reason: The series has moved to a bigger hall, the Fifth Avenue Theater, which can accommodate the large crowds these events draw. Put yourself on their mailing list for a season-ticket brochure (mailed in July for the fall season), or buy leftover tickets at the door. $15–$18 per event.

THE INDISPENSABLE LIBRARY

The Seattle Public Library is part of the family, a third hand, a shoulder to lean on, man's (and woman's) best friend. And the library stocks much more than printed matter these days. You can borrow music on CD, tape, and LP; videos (both feature films and educational ones); and books on tape, for those long drives.

You're eligible for a library card if you live, work, attend school, or pay property taxes in the city of Seattle. King County residents may check out materials in any branch if their local library system has an agreement with the Seattle Public Library. For others, there's a yearly fee of $50.

The library's holdings are cataloged in a computer database that you can access through one of the many computer terminals throughout the building (and at branches). If the item you want is already checked out, you can place a hold on it through the computer. You'll get a notice in the mail when the item has been returned and is ready for you to pick up.

The library offers other computer services too. The downtown branch has several computers with color monitors and printers. Computer equipment is also available at several branch libraries. You can reserve up to two hours of computer time up to a week in advance, in person or by phone, 386-4660. Most computers are equipped with word processing and spreadsheet software, and some have educational software for kids. Special software is available for those just learning to use computers;

some people have learned enough skills using the library's tutorials to secure word processing jobs.

All the Seattle public libraries offer on-line searches, which means they have access to several database services. For example, if you want to see articles on grizzly bears in the Rockies, the librarian will do a search for you and print out the articles—free. (For *The Seattle Times* and other major-city newspapers, you can also do on-line searches yourself, but for the *P-I* you'll need a librarian's assistance.) You need to do the search at the appropriate department, depending on your subject. Sometimes there's a wait.

AND NOW FROM HOME

You can access the library by computer from your home. For more information, pick up the library's instruction brochure.

Seattle Public Library fines

Item	Daily fine	Max. fine
Books, audiocassettes, record albums, magazine folders, artwork, posters, sculptures	$ .10	$4.00
Videocassettes (no grace period)	1.00	10.00
Reference items	.25	24.00

HOW 386-INFO WORKS

The library offers a truly exciting information service. Call 386-INFO and ask anything—from how to spell that suspicious word used by your Scrabble opponent, to who the third vice president of the United States was. You might have to wait on hold for a while, but the information specialists will unfailingly come through with your answer.

Four librarians answer the information line during the day and two work in the evenings. Fielding some 76,000 calls a year, they sit in a room at the downtown library, at a round table that has a lazy Susan–type bank of shelves in the center. The shelves are full of resource books, and when you ask your question the librarian spins it around to reach the right book. Voilà! The answer.

They get pretty weird calls sometimes. Bar bets are a popular item. And in Seattle, unlike some cities, they'll answer homework questions for kids who call. They figure if a kid has taken the time and made the effort to call, they may as well give him or her the answer.

Some popular and some unusual queries

- When is the full moon in August?
- When is the Seafair parade?
- How tall is the Columbia Tower?
- How many calories are in Juicy Fruit gum? (or anything else)
- What is the average rainfall in Seattle?
- How tall is the Statue of Liberty?
- What are the seven wonders of the ancient world?
- Who played the Wicked Witch in *The Wizard of Oz*?
- When did Mount St. Helens erupt?
- What legislative district am I in?
- Who's on the Supreme Court?
- Who were the members of the Doors?
- Who won the Best Picture Academy Award in 1969?
- What is the word for "cat" in French and Spanish?
- What is Ronald Reagan's middle name?
- When is the next solar eclipse?
- What are three English words ending in -gry?
- When does daylight saving time begin and end?
- What are the names of the Seven Dwarfs?
- What are the names of Santa's reindeer?
- When is Groundhog Day?
- What is the recipe for Play-Doh?
- When did the Hood Canal Bridge sink?
- When did Galloping Gertie (the Tacoma Narrows Bridge) fall?
- How do I get a ballpoint pen mark out of a white silk shirt?

Best times to call: Thursday mornings; or evenings.
Worst times to call: Lunch hours and between 10am and 4pm (peak hours). No service on Sunday.
Source: Seattle Survival Guide research

OTHER LIBRARY SERVICES

Two pamphlets listing all library services are available free from the library: *Your Seattle Public Library* and *A Guide to Your Downtown Library Resource Center*. Some highlights:

- Dial-a-Story: Recorded folktales for children, 386-4656.
- Directory service: Phone books and city directories for many cities. Call Info Line, 386-4636.
- Genealogy Collection: Resource for tracing family history. For staff schedule, call 386-4625.
- GED exams: Materials for studying for the high school equivalency exam available in the education department, second floor, downtown library.
- Literacy programs around the city for students and tutors.
- Media services: Films, slides, videotapes, and compact discs available; projectors may be borrowed and programs viewed in the library.
- Meeting rooms. (All meetings must be open to the public.)
- Multilingual Collection: Books in over 30 languages as well as newspapers and magazines from other countries.
- Newspapers and magazines: Back issues of Seattle papers and the *New York Times* available on microfilm; current issues of magazines and newspapers, second floor, downtown.
- Regional Foundation Center Collection: Help with seeking grants, second floor, downtown.
- Securities and Company Information: Stock and bond quotes, information on companies and nonprofit organizations. 386-4650.
- S.P.L.A.S.H.: Kids' after-school activities at Beacon Hill, High Point, Holly Park, Madrona–Sally Goldmark Library. Monday–Friday, 3–7pm.

Every Seattleite should have the library's quick-information number imprinted on the inside of his or her brain: 386-INFO.

- Tourist information: Free maps and advice, directions, etc.
- Voter registration: Available at branch libraries. The downtown history department has polling places listed too.

OVERDUE MATERIALS

Guilt, guilt, guilt. While your library books sit on the table at home, someone else is looking for them in the library. And if that's not enough incentive, refer to the table in this chapter that details the fines.

Yes, there is a grace period of seven days for overdue books. And yes, if you lose a book, you'll have to pay a replacement fee. And the library says there aren't any amnesty days (but we know better!).

SEATTLE PUBLIC LIBRARY LOCATIONS

Downtown
1000 Fourth Ave.
386-4636
Hours: 9am–9pm Mon–Thurs; 9am–6pm Fri–Sat; 1–5pm Sun. (Closed Sun. in summer)

Ballard
5711 24th Ave. NW
684-4089
Hours: 10am–9pm Mon; 10am–9pm Tues–Wed; closed Thurs; 10am–6pm Fri, Sat; 1–5pm Sun.

Beacon Hill
2519 15th Ave. S
684-4711
Hours: 2–6pm Mon, Wed, Fri; 10am–6pm Tues, Thurs; 1–6pm Sat; closed Sun.

Broadview
12755 Greenwood Ave. N
684-7519
Hours: 1–9pm Wed; 10am–9pm Mon, Thurs; 10am–6pm Tues, Sat; closed Fri, Sun.

Columbia
4721 Rainier Ave. S
386-1908
Hours: 10am–9pm Mon; 1–9pm Tues, Wed; 10am–6pm Fri, Sat; closed Thurs, Sun.

Douglass-Truth
2300 E Yesler Way
684-4704
Hours: 1–9pm Mon–Wed; 10am–9pm Thurs; 10am–6pm Sat; 1-5pm Sun; closed Fri.

Fremont
731 N 35th St.
684-4084
Hours: 2–9pm Mon–Tues; 4–9pm Wed; 10am–6pm Thurs; Noon–6pm Sat; closed Fri, Sun.

Green Lake
7364 Green Lake Dr. N
684-7547
Hours: 1–9pm Mon; 10am–6pm Wed, Fri, Sat; closed Thurs, Sun.

Greenwood
8016 Greenwood Ave. N
684-4086
Hours: 1–9pm Mon, Tues, Thurs; 10am–6pm Wed, Sat; closed Fri, Sun.

Henry
425 Harvard Ave. E
684-4715
Hours: 1–9pm Mon, Thurs; 10am–6pm Tues, Fri, Sat; closed Sun, Wed.

High Point
6338 32nd Ave. SW
684-7454
Hours: 10am–6pm Mon, Wed;
2–6pm Tues, Thurs, Fri; 1–6pm Sat;
closed Sun.

Holly Park
6805 32nd Ave. S
386-1905
Hours: 2–6pm Mon, Wed, Fri;
10am–6pm Tues, Thurs; 1–6pm Sat;
closed Sun.

Lake City
12501 28th Ave. NE
684-7518
Hours: 10am–9pm Mon, Tues,
Thurs; 1–9pm Wed; 10am–6pm Sat;
closed Fri, Sun.

Madrona–Sally Goldmark
1134 33rd Ave.
684-4705
Hours: 10am–6pm Mon, Wed;
2–6pm Tues, Thurs, Fri; 1–6pm Sat;
closed Sun.

Magnolia
2801 34th Ave. W
386-4225
Hours: 1–9pm Mon, Tues, Thurs;
10am–6pm Wed, Sat; closed Fri, Sun.

Montlake
2300 24th Ave. E
684-4720
Hours: 3–9pm Tues, Wed;
10am–6pm Thurs; noon–6pm Sat;
closed Mon, Fri, Sun.

Northeast
6801 35th Ave. NE
684-7539
Hours: 10am–9pm Mon, Tues, Wed;
10am–6pm Fri, Sat; 1–5pm Sun;
closed Thurs.

Queen Anne
400 W Garfield St.
386-4227
Hours: 1–9pm Mon, Wed, Thurs;
10am–6pm Tues, Sat; closed Fri,
Sun.

Rainier Beach
9125 Rainier Ave. S
386-1906
Hours: 1–9pm Mon, Tues, Thurs;
10am–9pm Wed; 10am–6pm Sat;
1–5pm Sun; closed Fri.

Southwest
9010 35th Ave. SW
684-7455
Hours: 1–9pm Mon, Tues, Wed;
10am–9pm Thurs; 10am–6pm Sat;
closed Fri, Sun.

University
5009 Roosevelt Way NE
684-4063
Hours: 1–9pm Mon, Wed, Thurs;
10am–6pm Fri, Sat; closed Tues,
Sun.

Wallingford-Wilmot
4423 Densmore Ave. N
684-4088
Hours: 2–6pm Mon, Wed, Sat;
2–9pm Tues, Thurs; closed Fri, Sun.

West Seattle
2306 42nd Ave. SW
684-7444
Hours: 10am–9pm Mon, Tues, Wed;
10am–6pm Fri, Sat; 1–5pm Sun;
closed Thurs.

Mobile Outreach/Bookmobile
425 Harvard Ave. E
684-4713
Hours: 8:30am–5pm weekdays;
closed weekends.
Remember those bookmobiles that
visited the schools when you were
a kid? They still exist, but not to the
same extent they did 20 years ago.
Seattle has one home-service book
van and three bookmobiles that
travel to people who do not have
access to libraries—the elderly, the
homebound, and day-care kids. If
you'd like to have a bookmobile
visit, just call.

WHAT GOOD SPORTS!

*F*ans of Seattle's professional sports teams saw their wildest dreams and their worst nightmares come true in the mid-'90s. The whole town fell in love with the "Refuse to Lose" Seattle Mariners as they clinched the 1995 American League West title, selling out the 58,000-plus seats in the Kingdome game after game and launching the Mariners on a successful bid for a new stadium.

The SuperSonics settled into the stylish new KeyArena and brought home a playoff title as well. And the Seahawks were abruptly "kidnapped" by owner Ken Behring and shipped off to Southern California, only to be ransomed by homegrown Microsoft billionaire Paul Allen and sheepishly returned to their Kirkland training camp amid threats of lawsuits and censure by the other NFL owners.

Will Paul Allen exercise his option to buy the Seahawks? Will the voters spring for another expensive stadium for the Hawks? Will Seahawks fans have to lie down in front of the semitrucks again to keep the Hawks in Seattle? These issues were in limbo at press time, but the way the Seattle sports scene keeps changing, they could be ancient history when you buy this book.

But the bright lights, fat TV contracts, and cliff-hanging politics of professional sports aren't for everyone in the Northwest. Maybe that's

As one sportswriter says, "NEVER pay to get into the Kingdome for a Seahawks game—they always look better on television."

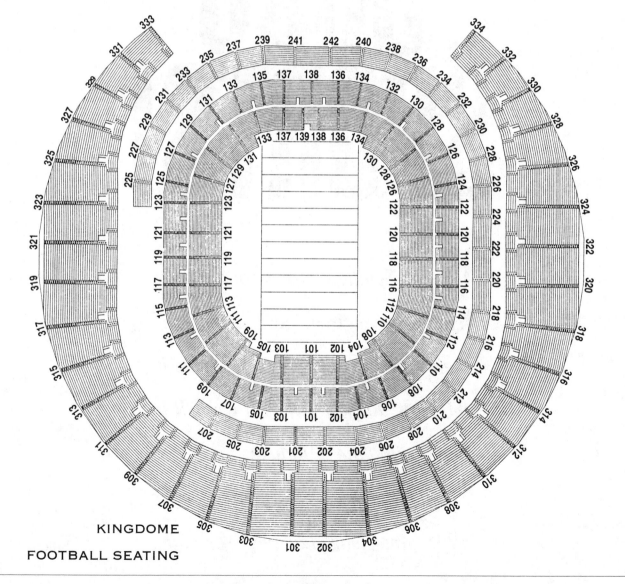

KINGDOME
FOOTBALL SEATING

why participant sports are so popular. Along with the fact that they satisfy the Northwest's self-image as fit, enthusiastic, and ultimately outdoorsy, you can be sure that no raiding party from Tampa or Colorado is going to try to buy away our multitudes of amateur soccer teams, over-40 basketballers, or down-and-dirty ruggers.

If you'd rather play the game yourself than watch others play, there are plenty of options: boats and bikes, swimming holes and golf courses, even lawn-bowling greens. There are countless beaches and parks large and small. And parents will find many places that delight kids: the zoo, the aquarium, the holiday-season carousel at Westlake Center.

THE TICKET TICKER

You don't decide at the last minute to go to a Seahawks game, at least not yet. You can still decide at the very last minute to go to a Mariners game—most of them, anyway (except you can't count on getting the best seats anymore). And at least now you know *where* to go if you want to watch the Sonics. Ticket savvy, in other words, is a sport in itself.

Occasionally, Seahawks ticket-holders who cannot attend a game donate their tickets to the Seattle Children's Home, which sells them at face value to fans who call at the right time. Seattle Children's Home: 283-3300.

THE HOT SEAHAWKS??

How times change. Couple years ago you couldn't get a Seahawks ticket even if you knew Ken Behring personally. Now they can't give 'em away. In fact, they can hardly give the team away—at least, last time we looked.

If a team's temperature is measured in terms of ticket sales, then the Seahawks need a doctor, so high and low does their temperature fluctuate. Fans hope that resolving the twin questions of ownership and whether or not to build a new stadium will turn out to be just what the doctor ordered.

Seattle plays in the Western Division of the American Football Conference. It plays home games each season against the Los Angeles Raiders, Denver Broncos, Kansas City Chiefs, and San Diego Chargers, and four other games against different teams from the NFL's other five divisions.

Seattle Seahawks
11220 NE 53rd St.
Kirkland, WA 98033
827-9777

Sonics Signing: The SuperSonics are hot, and that means their autographs are hot too. Best place to find your favorite hoopster after the game: south end of the KeyArena. Look for the fancy cars and the guys who seem to tower above everyone else. Hint: The Sonics tend to leave faster after a loss. For a Mariner's scribble? Try the northeast side of the Kingdome, where the players park their (very shiny and new) cars.

Home stadium: Kingdome,
64,981 seats for football
Ticket prices: $46, $41, $38, $33,
$28, $19/seat per game. Season tickets for eight regular-season home
games and two preseason games:
$460, $410, $380, $330, $280, $190.

THE ALMOST-
THERE SONICS

Established in 1967, the Seattle
SuperSonics of the National Basketball Association (NBA) are Seattle's
oldest professional sports franchise,
and thus occupy a special place in

the hearts of Northwest sports fans.

Better yet, they're the only Seattle
major sports franchise to win a
league championship, taking the
NBA crown in the 1978–79 season.
And against all Seattle sports traditions, they've shown signs that they
want to return to those lofty heights:
In 1996 they found themselves in the
thick of the division playoffs.

Which, of course, means it's getting harder to go see the Supes. And
when you do go, you might want to
rob a bank first. The NBA is becoming a pricey game—Sonics tickets
don't come cheap, and you can count
on them to be going up.

The SuperSonics play in the Pacific Division of the NBA's Western

Conference, in the new, improved
version of the old Seattle Center Coliseum, dubbed the KeyArena by its
major corporate sponsor, Key Bank.
Aside from the "eye pollution" controversy stirred up by Queen Anne
Hill residents when they got a look at
the huge, bright red KeyArena sign,
most Seattleites view the new arena
as a definite improvement. Seating capacity increased by 2,850 seats in the
new building, sightlines are better, the
upgraded bathrooms and concessions
are brand-new, and of course there
are those luxury suites with private
kitchens and seating for 16 for a mere
$135,000 per year. For the rest of us,
ticket prices went up—but not as
much as you might have expected.

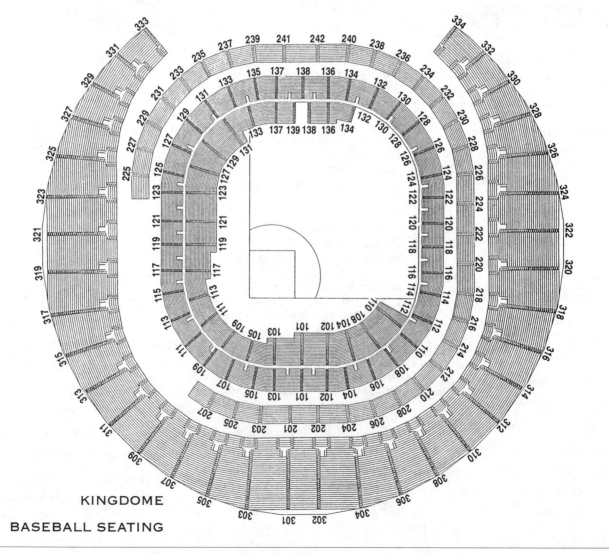

KINGDOME

BASEBALL SEATING

Seattle SuperSonics

190 Queen Anne Ave. N
P.O. Box 900911
Seattle, WA 98109-9711
283-DUNK
Home arena: KeyArena, 17,100 seats
41 home games per year
Ticket prices: $50, $45, $36, $28, $25, $15, $7
$65 club and courtside
Luxury suites $50,000 to $135,000 depending on location.
For season ticket prices, multiply the single-ticket price by 41 games (sorry, no price break).

HOW ABOUT THOSE M'S?

"You Gotta Love These Guys," says the Mariners' PR campaign—and all of a sudden Seattle DOES love the M's! The team gave the city a needed lesson in community boosterism, and

Fair warning about Mariners games: If you want to enjoy the game rather than spend the night engaged in aggressive self-defense, avoid Bat Night, one of the Mariners' most popular promotions. Just picture 20,000 or so pre-hormonal kids in the seats all around you, each armed with a full-sized M's bat, which constantly waggles dangerously close to your head or—worse—your cost-its-weight-in-gold King Beer.

the entire city and surrounding area flocked to see Randy, Junior, Bones, Sweet Lou, and the rest outdo themselves and win the AL West Championship in 1995. Announcers from other teams held their ears at the yells emanating from the Kingdome—and never again will people say we're not a baseball town!

The M's history was not always so happy. Founded in 1977, the M's, who play in the Western Division of the American League, compiled the losingest record in major league baseball history. Forget about contending for a championship; it wasn't until 1990 that they even had a season when they won more games than they lost. In 1992, the team was purchased for more than $100 million by a local group dominated by Nintendo and Microsoft bucks. It was the first time ever the Mariners hadn't been owned by outsiders. (Well, OK, it's true the biggest investor is Nintendo's president and he does live in Japan, but control rests solidly with certifiable locals, including such Puget Sound blue bloods as Boeing's Frank Shrontz, Puget Power's John Ellis, McCaw Cellular's John McCaw, etc.)

But even those insiders began to threaten to leave after the championship in '95. Wanted a stadium, and now they'll get one, thanks to help from the state legislature after city residents barely turned down a stadium measure. Even looks like it might have a retractable roof. My oh my.

Seattle Mariners

83 S King St.
P.O. Box 4100
Seattle, WA 98104
343-4600
Home stadium: Kingdome, 59,438 seats for baseball
Ticket prices: $20 for "box" seats (actually they're not boxes, just regular rows in the sections closest to home plate and along the two base lines). There's no longer a general admission section since the outfield seats are all reserved seating: adults, $7; kids in family or outfield sections

About six times a season on Mondays it's Family Night for the Mariners: Adult tickets are two for the price of one. That means in 1996 prices, for example, a family of four (or any other social group of the same size) could get box seats for a total of $40—and the really Skinflint family of four could settle for the peanut gallery seats for a total ticket outlay of $24. Beat that, sports fans. (Or movie fans, for that matter.)

$5. For the truly addicted, there are season ticket box seats at $1,620; outfield seats, $567.

WHAT ELSE GOES ON IN THE ORANGE JUICE SQUEEZER?

The Kingdome, a.k.a. King County Stadium, stages several other sporting events each year, to the delight of the hordes from the wilder corners of King, Snohomish, and Kitsap counties. The Kingbowl, held the first weekend in December, is the state high-school football championships in all five divisions: B-8 (8-man football), B-11, A, AA, and AAA. There's nothing quite like watching small-town America compete at football.

And it's not a sport exactly, but

the Promise Keepers, a Christian male-bonding group, meets at the Kingdome. In 1996, about 62,000 sensitive males turned up—the M's would love a turnout like that!

For the macho among us, there are three "dirt track" events per year at the dome:

- Supercross (motorcycles on dirt track)
- Mickey Thompson Grand Prix (trucks, tractors, buses, cars, cycles. . .various pulling and racing events)
- The Thrill Show (weird stuff à la Evel Knievel)

Kingdome behind-the-scenes public tours are available year-round, but are more frequent mid-April through mid-September, when they are held at 11am, 1pm, and 3pm Monday–Saturday. Cost is $4 for adults and teens, $2 for seniors and children under 12. Show up at Gate D, where tickets are sold 10 minutes prior to each tour; the tour lasts about an hour. You get a whiff of the locker room (and of the press box), visit the Kingdome Sports Museum (where you can eyeball Muhammad Ali's autographed boxing shorts) and (of course) the gift shop, and maybe even get a player's-eye view from the field. Call 296-3128 for tour info.

The Kingdome houses trade shows nonstop during the winter, including the Boat Show in January, the Sportsman's Expo in February, and the RV Show in March.

Kingdome
Office of Promotions
201 S King St.
Seattle, WA 98104
296-3126
Call for a complete schedule of events.

KINGDOME FACTS

- It opened in 1976.
- At 7 acres, it has the largest single-span concrete roof in the world.
- It was constructed with 443 tons of structural steel and 52,800 cubic yards of concrete.
- The concrete weighs 105,600 tons.
- The interior contains 67 million cubic feet of air.

Athletic stars:

- Seattle Mariners: Ken Griffey, Jr., Randy Johnson, and Edgar Martinez.
- Seattle SuperSonics: Shawn Kemp and Gary Payton.

Up-and-comers:

- Mariners: Alex Rodriguez.
- Sonics: Shawn Kemp (that's right, he's both).

CULT HOCKEY

Seattle's minor-league hockey franchise, the Seattle Thunderbirds of the Western Hockey League, has something of a cult following in the Northwest. Taking on such exotic rivals as the Brandon Wheat Kings, the T-birds play raucous, fight-bedecked, enthusiastic hockey in front of rabid fans, many of whom look like extras from the Paul Newman cult classic *Slap Shot.*

A hint for hockey fans: Stay sober—or at least stay peaceful. A fan who was drunk got in a fight at a Thunderbirds game; he suffered serious brain damage and his mother sued on his behalf. A jury ruled that nobody was liable but the fan, because of the choices he made for himself.

Seattle Thunderbirds
P.O. Box 19391
Seattle, WA 98109
728-9124
Home arena: KeyArena, 11,000 seats
Ticket prices: $20, $15, $12, $10, $8.

WHAT ABOUT SOCCER? AND THE PONIES?

It's said that soccer is the game of the future in America, just as it's the game of the present in the rest of the world. But don't hold your breath. Seattle's entry, Seattle Storm (of what was then the Western Soccer League), stopped kicking in 1990. There is some talk of resurrecting it, but you probably don't want to send for season tickets just yet.

As for horse racing, the venerable Longacres track closed in 1992, only to rise again as Emerald Downs in Auburn, opening spring of 1996. The new $60 milllion track and six-story grandstand is enticing old and new fans—and some familiar trainers and jockeys as well. Bring your cash card.

Emerald Downs
P.O. Box 617
Auburn, WA 98071
1-888-931-8400
Online: www.emdowns.com
To get there: Take I-5 south to Hwy. 18 exit at Auburn; turn north on Hwy. 167.
Post times: Weekdays at 4:30pm, weekends and holidays at 1pm. Tickets: $3 general; $5 clubhouse; children under 10 free.

AND DON'T FORGET THE HUSKIES

The University of Washington sells tickets for a number of intercollegiate sports. (For some sports, such as men's and women's crew, there is no admission charge).

The three major Husky sports are football (Division IA) and women's and men's basketball (Pacific-10 Conference). For women's basketball, which has been one of the better games in town in recent years, reserved seats are $8 per game; general admission, $6. "Family plan" tickets

(two adults and three children, or one adult and four children) are $13.

For men's basketball, reserved seats are $10; general admission, $6 for adults, $3 for children and senior citizens. "Family plan" tickets cost $13. Season ticket prices depend upon the number of home games.

Husky basketball's home arena is Hec Edmundson Pavilion.

The hottest ticket for UW sports is, of course, football. It has also provided the hottest news *off* the field, with big-time controversy earning the Huskies nearly as much national attention as their string of Rose Bowl appearances. Highest profile of several newsmaking flaps came in 1992 when star quarterback Billy Joe Hobert was suspended from the team after admitting that he had accepted a $50,000 personal loan from a Huskies supporter. For that, and other rules infractions, the Pacific-10 sports conference banned the football team from any bowl appearances for two years, took away its television revenue for one season, and imposed other sanctions. In response, long-time coach Don James resigned.

When playing action on the field gets dull, you can enjoy the stunning view of Lake Washington through the eastern open end of the stadium.

Home field: Husky Stadium, 72,000 seats
Football ticket-purchase options for the 1996 season included:

- Season ticket, $160 (6 games)
- Reserved seats: $26–$28
- Four-game package, called "Family plan," with seats in west end zone: $112
- General admission seats, in bleachers behind east end zone: $13–$14

Other Husky sports that charge admission include:

- Men's baseball
- Women's gymnastics
- Men's and women's soccer
- Women's softball
- Men's and women's swimming
- Men's and women's tennis
- Women's volleyball

Venues vary; call the ticket office.

University of Washington Huskies
101 Graves Bldg., 6C-20
Seattle, WA 98195
Ticket office: 543-2200

BASEBALL THE OLD-FASHIONED WAY

A midsummer night at the Everett Aquasox's outdoor ballpark is the stuff of American dreams. Every baseball fan should head to Everett to see the Rookie-League Everett Aquasox in action.

The Aquasox, who are part of the Seattle Mariners organization, play 38 games, from mid-June to early September. The stadium is like the major league teams' spring training parks. It's cozy and beautiful—the owners have a great eye for the aesthetics of ballparks. The grandstands sport chair seating with plenty of legroom. The ballplayers, in their first year of pro ball, are enthusiastic, earnest, and hungry. The stands are

The best seats in Husky Stadium can be had by making contributions of $100, $200, or $300 per seat per season to the Tyee Club. You'll still pay the regular season-ticket price, but you wind up with prime seats. The higher the contribution, the better the seat. Call 543-2234. But be warned: At last check there was a three-year waiting list.

packed with families, teenage groupies, and small children. The concessions are fabulous—one national magazine rated Everett's ballpark food as the best in the country. Parking is free. Sunday games begin at 2pm, other days at 7pm. The Aquasox also have a great PA system, a super announcer, and a fabulous selection of rock music. Stick around after the game to watch the groupies at work. Woo woo.

Everett Aquasox
2118 Broadway (just off I-5, Exit 192)
Everett, WA 98201
(206) 258-3673
Home field: Memorial Stadium (Everett), seats 3,600
Ticket prices: Reserved seats $7 for adults, $5 for children under 14; general admission tickets, which buy you bench seats in bleachers along the first- and third-baselines, are $5 and $4 (children).

BASEBALL DOWN SOUTH

Formerly called the Tacoma Tigers, the Rainiers are the Seattle Mariners AAA club, so you'll get a peek at the next generation of Mariners stars as you relax for some good, scrappy baseball in this 35-year-old family-oriented ballpark. That pitcher you see in Tacoma one week just might get called up to Seattle the next. Cheney Stadium boasts convenient concessions with good food, a souvenir and gift shop, batting cages, and a speed-pitch machine for the kids (and their parents), and it's an all-around fun place to spend an afternoon or evening.

Tacoma Rainiers
2502 S Tyler (take Hwy. 16 west toward Gig Harbor)
Tacoma, WA 98411
(206) 752-7707
Home field: Cheney Stadium, seats 10,000
Ticket prices: $8 boxes, $6 reserved,

$5 general admission, and a $2 discount for kids, seniors, and the military. Games start at 7:05pm Monday–Saturday, 1:35pm Sunday and holidays, and 12:30pm Wednesday.

THE HYDROS

Seattle's most established sporting event is the anachronistic hydroplane race, held early every August as the finale of the city's annual Seafair celebration. Hydroplanes are sperm-cell–shaped powerboats that skim along the top of the water. Most are powered by helicopter turbine engines enabling them to travel at speeds well in excess of 150 miles per hour over a 2-mile oval course south of the I-90 floating bridge on Lake Washington.

For years, the U.S. Navy's Blue Angels precision flying team added lots of noise and excitement to the race's ambience. But the Blue Angels were banned from the festivities in 1994 because the FAA shuddered every time the daredevil pilots made another high-speed, low-altitude pass over downtown Seattle and the highly populated areas around Lake Washington. Outraged Seafair backers and noise-addicted hydro fans lobbied for

the Blue Angels' return, and they're back—but limited to doing those heart-stopping dives and spins over Elliott Bay only.

The first races were held in 1950, making hydroplaning Seattle's oldest professional sport. While many fans watch from their own boats, moored the night before on a log boom east of the course, and others watch from homes and beachfronts along the lake, Seafair has its own section of prime viewing beach.

Par for the course

Golf course	Address	Phone	Holes	Fee
Bellevue Municipal	5450 140th NE Bellevue	451-7250	18	$18 $14 after 4:30pm
Jackson Park Municipal	1000 NE 135th	301-0472	18/9	$17.50 (18) $8.75 (9) $14 after 4pm
Jefferson Park	4101 Beacon S	301-0472	18/9	$17.50 (18) $8.75 (9) $14 after 4pm
Tyee Valley	2401 S 192nd	878-3540	18	$19 (18) $12.50 (9)
West Seattle	4470 35th SW	301-0472	18	$17.50 (18) $8.75 (9) $14 after 4pm

Source: Seattle Survival Guide research

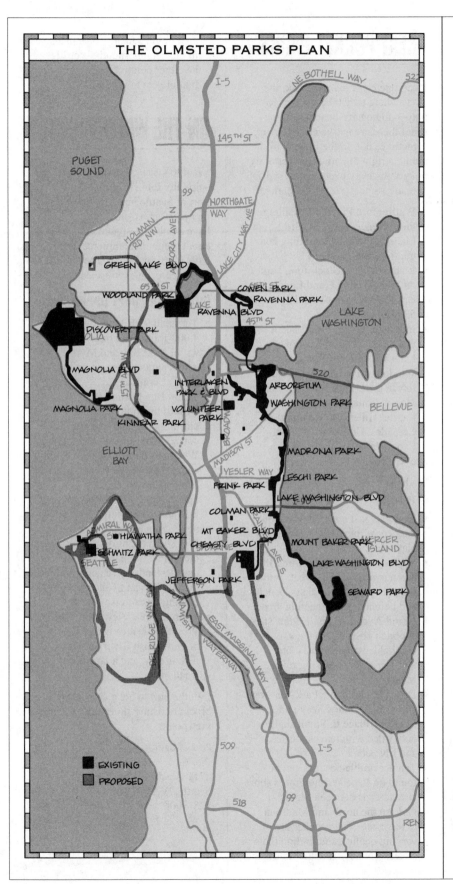

THE OLMSTED PARKS PLAN

Seafair

The Westin Building, Suite 2800
2001 Sixth Ave.
Seattle, WA 98121-2574
728-0123
Ticket prices: Admission to Seafair's official hydroplane race-viewing area is $10 for Saturday only. Sunday only prices are $8 in advance (at Texaco stations), $12 in advance (at Ticketmaster), or $16 at the gate. Two-day passes are $10 in advance (Texaco stations), $16 (Ticketmaster), $20 (gate). Bleacher seating on Sunday is $24, and $12 for kids under 12 and seniors. A one-day pit pass for any single day is $20, a three-day pit pass is $35.00. More privileged seating includes the Captain's Club, at $100 per person; the Sky Box, for $15,000 per box (seats about 100 people); Hospitality Suites at $10,000; and motorhomes (very limited) at $3,000 each.

A PARK PLACE

Seattle has over 5,000 acres of parkland, comprising more than 300 parks and playgrounds, everything from tiny pocket parks to huge wooded habitats such as Discovery Park. (Contact the Seattle Parks Department at 684-4075 for a map of the entire system.)

Frederick Law Olmsted Jr. and John Charles Olmsted had a profound influence not only on the city of Seattle but on landscape architecture in general. Here, the Olmsted firm designed a parks system connected by boulevards and including Volunteer Park, Lake Washington Boulevard, the Arboretum, and Seward Park. Wherever you go, you'll hear of the Olmsted parks.

PARK CHARACTERISTICS

Every park has its own character(s), and park atmospheres can change rapidly. But here's a brief rundown of some characteristics that have stayed pretty much the same over the years.

Alki Beach attracts throngs of young people in the summer. A law prohibiting car cruising is enforced.

The Burke-Gilman Trail, the "highway" for bicyclists and in-line skaters, has had no problems, according to park officials, except for the occasional flasher.

Camp Long is a great place for weddings.

Discovery Park is a habitat park. (See Chapter 19, "Green Grows the City.")

Freeway Park downtown is perceived as unsafe because there are lots of places to hide and it has a history of crime.

Golden Gardens is known for its intoxicating sunsets. It's a very romantic place, great for birthday parties and enjoying blustery winter weather.

Green Lake hosts the avid exercisers and the Sony Walkman crowd.

Doggie parks: Marymoor on the Eastside has a dog exercise area and you don't have to leash dogs, though they have to stay within voice range. (Also has fields where dogs aren't allowed.) Volunteer Park informally hosts dogs and owners at about dinnertime, 5–7pm, when you'll see lots of dogs being walked. Magnuson Park has big fields with lots of dog people and dog playmates.

Gay/lesbian hangouts: Madison Park Beach (north side, gay men; south side, families); Volunteer Park (gay cruising on west side, south of tennis courts, site of gay pride rally; also mixed with families, dog walkers, and everybody else); Denny Blaine Beach (used to be lesbians; now more mixed crowd except on north end where lesbians and gay men hang out); Woodland Park (gay cruising 1–3pm weekdays, signs outside bathroom from police and gay community discouraging sexual contact in parks).

GREAT POCKET PARKS

Everyone has a favorite park, the place where they take the kids to play—some have beaches. Sometimes these are marked on the map, sometimes not. In the interest of the public's right to know (but certainly not giving away every secret spot), here are some great pocket parks.

- Wallingford Playfield. Wallingford Avenue N and N 43rd Street. Elaborate wooden climbing contraption. Big playfield.
- Roanoke Park. Block-long park on 10th Avenue E and Edgar. Oasis of green between Highway 520 and I-5.
- Interlaken Drive E/Interlaken Boulevard, from E Roanoke to Lake Washington Boulevard E. Winding drive through dense forest, great for walking or biking.
- 15th Avenue E at Garfield, on Capitol Hill. Lake Washington, Cascades, University lookout. Exquisite view of the moon over the water.

Madison Park and Madrona have lots of pocket parks:

- Swingset just north of Madison Park (now joined by a children's play area).
- Al Larkins Park. Corner of 34th Avenue and E Pike Street. Winding path for child cyclists, bench, and neighborhood meeting area.
- Grand Avenue E and E Pine Street. Wooden observation deck, climbable wooden posts, big wooden steps, looks out over Madrona Drive.
- Denny Blaine Lake Park bus stop, corner of E Denny Way and Madrona Place E. Small shallow pool filled with leaves, turtles, and lily pads.
- Ten accessible beaches can be found on Lake Washington's shore at road ends between Madison Park on the north and Madrona to the south. The beaches are of varying quality, and finding them means you have to either know the

area or get a map. You can also ask in the neighborhood—you'll be either pointed in the right direction or sent toward Elliott Bay.

ON THE WATERFRONT

Want to know what those container ships are doing in Elliott Bay? The Port of Seattle manages several public access areas, and many of them have exhibits designed to teach you about seagoing commerce. Others have piers for fishing, footpaths, and, in one case, an exercise course.

Interesting port parks

- Terminal 91 Bike Path: This 4,000-foot paved path connects with Elliott Bay and Myrtle Edwards parks, Interbay, and Fishermen's Terminal.
- Elliott Bay Fishing Pier: Pier 86, west of the grain elevator, has fish-cleaning stations, bait and tackle concessions, and a 400-foot pier. Whether you should eat what you catch is debatable (see Chapter 19, "Green Grows the City").
- Elliott Bay Park and Myrtle Edwards Park: Enter these adjacent parks from either Elliott Avenue at Pier 86 on the north or Pier 70 on the south. The parks have more than 10 landscaped acres and more than 4,000 feet of shoreline, including an exercise course.
- Terminal 105 Viewpoint: This West Seattle area offers views of Duwamish River activities, a fishing pier, and a launch for small boats.

Call the port to get a copy of its slick brochure listing shoreline parks and viewpoints.

Port of Seattle
Pier 69
2711 Alaskan Way
Seattle, WA 98121
728-3000

684-7494
(Outdoor saltwater pool open summers only)

Evans Pool (Green Lake)
7201 E Green Lake Way N
684-4961

Madison Pool
13401 Meridian Ave. N
684-4979

Meadowbrook Pool
10515 35th NE
684-4989

Medgar Evers Pool (Garfield)
500 23rd Ave.
684-4763

Queen Anne Pool
1920 First Ave. W
386-4282

Rainier Beach Pool
8825 Rainier Ave. S
386-1944

Southwest Pool (West Seattle)
2801 SW Thistle St.
684-7440

SWIMMERS BEWARE

Seattle has a high incidence of drowning, especially when the weather gets hot. In general, saltwater beaches do not have lifeguards; most freshwater ones do. In 1994 (latest figures available), 22 of the 358 accidental deaths in Seattle–King County were drownings.

Non-lifeguarded beaches include: Alki Beach Park, Don Armeni Boat Ramp, Carkeek Park, Gas Works Park, Golden Gardens, Lincoln Park, Lowman Beach, Me-Kwa-Mooks, North Beach Community, and Washington School Site.
Lifeguarded beaches (mid-June to Labor Day) include: Green Lake Park, Madison Park, Madrona Park, Magnolia Park, Magnuson Park, Mt. Baker Park, Pritchard Island Bathing Beach, and Seward Park.
Particularly family-oriented beaches are Madrona Beach and Mt. Baker Beach; families also frequent the Matthews Beach, Green Lake, and Volunteer Park wading pools.

Parks department pools
(indoors unless otherwise noted)

Ballard Pool
1471 NW 67th
684-4094

Colman Pool (Lincoln Park)
8603 Fauntleroy Way SW

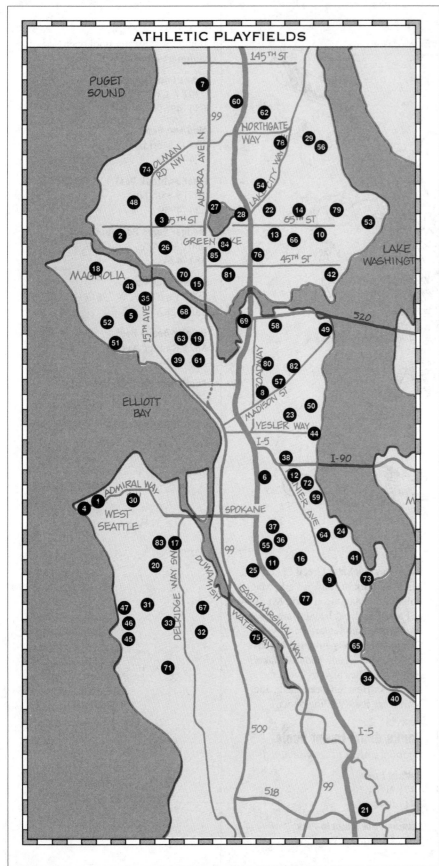

ATHLETIC PLAYFIELDS

Map key to athletic playfields

1. Alki Playground, 58th SW & SW Stevens; 1S, 1Sc, 2Tn*

2. Ballard Playground, NW 60th & 28th NW; 2S*, 1Sc*, 2R

3. Ballard Pool Courts, NW 67th & 14th NW; 4Tn*

4. Bar-S Playground, 65th SW & SW Hanford; 2L

5. Bayview Playground, 25th W & W Raye; 1L, 1Sc

6. Beacon Hill Playground, 14th S & S Holgate; 1L, 1S, 2TnR

7. Bitter Lake Playground, N 130th & Linden N; 1S*, 1B*, 1C*, 4Tn*

8. Bobby Morris Playfield, 11th E & E Pine; 1S*, 1B*, 1Sc*, 3Tn*

9. Brighton Playfield, 42nd S & S Juneau; 1S, 1B*, 1Sc*, 2Tn

10. Bryant Playground, NE 65th & 40th NE; 2

11. Cleveland Playground, 13th S & S Lucile; 1ScT

12. Colman Playground, 23rd S & S Grand; 1L, 1Sc

13. Cowen Park, University Way NE & NE Ravenna Blvd.; 1L, 3Tn

14. Dahl Playfield, 25th NE & NE 77th; 2S, 1S*, 1B, 1F, 1Sc

15. Day Playground, Fremont N & N 41st; 1S, 1S

16. Dearborn Park, S Brandon & 30th S; 2Tn

17. Delridge Playfield, SW Oregon & Delridge Way SW; 1S*, 1B*, 1Sc*, 2Tn

18. Discovery Park, 36th W & W Government Way; 2Tn

19. East Queen Anne Playground, Second N & Howe

20. Fairmont Playground, Fauntleroy SW & SW Brandon; 1S, 1Sc

21. Fort Dent Athletic Center, Interurban at Southcenter Pkwy., Tukwila; 4S*, 1S*, 1S, 2F, Cricket

22. Froula Playground, NE 72nd & 12th NE; 2Tn

23. Garfield Playfield, 23rd E & E Cherry; 1S*, 1S, 1B*, 1F*, 3Tn*

24. Genesee Playfield, 46th S & S Genesee; 2Sc, 2Tn*

25. Georgetown Playground, Corson S & S Homer; 1Sc*, 1Tn

26. Gilman Playground, 11th NW & NW 54th; 2L, 1Sc, 2Tn

27. Green Lake Park, N 73rd & W Green Lake Dr N; 2Tn

28. Green Lake Playfield, E Green Lake Dr N & Latona NE; 2S, 1B, 1C, 3Tn

29. Hale Playfield, 35th Ave NE & NE 110th; 1ScT

30. Hiawatha Playfield, California SW & SW Lander; 1S*, 1S/L, 1B, T*, 1Sc*, 3Tn*

31. High Point Playfield, 34th SW & SW Myrtle; 1S, 1B, 1Sc*, 2Tn

32. Highland Park Playground, 11th SW & SW Thistle; 1S, 1B, 1Sc, 1Tn

33. Hughes Playground, 29th SW & SW Holden; 2S, 1Sc

34. Hutchinson Playground, 59th S & S Pilgrim; 2S, 1Sc, 2Tn

35. Interbay Athletic Field, 17th W & W Dravus; 2S*, 1Sc, 1C*

36. Jefferson Park, 3801 Beacon Ave. S; 2Tn*

37. Jefferson Playfield, 16th S & S Dakota; 3S, 1B, 1C

38. Judkins Park & Playfield, 22nd S & S Charles; 1S, 1B, 1Sc, 1F

39. Kinnear Park, Seventh W & W Olympic Pl.; 1Tn

40. Lakeridge Playground, Rainier S btwn. 68th & Cornell; 1L, 1Tn

41. Lakewood Playground, 50th S & S Angeline; 1S, 1Sc

42. Laurelhurst Playfield, NE 41st & 48th NE; 2S, 1Sc, 4Tn*R

43. Lawton Park, 27th W & W Thurman; 1L

44. Leschi Park, 100 Lakeside S; 1Tn

45. Lincoln Park, Fauntleroy Way SW & SW Kenyon; 1S/L, 2B, 1F, 2Tn

46. Lincoln Park Annex, Fauntleroy SW & SW Webster; 6*R

47. Lowman Beach Park, 48th SW & Beach Dr. SW; 1Tn

48. Loyal Heights Playfield, NW 75th & 22nd NW; 1S*, 1B, 1F*

49. Madison Park, 43rd E & E Lynn; 2Tn*

50. Madrona Playground, 34th E & E Spring; 1L, 2Tn*

51. Magnolia Park, 31st W & W Garfield; 2Tn

52. Magnolia Playfield, 34th W & W Smith; 3S, 1S*, 1B, 2Sc, 1Sc*, 2*, 2Tn

53. Magnuson Park, Sand Point Way NE & 65th NE; 2S, 2Sc, 6

54. Maple Leaf Playground, NE 82nd & Roosevelt Way NE; 1L, 1Sc

55. Maple Wood Playground, Corson S & S Angeline; 2S, 1Sc

56. Meadowbrook Playfield, 30th NE & NE 107th; 2S, 1B, 6Tn*

57. Miller Playfield, 20th E & E Republican; 1S*, 1S/B*, 1Sc*, 2Tn*

58. Montlake Playfield, 16th E & E Calhoun; 1B, 1ScT, 2Tn

59. Mt. Baker Park, S McClellan & Lake Park Dr. S; 2Tn

60. Northacres Park, First NE & NE 130th; 1L, 1S, 1Sc

61. Observatory Courts, First N & W Lee; 2Tn

62. Pinehurst Playground, 14th NE btwn. 120th & NE 123rd; 1L

63. Queen Anne Playfield, First W & W Howe; 1B*, 1S*, 1L, 1Sc

64. Rainier Playfield, Rainier S & S Alaska; 1S*, 1B*, 1L, 1F*, 4Tn*

65. Rainier Beach Playfield, Rainier S & S Cloverdale; 2S, 1Sc, 4Tn*

66. Ravenna Park, 20th NE & NE 58th; 1S, 1Sc, 2Tn

67. Riverview Playfield, 12th SW & SW Othello; 4S, 1F, 1Sc, 2Tn

68. Rodgers Park/Queen Anne Bowl, Third W & W Fulton; 1ScT, 3TnR

69. Rogers Playground, Eastlake E & E Roanoke; 1S/L, 1Sc, 2Tn

70. Ross Playground, Third NW & NW 43rd; 2L

71. Roxhill Park, 29th SW & SW Roxbury; 2S, 1Sc

72. Seattle Tennis Center, 2000 M. L. King Jr. Way S; 10*4Tn

73. Seward Park, Lk. Wash. Blvd. S & S Juneau; 2Tn

74. Soundview Playfield, 15th NW & NW 90th; 2S, 1L, 1B, 1F, 1Sc, 2Tn

75. South Park Playground, Eighth S & S Sullivan; 2S, 1Sc, 2Tn

76. University Playground, Ninth NE & NE 50th; 1S, 1Sc, 2TnR

77. Van Asselt Playground, 32nd S & S Myrtle; 2S, 1Sc, 2Tn

78. Victory Heights Playground, NE 107th & 19th NE; 1Tn

79. View Ridge Playfield, NE 70th & 45th NE; 1S, 1B, 1C

80. Volunteer Park, 15th E & E Prospect; 2* 2Tn

81. Wallingford Playfield, N 43rd & Wallingford N; 1Sc, 2Tn

82. Washington Park, Lk. Wash. Blvd. E & E Madison; 1S*, 1S, 1Sc*

83. West Seattle Stadium, 35th SW & SW Snoqualmie; 1C*, T*

84. Woodland Park (Lower), Green Lake Way N btwn. N 50th & N 56th; 4S*, 1B, T, 2Sc*, 10Tn*

85. Woodland Park N 50th & Midvale N; 4Tn

Facilities key:

S = Softball
B = Baseball
L = Little League
F = Football
Sc = Soccer
C = Combination
T = Track
Tn = Tennis
R = Backboard (Tennis)
* = Lighted

TENNIS, ANYONE?

The parks department maintains almost 60 tennis sites—so why are the courts always full? Well, they aren't, they're just full when *you* want them.

- Busiest times at park tennis courts: 5:30–9:30pm weekdays (especially in summer), all day Sat. and Sun.
- Moderately busy times: early mornings in summer.
- Barren wastelands: dawn and midafternoon weekdays (especially in winter).
- Courts you might have a chance at getting onto (no crowds): Madrona Playground courts (two with lights) and 23rd and Cherry (Garfield Playfield) courts (three with lights). The two courts in Discovery Park are usually open, though not particularly well kept. Also, check your local high school.

Parks department courts are used on a first-come, first-served basis or reserved in advance. If you purchase a $15 reservation card, you can make phone reservations (684-4077); otherwise make reservations in person at the office of Seattle Parks and Recreation (5201 Green Lake Way N). Fees are $3 per 1½ hours or $4 for 2 hours of court time.

The Seattle Tennis Center (2000 Martin Luther King Jr. Way S, 684-4764) has 10 indoor courts; rates are $12 for singles, $16 for doubles for 1 hour and 15 minutes. In order to make reservations, you need a phone reservation card that costs another $25 per year. You can book up to six days in advance, but call by 7:15am if you want a court during prime hours. The Center also has four free outdoor courts.

The best times to get onto the Center's courts are between noon and 3pm. Also, summer is less busy because most people really want to play outdoors, which frees up the indoor courts—except when the Center hosts tournaments or when rain is falling. Lessons and organized competitive flights are available.

Selected courts

Ballard
14th Ave. NW and NW 67th St.

Bryant
40th Ave. NE and NE 65th St.

Laurelhurst Community Center
4554 NE 41st St. (lights)

Lincoln Park
Fauntleroy Ave. SW and SW Webster St. (lights)

Luther Burbank Park
2040 84th Ave. SE (Mercer Island)

Madison Park
43rd Ave. E & E Lynn St. (lights)

Madrona Playground
34th E & E Spring (2 courts with lights)

Magnolia Playfield
34th Ave. W and W Smith St.

Meadowbrook
30th Ave. NE and NE 107th St.

Miller Field
20th Ave. E and E Republican St. (lights)

Montlake Community Center
1618 E Calhoun St.

Rainier Playfield
Rainier Ave. S and S Alaska St. (lights)

Riverview
12th Ave. SW and SW Othello St.

Rodgers Field
Eastlake Ave. E and E Roanoke St. (bus fumes can be overwhelming at rush hour)

University of Washington
Montlake Blvd. (14 courts—5 with lights—and 6 more up on campus)

Volunteer Park
15th Ave. E and E Prospect St.

Woodland Park (lower)
W Green Lake Way N (lights)

PARK PROBLEMS

Seattle has less crime in its parks than other cities, but as the city grows, so do problems in the parks. The most persistent crime in parks is car prowls (theft from cars). All parks are patrolled with an overlapping system called "umbrella cars." In the summer, officers patrol all day; the horse patrol unit patrols all year. Downtown parks are patrolled by bikes all year.

The city doesn't have a list of what crimes have been committed at what parks, but unwelcome nighttime activities such as drug use, drinking, assaultive behavior, loud parties, and vandalism have resulted in most parks being closed at night. In addition, an anti-cruising ordinance is in effect at Alki Beach, Don Armeni Boat Ramp, and Lake Washington Boulevard.

A FEW MORE PRECAUTIONS

One night a Seattle police officer found 18 used condoms in Volunteer Park. Parents panic, understandably, when they find condoms and discarded syringes in parks and playgrounds. Used needles aren't exactly compatible with bare feet and little kids, but they are a fact of life in some of the area's parks, playgrounds, and beaches.

Teach kids not to pick up or play with certain discarded objects that they might find. If the kids are too young to understand about condoms, tell them not to pick up "balloons."

Used condoms should simply be thrown away in the garbage. Pick them up with a tool or by wrapping them in paper, plastic, etc.

The health department does not come out to pick up discarded syringes. You need to dispose of them yourself. Use gloves or tools to pick up the syringe and needle. Be very careful and handle the syringe only by the plunger or barrel, not the needle. Put syringes with needles in a wide-mouth plastic container or coffee can, and seal it. Then take it to any public health clinic for safe disposal; for locations, see Chapter 16, "The City Says Ahhhh."

The risk of disease transmission from a condom or discarded syringe is low. But if you have questions, call the Hazards Line at 296-4692. If you are stuck by a discarded needle, wash the injury with soap and water. Contact a doctor if any signs of infection occur, such as redness or fever. It's unlikely that a virus, such as hepatitis or HIV/AIDS, would be transmitted this way.

If needles are a recurring problem in an area, report it to the police. If you find hazardous items in a park, call the parks department.

King County Parks Division
296-4232
296-8100 (after-hours)

Seattle Department of Parks and Recreation
684-4075

Seattle/King County Health Department
Hazards Line: 296-4692

PARK POWER

The parks department, formally known as the Department of Parks and Recreation, is under the jurisdiction of the Board of Park Commissioners. So if you *really* want some improvement to the park nearest you, those are the folks to call. Seven commissioners serve three-year terms and meet twice a month.

Board members

Bill Arntz (chairperson)
Margaret Ceis
Susan Golub
John Hancock
John Little
Earl Sedlik

Grace Yuan
Board office: 684-5066
Parks superintendent: Ken Bounds, 684-8022

Seattle Department of Parks and Recreation (SDPR)
Information Office
5201 Green Lake Way N
Seattle, WA 98103
684-4075
Keyed maps of the system available.
Ballfield scheduling: 684-4077 (individual), 684-4082 (league)
Evening adult recreation: 684-7092
Maintenance/vandalism reports: 684-4075
Park use permits: 684-4080
Picnic permits: 684-4081
Tennis reservations: 684-4077

Other park resources

Adopt-a-Park
684-4557
Parks department–sponsored program to get community members involved in the city's parks.

Friends of Seattle's Olmsted Parks
P.O. Box 15984
Seattle, WA 98115-0984
The group schedules lectures, tours, and special events. Membership is from $7 to $50+.

King County Division of Natural Resources and Parks
2040 84th Ave. SE
Mercer Island, WA 98040
296-4232
Information on county parks, map, pamphlet.

U.S. Forest Service
915 Second Ave.
Seattle, WA 98104
220-7450
Maps, computerized trails information system (TRIS), brochures, walk-in help.

Washington State Parks and Recreation Commission
7150 Cleanwater Lane, KY-11
Olympia, WA 98504-5711
(360) 753-2027
Information on state parks, map, brochures.

Washington State Trails Directory
Interagency Committee for Outdoor Recreation
4800 Capitol Blvd., KP-11
Tumwater, WA 98504-5611
(360) 753-7140
Statewide map of trail resources.

MESSING ABOUT IN BOATS

Sailing is a tried-and-true tradition here, but beware—it can become addicting. Why else would anyone get up before dawn, rush to the boat in the rain, and spend the best part of a Saturday waiting for the wind to blow during the yacht club regatta? And why else would anyone pay the moorage fees that can at times rival your house payment? And then there's the problem of *where* to moor your boat. You probably don't want to wait for a slip at Shilshole; you'll be setting up a rocking chair on board by the time you get one.

If you'd like to sample the boating life before you commit to all this, here are some places to rent boats.

Center for Wooden Boats
1010 Valley St.
382-2628
Wooden rowboats and sailboats. Maritime museum.

Greenlake Boat Rentals
7351 E Green Lake Dr. N
527-0171
Paddle boats, rowboats, canoes, kayaks, sailboats, sailboards.

Northwest Outdoor Center of Lake Union
2100 Westlake Ave. N
281-9694
Kayaks.

Pacific Water Sports
16055 Pacific Hwy. S
246-9385
Kayaks and canoes. Teaches classes. Sea Kayak tours.

Map key

1. Shilshole Bay Marina
Located at the end of the fuel dock ("J" dock). Coin operated (24 hours).

2. Fishermen's Terminal
Located at the end of the fuel dock. Coin operated (24 hours).

3. Chandler's Cove
Dock will accommodate vessels up to 65 feet. Coin operated (24 hours).

4. Duke's Yacht Club
Dock will accommodate vessels up to 40 feet. Coin operated (24 hours).

5. Harbor Village
(north end of Lake Washington) Bilge pump-out and holding tank pump-out stations (24 hours).

6. Carillon Point Marina
(south of Kirkland) Located on the southernmost dock. Coin operated (24 hours).

7. Harbor Island Marina
Gain access to the pump-out facility and pay for its use at the Marina office. (Open 9am–5pm, 7 days a week.)

Source: Boaters Task Force

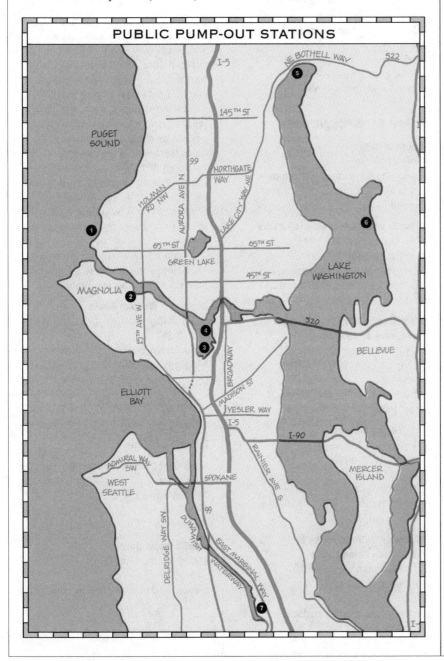

PUBLIC PUMP-OUT STATIONS

Seacrest Boat House
1660 Harbor Ave. SW
932-1050
Sixteen-foot aluminum boats.

Swallows Nest
2308 Sixth Ave.
441-8151
Belly boats, float tubes, camping equipment.

Swiftwater
4235 Fremont Ave. N
547-3377
Inflatable river rafts that hold from 1 to 10 people, nonmotorized. Kick-boats.

UW Waterfront Activities Center
SE corner of Husky Stadium parking lot
543-9433
Canoes, rowboats.

UNLOCKING THE LOCKS

There aren't really any regulations for taking a boat through Hiram Chittenden Locks, which raise and lower boats so they can pass between Lake Union and Puget Sound. But if you don't want to look like a fool to all the schoolkids and tourists watching, it's nice to have some idea of what you're doing. You don't have to have a motor to use the locks; kayaks and rowboats go through all the time.

Tips for the locks

Shortest wait: Weekdays, poor weather days, midwinter.

Hectic times: Just before three-day weekends, last day of the weekend, opening day of boating season, Fourth of July, before and after the Seafair hydroplane race.

How long it will take: The locks (but not the grounds) are open 24 hours a day. Average passage takes about 25 minutes through the large lock (which holds about 100 small boats in one lockage) and 10 minutes through the small one. Oceangoing vessels and log tows require a half-hour.

Most frequent mistakes boaters make in the locks: panicking, running engines full ahead, or letting engines die. **Hints:** Go down to the locks and watch the whole process from land before trying it in a boat. If you have a cruiser or sailboat, you need two 50-foot lines on board, bumpers for both sides of the boat, and at least two people on board (one for the bow and one for the stern).

A brochure, *Guidelines for Boaters,* is available from the locks visitors center on the main road through the grounds, or from the small or large lock-operating house. Tours at 2pm weekends.

Hiram Chittenden Locks

3015 NW 54th St.
Seattle, WA 98107
Locks: 783-7001
Visitors center: 783-7059
(Closed Tues.–Wed.)

Boating resources

Army Corps of Engineers (Seattle District)
4735 E Marginal Way S
Seattle, WA 98134
764-3750
Operates the locks, picks up debris from waterways, etc.

Boat Licensing Hotline
(800) 521-9319

U.S. Coast Guard
915 Second Ave.
Seattle, WA 98104
Emergency line: 217-6000 (24-hour)
Information: 220-7237
Handles vessel traffic system for Puget Sound and surrounding waters; involved in rescues and law enforcement on the water.

TOP ATTRACTIONS IN KING COUNTY

1. Kingdome: 2.5 million visitors annually
2. Lake Sammamish State Park: 1.7 million
3. Space Needle: 1.2 million
4. Woodland Park Zoo: 828,455
5. Pacific Science Center: 828,320
6. Seattle Aquarium: 619,060
7. Dash Point State Park: 382,860
8. Omnidome: 250,000
9. Pioneer Square Underground Tours: 144,148
Source: Downtown Seattle Association

KID PLEASERS

Seattle is renowned for its recreational opportunities for children, but kids aren't going to stumble upon them all by themselves. Parental imagination is a necessary ingredient—as, often, is the parental pocketbook. We've listed a few must-do activities for kids below—including some that are inexpensive or even free:

Camp Long
5200 35th Ave. SW
Seattle, WA 98126
684-7434
An absolute must. Run by the Department of Parks and Recreation, this 68-acre forested urban park offers all sorts of programs, and even some rustic cabins for getting away from it all without leaving town. The programs for adults and kids include stargazing sessions, introduction to rock climbing (seven-year-olds and up), bat culture classes, astronomy with the camp telescope, and more. There's even an outdoor recreation equipment and clothing exchange in December.

Seattle Parks and Recreation Department
684-4075
The parks department puts out a great summer calendar for kids, listing all kinds of activities. There's a kids' lip-sync contest (this one's free!) and an all-city high school dance (not free), as well as such artsy-craftsy things as clay-play, cartooning, and art history at community centers. There's even something for kids at that in-between age, called "Art for Almost Teens." And then of course there's the group piano lesson. The Parks Department has classes all year

round. For information on classes held near you, call the community center in your neighborhood.

Seattle Public Library
386-4675
Remember those summer reading clubs? Yes, they still exist. Some are for toddlers, others for kids in grades K–6. And the library has computer workshops for kids 8–12. Call the library to register.

DO THE ZOO— KIDSTYLE

The zoo offers grrr-eat strolling-around opportunities as well as special activities for kids. Here are some tried and true, proven thrill-makers:

Family Farm. Open Memorial Day to Labor Day. Kids can get up close to pet the animals and watch chicken eggs hatch.
Pony rides. For $2, kids can ride around and around a pony ring astride a tiny steed. Rides start weekends in April, then daily in the summer.
Raptors. The zoo has a Bird of Prey

Now that the zoo has what it calls bioclimatic zones (natural habitats for the animals), it's sometimes hard to see the lions in the savanna because they can hide in the tall grass. Our inside sources say the best time to see them is around 10am—when they're likely to be most active.

program on weekends all summer long where kids can watch raptors in flight. Check at the entrance gates for times.

Gorillas. Bobo's gone, but his memory (or is it some other essence of gorilla?) lingers on. The gorillas are usually right up front where kids can get a good look at them. And now kids can get a good look at the newest member of the primate family, a female gorilla born at the zoo on February 12, 1995. Nadiri (which means "rare") was born of two Seattle Zoo gorillas, but is essentially an orphan. Her father, Congo, died before she was born, and she was rejected by her mother, Jamoki, who gave birth under anesthesia and did not recognize the baby as her own. Not to worry, though—the little one was adopted by Nina, an experienced gorilla mom in another troop, and is doing just fine, thanks.

Elephant bath time. Show up at the delightful new elephant habitat at 10am, when keepers give the elephants their daily baths.

Penguin buffet. The penguins get their weekly dose of live fish (much different from the more mundane daily fare) at 11am Tuesdays. Fascinating, lively action when the underwater hunt is on.

Snake spectacular. Can a snake wink? You won't know for sure unless you show up at the Reptile House at noon on Wednesdays.

Bug moments. Meet a tarantula, and other equally interesting spiders and bugs, up close and personal at 11am Saturdays and Sundays.

The hippos. A personal favorite, they are usually wallowing in the mud close at hand on the savanna. Kids love talking about how much they look like Dad.

Discovery Tent. From 12:30 to 3:30pm on weekends (and weekdays during the summer), visitors can hold a tortoise shell, watch wildlife videos, and use the Zookeeper computer. At Discovery Carts also stationed around the grounds, you can feel the hair of a giraffe's tail and learn more about animal life.

The zoo also offers special activities:

Summer programs. Talks by zookeepers and naturalists are given at several locations. Signs announcing the next talk are posted at the different exhibits. Guess which are most popular? Elephants and raptors.

Classes. Except in winter, the zoo offers educational classes for children, families, and adults. Some are field trips, some are held at the zoo.

Summer concert series. Benefit performances by acoustical recording artists are given Wednesday nights during the summer.

Woodland Park Zoo
5500 Phinney Ave. N
Seattle, WA 98103-5897
Administration: 684-4800
Admissions: 684-4892
Hours are 9:30am–6pm, March 15–Oct. 15; 9:30am–4pm, Oct. 16–March 14; open daily including Thanksgiving and Christmas. Ticket prices: $7.50 adults, $5.75 seniors, $5 handicapped, $5 kids 6–17, $2.75 preschool; free for kids under 3. A yearly membership is a bargain at $50 for the family, with unlimited visits and two free guest passes. Individual memberships $35 yearly; AquaZoo (zoo and Seattle Aquarium) $80 family, $60 individual.

THE SEATTLE AQUARIUM

The Seattle Aquarium is another favorite, with a touch tank for the kids and an Underwater Dome perfect for tracking octopi. In spring and summer the Aquarium offers family classes—some are field trips, such as to Seattle's tidepools, others are held at the Aquarium. Longer "Outdoor Adventures" include canoe and kayak trips, and exploration of tidepools on the Olympic Peninsula.

Seattle Aquarium
Pier 59
Waterfront Park
386-4320 (recording)
386-4300 (live)
Hours: Labor Day–Memorial Day, 10am–5pm daily; Memorial Day–Labor Day, 10am–7pm daily. Ticket prices: $7.15 adults, $5.70 seniors, $4.70 handicapped, $4.20 kids 6–18, $2.45 kids 3–5, free for kids 2 or under. Discounts for groups and for King County residents.

SEATTLE CENTER

The Seattle Center has more than just the Fun Forest, though at times it's hard to tell. For example, when your youngster's gaze is turned upward to the brand-new old-fashioned roller coaster (the Wind Storm—one of only four of its kind in the world), it may be hard to lure him or her on to the cultural programs. The entire Fun Forest requires some allowance saving; the roller coaster, for one, is $3.50 (four 85-cent tickets) per ride. You can get eight tickets for $5.50, or 18 for $11, and at certain times you can get $12 bracelets that give you unlimited rides. In summer, you can get seven hours of unlimited rides for $15.

"More" includes a variety of public programs that would interest families with kids:

- Folklife Festival, Memorial Day weekend. International Children's Village and lots of music, storytelling, puppet shows, and other fun for kids. All activities free.
- Arts and Sciences Academy, for seventh- and eighth-graders. A two-week academy, held in July, which offers a choice of 23 classes taught by members of the Seattle Symphony, Pacific Northwest Ballet, and other experts in the arts and sciences. Apply during the school year; applications available at local schools. 233-3959.
- Peace Academy. High school students visit the center and learn peer mediation skills to reduce violence in their neighborhoods and schools. Apply through local schools during school year. 233-3959.
- Whirligig, an indoor winter carni-

val for families beginning at the end of February.

- Imagination Celebration/Arts Festival for Kids, which is usually held in April, with hands-on arts activities.
- Seattle International Children's Theater Festival, in May, with children's theater performances by internationally renowned entertainers.
- Artspring/Children's Handicapped Arts Festival, in May, a hands-on arts festival for and by handicapped children.
- KOMO KidsFair, in August, family day with entertainment, workshops, and sports.
- Bumbershoot, September, anything-goes entertainment.
- KING-5 Winterfest, December, holiday entertainment.

Seattle Children's Museum has tripled in size and taken over most of the first floor of the Center House. With its technology exhibit and a model volcano that pokes its head up through the main floor, you can't miss it. Kids can build a house in the "If I Had a Hammer" area, or (at an exhibit entitled "A Changed World") view artwork that reveals how kids in detention centers would like the world to be improved. They can walk through a health exhibit that has a doctor's office and shows the systems of the body in three dimensions and living color, or visit the Arts and Humanities area to make a video or play an electric guitar. The on-site Birthday Bashes are a great deal—you bring the food, the kids, and the presents, the museum does the rest—and your house doesn't get wrecked. Birthday Bash packages come in different price ranges, but they start at a very reasonable $75 for 15 kids for two hours. Call at least two weeks in advance to reserve a party room. And ask about the Bonanza ($140), which includes 20 invitations, all paper goods, etc.

Single admission is $4.50. Family memberships (parents, grandparents, and kids) are a measly $40/year with unlimited admission. Evening rentals for kid or grown-up parties as well.

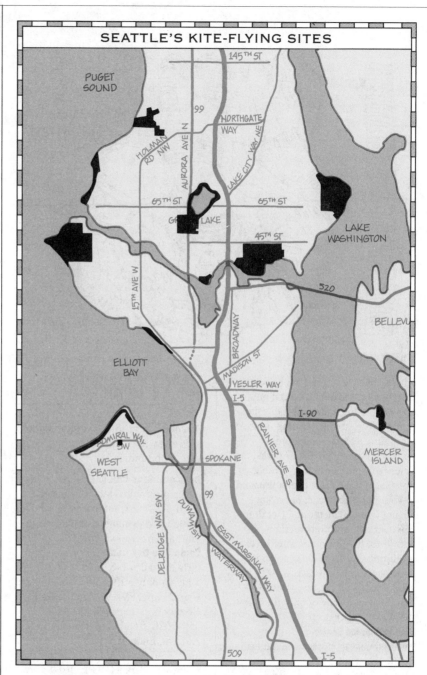

Seattle Center
Center House: 684-7200
Fun Forest Amusement Park: 728-1585
Seattle Center Monorail: 684-7340
Seattle Children's Museum: 441-1767
Space Needle: 443-2111

PACIFIC SCIENCE CENTER

A huge favorite with kids and adults alike is the Pacific Science Center—five buildings of otherworldly architecture filled with lots of hands-on permanent and traveling exhibits for all ages. Explore the "Tech Zone,"

where you can play virtual basket-ball, hang-glide over a virtual city, play tic-tac-toe with a 10-foot robot, or meet five moving, roaring, robotic dinosaurs. Spin a 2-ton granite ball with water power at Waterworks, the Science Center's outdoor exhibit, en-joy a laser light show choreographed to your favorite music, or go star-gazing in the planetarium. But don't trip over the new construction—in late 1996, the Science Center breaks ground for a 29.1 million dollar ex-pansion, which will add 56,000 square feet. and include a new 3-D IMAX theatre (one of only four on the West Coast).

Pacific Science Center
Located near the Space Needle in Seattle Center
General information: 443-2001
IMAX Theater: 443-IMAX
Laser Shows: 443-2850
Open daily except Thanksgiving and Christmas.
Hours: 10am-5pm, Mon-Fri; 10am-6pm, Sat-Sun.
Ticket prices: $7.50 adults, $5.50 ju-niors, $3.50 children, $5.50 seniors.
IMAX or laser matinee additional $2.

HAPPY CAMPERS

You don't have to go far to send the kids away to camp. Here are some in-city opportunities.

Boys and Girls Clubs. Day camp and overnight camps, too, for kids ages 6 to 16. Call the Central Seattle Club to get the phone number of the club in your neighborhood, 461-3890.

Camp Fire Day Camps. For boys and girls in grades 1–8, held in Southwest King County on Vashon Island and at Camp Long, 854-3676; East King County in Issaquah and Bothell, 453-7020; South King County in Auburn, Enumclaw, and the Kent area, 854-3676; and North King County at Carkeek Park, 461-8550.

Girls Club of Puget Sound, Martin Luther King Jr. Way and E Cherry Street, 720-2912.

Pacific Science Center Summer Camps. "Ages 9 to 99." Some day camps, some residential (family) camps. These camps examine every-thing from rocketry, light, and lasers to stones and bones. The residential camps include whale watching in the San Juans and hikes in the Cascades.

There are also "Science Celebration" classes for those under 9. For a cata-log, call 443-2925.

Totem Girl Scout Day and Resident Camps. The Girl Scouts have two resident camps in the area, for Scout and non-Scout girls, 7–17, and an extensive day camp program, 633-5600.

YMCA Day Camp. Forty locations in the area, with drop-off and pick-up sites in neighborhoods, for kids grades K–9. The YMCA also has two overnight co-ed camps, Camp Orkila and Camp Colman. To register, call 382-5003.

YWCA Summer Day Camp. Two groups, for children entering grades 1–5 and 6–8. Field trips to Seattle's parks and places of interest, and other activities, 461-8489.

QUINTESSENTIAL SEATTLE FUN

Some haunts are just as much a part of a child's life here as, well, chasing squirrels in the pocket parks or avoiding the duck poop at Gas Works.

Tradition: What's childhood in Seattle without memories of the summer Seafair Torchlight Parade? So it's crowded, and there are too many cars with waving dignitaries, and too many trucks with hydroplanes. So you can't park for miles and the curbs are packed eight deep with parade-goers. So it's dog-eat-dog juggling for a place that is suddenly shadowed by teenagers crowding in front of you. It's still the best place to be scared by a Seafair pirate and to see a purely anti-TV, real-life event. Yes, there are still baton twirlers and balloon hawkers; neighborhood communities still decorate floats with aluminum flowers and clowns still make kids laugh.

Get there early, take a blanket to sit on, and let the kids stay up late. They'll remember this until the time they take their own kids. The Torch-

WHAT GOOD SPORTS!

light Parade is held the Friday before the hydroplane race every year. More than 55 events take place during the entire three weeks of Seafair, from mid-July to early August. For more information, call Seafair at 728-0123.

A fishy lesson: Go to the Hiram Chittenden Locks when the salmon are leaping their way up the fish ladder. Keep a good hold on the kids' hands while crossing the locks, and make sure they don't lean too far over the ladder to watch the salmon from above. The underwater windows below give a closer view, but kids like the challenge of spotting a fish outside as it takes a grand leap. Best viewing time: Fourth of July weekend.

Carousel: Every Christmas season a huge antique carousel comes to Westlake Center, and crowds of children and adults climb aboard the 36 carousel horses and four chariots for a musical ride around and around. Rides are free, and donations of either canned food or money are accepted for Northwest Harvest's food bank.

The carousel belongs to the Perron family of Perron's Carousels Unlimited in Portland. In addition to the horses, many of which are original, the 1914 carousel has 800 lights on it. To find out when the carousel is open, call the Downtown Seattle Association (DSA), 623-0340, or pick up a holiday brochure beginning around Thanksgiving time at a downtown retail store.

Holiday cheer: DSA also sponsors free carriage rides downtown during the season, with a station at Fourth and Pine. And there is brunch with Santa, tree-lighting ceremonies at Pioneer Square and Westlake Center, the Jingle Bell Run, Great Figgy Pudding contest (caroling), strolling minstrels, and more—all are outlined in the holiday brochure available at retail centers during the holidays.

ETHNICITY: DIVERSITY AT WORK

They're singing in Welsh in Sand Point, meeting at Mama's in the Central District, and dusting off the new dragon in the International District. The school district includes the Indian Heritage School and the African American Academy.

Seattle has become increasingly diverse: In the last decade the white population actually declined by almost 10%, while the nonwhite population increased. Who's coming here in greatest number? Primarily Asians and Pacific Islanders, whose populations increased by 56%.

Aside from the stats, it's difficult to count the ethnic communities in Seattle; with almost as many as there are countries of the world, getting to know them makes for an excellent firsthand geography lesson.

The Ethnic Heritage Council comprises 270 member organizations, primarily based in the Seattle area, and most of them have at least one annual celebration to which the rest of the city is invited. Some groups have museums—the Nordic Heritage Museum and Wing Luke Asian Museum, for example—and all have individuals who have made their presence felt in politics, the arts, and social services.

With all that going for it, you'd think Seattle would be among the most progressive cities in accommodating ethnic cultures, but it is actually one of the most segregated cities in the nation in terms of housing distribution and employment for its communities of color. Consider this:

- The Central Area and southeast Seattle still house 72% of the city's African American population.
- While the city's total unemployment rate is 4.9%, unemployment in the black community is approximately 12.4%.
- In the American Indian community, unemployment is just slightly lower at 10%.

Seattle's ethnic diversity includes minorities of color—African Americans, American Indians, and Asians—as well as residents who have held on to the culture of their ancestors—the "Ya sure, y' betcha" Scandinavians of Ballard or the Irish who belong to the Friendly Sons of St. Patrick, for example.

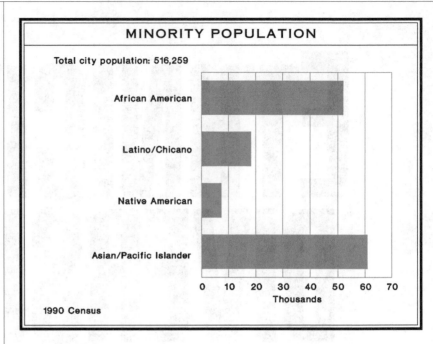

MINORITY POPULATION

Total city population: 516,259

1990 Census

The Ethnic Mix
Total city population: 516,259
African American: 51,948
Asian/Pacific Islander: 60,819
Latino/Chicano/Mexicano: 18,349
American Indian: 7,326
Source: U.S. census

Languages spoken at home
There are 75,122 Seattle residents who speak a language other than English at home. What they're speaking:

Spanish	18%
Chinese	10%
German	10%
Korean	9%
Tagalog	8%
Japanese	6%
French	5%
Vietnamese	5%
Scandinavian languages	4%

Source: U.S. census

Multicultural organizations
Atlantic Street Center
2103 S Atlantic St.
Seattle, WA 98144
329-2050
A multicultural agency providing support services, particularly counseling. Also deals with parenting and youth issues.

Ethnic Heritage Council
Center House, Seattle Center
305 Harrison, Suite 322
Seattle, WA 98109
443-1410
Board president: Joann Nicon
Executive director: Alma Plancich
The best resource for anything ethnic. Publishes a directory called *Contact: A Directory of Ethnic Organizations in Washington State* and a newspaper called *Fortelling*. The council sponsors events (WorldFest, Fourth of July Naturalization Ceremony), scholarships, and awards.

Northwest Folklife Festival
305 Harrison St.
Seattle, WA 98109
684-7300
Executive director: Scott Nagel
Folklife is an ethnic showcase held Memorial Day weekend at Seattle Center. The people wearing patchouli oil and camping in the parking lot in VWs may propel you back into the 1960s, but the real excitement is the music, dancing, food, and crafts from more than 100 countries.

The Folklife folks do more than put on the festival: they are a year-round resource for schools and community groups who would like to stage an ethnic event of their own. They have lists of what's available and what's needed in the way of space, stage, equipment, etc. The office also conducts multicultural teacher-training classes.

FROM WHENCE WE CAME

No wonder we're so polite in traffic. According to the U.S. census, Seattleites have a good dose of German cool stubbornness, followed by an English practicality, with the Norwegian penchant for silence not far behind.

An optional question on the census allowed us to specify up to two ancestries. Remember that this is not ethnic heritage but ancestry, which sometimes is a matter of family mythology; also, not everyone answered this question. For those reasons, the percentages do not match the more specific ethnic heritage figures elsewhere in this chapter and do not include groups distinguished elsewhere by race (Asian, Latino, etc.). Here are the groups that registered 1% or more of the population:

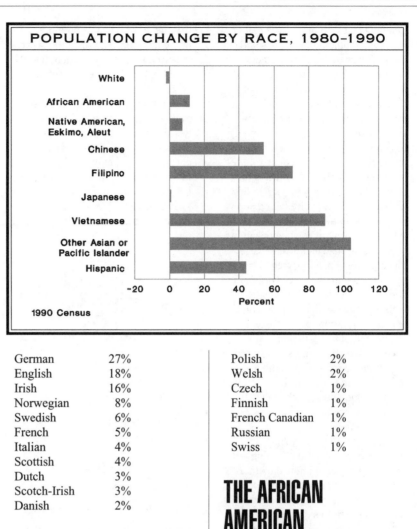

POPULATION CHANGE BY RACE, 1980–1990

1990 Census

German	27%	Polish	2%
English	18%	Welsh	2%
Irish	16%	Czech	1%
Norwegian	8%	Finnish	1%
Swedish	6%	French Canadian	1%
French	5%	Russian	1%
Italian	4%	Swiss	1%
Scottish	4%		
Dutch	3%		
Scotch-Irish	3%		
Danish	2%		

THE AFRICAN AMERICAN COMMUNITY

There's a movement afoot in Seattle's heretofore mellow African American community aimed at putting blacks in the boardrooms, shaking up the city's biggest corporations, integrating, as one community leader puts it, "the suites."

Economic injustice is the issue of the 1990s. It was no accident that the African American community gave Boeing the Bull Connor Anti–African American Community Service Award early in 1990. The "award" was bestowed because Boeing sold planes to South Africa and because historically there have been no blacks on its board of directors.

Boeing was the first target;

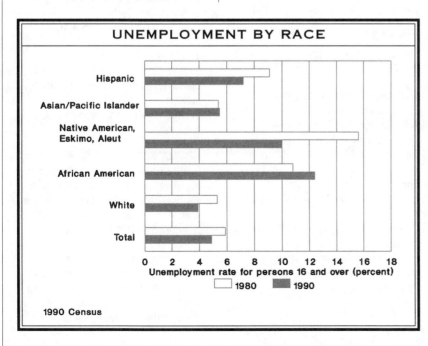

UNEMPLOYMENT BY RACE

1990 Census

Seattle's black community is gathering data on other corporations and their records of promoting blacks.

Why all the activity in a city that has never experienced the kind of riots and radical movements known elsewhere? Because black leaders would like to make Seattle a model of economic development for the rest of the nation. If there is to be true integration of African Americans in society, they say, it will happen first in Seattle, a literate city with a population open to the idea of inclusion. After all, affirmative action began in Washington state and Seattle has a black mayor. Then too, there's an openness within the black community here to developing new strategies.

It's fair to say that Seattle's black and white relations are not as volatile as they might be. Although it got tense and some businesses suffered smash-and-dash violence, the first Rodney King verdict in 1992 resulted more in eloquent sermons in Seattle's black churches than in riots on Seattle's streets.

That's not to say that Seattle is integrated. Neither side is going out of its way to get to know the other. (Some individuals are, though. No one's counting, but some in the city's black community say there are more interracial relationships in Seattle than in most other cities.) There's not necessarily discrimination on a one-to-one basis, but it's prevalent in the institutions. Private schools have low minority populations, whereas public schools have high ones.

And boardrooms, well, they're white (and mostly male).

African American leaders say the 1990s will be a time of self-criticism and self-help for the black community, combined with demands for less discrimination in the city's institutions. A potential gang confrontation in the late '80s, for example, resulted in the formation of Role Models Unlimited, a role model group for black male youths. And test scores showing the low scholastic achievement of black kids resulted in the formation of a black coalition that demanded

that the school district do more to improve learning. The resulting African American Academy opened in 1991. (See Chapter 15, "Seattle School Daze.")

Another aim is to develop a sense of community again in Southeast Seattle, which has been ravaged by drugs and gangs. Finally, large retailers are taking the plunge by moving in—something that the community has long been waiting for.

For survival, jobs are the key. At the Central Area Motivation

Want to get to know the black community? Go to church. The community heart lies in the very active Mt. Zion Baptist Church, the African Methodist Episcopal Church (both founded in the 1800s), the New Hope Missionary Baptist Church, and the Tabernacle Missionary Baptist Church.

Program (CAMP), employment experts assess job seekers' skills and find out what kinds of jobs they'd like—and they often recommend training or schooling. CAMP works with 125 companies who want black applicants. At any one time, CAMP has a pool of 50 to 100 applicants for jobs.

True success will come to African Americans who own their own businesses or become managers or entrepreneurs, says one Seattle community leader.

Names to know

Leon Brown, executive director, Central Area Motivation Program, 329-4111.

Adrienne Caver, development director of the United Negro College Fund.

Maya Denham, coordinator, Teen Housing Program, Central Area Youth Association, 322-6640.

Larry Gossett, King County Council member, 296-1010.

Girtherine Olivia Jackson, operator of Mama's Kitchen and community activist.

Reverend Robert Jeffrey, organizer, Black Dollar Days Task Force, and leader in community through New Hope Baptist Church, 323-4212.

Sandra Little-Berthé, executive director, Central Area Youth Association, 322-6640.

Reverend Dr. Samuel McKinney, pastor, Mt. Zion Baptist Church and community leader, 322-6500.

Norm Rice, mayor of Seattle, 684-4000 (office).

Millie Russell, community activist/educator.

Charlotte Watson Sherman, Franklin High grad, noted author, and recipient of several achievement awards.

Ron Sims, King County Council member, 296-1005.

Lacy Steele, president, NAACP, 324-6600.

Jeri Ware, community activist, 322-7902.

DeCharlene Williams, community activist.

Dr. Roz Woodhouse, executive director, Seattle Urban League.

Resources

Seattle's black community is rich in organizations. For example, almost every profession has its own association, such as the Association of Black Accountants, Black Professional Educators, and the Conference of Black Officials. And then there are social service groups, mainly centered in the Central Area and south Seattle. Business types network through four fraternities and four sororities, carrying on that college relationship much longer than other ethnic groups. Several groups say they are putting together a comprehensive list of organizations. Until then, here's a smattering of key African American community organizations:

African American Heritage Museum
2022 E Union
Seattle, WA 98122
324-3185
Fighting stereotypes and striving to get the old Colman School designated a heritage museum.

Black Achievers Program
East Madison YMCA
1700 23rd Ave.
Seattle, WA 98122
322-6969
Provides mentors for teen-age participants.

Black Dollar Days Task Force
124 21st Ave. S
Seattle, WA 98122
323-4212
President: Reverend Robert Jeffrey
Distributes an annual *African American Business & Service Directory.*
Also organizes Black Dollar Days in February—an effort to encourage patronage of African American businesses.

Black Heritage Society of the State of Washington
P.O. Box 22565
Seattle, WA 98122
325-7623
Contact: Mary Henry
Organized in 1977 to bring together people interested in the history, culture, and contribution of African Americans. Offers exhibits, speakers, photographs, slide/tape features, travel info, index to oral history interviews, ethnic crafts, archives, educational programs, genealogical materials, etc.

Carolyn Downs Family Medical Center
2101 E Yesler Way
Seattle, WA 98122
461-4587
Medical center for low-income people. Sponsored by private funds.

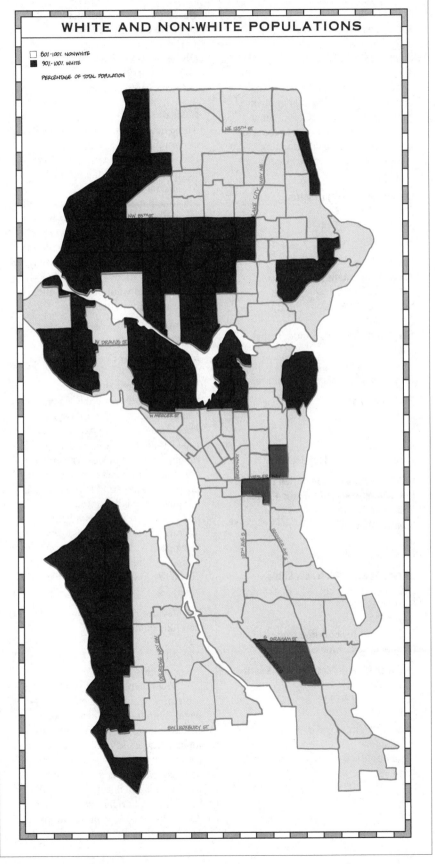

WHITE AND NON-WHITE POPULATIONS

Central Area Motivation Program (CAMP)
722 18th Ave.
Seattle, WA 98122
329-4111
Executive director: Leon Brown
Anti-poverty organization: housing, emergency services, employment assistance, energy assistance, minor home repair, outreach program for at-risk youth, rental space for meetings.

Central Area Senior Center
500 30th Ave. S
Seattle, WA 98144
461-7816

Central Area Youth Association (CAYA)
119 23rd Ave.
Seattle, WA 98122
322-6640
Executive director: Sandra Little-Berthé
Association providing youth with programs from tutoring to sports.

East Cherry YWCA
2820 E Cherry St.
Seattle, WA 98122
461-8480
Director: Patricia Hayden

NAACP (National Association for the Advancement of Colored People)
P.O. Box 22148
Seattle, WA 98122
324-6600
President: Lacy Steele

Odessa Brown Children's Clinic
2101 E Yesler Way
Seattle, WA 98122
329-7870
Health care for children from low-income families.

Urban League of Metropolitan Seattle
105 14th Ave.
Seattle, WA 98122
461-3792
Executive director: Dr. Roz Woodhouse
Social/political group of community activists.

Washington State Commission on African American Affairs
1210 Eastside SE
Olympia, WA 98504
(360) 753-0127
Director: Tony Orange

Media
Three newspapers serve the black community: *The Facts*, which has been around since 1961; *The Medium*, begun in 1970; and the newer *Seattle Skanner*, a business paper. The two old-time papers enjoy a semi-friendly competition; word is that if you get an announcement of your event in one paper, the other paper won't run it. *The Facts* has historically been read by everybody, *The Medium* by those who want objective, more professionally written news.

The Facts
2765 E Cherry St.
Seattle, WA 98122
324-0552
Editor: Elizabeth Beaver
"If you want to reach the black community, you have to use *The Facts*," says one activist. *The Facts*, founded in 1961, is known for running opinion pieces written by community members, but its founding editor, Fitzgerald Beaver, insists it's just a "weekly community newspaper." It includes a listing of community happenings. Anything goes—radical to conservative opinions—but if you want your article on the front page, you'll have to pay.

The Medium
2600 Jackson St.
Seattle, WA 98144
323-3070
Owner: Chris Bennett
The Medium, published weekly, is more of a straight, objective newspaper, with breaking news and features, than *The Facts*. But community leaders say you have to know somebody to get your issue or event covered. Bennett is a leader in the community and is active nationally in African American media affairs. *The Medium*'s sister publications, also owned by Bennett, are the

Tacoma True Citizen and the *Portland Medium*.

Seattle Skanner
P.O. Box 12770
Seattle, WA 98101-2604
233-9888
Editor: Bobbie Foster
Publisher: Bernie Foster
The *Skanner*, published weekly, has more of a business and professionals emphasis than the others.

Radio stations
KRIZ 1420-AM Seattle
KZIZ 1516-AM Tacoma
The only black-owned radio station in Seattle, KRIZ is an "urban station," offering soul music, news, and features about the African American community. Every Monday–Friday morning from 7am to 8am there's a community talk show with guests, and Sunday is all-day gospel-music programming.

Events
Martin Luther King Day Rally, January 15.
Festival Sundiata, Seattle Center. Takes place during February. Black History Month.
Black History Month programs, throughout the city during February.
Black Community Festival, the oldest cultural event in Seattle's African American community. Three days of carnival rides, concession booths, and candidate handshaking at Judkins Park; includes a Mardi Gras parade the last Saturday of July. Takes place during Seafair; some say it was the precursor to Seafair.
ROOTS (Relatives of Old-Timers) picnic is an annual gathering for pioneer families of the black community at Gas Works Park, usually in September.
Annual coat drive, sponsored by *The Medium* and KRIZ in October, just before the cold weather. One year 4,000 coats were donated to the city's needy.
Thanksgiving food drive, sponsored by KRIZ.

Kwanzaa, African celebration held December 26–31 at various locations in the Central Area.

THE AMERICAN INDIAN COMMUNITY

Seattle's first inhabitants recognized the region as a livable place long before the white settlers arrived in the 1850s. They had large cedar longhouses along the waterfront, and ate berries, grains, and the gifts from the sea: clams, salmon, and other fish. The Northwest Coast Indians were distinguished by their highly developed woodworking skills, an orientation toward the water, and an attention to wealth and status. These Seattle natives were basically pacifist. There were variations among the tribes, especially in language.

The Duwamish tribe lived where Seattle is now. The Suquamish were their neighbors to the north and west, and Chief Sealth, Seattle's namesake, was a leader of both tribes. The Indians welcomed the white settlers initially, and eventually were coerced into selling about 2 million acres of land, reservation sites, and the right to hunt and fish in their traditional sites for $150,000. Seattle-area Indians moved to Pierce and Kitsap counties. After a long, drawn-out treaty dispute, U.S. courts ruled in the 1970s that Indians may take half the yearly salmon catch in Northwest waters.

Once a depressed and disenfranchised people, Seattle Indians have in the last two decades revived pride in their culture. They have started schools and health care programs consistent with their culture, demanded treaty rights, and started to solve economic problems resulting from discrimination. The Seattle Indian community has a reputation for being creative and innovative in developing unique service delivery systems (such as the Department of Social

and Health Services Indian Unit, and the Indian Health Board).

According to U.S. Census Bureau estimates, there are 7,326 American Indians living in Seattle. People in agencies working with this population say the number is actually much higher than that.

Names to know

Letoy Eike, UW counseling center, 685-3456.
Adeline Garcia, member of the Seattle Indian Health Board.
Bernie Whitebear, director of United Indians of All Tribes.

Resources

American Indian Heritage School & Program (Seattle School District)
1330 N 90th
Seattle, WA 98103
298-7895
This unusual commitment on the part of the school district includes an alternative school primarily for American Indian students, but open to anyone who wants to learn about American Indians.

American Indian Women's Service League
113 Cherry St.
Seattle, WA 98104
621-0655
A longtime group whose main activity today is running an arts and crafts co-op gallery here in the old Broderick Building. Profits go to scholarships for American Indians.

Duwamish Tribe
212 Wells Ave. S, Suite 3
Renton, WA 98055
Tribal chairwoman: Cecile Maxwell, 226-5185

Muckleshoot Group Home
39015 172nd Ave. SE
Auburn, WA 98002
939-3311
Director: Terri Negri

Seattle Indian Center
Leschi Center
611 12th Ave. S, Suite 300
Seattle, WA 98144
329-8700
Director: Camille Monzon

Main provider of social services to the American Indian population. Low-income housing for Indian elders adjacent to the center.

Seattle Indian Health Board
Leschi Center
611 12th Ave. S, Suite 300
Seattle, WA 98144
324-9360
A full-fledged clinic, said to be the largest off-reservation health care facility for American Indians in the country. The Health Board also operates the Thunderbird Alcohol/Drug Treatment Center, 9236 Renton S, 722-7152.

United Indians of All Tribes (UIAT)
Director: Bernie Whitebear
Youth program director: Adrain Verzola
Provides educational, cultural, heritage, and some social service programs for American Indians.

• *Administrative Office*
Daybreak Star Arts and Cultural Center
Discovery Park
P.O. Box 99100
Seattle, WA 98199
285-4425
Head Start preschool and kindergarten classes are housed here. So is the Sacred Circle art gallery.

• *Pioneer Square Office*
102 Prefontaine Pl. S
Seattle, WA 98104
343-3111
Houses an outreach program for American Indian dropouts, street kids, and kids involved in the juvenile court system. It has a substance abuse and prevention program, tutoring, psychological evaluations, and counseling.

• *Lake Union Office*
1945 Yale Pl. E
Seattle, WA 98102
325-0070
Offers employment and family counseling services and a GED program. The *Daybreak Star Reader* is published here.

(CONTINUED ON PAGE 198)

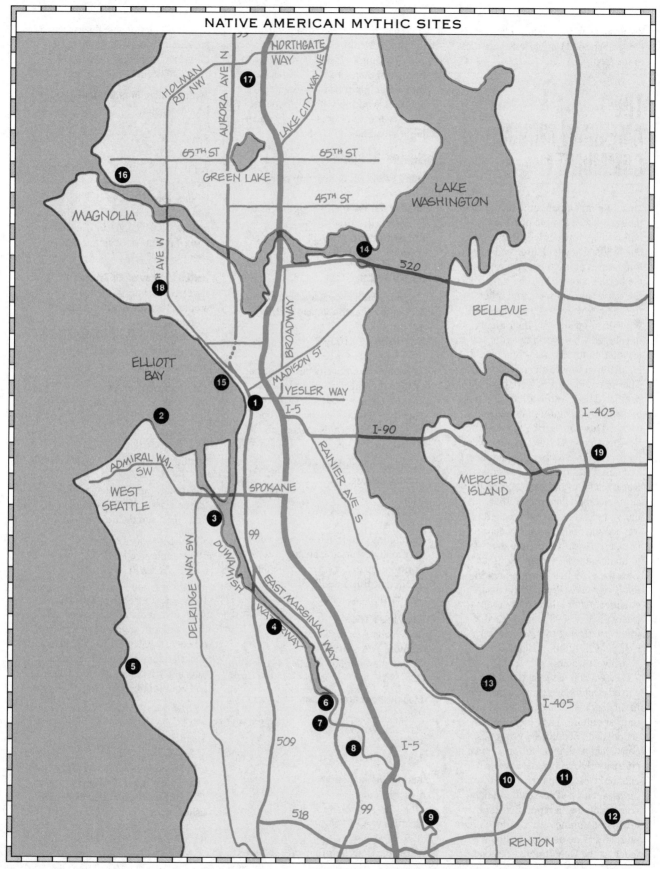

NATIVE AMERICAN MYTHIC SITES

Map key to notable Native American sites

Traces of Native American history can still be found in Seattle today, though many sacred sites have been paved over or otherwise used by the white newcomers for their own benefit.

1. Jijila'lich, "little crossing place." A native village existed at the current site of Pioneer Square, or, to be more precise, 20 feet below the current streets. A bust of Chief Seattle is, appropriately enough, prominent in the Square today.

2. Skwuduks, "below the point." At an Indian clamming beach and campsite just east of Duwamish Head, near the West Seattle boat ramp, Seattle's pioneers first met Chief Seattle in 1851.

3. Tola'ltu, "herring's house." Another native village site and the location of a large potlatch house. Part of the village site has been recently excavated by archaeologists.

4. Hucha'chee, "hand cut in two." A potent supernatural site on the Duwamish River near the South Park district. Legends tell of mutilated hands that rose from the river here and terrified passers-by, and of fighting giants who were turned into trees at the end of the mythic age, but who persisted in hurling fire at one another.

5. Psaiya'hus, "where there is an aya'hos." A supernatural site on the beach at Fauntleroy Cove south of the Vashon ferry dock, where a reddish beach was once thought to be an aya'hos, a horn-headed serpent believed to cause earthquakes and avalanches. The place may be the site of a buried village similar to Ozette on the Olympic Peninsula.

6. Kula'had, "the barrier." On the Duwamish River, near where the bridge crosses the river next to the old Duwamish Drive-in Theatre. In Puget Salish myth, it was the site of the climactic struggle between the icy wind of the north and the warm, wet wind from the south that announced the return of the salmon. The stone remains of a mythic ice fish weir can still be seen on the east bank.

7. Sbabade'el, "the little mountain." The center of the world, a rocky hill on the west bank of the Duwamish, just south of the kula'had. This is where the drama of creation, described in Duwamish mythology, was played out.

8. Skwoo'lach, "dirty face." Hill that was the weeping face of the Grandmother at Riverton. Maiden, Mother, and Hag are manifestations of the fertile earth in Puget Salish folklore, and the hill at Riverton was one of the more remarkable images of the nurturing Mother/Grandmother. Here, Duwamish Indians performed rituals designed to hurry the warm rains of spring.

9. Swawatee'htud, "earth beings." A race of supernatural dwarfs were believed to inhabit this hill near Longacres. Setting of an extraordinary melange of myths and legends.

10. Skate'lbsh, "where Skaitaw is." The lair of a powerful supernatural wealth-giving being that lived in a hole in the bottom of the now-vanished Black River in Renton.

11. The Mount Olivet Pioneer Cemetery. Here is the grave of William, the great chief of the Duwamish, and of Henry Moses, the last of a noble lineage of the Duwamish and a relative of Chief Seattle.

12. Su-whee'-whee-wud, "whistling place." The community of Eliot on the Cedar River, two miles east of Renton. The site of an important trade mart where people from as far away as British Columbia and Alaska traded slaves and copper for foodstuffs from the Columbia Plateau east of the Cascades.

13. Ha'chu, "the lake." In myth, Lake Washington appears as a great swallowing monster that consumes Mercer Island, its heart, each night and yields it up each morning to daylight.

14. Stetee'chee, "little island." Foster Island, at the north end of the Arboretum, was used as a burial ground for the people of Union Bay, the most powerful and numerous group on Lake Washington. The dead were placed in boxes that were hoisted into the trees.

15. Sh-chapau, "subterranean passage." On the shore of Elliott Bay beneath the present Seattle Aquarium was a mythical entryway to an underground stream that allowed whales to enter Lake Union.

16. Bitida'k, "spirit-canoe power." This supernatural being, which enable shamans to undertake the journey to the land of the dead, was believed to haunt a small stream in Ballard. A dance house was located there, just east of the village of Du Shi'l Shol, at the present site of the Hiram M. Chittenden Locks.

17. Liu'ktid, "colored." Reddish ooze still flows from Licton Springs in north Seattle, at about N 97th Street and Ashworth Avenue N, where shamans gathered mud for pigment to paint their paraphernalia.

18. Interbay. At two points on the slopes of Magnolia Bluff and Queen Anne Hill above Interbay, shell middens were found, denoting camps in which people hid to escape slaving parties coming down from Vancouver Island.

19. Sa'tsakal, "head of the slough." A village site near the modern community of Factoria, along 18th Avenue SE just west of the Factoria Interchange, was where hostile forces gathered to attack the fledgling community of Seattle in January 1856.

Source: David Buerge

Media

Daybreak Star Reader
1945 Yale Pl. E
Seattle, WA 98102
325-0070
Monthly publication for American Indian youth.

Events

Spring pow-wow, sponsored by the UW and the American Indian Student Commission.
Summer pow-wow, sponsored by the UIAT, during Seafair Days in July.
Chief Seattle Days, Suquamish. Across the water, the Suquamish Tribe puts on a weekend fest of canoe races, dances, and great food. It's usually held in mid-August. Call the tribe at (360) 598-3311.

THE ASIAN COMMUNITY

San Francisco's Chinatown doesn't hold a candle to Seattle's International District (ID), at least according to the ID's leaders. The reason? Our ID's residents are politically savvy, involved, and plugged into the powers that be in the city. They are a cohesive force with representatives in all leadership groups in the city and state.

The result is good health clinics, nutrition programs, child care centers, and the ownership of the Bush Hotel and other buildings by the Chinatown International District Preservation and Development Authority.

The community has been drawn together over the issue of Asian gangs, which the Seattle Police Department says number 45, with a total of 1,500 to 2,000 members. At the behest of city council members Cheryl Chow and Martha Choe and an active community group, the city has been trying to come up with programs—such as employment opportunities, a multilingual Little City Hall, and a late-night rec program—to combat the problem.

For specific information about each of Seattle's Asian communities, see the sections later in this chapter on the Chinese, Filipino, Japanese, Korean, Samoan, and Southeast Asian communities.

Elected names to know

Martha Choe, city councilwoman, 684-8802.
Cheryl Chow, city councilwoman, 684-8804.
Gary Locke, King County Executive, 296-4040.
Al Sugiyama, Seattle School Board member, 322-9080.

Resources

Asian American Journalist Association (Seattle Chapter)
333 Dexter Ave. N (KING-TV)
Seattle, WA 98109
448-3853
Contact: Lori Matsukawa
Encourages Asian Americans to enter journalism and promotes affirmative action in hiring and internships.

Asian Counseling and Referral Service
1032 S Jackson St., Suite 200
Seattle, WA 98104
461-3606
This United Way agency administers all kinds of social services to elderly and mentally ill Asians, Samoans, and Pacific Islanders.

Asian Pacific Women's Caucus
112 Fifth Ave. N
Seattle, WA 98109
722-3339
Contact: Vera Ing
Community organization founded in 1977 to deal with issues affecting Asian women.

Chinatown International District Preservation and Development Authority
409 Maynard Ave. S
Seattle, WA 98104
624-8929
Director: Sue Taoka
Low-income housing community development agency.

Commission on Asian American Affairs
501 S Jackson, Suite 301
Seattle, WA 98104
464-5820
State agency that advises the governor's office on Asian issues such as bilingual education and affirmative action.

Demonstration Project for Asian Americans
810 18th Ave., Room 201
Seattle, WA 98122
322-0203
Contact: Dorothy Cordova
Interpreters; demographic information on Asian Americans in Seattle and King County.

Interim
409 Maynard Ave. S
Seattle, WA 98104
624-1802
Community service organization.

International Drop-In Center
409 Maynard Ave. S
Seattle, WA 98104
587-3735
Director: Zenaida Guerzon
Recreation for senior Asians and other ethnic groups. Social service information center.

Kin On Nursing Home
1700 24th Ave. S
Seattle, WA 98144
322-0080

Northwest Asian-American Theatre
409 Seventh Ave. S
Seattle, WA 98104
340-1445
Artistic director: Judi Nihei

Wing Luke Asian Museum
407 Seventh Ave. S
Seattle, WA 98104
623-5124

Media

International Examiner
622 S Washington St.
Seattle, WA 98104
624-3925
Pan-Asian newspaper, published twice a month.

Street fair
Sponsored by Interim, a community service organization, usually in mid-July, in the International District between Maynard and King streets.

THE BRITISH COMMUNITY

Caledonian and St. Andrew's Society (Scotch)
P.O. Box 2727B
Seattle, WA 98125
284-1094
First Vice President: Ken Munro

Club Britannia
Contacts: Ethel Bull, 363-6189, and Eva Murphy, 938-3461

Daughters of British Empire
(206) 862-6599
Contact: Marie Collins

English Speaking Union of USA
362-8330
Contact: Mary Grace Schroeder

Misty City Morris
c/o Liz Dreisbach
6312 30th Ave. NW
Seattle, WA 98107
783-7639
Twenty-three–person morris dance team.

Mossyback Morris Men
Jim Rymsza
6823 30th Ave. NE
Seattle, WA 98118
526-0707
Morris dance instruction and performances.

THE CHINESE COMMUNITY

The Chinese came to the West Coast in 1849 for the gold, then to the Northwest for that gold measured in board feet: logs. Seattle's original Chinese settlement was on the tideflats south of Yesler.

Old-timers remember the huge dragon that wound through the International District during that neighborhood's Seafair parade. But sadly, the dragon slipped into the cave of a damp building and deteriorated over the years. Thanks to Kaohsiung, Seattle's sister city in Taiwan, a new one has proudly taken over.

When the 1882 Chinese Exclusion Act was passed to stop Chinese immigration, a group called the "Home Guard" fought to stop the Chinese from being forced out of the city. It was a bloody battle, but today the Chinese community in the Seattle area is large—about 35,000—and very active.

For years the community quietly took care of its own, but with population growth and now fourth-generation Chinese Americans coming along, it has achieved more of a presence in the mainstream—especially in the political and business arenas. There was a time 20 to 30 years ago when Chinese people could get jobs only in the laundry, grocery, or restaurant businesses; today there are Chinese American professional business organizations. But there are still few law-firm partners from the Chinese community, and fewer still Chinese politicians on the national level. As the younger generation learns to be more aggressive than its ancestors, that situation should change, community leaders say.

Family associations, benevolent societies, and tongs (social clubs) are still important elements in Seattle's Chinatown. The family associations, based on surname and ancestral origins, used to be a sort of city council of the community, but they no longer have the same influence. The benevolent societies are traditionally strong community support associations. Though active in these groups to some extent, younger people have also formed their own groups that are more geared to the world outside the immediate community.

Resources
For additional resources, see "The Asian Community" earlier in this chapter.

Chinese Information and Service Center
409 Maynard Ave. S, Room 203
Seattle, WA 98104
624-4062
Director: Daisy Lau-Leung
Provides language, advocacy, and other social services to the Asian elderly and new immigrants. Outreach group.

Chong Wa Benevolent Association
522 Seventh Ave. S
Seattle, WA 98104
623-2527
Provides service to the Chinese community.

Media

Chinese Post/NW Asian Weekly
414 Eighth Ave. S
Seattle, WA 98104
223-0623
Publisher: Assunta Ng
Editor: Deni Luna
Publisher Assunta Ng knows all about the International District. The *Post* is the only Asian legal newspaper and the only bilingual Asian paper in Washington state.

The World Journal
610 Maynard Ave. S
Seattle, WA 98104
682-8882

Events

Chinese New Year. Based on the lunar calendar, and celebrated by a parade and dinner, both open to the public.

Family associations have their own New Year's dinners.

Seafair Chinatown Parade, in late July.

THE FILIPINO COMMUNITY

The first Filipino in the state came to work at a sawmill on Bainbridge Island in 1883. Today the Filipino community constitutes the largest ethnic group among Asian/Pacific Americans in the nation. The term "Pinoy" refers to Filipino American males, "Pinay" to women (in the Philippines, it is sometimes used derogatorily). The community is growing in Seattle: in 1990, there were

16,223 Filipinos in the city compared to 9,510 in 1980—an increase of 41.4%—and the community is now larger than either the Chinese or Japanese communities citywide.

The Filipino community once centered near Immaculate Conception Catholic Church on 18th Avenue. Everybody knew everybody else and the power base was easy to trace. But with the high rate of immigration during the Marcos years, the old power base exists no longer.

The main issue for the local community is the animosity between the recent immigrants and the old-time community. One problem is that the newcomers speak one of the several dialects of the Philippines, and there are biases against those who speak a different dialect. There's even more

bias against those old-timers who have been in the U.S. for at least one generation who don't speak any of the dialects. For the community as a whole, English has become the common language, like it or not.

The newcomers see themselves as bringing progressive thinking to the community; the old-timers see the newcomers as snobbish and as rejecting their culture as soon as they get here in favor of materialistic values.

These subcultures within the community cause divisiveness, but attempts are being made to hold seminars with representatives from all the groups to talk about unity and political assertion.

While factionalism is the main issue, an equally important issue is education. The Filipino youth dropout rate hovers around 12% and of those who graduate, few plan to go on to college. "The kids," sighs one Filipino leader, "want immediate gratification."

As with other Asian youth, Filipino gangs have been a problem (there are still "barcadas," social groups of young people), but some say they aren't as violent as they once were.

Resources

You really need to know only one address to track Filipino affairs: 810 18th Avenue. In the old Immaculate School building there are more activities being juggled than there are commands for the famed Khordobah drill team. (It's not a big leap for the people working there; quite a few were students there in the old days and simply traded their student desks for business furniture. The blackboards are still present, as are the statues in the hallway.)

For additional resources, see "The Asian Community" earlier in this chapter.

Cabataan Folk Dancers
810 18th Ave.
Seattle, WA 98122
461-4870
A folk dance troupe for ages 2 through 19. Performs throughout Seattle.

Filipino American Citizens League
3434 Cascadia Ave. S
Seattle, WA 98144
Director: Sam Buyco, 722-0860

Filipino American National Historical Society
810 18th Ave., Room 202
Seattle, WA 98122
322-0203
Contact: Dorothy Cordova

Filipino Community of Seattle
5740 Martin Luther King Way S
Seattle, WA 98118
722-9372
President: Dr. Camillo de Guzman

Filipino Youth Activities (FYA)
810 18th Ave.
Seattle, WA 98122
461-4870

Director: John Ragudos
Provides outreach, job assistance, legal assistance, crisis intervention, liaison with school districts, and recreational activities for young people. Also houses an extensive Filipino library.

Khordobah Drill Team
810 18th Ave.
Seattle, WA 98122
461-4870
The Filipino Youth Activities agency sponsors this well-known drill team for children 9 to 19 years old. The team keeps from 65 to 125 kids busy practicing, traveling, and performing. They practice four hours every Saturday and perform in ethnic dress. Commands are given in Filipino dialects.

Media

Filipino-American Herald
2824 S Brandon St.
Seattle, WA 98108
725-6606
Editor: Emiliano Francisco
Oldest Filipino paper in the city, published monthly.

Events

Pista Sa Nayon ("Feast in Town"),
initiated by King County Councilman Ron Sims as a way to involve the Filipino community in Seafair. Sixty organizations from the community join in staging a street fair at Rainier Playfield including arts and crafts, food, and folk dancing. It's held in late July/early August.

THE GERMANS FROM RUSSIA COMMUNITY

American Historical Society of Germans from Russia, Greater Seattle Chapter
17767 14th Ave. NW
Seattle, WA 98177
542-8049
Group founded in 1968 to actively research the history of all Germans

from Russia in the Seattle area. Now has about 200 members.

THE GREEK COMMUNITY

The Greek Orthodox Church is the center of social life in Seattle's Hellenic community. The two main churches are St. Demetrios (2100 Boyer Avenue E) and the Church of the Assumption (1804 13th Street). Each has an annual festival featuring Greek food, dance, and music lasting several days—St. Demetrios in October and the Church of the Assumption in May. By unofficial (and probably high) estimate, there are 10,000 people of Greek descent in the Seattle area.

Resources

Daughters of Penelope
3704 Belvidere Ave. SW
Seattle, WA 98126
935-4688
Contact: Anna Rakus
The women's auxiliary to the Order of AHEPA. For high-school–age youth, there are two groups: Maids of Athena and Sons of Pericles.

Greek American Progressive Association
2825 W Jameson
Seattle, WA 98199
283-0286
Fraternal organization to preserve Greek language and social life for Hellenic community.

Order of AHEPA
American Hellenic Educational Progressive Association
313 NW 200th
Seattle, WA 98177
District governor: George Maroutsas, 542-3788
A nationwide men's group that promotes Hellenic culture and social ideals. You don't have to be Greek to join, but most are.

St. Demetrios Church Greek Language School and Dance Groups
2100 Boyer Ave. E
Seattle, WA 98112
325-4347
Language school for adults and children of Greek and non-Greek descent. Several groups for different ages and abilities perform dances for festivals and events.

THE HUNGARIAN COMMUNITY

Hungarian American Association of Washington
P.O. Box 84425
Seattle, WA 98124-5725
340-0706
Group of approximately 1,500 Hungarians; offers a language and folk dance school for children and adults, plus picnics and celebrations throughout the year.

THE IRISH COMMUNITY

If you think of pubs and a pint of Guinness when you think of Ireland, take note. According to an unofficial poll of true Irishmen, Kells in the Market has the most authentic kidney stew, while Murphy's Pub in Wallingford is supposedly the most genuine Irish watering hole in Seattle.

The Irish were a major presence in the early days of Seattle. The president of the Irish Heritage Club cites old land-claim records dating from 1852 that indicate that 1 in 12 settlers here were originally from Ireland. Like good Irish everywhere, they were natural politicians. Their descendants include U.S. Representative Jim McDermott and former governor John Spellman.

Resources

Irish Heritage Club
17043 Northup Way
Bellevue, WA 98008
865-9134
This 300-member club publishes a newsletter called *The Seanachie* and, among other services, can give you information about local Irish dancing and bagpiping groups.

Language Classes
547-2029
Tony Kavanaugh teaches classes in Gaelic, still the everyday language for many Irish citizens. Classes are popular with non-Irish as well.

Society of the Friendly Sons of St. Patrick
123 Third Ave. S
Seattle, WA 98104
623-5311
A men-only fraternal organization. The Seattle group is relatively new, but George Washington was one of the original founders of the society in this country. The Seattle members put on a big St. Patrick's Day banquet, which is the only time the society meets.

Events

Irish Week Festival, complete with St. Patrick's Day parade downtown and the laying of the John Doyle Bishop memorial green stripe along Fourth Avenue.
Annual summer picnic, where the local Gaelic football team competes against teams from California and Canada. (Similar to soccer, Gaelic football was banned in Ireland by the English in the 1500s because it was so very—Irish.)

THE ITALIAN COMMUNITY

Italian labor helped rebuild Seattle after the city burned down in 1889. Some early-day Italian immigrants were contractors; others were the bricklayers, masons, and skilled and unskilled laborers who built the streets, highways, and water and sewer systems of the city. They also worked on the railroads and in the mines.

In the early 1900s many Italians had truck farms in south Seattle, the area from Spokane Street to the Kent Valley. Until the Filipinos came along in 1929, the Italians were the major greengrocers at the Pike Place Market. Today there are about 106,000 Italians in Washington State.

Resources

Dante Alighieri Society
P.O. Box 80563
Seattle, WA 98108
762-6092
The local office of a worldwide organization formed to promulgate Italian culture, the society has a language school and a Montessori school for children. It meets twice a month for Italian programs, films, music, etc.

Sons of Italy Grand Lodge of the Northwest
8201 Third Ave. NW
Seattle, WA 98117
782-0824
State president: Eugene Mancini
This is the headquarters for the statewide group as well as the Seattle lodge, which numbers about 900 members; there is also a lodge in Bellevue. The Sons sponsor lots of social events and an annual Wine Festival.

Events

Festa Italia, held around Columbus Day; usually a weeklong celebration with events at Seattle Center and a bike race around Seward Park.

THE JAPANESE COMMUNITY

Early on, Japanese Americans operated many small farms in what is now Seattle and its suburbs; for years Japanese truck farmers were one of the largest groups of vendors at the Pike Place Market.

During World War II, Seattle's Japanese were sent to internment camps, primarily in California and Idaho, and many lost their land and assets. When they returned after the war, things were different. Where there had once been an identifiable "Japantown" cluster of shops and offices along Main Street and north of Jackson, there were now non-Japanese businesses. And there was no welcome home for the internees; they weren't wanted in the central city.

Many Japanese Americans settled on Beacon Hill and in the Rainier Valley, but they never established a central neighborhood again. Today many of Seattle's Japanese are moving out of the city and into the suburbs for education and job opportunities. There are about 20,000 Japanese Americans living in Seattle itself. If there is a hub to the community, it's probably Uwajimaya, and if there is a nominal leader, it's Akira Moriguchi, president of that incredibly successful Asian department store.

Two main issues drive the city's Japanese Americans today. The first is making sure that those eligible for redress from the government for internment receive their money. The second has to do with Japan-bashing because of the trade imbalance between that country and the U.S. In a familiar refrain, says one community member, the white community is having a hard time distinguishing Japanese Americans from "Japan Japanese," and is blaming the nisei and sansei here for taking over businesses in the United States even though many have never even been to Japan.

What's in a name? Plenty, if you're a member of Seattle's Japanese American community. You can hardly talk about the community without using the terms for different generations.

- **Issei: first-generation Japanese, born in Japan, now in the U.S.**
- **Kibei: born in Japan, living in the U.S., but returned to Japan at some point for education**
- **Nisei: U.S.-born children of issei**
- **Sansei: children of nisei**
- **Yonsei: fourth-generation children**
- **Gosei: fifth-generation children**

Resources

For additional resources, see "The Asian Community" earlier in this chapter.

Japan Shumy and Culture Society Dance Group
1724 S Hanford St.
Seattle, WA 98144
329-8769
Contact: Sayoko Boole
Adults perform Japanese folk dances in costume for cultural shows.

Japanese American Citizens League
District Office
671 S Jackson St., Suite 206
Seattle, WA 98104
623-5088
NW district director: Karen Yoshitomi
Regional director: Terry Yamada

Japanese American Citizens League (JACL)
Seattle Chapter
316 Maynard S
Seattle, WA 98104
622-4098
President: Elaine Akagi
JACL is considered the most active civil rights organization for Asians in the country, and the Seattle chapter is no slouch when it comes to radical moves. The movement for redress for interned Japanese Americans began in Seattle, as did the move to give aliens the right to own property and the move to rescind Executive Order 9066 (the internment order). Redress—making sure those eligible for funds get them— is still an issue for JACL, as are civil rights and leadership concerns. Seattle's JACL includes Doshi, a group of young sanseis, ages 25 to 45, who are beginning to get involved, and Tomono Kai, a social support group of widows and widowers. The chapter has 650 members.

Japanese Community Service
1414 S Weller St.
Seattle, WA 98144
323-0250
Assists visitors to America from Japan; provides leadership and fund-raising support to Japanese Language School; presents New Year's festivities. Has 350–400 members.

Japanese Garden Society
1819 129th Pl. SE
Bellevue, WA 98005
784-4209
Preserves and promotes the Japanese Tea Garden in the Arboretum.

Japanese Language School
1414 S Weller St.
Seattle, WA 98144
323-0250
Saturday schooling in culture and language for anyone interested.

Nikkei Concerns
1601 E Yesler Way
Seattle, WA 98122
323-7100
Umbrella organization that runs Seattle Keiro Nursing Home at this site and Kokoro-Kai, an adult day pro-

gram for Japanese elders at the Japanese Presbyterian Church.

Nisei Veteran Committee
1212 S King St.
Seattle, WA 98144
322-1122
Nutrition and social services for vets. Meiji Kai, a senior citizen center for Japanese, is also located in this building, affectionately called "Vets' Hall."

Seattle Japanese School
1408 140th Pl. NE
Bellevue, WA 98007
643-1661
Eastside school for children of Japanese businessmen living in Seattle temporarily. A way for the children to maintain ties to Japan's culture and education.

Media

North American Post
661½ S Jackson St.
Seattle, WA 98104
623-0100
Editor: Atiko Kusunose
The region's only Japanese-language newspaper, established in 1946 and published three times a week. (Henry T. Kubota, who arrived in Seattle from Japan in the early 1920s at age 21, was publisher for 30 years. He died in November 1989, on the day Congress approved reparation payments to West Coast Japanese.)

NW Nikkei
P.O. Box 3173
Seattle, WA 98114
624-4169
Editor: Sandee Taniguchi
A monthly newspaper started in 1989, owned by the *North American Post,* written in English for Japanese Americans.

Events
Cherry Blossom Festival, held in May.
Bon Odori, a festival of folk dances and foods, traditional costumes, and parades. It happens in July or August during Seafair, and is sponsored by the Seattle Buddhist Church.

THE JEWISH COMMUNITY

Seattle has a growing and very active Jewish community, traditionally centered in the Seward Park area and on Mercer Island, though that is less true today than in the past. The community has Northwest Yeshiva High School, the only Jewish secondary school north of Los Angeles and west of Denver. For younger children, the long-established Seattle Hebrew Academy still thrives, as does the Bellevue Jewish Day School.

To find out about local Jewish groups, visit the Jewish Federation of Greater Seattle. They have everything from a newspaper to a library and historical society.

Resources

American Jewish Committee
Joseph Vance Bldg., Suite 1414
1402 Third Ave.
Seattle, WA 98101
622-6315
Human relations agency since 1906.

B'nai B'rith
Greater Seattle, Unit #3003
2031 Third Ave., Suite 400
Seattle, WA 98121
441-3543
Local chapter of largest Jewish organization in the world.

Jewish Community Center
3801 E Mercer Way
Mercer Island, WA 98040
232-7115
Wide variety of religious, cultural, educational, and social events; also houses a Jewish theater.

Jewish Family Service
1601 16th Ave.
Seattle, WA 98122
461-3240
Social services, youth programs.

Jewish Federation of Greater Seattle
2031 Third Ave. #200
Seattle, WA 98121-2418
443-5400
Director: Michael Novick
Central organization for Seattle Jewish community, acting on public policy issues and serving as a sort of Jewish United Way.

Media

The Jewish Transcript
2031 Third Ave.
Seattle, WA 98121-2418
441-4553
Editor: Craig Degginger
A twice-monthly community newspaper.

Events

Community Hanukkah celebration, held each December at Jewish Community Center.

Jewish Film Festival, December 7 to 15, sponsored by the American Jewish Committee.

THE KOREAN COMMUNITY

The Korean Association of Washington estimates there are 30,000 Koreans living in King, Snohomish, and Pierce counties. About a third live in the Federal Way area. Assimilation has been swift, considering that Koreans began immigrating here in large numbers only following the Korean War. The Koreans have been very successful in small businesses such as the prototypical mom-and-pop grocery store or dry cleaner. (Grocers and dry cleaners have the largest representation in the Washington State Korean Chamber of Commerce.)

The Korean community in Seattle retains a strong sense of identity, fostered in the Korean schools (where schoolchildren take weekend classes in Korean culture, history, language, and manners) and in the churches.

Resources

For additional resources, see "The Asian Community" earlier in this chapter.

Korean Association of Washington State, Seattle Branch
1200 S Angelo St.
Seattle, WA 98108
767-8071
Executive director: Jung Ho Kim
Umbrella organization representing Koreans. It also sponsors the Seattle Korean School. Publishes a hefty phone directory listing Korean individuals and Korean-oriented agencies. The association hopes to become more politically active by registering voters and getting out the vote in the

Korean community. The statewide Korean Chamber of Commerce is also headquartered here, 241-1525.

Korean Counseling Center
302 N 78th St.
Seattle, WA 98103
784-5691
A nonprofit organization sited at Woodland Park United Methodist Church, providing after-school children's programs, parenting classes, interpretation and translation services, and legal and chemical-dependency counseling.

Korean Identity Development Society
8315 Lake City Way NE, Suite 120
Seattle, WA 98125
340-0937
President: Michelle Marshal
Promotes cultural awareness in American families who have adopted Korean children, providing an educational program for kids and their parents and a summer camp. About 600 families are members.

Media

Korea Central Daily News, Northwest Edition
13749 Midvale Ave. N
Seattle, WA 98133
365-4000
Editor: Dong Lee
Published daily.

Korea Times, Northwest Edition
430 Yale Ave. N
Seattle, WA 98109
622-2229
Editor: Song Hong
Published daily except Sunday. Also publishes a directory of Korean businesses.

Korean Journal
33110 Pacific Hwy S, Bldg. 4
Suite 4
Federal Way, WA 98003
661-1767
Published weekly.

THE LATINO, CHICANO, AND MEXICANO COMMUNITIES

If you speak Spanish and live in Seattle, you'll most likely be referred to by Anglos as Hispanic. But that's not really accurate. Here's the rundown:

- Latinos: from Central and South America
- Mexicanos: first-generation Mexican Americans
- Chicanos: second-generation Mexican Americans
- Hispanic: a word no longer favored

There are several different factions within the Latino community. Though the Spanish-speaking population in Seattle reaches almost 20,000, it does not have the cohesiveness and sense of identity that make well-established Chicano groups in the Southwest potent political forces. Recently there's been an effort to pull the various elements together in a new political coalition representing Chicano/Latino interests. The hope, according to some, is to "be as well organized as the black community" in Seattle.

Names to know

Roberto Maestas, longtime respected executive director of El Centro de la Raza.
Yolanda Martinez, director of the city's neighborhood office in Lake City.

Resources

Concilio for the Spanish Speaking of King County
157 Yesler Way, Suite 400
Seattle, WA 98104
461-4891
Umbrella organization founded in the 1970s as an advocate for Spanish-speaking groups. Was very political, now less active. Publishes *La Voz*.

Consejo Counseling and Referral Service

3808 S Angeline St.
Seattle, WA 98118
461-4880
Director: Dr. John Corey
The only mental health agency in Western Washington specifically for the Spanish-speaking population. Has contract with King County to provide mental health services; also receives United Way funding. Has treatment programs for chemical dependency. Consejo treats more than 200 clients of all ages each month. Satellite office at the Sea-Mar Community Health Clinic.

El Centro de la Raza

2524 16th Ave. S
Seattle, WA 98144
329-9442
Contact: Joanne Apont
Executive director: Roberto Maestas
Founded in 1972 to serve Spanish-speaking people, the center is now reaching out to other poor ethnic minorities as well, developing a sort of all-purpose Third World "rainbow" look. Still highly political, it has an international relations department and takes stands on Central American and international issues. It operates many programs: educational (ESL classes), cultural, day care (Jose Marti Child Development Center), food bank, housing, meals, and other social services, as well as an art gallery.

Sea-Mar Community Health Clinic

8720 14th Ave. S
Seattle, WA 98108
762-3730
Director: Rogelio Riojas
The major primary health care clinic for the Spanish-speaking population.

Media

Hispanic News

236 SW 153rd
Burien, WA 98166
241-2906
Publisher: Pedro Cavazos
Weekly bilingual newspaper, begun in 1984.

La Voz

157 Yesler Way, Suite 400
Seattle, WA 98104
461-4891
Editor: Raquel Orbegoso
Published 10 times a year by Concilio for the Spanish Speaking of King County.

Events

Cinco de Mayo, celebrating the defeat of the French occupation in Mexico, is a lesser event here (but big to Mexican restaurants).

Hispanic Seafair, held in July, is sponsored by the Concilio for the Spanish Speaking.

THE LATVIAN AND LITHUANIAN COMMUNITIES

Numerically these are minute ethnic groups in Seattle, but their sense of community is very strong, heightened no doubt by the drives for independence in their Baltic homelands. Most Lithuanians are Roman Catholic; many non-Russian Latvians are Lutherans.

There are approximately 100 Lithuanian families in Seattle, 70% of whom were born in the U.S., and an estimated 700 Latvian families in the Seattle/Tacoma area.

Resources

Latvian Association of Washington State

P.O. Box 75081
Seattle, WA 98125-0081
232-0984
President: Imants Ikstrums
Doubles as state and local headquarters.

Latvian Community Center

11710 Third Ave. NE
Seattle, WA 98125
362-9894
Also the location of the Latvian Evangelical Lutheran Church. All

important social, cultural, religious, and educational activities for the Latvian community take place here. There's a Saturday school for kids (culture, history, etc.), and a Latvian choir and dance group.

Lithuanian American Community, Inc.

3883 45th Ave. NE
Seattle, WA 98105
Seattle branch president: Ina Bertulyte Bray
The Seattle chapter of a national group involved in political as well as cultural and social activities.

THE NORDIC COMMUNITY

Seattle without Scandinavians would be like codfish without salt, lutefisk without aquavit. Scandinavians include Danes, Swedes, Finns, and Norwegians. And don't forget the Icelanders, the smallest Nordic community in Seattle. They had a small colony in Ballard around the turn of the century, and they had their own church, which is now called Calvary Lutheran Church. Then there are the Swede-Finns (Finns who speak Swedish).

Scandinavians from Norway and Sweden make up one of Seattle's largest ethnic communities. In case you're wondering why these immigrants flocked to Seattle, look around, especially at Puget Sound. Scandinavians already knew how to fish, log, build boats, and work in the shipping trade. The land and the resources were familiar, and the mild climate was an improvement over their homelands.

The Nordic immigrants settled primarily in Ballard, where many remain today, but their children and grandchildren can be found throughout the city. Scandinavians have become captains of industry, business, and politics here: the late U.S. senators Warren Magnuson and Henry "Scoop" Jackson; Ole Bardahl (Bardahl Manufacturing Corp.); the late Eddie Carlson (civic leader and former chief of United Airlines); and don't forget the Nordstrom family's retailing dynasty.

Several members of the state legislature are Scandies, including Seattle-area legislators Marlin Appelwick and Ken Jacobsen. The Viking crowd also founded some of Seattle's most venerable charitable organizations, such as the Millionair Club and the Lutheran Compass Mission.

The Nordic Heritage Museum in Ballard (the only museum in the United States that includes all five Scandinavian countries) helps keep Seattle's Nordic culture alive. The museum offers classes in Danish, Norwegian, Swedish, and Scandinavian handicrafts; it also has activities for children, and sponsors films, concerts, and art and historical exhibits.

Nordic Heritage Museum
3014 NW 67th St.
Seattle, WA 98117
789-5707
Director: Marianne Forssblad
Hours: 10am–4pm Tues.–Sat.; noon–4pm Sun. The museum publishes a booklet that lists all Nordic resources in the Northwest (Washington, Oregon, Idaho)—organizations, arts and crafts, speakers, university experts, consul staff, library holdings, etc.

Danish resources/media

Bien
1527 W Magnolia Blvd.
Burbank, CA 91506
(818) 845-7300
A weekly Danish newspaper available here.

Northwest Danish Foundation
1833 N 105th St., Suite 203
Seattle, WA 98133
523-3263
Publishes the *Little Mermaid* newsletter.

Finnish resources

Finlandia Foundation
17804 Third Ave. NE
Seattle, WA 98155
362-1869

Who gets the credit for inventing slimy lutefisk? The Norwegians (no one else wants it). According to a completely unofficial estimate, about 90,000 people of Norwegian descent live in Seattle and the surrounding region—and they all eat lutefisk! The annual Ballard Seafoodfest, held in late July as part of Seafair, features a lutefisk-eating contest; one year's winner downed 3½ pounds of the briny fish in under two minutes.

President: Fran Whitehill
The Seattle chapter of this group is the largest in the U.S. Mainly a social organization, but does charitable and cultural work as well. Regular newsletter.

Finnish American Chamber of Commerce
451-3983
President: Norman Westerberg
Small group that promotes business ties between Finland and the Pacific Northwest.

Icelandic resources

Icelandic Club of Greater Seattle
1826 Vernon Rd.
Lake Stevens, WA 98250
(206) 334-3763
President: Elias Langholt
Publishes a newsletter and offers social events celebrating major holidays such as Thorrablot (an ancient Icelandic winter festival) and Icelandic Independence Day in July.

Norwegian resources/media

Norwegian Commercial Club
Leif Erikson Hall
2245 NW 57th St.
Seattle, WA 98107
783-1274
President: Russ Oberg
Local businesspeople (fishing and shipping are big) of Norwegian descent. Meets twice monthly at Leif Erikson Hall.

Sons of Norway
Leif Erikson Hall
2245 NW 57th St.
Seattle, WA 98107
783-1274
The major Norwegian organization in Seattle, with about 2,000 members. The Ballard lodge is also the main gathering place for the Norwegian community.

Western Viking
2405 NW Market St.
Seattle, WA 98107
784-4617
Publisher/editor: Alf Knudsen
Weekly Norwegian-language newspaper published in Ballard. Includes listing of all local Norwegian groups and officers.

Swedish resources

Swedish Club
1920 Dexter Ave. N
Seattle, WA 98109
283-1090
Seattle's premier Swedish organization. There's a restaurant at the club and, before the high-rises started renting out their atriums and ballrooms, many a prom was danced away here. Meeting rooms too.

RUSSIAN AND UKRAINIAN COMMUNITIES

There are about 26,000 people from the former Soviet Union in the greater Seattle area, and as their homeland is racked with turmoil, their sense of community grows stronger. The hub is St. Spiridon Cathedral on Yale Avenue N, possibly the most distinctive church around with its blue-onion spires.

Resources

Russian Community Center & Hall
704 19th Ave. E
Seattle, WA 98112
323-3877
The center of social, cultural, and educational events, aside from the church.

THE SAMOAN COMMUNITY

One of the area's largest ethnic populations, the Samoan community numbers about 6,000 in the city; combined with Tacoma and Fort Lewis, it's closer to 10,000.

Older Samoans who were born in the Pacific Islands grew up in a culture where families formed the basic societal unit. The head of the family was king. Since that philosophy is not prevalent in the United States, some Samoans are having a hard time adjusting here.

The dropout rate among Samoan youth is close to 50%. The Seattle School District and a nonprofit group called Islanders Children and Youth Services provide an intervention program including tutoring, counseling, and after-school activities for at-risk Samoan students. Samoans and other Pacific Islander students number about 1,500 in the Seattle schools.

There's been a lot of press about Samoan gangs, and community leader Betty Patu has been a force behind pushing the city to provide resources for these kids.

Resources

For additional resources, see "The Asian Community" earlier in this chapter.

Islanders Children and Youth Services
8815 Seward Park Ave. S
Seattle, WA 98118
281-6529
Advisor: Betty Patu
Service organization that supports children and youth of the Pacific Islands.

Polynesian Intervention and Integration Services
281-6712

Events

Samoan Flag Day, in August, commemorates the signing of the treaty between the U.S. and Samoa in 1900.

THE SOUTHEAST ASIAN COMMUNITY

A flood of refugees from Southeast Asia came to the Seattle area between 1975 and 1980, most entering the country through the sponsorship of local churches. It's difficult to determine total population, but the census says Seattle has 5,309 Vietnamese alone, not to mention Laotians, Cambodians, and other nationalities. Families joining the original refugees have boosted the population.

The Laotians include the lowland Lao people as well as members of the highland tribes, Hmong, Mien, and Khmu. They all speak different languages. The Hmong people are accomplished textile artisans and have a stall in the Pike Place Market. It's estimated there are from 10,000 to 12,000 Laotians in the Seattle/King County area.

The Cambodians (Khmer) number 8,000 to 10,000.

The Vietnamese are the largest group of Southeast Asians; the unofficial population estimate for all of King County is 20,000.

Resources

For additional resources, see "The Asian Community" earlier in this chapter.

Indochinese Refugee Association
418 1/2 Eighth Ave. S
Seattle, WA 98104
625-9955

Vietnamese Buddhist Association of Washington
1651 S King St.
Seattle, WA 98144
323-2269

Vietnamese Catholic Community
Archdiocese of Seattle
1230 E Fir St.
Seattle, WA 98122
325-5626

THE WELSH COMMUNITY

Puget Sound Welsh Association
P.O. Box 19344
Seattle, WA 98109
President: Alan Upshall, 488-7288
Women's Club coordinator: Jackie Cedarholm, 282-5680
With about 1,000 names on the mailing list, this group coordinates Welsh cultural activities. Made up of Welsh Women's Club, Welsh Language Learners, and Seattle Welsh Choir. The choir sings a few impromptu hymns in the bar at La Fleur, a Sand Point restaurant, on Wednesday nights after rehearsal. It's also getting together a Welsh dance group to move to the tunes of the Red Dragon Band.

REFUGEE ASSISTANCE

The organizations listed below serve refugees of all nationalities. In addition, some ethnic communities sponsor organizations that help refugees from a specific ethnic group; they are listed in the section earlier in this chapter describing each community.

Eastside Multi-Ethnic Center
1811 156th Ave. NE
Bellevue, WA 98007
643-2221

Contact: Rudy Sanchez
Founded in 1982 for Southeast Asian refugees, the service center now helps refugees from all over the world. A million languages are spoken here, and the center provides all kinds of services (resettlement, housing, youth programs, etc.). Various Laotian, Cambodian, and Vietnamese organizations can be reached through the service center.

International Rescue Committee
318 First Ave. S, Room 210
Seattle, WA 98104
623-2105
Offers temporary housing assistance and other aid to refugees. Has resettled thousands of refugees from Southeast Asia, Central America, and Eastern Europe in the U.S. Local office of a worldwide organization originally founded to help people escape the Nazis.

Refugee Women's Alliance
3004 S Alaska St.
Seattle, WA 98108
721-0243
Group established in 1985 to help Southeast Asian refugee women establish self-sufficiency here. It has since widened its outreach to all refugee and immigrant women, including those from Eastern Europe. Sponsors classes in ESL, parenting, self-esteem, literacy, and employment awareness. Provides on-site child care. Also counsels residents of the nearby Rainier Vista housing project, helping them deal with family conflicts, violence, and health problems.

Washington Refugee Resettlement
464 12th Ave.
Seattle, WA 98122
322-0409
Helps find sponsors for refugees, mostly within churches. Some employment assistance for refugees who have been in the U.S. less than six months.

ENGLISH AS A SECOND LANGUAGE (ESL)

All three Seattle community colleges offer ESL classroom instruction and individualized tutoring. The following organizations also offer ESL classes.

Chinese Information/Service Center
409 Maynard Ave. S, Room 203
Seattle, WA 98104
624-5633
Beginning-level individual and small-group tutoring at the student's home or at the center. For all Asians.

El Centro de la Raza
2524 16th Ave. S
Seattle, WA 98144
323-6484
Beginning-level classroom instruction and individual tutoring for King County residents of color.

Employment Opportunities Center
4726 Rainier Ave. S
Seattle, WA 98118
725-8200
Free ESL classes.

Literacy Action Center
Greenwood Public Library
8016 Greenwood Ave. N
Seattle, WA 98103
782-2050
Free ESL conversation classes.

University of Washington
103 Lewis Hall
Seattle, WA 98195
543-6242
Individual on- or off-campus tutoring and campus classes for international students preparing to enter American colleges. Also for non-native speakers wishing to improve English skills. Fee required.

FOREIGN LANGUAGE RELIGIOUS SERVICES

Multilingual
First Slavic Full Gospel Church, Inc.
Ukrainian, Russian, and Polish:
783-0866

Specific languages
Arabic
Islamic Center, 363-3013

Cantonese
Chinese Baptist Church (American Baptist), 725-6363
Chinese Mission (Southern Baptist), 447-9529

Danish
St. John Lutheran Church, 784-1040 (Sunday before Christmas only)

Filipino
Cornerstone Baptist Church, 723-6211
Iglesia Ni Cristo, 723-0346
Seattle Filipino-American 7th Day Adventist Church, 767-7985

Finnish
Bethel Lutheran, 789-0864

German
German United Church of Christ, 325-7664

Greek
St. Demetrios Greek Orthodox Church, 325-4347

Hebrew
Bikur Cholim Machzikay Hadath, 721-0970
Congregation Ezra Bessaroth, 722-5500
Sephardic Bikur Holim, 723-3028

Japanese
Blaine Memorial United Methodist Church, 723-1536
Faith Bible Church, 322-8044
Japanese Baptist Church, 622-7351
Japanese Congregational Church, 325-4566
Japanese Presbyterian Church, 323-5990
Nichiren Buddhist Church, 323-2252
Seattle Buddhist Temple, 329-0800

Seattle Koyasan Church, 325-8811
Seward Park Seventh-Day Adventist
Church, 725-5253

Korean
Korean Community Presbyterian
Church, 547-7005
Korean United Presbyterian
Church, 367-5858

Latvian
Latvian Evangelical Lutheran
Church, 362-9894

Norwegian
Denny Park Lutheran Church,
623-7447 (Sept.–May, 2nd and 4th
Sundays)
Rock of Ages Lutheran, 783-4161
(twice a year)

Samoan
Samoan Community of Seattle,
725-7084

Spanish
Christ the King Catholic, 367-1136
Holy Family Catholic Church,
767-6220
Primera Iglesia Bautista Hispana,
241-8079
St. Mary's Catholic Church,
328-1613

Tongan
Rainier Beach United Methodist,
723-9700

Ukrainian
Ukrainian Orthodox Church,
524-3496

Vietnamese
Phien An Baptist Church, 935-4944
Vietnamese Alliance Church,
324-1865

Source: Church Council of Greater Seattle,
"Directory of Churches, Ministers and
Agencies," and Seattle Survival Guide re-
search

TRANSLATION HELP

Language Bank
American Red Cross
1900 25th Ave. S
Seattle, WA 98144
323-6565 x3203
Volunteer emergency service, 24

For those lost souls who don't
know their genealogy, there's hope.
The Pacific Northwest Regional
Archives, a branch of the U.S.
National Archives, 6125 Sand Point
Way NE, 526-6347, contains
thousands of microfilms of census
records for the years 1790–1910
for all states. The archives also has
Revolutionary War rolls, military
pension records, land records, tract
books, entries of settlers, and U.S.
District Court records. The other
thing that collects in the archives
is crowds: there's a full house of
ancestor-seekers daily. For that
reason, it's best to make an
appointment to do your research,
though walk-ins are welcome.
Volunteers and staff people are
on hand to guide you through your
own history.

hours a day. Offers written and oral
interpretation of 70 languages.

CONSULATES

Consulates represent their countries,
but they also offer services to Americans. For example, if you're planning
a visit to a foreign country, check
with the consulate for information.

For foreigners, of course, the consulate is invaluable. That's where you
get a passport or visa, take problems
facing you as a visitor, and find out
where to get in touch with your coun-
trymen in the area. If the consuls can't
help, they can direct you elsewhere.

Consulates

Austria
4131 11th Ave. NE
Seattle, WA 98105
633-3606

Belgium
3214 W McGraw St., Suite 301
Seattle, WA 98199
285-4486

Bolivia
5200 Southcenter Blvd., Suite 25
Seattle, WA 98188
244-6696

Britain
First Interstate Center
999 Third Ave., Suite 820
Seattle, WA 98104
622-9255

Canada
Plaza 600, Suite 412
Sixth Ave. & Stewart St.
Seattle, WA 98101-1286
443-1777
Immigration: 443-1372

Denmark
1201 Eastlake
Seattle, WA 98102
521-9719

Finland
Bellevue, WA
451-3983

France
P.O. Box 1249
Seattle, WA 98111
624-7855

Germany
One Union Square, Suite 2500
600 University St.
Seattle, WA 98101
682-4312

Guatemala
2001 Sixth Ave., Suite 3300
Seattle, WA 98121
728-5920

Iceland
5610 20th Ave. NW
Seattle, WA 98107
783-4100

Japan
601 Union, Suite 500
Seattle, WA 98101
682-9107

Korea
2033 Sixth Ave., Suite 1125
Seattle, WA 98121
441-1011

Mexico
2132 Third Ave.
Seattle, WA 98121
448-3526

Norway
Joseph Vance Bldg., Suite 806
1402 Third Ave.
Seattle, WA 98101
623-3957

Peru
7209 NE 149th Pl.
Bothell, WA 98011
488-4705

Russia
Westin Bldg.
2001 Sixth Ave., Suite 2322
Seattle, WA 98121
728-1910

Sweden
1215 Fourth Ave., Suite 1019
Seattle, WA 98161
622-5640

Taiwan
Westin Bldg.
2001 Sixth Ave., Suite 2410
Seattle, WA 98121
441-4586

SISTER CITIES

Another aspect of Seattle's multi-culturalism is its 20 sister cities. To get involved with the Sister City Committee for one of these cities, call the Office of Intergovernmental Affairs, 684-8055.

- Beer Sheva, Israel
- Bergen, Norway
- Cebu, Philippines
- Chongqing, China
- Christchurch, New Zealand
- Galway, Ireland
- Gdynia, Poland
- Kaohsiung, Taiwan
- Kobe, Japan
- Limbe, Cameroon
- Managua, Nicaragua
- Mazatlan, Mexico
- Mombasa, Kenya
- Nantes, France
- Pécs, Hungary
- Perugia, Italy
- Reykjavik, Iceland
- Surabaya, Indonesia
- Taejon, South Korea
- Tashkent, Uzbekistan

DEMOCRACY IN ACTION

Seattle has a chapter of everything from ACT UP to Zero Population Growth. We're such an activist city that several organizations have formed just to place volunteers in other organizations. Whenever two or more Seattleites get together, they're likely to call themselves a community action group, and when an issue arises, at least two groups immediately organize around it. Some call themselves Friends of Something, others use acronyms like WashPIRG or NARAL, and some string the cause out, like "Citizens Alliance to Keep the Pike Place Market Public."

Environmental groups continue to thrive in Seattle and, in some cases, vie with each other for money. And with a lingering recession, social service groups are begging for money as well as volunteers.

It may be hard to believe, but the groups listed in this chapter are just the tip of the iceberg. Groups come and go all the time, subject to the vicissitudes of funding, volunteer energy, and the political winds of change.

In addition to citizens' groups, there are boards and commissions beyond belief. But if you want to get involved in those, you have a lot of competition—especially for the prestigious jobs.

MAKING IT HAPPEN

Seattle is a clean town, but not devoid of wheeling and dealing. The business community uses its power in traditional ways, trading support for something it wants—a bus tunnel, for example. Citizens' groups can wield power too, but some methods of getting attention work far better than others. Here's what one activist recommends:

Have a central theme. Characterize the problem in some form.
Coalition-building between groups is a way to show that others believe in what you're doing. Sometimes it takes a little bit of smoke and mirrors to exaggerate support.
If you are a small minority, without direct connection to numbers of votes, popular appeal, or money, constant pressure is one of the only ways you can be effective.
Professional help is good if you can

Activist organizations are eager to have both your time and money. If you let them, the fund-raising brochures (not to mention the phone calls) can stack up. The best solution? When you sit down to pay your monthly bills, choose one group for that month and write a check. Some people choose the one handling the hot issue of the moment; others choose a longtime favorite. And if you want to be taken off a mailing list or phone tree, say so—repeatedly, if necessary.

get it. Get assistance from a public relations firm if you can.
Get someone in the legal community on your side. The law is a great way to drive a wedge into the system. Lawyers here are very willing to help free of charge; many firms have pro bono accounts, so ask.
Advertising is expensive; you can do a lot without it. Use volunteer resources instead.
Work the media: The establishment usually gets the coverage, but there are ways you can get heard. Meet with the editorial boards of newspapers, for example. Develop a relationship with reporters and give them tips. But don't lie to them.
Letters to the editor are easy and effective. Just use good sense and be truthful; the truth is always the best course and is hard to deny.
Don't forget radio. Try to get a 10-minute interview on a radio

talk show; it's all part of shaping public opinion, and people do listen to talk shows.
Graphic demonstrations can backfire. The media might think your stunt is silly; if you insult them, it can hurt. But sometimes it's the only way to get heard. For TV exposure, stunts are useful.
Petitions are a waste of time. They're dropped in the laps of officials with no noticeable effect—a lot of work and little payoff.
Lobby each key decision-maker (councilperson, committee member, etc.) several times, meeting with them individually.
If you have lots of support, filing an initiative is one of the most effective ways to get what you want. (The Pike Place Market was saved by an initiative.)

Source: Peter Steinbrueck, protector of Pike Place Market and resident thorn-in-the-side of local politicians

TAKING INITIATIVE

One way citizens can try to take the law into their own hands—or repudiate laws passed by their elected representatives—is by putting an initiative on the ballot. This can be done at the state or the city level. Since 1973, when the city started counting, there have been 42 initiatives filed with the city of Seattle. Some initiatives died before they began because of lack of signatures; others were defeated at the voting booth. Of the 42, eight passed and became city law. Here's how the process works:

1. File the proposed initiative with the city clerk's office, Room 104, Municipal Building.
2. The proposal is sent to the city attorney's office, where legal types review its language for legal problems. If there's no problem, they give it a ballot title.
3. Then you have 180 days to collect signatures supporting the petition from voters registered in the city of Seattle. The number of valid signa-

tures necessary to get your proposal on the ballot is 10% of the total votes cast in the latest mayoral election.

4. When you have enough signatures, send them in to the elections department to be verified. If there aren't enough valid signatures, you have another 20 days to get them.

5. If there are enough valid signatures, the initiative is sent to the city council, which can adopt it outright or place it on the ballot.

OUR REPS IN THE OTHER WASHINGTON

Here's how to contact the people who were elected to represent your needs and interests in the U.S. Congress. For local officials, see Chapter 7, "The Powers That Be."

U.S. House of Representatives

First District
Rick White (R)
116 Cannon House Office Bldg.
Washington, D.C. 20515-3007
(202) 225-6311 (Washington, D.C.)
640-0233 (Mountlake Terrace)
Committee: Commerce

Second District
Jack Metcalf (R)
507 Cannon House Office Bldg.
Washington, D.C. 20515-3007
(202) 225-2605 (Washington, D.C.)
(206) 252-3188 (Everett)
Committees: Banking and Financial Services; Resources; Small Business

Third District
Linda Smith (R)
1217 Longworth House Office Bldg.
Washington, D.C. 20515-3007
(202) 225-3536 (Washington, D.C.)
(360) 695-6292 (Vancouver, WA)
Committees: Resources; Small Business

Fourth District
Richard "Doc" Hastings (R)
1229 Longworth House Office Bldg.
Washington, D.C. 20515-3007
(202) 225-5816 (Washington, D.C.)

(509) 783-0310 (Kennewick)
Committees: National Security; Resources

Fifth District
George R. Nethercutt, Jr. (R)
1527 Longworth House Office Bldg.
Washington, D.C. 20515-3007
(202) 225-2006 (Washington, D.C.)
(509) 353-2374 (Spokane)
Committee: Appropriations

Sixth District
Norm Dicks (D)
2467 Rayburn House Office Bldg.
Washington, D.C. 20515-3007
(202) 225-5916 (Washington, D.C.)
(206) 593-6536 (Tacoma)
Committees: Appropriations; Intelligence

Seventh District
Jim McDermott (D)
2349 Rayburn House Office Bldg.
Washington, D.C. 20515-3007
(202) 225-3106 (Washington, D.C.)
553-7170 (Seattle)
Committees: Standards of Official Conduct; Ways and Means

You too can be an elected representative of the people. Precinct committee officers are elected every two years by the people who live within the city's voting precincts. All you have to do is file with the King County Office of Elections, pay a $1 fee, and campaign your heart out. If you have ambitions for higher office, the filing fee is 1% of the annual salary of the office.

Want to call the Prez? Here's his number: (202) 456-1111. Leave a message at the beep. Or do it the high-tech way: Send him some electronic mail at:

   president@whitehouse.gov

Or try Al Gore at:

   vice.president@whitehouse.gov

Eighth District
Jennifer Dunn (R)
432 Cannon House Office Bldg.
Washington, D.C. 20515-3007
(202) 225-7761 (Washington, D.C.)
450-0161 (Bellevue)
Committees: House Oversight; Ways and Means

Ninth District
Randy Tate (R)
1118 Longworth House Office Bldg.
Washington, D.C. 20515-3007
(202) 225-8901 (Washington, D.C.)
661-1459 (Federal Way)
Committees: Government Reform and Oversight; Transportation and Infrastructure

U.S. Senate
Slade Gorton (R)
730 Hart Bldg.
Washington, D.C. 20510
(202) 224-3441 (Washington, D.C.)
451-0103 (Seattle)
Committees: Appropriations; Budget; Commerce, Science and Transportation; Native American Affairs; Labor and Human Resources

Patty Murray (D)
111 Russell Bldg.
Washington, D.C. 20510
(202) 224-2621 (Washington, D.C.)
553-5545 (Seattle)

Committees: Appropriations; Budget; Banking, Housing and Urban Affairs; Veterans Affairs

AFFORDABLE HOUSING

HomeSight
3405 S Alaskan Way
Seattle, WA 98118
723-4153
Office coordinator: Patricia Montgomery
Turf: In cooperation with the City of Seattle and local banks, HomeSight provides ownership opportunities for first-time home buyers. Homes are located in revitalized neighborhoods in Central and Southeast Seattle. First-time home buyers with household incomes less than 115% of Seattle's median income are eligible. Priority is determined by a lottery system. Volunteers are needed for prescreening workshops and research on construction products and demographic statistics.

Operation Homestead
P.O. Box 22222
Seattle, WA 98122
443-1342
Contacts: Philip Thompson, Jon Gould
Turf: Organizes people to reopen closed downtown buildings. Works to prevent illegal abandonment of buildings. Prevention of illegal evictions and enforcement of housing code and building maintenance.
Membership: 150 activists on all levels, but rallies have attracted as many as 300–400.

Plymouth Housing Group
1305 Fourth Ave., Suite 417
Seattle, WA 98101
343-7838
Executive director: Cheryl DeBoise
Turf: Established in 1980 by members of Plymouth Congregational Church. Dedicated to preserving and developing low-income housing in downtown Seattle. Owns and/or manages over 360 units of housing in nine downtown buildings providing safe, decent, and affordable housing

to over 600 people. Call to volunteer time, furnishings (especially beds and dressers), or money.

Seattle Displacement Coalition
4759 15th Ave. NE
Seattle, WA 98105
523-2569
Contact: John Fox
Turf: Group organized to protest demolition of low-cost housing in the city.

Seattle Habitat for Humanity
306 Westlake Ave. N, Suite 210
Seattle, WA 98109
292-5240
President: Ed Choe
Turf: Part of a nationwide ecumenical organization that builds and refurbishes homes for sale to low-income families at cost. Office, committee, and construction work for volunteers.
Dues: No dues, but contributions welcome ($25 a month provides a square foot of decent housing for a family).

AIDS

Across the country, people have joined together to provide services and advocacy in response to the AIDS epidemic, and Seattle is no exception. Additional groups and services are listed in Chapter 16, "The City Says Ahhhh."

Chicken Soup Brigade
1002 E Seneca St.
Seattle, WA 98122
328-8979
Executive director: Chuck Kuehn
Turf: Meals, transportation, and other day-to-day services for people with AIDS. Especially need non-biased volunteers with daytime hours available who can make a four-hour commitment per week for six months. Retired people welcome. Training offered.
Dues: No fee for clients or volunteers
Membership: 1,400 volunteers serving 700 clients

Northwest AIDS Foundation
127 Broadway E
Seattle, WA 98102
329-6923 (info and referral, ext. 241)
Director: Terry Stone
Turf: Provides care services for people with advanced HIV/AIDS. Housing, medical access, insurance, legal assistance, home care, and emergency grant disbursement are but a few of their services. Other efforts include HIV University (a six-part workshop), quarterly community forums, aggressive ad campaigns, and education and prevention programs. Private donations make up more than half of total revenues. Utilizes more than 1,000 volunteers annually. Participation exceeds 27,000 hours annually. Training offered.

Shanti
P.O. Box 20698
Seattle, WA 98102
322-0279
Contact: Bev Williams, program manager
Turf: Emotional support and training for individuals and loved ones facing AIDS. Volunteers go through an interview and a two-weekend training session. Especially needed are good listeners who are nonjudgmental and in touch with feelings without being overwhelmed. In addition to three hours per week with a client, volunteers are expected to spend two hours per week dealing with their own feelings in a separate support group. A one-year commitment is requested. Some office volunteers needed.
Dues: $50 donation for training; scholarships available
Membership: About 150 volunteers

ANIMAL LOVERS

Seattle's animal lovers are a diverse lot, everyone from zoo docents to National Meatout activists.

Northwest Animal Rights Network
1704 E Galer St.
Seattle, WA 98112
323-7301

Contact: Jerry Esterly
Turf: Grassroots animal rights organization involved in issues dealing with everything from vivisection to vegetarianism to banning fur materials. Focus is on Northwest issues, but does not exclude national issues, e.g., National Meatout and Day for Lab Animals. Philosophy is to speak for those who cannot speak for themselves. Monthly newsletter.
Dues: $25
Membership: 300

Progressive Animal Welfare Society (PAWS)

15305 44th Ave. W
Lynnwood, WA 98037
787-2500
Executive director: Tim Greyhavens
Turf: Began in 1967 as an animal welfare and rights organization. PAWS has an animal shelter serving 10,000 abandoned or orphaned animals annually, and a wildlife hospital serving 5,000 animals annually. Also has an animal rights education program.
Dues: $20 individual and up
Membership: 10,000; volunteers are needed and welcome

Woodland Park Zoo

Volunteer Programs
5500 Phinney Ave. N
Seattle, WA 98103
684-4845
Turf: Not truly an activist group, but volunteers are needed for such things as assisting with veterinary records, special events, and docent tours. Docents must pass a four-hour-a-week training course offered from September to March and are asked for a two-year commitment. Has a formalized student intern program. And for the kids, pony leaders ages 12–16 help care for the ponies and operate the pony ring. Riding instruction provided. Will send brochure on program; there are waiting lists for most programs.

CONSUMER ADVOCATES AND GOVERNMENT WATCHDOGS

Watchdog groups are as much a part of local politics as are candidates shaking hands. Almost every political body has a watchdog group tracking its steps. These groups can be effective at times, dormant at others. One thing's for sure: They're listened to.

Allied Arts

105 S Main St., Suite 201
Seattle, WA 98104
624-0432
Director: Karen Taylor
Turf: A volunteer advocacy group for historic preservation, urban design, and arts legislation. Works to preserve and augment Seattle's general livability and to create a desirable working atmosphere for artists in the community. Avenues for citizen participation are a board and committees, which include Historic Preservation, Urban Environment, and Metropolitan Arts. Allied Arts has helped with design preservation in Pioneer Square and the Market; it assisted the King County Arts Commission in formulating guidelines for the use of hotel/motel tax revenues allocated to the arts, and continues to lead the fight to save historic downtown theaters.
Dues: $35 and up
Membership: About 800

Citizens to Save Puget Sound

P.O. Box 420
Seahurst, WA 98062
244-2394
President: Bruce Bowden
Turf: Formed to stop a sewage plant from being sited on the beach at Seahurst; active primarily in southwest King County. Works on water quality issues affecting Puget Sound.

Monitors Metro, the Department of Ecology, the legislature, and the Puget Sound Water Quality Authority. Recently the group has been involved in cross-Sound bridge, airport expansion, and creek restoration issues.
Dues: $10
Membership: 70–100

Common Cause
509 E 12th Ave., Suite 11
Olympia, WA 98501
(360) 352-4446
Executive director: Chuck Sauvage
President: Sarah Chandler
Turf: Nonpartisan citizens' group lobbying for good government. Issues include public disclosure and keeping the process of government open, accessible, and accountable. Focuses on state government, but works on federal, county, and local government, too.
Dues: $20; $30 family. Includes national membership, magazine, and newsletter.
Membership: 4,000 (8,000+ statewide)

League of Women Voters of Seattle
1402 18th Ave.
Seattle, WA 98122
329-4848
President: Dorothy Sale
Turf: Well respected for its research papers and doggedness in following issues. Publishes a free annual directory of public officials in King County —send a self-addressed stamped legal-size envelope. The league is well known for its *Primary Election Guide,* a review of key issues and candidates, produced for Seattle citizens prior to elections (they do not endorse candidates). Also coordinates a Voter Service Committee, a speakers bureau, and a variety of active subcommittees.
Dues: $0–$45
Membership: 650. Open to men as well as women.

Municipal League of King County
Central Bldg., Suite 604
810 Third Ave.
Seattle, WA 98104
622-8333
Executive director: Christine Cassidy

Turf: The 82-year-old Muni League is affectionately known as "a good-government watchdog." Nonpartisan and nonprofit in nature, it researches the knowledge, character, experience, and effectiveness of candidates. Also researches such issues as transportation, land use, and King County ballot measures. The league proposes alternative solutions to legislators, but is probably most listened to (and most feared) for its ratings of candidates at election time.
Dues: $50 for individuals. Corporate membership available. Publishes quarterly *Issue Watch,* monthly *Municipal News.*
Membership: About 1,200 countywide

Portwatch
2573 28th Ave. W
Seattle, WA 98199
283-0555
Contacts: Diana and Martin Swain
Turf: Port of Seattle. Portwatch works to involve the public in port processes and supports legislation requiring voter approval of the port's portion of the King County property tax. Monitors the port's marine division decision-making, focusing on financial accountability, how property tax levies are spent, port capital expansion, and the budget process.
Dues: $5–$15
Membership: About 200

WashPIRG (Washington Public Interest Research Group)
5200 University Way NE
Seattle, WA 98105
523-8985
Directors: Elizabeth Hull, Becky Lee, Jock Beveridge
Turf: An environmental and consumer protection citizens' lobby. Led the successful fight for a strong state toxic waste cleanup law, and helped push a strong Clean Air Act through Congress. Consumer issues include wasteful packaging, product safety, toxics, and consumer banking issues. Trained and paid canvassers visit area homes gathering financial and political support.
Dues: $35 household, $25 individual,

$2–$3 optional student fee per term. Quarterly newsletter.
Membership: 30,000 statewide

DOMESTIC VIOLENCE

Seattle has a number of shelters and other services to help those affected by domestic violence. For more services, see Chapter 13, "Lending a Hand."

Domestic Abuse Women's Network (DAWN)
P.O. Box 1521
Kent, WA 98035
656-4305 (to volunteer)
656-7867 (hotline)
Turf: Network of women helping other women, giving them information so they can help themselves. Services include emergency shelter, 24-hour crisis line, support groups. Volunteers needed; DAWN asks for a year's commitment, four hours per week answering the crisis line from home. A 40-hour crisis-intervention training program is provided.

Domestic Violence Hotline
(800) 562-6025
Turf: Refers volunteers to local domestic violence programs.

ENVIRONMENT

The environment may be Seattle's most popular cause, and it's no wonder why: From the Cascades to the Olympics, Lake Washington to Puget Sound, our area has some of the most spectacular surroundings in America.

Adopt-A-Beach
P.O. Box 21486
Seattle, WA 98111-3486
624-6013
Contacts: Ken Pritchard, Pat Buller, or Chrys Bertolotto
Turf: Nonprofit group that recruits and trains citizens to monitor beaches and wetlands. Also works with people who live near beaches to do

shellfish monitoring for the health department.
Dues: $25, but not required to volunteer
Membership: About 100, plus many volunteers

Adopt-A-Park

Seattle Parks and Recreation
100 Dexter Ave. N
Seattle, WA 98109
684-4557
Contact: Parks Coordinator
Turf: Developed in 1982 to enable citizens to participate in the maintenance of their own neighborhood parks. The coordinator sets up individual projects as needed in the parks, such as litter pickup, weeding, planting flowers. Affiliated with Treemendous Seattle's reforestation efforts. Approximately half of the 360 available parks are still waiting for adoption.
Dues: None
Membership: 200 individuals, 65 groups, 15 schools, and 10 businesses

Adopt-A-Stream Foundation

600 128th SE
Everett, WA 98208
(206) 316-8592
Contact: Tom Murdoch
Turf: Helps schools and organizations "adopt" streams and make them healthy environments for fish and human populations. New environmental education facility open to the public.
Dues: $25
Membership: 500

EarthSave Seattle

P.O. Box 9422
Seattle, WA 98109
781-6602
Contact: Sheila Hoffman
Turf: Provides education and leadership for transition to more healthy and environmentally sound food choices. Holds a monthly vegetarian potluck with educational speakers. Volunteers help with the newsletter, outreach, video screenings, special events, office work, and more.
Dues: $20 student/senior, $35 individual, $50 family
Membership: 500+

Friends of Discovery Park

3801 W Government Way
Seattle, WA 98199
285-6862
Contact: Bob Kildall
Turf: Protects Discovery Park as an urban wilderness. Includes ecology committee involved in planting and general park maintenance, work parties, field trips.
Dues: $10 individual, $5 low-income
Membership: 800

Friends of the Earth, Northwest Office

4512 University Way NE
Seattle, WA 98105
633-1661
EcoNet electronic bulletin board user name: "foewase"
NW director: David Ortman
Turf: Environmental lobbying group with the goals of restoration, preservation, and rational use of the earth. Issues include Elwha River watershed restoration, preservation of the Oregon and Washington coasts from offshore oil drilling, wetlands preservation, water conservation, and investigation of pollution at military bases in Washington.
Dues: $25 and up
Membership: 2,500 members in Northwest

Greenpeace

4649 Sunnyside Ave. N
Seattle, WA 98103
632-4326
Regional director: Bill Keller
Turf: International organization that combines nonviolent direct action, education, research, grassroots lobbying, and community organizing to protect the earth and promote environmental awareness. Issues include a halt to nuclear weapons production and testing, promotion of alternative energy and clean technologies, global warming, ozone depletion, toxics, and ocean ecology. Volunteers generally help with office work.
Dues: None. Supporters wishing to receive the quarterly newsletter contribute $30 or more. Because Greenpeace is a nonprofit 501(c)4 group (since its primary tool is grassroots lobbying), contributions are not tax-deductible. Tax-deductible donations

may be made to the separate Greenpeace Fund.
Membership: 4 million worldwide

Heart of America Northwest

Cobb Bldg., Suite 208
1305 Fourth Ave.
Seattle, WA 98101
382-1014
Executive director: Gerald Pollet
Turf: Dedicated to advancing the region's quality of life. Active in the effort to clean up the Hanford Nuclear Reservation in eastern Washington. Works for government accountability, responsible decision making, and protecting the public health as well as the economic and environmental quality of the region. Works closely with Hanford whistleblowers, scientists, lawmakers, and private citizens to educate the general public on issues surrounding toxic and radioactive wastes at the Hanford site. Helped prevent Hanford from becoming the nation's high-level nuclear waste dump.
Dues: $26; includes quarterly newsletter and monthly update to interested members
Membership: 16,800 statewide

Least competitive of city boards: Animal Control Commission. The city actually goes out looking for volunteers for this one. Half of the members have to be pet owners and half non-owners. The problem is how to find people who aren't pet owners who are still interested enough in animals to be on the board!

Lighthawk:
The Environmental Air Force
2915 E Madison
Seattle, WA 98112
860-2832
Contact: Les Welsh
Turf: Uses volunteer and staff pilots to fly small aircraft over national forests so people can see graphically what's going on with national forest and old-growth timber. Based in Santa Fe. Office volunteers and qualified pilots needed.

The Mountaineers
300 Third Ave. W
Seattle, WA 98119
284-6310
Executive director: Virginia Felton
Turf: Formed in 1906, the group's purpose is to "explore, study, preserve, and enjoy the natural beauty of the Northwest." Now the third-largest outdoor club in the nation, The Mountaineers has a 4,000-volume library specializing in outdoor topics and a publishing division with more than 200 titles. The club offers activities such as hiking, climbing, sailing, bicycling, photography, and kayaking. Publishes a monthly magazine of articles and a schedule of activities.

Dues: First year, $75 individual, $50 senior, $38 jr./student; drops to $41, $21, and $17 second year; special rates for spouses and out-of-staters
Membership: 15,000

The Nature Conservancy
Washington Field Office
217 Pine St., Suite 1100
Seattle, WA 98101
343-4344
State director: Elliot Marks
Turf: An international organization committed to the global preservation of natural diversity. It identifies lands that shelter natural communities and species, determining what is truly rare. Then it protects habitats through acquisition, and assists government and other conservation organizations in land preservation efforts.
Dues: $25 and up
Membership: 32,000 statewide

Northwest Conservation Act Coalition
217 Pine St., Suite 1020
Seattle, WA 98101
621-0094
Director: Sara Patton
Turf: Works for clean, low-cost regional energy solutions. Promotes widespread consumer involvement in Northwest Power Planning Council's regional power plan. Membership includes quarterly publication.
Dues: $20 individual, $200 nonprofit organization, dues for businesses negotiable
Membership: Umbrella group of 60–70 organizations; plus several hundred individuals

Northwest Environment Watch
1402 Third Ave., Suite 1127
Seattle, WA 98101-2118
447-1880
Executive director: Alan Thein Durning
Turf: Founded in 1993—largely by researchers from Washington D.C.'s Worldwatch Institute—Northwest Environment Watch (NEW) is a not-for-profit research center that seeks to promote the concept of sustainable living in the Northwest. Issues include creating green jobs, biodiversity, reversing sprawl, sustainable economies, pollution, cars and cities, and the health of ecosystems.

Through research, grass-roots lobbying, interaction with community and business leaders, and a series of publications, NEW seeks to foster an environmentally sound economy and way of life in the Pacific Northwest.
Dues: $25 (subscriber) and up
Membership: Governed by a 7-member board of directors; the work is carried out by a small staff and a large corp of volunteers.

People for Puget Sound
1326 Fifth Ave., Suite 450
Seattle, WA 98101
382-7007
Executive director: Kathy Fletcher
Turf: Works to eliminate the contamination of Puget Sound and the Strait of Juan de Fuca, to halt the destruction of natural habitats, and to sustain the Sound and Strait as healthy sources of people's livelihood, enjoyment, and renewal. Group has asked residents to take 12 "Sound Resolutions" to "turn the tide against water pollution."
Dues: $5 adult, $1 children, $15 family
Membership: 20,000
(Puget Sound area)

PlantAmnesty
906 NW 87th St.
Seattle, WA 98117
783-5660
President: Cass Turnbull
Turf: Works to end mutilation of trees and shrubs caused by mal-pruning through educating the public. Aims to create a vision of beautiful yards and nurture respect for photo-synthesizers.
Dues: $10, includes newsletter
Membership: 500 in 44 states

Puget Sound Alliance
1415 W Dravus
Seattle, WA 98119
286-1309
President: Tom Putnam
Turf: Formed in 1984, a nonprofit network of organizations and individuals concerned about the future of Puget Sound. Major program is the Puget Soundkeeper, which employs an environmental ombudsperson who trains and works with citizens

as well as businesses and agencies to identify and stop sources of pollution to the Sound. Based on programs on Long Island Sound, San Francisco Bay, and the Hudson River.
Dues: $10 student/fixed income, $15 individual, $25 family
Membership: 1,200

Rivers Council of Washington
1731 Westlake Ave. N, Suite 202
Seattle, WA 98109-3043
283-4988
Executive director: Joy Huber
Turf: Formerly Northwest Rivers Council, the group focuses on local organizing for river stewardship in the 62 watersheds of Washington State. Besides educational and advocacy work, the group takes legislators and other leaders on river-running trips and publishes a quarterly newsletter. Volunteers are needed for office and outdoor work.
Dues: $15/$25
Membership: 700 statewide

Seattle Audubon Society
8028 35th Ave. NE
Seattle, WA 98115
523-4483
President: Robert Sieh
Turf: Formed to enjoy and conserve nature, and to educate people about the natural world.
Dues: $20 introductory
Membership: 5,000

Sierra Club
Cascade Chapter
8511 15th NE
Seattle, WA 98115
523-2147; Sierra Singles, 781-5704
Chair: Dan Cantrell
Turf: Grassroots environmental organization involved in conservation activities, especially lobbying for environmental legislation at federal and local levels. Also sponsors outings. All sorts of volunteers needed, from mail crew to air- and water-quality experts. "We are looking for people with enthusiasm, not necessarily with technical backgrounds. We'll find something for them to do and help them be effective."
Dues: $33
Membership: 13,000 members in

Cascade Chapter, which includes most of Washington State.

The Trust for Public Land
Northwest Regional Office
Smith Tower, Suite 1510
506 Second Ave.
Seattle, WA 98104
587-2447
Contact: Mary Rolston
Turf: Nonprofit land conservation organization that protects open spaces, especially near urban areas where people work and live. Since establishment of its Northwest office in 1979, has acquired almost 40,000 acres of land in six states. Holds threatened lands until they can be conveyed to public agencies or nonprofit land stewards. Helps community groups preserve local open space resources. Publishes regional newsletter.
Dues: Gifts of $25 or more
Membership: 6,000 contributors

Union Bay Foundation
5026 22nd Ave. NE, Suite 2
Seattle, WA 98105
525-0716
Coordinator: John Huskinson
Turf: Works to create a management umbrella for Union Bay and its shorelines, including Foster Island and adjacent wetlands. Includes a program for wildlife enhancement and maintenance of open space. Is fighting proposed development in a critical wildlife habitat area. "In 1880, there were 2,300 acres of wetlands on Lake Washington. This is one of the last remaining."

Volunteers for Outdoor Washington
8815 15th NE
Seattle, WA 98115
517-4469
Volunteer facilitator: Suse Altengarten
Turf: Helps maintain outdoor recreation areas, such as city, state, and national parks as well as state and national forests. Provides trail maintenance and training workshops.
Dues: $25 adult, $30 family, $10 low-income, $5 for newsletter only

Washington Citizens for Resource Conservation
157 Yesler Way, Room 309
Seattle, WA 98104
343-5171
Executive director: Mariann Mann
Turf: Works to reduce waste and conserve natural resources. Educational public programs and "earth-friendly" packaging awards/endorsement program. Also involved in hands-on pilot programs such as setting up sites where people can take used motor oil. Quarterly newsletter.
Dues: $25 and up
Membership: 2,500

Washington Environmental Council
1100 Second Ave., Suite 102
Seattle, WA 98101
622-8103
Executive director: Joan Crooks
Turf: Provides information, policy, and advocacy on environmental issues in the state. An umbrella group for more than 100 environmental organizations. Volunteers are needed to work on issues such as growth, wetlands, forestry, and transportation. Work includes collecting signatures, writing for the newsletter, or serving on research committees.
Dues: $25 individual; $15 student/senior
Membership: About 2,000 statewide

Washington Toxics Coalition
4516 University Way NE
Seattle, WA 98105
632-1545
Contact: Phillip Dickey
Turf: Has been working since 1981 to reduce society's reliance on toxic chemicals. Issues include pesticides, industrial toxics, groundwater protection, and toxic household products. Provides technical information, strategies, and alternative management policies to communities. The Home Safe Home program identifies and promotes safe alternatives to toxic household products; a series of fact sheets is available for a nominal charge. A slide show is also available.
Dues: $20; includes *Alternatives,* a quarterly newsletter, and issue alerts

and invitations to events
Membership: 1,500

Washington Trails Association
1305 Fourth Ave., Room 512
Seattle, WA 98101
625-1367
Contact: Dan Nelson, editor of
Signpost
Turf: Working to create an inter-
connected network of trails linking
communities and providing access to
the natural world for the enjoyment
of all. Publishes a monthly magazine
called *Signpost for Northwest Trails*.
Dues: $25 new members, $35
renewals; includes subscription
to monthly magazine
Membership: 2,500

Washington Wilderness Coalition
4649 Sunnyside Ave. N, Suite 242
Seattle, WA 98103
633-1992
Executive director: Cathy Currie
Turf: Works to protect the natural
splendor of Washington's public
lands, including forests, rivers,
and wilderness areas. Welcomes
volunteers.
Dues: $25
Membership: 1,000+

Wilderness Society
1424 Fourth Ave., Suite 816
Seattle, WA 98101
624-6430
Regional director: Steven Whitney
Turf: Protection of federal lands
(national parks, forests, wildlife
refuges, etc.) and major ecosystems.
Highest priority is protection of
the Northwest's ancient forests.
Dues: $15 introductory, $30 individual, $15 senior/student/fixed-income
Membership: 11,000 statewide

Zero Population Growth
4426 Burke Ave. N
Seattle, WA 98103
548-0152
Co-chairs: R.T. Vance, Paul Shelton
Turf: Believes the survival of human-
kind depends on the attainment of
equilibrium between population and
environment. Seeks to stop global
population growth and overconsump-
tion of natural resources by changing
U.S. policy. Runs the Rubber Tree, a

Want to get paid for doing good?
Sound Opportunities newsletter,
published every two weeks, lists
jobs available in Seattle's nonprofit
community. Call 933-6556 for a free
copy. Subscribe for three months
($13), six months ($19), or one year
($34), depending on how fast you
think you can find the job you want.
"Most people sign up for six
months," say *Sound Opportunities*
staffers. "Optimists go for three,
pessimists—a year." They also
publish the *Nonprofit Community
Resource Directory*, which lists more
than 1,500 nonprofit groups in the
state. If you'd like to work for the
Seattle Housing Authority, a public-
housing provider, try their jobline:
615-3535.

nonprofit project that provides non-
prescription contraception and safer-
sex supplies, at the same address.
Dues: $20
Membership: 2,100 in Northwest

PEACE AND JUSTICE

Like environmentalists, peace
activists in Seattle have only one
problem: deciding which group gets
their time and money. Many of the
groups cluster around "Peace Alley"

(45th and University Way NE). Some
don't have offices but instead have
regional representatives who handle
the organizational end of things.

American Civil Liberties Union (ACLU)
705 Second Ave., Suite 300
Seattle, WA 98104
624-2184 (administrative)
624-2180 (complaint line)
Contact: Doug Honig
Turf: Works to protect the civil liberties of all Americans through public
education, legislative advocacy, and
litigation. Issues include reproductive
freedom, privacy, due process, freedom of speech, and all other First
Amendment rights. Volunteers do
outreach at public events, advocate
on civil liberties issues, and help with
office tasks.
Dues: $20 individual, $30 group,
$5 low-income
Membership: 10,000 statewide

American Friends Service Committee
814 NE 40th St.
Seattle, WA 98105
632-0500
Turf: Believes in the dignity and
worth of each person, and in the
power of love and nonviolence to
bring about change. Active in many
issues, including peace and Native
American fishing rights. One of five
organizations supporting Lambert
House, a community center for gay/
lesbian/bisexual youth. Founded by
Quakers.
Dues: Contributions

Committee in Solidarity with the People of El Salvador (CISPES)
P.O. Box 20091
Seattle, WA 98102
325-5494
Contact: Tom Leonard or Chris
Ferlazzo
Turf: Works with Salvadoran
people for peace and social justice.
Welcomes anyone committed to
achieving the goals of the group with
any amount of money or time.
Dues: Contributions

Evergreen State Peace Mission
225 N 70th St.
Seattle, WA 98103
632-3777

Contact: Mary Hanson
Turf: Nuclear proliferation and foreign policy are major issues. Umbrella group that coordinates citizen lobbying of state's congressional delegation in D.C. or at-home offices. Representatives from its 20 member organizations are briefed on issues and trained for lobbying visits. Helps citizen lobbyists prepare for D.C. visits, provides materials and debriefing sessions in Seattle on return. Has information on state delegation members' voting patterns and policy positions.

Nonviolent Action Committee of Cascadia

4554 12th Ave. NE
Seattle, WA 98105
547-0952
Coordinator: Geov Parrish
Turf: Dedicated to nonviolent direct action for change. Issues include anti-militarism, budget priorities, and social justice. Provides information and counseling on war tax resistance and redirection. Administers the largest escrow account of refused military taxes in the U.S. Volunteers are needed to do office work, write articles and help with newsletter production, do outreach, and help organize public protests.
Dues: No dues, but subscriptions to newsletter are $10.
Membership: 600 escrow account holders nationwide and 1,000 subscribers to newsletter in the Seattle area (2,000 nationwide)

Peace Action of Washington State

5828 Roosevelt Way NE
Seattle, WA 98105
527-8050
Turf: Statewide organization mobilizing citizens through legislative and educational activity. Issues include violence in the community and gun control, federal budget priorities, economic conversion, and nuclear weapons production and testing. Volunteers can help with the legislative action network, the newsletter, special events, lobbying, community outreach, and office work.
Dues: $25 or more includes one-year subscription to newsletter. Tax-

deductible.
Membership: 13,500

Physicians for Social Responsibility

4554 12th Ave NE
Seattle, WA 98105
547-2630
Executive director: Martin Fleck
Turf: Nonprofit, nonpartisan group doing educational work with issues related to the arms race, nuclear war, and military spending.
Dues: $90 physicians, $50 public
Membership: About 1,600 in Western Washington, 60%–70% physicians

Washington State Peace Corps Association

c/o Peace Corps Recruitment
2001 Sixth Ave., Suite 1776
Seattle, WA 98121
553-5490
Turf: Alumni group of returned Peace Corps and VISTA volunteers. Works on global education in local schools and raises funds for international and local development projects.
Dues: $15 local, $35 local and national
Membership: 300

Western Washington Fellowship of Reconciliation (FOR)

225 N 70th St.
Seattle, WA 98103
789-5565
Turf: Pacifist group educating people and promoting nonviolent actions to create peace and social justice. Annual conference at Seabeck every Fourth of July weekend draws over 200 people from the Northwest.
Dues: Tax-deductible contribution. Subscription to FOR's national *Fellowship* magazine is $15.
Membership: 1,000 in Western Washington

Women's International League for Peace and Freedom

2524 16th Ave. S
Seattle, WA 98144
329-3666
Turf: More than 75-year-old peace and justice organization concerned about such issues as a comprehensive nuclear test ban, undoing racism,

ending the arms race, and opposing U.S. intervention in affairs of other nations. World headquarters is in Geneva.
Membership: 250 women and men locally

POLITICAL PARTIES AND PARTISAN GROUPS

Left, right, or center—if party politics is your thing, Seattle offers a range of choices. And which way have the political winds been blowing lately? Consider these facts:

- As of fall 1992, all Congressional representatives from the Seattle area were Democrats. As of 1996, all but two were Republicans
- In 1992, Bill Clinton carried King County. This was the second time in 20 years a Democrat carried the county in a presidential election. (Dukakis in 1988 was the first.)
- Clinton also carried Washington State in 1992.

Democrats and Republicans

Democratic Central Committee of King County

1411 Fourth Ave., Suite 1106
Seattle, WA 98101
622-9157
Executive director: Heather Hamill

Democratic State Central Committee of Washington
Smith Tower, Room 1701
506 Second Ave.
Seattle, WA 98104
583-0664
Executive director: Linda Medcalf
Chairperson: Charles Rolland

King County Republican Party
1305 Republican St.
Seattle, WA 98109
467-1990
Chair: Nona Brazier

Republican State Committee of Washington
16400 Southcenter Pkwy., Suite 200
Tukwila, WA 98188
575-2900
Chair: Ken Eikenberry

Other parties and groups

Metropolitan Democratic Club
1388 Alki Ave. SW, #404
Seattle, WA 98116
937-5088
Executive secretary: Mary Jo Heavey
Turf: Established in the early 1950s as a liberal alternative to the mainstream party apparatus. Since then it has remained an independent, progressive organization. "Although outside the Democratic Party structure, the members are part of the progressive Democratic Party tradition." Sponsors debates, speakers, and forums on topics of concern to Seattleites. Endorses candidates at election time. Events are held downtown and are open to the public.
Dues: $20
Membership: About 220. Conservatives need not apply.

Revolutionary Communist Party of America
c/o Revolution Books
1833 Nagle Pl.
Seattle, WA 98122
325-7415
Spokesperson: Terri Timms
Turf: Spokesperson hosts regular discussions at bookstore.

Socialist Workers Party
1405 E Madison
Seattle, WA 98122
323-1755

Catch new bands and old favorites this summer at free Sunday afternoon concerts presented by the Peace Movement Northwest coalition, which has put on concerts every summer since 1980. Concerts take place in a different park each Sunday during the summer; admission's free, but bring a food bank donation. Call 789-5651 for information or watch for posters in June.

Turf: Supports the abolition of capitalism worldwide.

SOCIAL SERVICES

Social service groups work on everything from disaster preparedness to tenants' rights. For additional services for the homeless, domestic violence victims, children and parents, seniors, and the disabled, see Chapter 14, "Lending a Hand."

American Red Cross
1900 25th Ave. S
Seattle, WA 98144
323-2345
Turf: Strives to improve the quality of human life; to enhance self-reliance and concern for others; and to help people avoid, prepare for, and cope with emergencies. Volunteers can do office work, receive training to aid in disaster relief, or become involved with other Red Cross services, including the language bank. Offers services to military families and first aid/CPR, babysitting, HIV/AIDS education for individuals or groups. Administers Retired Senior Volunteer Program. Youth volunteer training and opportunities available.
Dues: Donations
Membership: 6,000 volunteers countywide

Community Services for the Blind and Partially Sighted
9709 Third Ave. NE, Suite 100
Seattle, WA 98115-2027
525-5556 (V/TDD)
(800) 458-4888 (V/TDD)
President: June W. Mansfield
Turf: Provides support services for blind and visually impaired persons to enable them to work, study, and live independently. Volunteers provide one-on-one assistance to blind people in their neighborhoods, visiting once a week to help with basic needs: mail, shopping, errands, walks.
Membership: 315 volunteers serving 450 clients

Court Appointed Special Advocates (CASA)
Family Court of King County
King County Superior Court
Third and James, Room C205
Seattle, WA 98104
296-9320
Turf: Volunteers represent the interests of children in divorce court proceedings. Training is provided. Call for information packet in order to volunteer.

Crisis Clinic
1515 Dexter Ave. N, Suite 300
Seattle, WA 98109
461-3222 (crisis hotline)
461-3200 or (800) 621-INFO (information line)
461-3210 (for publications and to volunteer)
Turf: The Crisis Clinic has two distinct services: the Crisis Hotline and the Community Information Line. The hotline operates 24 hours a day and receives 80,000 calls a year from people who are in an emotional crisis. The information line receives 38,000 calls a year and is operated from

8:30am–6pm, Monday–Friday. The info line serves all of King County and provides referrals for human services—needs such as parenting programs, shelter, food, etc. The database lists about 2,400 services. The Crisis Clinic also publishes two magazines, *Where to Turn* and *Where to Turn Plus*.

Volunteers: Phone lines are staffed by volunteers. Each volunteer is required to participate in an extensive crisis intervention training program involving about 40 hours of classroom work, problem-solving skills, independent study using the computer system, and practice in a simulated phone room. A one-year commitment is required, and volunteers usually spend 4½ hours per week on the phones.

Easter Seal Society
521 Second Ave. W
Seattle, WA 98119
281-5700
Contact: Jennifer Roberson
Turf: Aims to increase the independence of people with disabilities. Programs include housing assistance and modification, camping, therapeutic

horseback riding, respite care, and information and referral. Volunteers do everything from administrative tasks to working in camping programs.

Seattle Tenants Union
3902 S Ferdinand St.
Seattle, WA 98118
723-0500
Hotline: (800) 752-9993
Turf: Runs a hotline for landlord/tenant questions that receives 25,000 calls per year. Sends people to organize tenants at housing projects and apartment buildings, and inform them about their collective bargaining rights. Also lobbies for such things as mandatory inspections and sells a Renter's Kit that includes information on landlord-tenant laws.
Dues: $0–$25 depending on income
Membership: Over 1,000

Urban League of Metropolitan Seattle
105 14th Ave.
Seattle, WA 98122
461-3792
President: Dr. Roz Woodhouse
Turf: Community service agency founded in 1930 to eliminate racism and secure equal opportunities for

ethnic minorities. Trains people in wise home buying, rental searches, fair housing, and avoiding foreclosure. Also scholarship assistance for college-bound students, employment and job placement assistance, a school program for at-risk youth, and a literacy/parenting program for adults. Volunteers can assist with housing or education programs or office tasks.
Dues: $10 student/senior, $25 individual, $500+ corporate

Washington Coalition of Citizens with Disabilities
4649 Sunnyside Ave. N, Suite 100
Seattle, WA 98103
461-4550
Executive director: Kerry Klockner
Turf: For people with disabilities, this coalition of groups offers self-empowerment programs, self-advocacy training, peer counseling, a job-seeking support group, legal services, and support for independent living. For the community at large, offers disability sensitivity training, a consultant service, and access reviews. Sends a newsletter to 1,000 people quarterly. Welcomes volun-

teers, with and without disabilities. Volunteers can do office tasks; those with disabilities can be trained to help agencies meet the requirements of the Americans with Disabilities Act. Dues: $15; services are free.

Washington Literacy
220 Nickerson
Seattle, WA 98109
461-3623
(800) 323-2550 (Literacy Hotline)
Turf: Provides many literacy services, including training literacy volunteers and lending educational materials. Operates the Literacy Action Center, which tutors adults at or below a sixth-grade reading level; Literacy Bookstore; a workplace literacy program; and the Washington State Literacy Hotline, a referral service for students, tutors, and volunteer-based programs. Coordinates children's summer day camp and inner-city day-care reading program.

WOMEN'S ISSUES

National Abortion Rights Action League (NARAL)
811 First Ave., Suite 456
Seattle, WA 98104
624-1990
Executive director: Karen Cooper
Turf: Dedicated to protecting a woman's constitutional right to choose a safe, legal abortion. NARAL lobbies legislators and researches candidates for pro-choice stances before endorsing. About 3–20 volunteers a day help out in NARAL's office. Volunteer work includes office tasks, special events/fund-raising, and legislative affairs.
Dues: Donations accepted
Membership: 14,000 statewide

National Organization for Women (NOW)
4649 Sunnyside Ave. N, Room 222
Seattle, WA 98103
632-8547
Co-presidents: Louise Chernin and Hannah Bennett
Turf: Works on issues such as women's health and reproductive choice, lesbian/bisexual rights, elimination of violence against women, and workplace equity. Regular meetings. Gives referral numbers for women's health, domestic violence, and legal services. Volunteers needed for administrative work, community actions, mailings, and special projects. Local chapter of the largest multi-issue feminist group in the nation.
Dues: $20–$40; includes local, state, and national newsletter.
Membership: About 1,000 (6,000 statewide). Open to both men and women.

Northwest Women's Law Center
119 S Main St., Suite 330
Seattle, WA 98104
621-7691 (legal referral service)
682-9552 (office)
Executive director: Kelly Maguire
Turf: Specializes in legal issues and legal action to advance women's rights. Has a lobbying program and a litigation program that represents classes of women or individual women whose cases affect overall women's rights. Offers free family-law seminars, sexual harassment response training, domestic violence information, and books and videotapes, including a family-law book in Spanish. Information and referral service offers free information to the public on all legal topics and refers callers to appropriate attorneys. Volunteers with legal background are especially needed, but anyone interested should call.
Dues: $35, less for low-income
Membership: About 2,000. Open to all who support women's rights.

Planned Parenthood of Seattle/King County
2211 E Madison
Seattle, WA 98112
328-7713
Volunteer coordinator: Samantha Bowley
Turf: Provides clinical and educational reproductive health services. Volunteers can assist in the clinic or bookstore, on the sexuality information hotline, or as an outreach educator. Volunteers are asked for a six-month commitment of at least four hours per week. Training provided. The University District office, 632-2498, also welcomes volunteers.

If you want to work abroad, consider the Peace Corps, which celebrated its 35th anniversary in 1995. Volunteers serve in 90 countries worldwide—including Eastern Europe, a relatively new addition. The University of Washington ranks second in the nation as a producer of Peace Corps volunteers. Since 1961, 5,000 people from Washington state have volunteered, with 336 overseas now. Most-sought are people with backgrounds and/or degrees (degrees are preferable) in agriculture, forestry, freshwater fisheries, math, science, education, secondary education, industrial arts, health, or nutrition. A background in linguistics or experience teaching English as a foreign language can be utilized in teaching secondary-level English. Average age is 29; there's no upper age limit, but good health is a requirement. The application process takes 4 to 12 months. For more information, contact Peace Corps Recruitment, 553-5490.

Radical Women

5018 Rainier Ave. S
Seattle, WA 98118
722-6057
Organizer: Ann Slater
Turf: A socialist feminist organization dedicated to achieving the full equality of women by making radical changes. Advocates "the overthrow of both capitalist rule and Stalinist bureaucratism." Formed in Seattle in 1967.

Soroptimist Club

P.O. Box 2676
Seattle, WA 98111
523-5375
Contact: Lora Holzer
Turf: Soroptimist means "the best for women," and the Puget Sound area has six clubs, each with its own projects. Community service is the focus, and every club gives scholarships to mature women who need to re-enter the workforce as well as to outstanding high school students. Members are professionals who work full- or part-time. It's possible to participate both locally and worldwide.
Dues: $50 and up
Membership: About 300 locally

Washington State Women's Political Caucus

P.O. Box 21767
Seattle, WA 98111
654-4165
Contact: Dawn Wylen Bogart
Turf: The political arm of the feminist movement. Main focus is on electoral politics and public policy roles. A bipartisan group, the caucus considers itself pragmatic, focusing on getting women into elective and appointive offices for more balanced representation. May's List, a project of WPC, endorses candidates locally and nationally. "We are a political organization as opposed to an issue organization." Needs volunteers for campaign work with endorsed candidates and to chair committees, lead task forces, etc.
Dues: $40
Membership: 1,500 statewide

STILL LOOKING?

If you still can't decide where to put your time, perhaps one of these agencies can channel your energies. They each work to place volunteers where their talents are needed.

The Benefit Gang

P.O. Box 1989
2601 Elliott Ave.
Seattle, WA 98111
443-3277
Executive director: Marion Dobson De Forest
Turf: Volunteer recruitment, training, and placement of Puget Sound's young adults. Contracts with nonprofit groups in the city to provide volunteers. Opportunities range from one-time events to ongoing commitments. Sends out a regular listing to potential volunteers so they can pick the position they want; just call to be placed on mailing list. Service is free to volunteers and nonprofits.
Dues: None
Membership: Over 4,500 volunteers

United Way Volunteer Center

107 Cherry St.
Seattle, WA 98104
461-6906
Contact: Diane Kuhn
Turf: A free community service provided by United Way, the Volunteer Center maintains a database of people interested in volunteering and connects them with 400–450 organizations in need of volunteers. Receives 3,500 calls from would-be volunteers each year. Volunteer opportunities tend to be health- and human services–related, but there are some arts, environmental, and school volunteer opportunities as well. Also does training in volunteer management for corporations.

Want to support women-owned businesses and organizations? Get a copy of the annual *Women's Resource and Business Directory*. It's available for $9 from the publisher at P.O. Box 58876, Renton, WA 98058. For more information, call 726-9687.

COMMISSIONS AND BOARDS

If working *within* the city structure is your thing, you may be interested in one of the more than 90 city boards and commissions that recruit volunteers from the community (sometimes a small stipend is offered). You can get a list of all the boards and commissions from the mayor's office, 684-4000. Here are just a few:

Animal Control Commission
Arboretum and Botanical Garden Committee
Arts Commission
Bicycle Advisory Board
Capitol Hill Housing Improvement Program Council
Chinatown–International District Preservation and Development Authority Council
Civil Service Commission
Historic Seattle Preservation and Development Authority Council
Landmarks Preservation Board
Museum Development Authority Council
Pike Place Market Historical Commission

How do you get on a city board or commission? It can help to know someone, depending on the prestige of the board position. Here's how it works: The mayor usually sends out a press release about the opening. Then someone in city hall interviews the potential candidates. Usually the person picked represents a particular neighborhood or group affected by the issue or has relevant expertise.

You can also sign up for county and state boards and commissions.

Office of King County Executive
400 King County Courthouse
Seattle, WA 98104
296-4040

Office of the Governor
Assistant for Boards and Commissions
P.O. Box 40002
Legislative Bldg., AS-13
Olympia, WA 98504-0413
(360) 753-6780

LENDING A HAND

CRISIS CLINIC

LOW-INCOME HOUSING

SHELTERS

FOOD BANKS

DRUG ABUSE

DOMESTIC VIOLENCE

RUNAWAYS

FOSTER CARE

ADOPTION

CHILD CARE

*A*long with Seattle's growth during the past decade came a rise in social problems. The 1985 documentary Streetwise *brought national attention to the number of youths living on Seattle's streets, and in the 1990s the number of homeless people camped* on city sidewalks drew increasing ire. But true to Seattle's reputation as a caring city, the number of social service organizations ministering to those in need multiplied as well.

There's a good share of help with less visible social needs, too: literacy and employment services, assistance for the stressed-out parent, help with adoption and foster care. And the city's seniors and disabled have a number of organizations to turn to for support.

Aside from the politics of social service, there is the problem of gaining access to the dizzying array of social programs that are out there to help people. (If you are lucky enough not to be in need, look at it as an opportunity to volunteer to help those who *are*.)

WHEN IN CRISIS...

The social service network in Seattle consists of 600 private and nonprofit organizations as well as hundreds of city, county, state, and federal employees who administer a wealth of services. The churches are picking up more than their share; almost every denomination is heavily involved in services for needy people. Add to these the large numbers of social workers in private practice running small clinics and group therapies, and the network soon takes on the appearance of a maze.

Getting access to that maze can be tough. If you don't know whether a program exists to meet your needs, be persistent in your research. It probably does. And if you can't pay, or can't pay much, speak up. Most agencies operate on a sliding-scale basis.

Here's the first resource you need to know about: the Crisis Clinic. Begun as a crisis intervention hotline in the socially conscious sixties, the Crisis Clinic started keeping a Rolodex file of referral numbers for all kinds of mental health and emergency services. The list was eventually indexed, cross-referenced using a decimal numbering system, and entered into a computer database.

In addition to 24-hour crisis intervention, the Crisis Clinic is now under contract to provide general information and referral services for all United Way agencies through this data bank, and refers clients to non–United Way agencies as well. (Even the telephone directory listing for the King County Human Services Mental Health Division gives the Crisis Clinic's hotline number under "Crisis Referral/Emergencies.")

The Crisis Clinic can refer you to agencies in any one of 60 categories, from family planning to employment services, from divorce lifelines to home care providers.

The clinic's database provides information not only to its own line, but also to the downtown branch of the Seattle Public Library. The library has the Resource File index, which refers you to an 850-page volume of lists of agencies and services. Major listings in the index are education, environmental quality, and health care.

A smattering of the Crisis Clinic's broad, diverse, and unique listings:

- Agent Orange Hotline (State Dept. of Veterans Affairs): (800) 225-4712.
- Dial-a-Complaint (billing disputes with privately owned telephone and power companies): (800) 562-6150.
- Eastern European Clinic (HMO-type care for immigrants): 521-1770.
- Ingersoll Gender Center (counseling, support, referral for transsexuals): 329-6651.

Crisis Clinic

1515 Dexter Ave. N, Suite 300
Seattle, WA 98109
461-3222 (crisis hotline)
461-3200 or (800) 621-INFO
(information line)
461-3210 (for publications and to volunteer)

LOW-INCOME HOUSING

One reason for the large numbers of homeless is the gentrification of traditional low-income–housing areas. With the problem has come a plethora of emergency service centers, housing activists, and downright angry citizens.

Downtown Seattle lost 15,000 housing units between 1960 and 1990. But the city says that trend is changing, with an average of 500–1,000 units being added per year. The city isn't building new units, but is turning existing buildings into low-income housing (which, according to groups like SHARE, happens only when the homeless rise up in anger).

The federal government's policy hasn't made things easier: Federal block grants, which support shelters and other social services, dropped from $17.2 million in 1980 to $14.2 million in 1993. (City housing services get another $9.1 million from local and city contributions to block grants. Of the total $23.3 million in block grants, $8.2 million goes toward housing.)

There is some—not enough, but some—housing help out there for those who are considered low income. And there are a lot of low-income folks out there. Seattle's poverty rate is higher than both the state and county rate: 12.4% of the population is poor. (That percentage goes up dramatically for nonwhite residents: the Hispanic poverty rate is 22.3%, African American 25.5%, American Indian 32.9%.)

Low-income housing is available to anyone in one of three categories:

- Involuntarily displaced or homeless (no permanent nighttime address).
- Those living in substandard housing or paying more than 50% of their gross income for rent and utilities (often elderly or handicapped).
- Everyone else whose low level of income makes them eligible

(typically includes the mentally ill or those with family dysfunction).

Clients are rated by need: homeless first, then those paying a disproportionate amount of income for housing, then everyone else.

What are the income levels for low-income housing? It depends on which housing authority you're dealing with—there are seven in the Greater Seattle area. What the federal Housing and Urban Development Department (HUD) calls "low income"—which would make someone eligible for low-income housing—is 80% of the median income in the county, or $26,900 per year for one person. Another category, "very low income," is set at 50% of the median income, or $16,800 for one person living in King County.

A number of local organizations advocate for low-income people and for more affordable housing. Many are listed in Chapter 12, "Democracy in Action." Here are a few others:

Common Ground
107 Cherry St., Suite 410
Seattle, WA 98104-2214
461-4500
Pulls together sponsors, buildings, and funds for low-income housing. Negotiates agreements, arranges repairs, and develops new methods of financing. Works primarily with churches, community groups, agencies, and nonprofit organizations.

Downtown Human Services Council
115 Prefontaine Pl. S
Seattle, WA 98104
461-3865
Advocacy for low-income population in downtown area.

HOW TO APPLY

The Seattle Housing Authority (SHA) accepts applications and verifies all the information. If the applicant is qualified and homeless, SHA must provide transitional housing until permanent housing becomes

The Seattle Housing Authority waiting list

Unit size	Families waiting, 1996	Families waiting, 1993	Length of wait
1 bedroom	946	1,528	4 months
2 bedroom	3,347	1.303	6 months
3 bedroom	751	706	18 months
4 bedroom	372	185	24 months

Source: Seattle Department of Human Services

available. This transitional housing, sometimes in low-cost hotels or motels, is often used from three to four weeks to a couple of months before permanent housing is secured.

The truth is that of the 5,416 families on the waiting list for a home, many are spending their nights in shelters or on the streets. If qualified but not homeless, the applicant is added to the waiting list for the first available housing.

BUT WHERE TO SLEEP?

How much low-income housing is available in Seattle? The answer is difficult to pin down and depends on how much help you need as well as whether you're dealing with one of the seven separate housing authorities in King, Snohomish, and Pierce counties or with HUD. Each of these agencies has a variety of rental and rent subsidy programs. Keep after them until you get help, if you feel you may qualify. And check around; it could be well worth the time you spend.

Seattle Housing Authority owns 11,154 units; King County Housing Authority owns 3,500 units (1,700 elderly, 1,800 family); and Renton Housing Authority owns 398 units. Total owned units: 15,052. Turnover rate: 25%–30% per year.
Source: Seattle Housing Authority, King County Housing Authority, Renton Housing Authority, December 1992

Everett Housing Authority
1401 Poplar St.
Everett, WA 98201
(206) 258-9222

King County Housing Authority
15455 65th Ave. S
Seattle, WA 98188
244-7750

Pierce County Housing Authority
603 S Polk St.
Tacoma, WA 98445
(206) 535-4400

Renton Housing Authority
970 Harrington Ave. NE
Renton, WA 98056
226-1850

Seattle Housing Authority
120 Sixth Ave. N
Seattle, WA 98109
443-4400

Snohomish County Housing Authority
12625 Fourth Ave. W, Suite 200
Everett, WA 98201
(206) 258-4357 (24 hours)

Tacoma Housing Authority
1728 E 44th St.
Tacoma, WA 98404
(206) 207-4400

OTHER HOUSING HELP

Seattle and King County issue rent certificates to low-income residents so they can rent private housing at 30% of their total income. The feds pick up the tab for the balance of the private rents. The federal government allocates money to states, which in turn allocate it to counties to fund the program. There's a substantial waiting list; for info, call Seattle Housing Authority's applications department, 443-4411.

HUD also has a number of subsidy contract programs with private apartment-house owners. These owners have borrowed money from HUD under various loan programs and are under contract to make a certain number of the units (sometimes all of them) available for low-income housing.

The prospective tenant applies directly to the landlord, who "keeps his own waiting list, has the right of tenant selection, processes applications, verifies income, assets, allowances and eligibility, and determines rent by completing the Tenant Certification as required by HUD regulations."

But HUD periodically publishes a list of private apartment houses in its program; interested tenants can get it by requesting the "subsidized housing list" from the HUD office in Seattle, 220-5140. HUD doesn't know which have vacancies; it's up to the prospective tenant to find them, which can pose a problem for those who can't afford a phone. The list includes apartment-building addresses, phone numbers, unit sizes, and programs for which the units are eligible.

THE HOMELESS

Conservative estimates say that between 3,000 and 5,000 people in Seattle are homeless. Tonight, more than 800 families who call Seattle home are spending the night on the streets or in shelters. One shelter for abused women turned away over a thousand women in just eight months.

Sound bleak? It's actually better than it was a few years ago, before a tent city of homeless people near the Kingdome brought to light the plight of less fortunate city residents.

Lots of people are trying to help the homeless in some way—feeding programs, shelters, health services—but only *Real Change* is actually setting the homeless up in business for themselves. *Real Change* (whose name is a play on the plaintive "Spare change?" heard everywhere on the streets each day) bills itself as "Seattle's Homeless Newspaper." And in fact, it is largely written and exclusively sold (for $1) by homeless vendors, who keep 100% of the money they earn. Vendors must wear an ID badge, and cannot drink while they're selling. Most vendors will tell you they hope to earn enough money to get a place to live. Some just want to earn enough to buy a pager, which sounds frivolous but is the best way for them to be reached by prospective employers, landlords, etc. Lots of Seattleites buy *Real Change* regularly, either to help the homeless or just because they like the gritty, honest quality of the paper. Contact: *Real Change*, 2129 Second, Seattle, WA 98121; 441-3247.

In 1990, a group of homeless people calling themselves Seattle Housing and Resources Effort (SHARE) settled into 35 tents and grabbed the attention of the national media, prompting the city to sit up and take notice of the inadequacy of existing homeless shelters and services.

But publicity aside, today there are still a whole lot of residents living in boxes under the viaduct—or in a forest of bushes under the Yesler overpass—or on a cold piece of view property in a park corner overlooking Puget Sound.

WHO ARE SEATTLE'S HOMELESS?

When you think of the homeless, you might be thinking of the lines of men under the Alaskan Way viaduct trying to get into the missions on a cold winter night. But the city's homeless are a broad mix of the very young, the very old, families, individuals, disabled, nondisabled, and the mentally ill. The common characteristics are lack of a permanent nighttime address and being flat broke.

Homeless facts

- Conservative estimates show that 1,500 to 3,000 homeless are served by the shelter network on any given day, one-third of whom are children. Other estimates show from 3,000 to 5,000 homeless on Seattle's streets per day.
- The shelters serve 15,000 people every year. Not all homeless are served by the shelter network, particularly the mentally ill.
- At least 7,000 homeless are single adults: 90% men, 10% women.
- As a group, the homeless have high levels of disability, which include alcoholism (50%–60% of men), drug abuse, mental illness (10% of men), and physical impairment.

- Forty-five percent of single homeless women are victims of domestic violence or other abuse, 30% of single women shelter clients are mentally ill, and the percentage outside the shelters is considered to be much higher.
- At least 5,000 of the homeless who come to shelters are parents with children. It used to be that the majority were single mothers with children, but two-parent families are now in the majority. The average family includes 2.2 children.
- Over half of all homeless families are minorities.
- The vast majority of families are public assistance recipients whose grants do not enable them to afford housing, or who are new to the area and seeking employment, or who are fleeing domestic violence.
- Shelters serve 4,000 children under the age of 18, over half of whom are under the age of 6.
- At least 3,000 are street kids—youths not part of any family structure. Some are as young as 11 or 12; most are 15–19.
- There are about 200 shelter beds available for youths, but the majority require referrals by the Department of Social and Health Services. A total of six shelter beds are available for youths on a drop-in basis.
- Seattle has over 1,500 emergency shelter beds.

Source: Various social service agencies and reports

THE HOMELESS MENTALLY ILL

State mental hospital populations dropped from 5,000 in the 1970s to 1,436 in 1992. According to shelter managers in Seattle, many of those released are now among the homeless on Seattle streets. No emergency shelters exist specifically for the mentally ill. At any given time, 100 to 120 mentally ill people are in the county jail.

Source: State Division of Mental Health, DSHS

BUDDY, CAN YOU SPARE A DIME?

Panhandling in Seattle peaked dramatically a few years ago for several reasons. First, police drunk checks were phased out when public drunkenness was no longer considered a crime. Second, the Police Crime Prevention Unit at the SPD believes the Pioneer Square and Market areas fostered a "seedy" atmosphere that attracted panhandlers. The third reason involved a now-defunct federal program to help alcoholics by giving them grants of $300 a month. The recipients quickly drank their way through the money and panhandled to make ends meet. Attracted to this area by the program, the indigents made Seattle the Panhandler Capital for a while.

Reports suggest our area's mild weather now has the most to do with it. Whatever the reason they're here, panhandlers work areas where there is lots of foot traffic, so it seems as if they're everywhere.

It's difficult to tell how much a panhandler in Seattle makes, but some street people estimate it's between $20 and $30 a day.

Most panhandlers are not danger-

The most welcome donations to homeless shelters: appliances, bedding and linens, clothing, children's items, nonperishable food, furniture, personal hygiene supplies, office equipment, and cash.

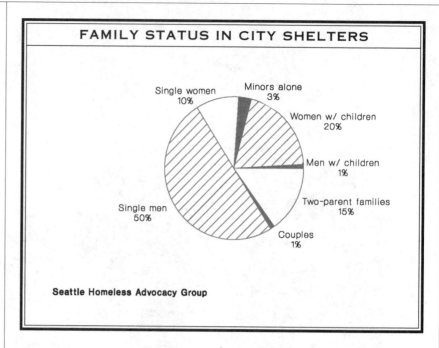

FAMILY STATUS IN CITY SHELTERS

- Single women 10%
- Minors alone 3%
- Women w/ children 20%
- Men w/ children 1%
- Two-parent families 15%
- Couples 1%
- Single men 50%

Seattle Homeless Advocacy Group

ous. Most are alcoholics and homeless; many are mentally ill.

Seattle has an aggressive anti-panhandling law; harassing anyone for money or any other reason is a misdemeanor on Seattle streets. Most panhandlers know this and will leave you alone rather than risk arrest.

WAYS TO HELP

Should you give that change in your pocket to a panhandler? Nothing produces more guilt than passing someone by who wants just a nickel (or 13 cents, which the guy nicknamed "Thirteen" down by the Market always requests). Some panhandlers have dogs and beg for "money for dog food"; some have signs asking for money for the kids left behind; and some have a sob story about how they wound up in Seattle without a dime and they could get home to Bellingham if you'd just part with your pocketbook. . . . You get the idea. One guy at least uses humor: "No refunds," his sign says.

What to do? Some people give and some don't. Some buy soup or coffee and give it to the panhandlers—an effort met with mixed results. The big question is, are you destroying their livers with your hard-earned pocket change?

Some groups have been very successful with voucher programs for panhandlers. Caring Neighbors sells a package of four 25-cent vouchers that can be redeemed at various Capitol Hill businesses (listed on each voucher) for laundry, food, showers, or Metro buses. What's most used? The laundry vouchers.

While these programs are generally considered successful, there have been more vouchers sold to caring residents than redeemed by the homeless. Why is a mystery, but on Capitol Hill it could have something to do with the fact that the hill's major supermarkets won't participate in the Caring Neighbors program. Strange, since it was modeled after a program in Berkeley, where the Safeway was the first to sign up.

Voucher programs
Caring Neighbors
329-8601

EMERGENCY SHELTERS

While giving or not giving to pan-handlers may be the source of angst, many emergency shelters have no qualms about accepting donations and/or offers of volunteer time. In fact, most have volunteer coordinators who will tell you how you can best help.

One caution: At Thanksgiving everyone wants to help. One volunteer said she showed up to feed the hungry along with many others doing the same thing. They were jostling elbows to get to the needy—who were in the minority—and under their breath saying, "That's *my* needy person, that's *my* needy person." Volunteers are still needed on holidays, but they're needed throughout the year, too. Many groups have daily soup kitchens and welcome help.

Shelters for adults and families

(Shelters for youths and victims of domestic violence are listed separately later in this chapter.)

Bethlehem House
West Seattle
937-7521
Serves women with children.

Bread of Life Mission
97 S Main St.
Seattle, WA 98104
682-3579
Serves single men.

Broadview Emergency Shelter
P.O. Box 31151
Seattle, WA 98103
622-3108
Women with children and single women.

Downtown Emergency Service Center
210 Jefferson St.
Seattle, WA 98104
464-1570
24-hour homeless shelter for single men and women.

Immanuel Lutheran
1215 Thomas St.
Seattle, WA 98109

The Crisis Clinic has an incredible directory of human resources called *Where to Turn* and an even more complete one called *Where to Turn Plus.* They are available for $5 and $20 respectively from Where to Turn, 1515 Dexter Avenue N, Suite 300, Seattle, WA 98109; 461-3210.

622-1930
Single men. Operates Nov.–Mar. only.

Lutheran Compass Center
77 S Washington St.
Seattle, WA 98104
461-7837
Single men and women.

Noel House
2301 Second Ave.
Seattle, WA 98121
441-3210
Single women.

Operation Nightwatch
P.O. Box 21181
91 Wall St.
Seattle, WA 98111
448-8804
Two-parent and single-parent families with children, couples, and single adults. Makes referrals and places in shelters people who haven't found a place to stay by 10pm.

Peniel Mission
2421 First Ave.
Seattle, WA 98121
441-7700
Single men and women.

Providence Hospitality House
P.O. Box 22382
Seattle, WA 98122

322-2107
Women with children.

Sacred Heart Shelter
232 Warren Ave. N
Seattle, WA 98109
285-7489
Two-parent and single-parent families and single women.

Seattle Emergency Housing Service
905 Spruce St., Suite 111
Seattle, WA 98104
461-3660
Two-parent and single-parent families with children.

St. Martin de Porres
1561 Alaskan Way S
Seattle, WA 98134
323-6341
Single men over 50.

Traveler's Aid Society
909 Fourth Ave., Suite 630
Seattle, WA 98104
461-3888
Two-parent and single-parent families, couples, and single adults who are not Seattle residents or who are new to or leaving the area.

Union Gospel Mission
318 Second Ave. Extension S
Seattle, WA 98104
622-5177
Single men.

Union Gospel Mission Family Shelter
520 S King St.
Seattle, WA 98104
628-2008
Two-parent and single-parent families, married couples, and single women.

YMCA Downtown— Young Adults in Transition
909 Fourth Ave.
Seattle, WA 98104
382-5018
Men and women, 18–22 years old.

YWCA Downtown Emergency Shelter
1118 Fifth Ave.
Seattle, WA 98101
461-4888
Women with children and single women. Call in advance.

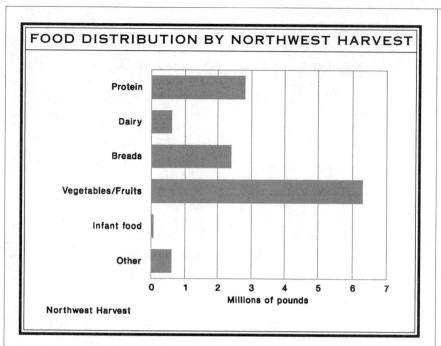

FOOD DISTRIBUTION BY NORTHWEST HARVEST

Millions of pounds

Northwest Harvest

YWCA—
East Cherry Emergency Shelter
2820 E Cherry St.
Seattle, WA 98122
461-8480
Two-parent and single-parent families with children.

Other assistance

Catholic Community Services
Emergency Assistance Program
100 23rd Ave. S
Seattle, WA 98144
323-6336
Motel vouchers for families with children, rent and eviction prevention assistance, child-care supplies, and referrals.

Central Area Motivation Program
722 18th Ave.
Seattle, WA 98122
329-4248
Rent and voucher assistance.

El Centro de la Raza
2524 16th Ave. S
Seattle, WA 98144
329-3837
Telephone and list of area shelters available.

First Avenue Service Center
2015 Third Ave.
Seattle, WA 98121

441-8405
Day center; must pick up vouchers. ID card needed to use center. Cards are distributed first Sunday of each month, 6:30 to 8am. Vouchers can then be exchanged for services, including laundry, mail, and shower facilities and clothing distribution. Open all night in life-threatening, subfreezing weather, as backup for shelters.

Food Lifeline
15230 15th Ave. NE
Seattle, WA 98155
545-6600
Distributes food to food banks and meal programs. Volunteers and donations welcome.

Fremont Public Association
P.O. Box 31151
4001 Aurora Ave. N
Seattle, WA 98103
634-2222
Housing voucher program for families with children; offers eviction and mortgage default counseling; operates a food bank and soup kitchen.

Homeless Donation Service
461-3200
A joint project of the city and the Crisis Clinic, this is a referral service for those who want to donate such

things as bedding, clothing, toys, and furniture to the homeless. Call to learn how to contact the shelter most in need of your donations.

Lazarus Day Center
416 Second Ave. Extension S
Seattle, WA 98104
623-7219
Day center for men and women over age 50. Meals, shower and laundry facilities, and clothing distribution.

Millionair Club Charity
2515 Western Ave.
Seattle, WA 98121
728-5600
Job Service Line: 728-5627
Serves breakfast Mon.–Fri.; dinner Mon.–Sat. Also offers employment placement, counseling, and an eye clinic.

And why does the Millionair Club spell its name without an "e" on the end? Because it's not associated with any millionaire. It operates on a million-dollar budget, which it receives in donations from a variety of sources.

Neighborhood House
905 Spruce St.
Seattle, WA 98104
461-8430
Provides social services to residents of five Seattle-area public housing communities. Services include legal advocacy, food and clothing referrals, five Early Childhood Education programs, and transportation.

Northwest Harvest
711 Cherry St.
Seattle, WA 98102
625-0755
Northwest Harvest is a center for food collection. It distributes food through community hunger programs as well as directly to senior citizen centers and relief missions. Call Northwest Harvest (or local food banks) if you have food to contribute, or watch for food drives. Items most needed are powdered milk, food staples, packaged goods, and dietetic and baby foods. And, of course, money.

Seattle Food Committee
P.O. Box 31151
Seattle, WA 98103-1151
633-6405
Provides referrals (to people in need or people who want to donate) to food banks, feeding programs, and the Food Resources program of the Fremont Public Association.

Seattle Indian Center
611 12th Ave. S
Seattle, WA 98144
329-8700
Motel vouchers and referrals.

The Sharehouse
Associated Program of Church Council of Greater Seattle
4759 15th Ave. NE
Seattle, WA 98105
527-5956
Central warehouse project where surplus items from manufacturers are stored for distribution to Seattle shelters. Specializes in collecting *new* as opposed to used items, and targets local manufacturers for donations. Also accepts used furniture and other household items from individuals and businesses; limited pickup service. Donations accepted at Pier 36, 10am to 7pm, Tuesdays, Thursdays, and last Saturday of each month.

St. Vincent de Paul
909 Eighth Ave.
Seattle, WA 98109
767-6449
Vouchers for clothing, furniture, etc.

Strand Helpers
5747 Martin Luther King Way S
Seattle, WA 98118
723-6082
Almost legendary service for street people. Serves food, distributes blankets, provides transportation, does almost anything else needed. Every day from 3pm on, Strand Helpers serves food to 300–1,000 people downtown at the Fourth Avenue side of the Public Safety Building.

ALCOHOL— AND OTHER DRUGS

Alcoholics Anonymous (AA) sponsors 1,200–1,300 meetings each week in King County—and it's only one service out there offering help to those addicted to alcohol. The Crisis Clinic has a long list of facilities and services, and there's a 24-hour hotline for drug and alcohol abuse help: 722-3700. That line serves thousands of people each year seeking help for themselves or someone else.

Some county services

The King County Division of Alcoholism and Substance Abuse supplies most of the abuse services in the Seattle area. Call 296-7615 for information about these programs:

Alcoholism and Drug Abuse Treatment and Support Act (ADATSA): Assessment and case management services.

Alcohol Involuntary Treatment Services: Changes in the laws that govern involuntary treatment have turned procedures upside down and the county is scrambling to respond—in general, most people can't be treated involuntarily unless they're "a high-profile public nuisance," according to Luis Rosada at the Division of Alcoholism and Substance Abuse. Call 296-7612 for information.

Cedar Hills: A 208-bed inpatient residence for long-term and intensive treatment.

"Detox": There've been big changes in the way Seattle handles acute and chronic alcoholics. The King County Detoxification Center, a 105-bed facility that recycled Seattle drunks for years (it had a return rate of 75%), no longer exists. In its place, King County now contracts with Central Seattle Recovery Center (CSRC) and South King County Recovery Center, two private agencies that provide detoxification services with an emphasis (as their name indicates) on recovery.

Under the new rules, if you're picked up drunk or drugged on the streets in Seattle, or while driving, you're sent to a 20-bed "sleep-off" center run by Sound Recovery at 63 Clay Street. When you're sober, you'll be released with or without a ticket (since public drunkenness is not a crime in Seattle unless you're driving). At that time, you can ask to be evaluated for treatment and referred to CSRC or its equivalent in south King County. Or you can call CSRC after you get home and think it over.

CSRC has 15 beds for "medical detox" (acute care) and 13 beds for subacute care. And they don't recycle drunks more than once. If you're admitted to the program and drop out, you get a second chance (just one) to complete the program. After that, they won't accept you. "We offer them a continuum of care, which includes referrals to AA and BA—we have four AA meetings on the premises. We treat this like the primary illness it is, not as a secondary illness. Our staff are former addicts who've 'been there.' It's a tougher program, but it comes from the heart because we can't stand to see them killing themselves" (CSRC staff member).

How is the new program working? The old-style detox facility evaluated 1,000 people each month at an annual cost of $4.2 million per year to the taxpayers—and 75% of those evaluated were the same people over and over. CSRC evaluates about 200 people each month at their own request, and admits about half to treatment. Costs have dropped to $1.3 million per year for CSRC and about $1 million for the South King County Recovery Center.

Emergency Service Patrol: Assists downtown Seattle police in picking up, screening, and referring people found inebriated or high on drugs on the streets or while driving.

Methadone Services: Provides methadone and monitoring to rehabilitate heroin addicts.

North Rehabilitation Facility: A minimum-security county jail facility that provides rehab and education for those convicted of DWI.

Outpatient and Youth Treatment Clinics: Five clinics serve a population of 400 to 900 each. Sliding-scale fees.

Prevention Services: Drug- and alcohol-abuse prevention education.

Other substance abuse help

Alcoholics Anonymous
587-2838

Al-Anon Information Service
625-0000
For friends and relatives of alcoholics.

Alcohol-Drug Helpline
722-3700

Crisis Clinic
461-3200

King County Division of Alcoholism and Substance Abuse
296-7615

Lesbian Resource Center
322-3953
Substance-abuse support groups.

Mothers Against Drunk Driving (MADD)
364-6233
Victims' advocate. Monitors courts and enforcement policies; active in government relations and public education.

Narcotics Anonymous
329-1618
Regular support groups for recovering addicts.

Seattle Poison Center
525-2121, (800) 732-6985
Formerly part of Children's Hospital, the Poison Center is now independent and is located at the Northgate Executive Center. The Poison Center is still staffed 24 hours a day by professionals who answer more than 75,000 calls annually. They identify proper medical treatment for over 400,000 toxic substances.

United Way Agency
386-0220
Eighty- to 100-person waiting list for treatment. Many payment options, including free treatment for the indigent (28% of referrals are homeless).

Washington State Substance Abuse Coalition
637-7011
Maintains a clearinghouse of drug- and alcohol-related infor mation for the public.

Women in Recovery
722-6117
(800) 562-1240 (inside Washington state)
Women helping other women to cope with life without drugs or alcohol; regular meetings.

DEADLY DRUGS

The fact that drugs can kill is illustrated most dramatically by the Medical Examiner's annual report. In 1994, 68% of drug-related deaths involved cocaine or heroin/opiates. The number of deaths from cocaine has continued to increase by about 25 deaths each year since 1987. And the number of deaths from all drugs has increased by 45% since 1985. Seventy-five percent of drug deaths were in the 30-to-49 age group— of those, three out of four were males.

HOME SWEET HOME?

More than 8,000 domestic abuse cases are reported in Seattle annually, and the FBI estimates that only 1 in 10 domestic violence assaults is reported to police.

If you think that's depressing, consider these facts:

- Just one shelter, New Beginnings, turned away 1,033 women in eight months. Seattle's shelters for battered women turn away an estimated 5,500 victims of domestic violence per year.

The most important thing when confronted by a panhandler is to at least give an answer, say shelter operators. Whether or not to give is a decision each person has to make. If you want to give, go ahead—often panhandlers really do need the money for food; they aren't all out there for sinister reasons. And if you don't want to give, don't just look away and keep walking. Say no— treat the panhandler as a person. When you ignore panhandlers, it perpetuates the idea that they're not fully human.

- 25%–40% of battered women are pregnant.
- Nearly half the homeless women with children and homeless single women in Seattle are without a home due to domestic violence.
- Arrests for domestic violence increased from 387 in 1983 to 2,475 in 1985 to 2,500–3,000 currently. Of the total cases investigated each year, about 5,000 are cases in which the assaulter has left the scene by the time the police arrive, according to the Seattle Family Violence Project.

Domestic violence resources

Catherine Booth House
P.O. Box 20128
Seattle, WA 98102
324-4943
Shelter for women with children and single women. Children's advocacy.

City of Seattle Law Department, Criminal Division
Family Violence Project
Dexter Horton Bldg., Room 1414
710 Second Ave.
Seattle, WA 98104
684-7770 (TTY)
Assists victims of domestic violence in cases where criminal charges have been filed.

Domestic Abuse Women's Network (DAWN)
Hotline: 656-7867
South King County network of women helping other women. Emergency shelter, 24-hour crisis line, support groups.

Domestic Violence Hotline
(800) 562-6025
Statewide hotline. Referrals to shelters, and a sympathetic ear.

Hickman House
P.O. Box 20128
Seattle, WA 98102
932-5341
Transitional housing for women with children and single women. May stay up to six months. Offers counseling, case management, follow-up after women obtain permanent housing.

King County Sexual Assault Resource Center
226-5062
For adults, ongoing legal advocacy; 24-hour crisis information line. For children, legal advocacy, medical exams, and therapy.

Lesbian Resource Center
322-3953
Support groups for battered lesbians; library; therapist referral book available in office.

New Beginnings Shelter
P.O. Box 75125
Seattle, WA 98125-0125
522-9472 (24-hour crisis line)
Confidential-location shelter for battered women and children, including teenage boys. May stay up to four weeks. Provides food and bus fare; community, legal, and children's advocacy.

Planned Parenthood
328-7700
Referrals to other community services.

GETTING BACK ON YOUR FEET

A few of the local agencies offering employment and literacy services:

Employment assistance

Belltown Multi-Service Center
2106 Second Ave.
Seattle, WA 98121
464-6449
State-funded employment service; also, homeless employment project.

Employment Opportunities Center
4726 Rainier Ave. S
Seattle, WA 98118
725-8200
Free services include direct placement, referral, ESL and GED classes, and a learning center for AFDC clients.

Goodwill Industries
1400 S Lane
Seattle, WA 98144
Nine-month training program in plant or store.

Workforce Services
4142 Brooklyn Ave. NE
Seattle, WA 98105
547-8354
Assists chronically unemployed and underemployed people. Three-stage program includes employment readiness seminar, one-to-one help with job search, and follow-up.

Literacy

Goodwill Literacy
1400 S Lane
Seattle, WA 98144
329-1000 ext. 291
Reading, writing, and math classes for English-speaking adults, from basic literacy to college prep. Individual and small group tutoring.

Washington Literacy
220 Nickerson
Seattle, WA 98109
461-3623
(800) 323-2550 (Literacy Hotline)
Trains literacy volunteers and lends educational materials. Operates Literacy Bookstore and the Literacy Action Center, which tutors adults at or below a sixth-grade reading level; Workplace Literacy consultants for employers; and the Washington State Literacy Hotline, a referral service for students, tutors, and volunteer-based programs. Coordinates children's summer day camp and inner-city day-care reading program.

KID STUFF

In the 1980s, then-mayor Charles Royer started a program called "KidsPlace." It was supposed to arrest the exodus of children and families from the city and turn Seattle into a giant playground. Some critics charged that Royer's actions were inspired political moves of no substance; the former mayor bristled. The old saying "time will tell" comes into play here. What's the status of KidsPlace?

It's defunct. So much for politics.

But not to worry. City government in all its guises still provides services. The parks department even borrowed the name KidsPlace for its after-school and summer program. It's available at many community centers, including Ballard, Delridge, Garfield, High Point, Miller, Rainier, Rainier Beach, South Park, Van Asselt, and Yesler. Contact your local center for details.

The city still has a summer youth employment program (though the demand for jobs always far exceeds the supply), and there's help with child-care expenses through the Department of Housing and Human Services. Seattle's community YMCAs do their part with an extensive array of classes, lessons, recreational opportunities, and more.

Department of Housing and Human Services

618 Second Ave.
Seattle, WA 98104-2232
386-1375
Summer youth employment program for youths ages 14–21, from low-income families. Applications become available in March.

Fauntleroy YMCA

9260 California Ave. SW
Seattle, WA 98136
937-1000
After-school recreation program, nursery, day camps, Indian guides, etc.

Seattle's Child

2107 Elliott Ave., Suite 303
Seattle, WA 98121
441-0191
A monthly newspaper that's *the* local resource for kids' services, things to do, children's issues, directories. Annual readers' poll called Golden Bootie Awards, for best kids' stuff. Publishes *Eastside Parent* and *Puget Sound Parent* as well.

West Seattle Family YMCA

4515 36th Ave. SW
Seattle, WA 98126
935-6000
Indian guides, parent-child programs, youth activities.

HOW ABOUT A PARENTSPLACE?

Being a parent sounds easy—until you become one. First parenting means getting up all night, then it's shivering at Little League games, and then adolescents-from-hell take over your life. But there's help out there—in the form of helplines, parenting workshops, and classes.

The most prolific in terms of services for parents is Children's Hospital and Medical Center, a 200-bed medical facility serving a four-state region. Eighty percent of its patients are under 3 years old. It's a big operation, with 59 pediatric

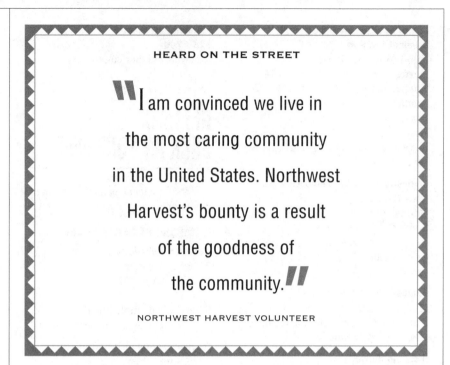

subspecialty clinics and the largest auxiliary in the U.S. (15,000 guild members). The board of trustees is all women. Here's a partial rundown on what Children's offers:

Children's Resource Line: 526-2500. Staffed seven days a week, 7am–11pm, by pediatrics registered nurses: provides parents with information on development and health-care issues, and treatment of injuries and illnesses. Will refer you to physicians if needed.

Good Growing: A series of monthly programs and newsletter focusing on the most requested parenting and child health topics. Designed for adults, teens, and children. Call Resource Center (526-2201) for free series schedule and to pre-register. Also sponsors health fairs and support groups.

Parents Resource Center: Fifth Floor, Wing A of the hospital, 526-2201. Open to the public as well as to parents of children at the hospital, the Resource Center has books, brochures, and articles on diverse topics such as preventive health care, child safety, childhood illnesses, parenting, and growth and development.

The Parents Center library contains 1,000 books and 1,500 pamphlets on everything from how to form a babysitting co-op to dwarfism. If you want information on a medical problem, you can look at the same books the doctors use in the hospital's medical library. There is also information on Seattle-area activities for children.

Seattle Poison Center: Formerly part of Children's Hospital, the Poison Center is now independent and is located at the Northgate Executive Center. The Poison Center is still staffed 24 hours a day by professionals who answer 75,000+ calls annually. They identify proper medical treatment for more than 400,000 toxic substances;
526-2121, (800) 732-6985.

Children's Hospital and Medical Center

4800 Sand Point Way NE
Seattle, WA 98105
526-2000

MORE PARENTING HELP

In case that isn't enough help, there's more:

Atlantic Street Center
7301 Beacon Ave. S
Seattle, WA 98108
723-1301
This nonprofit family center, located in the lower level of the Beacon United Methodist Church, offers multicultural parenting classes at no charge. Visit first, or call to be put on the mailing list for brochures and flyers. Free parking. Open Mon.–Fri. 9am–5pm.

Children's Home Society
524-6020
Parent Development program offers support groups and a newsletter. To join the program, you must be enrolled in the society's "Families First" program.

**Council for Prevention of
Child Abuse and Neglect (COPCAN)**
1305 Fourth Ave., Room 202
Seattle, WA 98101
343-2590
Parent Line—a support and information service during business hours for people needing information or referral on child-related matters. Library open to the public.

Family Life Education Network
524-6020 (Children's Home Society)
A coalition of social service agencies that puts out *Family Life Connections,* a guidebook on parenting (and youth) classes. The classes are offered by various organizations such as Youth Suicide Prevention Group, Seattle Children's Home, and Ryther Child Center.

Northwest Hospital
364-BABY (364-2229)
Offers parenting classes, as do many hospitals in the area. Check with yours.

Parents Anonymous
233-0139 (24-hour hotline)
A support group for stressed-out parents to prevent them from taking their frustrations out on their kids. Evening calls are fielded by parent volunteers. Parent info line for parenting classes, support, and activities.

Program for Early Parent Support (PEPS)
547-8570
Trains volunteers to lead support groups for parents of infants throughout King County.

Ruth Dykeman Center
242-1698
Residential treatment center for emotionally disturbed elementary-age children.

Ryther Child Center
525-5050
Offers a parenting class for parents of emotionally disturbed children.

THE DAY-CARE MAZE

About 2,500 licensed day-care operators have set up shop in the Seattle/King County area; more than 75% are based in their own homes (up to 6 kids), and the vast majority of the remainder are mini-centers (up to 12 kids). The average weekly cost of day care in Seattle in 1995:

- Infants (1–11 months): $159
- Toddlers (12–29 months): $131
- Preschoolers (30 months+): $111
- School-age children: $63 (before school), $88 (before and after school)

Although there seem to be lots of providers, more are needed. And prices vary, depending on the type of facility and its location.

The real trick is finding *conveniently located* day care. The state's Department of Social and Health Services (DSHS) does licensing, but doesn't give out lists of day cares in the normal course of business. The Crisis Clinic and the city combined to form Child Care Resources, which provides a list of day-care options in your zip-code area or near your work. In 1995, 8,075 people called.

Child Care Resources
2915 E Madison, Suite 305
Seattle, WA 98112
461-3207 (for parents)
461-3708 (for day-care providers)
Day-care referral service,
Mon.–Thurs., 9am–3pm and
6:30–9:30pm; Fri., 9am–1pm.
Also produces a consumer guide for parents called *Choosing Child Care.*

Other day-care resources

Camp Fire's Phone Friend
Seattle/King County Council
8511 15th Ave. NE
Seattle, WA 98115
(800) 543-8255
An after-school helpline for latchkey children, Mon.–Fri., 3–6pm.

**Family Child Care Association
of King County**
1225 Fourth Ave. S, Suite A
Seattle, WA 98134
467-1552
Licensed providers who make referrals for parents.

Gentle Care Program
Auburn General Hospital
20 Second St. NE
Auburn, WA 98002
833-7711, ext. 350
Offers day care for mildly ill children, as beds available. Ask for the nurse's office.

Neighborhood House
905 Spruce St.
Seattle, WA 98104
461-8430
Administers a child-care program with conveniently located branch centers.

**Seattle Dept. of Housing
and Human Services**
Division of Family and Youth Services
618 Second Ave.
Seattle, WA 98104
386-1050
Child-care subsidy program for working parents.

Tender Loving Care
Virginia Mason Hospital
1201 Terry St.
Seattle, WA 98111
583-6521
Offers day care for mildly ill children, as space in the napping room is available.

THE NOT-SO-BRIGHT SIDE

So how do kids fare in Seattle?

- In 1990, the percentage of pregnant women in King County receiving prenatal care was 27% below the national average. Due partially to expansion of Medicaid eligibility for pregnant women, increased provider payments, and enhanced support services, this has turned around: In 1992, the number receiving care was 6% higher than the national average.
- Number of teen births in King County (1991): 2,153 or 9.4% of all live births. Number of births the same year to mothers under 15 years old: 23. Between ages 15 and 17: 551.
- Number of homeless youths in the city: 1,000.
- Number of emergency beds in King County for youths: about 200.
- Types of child abuse cases reported to Child Protective Services: physical abuse, 25%; sexual abuse, 15%; neglect, 48%; emotional maltreatment, 6%; other, 6%.

Resources for children/families in crisis

Atlantic Street Center
2103 Atlantic St.
Seattle, WA 98144
329-2050
Refuge for individuals, children, youth, and families in need. Includes adolescent services, counseling, haven for homeless schoolchildren, parent co-op, etc. Volunteers welcome. Family center offers training in parenting skills; call 723-1301.

Big Brothers of King County
2719 E Madison, Suite 200
Seattle, WA 98112
461-3630
Links adult mentors with boys in need.

Big Sisters of King County
1100 Virginia St.
Seattle, WA 98101
461-8502
Links adult mentors with girls in need.

Child Protective Services (CPS)
Washington State Dept. of Social and Health Services
2809 26th Ave. S
Seattle, WA 98144
721-4115 (to make a report)
721-4225 (caseworkers)
Investigates reports of child abuse, neglect, and exploitation. Names confidential.

Childhaven
316 Broadway
Seattle, WA 98122
624-6477
Day treatment center for abused children. Free.

Committee for Children
2203 Airport Way S
Seattle, WA 98134
343-1223
Started by Dr. Jennifer James, this group provides training, education materials, and curricula on child-abuse prevention and personal safety.

Council for Prevention of Child Abuse and Neglect (COPCAN)
1305 Fourth Ave., Room 202
Seattle, WA 98101
343-2590
Abuse-prevention programs, a referral service, and a library open to the public. Also a Parent Line—a support and information service during business hours for people needing information or referral on child-related matters.

Court Appointed Special Advocates (CASA)
Family Court of King County
King County Superior Court
Third Ave. and James St.,
Room C205
Seattle, WA 98104
296-9320
Represents the interests of children in divorce court proceedings.

Friends of Youth
P.O. Box 12
414 Front St. N
Issaquah, WA 98027
392-KIDS
Outpatient counseling, teen mom program. Serves Eastside, Renton to Bothell. Two shelters for runaways ages 11–17.

Guardian ad Litem Program
King County Superior Court
1211 E Alder St.
Seattle, WA 98122
296-1120
Uses trained laypeople within the courts to act as independent advocates for children. Makes recommendations to the court in the best interest of the child.

Medina Children's Service
123 16th Ave.
Seattle, WA 98122
461-4520
Administers Teen Age Pregnancy Project (TAPP) and adoption services in cooperation with the City of Seattle, the Seattle/King County Public Health Department, and the Seattle School District. Adoption searches.

Youth Advocates
2317 E John St.
Seattle, WA 98112
322-7838
Services for high-risk adolescents, teen pregnancy counseling, residential crisis centers, resource for gay and lesbian youth.

EVERY PARENT'S NIGHTMARE

Your teenager doesn't come home on time, and dawn finds you wringing your hands. Could it be that he or she has run away? What to do? The people at Friends of Youth, an Eastside agency that helps runaways and their families, say there's not a lot you can do. But here's where to start:

- Be your own detective. Check with the child's friends about where he or she might be and when your child was seen last.
- Check with school counselors to see if your child was in school that day. In other words, determine how long he or she has been gone.
- If you do find your child, he or she doesn't have to come home—it's a child's legal right to make his or her own choices.
- If your child refuses to come home and you feel he or she is in a bad or dangerous situation, call Child Protective Services. They may investigate.
- Call the police if your child has been gone for more than 24 hours. But don't expect much—they will only investigate if there's a specific problem, such as your child hanging out at a crack house.
- Once you have found your child, get outside help. Try the family counseling Friends of Youth and other agencies provide. They try to get your child to talk to you—if the child won't talk, be prepared to wait him or her out.

Runaway hotlines

Runaway Hotline Service
(800) 231-6946
Relays messages between runaway children and parents. Nationwide information referral.

The Teen Hotline
722-4222
State-sponsored hotline staffed by trained teens, 24 hours a day. Crisis counseling and referrals to long-term counselors and shelters.

Youth shelters

Denny Place Youth Shelter
210 Dexter Ave. N
Seattle, WA 98109
328-5693
Youth ages 12–17. Meals, referrals, counseling.

Friends of Youth
P.O. Box 12
Issaquah, WA 98027
392-KIDS
Two shelters, in Issaquah and in Bothell/Kenmore, for runaways ages 11–17.

The Shelter
6201 46th Ave. S
Seattle, WA 98118
725-8888
Outreach program, with beds, for street kids and homeless young men and women, 12–17 years old. Operated by Orion Multi-Service Center.

How Seattle eats:

- **Northwest Harvest distributed 728.8 tons of meat in 1992: 651,548 pounds of chicken backs and necks, and 806,000 pounds of turkey meat.**

- **Metropolitan Grill (hangout for stockbrokers, businesspeople, and politicians) serves in a year: 196,000 pounds (98 tons) of steak.**

Source: Consolidated Restaurants, Northwest Harvest

YMCA Downtown— Young Adults in Transition
909 Fourth Ave.
Seattle, WA 98104
382-5018
Young men and women, 18–22 years old.

PROFILE OF A RUNAWAY, KING COUNTY

Average age: girls, 15.6; boys, 16.2.
Sex: 54% male; 46% female.
Racial makeup: 58% white; 18% native American; 9% African American; 4% Samoan; 4% Hispanic; 3% Asian; 4% other.
Abuse: More than 50% of runaways have a history of sexual or physical abuse.
School: More than 50% have dropped out or been suspended.
Drugs: 63% have been involved with drugs and alcohol.
Involvement in juvenile justice system: 43%.
Reasons for leaving: abandonment, rejection, boredom, unhappiness, serious family or school problems, conflict over sexual identity.

Source: Seattle Human Services Strategic Planning Office, "Homeless Youth in Seattle"

FOSTER CARE AND ADOPTION

At any one time, more than 50 kids are on a waiting list for group foster care in the city.

The state funds foster care in two ways: direct payment to foster parents, and payment to volunteer agencies (such as the Children's Home Society) that fund group facilities for foster kids.

In the Seattle area, as in any city, there's always a need for adoptive parents for older or special-needs

What can middle-class Seattle do about the homeless? Volunteer. Almost every shelter or social service agency maintains a list of volunteers they can call on. With Strand Helpers you can wash dishes and serve meals. Also, Strand Helpers is one of many homeless agencies that accept donations of blankets and coats. If washing dishes isn't your style, try giving those odd jobs around the house to someone from the Millionair Club Charity. They screen and place casual laborers in temporary jobs on a first-come, first-served basis.

kids. The only figures on how many kids are available overall for adoption are national estimates. Of the 500,000 children needing foster care in the U.S., 300,000 are legally available for adoption.

One Seattle agency, Adoption Services of WACAP (World Association for Children and Parents), places 50 to 100 babies per year under the Options for Pregnancy program, a system whereby birth parents choose adoptive parents for their newborn and remain in contact with the child as he or she grows.

WACAP reports a two-year waiting period for a young, healthy child. Minority couples might be able to adopt a child more quickly.

Foster care resources

The Casey Family Program
300 Elliott Ave. W, Suite 110
Seattle, WA 98119
286-4450

Catholic Community Services
100 23rd Ave. S
Seattle, WA 98144
323-6336

Children's Home Society of Washington
3300 NE 65th St.
Seattle, WA 98115
524-6020

Friends of Youth
2500 Lake Washington Blvd. N
Renton, WA 98056
228-5776
or
P.O. Box 12
Issaquah, WA 98027
392-KIDS

Jewish Family Service
1214 Boylston Ave.
Seattle, WA 98101
461-3240

Lutheran Social Services
6920 220th SW
Mountlake Terrace, WA 98043
672-6009
Children ages 8 and under. Refugee foster care program also.

Washington State Dept. of Social and Health Services
2809 26th Ave. S
Mail Stop N56-1
Seattle, WA 98144
721-4527

Youth Advocates
2317 E John St.
Seattle, WA 98112
322-7838

Agencies providing adoption services

Adoption Services of WACAP
543 Industry Dr.
Tukwila, WA 98188
575-4550

Catholic Community Services
100 23rd Ave. S
Seattle, WA 98144
323-6336

Children's Home Society of Washington
3300 NE 65th St.
Seattle, WA 98115
524-6020
Also offers support for those touched by adoption, including the Adoption Shop, a bookstore with materials on adoption.

Hope Services
424 N 130th St.
Seattle, WA 98133
367-4604

Jewish Family Service
1214 Boylston Ave.
Seattle, WA 98101
461-3240

Lutheran Social Services
6920 220th SW
Mountlake Terrace, WA 98043
672-6009

Medina Children's Service
123 16th Ave.
Seattle, WA 98122
461-4520

Other adoption resources

Adoption Information Service
P.O. Box 55183
Seattle, WA 98155
325-9500

Becoming Adoptive Parents
c/o Childbirth Education Association
485-5649 (Mary Sutton)
Class for families waiting for arrival of an infant.

Korean Identity Development Society (KIDS)
8315 Lake City Way NE, Suite 120
Seattle, WA 98125
340-0937
Teaches Korean culture to Korean-American children and adoptive families. Culture camp each July.

Northwest Adoption Exchange
1809 Seventh Ave., Suite 409
Seattle, WA 98101
292-0082

**One Church One Child
of Washington State**
6419 Martin Luther King Jr. Way S
Seattle, WA 98118
723-6224
Recruits African American families
to adopt African American children.

ACCESSING SEATTLE

People say that Seattle is one of the
best cities for the disabled to live
in. Accessibility guides and other
services proliferate—primarily
because the disabled community
here is outspoken and assertive.
Some resources:

Access Seattle
Easter Seal Society of Washington
521 Second Ave. W
Seattle, WA 98119
281-5700
Publishes guidebook to handicapped-
accessible places in Seattle. Programs
include housing assistance and modification, community access and
Americans with Disabilities Act
(ADA) consultation and education,
Stroke Association, polio outreach,
camping, therapy, therapeutic horseback riding, respite care, durable
medical equipment, and information
and referral.

**Community Services for
the Blind and Partially Sighted**
9709 Third Ave. NE, Suite 100
Seattle, WA 98115-2027
525-5556 (V/TDD)
(800) 458-4888
Teaches skills and provides support
services to help blind and partially
sighted people to work, study, and
live independently. Low-vision rehabilitation is provided at minimal cost;
other services are free. Provides
instruction in safe movement and
travel, counseling, and support
groups. Runs Adaptive Aids and
Appliances Store.

**Dental Education
for Care of the Disabled**
543-4619
Lower-cost dental clinic serving

the disabled, operated by the UW
School of Dentistry. Acceptance
based on dental needs and teaching
applicability.

**Governor's Committee on Disability
Issues and Employment**
P.O. Box 9046
Olympia, WA 98507-9046
(360) 438-3168
Offers publications for a fee,
including *Accessible Meetings in
Washington State* and *Reasonable
Accommodation,* which covers how
to make workplaces accessible.

Mayor's Office
618 Second Ave., Suite 250
Seattle, WA 98104
684-0500
Disabled people not living in subsidized housing can apply for
discounts on utilities (Seattle City
Light and water, sewer, and garbage
services) through this office.

Seattle Public Library Bookmobile
684-4713
Bookmobiles travel to homebound
people who do not have access to
libraries. Call to request a visit.

**Washington Coalition
of Citizens with Disabilities**
4649 Sunnyside Ave. N, Suite 100
Seattle, WA 98103
461-4550; 461-3766 (TTD)
Offers a quarterly newsletter, self-
advocacy training, peer counseling,
a job club, legal services, ADA and
disability sensitivity training, consulting, access reviews, and support
for independent living.

**Washington Library for
the Blind and Physically Handicapped**
821 Lenora St.
Seattle, WA 98129
464-6930
Hours: 8:30am–5pm weekdays;
closed weekends. Phono records,
cassettes, braille, large print, and
print reference collections.

FOR SENIORS...

It would take a whole book to list
all the services, programs, and discounts available to seniors in the
Seattle/King County area, but here
are a few to get you started. For local
senior newspapers, see Chapter 9,
"Film at Eleven"; for senior services
offered by Seattle's ethnic communities, see Chapter 12, "Ethnicity:
Diversity at Work."

**Alzheimer's Association
of Puget Sound**
783-6600, (800) 848-7097
Referrals, annual conference.

**American Association
of Retired Persons**
526-7918

City of Seattle Division on Aging
684-0660
Senior support.

Homesharing for Seniors
448-5725
Intergenerational program that helps
seniors stay in their own homes while
gaining companionship and help with
daily living.

Mayor's Office for Senior Citizens
684-0500
Senior Joblines: 684-0477 and
684-0495
Offers an employment program
and advocacy services. Low-income
seniors not living in subsidized housing can apply for discounts on
utilities (Seattle City Light and
water, sewer, and garbage services)
through this office.

**Nursing Home Patient
Abuse and Neglect Reports**
(800) 562-6078
Office of the state's Long-Term
Care Ombudsman.

**Seattle/King County
Advisory Council on Aging**
684-0662

Seattle Public Library Bookmobile
684-4713
Bookmobiles travel to homebound people who do not have access to libraries. Call to request a visit.

Senior Citizen Information and Assistance
448-3110
City-funded service offering referrals; has free brochure on low-income housing programs for seniors in Seattle. Can direct you to the senior center nearest your neighborhood.

UW Senior Citizen Access Program
543-2320
Seniors 60 years or older can audit (sit in on) two UW classes per quarter for just $5.

SEATTLE SCHOOL DAZE

They're not exactly clicking their heels together and saluting, but the 46,225 students in Seattle's schools began getting a taste of the military way in 1995, when an exasperated school board turned away from tradition and appointed a retired

How does the school district determine which students get their first-choice schools? If too many students apply to one school, the district has set up the following list of considerations to guide the difficult decision-making:

- Students who have sisters or brothers attending the school receive first priority.
- Students who have attended special programs may receive priority over those who have not.
- A child whose race will help provide racial balance at a school will be given priority. (Kindergarteners are exempt from this rule; they almost always get their first-choice school.)
- Students living closer to a school are assigned before those living farther away.
- If none of the above considerations applies, students are given a random three-digit lottery number, and those with with lower numbers receive priority.

Army major general to the post of superintendent.

As for the new supe, John Stanford, he swept onto the school battlefield much as he tackled deliveries to the front lines in the Gulf War. As in:

Attenshun! There's now a rule that administrators spend at least one day a week in the classroom.

About face! The school is looking at charging parents if a child brings a weapon to school (and weapons include everything: toy guns, wicked-looking rings, etc.).

March! Parents have homework. Parents of grade school children must read to their children at least 30 minutes each evening.

Salute! Tests in third, fifth, eighth, and eleventh grades will show if a student should be kept back a grade instead of being designated as operating "below grade level" and going right on through school to the end.

There's more, and so far Stanford is on a honeymoon with parents, teachers, and principals (whom he calls CEOs) alike. The honeymoon is not all wine and roses, though. Stanford arrived just as the voters scoffed at a $150 million operations levy, defeating the voting measure for the first time in 20 years. It passed the second time around, thanks partially to his strong campaigning.

UNDER CONTROL

Under the new superintendent, the school board is proposing to change the way students are assigned to school. Beginning in the 1997–98 school year, it seems likely that some alternative to the controlled-choice system will be in place. The board is leaning toward a "regional choice" alternative, in which parents could choose among schools in the region where they live, with priority to neighborhood schools. The danger? Resegregation of the schools. If the minority cap set by the state (82%) is surpassed, the district could lose up to $27 million in construction funds.

Why all the flap? In 1995, 73% of the kids in elementary school were assigned to their first-choice schools. The district wants that figure to be 100%.

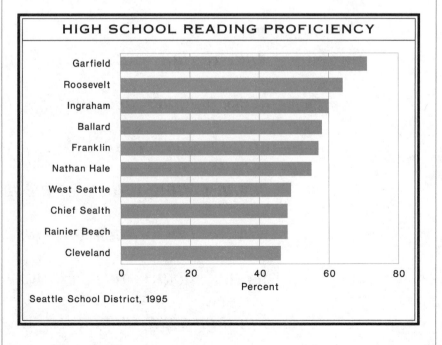

HIGH SCHOOL READING PROFICIENCY

Seattle School District, 1995

Tips from parents for getting through the public school maze:

- **Request a hearing.**
- **Turn in applications on time.**
- **To expand your options, have your child tested for special programs.**
- **Talk to more than one person.**
- **Don't take no for an answer.**
- **Don't wait for people to call you back. Keep calling them.**
- **Refuse to leave the office until you get who or what you want.**
- **Get to know a school board member.**
- **Get to know the principal at the school of your choice.**
- **Talk frequently with staff at Parent Information Centers or the student placement office, and talk with as many staffers as possible.**
- **Don't whine. It doesn't help to tell employees that your child's needs can't be met anywhere else.**
- **Don't threaten to take your child out of the system. Promise instead to stick around and be a problem.**
- **Understand "tiebreaker" rules, i.e., siblings in the same program, distance from school, etc.**
- **Go public. Be visible and vocal with your concerns.**

How choice works

Here's a short primer on the controlled-choice process:

Clusters: Students are assigned to a cluster based on their home address. Clusters are groupings of five to eight elementary schools, including a student's neighborhood school. Note: Your neighborhood school is determined by the cluster boundaries, not by the school that is necessarily closest to your home. When selecting a school, you'll receive a "Choices, Choices" booklet that briefly describes the schools in your area.

Zones: The city is divided into three zones for elementary school assignment purposes. Each zone includes certain clusters.

Elementary school: As your child enters kindergarten or enters a new cluster, you can pick your first, second, and third choice of schools. After your child is given an assignment, he or she will be able to keep attending that school until graduation to middle school. The program is designed so that if you choose your neighborhood school as your first choice for your kindergartener, you will be guaranteed a spot there.

Middle school: You are offered a choice between two base schools determined by which elementary school your child attended. A student is guaranteed a spot in one of the two base schools if the base school is his or her first-choice school. You can also pick any middle school in the city, but, unlike the base schools, you may not get transportation paid for and there may not be a place for your student. You choose a middle school when your child is in the fifth grade.

High school: The same formula is applied to high schools. The school district assigns two base schools from which to choose, though you can choose any of the city high schools. Admission is based not only on racial balance but on how many kids can fit in the school;

Just as students have their favorite teachers, teachers have their favorite schools. We checked with education administrators to come up with this list of schools considered plums:

- **Garfield High School**
- **Gatzert Elementary**
- **Laurelhurst Elementary**
- **Lawton Elementary**
- **Roosevelt High School**
- **Viewlands Elementary**
- **Wedgwood Elementary**
- **Whitworth Elementary**

some schools (e.g., Garfield) are tough to get into simply because they are so popular.

Application times: For choosing elementary schools, February; middle schools and high schools, March.

Appeals: You can appeal if you're unhappy with the school your child has been assigned to. The district's Parent Information Centers have information about the process and appeal forms you can mail in. You'll then be notified by mail of the Appeals Board's decision; if you disagree with it, you can request a hearing before the board. That decision will be final.

English as a second language: In addition to helping parents select schools for their children, PICs can provide assistance to students and parents who have trouble speaking English. Seattle public

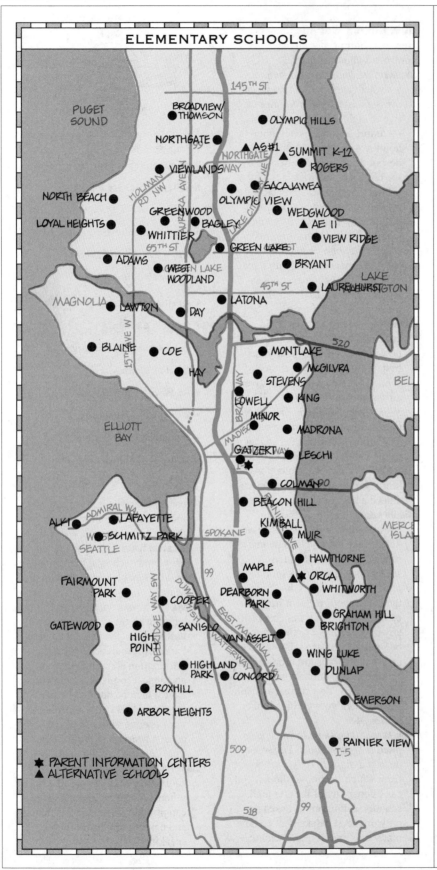

ELEMENTARY SCHOOLS

145TH ST

PUGET SOUND

BROADVIEW/THOMSON
OLYMPIC HILLS
NORTHGATE
AS #1
SUMMIT K-12
ROGERS
VIEWLANDS
SACAJAWEA
NORTH BEACH
OLYMPIC VIEW
GREENWOOD
WEDGWOOD
LOYAL HEIGHTS
BAGLEY
AE II
WHITTIER
VIEW RIDGE
GREEN LAKE
ADAMS
BRYANT
WEST LAKE WOODLAND
LAURELHURST
LAKE WASHINGTON
LATONA
MAGNOLIA
LAWTON
DAY
BLAINE
COE
HAY
MONTLAKE
McGILVRA
STEVENS
ELLIOTT BAY
LOWELL
KING
MINOR
MADRONA
GATZERT
LESCHI
COLMAN
BEACON HILL
ALKI
LAFAYETTE
KIMBALL
SCHMITZ PARK
MUIR
SEATTLE
HAWTHORNE
MAPLE
ORCA
FAIRMOUNT PARK
WHITWORTH
DEARBORN PARK
GATEWOOD
COOPER
GRAHAM HILL
HIGH POINT
SANISLO
BRIGHTON
VAN ASSELT
WING LUKE
HIGHLAND PARK
DUNLAP
CONCORD
ROXHILL
EMERSON
ARBOR HEIGHTS
RAINIER VIEW

★ PARENT INFORMATION CENTERS
▲ ALTERNATIVE SCHOOLS

---

schools serve over 9,900 students who speak a language other than English. An estimated 77 languages and/or dialects are represented.

More information: The district has two Parent Information Centers, or PICs. Parents should contact a PIC well before the winter application deadlines to familiarize themselves with the process. Parents can currently scan the schools in the district at the two PICs with the help of computers. Soon that school shopping may be easier than ever. The PICs may be disbanded altogether, with mini-PICs created at each school, all networked by computer. The idea is that parents can go to the school nearest them and peruse all the school profiles (complete with pictures) on a computer right there.

Northeast PIC
11530 12th Ave. NE
281-6989

Southeast/Central PIC
3928 S Graham St.
281-6456

PIC hours: Monday–Friday, 8am–4:30pm.

BEYOND THE SNIFF TEST

So how do you tell which is the best school for your student?

A friend of ours swears by what he calls "the sniff test." He maintains there's no substitute for personal presence in the classroom and suggests just walking into a school and asking, unannounced, to visit a class. He literally sniffs out what's going on and, more by osmosis than by any real scientific analysis, decides if this is a place that he—and his kids— would want to spend almost a third of their lives.

As an alternative to sniffing around classrooms, refer to the tables at the end of this chapter. Listed there are reams of facts and factoids about Seattle's public and selected private schools, designed to help parents evaluate the schools. Although the tables are not meant to rate the schools in any way, they give a good overview of what the choices are.

ACCELERATED PACE

The Seattle School District offers two special enrichment programs—Spectrum (formerly known as Horizon) and the Accelerated Progress Program (APP)—for high-potential students. Test scores, teacher input, and a parent questionnaire are used to determine which students qualify (generally the top 5% of test scores for Spectrum; the top 1% for APP). One elementary school in each controlled-choice cluster offers a Spectrum program; all middle schools offer some Spectrum classes in core subjects. The APP curriculum is available at Madrona Elementary, Washington Middle School, and all high schools.

ALTERNATIVE SCHOOLS

Alternative programs within the Seattle schools differ from the district's typical fare both in teaching philosophies and in techniques. They use methods and materials not usually found in regular programs—open-concept and multigraded classes and experiential approaches, for example. Alternative schools also provide opportunities for children who have special barriers (language, cultural, or social) and needs that can't be met elsewhere in the system (teenage parent programs with day care, night classes, etc.).

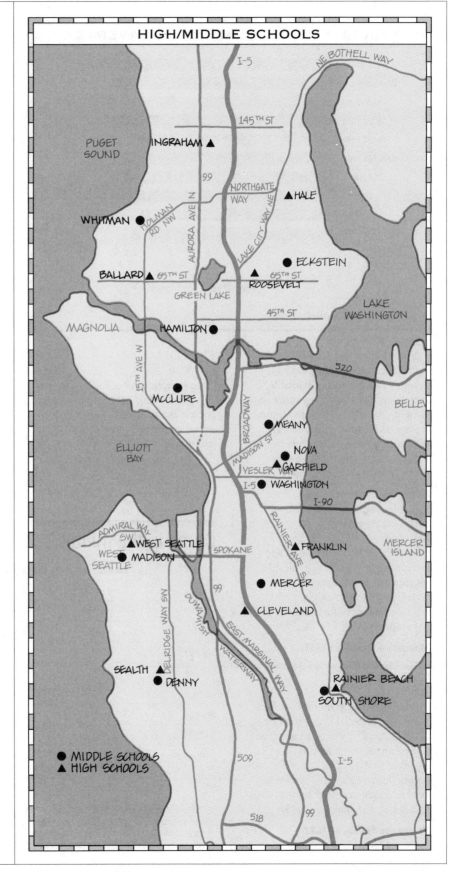

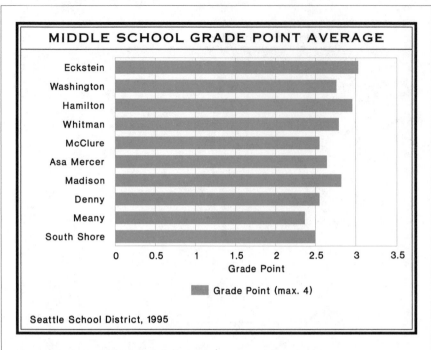

MIDDLE SCHOOL GRADE POINT AVERAGE

Eckstein
Washington
Hamilton
Whitman
McClure
Asa Mercer
Madison
Denny
Meany
South Shore

0   0.5   1   1.5   2   2.5   3   3.5
Grade Point

Grade Point (max. 4)

Seattle School District, 1995

Some alternative programs are more "alternative" than others in structure and in choices available to students. More than any other segment of the district, these programs require firsthand investigation via talks with principals, teachers, parents, and students before you consider them for your child.

African American Academy
Magnolia Elementary School
2418 28th Ave. W
281-6755
Opened in 1991; K–8; plan to add one grade per year up to grade 12; coursework taught from an Afrocentric perspective; children of any race can apply for this school; 265 students (1995).

Alternative School #1 (AS1)
Pinehurst Building
11530 12th Ave. NE
281-6970
Open-concept program for K–8 focusing on "experiential learning for nonlinear learners"; parents are involved in program development and in teaching; over 80 days of field trips for "adventure-based education"; pre-enrollment interview required; serves Zones 1, 2, and 3; 155 students (1995).

Alternative School #2 (AS2)
Decatur Elementary

7711 43rd Ave. NE
281-6770
Open-concept school for K–6 emphasizing individual instruction; no letter grades; evaluation via parent conferences; currently serves Zone 1; 300 students (1995).

Alternative School #3/ Escuela Latona (AS3)
Latona Elementary
401 NE 42nd St.
281-6530
Structured program emphasizing basic skills and the study of the Spanish language and Latino culture for K–5; serves Zone 2; 284 students (1995).

Alternative School #4 (AS4)
5012 S Genesee St.
281-6735
Focus on Native American culture and heritage; evaluation through narrative reports to parents; K–5; Zone 3; 179 students.

Alternative School #5/Coho (AS5)
Broadview Elementary
13052 Greenwood Ave. N
281-6280
Focus on whole child, cooperative school, de-emphasis on academic competition with evaluation through conferences and portfolios of student work; K–5; serves Zones 1 and 2; 111 students (1995).

Crime in the middle schools

	Assaults	Drugs	Disturbances	Weapons	Total cases*
Denny	5	2	4	8	29
Eckstein	2	1	1	2	18
Hamilton	14	4	5	0	28
Madison	11	4	8	2	36
McClure	2	0	1	4	16
Meany	22	5	32	7	116
Mercer	8	3	7	4	53
South Shore	12	1	7	6	54
Washington	43	9	35	4	134
Whitman	1	0	6	2	14

*Also includes false alarms, arson, burglaries, car prowls, fraud, injuries, kidnapping, property damage, service calls, sexual incidents, suspicious circumstances, and trespassing.
Source: Seattle School District Security System, Incident Report Summaries, Sept. 1995–May 1996

A few teacher facts:

• Beginning wage for a Seattle School District teacher with a B.A. or B.S.: $22,302.

• Beginning wage for a teacher with an M.A. or M.S.: $26,714.

• Top pay for a teacher with over 13 years of experience and a Ph.D.: $47,542.

• Degrees: 47% of Seattle teachers have a master of arts or science degree; 2% have a Ph.D. or Ed.D. degree. The remaining 51% have a bachelor of arts or science degree.

• Racial mix of teachers in SSD: 79% white, 10.5% black, 8.3% Asian, 1% Chicano/Latino, 1.1% Native American.

American Indian Heritage School
1330 N 90th St.
298-7895
Emphasis on Native American history, literature, and culture; academic and vocational courses; social-support services; 122 students (1995); grades 6–12; open to all races.

Kimball Elementary
3200 23rd Ave. S
281-6870
Open-concept school using team teaching for K–5 students; reading and language arts emphasis; outreach to bilingual students; serves Zones 1, 2, and 3; 531 students (1995).

Marshall Alternative High School
520 NE Ravenna Blvd.
281-6115
281-6146 (Evening High School)
Provides special programs for high-risk secondary students who live north of the ship canal: dropouts, underachievers, teenage parents (day care provided), students re-entering school after suspension or expulsions; also offers GED focus, evening high school for those who can't attend school during the day; 400 students (1995).

Middle College High School
1701 Broadway Ave., PC303
587-2015
Provides programs for at-risk 16- to 20-year-olds, with a focus on high school completion and higher education; 168 students (1995); grades 9–12.

New Option Middle School
Old Hay Elementary
411 Boston St.
281-6226
Global citizenship is central theme; cooperative learning; students go out into the community and assist in social service programs; 260 students (1995). Grades 6–8. Open to students districtwide.

1996 Excellence in Education Awards

• Betty Gray, assistant principal, Cleveland High School

• Joan Northfield, teacher, Nathan Hale High School

1996 A+ Educator Awards

• Chuck Chinn, principal, Ballard High School

• Don Bloedel, science teacher, TOPS

• David Kim and Patricia Costa Kim, music teachers, Chief Sealth High School

• Betty Patu, coordinator, Rainier Beach High School

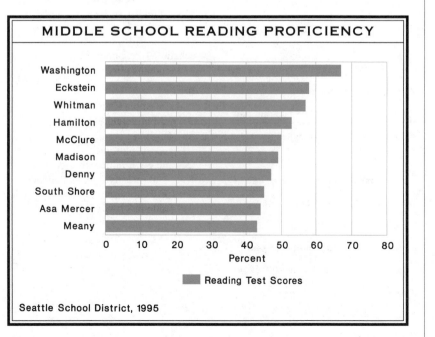

MIDDLE SCHOOL READING PROFICIENCY

Reading Test Scores

Seattle School District, 1995

Checkmate! More than 3,000 students in 65 Seattle public elementary and middle schools play chess after school one day a week. The free program is sponsored by the Chess Mates Foundation and is the brainchild of Henry Eisenhardt, a retired Seattle businessman. The program was started at Madrona Elementary in 1989. Call 789-9614 and ask if there is a chess club at your child's school.

NOVA
2410 E Cherry St.
281-6363
Individualized, flexible high school program in which students may earn credits toward a diploma at NOVA or at another Seattle public school or community college, or through tutorials; students sign contracts outlining a plan of instruction and schedule of evaluations; ungraded; 124 students (1995).

Orca
Old Columbia Elementary
3528 S Ferdinand St.
281-6310
Basic skills plus special emphasis on arts and environmental sciences for K–5; parental involvement encouraged; currently serves Zones 2 and 3; 249 students (1995).

Pathfinder
5012 SW Genesee St.
281-6735
Focus on Native American culture and heritage; evaluation through narrative reports to parents; K–5; serves Zone 3; 179 students (1995).

Sharples Alternative High School
Sharples Building
3928 S Graham St.
281-6910
Program similar to Marshall's, for students who live south of the ship canal; 254 students (1995).

Summit K–12
11051 34th Ave. NE
281-6880
Currently the only K–12 alternative in the district; multicultural curriculum; cross-age tutoring; multigrade classrooms; emphasis on arts and physical education; 632 students. Open to students districtwide.

TOPS
(The Option Program at Seward)
Seward Elementary
2515 Boylston Ave. E
281-6912
Basic skills emphasis, plus exploration of the urban environment outside of school; K–8; waiting list in some grade levels and for racial balance; currently serves Zone 2; 508 students (1995).

Other programs

Huchoosedah Indian Education Program
1330 N 90th St.
298-7945
The program, available in nine schools, offers home/school coordination and volunteer tutoring for Native American students and families.

Proyecto Saber
2600 SW Thistle St.
281-6066
Tutoring and support services and a limited number of classes for Latino/Chicano students. Schools served may change, but in 1994–95 served Ballard, Ingraham, and Chief Sealth high schools; Denny, Madison, and Hamilton middle schools; Concord, Cooper, Roxhill, and Viewlands elementaries. Bilingual/bicultural staff.

Graduation percentage by school district

Bellevue	76.96%
Everett	78.94%
Federal Way	79.74%
Mercer Island	96.11%
Seattle	**83.17%**
Spokane	82.52%
Tacoma	81.24%

Source: Superintendent of
Public Instruction, 1993–1994

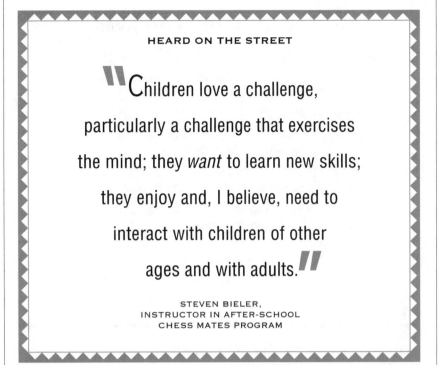

HEARD ON THE STREET

"Children love a challenge, particularly a challenge that exercises the mind; they *want* to learn new skills; they enjoy and, I believe, need to interact with children of other ages and with adults."

STEVEN BIELER,
INSTRUCTOR IN AFTER-SCHOOL
CHESS MATES PROGRAM

SEATTLE'S SCHOOL DAZE

Seattle public schools carry a heavy load. The average teacher/student ratio in high school classes is 1 teacher to 30 students. (The teachers' union stipulates a high school teacher is not to have more than 150 students a day, so a teacher responsible for five classes of 30 students each has reached the limit.) By way of comparison, Bellevue high schools average 27.3 students per class, and Edmonds schools average 23 students. In general, each Seattle high school has one principal and two assistant principals; one counselor per 400 students is available, as is one librarian.

All Seattle middle schools include sixth grade. Average middle-school class size is 29.5 students, compared to an average of 25 students in Bellevue classrooms and 23 in Edmonds. The teacher/student ratio in Seattle elementary schools is 1 to 28.

The Seattle School District says its dropout rate in 1994–95 for high schools was 14.7%; and middle schools, 7%. (The Superintendent of Public Instruction's office gives different figures, but the district contests those, arguing that the state figures incorrectly count as dropouts students who transfer to other schools or who leave and return several times.)

In addition to academics, all Seattle public high schools offer the following sports: football, volleyball, cross country, golf, swimming, wrestling, gymnastics, baseball, softball, tennis, girls' and boys' soccer, girls' and boys' basketball, and girls' and boys' track.

SCHOOL DISTRICT RESOURCES

The Seattle School District Board of Directors meets two Wednesdays a month, usually in the Administrative and Service Center auditorium, 815 Fourth Avenue N. Call the Board office, 298-7040, for date and time or to contact a board member.

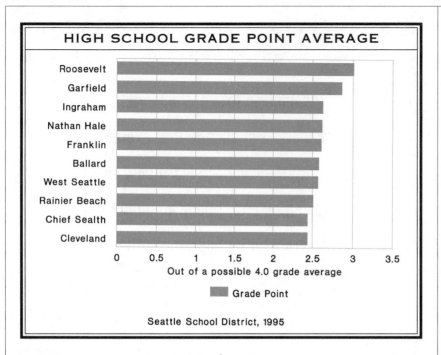

HIGH SCHOOL GRADE POINT AVERAGE

Roosevelt
Garfield
Ingraham
Nathan Hale
Franklin
Ballard
West Seattle
Rainier Beach
Chief Sealth
Cleveland

0   0.5   1   1.5   2   2.5   3   3.5

Out of a possible 4.0 grade average

■ Grade Point

Seattle School District, 1995

The members of the School Board hire the school superintendent, set policy, and control the school district's budget. School board members, who are elected to serve four-year terms, are listed below.

Ellen Roe (District 1)—term ends 1999.
281-6179
Scott Barnhart (District 2)—term ends 1999.
281-6724
Linda Harris (District 3)—term ends 1999.
281-6721

Don Nielsen (District 4)—term ends 1997.
292-1193
Michael Preston (District 5)—term ends 1997.
281-6553
Barbara Schaad-Lamphere (District 6)—term ends 1999.
281-6375
Al Sugiyama (District 7)—term ends 1997.
281-6476
Superintendent: John H. Stanford
298-7100

Other school district resources

Bilingual education office
298-7070

Facilities office
298-7500

Food services
298-7675

Gifted students
298-7130
Info on advanced placement.

Hearing office
298-7780
To appeal district decisions regarding your child.

Looking for after-school activities for your kids? *Seattle's Child* newspaper publishes an annual *After-School Guide* that's a great introduction to all the options out there. Also check with your local community center; many offer classes, sports, and other programs.

Crime in the high schools

	Assaults	Drugs	Disturbances	Weapons	Total cases*
Ballard	24	25	52	11	190
Cleveland	2	1	8	5	32
Franklin	18	13	15	3	109
Garfield	5	7	7	5	55
Ingraham	18	23	34	9	161
Nathan Hale	11	14	27	13	144
Rainier Beach	10	1	21	2	66
Roosevelt	6	24	9	9	105
Chief Sealth	8	4	8	4	42
West Seattle	6	6	9	5	54

*Also includes false alarms, arson, burglaries, car prowls, fraud, injuries, kidnapping, property damage, service calls, sexual incidents, suspicious circumstances, and trespassing.
Source: Seattle School District Security System, Incident Report Summaries, Sept. 1995–May 1996

Homework hotline
281-MATH
For help with math homework.
Monday through Thursday, 6–8pm.
Sponsored by the University of
Washington MESA (Math, Engineer-
ing, Science Achievement) Program
and the district.

Parent Teacher Student Association
364-7430
Sponsors parenting workshops,
fund-raising, etc.

School district archives
281-6564
Call for appointment.

Special-education preschool info
298-7805

Transportation office
298-7900

YET MORE RESOURCES

Citizens Education Center Northwest
310 First Ave. S, Suite 330
624-9955
Nonprofit organization dedicated to
excellence in public education for all
children. Members get legislative updates, discounts on publications, etc.

Educational Referral Services
2222 Eastlake Ave. E
323-1838
Director: Yvonne Jones
A private consulting company matching children ages 2½–18 to local private and public schools, national
boarding schools, and treatment centers. Handles about 40 requests per
month. Fees vary.

Seattle Alliance for Education
500 Union St., Suite 320
Seattle, WA 98101
343-0449
President: Robin Pasquarella
A business group monitoring the
school district. Interested in teacher
accountability.

Seattle Education Association
720 Nob Hill Ave. N
Seattle, WA 98109
283-8443
President: Verlita Wooten
Teachers union. Annual contract ne-
gotiations usually come to a climax
two weeks before school starts in
September.

Seattle's Child
2107 Elliott Ave., Suite 303
Seattle, WA 98121
441-0191
Monthly newspaper. Prints annual
free *Education Directory* and *After-
School Guide* supplements.

Grade 8 CTBS* scores

School district	Reading	Language	Math	Total
Bellevue	66	66	71	66
Federal Way	56	58	58	56
Lake Washington	68	61	66	64
Mercer Island	78	82	85	80
Renton	53	50	55	51
Seattle	**49**	**50**	**48**	**48**
Shoreline	66	63	58	61
Washington State average	55	53	53	54

*CTBS (Comprehensive Test of Basic Skills) scores are mean percentile scores
(average of all students' scores converted to national percentile equivalent).
Source: Office of Superintendent of Public Instruction, 1995

MAKING YOUR WAY THROUGH THE SCHOOL MAZE

Sometimes it seems you need an advanced degree just figure out the Seattle school system and make the best decisions for your kids. In an effort to help guide you through this perplexing maze, we've compiled the tables on pages 260–276. There you'll find summarized the key information about Seattle public schools and a representative sampling of Seattle private schools.

INTERPRETING THE PUBLIC SCHOOL TABLES

Except where noted, **figures** on pages 260–276 are for the 1994–1995 school year and come from school district records.

We compiled the **hot programs** list for each school by asking school personnel and by perusing the 1994–95 annual reports. These reports are published for every school and are provided by the school district to the public. It should be noted that the funding for some listed magnet programs may not be renewed; check with the individual schools.

In the elementary schools' hot programs listings, you may see the following terms:

- Central Area Mothers for Peace and Improvement (CAMPI) is a preschool program for four-year-olds in Brighton, Leschi, and Muir schools.
- Direct Instructional Teaching of Math and Reading (DISTAR) is used in grades K–5 at the schools indicated.
- The Early Childhood Model program provides small-group instruction at levels appropriate to the needs of individual students.

Seattle's schools have struggled toward racial equality, succeeding in some instances more than in others. We've listed the percentage of **minority students** in each school.

Dropout rates are school district figures for the 1994–95 school year. The district counts as drop-outs students who leave without graduating or transferring to another school and who do not return the following fall.

Test scores are one indication of the strength of programs offered in a school, but are a bit difficult to understand. They are from the April 1995 California Achievement Tests administered in the schools. The scores show how a midmost student in each school performed in relation to other students across the nation. A school mean score above 50 indicates that students are performing above the national average, and vice versa.

We included the number of students in various **lunch programs** to help you judge whether a school includes a cross-section of Seattle society. You can get a feel for the percentage of low- or lower-middle-income families at a particular school from looking at the number of students who qualify for reduced-cost or free lunches. A student from a family of four, for example, qualifies for reduced-cost lunches if the family's annual income is $28,028 or less; for free lunches, if the family's income is $19,695 or less.

A caution: Public schools are required to report certain things that

private schools are not, such as **weapons confiscated** ("weapons" include items such as toy guns, BB guns, scissors, and pocketknives) and other **security incidents.** (Private schools have only to turn to the next name on the waiting list to relieve themselves of troublemakers—a luxury not allowed public schools.) Security incidents include arson, assault, bombs, burglary, disturbances, drugs, harassment, robbery, sex offenses, theft, trespassing, and vandalism.

Disciplinary action stats are 1994–95 school district figures, and comprise suspensions and expulsions.

PRIVATE SCHOOL TABLES

Seattle has 14,114 students attending its 67 private and parochial elementary and secondary schools. Those listed in the following tables are a representative sampling. School enrollments range from a dozen students to more than 700; some schools base their programs on strongly held religious beliefs, while others' curricula are based on specific academic theories and methods.

Parents considering private schools have other elements to consider: tuition, waiting lists, and a sometimes involved application process. Although each school's process is different, most involve testing, school visits, interviews, and an application fee; some begin the process as early as November.

Private schools collect records differently than the public schools do—which accounts for the variations in statistics here.

Public elementary schools

	Adams Elementary School 6110 28th Ave. NW 281-6210	Alki Elementary School 3010 59th Ave. SW 281-6220	Arbor Heights Elementary School 3701 SW 104th St. 281-6230	Bagley Elementary School 7821 Stone Ave. N 281-6240
Students	503	343	418	221
FTE classroom teachers	17	11.5	15	7.5
School built/remodeled	1988	1951/1965	1949	1931
Principal	Barbara Nielsen	Kathy Lindsey	Carl Leatherman	Maribeth Phair
Hot programs	DISTAR K–1	Academic Achievement; Early Childhood Model	Early Childhood Model	Academic Academy magnet; ESL
Minority students	50%	54.7%	44.3%	58.7%
Test scores	Reading 51% Language Arts 55% Math 54%	Reading 51% Language Arts 54% Math 61%	Reading 51% Language Arts 53% Math 56%	Reading 51% Language Arts 50% Math 49%
Free or reduced-cost lunches	45.4%	41%	41.3%	55.1%
Disciplinary action	0%	3%	0%	0%

	Beacon Hill Elementary School 2025 14th Ave. S 281-6250	Blaine Elementary School 2550 34th Ave. W 281-6260	Brighton Elementary School 4425 S Holly St. 281-6270	Broadview Elementary School 13052 Greenwood Ave. N 281-6280
Students	260	353	240	521
FTE classroom teachers	8.5	11.5	8.5	22
School built/remodeled	1971	1962	1922/1945/1953	1961/1981
Principal	Margie Kates	Kathryn Bledsoe	Beverly Raines	Zoe Jenkins
Hot programs	Early Childhood Model; Chapter 1	Math and reading labs; instrumental music	CAMPI; Early Childhood Model	Head Start; Spectrum
Minority students	76.2%	35.8%	82.5%	48.1%
Test scores	Reading 52% Language Arts 57% Math 67%	Reading 55% Language Arts 56% Math 55%	Reading 42% Language Arts 47% Math 46%	Reading 59% Language Arts 61% Math 67%
Free or reduced-cost lunches	67.3%	23.9%	53.1%	37.9%
Disciplinary action	1%	1%	1%	2%

General note: The Horizon Program has become the Spectrum gifted education program.
Source: Seattle School District records; school surveys

	Bryant Elementary School 3311 NE 60th St. 281-6290	Coe Elementary School 2433 Sixth Ave. W 281-6940	Colman Elementary School 2401 S Irving St. 281-6603	Concord Elementary School 723 S Concord St. 281-6320
Students	539	364	308	253
FTE classroom teachers	18.5	12.5	8.5	9.5
School built/remodeled	1926	1906/1973	1989	1914/1971
Principal	Terry Acena	William Cuthbert	Ed Jefferson	Claudia Allan
Hot programs	Early Childhood Model; World Cultures magnet	Early Childhood Model; Chapter 1	DISTAR K–2; Early Childhood Model; Spectrum	Early Childhood Model; Proyecto Saber tutoring
Minority students	40.1%	50.4%	75..2%	66.9%
Test scores	Reading 58% Language Arts 61% Math 64%	Reading 57% Language Arts 61% Math 64%	Reading 43% Language Arts 42% Math 43%	Reading 43% Language Arts 45% Math 48%
Free or reduced-cost lunches	26.2%	44.6%	55%	61.4%
Disciplinary action	0%	0%	0%	0%

	Cooper Elementary School 5950 Delridge Way SW 281-6330	B.F. Day Elementary School 3921 Linden Ave. N 281-6340	Dearborn Park Elementary School 2820 S Orcas St. 281-6350	Dunlap Elementary School 8621 46th Ave. S 281-6370
Students	418	307	250	206
FTE classroom teachers	13	11.5	8.5	8.5
School built/remodeled	1964	1892/1992	1971	1924/1963
Principal	Sharon Aune	Carole Williams	Ed James	William Cook
Hot programs	Early Childhood Model; Proyecto Saber tutoring	World Cultures magnet (focus on Africa); Early Childhood Model	Early Childhood Model; PIPE partner: KOMO	Academic Academy program; Early Childhood Model
Minority students	77.2%	58%	84.4%	82.5%
Test scores	Reading 39% Language Arts 40% Math 42%	Reading 50% Language Arts 51% Math 54%	Reading 45% Language Arts 51% Math 49%	Reading 43% Language Arts 52% Math 48%
Free or reduced-cost lunches	75.4%	60.1%	69.2%	72.8%
Disciplinary action	4%	0%	0%	1%

continued▶

Public elementary schools

	Emerson Elementary School 9709 60th Ave. S 281-6380	Fairmount Park Elementary School 3800 SW Findlay St. 281-6390	Gatewood Elementary School 4320 SW Myrtle St. 281-6950	Gatzert Elementary School 1301 E Yesler Way 281-6410
Students	279	294	400	375
FTE classroom teachers	10.5	10.5	13.5	13
School built/remodeled	1909/1930	1963	1991	1988
Principal	Gloria Warren	John Miner	Daniel Barton	Patricia Sander
Hot programs	Early Childhood Model; PIPE partner: KOMO TV	School for 21st Century; Chapter 1	DISTAR K–2; child development center	Early Childhood Model; Head Start
Minority students	81.2%	50.7%	50.1%	83.2%
Test scores	Reading 47% Language Arts 45% Math 47%	Reading 52% Language Arts 59% Math 51%	Reading 48% Language Arts 50% Math 50%	Reading 37% Language Arts 44% Math 42%
Free or reduced-cost lunches	67.4%	54.6%	48.6%	85.2%
Disciplinary action	0%	3%	4%	2%

	Graham Hill Elementary School 5149 S Graham St. 281-6430	Green Lake Elementary School 2400 N 65th St. 281-6440	Greenwood Elementary School 144 NW 80th St. 281-6450	Hawthorne Elementary School 4100 39th Ave. S 281-6664
Students	357	325	321	467
FTE classroom teachers	14	10.5	11.5	17
School built/remodeled	1960	1970	1909/1921	1989
Principal	Birgit McShane	Harvey Deutsch	Joanna Cairns	John Morefield
Hot programs	Spectrum; Early Childhood Model	Arts specialist; Early Childhood Model	Early Childhood Model; Artist-in-Residence	Early Childhood Model; PIPE partner: Woodland Park Zoo
Minority students	72.2%	45.7%	51.4%	68.5%
Test scores	Reading 50% Language Arts 53% Math 51%	Reading 56% Language Arts 59% Math 57%	Reading 58% Language Arts 61% Math 63%	Reading 50% Language Arts 52% Math 57%
Free or reduced-cost lunches	58%	35.6%	40.2%	53.9%
Disciplinary action	3%	0%	2%	0%

	Hay Elementary School 201 Garfield St. 281-6460	High Point Elementary School 6760 34th Ave. SW 281-6470	Highland Park Elementary School 1012 SW Trenton St. 281-6480	Kimball Elementary School 3200 23rd Ave. S 281-6870
Students	488	261	472	531
FTE classroom teachers	16.5	6.5	16	18
School built/remodeled	1989	1988	1921/1926/1936	1971
Principal	Kathleen Wayne	Guadalupe Barnes	Jim Oftebro	Victoria Foreman
Hot programs	Early Childhood Model; PIPE partner: KCTS; Child Development Center	Early Childhood Model; PIPE partner: EPA Tutors	World Cultures magnet (focus on Russia)	Open-concept classrooms; reading and language arts emphasis
Minority students	36.3%	75.2%	64.3%	68.6%
Test scores	Reading 60% Language Arts 59% Math 57%	Reading 39% Language Arts 45% Math 46%	Reading 43% Language Arts 49% Math 49%	Reading 53% Language Arts 54% Math 58%
Free or reduced-cost lunches	22.8%	89.7%	60.7%	38%
Disciplinary action	1%	2%	3%	0%

	Martin Luther King Elementary School 3201 E Republican St. 281-6510	Lafayette Elementary School 2645 California Ave. SW 281-6520	Latona Elementary School 401 NE 42nd St. 281-6530	Laurelhurst Elementary School 4530 46th Ave. NE 281-6540
Students	137	454	284	359
FTE classroom teachers	5.5	15.5	11	11.5
School built/remodeled	1913/1958	1950/1953	1906/1918	1929/1950
Principal	Euhania Hairston	Los Freeborn	Lisa Bowman-Gordon	Nancy Chin
Hot programs	Early Childhood Model; DISTAR	Spectrum	Alternative Elementary 3 (Escuela Latona)	Multi-Arts magnet; bilingual center
Minority students	66.2%	51.3%	46.6%	46.5%
Test scores	Reading 40% Language Arts 43% Math 40%	Reading 59% Language Arts 59% Math 63%	Reading 58% Language Arts 49% Math 60%	Reading 61% Language Arts 64% Math 68%
Free or reduced-cost lunches	40.3%	35.7%	32.8%	22.7%
Disciplinary action	1%	1%	0%	0%

continued▶

Public elementary schools

	Lawton Elementary School 4000 27th Ave. W 281-6550	Leschi Elementary 135 32nd Ave. 281-6560	Lowell Elementary School 1058 E Mercer St. 281-6570	Loyal Heights Elementary School 2511 NW 80th St. 281-6580
Students	366	364	206	374
FTE classroom teachers	14	13	7.5	13
School built/remodeled	1990	1988	1911/1960	1931/1946
Principal	Larry Jacobs	Patricia Newton	Ken Seno	David Ackerman
Hot programs	Early Childhood Model; Artist-in-Residence	CAMPI; DISTAR in K; Spectrum	DISTAR K–5; Chapter 1	DISTAR K–2; LAP 1–5*
Minority students	40.9%	75.1%	73%	42%
Test scores	Reading 59% Language Arts 62% Math 62%	Reading 49% Language Arts 45% Math 49%	Reading 46% Language Arts 53% Math 53%	Reading 59% Language Arts 61% Math 60%
Free or reduced-cost lunches	24.9%	63.5%	57%	34.9%
Disciplinary action	0%	0%	0%	0%

*Learning Assistance Program (a state-subsidized remedial education program for low-income kids, similar to Title I)

	Madrona Elementary School 1121 33rd Ave. 281-6590	Maple Elementary School 4925 Corson Ave. S 281-6960	McGilvra Elementary School 1617 38th Ave. E 281-6610	Minor Elementary School 18th & Union streets 281-6620
Students	657	441	183	261
FTE classroom teachers	24.5	14	6	9
School built/remodeled	1917/1961	1971	1910/1942/1972	1890/1941/1960
Principal	Jill Hearne	Ellie Weisenbach	Janice Perry	John Willson
Hot programs	Early Childhood Model; Accelerated Progress Program	World Cultures magnet (funding pending: focus on Latin America)	Music program; Early Childhood Model	Early Childhood Model; Academic Academy magnet;CAMPI
Minority students	45.3%	78.7%	48%	76.3%
Test scores	Reading 74% Language Arts 75% Math 75%	Reading 50% Language Arts 59% Math 59%	Reading 57% Language Arts 60% Math 63%	Reading 42% Language Arts 43% Math 46%
Free or reduced-cost lunches	26.1%	45%	38.6%	79.5%
Disciplinary action	3%	0%	2%	0%

	Montlake Elementary School 2409 22nd Ave. E 281-6860	Muir Elementary School 3301 S Horton St. 281-6630	North Beach Elementary School 9018 24th Ave. NW 281-6640	Northgate Elementary School 11725 First Ave. NE 281-6650
Students	228	356	284	371
FTE classroom teachers	7.5	14	10.5	11
School built/remodeled	1913	1910/1924/1971	1958	1953/1956
Principal	Christi Clark	Beverly Walker	Venus Placer-Barber	Dorothy Woods
Hot programs	Computer classes; art; specialized students integrated into regular curriculum	CAMPI; DISTAR K–1; Spectrum	Early Childhood Model; music program	DISTAR in K; Early Childhood Model
Minority students	39.9%	69.9%	35.7%	64.5%
Test scores	Reading 64% Language Arts 63% Math 68%	Reading 52% Language Arts 58% Math 52%	Reading 56% Language Arts 57% Math 58%	Reading 49% Language Arts 51% Math 52%
Free or reduced-cost lunches	21.1%	54.1%	23.2%	53.9%
Disciplinary action	0%	0%	2%	0%

	Olympic Hills Elementary School 13018 20th Ave. NE 281-6660	Olympic View Elementary School 504 NE 95th St. 281-6670	Rainier View Elementary School 11650 Beacon Ave. S 281-6680	Rogers Elementary School 4030 NE 109th St. 281-6690
Students	310	437	210	335
FTE classroom teachers	11.5	14	6.5	11.5
School built/remodeled	1954	1989	1961	1956
Principal	Evelyn Fairchild	Margaret Reeder	Cothron Huey-Ray	Evette Mardesich
Hot programs	Early Childhood Model; science; Spectrum	Early Childhood Model; music program	DISTAR K–1; Early Childhood Model	Early Childhood Model; Artist-in-Residence
Minority students	55.2%	42.9%	83.2%	44.6%
Test scores	Reading 47% Language Arts 48% Math 47%	Reading 57% Language Arts 58% Math 60%	Reading 36% Language Arts 39% Math 35%	Reading 59% Language Arts 61% Math 60%
Free or reduced-cost lunches	54%	29.8%	64.1%	24.7%
Disciplinary action	1%	2%	4%	2%

continued▶

Public elementary schools

	Roxhill Elementary School 9430 30th Ave. SW 281-6980	Sacajawea Elementary School 9501 20th Ave. NE 281-6710	Sanislo Elementary School 1812 SW Myrtle St. 281-6730	Schmitz Park Elementary School 5000 SW Spokane St. 281-6740
Students	337	262	309	333
FTE classroom teachers	10.5	9.5	11.5	11.5
School built/remodeled	1959	c. 1950	1970	1962
Principal	Luevennie Bridges	Harry Nelson	Karen Ho'o	Joan Armitage
Hot programs	Music; computer lab; developmental preschool and kindergarten; Proyecto Saber tutoring	Early Childhood Model; music program	Open-concept classrooms; SCATS (aerobic and circus acts performing group)	Early Childhood Model; science and computer teacher; music program
Minority students	60%	39.9%	66.9%	40.6%
Test scores	Reading 44% Language Arts 47% Math 44%	Reading 53% Language Arts 54% Math 52%	Reading 44% Language Arts 54% Math 52%	Reading 57% Language Arts 58% Math 60%
Free or reduced-cost lunches	59.7%	37.5%	51.3%	29.4%
Disciplinary action	1%	0%	0%	1%

	Stevens Elementary School 1242 18th Ave. E 281-6760	Van Asselt Elementary School 7201 Beacon Ave. S 281-6780	View Ridge Elementary School 7047 50th Ave. NE 281-6790	Viewlands Elementary School 10525 Third Ave. NW 281-6990
Students	256	281	332	430
FTE classroom teachers	9.5	9.5	9	15
School built/remodeled	1906/1928	1862/1907/1951	1948	1953
Principal	Joanne Franey	Hajara Rahim	Ed Brown	Larry Bell
Hot programs	Early Childhood Model; Artist-in-Residence	Early Childhood Model; Academic Academy magnet	Classes for hearing-impaired and dyspraxic students	Early Childhood Model; Proyecto Saber tutoring
Minority students	55.9%	88.9%	48.7%	53.3%
Test scores	Reading 48% Language Arts 50% Math 56%	Reading 41% Language Arts 50% Math 58%	Reading 61% Language Arts 62% Math 57%	Reading 49% Language Arts 52% Math 54%
Free or reduced-cost lunches	43%	78.5%	24.9%	47.4%
Disciplinary action	0%	1%	1%	0%

	Wedgwood Elementary School 2720 NE 85th St. 281-6810	West Woodland Elementary School 5601 Fourth Ave. NW 281-6820	Whittier Elementary School 7501 13th Ave. NW 281-6830	Whitworth Elementary School 5215 46th Ave. S 281-6840	Wing Luke Elementary School 3701 S Kenyon St. 281-6850
Students	362	471	357	432	242
FTE classroom teachers	13	16	13.5	15.5	9.5
School built/remodeled	1954	1991	1908/1928	1989	1971
Principal	Dan Peterson	Dan Hailey	Ellen Punyon	Susan McCloskey	Pauline Hill
Hot programs	Spectrum; Early Childhood Model	Early Childhood Model; bilingual program	Spectrum; Early Childhood Model	Chapter 1; Early Childhood Model	Spectrum; Early Childhood Model
Minority students	34.6%	44.4%	33.3%	74.9%	77.2%
Test scores	Reading 71% Language Arts 73% Math 73%	Reading 55% Language Arts 57% Math 61%	Reading 65% Language Arts 68% Math 70%	Reading 48% Language Arts 45% Math 48%	Reading 47% Language Arts 52% Math 54%
Free or reduced-cost lunches	20.6%	27.6%	22.6%	57.6%	69.8%
Disciplinary action	0%	0%	0%	0%	1%

Public middle schools

	Asa Mercer Middle School 1600 Columbian Wy S 281-6170	Denny Middle School 8402 30th Ave. SW 281-6110	Eckstein Middle School 3003 NE 75th St. 281-6120	Hamilton Middle School 1610 N 41st St. 281-6130	Madison Middle School 3429 45th Ave. SW 281-6140
Students	849	869	1,111	700	923
FTE certified staff	47.4	50	62	40	49.9
FTE classroom teachers	32.2	33	42.4	25.4	34.4
School built/remodeled	1957	1952	1950/1968	1926/1970	1929/1931/1972
Principal	Dean Sanders	Pat Batiste-Brown	Lynn Caldwell	Allen Nakano	Marella Griffin
Foreign languages offered	Chinese (Mandarin), French, Spanish	French, Spanish	French, German, Japanese, Spanish	French, Spanish	French, Spanish
Hot programs	Music, vocal, computers	Strong math department (teachers use team approach); Proyecto Saber tutoring	Satellite and cable television in each classroom; orchestra and band; only middle school with TV and radio studio	Drama program; bilingual program; Spectrum; Proyecto Saber tutoring	Bilingual program; multimedia lab; concert band
Minority students	82.2%	58.1%	53.1%	57.9%	62.9%
Test scores	Reading 44% Language Arts 51% Math 50%	Reading 47% Language Arts 49% Math 51%	Reading 58% Language Arts 59% Math 57%	Reading 53% Language Arts 53% Math 54%	Reading 49% Language Arts 52% Math 54%
Grade point average	2.68	2.65	3.11	2.97	2.87
Disciplinary action	18.1%	14%	8.7%	17.3%	6.4%
Dropout rate	4.1%	8.1%	1.7%	5.8%	4.2%
Free or reduced-cost lunches	531 (61.3%)	531 (56.6%)	415 (35.5%)	339 (48.4%)	474 (49.5%)
Sports	After-school intramurals	Intramurals before and after school and at lunch	After-school intramurals	After-school intramurals four nights a week	After-school intramurals, soccer, basketball
Security incidents	53	29	18	28	36
Weapons confiscated	4	8	2	0	2

Source: Seattle School District records; school surveys

	McClure Middle School 1915 First Ave. W 281-6150	Meany Middle School 301 21st Ave. 281-6160	South Shore Middle School 8825 Rainier Ave. S 281-6180	Washington Middle School 2101 S Jackson St. 281-6190	Whitman Middle School 9201 15th Ave. NW 281-6930
Students	741	543	763	959	1,027
FTE certified staff	35	38	47.4	51	56.9
FTE classroom teachers	27.6	22	31.2	37.2	42
School built/remodeled	1964	1902/1945/1951/ 1955/1962/1995	1973	1964	1959
Principal	Beatrice Cox	Joanne Testa-Cross	Dr. John German	Bruce Hunter	Bi Hoa Caldwell
Foreign languages offered	French, Spanish	French, Spanish	French, Spanish	French, Spanish	French, Spanish
Hot programs	Art magnet; science; music; math honors	English as a Second Language; math honors	Team approach; health sciences; Spectrum; CAD lab	Band; math-science; high-tech; Accelerated Progress Program; Spectrum	Strong guidance program; MESA; bilingual program
Minority students	59.4%	75.8%	71.4%	54.1%	45%
Test scores	Reading 50% Language Arts 49% Math 51%	Reading 43% Language Arts 45% Math 44%	Reading 45% Language Arts 48% Math 49%	Reading 67% Language Arts 63% Math 63%	Reading 57% Language Arts 57% Math 58%
Grade point average	2.66	2.43	2.62	2.91	2.88
Disciplinary action	16.8%	12.8%	15.3%	12%	16.7%
Dropout rate	11.4%	10.4%	9%	7.1%	4.9%
Free or reduced-cost lunches	357 (46.6%)	296 (54.7%)	478 (54.6%)	340 (34.4%)	372 (33.2%)
Sports	After-school intramurals; swimming	After-school intramurals	Strong intramural program before and after school, with swimming option	Some after-school programs	Before- and after-school intramurals
Security incidents	16	116	54	134	14
Weapons confiscated	4	7	5	4	2

Public high schools

	Ballard High School 1418 NW 65th St. 281-6010	Cleveland High School 5511 15th Ave. S 281-6020	Franklin High School 3013 S Mt. Baker Blvd. 281-6030	Garfield High School 400 23rd Ave. 281-6040	Ingraham High School 1819 N 135th St. 281-6080
Students	1,089	643	1,420	1,531	936
FTE certified staff	66.6	43.7	73.8	74.3	59.1
FTE classroom teachers	34.4	24	50.2	57.1	34.2
School built/remodeled	1915/1925/1941/1959	1927/1957/1993	1990 (historic renovation)	1920/1923/1928	1959
Principal	Charles Chinn	Ted Howard	Sharon Green	Ammon McWashington	Gloria Izard-Baldwin
Foreign languages offered	French, German, Spanish	French, Japanese, Mandarin, Spanish	Four years of French and Spanish; three of Japanese	French, German, Japanese, Latin, Russian, Spanish	French, German, Japanese, Spanish
Seniors who graduate	73.9%	78.7%	87.7%	96%	81.1%
Hot programs	Academy of Finance, a junior-senior program on career options for 30 qualified students; "very modern computer lab"; marketing education program with student store and marketing studies; Proyecto Saber tutoring for Spanish-speaking students; Principles of Technology class; electronics class offered by NSCC for college credit; visual and performing arts center for the school district; College Prep 101 course; Accelerated Progress Program.	All-city International Focus Magnet, with international education courses incorporated into regular curriculum and specialized classes; national computer link with selected schools throughout the nation that are participating in education reform projects; business programs; DECA marketing program; in-house drama classes during the day; Accelerated Progress Program.	Strong humanities program for all-city students; Multi-Arts program; science emphasis for ninth graders; commercial arts program; extensive drama program including touring company; FAME performing arts theater; BelCanto choir/vocal ensemble; participation in Law and Society competition; Mock Trial Competition; Academy of Finance trains students specializing in business and includes a summer intern program; Accelerated Progress Program.	Magnet Science Program including marine and health science, with field trips to Papua New Guinea, Kenya, Great Barrier Reef, and Hawaii; award-winning jazz band and chamber orchestra; noted marching band; black literature collection; technical education including commercial kitchen; fashion merchandising; Accelerated Progress Program.	Advanced placement program in art; bilingual and newcomer programs; MESA; FBLA; internship program with Boeing; Accelerated Progress Program.
Minority students	43.2%	83%	68.5%	49.7%	61.5%
Test scores	Reading 58% Language Arts 53% Math 60%	Reading 46% Language Arts 46% Math 52%	Reading 57% Language Arts 51% Math 58%	Reading 71% Language Arts 61% Math 69%	Reading 60% Language Arts 51% Math 59%
Grade point average	2.64	2.50	2.59	2.95	2.67
Disciplinary action	12.5%	5.6%	6.1%	7.4%	22.1%
Dropout rate	15.4%	11.9%	5.1%	3.8%	8.1%
Free or reduced-cost lunches	366 (32%)	321 (43.2%)	470 (30.4%)	275 (17.2%)	447 (37.5%)
Security incidents	190	32	109	55	161
Weapons confiscated	11	5	3	5	9
Notable	Very strong PTSA.	"The best-kept secret in the SSD"; only steel drum band in the city; teen clinic.	Playoff contenders for all major sports; new teen clinic.	Highly rated school newspaper; strong career center; teen clinic.	Advanced placement classes; solar car and boat team; award-winning band.

Source: Seattle School District records; school surveys

	Nathan Hale High School 10750 30th Ave. NE 281-6920	Rainier Beach High School 8815 Seward Park S 281-6090	Roosevelt High School 1410 NE 66th St. 281-6050	Chief Sealth High School 2600 SW Thistle St. 281-6060	West Seattle High School 4075 SW Stevens St. 281-6070
Students	966	762	1,552	790	740
FTE certified staff	62.8	52	78.9	53.8	48.8
FTE classroom teachers	31.8	29.8	53.4	28.8	25.8
School built/remodeled	1963/1970/1972	1960	1922/1927/1960	1956/1993	1917/1924/1954
Principal	Eric Benson	Marta Cano-Hinz	Marilyn Day	Joan Butterworth	James McConnell
Foreign languages offered	French, Japanese, Spanish	French, Spanish	French, Latin, Spanish, Japanese	French, Japanese, Spanish	French, German, Spanish
Seniors who graduate	83.8%	82.1%	90%	80.4%	88.5%
Hot programs	Three-year humanities program, with language arts and social studies courses in a two-hour sequence; child and family psychology classes; hands-on technology course; satellite telecommunications; horticulture magnet program; fine arts program; computer lab. Accelerated Progress Program.	College Into High School program offering college credit in several subjects; Writing Project; Principles of Technology, for careers in engineering and technology; Roads to Success career paths program; Accelerated Progress Program.	Award-winning concert orchestra, chamber orchestra, and jazz band whose members have traveled extensively in competition; Computer Team; science seminar; extensive honors and advanced placement program; culture and arts center for district; Accelerated Progress Program.	Proyecto Saber tutoring; MESA program with emphasis on college training in math and science; avionics and aerospace work training for specialized students; hospitality and tourism field study; Accelerated Progress Program.	Gemologist-taught jewelry-making course; technology grants received for two computer labs; auto shop; music; fashion illustration; genetics and biotechnology; Principles of Technology program; Accelerated Progress Program.
Minority students	57.5%	82.3%	55.1%	68.7%	51.6%
Test scores	Reading 55% Language Arts 48% Math 55%	Reading 48% Language Arts 43% Math 47%	Reading 64% Language Arts 57% Math 65%	Reading 48% Language Arts 45% Math 49%	Reading 49% Language Arts 44% Math 49%
Grade point average	2.67	2.57	3.05	2.43	2.59
Disciplinary action	31.5%	22.6%	6.6%	13.4%	19.4%
Dropout rate	11.7%	11.2%	3.9%	11.3%	15.6%
Free or reduced-cost lunches	396 (36.3%)	410 (45%)	456 (27.4%)	464 (49.9%)	301 (36.1%)
Security incidents	144	66	105	42	54
Weapons confiscated	13	2	9	4	5
Notable	Won National Council of Teachers of English Writing Award nine times in 13 years; Naha (Japan) exchange program.	The first school with a Site Council, a goal-setting body made up of students, parents, teachers, and community members; first school teen health clinic in the state.	College prep school; tai-chi classes in physical education department.	Senior projects with individual responsibility; Environmental Education prototype school.	Ivar Haglund was a student here, as were Dyan Cannon and the Whitaker brothers of mountain climbing fame; active alumni organization and revitalized, active parent club.

Private schools

	Bertschi School 2227 10th Ave. E Seattle, WA 98102 324-5476	Blanchet High School 8200 Wallingford Ave. N Seattle, WA 98103 527-7711	Bush School 405 36th Ave. E Seattle, WA 98112 322-7978	Epiphany School 3710 E Howell St. Seattle, WA 98122 323-9011	Evergreen School 15201 Meridian Ave. N Shoreline, WA 98133 364-0801
Type	K–5	High school, coed, Roman Catholic	K–12, coed	Preschool–6	Preschool–8
Enrollment	175	970	530	135	315
Class size	14–18 (larger classes in older age groups)	26	Varies	Preschool, 12 students per class; K–6, 16–18 per class	15–18, depending on age and grade level
Minority students	15%	17%	16%	16%	14.2%
Teacher/student ratio	1:9	1:26	1:9	1:13	1:12
Academic emphasis	Strong academic emphasis; children work at own speed in classroom; group work encouraged; "We encourage the kids to take risks."	College preparatory	College preparatory; experiential learning	Traditional elementary school with a strong curriculum of basic academic skills enriched with programs of art, music, French, PE, science, computers, library, and drama; self-esteem, problem-solving, and critical thinking stressed	Individual curriculum for gifted students encouraging self-motivation and problem-solving; writing and computer skills; French, German, Spanish, and Chinese; global awareness; science; music and drama; enrichment activities
Sports	PE teacher; after-school activities (swimming, gymnastics, soccer, basketball, T-ball, baseball)	All boys' and girls' sports, Metro AA League	All interscholastic sports, Sea-Tac B League (all non-public schools)	Daily PE activities for all grades	PE for younger students, basketball, cross-country running, track and field, family ski program, and baseball for ages 9 and up
Waiting list	For all grades	Yes	Yes	Nearly all grades	Yes
Tuition (annual unless noted)	$8,200	Catholics $4,587; non-Catholics $5,170	K–2 $9,970; 3–5 $10,400; 6–8 $11,900; 9–12 $13,050	Preschool $4,828 (half-days); K–6 $6,908	Preschool $4,230; pre-primary $8,950; K–3 $9,450; 4–8 $9,925
College bound	—	95%	100%	—	A small number go on to the University of Washington's Early Entrance Program.
Application procedure	School tour required before applying by March 1 for coming year; $50 application fee; first-grade children visit school, meet with teacher and school director in small class situation; older children sit in on classroom for a half-day.	Written application and placement/scholarship exam.	Parent interviews, academic testing, student visit required; administers joint admissions test with four other private schools; major entry points, grades K, 6, and 9; looking for students who are responsible, for commitment to the school, sense of personal worth.	Open house for prospective parents (mid-January); school tours December–March; testing and student visits grades 1–6; interviews for preschool and kindergarten applicants; admissions information available November 1.	IQ testing required for K and above; student visit; application deadline is late February for fall entrance; open house and tours available.
Notes		Teachers are religious and lay professionals with bachelor's degrees or higher.	Students must do a community service, sport, or theater "action module" to graduate; much personal freedom.	Nonsectarian independent school; tutoring available for children with specific language disability (dyslexia); founded in 1958.	Individual and small-group instruction; non-graded; 8th-grade trip to non-Western country; parent involvement; licensed day care center for 6 weeks and above; summer program.

Source: Seattle Survival Guide research

	Holy Names Academy 728 21st Ave. E Seattle, WA 98112 323-4272	Islamic School of Seattle 720 25th Ave. Seattle, WA 98112 329-5735	King's Elementary School 19531 Dayton Ave. N Seattle, WA 98133 546-7258	King's High School 19303 Fremont Ave. N Seattle, WA 98133 546-7241	Lakeside Schools 13510 First NE (Middle) 14050 First NE (Upper) Seattle, WA 98125 368-3600
Type	High school, girls, Roman Catholic	Preschool–8	K–6	7–12	Middle, 5–8; Upper, 9–12
Enrollment	380	60	600	600	690
Class size	Varies	10	Varies, 22–25 max.	24	14–18
Minority students	36%	—	15%	15%	27%
Teacher/student ratio	1:12	1:10	1:24	1:15	1:9
Academic emphasis	College preparatory; advanced placement courses; honors program; women's leadership courses and programs	Islamic perspective, Qu'ran, Arabic language; emphasizes whole language and hands-on math and science; ungraded classrooms	Regular elementary curriculum with the addition of Bible and chapel	College preparatory	Liberal arts
Sports	Very active program, Metro AA League — track, soccer, volleyball, basketball, cross-country, swimming, softball, tennis, crew	Gymnasium; seasonal sports; swimming year-round	PE program	Football, volleyball (fall); basketball (winter); track/field, golf (spring); cross-country running	Most interscholastic sports, Metro AA League
Waiting list	Yes	Yes	None	None	Alternate pool
Tuition (annual unless noted)	$5,568	$2,200 (reduced for additional children)	Half-day kindergarten $2,725; full-day kindergarten $3,900; 1–3 $4,250; 4–6 $4,570	$5,450 (reduced for additional children)	Grades 5–8, $12,100; grades 9–12, $12,600
College bound	99%	—	—	4-year, 75%; 2-year, 20%; 95% total	99%
Application procedure	Open house (early October and early January); application; school recommendation; transcripts; visit to the school.	School visit, interview, referral from last school.	Fill out application; $35 application fee; interview; notified if accepted; $150/family registration fee.	Call the office for an application kit; $35 application fee; recommendations; if accepted, must pay registration fee (goes toward first-year tuition).	In November through February for following fall; independent school entrance exam required; 30% acceptance rate, no carry-over.
Notes	Two-time winner of U.S. Department of Education Exemplary School Award; 35% of senior class receive college admission honors and/or scholarships.	On-site day care.		Spectacular campus; serves families who desire integration of Christian faith and learning; excellent music programs and missions emphasis.	Commitment to diversity; excellent facilities; community service; outdoor program; financial aid available.

continued▶

Private schools

	Morningside Academy 1633 12th Ave. Seattle, WA 98122 329-9412	Northwest School 1415 Summit Ave. Seattle, WA 98122 682-7309	O'Dea High School 802 Terry Ave. Seattle, WA 98104 622-6596	Perkins Elementary School 4649 Sunnyside Ave. N Seattle, WA 98103 632-7154	St. Joseph School 700 18th Ave. E Seattle, WA 98112 329-3260
Type	K–9	Grades 6–12	High school, boys, Roman Catholic, Christian Brothers	K–5	K–8
Enrollment	40	350	450	165	621
Class size	7	12–18	25	15–20	Varies by grade; 20–25
Minority students	35%	20%	28.4% (1993)	8.5%	19%
Teacher/student ratio	1:7	1:9	1:16	1:12	Varies by grade
Academic emphasis	Individuals with learning and attention problems	College preparatory	College preparatory	Strong academic emphasis; French, computers, music, and art are part of the daily curriculum	Arts and sciences
Sports	Soccer	Soccer, basketball, skiing, volleyball	All boys' sports, Metro AA League	Basketball and physical fitness; after-school sports through Wallingford Boys and Girls Club	Catholic Youth Program (all sports except football)
Waiting list	Yes	Yes	No carry-over	Yes; waiting pool	Yes
Tuition (annual unless noted)	$8,500	$9,700–$10,000 (includes lunches and books if avail.)	Catholics $3,608; non-Catholics $4,125	$5,800, includes $500 deposit; financial aid available	$4,284; financial aid and parish subsidies (for parishioners) available
College bound	—	100%	95%	—	—
Application procedure	Interview with director; testing.	School tour or interview, admission test, transcript with recommendations required.	Open house in November and late January; entrance exam for incoming ninth-grade students.	Make appointment to tour school; open house in February; apply by March for the coming year; $500 deposit required with application; notification within three weeks.	Application and interview; process over by end of February.
Notes	Ungraded school, daily individual progress reports; monthly field trips.	Core curriculum in integrated humanities, international studies; exchange programs; arts; environmental program; honors science. In 1992 10% of students were National Merit finalists.	SAT scores above average; religious studies and foreign language required; most students come from Catholic elementary schools, though this is not a prerequisite; state-of-the-art computer and math labs; student-to-computer ratio is 4:1; complete honors program.	Perkins accepts a small proportion of children with slight learning or physical disabilities who can be readily assimilated into the classroom and who can adapt to the building's limitations; before- and after-school summer program.	Student body is 70% Catholic; strong music program; good computer lab and computer program; new library; most students go on to private or parochial high schools.

	Seattle Academy of Arts and Sciences 1432 15th Ave. Seattle, WA 98112 323-6600	Seattle Country Day School 2619 Fourth Ave. N Seattle, WA 98109 284-6220	Seattle Hebrew Academy 1617 Interlaken Dr. E Seattle, WA 98112 323-5750	Seattle Preparatory School 2400 11th Ave. E Seattle, WA 98102 324-0400	Spruce St. School 411 Yale Ave. N Seattle, WA 98109 621-9211
Type	Grades 6–12	K–8	Preschool–8	High school, Roman Catholic, Jesuit	K–5
Enrollment	215	290	282	650	44
Class size	16	16	20	Varies by subject	15
Minority students	16%	15%	—	19%	19%
Teacher/student ratio	1:8	1:16	1:12	1:15	1:10
Academic emphasis	College preparatory	Special education for highly capable children with creative strengths	Dual curriculum—complete secular program plus Judaic studies and computer science	College preparatory, religious	Integrated learning with an emphasis on humanities; literature, drama
Sports	Member of Sea-Tac League; field soccer, basketball, and track	PE program, intramural sports grades 3–8	Full PE program, including basketball and soccer	Metro AA League; compete in nearly all sports	Gymnastics and ball sports
Waiting list	Yes	For summer only	None	Yes	None
Tuition (annual unless noted)	Grades 6–8, $10,900; grades 9–12, $11,775	Kindergarten $8,210; grades 1–3 $8,500; grades 4–8 $8,810	$6,000	$6,375	$6,400
College bound	100%	—	—	99%–100%	—
Application procedure	Written application; admission exam; student all-day visit; parent interview; March 1 deadline for fall admission.	Student visit, student exam (Wechsler Intelligence Scale for Children); recommendations, transcripts, and achievement tests for older students; begin application process October, end mid-March; most openings at K–1 level; serves children who fall in top 1%–3% intellectually with strong creative problem-solving skills; nurtures children emotionally, socially, creatively, and academically; individualized program; strong multicultural program; commitment to diversity; $40 application fee.	Letter of application, application filled out by parents; interview; rolling applications; most apply February–April for coming year.	Open house in November; teacher references; grades; standard tests; $200 registration fee; late January deadline.	Call for information; morning visit; fill out application, $65 application fee; those accepted will be notified by late March with acceptance letter; candidates have until April 10 to send back contract with 10% deposit; revolving registration.
Notes	Offers a demanding college preparatory curriculum, including a full-range arts program and seven years of lab science; outstanding writing and speech program; integration of technology into all disciplines, and a emphasis on a global perspective; financial aid available.	Strict profile for acceptance—top 1%–3% intellectually, plus creative gifts; stresses challenge to imagination, self-discipline for maximum use of gifts, social and emotional maturity; students often go on to Lakeside, Bush, Seattle Prep, or public high schools with accelerated programs.	Accepts only Jewish students ("While we're an Orthodox Jewish school, we accept children of any Jewish background"); fairly intense academic program; students generally score one to two grades ahead of national norm; students go on to Jewish (Yeshiva High School) and secular private and public high schools.	Scholarship exams and financial aid; endowed school.	Students can publish own works with own press.

continued

Private schools

	University Prep 8000 25th Ave. NE Seattle, WA 98115 523-6407	Villa Academy 5001 NE 50th St. Seattle, WA 98105 524-8885	West Seattle Christian School 4401 42nd Ave. SW Seattle, WA 98116 938-1414	Westside Place 1310 N 45th Seattle, WA 98103 634-0782	Zion Academy 4730 32nd Ave. S Seattle, WA 98118 723-0580
Type	Grades 6–12	K–8, Catholic	Preschool–8	8–18 yrs.	Preschool–8
Enrollment	385	488	250	60	615
Class size	16 maximum	K, 1–14; 1–8, 1–18	Varies	8–12	24–27
Minority students	16%	13%	15%	30%	95%
Teacher/student ratio	1:10	K, 1:14; overall, 1:18	K–8, 1:18	1:8	1:12
Academic emphasis	College prep; traditional liberal arts and sciences with emphasis on writing skills; sciences are lab-oriented	General elementary	Christian elementary	Work with students who have average or above-average abilities who have not had success in traditional school setting; math, history, science, fine arts, wood shop, and language arts offered	"Open Court" method — heavy emphasis on phonics and Marva Collins' teaching
Sports	Basketball, soccer, tennis, volleyball, cross-country teams; competes in Sea-Tac League	PE program, participates in Catholic Youth Organization sports program	None	PE program	PE and playground sports
Waiting list	Grades 6–9	Yes	Rarely	None	None
Tuition (annual unless noted)	Middle school $10,975; high school $11,185; books $200; deposit $500	K–5 $5,825; 6–8 $6,130	Preschool $620–$940; K $1,490; 1–5 $2,470; 5–8 $2,590	$10,000	$2,000
College bound	100%	—	—	—	—
Application procedure	Open house in November and January; February 1 deadline; administers ISEE admission tests with five other schools; visit; interviews, and two teacher evaluations; notification by April 1.	K: Readiness tests; open house in February, apply by March 5.	Register in March; interviews with parent and child.	Call for application and they will direct you through application process.	Interview older students; open registration.
Notes	Financial aid available.	Three-fourths of all students go on to Seattle Preparatory.	Run by West Seattle Christian Church since 1969; does not accept children with behavior problems.	State-approved special education program; programs for students with attention deficit disorders, learning disabilities; main goal is to develop academic and social skills so students will have more choices in terms of school placement.	High expectations; parent involvement mandatory; majority go on to private schools' feed-in program with Bush; tuition includes students' meals.

THE CITY SAYS AHHHH

You'd think, with all those hiking boots and four-wheel-drive vehicles around town, that Seattleites would be the healthiest of people around. Let's find out! Lie down on the X-ray table, Seattle, and let's examine the state of your health. It's true you have a whole hill of hospitals—Pill Hill—and a whole bunch of people who swear they know CPR. Despite those huddled knots of smokers puffing away outside downtown office buildings, you have more non-smokers than elsewhere, and you are the #6 city in the nation in apple consumption—a true believer in the old apple-a-day theory. Your chart says people who live here live longer and are healthier than Americans as a whole.

But, while on the surface the prognosis seems hopeful, there are threats lurking. A visit to the doctor may be in order.

WHAT AILS YOU

Judging by walk-in and call-in complaints at Group Health Cooperative's central hospital, Seattle's top 12 health complaints have to do with:

- Stomachaches
- Back pain
- Congestion
- Coughs
- Earaches
- Headaches
- Fever in kids
- Rashes
- Sore throats
- Urinary tract infections
- Vaginitis or sexually transmitted diseases
- Injuries

FOOD COMPLAINTS

Got a stomachache? Eight hundred people per year call the Environmental Health Department with complaints about aches and pains they think came from having eaten at restaurants. In 1993, the big E. coli scare made everyone nervous, at least about eating hamburgers at fast-food places.

- Food establishments with permits in Seattle: 8,500
- Number temporarily closed for health violations annually: 92

- Closed "fixed food establishments" (groceries, restaurants): 44
- Closed "mobile food, carts, or vehicles": 48

Environmental Health Department
Central office: 296-4632
North office: 296-4838
South office: 296-4666
Eastside: 296-9791
To report food complaints about establishments in various areas of King County.

MORE TO YOUR WATER

There's more to your drinking water than you might think. Seattle has fluoridated its water since 1970, and the dental community says tooth decay has been reduced by as much as 50% to 70%. Although controversial in some cities for supposed side effects, fluoridation is widely accepted in the U.S. In Washington State, 39.1% of the population uses fluoridated water, which gives the state a national ranking of 36th. The places with the largest percentage of population drinking fluoridated water? Washington, D.C., followed by Illinois.

PUFF STUFF

In Washington State, 21.8% of adults smoke. Surprisingly, this percentage has decreased since the 25% of 1992. The state is doing better than the national average, which is about 25% of the adult population.

About 401.3 million packs of cigarettes are sold in Washington annually. If you were to dump all those cigarettes into the Kingdome, they'd make a pile 20 inches deep.

Here's some more smokin' stuff:
- 80% of adults who smoke started before they were 18.
- 8,061 people in Washington died from tobacco use in 1993.
- $120 million is spent in Washington promoting tobacco products annually.

- 27% of expectant girls, ages 10-19, smoke during pregnancy.

Source: American Lung Association; Seattle/King County Department of Public Health

American Lung Association of Washington
2625 Third Ave.
Seattle, WA 98121
441-5100
Focuses on asthma, environmental health, and smoking cessation. Summer camps for children with asthma, "lung clubs" for people with chronic lung disease, smoking cessation clinics, and anti-smoking school curricula. Call to get on the mailing list.

Fresh Air for Non-Smokers (FANS)
932-7011
Activists dedicated to the banning of smoking in public places.

KICKING THE HABIT

For help in quitting smoking, try these resources:
Evergreen Hospital, Kirkland, "Fresh Start" program, 899-3300.
Seventh-Day Adventist Church's "Breathe Free Plan," 481-7171.
American Lung Association's "Quit Kit," 441-5100.

Want to live longer? Move to Mercer Island. The Seattle/King County Health Department reports that life expectancy on Mercer Island is 81 years, compared to 71 years in central Seattle and 79 years in Fremont and Ballard.

For help in quitting drinking, try these:

Alcoholics Anonymous, 24-hour line, 587-2838.

Alcohol and Drug 24-Hour Help Line, 722-3700 (teen line: 722-4222).

HEART CITY

If you're going to have a heart attack, have it in Seattle, the city where you're most likely to receive cardio-pulmonary resuscitation (CPR), according to the American Heart Association's national office. The city does have the highest rate of citizens trained in CPR, according to the Medic Two program, which oversees CPR training in King County. (One in three Seattleites has been trained in CPR, and over 24,000 people are trained—or retrained in a refresher course—in King County every year.)

American Heart Association
632-6881
Information, memorials, gifts.

American Red Cross
1900 25th Ave. S
Seattle, WA 98144
323-2345
The Red Cross trains people in CPR, first aid, water safety, and HIV/AIDS education. Call for course schedule.

Medic Two
684-7274
Information on CPR training.

WOMEN'S HEALTH

Seattle has many clinics offering women's health care, pregnancy testing, birth control, and abortion services. Here are a few places to start:

Aradia Women's Health Center
1300 Spring
323-9388
Health care for women by women.

Teens and Tobacco

Percentage of eighth-graders who admit	1992	1995
Experimenting with smoking	31%	48%
Experimenting with smokeless tobacco	13.1%	22.9%

Source: American Lung Association

Seattle-area hospitals' cesarean section rates

	Cesarean births	Total deliveries	Cesarean rate
Group Health Cooperative*	120	599	20.0%
Group Health Eastside	141	851	16.6%
Highline Community	159	836	19%
Northwest*	267	1,138	23.5%
Providence	43	280	15.4%
Swedish*	467	1,862	25.1%
Swedish at Ballard*	40	216	18.5%
University*	300	1,500	20%
Virginia Mason*	113	660	17.1%

*Hospitals with neonatal units.
Source: Public Citizen Health Research Group

Planned Parenthood of Seattle/ King County
Central Seattle: 328-7700
University District: 632-2498
Affordable birth control and gynecological services.

University YWCA Abortion & Birth Control Referral Service
543-4635 ext. 38

TOO MANY CESAREANS?

In the late 1980s, there was a growing concern in the U.S. about the number of cesarean deliveries in hospitals. Thanks to a consumer revolution, the national rate of C-section births declined for the first time from 1989 to 1990. But cesarean sections are still the most frequently performed major surgical operations and, according to the Public Citizen's Health Research Group, the most frequently unnecessary.

The ideal ratio of C-sections to total births in any one hospital is not carved in stone, but the Research Group says the appropriate range for C-section rates—"if the operation were used only when medically indicated"—is between 7% and 17%. For a state, the figure used is 12%. The Research Group suggests that pregnant women ask hospital administrators what the rate of C-section births is. If it's a community hospital, the rate should be close to 7%; if it's a hospital with a neonatal care unit (which handles more difficult cases), the rate will be closer to 17%.

Doctors keep track of their vaginal vs. C-section birthrate too, sometimes pushing prospective C-section births off onto another doctor to keep their own ratio low.

Seattle-area hospitals' C-section rates seem high when compared to the activist group's recommended rate, but our state still does better than the national average—24.4%, versus Washington's 21.7%.

THE TRUTH ABOUT STDS

You probably didn't know it, but the faculty at Harborview's Sexually Transmitted Disease facility is famous in certain circles. The standard medical text on the subject is edited here and almost all experts on STD are trained here. And Seattle's experts set national and international standards for diagnosis and treatment. Does that mean we're the herpes capital of the world? Not really. In fact, one STD—gonorrhea—has been all but wiped out locally. What is on the rise is chlamydia, the most common STD in the U.S. today—as many as 5 million people nationwide have it without even knowing it. It's caused by a bacteria and is treatable.

Sexually Transmitted Disease Clinic
Harborview Hospital
223-3590

Washington State Dept. of Health
Office of STD Services
Airdustrial Park, Bldg. 14
P.O. Box 47842
Olympia, WA 98504-7842
(360) 753-5810

PUBLIC HEALTH CLINICS

At Seattle's public health centers, fees are based on family size and income, and no one is denied service due to inability to pay. The centers accept medical coupons and can bill third-party insurance companies. Some services have eligibility requirements such as age, income, or medical need.

Columbia Health Center
4400 37th Ave. S
205-6060
Services include family planning, pediatrics, WIC clinic.

Downtown Public Health Center
2124 Fourth Ave.
296-4755
Services include child care, dental care, family planning, pharmacy, refugee health, travelers' health care, WIC program.

North Public Health Center
10501 Meridian Ave. N
296-4765
Services include family health, STD and WIC clinics, immunizations, dental care.

GUIDE TO SEATTLE HOSPITALS

The aptly named Pill Hill, located between Ninth Avenue and Broadway, is not the only place to find Seattle's hospitals. Hospitals and clinics are big business in both hills and valleys in the city, and on the Eastside too. In fact, they now compete for patients to inhabit their beds. That competition results in heavy advertising, but also in more and varied services. For example, many hospitals offer services such as sleep disorder or sports clinics. Many also offer "well-care" seminars and activities, sponsoring such programs as mall walks for senior citizens.

It's best to shop around for a hospital when you're well; office-based doctors are usually connected to one or more hospitals and can recommend an appropriate facility for you.

Rising Costs

The Washington State Hospital Commission in Olympia notes a dramatic increase in use and cost of medical care over the past decade in the state. Some of the reasons for the increase are obvious, such as a growing elderly population, but others are worth noting.

Overuse of health care. The commission says many payment systems encourage overuse of the doctor's office, emergency room, and prescriptions.

Defensive medicine. Malpractice suits have increased (as have insurance rates), which can result in physicians ordering unnecessary tests, the commission says.

Technology. Hospitals believe in having the latest in medical technology. But if the hospital doesn't have enough patients to keep the equipment busy, the cost is often passed on to other patients in the hospital.

Medical insurance that hides the true cost of medical care from the consumer.

Little incentive for physicians or hospitals to hold down costs.

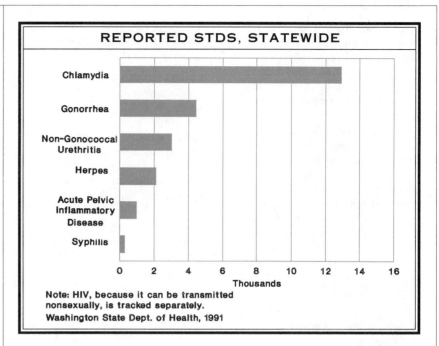

REPORTED STDS, STATEWIDE

Note: HIV, because it can be transmitted nonsexually, is tracked separately.
Washington State Dept. of Health, 1991

The Hospital Tables

And so, on to hospital shopping. In the hospital tables that appear on the following pages, the figures about **number of beds**, **occupancy rate**, **admissions**, and number of **physicians** and **registered nurses** were provided by the individual hospitals. The charges for treating various **illnesses** are from the annual *Health Care Users Guide*, a free booklet available from Washington State Department of Health, Office of Hospital & Patient Data, P.O. Box 47811, Olympia, WA 98504-7811.

Here's some basic information about the Seattle hospitals in our tables. For comparison purposes, we've also included in the tables Overlake Hospital Medical Center, located in Bellevue.

Children's Hospital and Medical Center
4800 Sand Point Way NE
Seattle, WA 98105
526-2000
Special services: Renowned pediatric medical center, Children's Resource Line, Resource Center (library for patient and family education).

THC Seattle
10560 Fifth Ave. NE
Seattle, WA 98125
364-2050
Special services: In-patient acute care.

Group Health Cooperative Central Hospital
201 16th Ave. E
Seattle, WA 98112
326-3000
Group Health is the Northwest's largest consumer-governed health

Problems with health insurance? Contact the State Insurance Commission, 800-562-6900. That office has information for the consumer, including consumer tips and rights.

maintenance organization (HMO), providing complete and coordinated care for a fixed, prepaid fee with minimum co-payments and deductions. It's the nation's 11th-largest HMO overall, and the third-largest nonprofit HMO.

Special services: Maternity, immediate care nursery, pediatrics, adolescent care center, neurosurgery, orthopedic surgery, ambulatory surgery program, cardiac intensive care, comprehensive geriatric, hospice, and other intensive care. Group Health is affiliated with UW teaching, research, and patient care programs.

Cost for individual cases is covered by co-op individual dues, which vary according to age and level of coverage.

Harborview Medical Center

325 Ninth Ave.
Seattle, WA 98104
731-3000
Special services: Emergency/trauma center, regional epilepsy center, center for anxiety and depression, Northwest Lipid Research Clinic, sexual assault center, injury prevention and research center, Northwest regional burn center, major clinical site for UW Center for AIDS Research (one of seven such programs in the country).

Highline Community Hospital

16251 Sylvester Rd. SW
Seattle, WA 98166
244-9970
Special services: Barney Clark special care unit, comprehensive geriatric program.

Northwest Hospital

1550 N 115th St.
Seattle, WA 98133
364-0500
Special services: Northwest Tumor Institute, Hospice Northwest, cancer care, rehab center, MED-INFO (medical information and physician referral line).

Providence Medical Center

500 17th Ave.
Seattle, WA 98122
320-2000
Special services: Heart center, respiratory care center, CancerCare, rehabilitation services, mental health, Family Childbirth Center.

Swedish Hospital Medical Center

747 Summit Ave.
Seattle, WA 98104
386-6000
Special services: Antepartum unit for high-risk pregnancies, neonatology (special care nursery), 24-hour renal transplant service, Tumor Institute, two bone-marrow transplant units available in affiliation with Fred Hutchinson Research Center. Also surgical specialties with over 24,000 procedures performed each year, etc.

University Hospital

1959 NE Pacific St.
Seattle, WA 98195
548-3300
A teaching facility for the UW School of Medicine, University Hospital is also part of the Warren G. Magnuson Health Sciences Center, which has 12 major units including dentistry, medicine, nursing, pharmacy, public health, community medicine, and social work; four centers (Alcohol and Drug Abuse Institute, Child Development and Mental Retardation Center, Regional Primate Research Center, Research Center in Oral Biology); and two medical centers (University of Washington Medical Center and Harborview Medical Center). The hospital also features a regional clinical referral center and a major research institution.

Special services: Cardiac diagnostic services, cardiac surgery, cancer care services, bone and joint center, neonatal intensive care unit, multidisciplinary pain services, and Northwest Spinal Cord Injury Center.

Virginia Mason Hospital

925 Seneca St.
Seattle, WA 98101
624-1144
Special services: Critical care, diagnostic medicine, immunology research, diabetes, cancer, heart, women's health, specialty medicine, lithotripsy, MRI.

Cancer research

Fred Hutchinson Cancer Research Center

667-5000
Cancer Information Service: (800) 4-CANCER
Fred Hutchinson is a research center rather than a hospital—one of 24 comprehensive cancer centers in the nation and the only federally designated center in the Northwest. Bone marrow transplants are the only patient service the center offers, and it accepts patients from all over the world, performing more transplants than at any other location.

More than 200 research projects are under way at the center. They focus on three areas: basic sciences, public health sciences, and clinical research. Eventually, all operations will move from First Hill to the new center on southeast Lake Union, which currently houses a clinical research lab.

The center operates the Cancer Information Service to answer questions from the public and publishes a number of booklets on cancer risks, avoiding cancer, and how to seek the most appropriate diagnosis and treatment.

SUBSTANCE ABUSE SPECIALISTS

Highline Recovery Service

12844 Military Rd. S
Seattle, WA 98168
248-4790
Substance abuse program director: Mary Beth Foglia

Schick Shadel Hospital

12101 Ambaum Blvd. SW
Seattle, WA 98146
244-8100

(CONTINUED ON PAGE 286)

Hospitals

	Children's Hospital and Medical Center	THC Seattle	Group Health Cooperative Central Hospital	Harborview Medical Center
Ownership	Private, non-profit	Private, for profit	Private, non-profit	Local government
Beds	208	55*	222	413
Occupancy rate	70%	30%*	65%	90%
Admissions/year	9,379	672*	11,573	11,930
Physicians	918	73*	245	729
Registered nurses	691	31*	440	650

*1993 figures

Illness category	Regional average charge	Average charge	Average charge	Average charge	Average charge
Stroke	$ 6,559	NA	$ 13,249	NA	$ 8,486
Pneumonia	6,014	NA	4,197	NA	4,931
Heart failure and shock	5,467	NA	7,372	NA	5,189
Chest pain	3,547	NA	NA	NA	3,971
Digestive disorders	4,117	NA	NA	NA	4,310
Joint replacement and limb reattachment	14,261	NA	13,773	NA	19,994
Medical back problems	4,451	NA	5,135	NA	5,773
Cesarean section	4,620	NA	NA	NA	NA
Normal childbirth	2,518	NA	NA	NA	1,854
Normal newborn	612	NA	NA	NA	NA
Chemotherapy	5,294	NA	NA	NA	5,752
Psychoses	6,314	NA	6,520	NA	6,747

Sources: "Health Care Users Guide, 1995,"
Washington State Department of Health, and individual hospitals

continued ▶

Hospitals

	Highline Community Hospital	Northwest Hospital	Overlake Hospital Medical Center (Bellevue)	Providence Medical Center
Ownership	Non-profit	Private, non-profit	Non-profit	Church. non-profit
Beds	279	247	225	334
Occupancy rate	75%	60%	67%	71%
Admissions/year	8,954	10,608	12,586	16,249
Physicians	164	295	375	480
Registered nurses	300	400	357	738

Illness category	Regional average charge	Average charge	Average charge	Average charge	Average charge
Stroke	$ 6,559	$ 6,492	$ 6,445	$ 5,759	$ 6,999
Pneumonia	6,014	6,262	6,411	5,703	6,356
Heart failure and shock	5,467	5,340	5,312	5,787	6,755
Chest pain	3,547	2,854	3,237	3,522	4,790
Digestive disorders	4,117	4,365	4,376	3,362	4,696
Joint replacement and limb reattachment	14,261	15,268	14,979	15,518	14,068
Medical back problems	4,451	4,183	3,892	3,598	5,601
Cesarean section	4,620	5,245	4,944	4,132	4,837
Normal childbirth	2,518	2,632	2,575	2,482	2,661
Normal newborn	612	524	506	702	659
Chemotherapy	5,294	3,869	4,432	3,613	4,858
Psychoses	6,314	7,505	10,639	4,628	7,044

	Swedish Hospital Medical Center	University Hospital	Virginia Mason Hospital
Ownership	Private, non-profit	State government	Private, non-profit
Beds	697	450	336
Occupancy rate	65%	73%	80%
Admissions/year	25,400	14,425	11,240
Physicians	1700	400	400
Registered nurses	1136	800	377

Illness category	Regional average charge	Average charge	Average charge	Average charge
Stroke	$ 6,559	$ 6,234	$ 7,847	$ 6,691
Pneumonia	6,014	6,132	5,738	5,417
Heart failure and shock	5,467	5,592	5,300	4,935
Chest pain	3,547	3,917	3,298	3,564
Digestive disorders	4,117	4,130	4,431	4,093
Joint replacement and limb reattachment	14,261	12,941	18,288	14,742
Medical back problems	4,451	3,990	5,986	3,787
Cesarean section	4,620	4,704	5,882	4,791
Normal childbirth	2,518	2,670	2,702	2,285
Normal newborn	612	720	695	582
Chemotherapy	5,294	5,340	6,302	4,527
Psychoses	6,314	7,646	6,279	6,077

Seattle Indian Health Board
611 12th Ave. S
Seattle, WA 98114
Outpatient clinic: 324-9360
Thunderbird Treatment Center:
722-7152 (inpatient)

Swedish Medical Center/Ballard
NW Market and Barnes Sts.
Seattle, WA 98107
781-6209
Substance abuse program director:
Joe Lucey

DEATH AND DYING

In King County, heart disease is the leading cause of death, closely followed by cancer. The statistic that's really startling, however, is that in the 25–44 age group AIDS is now the leading cause of death. Since 1987, 2,247 people in King County, most of them young men, have died of AIDS.

The King County Medical Examiner has the unenviable job of investigating sudden, violent, unexpected, and suspicious deaths. In 1994, for example, he investigated 1,501 of the 12,235 deaths in the county.

In an annual report, the examiner comments on outstanding factors noted in investigations during the year, primarily the use of alcohol, drugs, and firearms in violent deaths. In 1994 he noted that of all the traffic fatalities in which blood alcohol tests were performed, 30% of drivers tested positive. Firearms accounted for 67% of homicides and 59% of suicides. Of drug-caused deaths in 1994, 38% involved cocaine—up from 29% in 1991. There was an 11% increase in overall drug-caused deaths in 1994 compared to the previous year.

COUNTY MORTALITY STATISTICS

- Traffic fatalities, 1994: 178
- People who died in an automobile: 113
- People who died wearing seatbelts: 37
- Deaths involving motorcyclists: 13
- Percentage of motorcyclists killed who were wearing helmets: 62%
- Murders: 118
- Suicides: 216

- Drownings (does not include homicide or suicide): 22
- Drug-caused deaths: 166 (cocaine- or opiate-related: 68%)

Source: King County Medical Examiner, 1994 annual report

King County Medical Examiner
850 Alder St.
Seattle, WA 98104
731-3232

INFANT MORTALITY RATES

Seattle's infant mortality rate is 7.9 for every 1,000 live births—about equal to the state's rate of 7.8, and considerably better than the U.S. rate of 9.1. (King County's rate has dipped from 1985's high of 9.5 to 6.8.)

If that sounds like good news, look again. The infant mortality rate was three times greater for African Americans than for Caucasians. And Seattle's average African-American infant mortality rate is worse than 16 of 23 major U.S. cities. The rate varies according to where in the city the mothers live. In central, north, and southeast Seattle, the rate is significantly higher than elsewhere.

Source: "Health of King County" report, Seattle/King County Department of Public Health

AIDS: THE STAGGERING FACTS

The figures are earthshaking: One in every 100 people in the Seattle/King County region might be infected with the human immunodeficiency virus (HIV).

That statistic from the AIDS Prevention Project of the Seattle/King County Department of Public Health makes a few assumptions, such as that about 15% of the Seattle/King County population is gay, that half

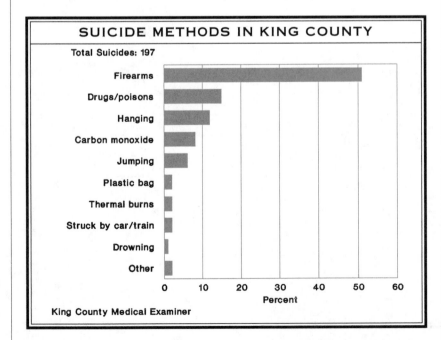

SUICIDE METHODS IN KING COUNTY

Total Suicides: 197

Firearms
Drugs/poisons
Hanging
Carbon monoxide
Jumping
Plastic bag
Thermal burns
Struck by car/train
Drowning
Other

0   10   20   30   40   50   60
Percent

King County Medical Examiner

LEADING CAUSES OF DEATH IN KING COUNTY

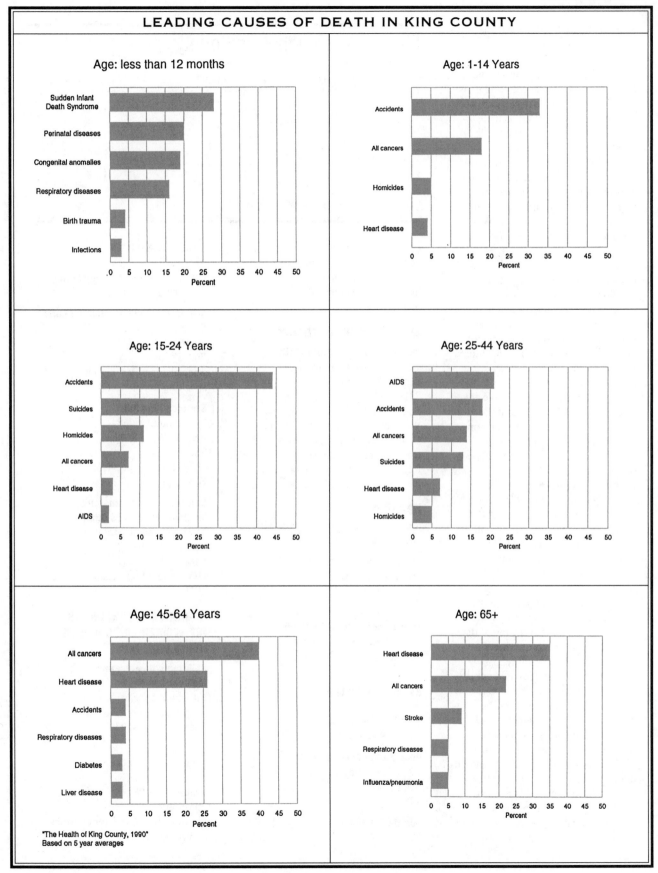

Age: less than 12 months
(Percent)
- Sudden Infant Death Syndrome
- Perinatal diseases
- Congenital anomalies
- Respiratory diseases
- Birth trauma
- Infections

Age: 1-14 Years
(Percent)
- Accidents
- All cancers
- Homicides
- Heart disease

Age: 15-24 Years
(Percent)
- Accidents
- Suicides
- Homicides
- All cancers
- Heart disease
- AIDS

Age: 25-44 Years
(Percent)
- AIDS
- Accidents
- All cancers
- Suicides
- Heart disease
- Homicides

Age: 45-64 Years
(Percent)
- All cancers
- Heart disease
- Accidents
- Respiratory diseases
- Diabetes
- Liver disease

Age: 65+
(Percent)
- Heart disease
- All cancers
- Stroke
- Respiratory diseases
- Influenza/pneumonia

"The Health of King County, 1990"
Based on 5 year averages

of those are male, and that those males who are tested for HIV are representative of the rest of the population. The Project people say the figure is as close to a true number as they can get because doctors are not required to report HIV-positive statistics to any agency (although they must report AIDS cases).

Testing HIV-positive means a person has been exposed to the virus at some point. He or she may have slight symptoms or may not even become sick. Researchers think that the average time it takes to develop full-blown AIDS is between 9 and 14 years, and they think a small percentage of people who test positive never develop AIDS symptoms.

Acquired Immune Deficiency Syndrome (AIDS) is actually the end stage of the HIV virus, the point at which a person catches pneumonia or develops cancer or contracts another, fatal, infection.

Those who are HIV-positive are infected and able to transmit the virus to other people through sexual contact or transmission of blood.

As of March 1996, there had been 6,392 cases of AIDS reported in King County; 2,247 deaths from AIDS were reported. Nationwide, over 311,381 people have died of AIDS. To track the depressing stats, call the Washington State AIDS Hotline, (800) 272-AIDS, where you can get an up-to-date report.

A word on AIDS statistics: Physicians are required to report AIDS cases to the county, but may take up to six months after the initial diagnosis to file their report. Therefore, statistics lag behind reality.

AIDS death statistics are kept in a unique way. For each period (i.e., a quarter), there is a figure for the number of AIDS cases diagnosed, followed by the number of those diagnosed in that period who have died. If more of the people diagnosed during that period die, the death statistic for that period is revised.

One more caution: Statistics from the public health system versus those from AIDS foundations differ be-

Birth and death in King County
Rates are per 1,000 population

Year	County population	BIRTHS		DEATHS	
		Number	Rate	Number	Rate
1994	1.6 million	21,972	13.7	11,241	7.03
1993	1.59	23,236	14.1	11,524	7.26
1992	1.56	23,036	14.7	10,899	6.97
1991	1.54	22,799	14.8	11,616	7.5

Source: Seattle-King County Department of Public Health

cause the health system counts only deaths from AIDS itself; foundations often count deaths of those with the AIDS virus for any reason, including suicide.

Experimental treatment

AIDS Clinical Trial Unit (ACTU)
1001 Broadway, Suite 218
Seattle, WA 98122
731-3184
Sponsored by the University of Washington/Harborview Medical Center. Screening tests, study medications, lab, and clinical monitoring free to HIV-positive persons who participate in ACTU studies.

Health care
Seattle clinics with a focus on HIV and a sliding fee schedule:

Country Doctor Community Clinic
500 19th Ave. E
Seattle, WA 98112
461-4503

45th Street Community Clinic
1629 N 45th St.
Seattle, WA 98103
633-3350

Harborview HIV Clinic
325 Ninth Ave.
Seattle, WA 98104
731-4394

Pike Market Community Clinic
1930 Post Alley
Seattle, WA 98101
728-4143

Seattle Gay Clinic
500 19th Ave. E

Seattle, WA 98112
461-4540
Nurse practitioner, limited clinical monitoring, and referrals.

Sea-Mar Community Health Center
8720 14th Ave. S
Seattle, WA 98108
762-3730
Specializes in serving the Spanish-speaking population.

Swedish Hospital
747 Summit Ave.
Seattle, WA 98104
386-6000
HIV Patient Supervisor: Margo Bykonen

University of Washington Medical Center AIDS Clinic
1595 NE Pacific St.
Seattle, WA 98159
548-4728
HIV Patient Supervisor: Connie O'Hara

Health care specialists for women and children living with HIV

Children's Hospital and Medical Center
Infectious Disease Specialty Clinic
4800 Sand Point Way NE
Seattle, WA 98105
526-2116

Columbia Health Center
4400 37th Ave. S
Seattle, WA 98118
205-6060
Medical/dental care for children and adolescents.

Harborview Pediatric Clinic
325 Ninth Ave.
Seattle, WA 98104
731-3335
Medical services for HIV-positive children.

Harborview Women's Clinic
325 Ninth Ave.
Seattle, WA 98104
731-3367
Medical and prenatal care for HIV-positive women.

Odessa Brown Children's Clinic
2101 E Yesler Way
Seattle, WA 98104
329-7870
Medical/dental care for children and adolescents.

Hotlines

AIDS Prevention Project Hotline
296-4999

U.S. Health Service AIDS Hotline
(800) 342-AIDS

Washington State AIDS Hotline
(800) 272-AIDS

Other resources

Most AIDS- and HIV-related resources can be found by contacting the Northwest AIDS Foundation or the AIDS Prevention Project Hotline at 296-4999.

AIDS Housing of Washington
448-5242
Develops housing for people living with AIDS. Past projects include the Bailey-Boushay House, a nationally acclaimed nursing-care facility in Madison Valley for people in the last stages of AIDS. Bailey-Boushay is run by Virginia Mason Medical Center.

American Civil Liberties Union of Washington
624-2180
Legal services for AIDS victims.

Chicken Soup Brigade
328-8979
Meals, transportation, and other services to people with AIDS.

Delta Society
226-7357
Information for people with HIV who own pets.

Health Education and Training Center
University of Washington
720-4250
Provides AIDS education and training for health care providers.

Health Information Network
784-5655
Education and referral.

Humane Society
641-0080
Special assistance for pet owners with HIV, including free pet food and kitty litter.

In Touch
328-2711
Massage therapy for people with AIDS.

National Lawyers Guild, Seattle Chapter
622-5144
Legal aid.

Northwest AIDS Foundation
329-6923
329-6963 (referrals)
Social work, case management, housing issues, education.

Northwest Family Center
720-4300
Health services for HIV-positive women and their families; pediatric and obstetric clinic.

AIDS cases and deaths in King County

Year	Cases	Deaths
1996	Through May–58	Through April–100
1995	436	426
1994	525	421
1993	613	414
1992	259	181
1991	394	186

Source: Seattle–King County Department of Public Health Epidemiology, 1996

Parents and Friends of Lesbians and Gays
325-7724
Support services for gays, lesbians, families, friends, mates, and spouses.

People of Color Against AIDS Network (POCAAN)
322-7061
Education and referral for blacks, Haitians, Latinos, native Americans, and Asian/Pacific Islanders.

Rise 'n' Shine
628-8949
Emotional support services for children affected by AIDS.

The Rubber Tree (Zero Population Growth Seattle)
633-4750
Low-cost condoms, spermicides, and lubricants; educational materials.

Seattle AIDS Support Group
322-AIDS (322-2437)
Support groups and drop-in center.

Seattle Gay Clinic
461-4540
Health care and info for gay males.

Seattle Treatment Education Project
329-4857
Info on alternative and experimental treatment for people with HIV.

Shanti
322-0279
Emotional support and training for individuals and loved ones facing AIDS.

Stonewall Recovery Services
461-4546
Drug and alcohol counseling and education for gays and lesbians.

Tel-Med
621-9450 (recording)
Information on AIDS and HIV.

Washington State Human Rights Commission (Seattle)
464-6500
Investigates complaints of discrimination against persons with AIDS/HIV; information and referral.

IT'S A CRIME

What are the chances that your car will be stolen in Seattle in the next year? Pretty darn good, say the 6,800 people whose cars were ripped off in 1995. And if the thieves don't take the whole *car, chances are they'll take the tape deck, at least. If they* do *take your*

car, there's a good chance you'll get it back; but if they take your stereo, you can kiss it goodbye.

In Seattle, you don't have to worry quite as much about getting murdered, raped, robbed, or assaulted as you would in another city. But hold onto your mountain bike, your Honda, and Grandma's silverware. The city's main crime problem is people taking things, not hurting each other.

The rate of property theft is so high that when serious property crimes (such as burglary, larceny, and auto theft) are combined with violent crime, the resulting overall crime rate puts Seattle on par with other mid-sized metropolises.

Property crimes aren't the ones that keep residents awake. However, in recent years, there has been a decrease in murders in the city. Seattle had 47 murders in 1995, down from 69 in 1994—an decrease of 46% in just one year.

Although there has been a decrease in homicides, guns are still the weapon of choice in Seattle for murderers. And whether for protection or aggression, more than 5,000 people carry a gun by permit from the city.

Unless otherwise specified, statistics in this chapter have been provided by the Seattle Police Department.

HOW, WHEN, AND WHY THE POLICE RESPOND TO CALLS

To report a crime in Seattle, call 911—even if the crime is not in progress. Our city's 911 service is unusual in that it is used for both emergency and nonemergency police access. When you call 911, you are routed to one of 19 telephone lines leading to the police department's communications center.

A certain number of lines are allocated to different regions of the city, so if it's a particularly busy night in your part of town, you may wait a while before your call is answered. Waiting is rare, however; the average 911 call is picked up within 4 to 5 seconds.

If you're calling to alert the police of an emergency, your call is given a priority rating, which determines how fast the cops will respond to your call. The priorities are:

Critical Dispatch. Acute need for dispatch. The life of a citizen or officer is in obvious danger; this call goes out for crimes-in-progress like shootings and stabbings.

Immediate Dispatch. Dispatch at once; nearly critical. Other crimes-in-progress, or ones that are imminent or have just occurred. Includes major disturbances with weapons, serious injury accidents, most alarms.

Urgent Dispatch. Nearly immediate dispatch. Circumstances where quick police response could nab the suspects; altercations that could really get out of hand if not policed quickly; incidents where there is a threat of violence, injury, or damage to property. Also, unknown injury or minor-injury accidents.

Prompt Dispatch. Dispatch as soon as possible. Most noise and traffic complaints are "prompt dispatch." Also used for investigations or minor-incident complaints in which response time is not a critical factor.

Dispatch as Available. Self-explanatory. Mischief or nuisance complaints such as snowballing, firecrackers, etc. Lowest priority calls; dispatched after all others are taken care of.

FOLLOW-UP

After the initial dispatch, cases are assigned to a police investigator on a priority basis, starting with the most serious felonies and ending with the least serious. After that, a number of factors determine whether your case will be assigned to an investigator— let alone solved:

- If the perpetrator has been identified, or can be.
- If a gun or dangerous weapon was used.
- If serious injury took place.
- If there's an unusual, unique *modus operandi* or obvious pattern to the crime.
- In the case of a residential burglary, if the house was occupied at the time.
- If the crime took place on a unique premise (church, community institution, etc.).
- If a large loss occurred.
- If a gun without a serial number is reported stolen.
- If you were the victim of a similar crime within the past six months.
- If there are leads or evidence to follow up.
- If the crime has the potential for creating unusual community or police interest.

When the case is assigned, the detective takes statements and examines leads (mainly on the phone). A suspect may be determined.

The case is then either submitted to the prosecutor for action, referred to the court unit for possible prosecution as a misdemeanor, or filed in the records as "Inactive." You will be notified of the case status in a letter from the department.

GOT A HOT TIP?

Several areas have hotlines you can call to report crimes that don't necessarily need immediate police response (e.g., to report graffiti, crack houses, or drug dealing on the corner). Volunteers record the information and let the police know about problem houses and areas.

South Seattle Crime Prevention Council
625-0577

East Precinct Crime Prevention Coalition
625-0577

West Seattle Crime Hotline
937-CLUE

CAR 54, WHERE ARE YOU?

The Seattle Police Department's (SPD) patrol officers are housed in four precincts: North, South, East, and West. Each precinct has a captain as precinct commander and a lieutenant as commander of all activity on a shift.

The precincts operate on three shifts. First shift (4am–noon): 122 officers. Second shift (noon–8pm): 241 officers. Third shift (8pm–4am): 200 officers.

The following precinct information is taken from 1995 figures.

North Precinct
10049 College Way N
684-0850
North Precinct Commander:
Capt. Dan Bryant

Located west of I-5 and the Northgate shopping mall, just across the street from North Seattle Community College.
North Precinct population: 229,303 (43.03% of city)
Percentage of serious offenses (murder, rape, robbery, burglary, aggravated assault, larceny, auto theft, and arson) committed in North Precinct: 31.68%
Number of serious crimes (1995): 17,555
Number of serious crimes (1994): 17,454
Change in serious crime (1994–1995): +0.58%
Number of officers (1996): 147

South Precinct
3001 S Myrtle St.
386-1850
South Precinct Commander:
Capt. Nick Metz
Located on south Beacon Hill, east of Boeing Field and I-5, across the street from the Van Asselt Community Center.
South Precinct population: 156,219 (29.31% of city)
Percentage of serious offenses committed in South Precinct: 24.1%
Number of serious crimes (1995): 13,356
Number of serious crimes (1994): 14,555
Change in serious crime (1994–1995): –8.2%
Number of officers (1996): 147

East Precinct
1519 12th Ave.
684-4300
East Precinct Commander:
Capt. John Diaz
Located at the corner of 12th Avenue and Pine Street, two blocks east of Broadway.
East Precinct population: 82,497 (15.48% of city)
Percentage of serious offenses committed in East Precinct: 15.48%
Number of serious crimes (1995): 9,476

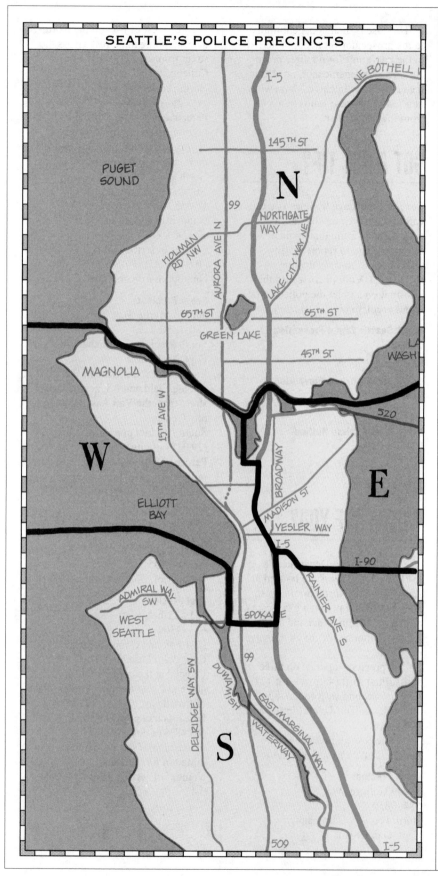

SEATTLE'S POLICE PRECINCTS

Number of serious crimes (1994): 10,658
Change in serious crime (1994–1995): –11.1%
Number of officers (1996): 138

West Precinct
610 Third Ave.
684-8917
West Precinct Commander: Capt. Gene Hunt
Located on the third floor of the Public Safety Building (SPD headquarters) at Third Avenue and James Street.
West Precinct population: 64,881 (12.18% of city)
Percentage of serious offenses committed in West Precinct: 27.12%
Number of serious crimes (1995): 15,027
Number of serious crimes (1994): 15,175
Change in serious crime (1994–1995): –0.01%
Number of officers (1996): 154

SPECIAL OPERATIONS DIVISION

This division contains the Traffic and Metropolitan sections, which include the Special Patrol Unit, the Harbor Patrol Unit, the Mounted Unit, and the Canine Patrol Unit. It is headquartered in the Public Safety Building.

Canine Patrol Unit
684-7472
There are 14 officer-and-dog teams. One dog is trained to sniff out explosives, and several can locate narcotics.

Harbor Patrol Unit
684-4071
The Harbor Patrol polices Lake Union, Puget Sound north of the West Point Lighthouse, Lake Washington (within city limits), and the Ship Canal. The unit has 23 staff members and eight boats (two

Zodiacs, one Boston whaler, one 20-ft. jet boat, and two 34-ft. and two 38-ft. patrol boats).

In addition to keeping the law on the water, these floating police respond to distress calls. They also help clear floating debris (800 tons annually) and have shored up a house-boat or two. The unit operates out of a dock and maintenance area at 1717 N Northlake Place on Lake Union.

Who patrols south of West Point? The Seattle Fire Department, which has fire boats on Elliott Bay, will respond to fire calls south of West Point, but other than that, there is no law enforcement in the city waters south of the lighthouse. If you're in real trouble on the Sound, call the

Coast Guard:
24-hour Command Center: 220-7000
Channel 16, VHF, for emergencies
Channel 22, VHF, for non-emergencies

The speed limit is 7 knots on Lake Union, through the Lake Washington Ship Canal to the Sound, and through Portage Bay and Montlake Cut to Lake Washington. At the north end of Lake Union is a small area bounded by yellow buoys where there's no speed limit. It's a test course for ship-yards to run engines and test boats. They have to shut down to 7 knots at either end of the course.

Lake Washington has no speed limit except within 100 yards of the shore or bridges, where the limit is 7 knots.

Mounted Patrol Unit
386-4238
Cops on horses—one sergeant and four officers (eight officers during summer)—patrol events such as Seahawks games and big concerts, and trot through Pioneer Square on a regular basis. As anachronistic as this idea seems in the high-tech age, patrolling on horseback is extremely effective in crowd control. Various city agencies say that public use of beaches and parks noticeably increases when the mounted patrols make regular appearances—a cop-and-horse team lowers the fear of crime. Some estimate one officer in the saddle is equal, in terms of crowd

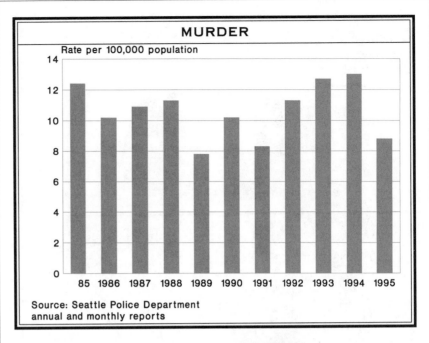

MURDER

Rate per 100,000 population

Source: Seattle Police Department annual and monthly reports

control, to four on foot. Stables are at Discovery Park (944 Kansas Avenue).

Special Patrol Unit
684-8755
The largest of the units in the Metro Section, this is the unit that protects dignitaries who come to town. They also work special situations like labor strikes and other demonstrations, and provide backup to patrol units. But the primary job of the Special Patrol Unit is serving warrants where the arrestee is apt to be less than cooper-ative, and assisting narcotics units in executing search warrants.

POLICE FACTS

- Average number of calls received per day: 2,429 (first shift, 22% of calls; second shift, 41%; third shift, 37%).
- Ratio of police officers to pop-ulation in Seattle: 1 to 423. In nation: 1 to 446.
- Number of police officers per 1,000 population in Seattle: 2.37. In nation: 2.24.
- Average number of officers walking or biking beats during the day: 241.

VIOLENCE: NOT QUITE A WAY OF LIFE

Relative to other metropolitan regions, Seattle is not a killing town. Most murders occur in the downtown area and in parts of central and south Seattle.

- Number of murders (1995): 47
- Number of murders (1994): 69
- Murders per 100,000 population (1995): 8.8
- Percentage of murders solved (police arrest suspect and turn over to prosecutors) (1995): 70%

SPD Homicide/Assault Unit
684-5550

RAPE

The Police Department's Special Assault Unit handles rape, child abuse, and missing persons cases.

- Number of rape incidents (1995): 260

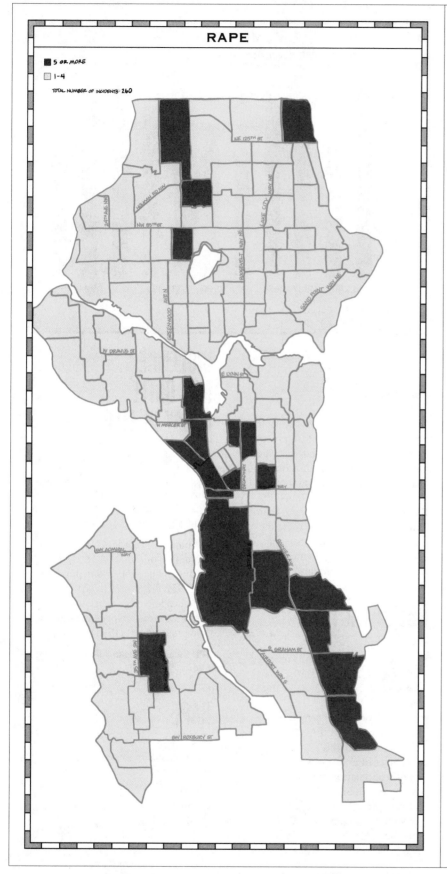

RAPE

■ 5 OR MORE

□ 1-4

TOTAL NUMBER OF INCIDENTS: 260

- Number of rape incidents (1994): 318
- Rapes per 100,000 population (1995): 48.8
- Percentage of rape cases solved (1995): 44%

SPD Special Assault Unit
684-5575

Other resources
Additional services are listed in Chapter 14, "Lending a Hand."

Harborview Sexual Assault Center
521-1800

Seattle Rape Relief
Crisis Line: 632-7273
Business: 325-5531 (TTY)

AGGRAVATED ASSAULT

Most aggravated assaults are handled by the Homicide/Assault Unit; cases are screened for immediate need before assignment.

- Aggravated assaults (1995): 2,392
- Aggravated assaults (1994): 3,615
- Assaults per 100,000 population (1995): 449
- Percentage of assault cases solved (1995): 55%

SPD Homicide/Assault Unit
684-5550

Domestic violence resources
Additional services are listed in Chapter 14, "Lending a Hand."

Battered Women's Shelter Information
461-3200

City of Seattle Law Department, Criminal Division
Family Violence Project
710 Second Ave., Room 1414
Seattle, WA 98104
684-7770 (TTY)
Assists victims of domestic violence in cases where criminal charges have been filed.

SPD Domestic Violence Unit
684-0330

Domestic Violence Hotline
(800) 562-6025

ROBBERY

Robbery statistics include extortions, strong-arm robberies, and purse snatches.

- Number of robberies (1995): 2,212
- Number of robberies (1994): 2,536
- Rate per 100,000 population (1995): 415
- Percentage of robbery cases solved (1995): 27%

SPD Robbery Unit
684-5535

GOODBYE TO THE VCR: PROPERTY CRIMES

To get an idea of the chances of the police department catching the thief who has just burglarized your home—let alone getting back the

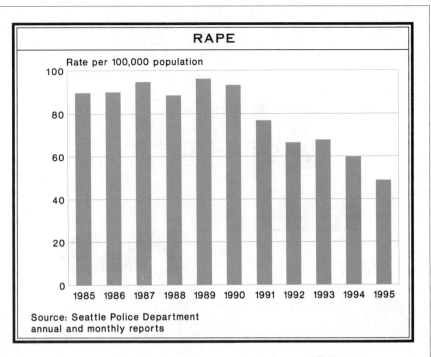

RAPE

Rate per 100,000 population

Source: Seattle Police Department annual and monthly reports

swiped VCR, stereo, and silver— take a look at some numbers:

- Number of burglaries and thefts reported (1995): 43,671
- Number cleared: 7,051

In other words, 16% of all burglaries and thefts are solved.

A large percentage of burglaries are connected to narcotics; users steal the stuff, then sell or trade it to sup-

The only way to increase the chance that your stolen property will be found and returned is by knowing the serial number of the VCR, stereo, etc., or some unique identifying symbol (a scratched-in social security number, for example). If a thief just ripped off your Toshiba, the police can enter the serial number into a computer file and notify you if it turns up. Otherwise, you're out of luck.

port a habit. One cop who regularly busted rock houses (where crack cocaine is sold and used) says it's not uncommon to find the house bare—

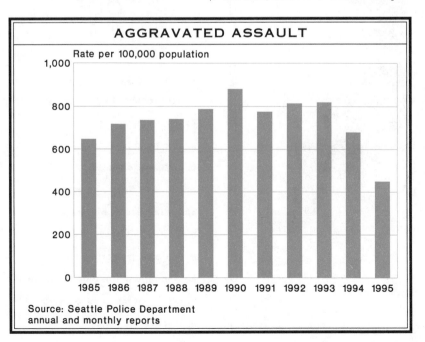

AGGRAVATED ASSAULT

Rate per 100,000 population

Source: Seattle Police Department annual and monthly reports

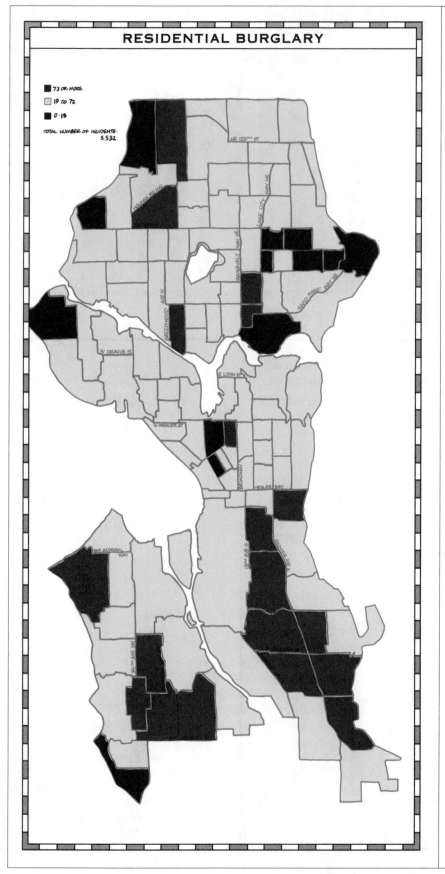

RESIDENTIAL BURGLARY

■ 73 OR MORE
□ 19 TO 72
■ 0-18

TOTAL NUMBER OF INCIDENTS:
5,532

except for the hot VCRs and stereos stacked in the closet. In a typical *month*, about $700,000 worth of electronics (stereos, televisions, etc.) is reported stolen; just under $30,000 worth is recovered.

And just when do burglaries happen? Residential burglaries happen slightly more frequently in the daytime than at night; the reverse is true of non-residential.

Burglary and theft incidents are handled by each precinct, not by a centralized unit. The department also has a Property Inspection Squad—a sergeant and four detectives—that investigates pawnshops and scrap yards and monitors gun shops.

- Value of property stolen (1995): $56.3 million
- Amount recovered: $30.6 million

SPD Property Inspection Squad
684-5737

Because the police department
is flooded with theft and burglary
cases, each case is handled
according to how much information
is available to identify the thief.
If your case has some good leads
and witnesses, it will probably
make it to the hands of a detective.
If your case is short on leads,
bet the farm that it'll be dispatched
to police purgatory, also known
as inactive file status.

HAPPINESS IS A "BORROWED" CAR

The auto theft rate just keeps going up—from 6 per day in 1983 to 18.6 per day in 1995. So far the police recover most of the cars nicked, though they don't usually find the thieves. We checked to see if Seattle is unusual in the number of car thefts in cities of comparable population. In 1995, there were 6,800 cars stolen in Seattle; 10,036 in Boston (population 572,454); 7,103 in New Orleans (population 500,791), and 5,435 in Long Beach (population 438,378). The reason for the high recovery in Seattle is that, for the most part, cars around here are stolen for joy rides; there isn't a big market for hot automobiles.

But "recovered" doesn't mean your Volvo will come back to the garage untouched. Recovered cars are generally damaged to some extent, and if the stereo was anything more than a factory AM-only system, it'll be gone. Double ditto for the car phone.

What can you do to prevent your car from being stolen? Car alarms

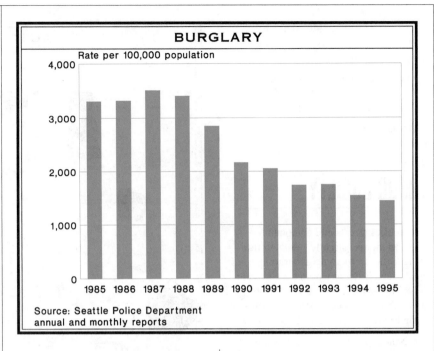

BURGLARY

Rate per 100,000 population

Source: Seattle Police Department annual and monthly reports

help—but most thieves know how to disarm them. Those bars for the steering wheel look good and may scare some off, but those who know say they almost present a welcome challenge for a tool-wielding thief. Park in a garage, says the police department wryly.

- Number of cars stolen in Seattle (1995): 6,800
- Dollar value of cars stolen (1995): $35,360,000
- Dollar value recovered (1995): $34,652,800
- Percentage of car thefts solved (arrests made): 11.3%

Car prowls are as common as slugs in the marigolds—there were

What kinds of cars get stolen most often? VW Rabbits are popular with thieves—probably because they're easy to break into. Ditto with Hondas. Toyota Corollas too are apparently easy to break into. (And owners of old Toyota Tercels very often cruise the more sordid parts of town to find their stolen cars—hot-wiring the little beaters seems to be a piece of cake.)

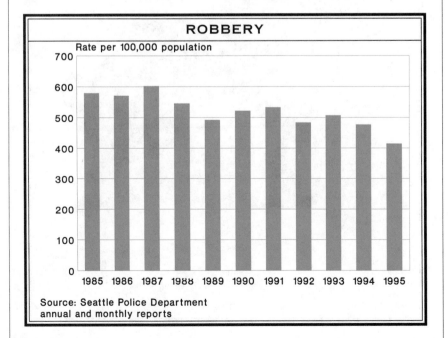

ROBBERY

Rate per 100,000 population

Source: Seattle Police Department annual and monthly reports

13,159 of them in 1995 alone. In case you think this means small change was stolen, think again.

- Value of property stolen during car prowls (1995): $5,350,814
- Value recovered: $146,115

SPD Auto Theft Squad
684-8940

DRUG SOCIETY

Narcotics arrests and complaints are on the rise slightly—something that is not news to neighborhood activists. But you would have trouble convincing neighborhood activists that drug use is decreasing. According to the Seattle Police Department:

- Number of felony narcotics arrests (1995): 3,135; in 1994: 3,025; in 1993: 2,934.
- Number of search warrants (1995): 254; in 1994: 281; in 1993: 318.

If there's drug dealing in your neighborhood, what can you do? A number of things:

- Call the police, either 911 or the Narcotics Section, and let them know about it.
- Call your local Crime Hotline (listed earlier in this chapter) to report drug activity. Volunteers record information from the calls and let the police know about problem houses and areas.
- Watch the area. Try to determine if activity is going to a specific house. Record the makes and license numbers of cars that visit the house, the traffic through the house during any given day, and any names you can get.
- Find out who the owner of the house is. He or she is probably not the person doing the dealing. One place to go to determine the owner is the King County Tax Assessor's Office on the seventh floor of the King County Administration Building at Fourth and James. Punch in the address on the public access computer terminals there,

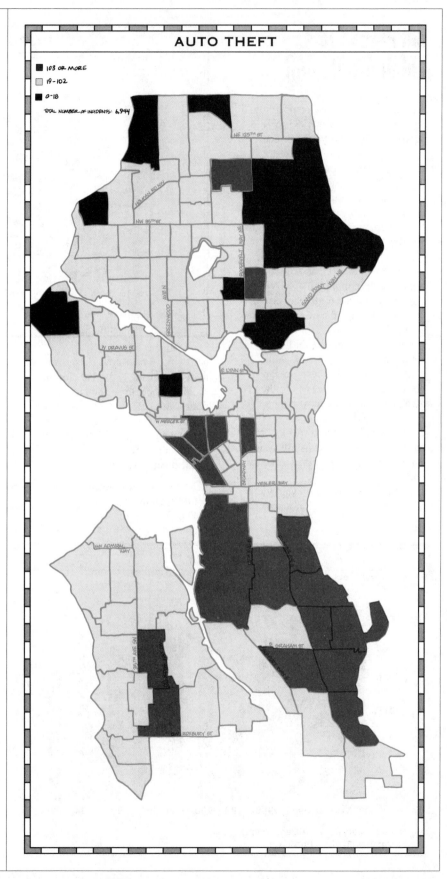

AUTO THEFT

- 103 OR MORE
- 19-102
- 0-18

TOTAL NUMBER OF INCIDENTS: 6,944

and the database will tell you who's paying taxes on the property.

Let the owner know what's happening and that abatement proceedings (where the city takes over the property) might be in the offing if the house isn't cleaned up. You'll probably see action.

• Find out if the utility bills—especially the water bill—are in arrears. If the city can shut off water, it can shut the house down.

SPD Narcotics Section
684-5797

GANG ACTIVITY

Police have identified over 1,200 gang members and hangers-on in the city. In the past few years, Seattle has seen a dramatic rise in the number of Asian gangs.

Police won't say how many murders gangs were responsible for, but since it is increasingly young people getting murdered, it's safe to say gang members are still killing other gang members—mostly with guns. One reason the cops may be reluctant to talk about it is that there is a feel-

ing in the air that letting the media in on the gang culture tends to glorify it.

There have been community efforts to curb the killing, with gun buy-back programs (the Stop the Violence Committee collected 1,772 guns in five days, paying $50 each) and a drug-traffic loitering ordinance.

SPD Gang Section
684-8679

THE SEARCH FOR PERRY MASON

If you find yourself collared by the heavy hand of the law, you'll need a defense attorney. Fortunately (or unfortunately, depending on your point of view), Seattle is full of attorneys. They're not all defense attorneys, but the pickings for a defendant aren't slim. Here are a few helpful resources.

Columbia Legal Services
464-5911
Free legal advice for low-income citizens.

Lawyers Referral Service
623-2551
Sponsored by the Washington State Bar Association.

Neighborhood Legal Clinic
340-2593

Northwest Women's Law Center
621-7691
Legal referral service offering free information to the public on all legal topics.

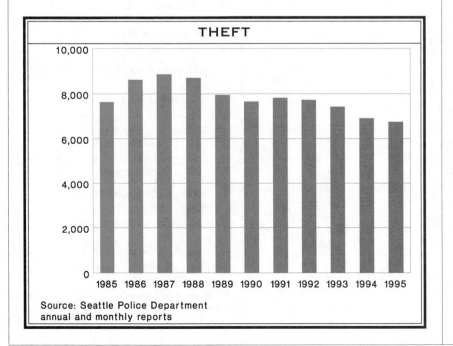

THEFT — Source: Seattle Police Department annual and monthly reports

If you don't pay your parking tickets, the police will put a hold on your vehicle license. And driving with expired tabs is one sure way to be pulled over by police, who will immediately let you know that you are wanted on an outstanding warrant. If you're curious about your current bill, call the Municipal Court office (684-5600) and give them either your vehicle license or a case number. They'll look up your file on computer and read you the list of your individual tickets, along with the grand total.

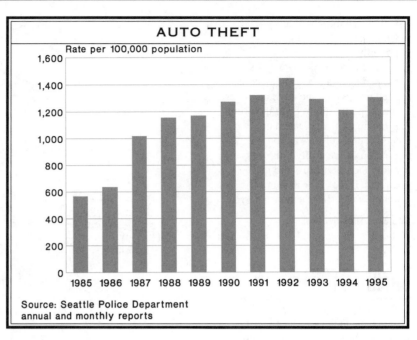

AUTO THEFT

Rate per 100,000 population

Source: Seattle Police Department annual and monthly reports

PUBLIC DEFENDERS

The public defender's office in Seattle is actually made up of four organizations: Associated Counsel for the Accused (ACA), Society of Counsel Representing Accused Persons (SCRAP), Northwest De-

fenders Association (NDA), and the Public Defenders Association (PDA). Seattle and King County contract with these agencies to provide attorneys when you need free legal defense. The King County Office of Public Defense assigns your case to one of the four, and they take it from there.

King County Office of Public Defense
Smith Tower, Room 321
506 Second Ave.
296-7662
Assigns cases to one of four public defense agencies.

Associated Counsel for the Accused (ACA)
401 Terrace St.
624-8105
Seventy-five attorneys. Handles felonies, juveniles, municipal court cases, and most of the public defense cases in district court.

Northwest Defenders Association (NDA)
157 Yesler Way, Suite 203
623-5091
Twenty-seven attorneys. Handles juveniles, felonies, municipal court cases; also does some district court work.

NARCOTICS COMPLAINTS VS. ARRESTS

Thousands

Narcotics Complaints ■   Narcotics Arrests ☐

Source: Seattle Police Department annual and monthly reports

Public Defenders Association (PDA)
Central Bldg., Eighth Floor
810 Third Ave.
447-3900
Largest of the four defense organizations; has 90 attorneys. Handles felonies, juveniles, involuntary commitments (mental health and alcohol), municipal court cases, and a few district court cases.

Society of Counsel Representing Accused Persons (SCRAP)
1401 E Jefferson St., Suite 200
322-8400
Fifty-three attorneys. Handles felonies and juvenile cases. Does not operate in municipal court.

LOWLIFE

The SPD's Vice Section handles the city's lowlife, everything from the world's oldest profession to gambling and pornography. Prostitutes frequent certain corners of the city, most notably near downtown's Yesler Way overpass, and Pacific Highway S, near Sea-Tac Airport.

They used to hang out downtown at Sixth and Pike, but the cops put a stop to that. Second and Pike is popular for all sorts of lowlife after midnight, when it comes alive with drug dealers and kids looking for action. Aurora Avenue N, once made lively after dark by the prostitutes, has calmed down in recent years after the merchants and residents posted signs asking people to report the license numbers of "johns" stopping along the strip. Most of the signs ended up in teenagers' bedrooms, but increased patrolling of the area helped.

SPD Vice Section
684-8660

PISTOL PACKIN' CITY

It's not only the police who carry guns in Seattle. And it's not only those with gun permits from the city who carry guns. But the number of those conscientious enough to get a permit seems to be decreasing. Of course, that could mean that everyone who wants a gun already has one.

More women are carrying guns than ever before. In Seattle, local gun/sporting goods stores report handgun sales to women have increased 50% since 1985. Most of the buyers are first-time gun owners.

Gun permits issued by the city in recent years:
1993: 4,985
1994: 3,309
1995: 2,322

ALTERNATIVES TO FEAR

For women who want to defend themselves without packing a rod, here are some other options:

Alternatives to Fear
328-5347

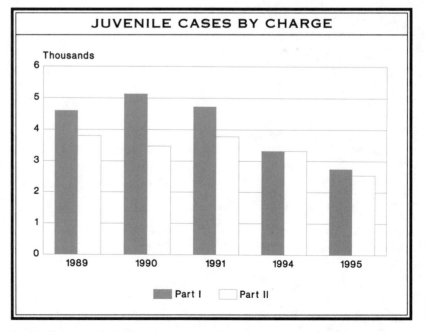

JUVENILE CASES BY CHARGE

Thousands

(Bar chart showing Part I and Part II juvenile cases for years 1989, 1990, 1991, 1994, 1995)

Legend: Part I (shaded), Part II (white)

Part I offenses *include the most serious crimes: murder, manslaughter, rape, robbery, aggravated assault, burglary, theft, auto theft, and arson.*

Part II offenses *include assault, forgery, fraud, stolen property, vandalism, weapons violations, prostitution, sex offenses, narcotics violations, gambling offenses, liquor violations, and disorderly conduct.*

Self-defense classes; curriculum and teaching aids; educational programs for teenagers (boys and girls), schools, churches, community groups, the workplace, and blind and partially sighted women.

Powerful Choices
P.O. Box 30918
Seattle, WA 98103
782-5662
Nonprofit organization offering 27 hours of full-contact, full-force training specifically designed for women. Also offers boundary-setting workshops as well as weekend self-defense seminars for men.

CRIME VICTIM RESOURCES

Families and Friends of Missing Persons and Violent Crime Victims
P.O. Box 27529
Seattle, WA 98125
362-1081

King County Prosecutor's Victim's Assistance Unit
King Co. Courthouse, Room E542
516 Third Ave.
Seattle, WA 98104
296-9552

Mothers Against Drunk Driving
929 N 130th St.
Seattle, WA 98133
364-6233

SPD Victim Assistance Section
Dexter Horton Bldg., Room 801
710 Second Ave.
Seattle, WA 98104
684-7777

CHAPTER

18

HAMMERS SAWS AND PERMITS

PERMITS

ARCHITECTS

CONTRACTORS

TREES

ZONING

INSPECTORS

UTILITIES

TOOLS

Weekend warriors—that's how contractors and architects snidely refer to the do-it-yourselfers who don't listen to the experts. But urban weekend warriors thrive here, where 70% of the city's land is zoned for single-family residences. In 1995, the city's building department issued 5,329 permits for additions and alterations to old homesteads—and that figure doesn't include the changes wrought by those who ran the saw out of earshot of city inspectors.

While it's true that contractors know how to avoid waiting in city permit lines when they're aching to hit the plumb lines, particular weekend projects may not even need a permit. To find out if yours does, contact the Permit Center at the city's Department of Construction and Land Use (DCLU). The rule of thumb is that if there is no structural change, and if access and ventilation are not reduced, you probably don't need a permit. You always need a permit to add plumbing and wiring.

The city doesn't list the remodeling projects that require a permit, so before you pound in a nail you should check. But take heart—such things as constructing oil derricks are exempt from the permit process. And the city trusts you to paint and put up wallpaper all by yourself.

NAILS AND GLUE

What you can hammer without city hall looking over your shoulder:

- Tool sheds and other sheds less than 120 square feet and under 12 feet in height
- Playhouses less than 120 square feet
- Playground equipment
- Sculptures
- Fences under 6 feet in height
- Movable counters and partitions under 5 feet 9 inches
- Retaining walls not over 4 feet high
- Water tanks holding less than 5,000 gallons
- Walkways and driveways not more than 30 inches above grade and not over any basement or lower story
- Temporary motion picture, television, and theater stage sets and scenery
- Window awnings that don't extend more than 54 inches from exterior walls

- Prefabricated swimming pools not exceeding 5,000 gallons
- Hot tubs
- Minor repairs or alterations that cost less than $2,500 and do not require structural changes

If your project isn't exempt, pull out your checkbook. For starters, Seattle's DCLU wants $110 to begin the permit process—and it can take up to six weeks just to get the application appointment!

SINGLE-FAMILY ZONING REGS

Sometimes it seems like there's a regulation for almost everything:

Lot coverage. You can cover only 35% or 1,750 square feet of your lot, whichever is greater, including house, garage, and any other buildings. This does not include decks under 18 inches high or below-ground swimming pools. You could cover your whole lot with playground equipment, as far as the city is concerned.

Height limits. Maximum permitted height for any residential structure is 30 feet, with some exceptions for things like peaked roofs, solar collectors, and chimneys. Maximum height for garages and sheds is 12 feet.

View corridors. Despite Seattle's hilly neighborhoods and incredible views, view regulations apply only to the downtown and to shoreline areas. Anywhere else neighbors are left to squabble in court over who's blocking what view. On the shoreline, views are protected for motorists and pedestrians first. Regulations vary per zone; e.g., in some areas, if you live on the water, you can't build on more than 35% of the width of your property.

Yards. A minimum-size front, side, and back yard are required of every single-family lot in Seattle. There must be at least 20 feet from the property line to the house for the front yard, or the average of the two

adjoining neighbors' front-yard sizes, whichever is less. The back yard must be a minimum of 25 feet from the rear lot line to the foundation, and side yards must be at least 5 feet in width. If you build a chicken coop or whatever in the back yard, you can't cover more than 40% of the total back yard space.

If you get to the point where you want to give up and tear the whole darn thing down, wait! You have to have a permit to demolish anything that required a building permit in the first place. For this privilege you pay from $71 to $213, based on square footage.

Seattle Dept. of Construction and Land Use
Permit Center
Dexter Horton Bldg., Second Floor
720 Second Ave.
Seattle, WA 98101
684-8850 (application, permit info)
684-8600 (24-hour info)
Open 8am–5pm Mon., Wed., Thurs., Fri. and 10am–5pm on Tues.

Seattle-King County Dept. of Public Health
Smith Tower, Room 201
506 Second Ave.
Seattle, WA 98101
296-4732 or 296-4727
For plumbing inspection. Call between 7:30 and 8:30am to talk to inspector, or bring your plans in during the same hours, no appointment necessary. When the job is done, make an appointment for yet *another* inspection.

DOWN ON THE (CITY) FARM

Urban farmers should cry foul on Seattle's hog discrimination. The only animal you can't keep in your yard is the poor, unfairly maligned swine—with the exception of pot-bellied pigs, the darling pet of the yuppie set, which are legal. There's no reason for the prohibition, city

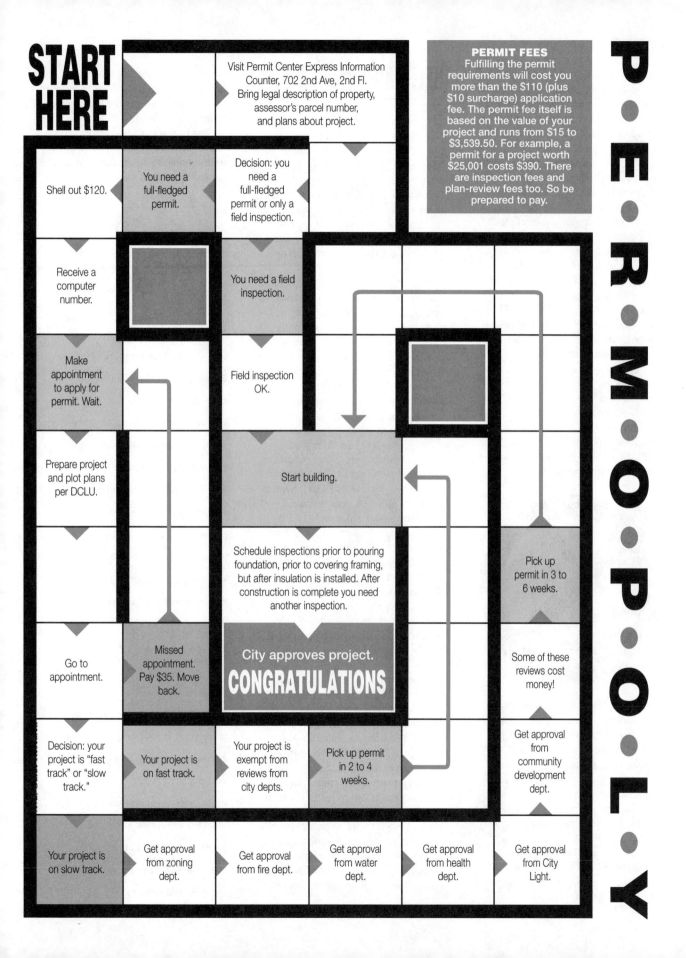

START HERE

Visit Permit Center Express Information Counter, 702 2nd Ave, 2nd Fl. Bring legal description of property, assessor's parcel number, and plans about project.

PERMIT FEES
Fulfilling the permit requirements will cost you more than the $110 (plus $10 surcharge) application fee. The permit fee itself is based on the value of your project and runs from $15 to $3,539.50. For example, a permit for a project worth $25,001 costs $390. There are inspection fees and plan-review fees too. So be prepared to pay.

Shell out $120.

You need a full-fledged permit.

Decision: you need a full-fledged permit or only a field inspection.

Receive a computer number.

You need a field inspection.

Make appointment to apply for permit. Wait.

Field inspection OK.

Prepare project and plot plans per DCLU.

Start building.

Schedule inspections prior to pouring foundation, prior to covering framing, but after insulation is installed. After construction is complete you need another inspection.

Pick up permit in 3 to 6 weeks.

Go to appointment.

Missed appointment. Pay $35. Move back.

City approves project.
CONGRATULATIONS

Some of these reviews cost money!

Decision: your project is "fast track" or "slow track."

Your project is on fast track.

Your project is exempt from reviews from city depts.

Pick up permit in 2 to 4 weeks.

Get approval from community development dept.

Your project is on slow track.

Get approval from zoning dept.

Get approval from fire dept.

Get approval from water dept.

Get approval from health dept.

Get approval from City Light.

PERMOPOLY

folks say—it's just historic bias. It could have something to do with a pig's love of mud. Take one Seattle pig, one Seattle yard, and one Seattle winter and—well, would you want to live next door?

But don't throw away those overalls yet. Right there in Wallingford, or any other neighborhood zoned for single-family residences, you can have a chicken coop. In most cases you can have no more than three chickens, but if you have an especially large lot, you can raise more. Single-family zones are designated by minimum lot size in square feet (S.F.) for different zones: S.F. 9,600, S.F. 7,200, or S.F. 5,000. For every extra 1,000 square feet of lot area, you can have one extra chicken (or duck—it's the same for all domestic fowl).

As for the lady down the street with three dozen cats, she's probably breaking the law. The city allows up to three small animals per house in a single-family zone. Only if you have a 20,000-square-foot lot can you have four small animals.

Cows, sheep, horses, and other farm animals (except, remember, pigs that aren't pot-bellied) are permitted only on lots of at least 20,000 square feet, and only at the rate of one per every 10,000 square feet of lot area. Barns have to be at least 50 feet from property lines. With 20,000 square feet you can even have a goat (which smells a lot worse than a pig, with or without the mud).

Go ahead and keep bees, but no more than four hives on lots of less than 10,000 square feet.

HELP! ARCHITECTS

Only 10% of home builders in Seattle actually use an architect to draw up plans for remodels or new buildings. Most use a builder, contractor, or architectural designer, primarily because of cost. Architects' fees vary from $9 to $65 an hour depending on the firm and the project. In general you can figure on spending 10% to 15% of the cost of construction on an architect.

Architects simply hate people who call themselves architectural designers. Designers charge less than architects; some have good reputations and some don't—just like architects themselves. The difference is that an architect is licensed, has had five years of college, and has passed architectural boards. A designer is basically anyone choosing to call him- or herself that.

In Seattle it seems there's an architect behind every tree. There are 1,600 members of the American Institute of Architects (AIA), Seattle Chapter. The AIA does not make referrals, but its office at 1911 First Avenue has a Resource Center for Architecture. Visitors can use the visually oriented and indexed system of access to architects' work. In addition, they can peruse the "Firm Pro-File," a roster of 350 local architectural firms. It includes a brief description of the firm, type of work, and its history. The Firm ProFile can be purchased for $30.

You can also look at a pamphlet of outstanding work by local architects selected by a professional jury. The pamphlet, from the Honors Award Program, includes photos of projects, along with the address of the house or structure, and the name of the contractor and consultant—a good source of hiring leads. (In addition, AIA will file resumes from people looking for a job with architects.)

The big problem in choosing an architect is in making the best "fit." You want someone you feel comfortable talking to. Remember, this pro is going to be hanging around the house a lot; you don't have to wonder if he or she squeezes the toothpaste tube from the bottom, but almost.

The best way to find a good architect is by word of mouth. Ask owners whose houses you admire who designed them, then get a client list

Get a permit for a remodel? "Well, you could go that route...," says one builder we know. Only the incredibly naive think the city's building permit stats reflect how many building projects there are in the city. City officials estimate only half the projects that should have a permit have one. If you get caught without one, usually due to tattle-tale neighbors, you have to pay up for an "investigation fee." So should you take your chances? Maybe, if you know what you're doing and are only building a deck. But insurance companies are sticklers on knowing that things are up to code and inspected. If your house burns down because of your makeshift wiring, you might be in trouble. And real estate agents sometimes question whether remodels are up to code. There's a safety factor too, so remodeling without a permit is a calculated risk.

from the respective architect. Get on the phone and ask questions of those clients. And don't be intimidated by the vocabulary: "Arch-speak" can rival the chatter of doctors.

Be sure an architect can develop plans tailored to specific clients; if all his or her work looks the same, you can bet the architect isn't listening to the individual needs of the client. (Of course, if you like the style, there is a certain security in knowing that what you see is what you'll get.) Ask first: Architects should give free initial consultations. If they don't, walk.

Names to know

Architects of some distinction in the world of Seattle residential architecture, chosen for awards won, work featured in glossy upscale mags, and recognition by peers:

- Ralph Anderson
- Tom Bosworth
- Arne Bystrom
- Jim Cutler

- Miller Hull Partnership
- Mark Millett
- Jim Olson
- Stuart Silk

Where, one might ask, are the women? There are only 186 women members of the local AIA (11.8% of total membership).

American Institute of Architects/ Seattle Chapter
1911 First Ave.
Seattle, WA 98101
448-4938
Executive director:
Marga Rose Hancock

HELP! CONTRACTORS

It's not enough to drive a pickup to call yourself a contractor in Seattle. You're a carpenter or builder or simply a pickup driver unless you are licensed and bonded.

Someone building a monstrosity next door without a permit? Neighbor littering the yard with offensive junk? You can rat on the neighbors by calling 684-8420 with construction complaints, or 684-7899 with housing code violations and junk storage gripes. To complain about excessive noise, call the DCLU at 233-7224. But don't say we sent you.

The AIA provides something called a "contractor's qualification statement" for evaluating the expertise of contractors. It asks questions about experience, where the contractor is licensed to do business, trade references, financial assets, and other potentially embarrassing questions.

There are organizations, such as Seattle Master Builders, where you can get referrals. The trouble is that the group recommends members, and all you have to do to be a member is pay dues. Only 10% of all Seattle contractors belong to the Master Builders.

Tips for choosing your contractor

- Check with Department of Labor and Industry, (800) 647-0982, for the credentials or record of a contractor.
- Ask for references, call them, and try to see their work. If a contractor balks at giving references, find another.
- If you have the time and money, get a second opinion from a disinterested designer or inspector on the advice or bid a contractor is giving you.

Master Builders Association
2155 112th Ave. NE, Suite 100
Bellevue, WA 98004
451-7920

INSPECT YOUR INSPECTOR

There was a time when somebody at the city issued a policy statement declaring that inspectors must be professional engineers. Slap! A lawsuit. The policy was retracted.

Building inspectors now come in all shapes and sizes, competencies, and lack thereof. Private inspectors don't need to have *any* qualifications—they *give* themselves qualifications in order to get work. (The law outlines some

Beware of trigger-happy pest inspectors who are eager to treat the symptom (the bugs) rather than the causes of infestation. Be leery of insecticides, especially a suspect method called "tenting" where plastic is literally draped over the entire home and then the place is fumigated to death. Replacing portions of the house that invite pests, like damp wood, should take care of the problem, maybe with the help of a little localized, low-key pest control.

qualifications, but they're so vague as to be virtually unenforceable.) There are 60 or so inspection agencies around, but only five are registered with the engineering department.

To find a private inspector you can close your eyes and take a stab in the Yellow Pages, or you can ask your favorite realtor. For a pre-purchase real estate inspection, either the buyer or seller hires an inspector to assess the overall structural integrity of a house, determine how it was built and maintained, and generally check out all conditions that might invite problems, such as the dreaded soil/wood contact. The going rate for a general pre-purchase inspection is about $300–$325. Some inspectors also act as "owner representatives," looking at proposals from contractors to determine whether things are on the up-and-up.

RX FOR THE SEATTLE HOUSE

Here's the lowdown on a few typical Seattle house ailments.

Mildew and rot

Causes: Weather from outside seeping in through leaks, especially in basements that aren't sealed, and moisture generated from inside that can't get out.

Signs of impending doom: Blistering paint, mildew or dampness on walls, and sweaty windows. If you aren't sure if you have rot, push an ice pick into suspect wood and see if it goes in too easily.

Solution: You need ventilation, especially in the attic, kitchen, bathroom, and crawl spaces. Try fans in the living areas and vents in the crawl space and attic. And get that basement sealed. Also, cut back on houseplant watering and aquariums in the winter.

Some private building inspectors have a business on the side setting the "wrongs" they discover "right." For example, a pest inspector might be able to exterminate imaginary critters that were never a problem until he or she diagnosed them. The inspection might be cheap, but wait until you get the bill for the treatment. Ask inspectors if they have a repair business and if they do, find someone who doesn't.

Bugs, pests, and critters

Termites generally prefer a warmer clime, but that doesn't mean there aren't problems with pests such as the lowly powderpost beetle and the carpenter ant, which loves mold.
Causes: Moldy basements, damp wood.
Signs: Little sawdust piles at the base of wood studs. Powderpost beetles are usually found in older homes.
Solution: Call a pest control company and repair structural damage the little critters caused.

Asbestos angst

Your furnace and ducts may be insulated with materials containing asbestos; and siding and sprayed ceilings applied before 1978 may also contain the deadly stuff. Don't touch it—have an inspector look at it. Or call the Hazardous Waste Hotline, 296-4692, a service of the Seattle/King County Health Department. The hotline, which acts as a clearinghouse, can tell you how to get your house tested and whether you have a problem. They can also tell you how and where to dispose of asbestos. And by the way, not all asbestos has to be removed.

Moss on the roof

Roofs in shaded areas should have a zinc strip installed at the ridge to reduce damage from moss.

HIP, HIP, HOORAY— FOR CITY LOANS

The City of Seattle Department of Housing and Human Services provides low-interest home improvement loans to low-income residents. The program is called REACH (Rehabilitation and Emergency Assistance for City Homeowners). The loan rates are 3%.

REACH's 1996 income limits:

- 1-person household: $29,100
- 2-person household: $33,300
- 3-person household: $37,450
- 4-person household: $41,600
- 5-person household: $44,950
- 6-person household: $48,250
- 7-person household: $51,600
- 8-person household: $54,500

The city also has an Emergency Code Repair loan program to help low-income homeowners correct hazardous or deteriorated conditions.

Department of Housing and Human Services
618 Second Ave.
Seattle, WA 98104
684-0355

Still renting? There are resources out there for you too. The Seattle Tenants Union operates a renters' hotline, (800) 752-9993, and sells a "Renter's Kit" that includes information on landlord-tenant laws, sample letters, etc. For info, call 723-0500. The State Attorney General's office will send you a sample room-by-room checklist and a brochure on the landlord-tenant laws; call 464-6684. The Department of Construction and Land Use, 684-7899, accepts complaints/inquiries about Seattle's just-cause eviction ordinance, repair problems, and code violations.

CAVEAT EMPTOR

There are approximately 13,000 real estate agents prowling around the Puget Sound area, and to give you an idea of how busy they are (or aren't), they sold about 3,159 houses in April 1996. It's a tough sell out there.

When you're looking to buy or sell your house, don't go into the savage market unarmed. Jim Stacey, a Seattle real estate agent, teaches savvy classes in buying a home and investing in real estate. He's a big advocate of buyer representation (or "buyer brokers") and laces his advice with plenty of good humor. Call the Experimental College for information on the classes, or call Jim himself. Or take a look at his thorough book *Washington Homes: Buying, Selling, and Investing in Seattle and Statewide Real Estate*.

Other outlets for real estate education are Michael Martin's Sunday morning show on KING radio and Tom Kelly's Sunday morning show on KIRO AM.

Experimental College
University of Washington
543-4375

Jim Stacey Real Estate Services
6307 Phinney Ave. N
Seattle, WA 98103
784-1426

YURTS AND DREAM BOATS

Yurts and other eccentric structures are allowed, and thrive, in Seattle, but check with the DCLU before you build or draw up plans, to make sure you comply with local codes. The *Uniform Building Code* or "builder's bible," as it is called, is available at bookstores for $54.95, or can be found in the architectural library at the UW's Gould Hall (though you can only read it there for two-hour stints).

The most popular alternative home in the city is the houseboat, more correctly known as a floating home. About 480 floating homes are docked in Seattle, divided among 50 docks on Portage Bay and Lake Union. They are so popular that the prices are soaring: with luck, you can still find a very small, very rundown houseboat for $60,000; a designer one goes for around $1.5 million. Since no new moorage is to be found, people are buying old houseboats, tearing them down, and building new ones.

Want one? The Floating Homes Association recommends several ways to find one:

- Visit a realtor.
- Walk around the docks to get a feel for the different areas and to look for "For Rent" or "For Sale" signs.
- Put up a "Want to Buy" sign at Pete's Grocery on Fairview Avenue near Lake Union and at Canal Market on Fuhrman Avenue E, Portage Bay. Floating-homers frequent both places.

A couple of things you should know: Banks considering loans sometimes categorize a houseboat as personal property rather than real estate, which makes for financing problems.

Insurance is tough too. Some insurance companies consider houseboats a bad risk, and either charge an arm and a leg or don't offer coverage at all.

If you're thinking of building a houseboat, find someone who's experienced with the idiosyncrasies of plumbing and electrical matters at sea.

The city has from time to time tried to do away with houseboats altogether, but floating home aficionados organized the Floating Homes Association to fend off such threats.

There are two ways to own a houseboat: either lease space on a dock or join a cooperative that owns the dock. Some houseboats do not comply with city shoreline law and are only floating because of their historic (or grandfathered) use.

The big houseboat issue today is that houseboats appear to be as upwardly mobile as their owners. As most of the one-story homes are becoming two-story, they grow in value. The city recently raised the height limit for grandfathered houseboats from 16 feet to 18 feet, so second stories are blossoming along the water. (Height limit for conforming houseboats is 21 feet.) This growth means that views and light are being cut, and there's even a tunnel effect between some docks.

Another Lake Union houseboat owners' gripe is noisy seaplane takeoffs. The seaplane companies have compromised somewhat and the planes no longer take off at the crack of dawn.

Floating Homes Association

2329 Fairview Ave. E
Seattle, WA 98102
325-1132
President: Bill Keasler
Live-aboards are people who live on boats rather than houseboats. The distinction is that live-aboards' boats are not on floats, as houseboats are. At Shilshole Marina, for example, over 250 people live aboard. Aside from moldy shoes and fights with marinas over rates and sewage, these folks love the life on board and develop small communities within the marinas. Property taxes—nonexistent of course—are a pleasure to talk about. Not all marinas allow live-aboards, and there are strict requirements for holding tanks and other water and power systems.

THE SUNSET OF SOLAR POWER

Several years back, solar power companies were on every city corner, but there aren't many left now. Perhaps some decided this isn't the greatest part of the country for solar power, but the most probable reason for their absence is that the federal tax credit for solar anything was

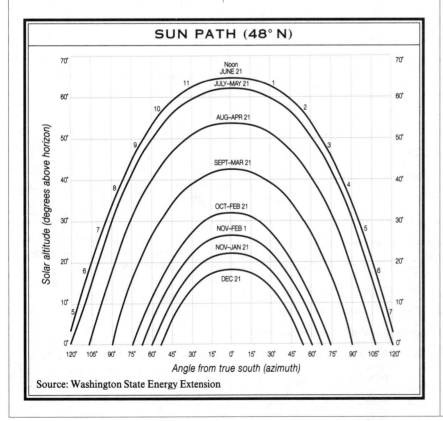

SUN PATH (48° N)

Solar altitude (degrees above horizon)

Noon
JUNE 21
JULY–MAY 21
AUG–APR 21
SEPT–MAR 21
OCT–FEB 21
NOV–FEB 1
NOV–JAN 21
DEC 21

Angle from true south (azimuth)

Source: Washington State Energy Extension

abolished by the Reagan administration. When financial incentives went, businesses went too. Some people still heat hot water with solar water heaters, however. Most solar water systems in Seattle utilize a system of rooftop panels that use black metal with glass glazing for collector areas. A small electronic pump circulates water between the panels and the hot water tank.

Washington's latitude is about 48°N. Since latitude affects both the intensity of solar energy and the amount of time it's available, looking at a sun path chart for our latitude helps you choose the best site and angle for solar panels. Climate affects the amount of solar radiation delivered to a site too, of course.

STREET-TREE WISE

There's a guy who works for the City of Seattle named Jerry Clark who practically wears leaves in his hair. As city arborist, he is a kind of

Very few contractors in Seattle are qualified to install solar panels for heating water. Check with the Energy Extension Service for what you need to know about installation and then carefully assess dealers and installers. Ask how long the company's been in business, if they can provide references, and what sort of warranty they provide.

Your planting strip along the street is the only sunny place in your yard? Go ahead and plant your vegetable garden there. The city won't care unless your corn grows so high it blocks visibility. And then they only care if someone complains. Whatever you do, don't pave the strip—that's verboten under the city's new push to combat the greenhouse effect by creating an urban forest.

social worker for trees, calling himself a "spokesperson for good tree policy." Clark is developing an urban forest which he hopes will number 200,000 street trees.

A city arborist has been around in one form or another for 50 years. After a landscape beautification effort by Mia Mann and Victor Steinbrueck, among others, the arborist's office was officially established in 1968. Since then, 28,000 trees have been planted in planting strips—the area between the sidewalk and the curb. The most popular trees are maples and ash.

You may not know it, but you own up to 30 feet out into the 60-foot right-of-way of the street in front of your house. But, though you own it, the city manages the right-of-way for the general public. So you have to obtain permits to repair your sidewalk or to plant on the strip. (And, since you have the privilege of owning it, you have to pay for the repairs or tree pruning, etc.) There's no

fee for a planting permit, but you'll receive advice from the arborist about the proper tree selection to minimize conflicts with such things as utility poles. And you'll learn how to locate trees properly and how to maintain them. The city did a survey of historic urban trees—mostly maple, horse chestnut, ash, cedars, and poplars—and tries to match new trees to them to preserve the character of the streets.

City Arborist
710 Second Ave.
Seattle, WA 98104
684-7649
Hours: 7am–3:30pm (early morning is the best time to call)

CURBSIDE GARDENS

People plant lots of things in the planting strips between the sidewalk and curb, including vegetable gardens. The only time that's a problem is if something like corn or hay limits visibility. Vegetation under 2½ feet is officially allowed. Trees can only be planted along city streets when there is a curbed roadway and the planting strip is at least 5 feet wide.

TO THROW YOUR OWN NEIGHBORHOOD PLANTING PARTY

1. Call the arborist at 684-7649. He'll come talk to your group.
2. Find money through neighborhood matching funds, from Department of Neighborhoods small and simple grants (684-0464), or from City Light (386-1902).
3. Get a permit and choose the type of trees, with the arborist's help.

4. Choose only small-scale street trees when planting underneath power lines.

5. Call (800) 424-5555 to locate all underground utilities.

6. Plant small-scale trees between 15 and 25 feet apart. Plant all medium-size trees between 25 and 35 feet apart. Do not plant a tree any closer than 5 feet to any utility line or power pole, 10 feet from a driveway, and 20 feet from a streetlight or existing trees.

7. Don't plant between June and September when water is at a premium. The arborist recommends drought-tolerant trees, but even those need water, usually about 5 gallons once or twice a week.

TREES SUITED TO A SEATTLE URBAN FOREST

Looking to re-create Yosemite in your yard? Here are some suggestions.

Big shade trees

- Oaks and ash are generally drought resistant and grow well. (Maple is not recommended because it suffers from drought.)

Medium shade trees

- Flame ash (35–40 feet, classic look, fruitless). View them along 35th Avenue NE, north of NE 85th Street.
- Pyramidal European hornbeam (30–35 feet, pyramidal shape, slow grower). See along 19th Avenue E, north of Madison.
- Ruby red horse chestnut (30 feet, red flowers in spring, nearly fruitless). See at Hiram Chittenden Locks to west of walkway.
- Crimean linden (45–50 feet, bright green, small foliage). See on 35th Avenue SW between SW Snoqualmie and SW Morgan streets.
- Katsura (40 feet, light and dainty branch structure, fall color, needs moisture). See near 35th Avenue E and E Mercer Street.

- Cleveland Norway maple (40–50 feet, yellow fall color, smaller than Norway maple). See along Fifth Avenue downtown.
- Red maple (40–45 feet, fall color, requires most water). For narrow streets, columnar variety of red maple is best. See columnar along Madison Street near Boren.
- Sweetgum (50–60 feet, semievergreen, fall color). See along Fourth Avenue downtown.
- Zelkova (40–50 feet, fine-textured, slightly serrated leaf, use as substitute for American elm). See along 24th Avenue NW, north of Market Street.

Small-scale shade trees

- Flowering ash (good tree with fragrant flower, dark green foliage, round head, grow in minimum 8-foot strip).
- Flowering cherry: *Prunus serrulata* (blooms April and May, full sun, moist soil). Selections include Shirofugen (25 feet), Shirotae (20 feet), Akebono (25 feet).
- Other flowering cherries include Yoshino and Sargent (both 40 feet, 30-foot spread), and Kwanzan (30 feet, 20-foot spread).
- Flowering crabapple: Select only those resistant to scab, cedar apple rust, mildew, and fireblight. Most grow 18 to 20 feet high. Recommended are Baccat Jackii, Donald Wyman, Doubloons, Red Baron, Floribunda, Snowdrift, Veitch's Crab.
- Goldenrain tree (35 feet, intense sulphur yellow flower, blooms late spring into summer, fruit until fall; drought tolerant).
- Hawthorn: Recommended are Lavalle hawthorn (30 feet, shining green foliage, white flowers, and coral-colored berries); Washington hawthorn (25 feet, white flowers, orange fruits, tolerant of pollution and extreme urban conditions).
- Flowering plum: Recommended are Krauter's Vesuvius plum (35 feet, 25-foot spread); Thundercloud plum (25 feet, same spread).

- Flowering pear: Recommended are Chanticleer (upright, 30 feet high, 15-foot spread, fall color); Aristocrat (very upright, 30 to 35 feet, 20–25-foot spread, fall color); Redspire (upright, pyramidal, 35 feet, 25-foot spread, fall color).

Source: City Arborist

POTHOLES AND MORE

Another part of your household, whether you know it or not, is the city itself. Sure, your sidewalk is your responsibility, but the city certainly wants to know what goes on there. Ditto the pothole, the alley behind your house, or the street that just flooded. Contact the city road maintenance department; it's divided into two offices, one north of Denny Way, one south.

Road Maintenance Office, North
12555 Ashworth Ave. N
Seattle, WA 98133
684-7508

Road Maintenance Office, South
714 S Charles St.
Seattle, WA 98134
386-1218
Streets and alleys 24-hour line: 386-1218. Handles repair and maintenance, potholes, drainage, and surface street flooding.

Specific road problems

Sign and signal requests: 684-7623
Sign and signal repair: 386-1206

Weeds and more

Department of Construction and Land Use
Housing Enforcement Division
Weeds, hazardous overgrowth, debris on private property: 684-7899

LET THERE BE LIGHT

Seattle City Light is the reason your refrigerator refrigerates and your dishwasher washes. Oddly enough, city electric rates rise when the rain doesn't fall. In 1993 the city council glanced toward the clouds and approved a rate increase, boosting rates by 17% that year and 15% again in 1994.

City Light does more than send out bills, however:

- Seattle City Light Service and Info: 625-3000. Telephone hours are 7:30am–6pm Mon.–Fri., 8am–5pm Sat.
- Outage report: 625-3000
- Appliance repair: 684-3800
- Clearing trees near power lines: 386-1663
- Commercial and industrial energy management: 684-3254
- Community relations: 684-3112
- Conservation hotline: 684-3800. Information about energy conservation and home weatherization programs.

Seattle City Light will answer your questions about home weatherization and insulation, hot water heaters, energy consumption of appliances, alternative energy sources, and available discount loan or grant programs. If your house is heated electrically you qualify for a free energy audit telling you how to reduce energy usage (and bills). Free water-heater insulation blankets can be installed during the check. Call 684-3800 and ask about these and other City Light programs.

- Electric service: 517-3272 (north of Mercer Street); 654-2720 (south of Mercer Street). New wiring, rewiring, conversion to electric heat.
- Streetlight repair: 386-1661
- Skagit tours: 684-3112. Tours of City Light's Skagit hydroelectric project in the North Cascades.

WATERWORKS

Information on your water meter, water-efficient gardening, how to find leaks—Seattle's water department is a fount of information, so to speak.

The department puts out numerous publications that you can order by calling 684-5900 and requesting them by number. Here's a sampling:

#102 Information for Rental Property Owners
#104 If the Building on Your Property Is Vacant
#105 Utility Credit Program
#107 Payment Stations
#201 How to Locate and Read Your Meter
#203 Protect Your Pipes in Winter
#206 Fix That Faucet
#207 Repairing Toilet Leaks
#211 Inspection Requirements for Private Water Line Repair or Construction
#401 Single-Family Residence Sewer Charge
#402 Duplex Sewer Charge
#404 Drainage Fee
#501 Free Water Conservation Kit
#503 Energy Costs Going Through the Roof
#510 Are You Wasting Water?
#511 Water-Efficient Gardening

Seattle Water Department
Dexter Horton Bldg., 10th Floor
710 Second Ave.
Seattle, WA 98104
684-5885
The water department also offers a free conservation kit to help you save up to 20% of your water usage. Request one by calling 684-5879.

Billing information: 684-5900
Conservation office: 684-5879
Credit and collections: 684-5888
Drainage (general information): 684-7560
Emergency service: 386-1800 (24 hours)
Service and inspection: 684-5800
Sewers (backups, permits, and inspection): 684-5253
Surface street flooding: 386-1218 (24 hours)
Water quality information: 684-7404

RENT IT

Lack the tools to be a weekend warrior? Try these resources:

AA Rentals
12558 Lake City Way NE
Seattle, WA 98125
362-5544
Thirteen locations all over the city. Rent all kinds of building equipment, large to small: paint sprayers, loaders, jackhammers, saws, floodlights, etc. Most equipment rents by the day, but some by the hour.

40 Rentals
430 SW 153rd St.
Burien, WA 98166
244-1655
Four locations. Large and small equipment rental.

Handy Andy Rent-a-Tool
10711 Aurora Ave. N
Seattle, WA 98133
367-5050
NE 45th and First NE
Seattle, WA 98105
632-0404

More homeowner resources
Home Owners Club
1202 Harrison St.
Seattle, WA 98109
622-3500
Membership organization of about 2,000. Dues are $42 per year. Provides referrals for plumbing, electrical, TV repair, contractors, etc. Will even dispatch someone to your home to assess damage.

Phinney Neighborhood Association
Phinney Neighborhood Center
6532 Phinney Ave. N
Seattle, WA 98103
783-2244
Classes on home repair, wiring, etc.;
a tool bank from which they loan
tools, $10 for nonmembers, $5
for members.

Seattle Conservation Corps
684-0191
This section of the city's Department
of Human Resources has teams
that provide neighborhood cleanup
and recycling; they also assist with
stream rehabilitation and waterfront cleanup.

Washington Energy Extension Service
914 E Jefferson St., Suite 300
Seattle, WA 98122
(800) 962-9731 or 296-5640
Answer questions on energy conservation. Have 50 free publications on
energy conservation available.

CHAPTER

19

GREEN GROWS THE CITY

BIRDS

FISH

CRITTERS

WATER

WILDLIFE

P-PATCHES

POLLUTION

RECYCLING

WASTE

CONSERVATION

Old-growth forests in Schmitz Park, coyotes in Ballard, eagles in Seward Park. Amid the hustle of city life, nature takes its course, setting up housekeeping in our urban habitat. Of the major cities in the United States, Seattle may have the most abundant wildlife. While we listen to the call of Canada geese over Lake Union and applaud the orcas in Elliott Bay, most American city dwellers have only pigeons and the occasional rat to liven up their surroundings. In Seattle, no need to pack up the car with camping gear—you can get a taste of the wilds without ever leaving the city.

BIRD'S-EYE VIEW

A variety of bird species use the Puget Sound region as a resting ground during their migration along the Pacific flyway. Many of these birds and waterfowl, figuring this is far enough south (or north) to travel, spend the entire winter (or summer) in this area.

Seattle itself is certainly not lacking in feathered friends. In fact, members of two endangered species—as well as some not-so-endangered raptors—have been seen within the city limits:

Peregrine falcons. These swift flyers have been spotted near the closed-off smokestacks in the south end of Ballard; the smokestacks could substitute for natural snags, and rumor has it a pair has nested. Another pair may be overwintering here. The sightings prompted the Department of Wildlife to anchor nesting platforms on downtown high-rises, in the hope that if the pair decide to nest, they'll choose a safe spot.

Seattle has adopted one pair of peregrine falcons, named Stewart and Bell, and made video stars of them. In the spring, march into the Washington Mutual Tower bank lobby, and watch the couple and their chicks on TV, thanks to a video camera focused on their nest far above. It's fascinating viewing, but also educational. The Falcon Research Group analyzes the birds' behavior. There's even a Peregrine Hotline, 654-4423.

What brings the peregrines to Seattle? A steady diet of their favorite food: pigeons. And the fact

that the buildings create walls as steep as the cliffs where they normally dwell.

Purple martins. Plentiful in Seattle until the 1950s, they have now reached endangered species status. They have been seen nesting near the skybridge next to the Bon Marché, where they've found niches similar to natural tree cavities.

Though not endangered, nighthawks (members of the goatsucker family—not really hawks) have dwindled in number in recent years, but still can be seen in the city. They feed on insects at higher altitudes than do swallows and swifts.

Other raptors. Also downtown, watch for such birds of prey as red-tailed hawks, merlins (also called pigeon hawks), and kestrels. Redtails have been seen nesting at the King Street train station. Accipiters (sharp-shinned hawks and Cooper's hawks) can also be spotted in the downtown core. These wild-area nesters pass through the city on the lookout for prey—often pigeons on the wing or small birds.

AND THEN THE "SEAGULLS"

Not so endangered are the gulls, which you'll find nesting on many a downtown building. But guess what? There's no such thing as a "seagull."

We have five or six species of gull: the glaucous-winged, which is the largest and most common, as well as the California, mew, ring-billed, and black-headed gulls—and sometimes little gulls.

BIRD-WATCHING

There are three main birding spots in Seattle—the downtown core, Discovery Park, and the Montlake Fill. Any of the birds mentioned above can be spotted downtown,

but for serious bird-watching, take your binoculars and field guides to one of the following spots.

Discovery Park. This "island of habitats" comprises sandy and rocky beaches; sand cliffs; open meadows facing both north and south; conifer forests, conifer mix, and major deciduous areas; and marshy areas. Such a variety affords both nesting and "drop-in" habitats for species passing through on their migration routes. The park is also a hangout for birds wintering over.

If you want to see one of Seattle's three nesting pairs of bald eagles, head to the meadow area in the center of the park and scan the trees behind the maintenance building. A pair of eagles nests in a very large grand fir there. In this sweeping meadow you may spot goldfinches, red-tailed hawks, a variety of sparrows, migrating osprey (if you're lucky), and members of the falcon family: merlins, peregrines, and kestrels, as well as accipiters. Also in these transition understory/meadow areas, look for the rufous humming-

bird and Anna's hummingbird.

Head for West Point to see seabirds. Here are two miles of wonderful beach habitat—to the north the beach is rocky, to the south sandy. Migrating species pass by West Point because of the narrow passage between the point and Bainbridge Island—about three miles of water allow you a good look at anything flying by.

What's likely to be seen here?

Know your chums

Type	Numbers going through the locks	When
Sockeye (reds)	250,000–350,000	Early June–Aug.
Coho (silvers)	60,000	Early Aug.–late Oct. Peak end Sept.
King (chinook)	25,000–30,000 (70% hatchery)	Early June–Sept.
Chum (dogs)	Very few	Late Oct.–Nov.
Steelhead trout	+/–2,100	Early Nov.–Apr.

Source: Washington State Departments of Fisheries and Wildlife

A variety of gulls, as well as Caspian and common terns, plus a variety of shorebirds, including harlequin ducks in the fall and winter. Look carefully along the cliffs from the beach area and you'll see a most exciting species, pigeon guillemots, which nest in burrows.

Lake Union. If you enjoy feeding Canada geese…well, please don't. It only makes an already messy problem worse. But if you just want to see some, head to the south end of Lake Union. Herds of grunting and honking geese will practically trample you.

In recent years, the local goose population has multiplied to problem proportions. Like other population boosters, the geese are not native to Seattle; they're a Great Basin subspecies from eastern Washington. A few were released in Seattle in the 1930s for a duck club, and others were transplanted here in the 1960s from the Potholes area when a new dam displaced a breeding population and the Department of Wildlife brought the goslings to Lake Washington. Now that generations of them have been comfortably fed by residents, they're here to stay.

Some of the geese wander within King, Snohomish, and Pierce counties, but they can be considered year-round regional residents, unlike the Aleutian geese or other species that migrate over the city.

Montlake Fill. An area of fill dirt created from dredging the Montlake Cut, and once the site of a garbage dump, the Montlake Fill is a haven for birds that nest and feed in marshy scrub and wetland. You're likely to see an array of shorebirds—yellowlegs, dunlin, sandpiper—and those species preferring freshwater: wood ducks, gadwall, and teal. This meadow-marsh system—the Fill, the Arboretum, and the linking waterway in between—comprises a complete ecosystem of wetland, scrubby shrubs, and forested swampland.

The Arboretum also provides tangles of blooming red currant, salmonberry, and blackberry bushes that attract hummingbirds—rufous and, on rare occasions, Anna's hummingbirds. Coots, mallards, great blue herons, and other varieties can be seen along marshy shore and waterfront areas. A nature trail runs along this area, where from a wooden walkway you can observe birds feeding and diving. The trail starts at the Museum of History and Industry and winds along the water. Great for kids.

Seward Park. A pair or two of breeding bald eagles nest here. Look for tall snags.

Other Areas for Birding. Try Magnuson Park and Frink Park (Lake Washington Boulevard S and S Jackson) and those hidden corners of "greenbelt"—tiny islands of habitat where you're likely to hear or see olive-sided flycatchers, black-headed grosbeaks, and western flycatchers among the slide alder, maple, and mixed forests. These greenbelt areas are vital nesting habitats within the city.

Birding resources

Audubon Society
8050 35th Ave. NE
Seattle, WA 98115
523-4483
933-1831 (to report rare bird sightings)
Audubon Society has birding checklists for your sightings covering Seattle parks and other areas. The group also provides birding field trips in Seattle parks and downtown strolls. It also has an ornithologic/nature library and offers classes in bird identification. The Audubon Society has a list of 11 "seed depots" in the city where you can buy bulk wild birdseed. The mix, which is designed especially for birds of the area, includes black oil sunflower seeds, thistle seed, and suet.

Flora and Fauna Books
121 First Ave. S
Seattle, WA 98104
623-4727
A bookstore with a staggering variety of birding guidebooks. Also a hangout for Audubon birders.

PAWS HOWL Shelter
787-2500
To report sick or injured birds or take them in for care. Call first.

FRUSTRATING HERSCHEL

Those sea lions at the locks are actually social and sexual rejects from California.

The name Herschel was given to the first California sea lion who wreaked havoc on the fish runs at Hiram Chittenden Locks in the early 1980s. Since then, the collective population of sea lions at the locks has been given the nickname "Herschel," a lovable moniker for the mammals who spend the winter gorging themselves on steelhead trout at the entrance to the locks.

The immature males arrive in Seattle in early November and stay

until about mid-May, when the steelhead run ends. Too weak sexually or socially to establish their own breeding "turf" in California, the sea lion bachelors' club formed out of sexual frustration.

They've spread their own frustration to the Department of Wildlife, which, with the help of a group of marine mammal experts, has been trying every conceivable scheme to rid the locks of this pack. In 1989, 39 sea lions were deported to Long Beach, California, and 29 swam the 1,300 miles north back to the Sound. Biologists have tried rubber-tipped arrows, nets, firecrackers, ultrasound machines, and—finally—decided to outright
kill the creatures. But Sea World of Florida came to the rescue of the sea lions (and the biologists, since animals rights' groups were preparing for war) and three of the worst offenders were carried off in 1996 to the sunny southeast to live out their days. (No one says how many of these 500 to 900-pound monsters they're prepared to adopt.)

Stay tuned. The Herschel saga continues. The collective Herschels consume 64% of the steelheard run in a year, enough to create a threat to the run's continued existence.

SALMON CULTURE

The two most exciting fish to see in Seattle are salmon and steelhead, and the best place to see them is at the locks (or maybe in the Pike Place Market).

Let's get this straight right off: Salmon and steelhead are two different fish, although both belong to the Salmonidae family—sort of kissing cousins. Some steelhead are wild; some are hatchery fish. Hatchery steelhead have been genetically programmed to migrate earlier than their wild counterparts, and there's a limited fishery on them. But wild steelhead are completely protected from commercial fishing. The hatchery steelhead begin returning in November and run through January, heading up the Cedar River and Sammamish Slough to spawn. The wild run begins in mid-January and goes through early April. There are about 2,100 wild steelhead B.S. (before sea lions); about 800 after Herschel gets his fill. Sea lion migration is tied to the steelhead run—they prefer steelhead to salmon, for some reason.

Four species of salmon migrate through the Puget Sound area: sockeye, coho, king, and chum. King salmon are the mature adults, while chinook are the baby kings or "blackmouths." There is a good-sized salmon run of 30,000 to 50,000 kings up the Duwamish to the Green River.

GOING FISHING?

You see people fishing in Elliott Bay, but should they actually *eat* what they catch? No way, say the people at the Seattle–King County Health Department. Elliott Bay is an estuary system, where the freshwater currents of rivers reach the tides of the bay.

Researchers have found tumored, diseased species there, especially pollock, cod, and other bottomfish. Diseased fish with such afflictions as kidney tumors tend to migrate to estuary systems where salinity levels are lower.

This phenomenon of diseased fish migrating to estuary systems has given rise to many theories. One is that saltwater parasites are shed due to the freshwater influx; another is the notion that freshwater may ease the pain and suffering of the diseased and tumor-infested fish. Yum!!

But who is that fishing out in Lake Union? Most likely Native Americans who have a historic right to the fishing grounds there. Fishing for chinook, coho, and sockeye is allowed on Lake Union for the Muckleshoot tribe, in keeping with their traditional tribal practice. They fish now with fixed gillnets.

CITY WHALE WATCHING

Every once in a while on one of the ferries plying the waters between Seattle and points west, someone yells, "Whale!" and all the passengers run to the rail to watch these marine mammals—usually orcas—cavort. Sometimes the whales swim along with the ferry, putting on a show all the way across the Sound. (And sometimes someone yells, "Whale!" only to have someone else point out that the shiny backs are really Dall's porpoises. You can tell them from orcas because the porpoises are smaller and surface more often than the orcas. Sometimes they ride the bow wave of the ferry.)

The ferry is also a great place to see other marine mammals such as harbor seals and harbor porpoises. But it's a bit like the lottery: You take your chances which ferry run will be the lucky one to be followed or led by marine mammals. You can also see whales from the central waterfront, West Seattle, and Discovery Park.

There are three pods of orca in Puget Sound, but two—called J and K pods—are most likely to pass by downtown Seattle. They travel a 200-mile range north and south, with the San Juan Islands in the center, and come to this part of the Sound as frequently as once a month, year-round. You might see them more often—about three times a month—in September and October when they're following the salmon runs.

In summer the orcas move north to the San Juan Islands. June is the best time to see them there (try Limestone Point on San Juan Island). During the winter, L pod moves through the Sound north to the Fraser River in British Columbia to feed on spawning salmon.

SQUID AND OCTOPI

They should make a movie called "The Octopus That Ate Seattle." Rumors have it that an octopus was found in Puget Sound that weighed 600 pounds! And that there are giant squid 65 feet long!

Most octopi here are much smaller than that (average size: 40 pounds, 8 feet across), but they are plentiful. To see them you need to go diving (or go to the Aquarium). They like to hang out under piers in Elliott Bay, where they are attracted to the concrete rubble of crumbling finger piers. Unfortunately, it's not a great idea to dive in Elliott Bay because the bottom sediment makes visibility so poor. But you can go to the Don Armeni Boat Ramp at Duwamish Head at night to see benthic and stubby squid.

FISHY RESOURCES AND SITES

Hiram Chittenden Locks
315 NW 54th St.
Seattle, WA 98107
783-7059
The best time to see the spectacular sockeye salmon run at the Hiram Chittenden Locks in Ballard is the Fourth of July weekend. Thousands upon thousands of sockeye fight their way into Lake Washington and head for the spawning grounds in the Cedar River and other streams that empty into the lake. You can cheer them on from viewing rooms at the locks or from up above the fish ladders.

There are two professional fish counters at the locks. They count only the sockeye salmon by taking a "subsample," meaning they count for 10 minutes every hour for 12 hours, seven days a week, when the sockeye are running. Then they extrapolate the totals.

Marine Animal Resource Center
285-7325
To report stranded seals.

Salmon Days Festival
Another good way to watch the fish is at the Salmon Days Festival in Issaquah the first week of October. Issaquah has a huge run in Sammamish Slough and Issaquah Creek.

Seattle Aquarium
1483 Alaskan Way
Seattle, WA 98101-2059
386-4300
Marine education specialist: Buzz Shaw

Whale Hotline
(800) 562-8832
To report whale sightings and strandings in the Sound. Whales have been tracked via the hotline since the '70s.

BIG GAME

Well, OK. There's not a lot of big game right in Seattle, but there's small game that seems big when it decides to hide in your attic.

First, let's consider our wild neighbors that sometimes seem more like pests than nature's blessings.

Take squirrels, for instance. Those cute little frisky gray squirrels that run along the phone lines are actually non-natives who have aggressively driven away Seattle's native squirrels. Someone thought it would be cute to bring them to the Arboretum from New York 60 years ago, and today they are the dominant force in the city's squirreldom. And they are driving natives and non-natives nuts.

The eastern gray squirrel should not be confused with the Douglas gray, red, or flying squirrel, or chipmunk—all of which are native and now hide out in the forests (squirrel suburbs?) outside the city. The eastern grays, which adapt easily to a variety of habitats, are prolific, outnumbering the city's natural predators and having few enemies.

They nest in attics, blow up transformers, eat fruit and nuts from trees, dig holes in yards, eat birdseed from feeders, and can be vicious. They'll bite the hand that feeds them, especially if they've been fed and then the feeder stops the handouts.

Some people think squirrels are almost as bad as rats, and Seattle does have a healthy population of squirrels. They aren't known to be rabid, although their bites can cause nasty infections.

Declaring war on squirrels

- If a squirrel gets in your attic, try putting mothballs up there. Sometimes they'll leave in disgust. Or try flashing lights or playing transistor radios (set to your teenager's favorite station).
- If you have trees, be sure the limbs are trimmed away from the house, so it's not so easy for the squirrels to get on the roof.
- The last resort is a brutal one. The Department of Wildlife will loan you a trap for the squirrels. Once they're caught, the department (remember, it's those people, not us!) recommends that you drown the squirrels in a garbage can filled with water.

Why not just move them out to the woods? Because they aren't native and upset the balance so badly. No one wants them to spread any farther.

IT'S THE RAT PATROL

"Rat patrols"—teams of 15 to 20 ratcatchers—are a thing of the past, but not because there aren't rats in Seattle. The creepy rodents aren't a health hazard—the last case of bubonic plague was in Tacoma in 1921. Although it seems rats are always scrounging for garbage, they don't need "three squares" to keep alive, only 2 to 4 ounces of food a day. Unfortunately, their quest for food sometimes leads them up the sewer lines and into toilets, where they like to surprise the unsuspecting. The rats can be as much as 3 inches in diameter—no small mouse, that—but most are long and skinny, not the large Norwegian rats you sometimes see on the waterfront.

Big or small, Ratty still upsets folks. Here are the number of rat complaints received by the Seattle–King County Health Department for the Seattle area alone:

- 1994: 1,010
- 1995: 1,089
- Rat in toilet complaints, 1994: 129
- Rat in toilet complaints, 1995: 113

Rat in your toilet?

The health department gets almost 10 "toilet complaints" a month—panicky residents want to know what to do about the rat smiling at them from the toilet bowl. Here's what to do:
1. Put the lid down and pile some heavy books on it (make sure the books are heavy—rats are strong!).
2. Flush the toilet three or four times.
3. Do NOT try hitting the rat with a broomstick—they're agile and have been known to climb right up the broomstick.
4. If the rat still hasn't gone away, leave the lid shut and wait several hours. Since he's looking for food, he'll probably just go back down into the sewer.

HEARD ON THE STREET

"People think of wildlife as living in hollow trees. There aren't any hollow trees left. Wildlife lives in your house. Raccoons are having their litters in your attic. Opossums are in your crawlspace."

"TRAPPER" JOHN CONSOLINI

5. Call the health department, 296-4632 south of ship canal; north of ship canal, 296-4838. If you're *really* panicky, they'll come help. Otherwise, they'll bait the sewer in a four-block radius around your house and get the nasty rodent that way.

WINGED CRITTERS

And rats aren't the only critters attracting attention. Judging from the average number of bat complaints per year (125 in King County), those aren't just late-night swallows winging through the evening sky.

There have been cases of rabies reported in bats in the area, so don't fool with these guys. Usually they enter your house through the chimney. What to do? Close all doors, open all windows, and get out of there. If they've nested in your attic, close outlets, open vents, and bang on the ceiling to get them out; then cover openings with something they can't chew through.

OTHER CRITTERS

Opossums are pretty common in city yards, especially if you leave your cat—or dog—food out. (Same with raccoons. An estimated 15,000 raccoons share the city with us. They're everywhere, but West Seattle takes the prize for most raccoons.)

Opossums are cat-size, usually grayish brown, with pointy faces. They have the fur of a cat and the tail of a rat. They like to burrow in woodsheds.

The Department of Wildlife (DOW) has traps in which you can catch both opossums and raccoons, and then relocate them in the forests outside the city.

People who live near hillsides (and who doesn't in Seattle?) have a chance of seeing mountain beavers, or at least of seeing their marks. They like to eat rhododendrons and ferns

and otherwise destroy landscaping. They are the size of a cat, brown, and tail-less. They develop an extensive trail system underground so that people are led to think several are around, when it's usually just one. They don't leave a mound the way moles do.

The DOW offers traps to catch beavers alive. You set the trap right over the hole so the beaver has nowhere to go, and then move it to a forest service road where there's a hillside and let it go.

Every once in a while, someone will see a coyote running down Greenwood Avenue. An estimated 50 coyotes live in or near Seattle. They also like to move along the old Burlington Northern right-of-way from Richmond Beach down through Carkeek Park to Golden Gardens. And, along with the bike riders, they use the Burke-Gilman Trail to access certain neighborhoods, like Laurelhurst and the UW campus. They like the Arboretum too, and several years ago one was spotted downtown at the corner of Third and Cherry. They are mostly nocturnal and will eat cats or small dogs (and they like pet food). You can't live-trap coyotes, only fence them out. Keep dogs and cats in at night to protect them.

CRITTERS, GOOD AND BAD

- There are 47 mosquito species in the Seattle area.
- There are 12 species of bats in the city, from the hoary bat with a 15-inch wingspan to the 9-inch western small-footed bat.
- Seattle has no dangerous snakes (except for a few in downtown high-rises).
- Seattle has two lizards: the western fence lizard (tannish, blue-bellied, about 6 inches long) and the northern alligator lizard (slender, with gray to brown coloring and short legs, about 10 inches long).

Honking cars, jets overhead, and the peace of a huge, ancient tree dripping with grass-green moss—they all mix together in a few sites. The best place to see old-growth trees is Schmitz Park in West Seattle. Next is Seward Park on Lake Washington: Turn left at the park entrance and park in the lot at the crest of the hill. Cross the road and follow the trail. In Tacoma, drive into Point Defiance Park on Pearl Street. Follow signs for Five-Mile Drive to the really big trees on the north end of the peninsula.

- There are an estimated 200,000 feral (homeless and bordering on wild) cats living in the city.
- In some neighborhoods, the Norwegian rat outnumbers people by as many as 40 to 1.
- Snapping turtles in Lake Washington and Green Lake (left there by pet owners who tired of the little darlings) weigh up to 30 pounds.

Critter complaints
**Seattle–King County
Health Department**
Environmental Health Project
South of Montlake Cut: 296-4632
North of Montlake Cut: 296-4838

ON THE OUTSKIRTS

There is wildlife closer to the city than most people think, or want to believe. Cougar and other big game can be seen 20 minutes from Seattle in a fringe area between the city limits and the last remaining wilderness area nearby. Mount Si, Tiger Mountain, and Cougar Mountain form an oasis that includes Department of Natural Resources (DNR) state trust and forest management lands.

Mount Si was purchased by the state in 1977 and has a conservation status. Cougar Mountain Regional Wildland and Squak Mountain are shoulder-to-shoulder with Tiger Mountain State Forest, a multiple-use area where visitors can observe wildlife and enjoy other recreational activities. Efforts are being made to preserve an east/west corridor for wildlife around Cougar, Squak, and Tiger mountains—but there is development pressure as Seattle spreads to the east.

What animals can be found there? Deer, cougar, and coyote wander among the trees. Issaquah Creek serves as watering ground for elk, and Tiger Mountain is home to black bears.

Peak times at the Arboretum: To see the camellias and rhodies in bloom, go anytime from the end of March to the end of June. Flowering cherries and plums peak in April and May, followed by the azaleas.

The best time to get to the Arboretum Plant Sale is before it begins. Only members can get in the day before the sale. Not a member? Get there right at the beginning of the sale (usually at 10am sharp) for best selection. For best prices, go around 4 or 5pm. Some prices are lowered as the crowd thins out. To become a member of the Arboretum Foundation, call 325-4510.

Wildlife resources

Department of Fish and Wildlife
16018 Mill Creek Blvd.
Mill Creek, WA 98012
774-8812

Department of Natural Resources
Regional Office
857 Roosevelt Ave. E
Enumclaw, WA 98022
(800) 527-3305
This office has brochures, maps, and info on Tiger Mountain State Forest and Mount Si DNR land.

Issaquah Alps Trail Club
328-0480
24-hour hotline listing events and how to participate. This is *the* group working on this regional park area.

King County Parks
General Info: 296-4232
Recreational and interpretive info:
296-4171
Has brochures and info about the area.

SEEDY CITY

Whether it's countering the greenhouse effect or just plain love of leaves, Seattleites and seeds go together like lawyers and oil companies.

The Arboretum is the center of flora culture in Seattle, with thousands of plant species maintained by the UW Center for Urban Horticulture but owned by the city's parks department.

The best global effort in town is the Seed Exchange at the Arboretum. The volunteers there collect seeds from plants in the gardens and exchange them with other arboretums from around the world.

The fall color display at the Arboretum is spectacular, mostly because Eastern trees such as sugar maples have been transplanted here.

Arboretum Plant Sale. Each spring, usually in April or May, the Arboretum holds a plant sale at the visitors center, where they sell cuttings, seeds, plants, grafts, and more. This is a wildly popular event. The Arboretum gets donations from members' gardens and various greenhouses in the area. The best-selling plants? Rhododendrons (they have a huge variety) and trees. There's also a bulb sale in October, held in the Arboretum.

The best way to get into a P-Patch is to see that one gets opened close to your home. Call the P-Patch office (684-0264) to get into the network, suggest an empty lot, and work with your community council.

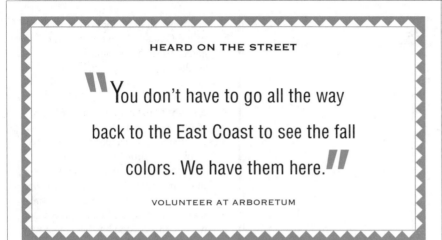

"You don't have to go all the way back to the East Coast to see the fall colors. We have them here."

VOLUNTEER AT ARBORETUM

P-PATCH PROGRAM

Seattle has 36 different P-Patch sites with 1,600 garden plots in all. Each spring, 4,500 gardeners plant their hearts out and each fall they reap the benefits. Seattle's P-Patches are for organic gardening only.

These communal gardens are very popular, and you'll need to worm your way in via a waiting list. There are always hundreds of P-Patch wannabes waiting for space, but don't be discouraged: new sites are being added. The P-Patch Program monitors the garden plots to make sure they are being used; if they aren't, the program sends out a "weedy letter" to ask the gardener's intentions. The gardener has one week to stick a shovel in the ground and get to work, or the plot is given over to the next person on the waiting list.

Of the sites, some belong to the city, and the rest are privately owned.

P-Patch gardeners usually grow vegetables; most grow for their own use, but many gardeners contribute to the Lettuce Link project, which coordinates delivery of surplus fresh produce to Seattle food banks. The generous gardeners usually deliver 3,300 pounds a year.

P-Patch Program
Community Services Division
618 Second Ave.
Seattle, WA 98104-2222
684-0264

HOW DOES YOUR GARDEN GROW?

Need compost? Try ZooDoo Compost from Woodland Park Zoo, "where every day is Earth Day" (call 625-7667). You have to pick it up yourself and it sells out fast, so call early in spring or fall. "Down-to-earth prices": $1–$3 per garbage bag, $45 for a truckload. The zoo offers composting classes too; info from same number.

For other manure, look in the Yellow Pages and classified ads for dairies and stables with low-cost or free manure.

And don't say the police never did anything for you: You can get horse manure and wood shavings free from the police department (386-4238). Go out to Discovery Park to get the goods.

And the engineering department has leaves, though not for food crops (684-7508, north end; 386-1218, south end).

You can get coffee chaff from Starbucks by calling their roaster desk (447-7950). The chaff's free, but in limited supply. They also have burlap bags for waste or to help control soil erosion.

Gardening resources

Master Composter Program
Compost Hotline
633-0224

There are few ancient trees left in Seattle, because Henry Yesler and his crew stripped the land when they got here. Some of the oldest are in Schmitz Park in West Seattle and in older graveyards. Although a very few cedars and grand firs may presently reach 200 feet in the city, only Douglas firs are definitely known to be that tall, with a few even topping more than 250 feet! The tall exotics (non-natives) in Seattle were measured in 1988, and presumably have grown even taller since then. But in '88 the tallest were as follows:

- 141' Coast Redwood
- 139' Lombardy (Black) Poplar
- 122' American Elm
- 120' European Beech
- 118' Tulip Tree
- 115' Certines Poplar
- 114' Deodar Cedar
- 114' 'Eugenei' Hybrid Poplar
- 113' English Elm
- 112' Sierra Redwood
- 112' Pin Oak
- 112' Ghost (Black) Poplar
- 109' 'Regenerata' Hybrid Poplar

Source: Arthur Lee Jacobson, *Trees of Seattle*

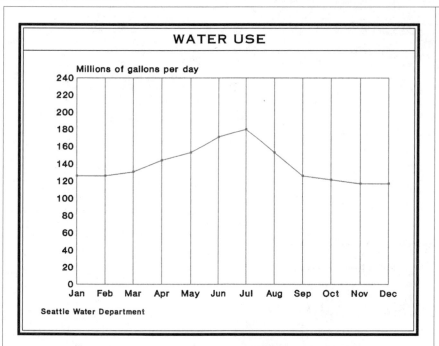

WATER USE

Millions of gallons per day

Seattle Water Department

Composting and recycling information sponsored by Seattle Tilth and the Seattle Solid Waste Utility. Call for free map of compost demonstration sites and information about guided group tours.

Seattle Tilth Association
4649 Sunnyside Ave. N
Seattle, WA 98103
633-0451
Volunteer organization of gardeners interested in ecological food production. An urban chapter of the non-profit Western Washington Tilth Association. Demonstration garden is open to the public and there are tours, lectures, and two annual events: the Edible Landscape Sale and the Fall Harvest Festival.

Washington Park Arboretum
Washington Park
Lake Washington Blvd. E
   and Madison St.
543-8800
The support group for the Arboretum is the Arboretum Foundation. The foundation puts on events, runs school workshops, trains volunteers, and generally raises funds for the gardens. The Foundation number is 325-4510.

WATER, WATER EVERYWHERE . . .

Puget Sound holds 31 cubic miles of water; 1.5 cubic miles move with each change of the tides. Lake Union and Lake Washington combined have about 25,000 surface acres of water. It rains a lot, and the city's water-

When you plant your own garden, you might want to plant an extra row for someone else. Northwest Harvest, 625-0755, accepts donations of vegetables for food banks, thereby supplementing their usual offerings of canned and dried goods with fresh produce.

sheds are right on the western slopes of the Cascade Range, where they can capture the snowpack melt.

Plenty of water, right? Wrong—at least in the last few years. Scientists say we did not exactly have a drought in the summer of 1992, but to the lawns that became crunchy and dry under strict watering restrictions, it felt like a drought. It all gets blamed on the dwindling snowpack in the mountains, but whether it's the weather or a lack of planning on the part of the city, the fact remains that water conservation has become a way of life in the Rainy City.

CONSERVE OR PAY

We did learn to conserve during that famous summer of 1992; therefore, the city decided to increase water rates to make up for the revenue it lost because we learned to conserve. Got that? The rates went up 19.9%, phased in over two years. Your bill is based on actual water use. (Who knows, if you really conserve, maybe the rates will go up again?)

An average single-family residence pays $10.44 per month for water in the winter, and $20.08 in the summer. Average annually is $13.65/month.

A DROP TO DRINK

Thirsty? Before turning on the tap, consider these facts about Seattle's water:

- The Seattle Water Department supplies nearly 1.1 million people with water.
- On an average day, 166 million gallons of water are used by consumers in the Seattle area.
- An average Seattle family uses 5,200 gallons of water a month.
- Virtually all of Seattle's water comes from the Cedar River and Tolt River watersheds.
- Demand on the two watersheds

isn't just from thirsty people: The Cedar River provides the freshwater needed to keep the level of Lake Washington stable and to keep saltwater from entering the lake.

- Residential users consume about 50% of the water supplied by the system. Consumption more than doubles in the summer, when precipitation is at its lowest.
- During summers, about 2% of Seattle's water comes from deep protected wells.
- Treatment of the city's water includes a low level of chlorination for disinfection; fluoridation; and the addition of a small amount of natural minerals.

SOFT OR HARD?

For some reason people are always curious whether they have soft or hard water—whether their shampoo will lather or just sit there in a slimy mass. Seattle's water is very soft and low in dissolved minerals such as sodium. So lather away.

And about quality: The water contains low levels of compounds called trihalomethanes, formed during disinfection, but the levels are within federal and state limits. No synthetic organic compounds indicating industrial or pesticide contamination have been detected.

Water from Seattle's taps has shown lead concentrations higher than the federal goal of 15 parts per billion or less. Some suggest we should run water until it's cold before drinking it and avoid running the hot water for drinking water.

The city's water is sampled daily after being collected at representative points in the city.

Seattle Water Department
710 Second Ave., 10th floor
Seattle, WA 98104
General info: 684-5900
Conservation: 684-5879
Conservation brochures: 684-5849
Quality info: 684-7404

WAVES OF TROUBLE

We've got trouble, my friends, right here in water city. Those lovely sparkling waters viewed from almost

every spot in Seattle are home to fish, aquatic plants—and pollution.

Thanks to an extensive effort beginning in the 1950s, Lake Washington is as clean as it looks, safe for swimming, and free from sewer overflow most of the time. But the city's other bodies of water—including Puget Sound—are depositories for all sorts of things, including bacteria.

Somehow you'd never think that in this high-tech age we would still be discharging raw sewage into waterways, but we are. Buckets of money are being spent on decreasing the amount of raw sewage that gets dumped into our water, and hopefully someday storm water will be the only runoff expanding the lakes, rivers, and Sound.

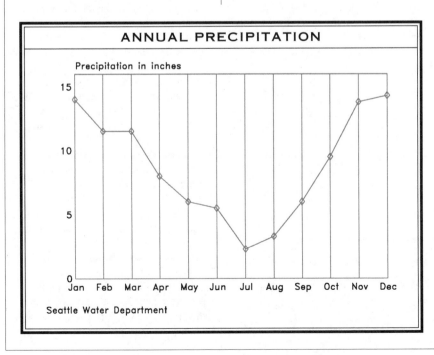

ANNUAL PRECIPITATION

Precipitation in inches

Seattle Water Department

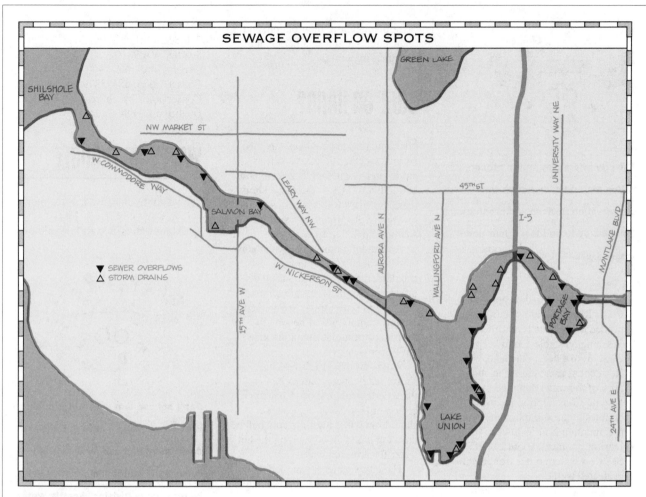

SEWAGE OVERFLOW SPOTS

THE RAW TRUTH ABOUT SEWAGE

There are hundreds of overflow pipes all over the city that often spew forth something called Combined Sewer Overflow (CSO). Don't we have sewage treatment plants? We do, but when the heavy rains come, the raw sewage is allowed to overflow with storm water into Lake Union, Portage Bay, Elliott Bay, and the Duwamish River. If there weren't overflows, the sewage would back up into houses—an unpleasant thought that makes the overflow system the lesser of two evils.

In Elliott Bay, for example, the Denny Way CSO lets loose as many as 50 times per year with discharges of combined runoff and raw sewage.

Consequently, Elliott Bay is a toxic hotspot. The contaminated sediments in the bay are being capped with sand and monitored for five years to see if the contaminants can be kept from spreading.

The best time to visit a wetland is near either dawn or dusk when wildlife are most active. These quiet hours are feeding times for many birds, fish, and animals.

Everyone knows that Elliott Bay is no place to take the kids for a Saturday swim, and you wouldn't swim in the Duwamish River either. But the truth is that Lake Union—which has overflows everywhere dumping combined sewage and storm water into the lake—is worse, as far as polluted sediments are concerned, than either Elliott Bay or the Duwamish.

Portage Bay has its share of overflows too. So next time you step outside the door of that houseboat, think twice before dangling your feet in the water.

What to do? Consider two options, both expensive. One is to build storm drains that take off only street runoff, leaving the existing pipes for sewage. That plan is in process.

The other possibility is to build huge storage tanks for the overflow and then pump it back during non-storm hours—an expensive proposition.

In the meantime, it's a good idea not to go swimming anywhere but Lake Washington for about five days after a heavy rainstorm.

THE GREEN LAKE SCUM PUZZLE

Green Lake isn't green in name only. Every summer it blooms with a scummy green algae.

The lake's bottom soils naturally contain phosphorus, and the duck poop adds more until the bottom sediments are so full of the stuff that when the warm months hit, the green algae grows like crazy. It's not a health problem; parasites on the ducks, not the algae, cause the swimmers' itch you can occasionally get in

Wetlands fanatic? You can get free copies of *Wetland Walks*, a guide to wetlands with public access throughout the state. Order by contacting Publications Office, Washington State Department of Ecology, Mail Stop PV-11, Olympia, WA 98504; (206) 459-6000.

the lake. But the algae seems pretty unappetizing, and if left alone the lake would eventually be covered with it.

The city may flush out the lake with fresh water from Lake Washington periodically, or may end up using alum. Either way, there's someone who doesn't like the solution.

Worried about what you're pouring down the sink? The Master Home Environmentalist program teaches such things as using baking soda, salt, and vinegar to clean house. Volunteers work with community groups and members of households educating them about environmental dangers at home. For information, call the American Lung Association, 441-5100.

And there's another problem, this one caused by algae removal. As the algae is cleaned out, light penetrates down into the lake, stimulating bottom weeds that plug up the lake and act like tentacles grabbing unsuspecting swimmers.

WETLAND WASTELAND

Ninety-eight percent of the wetlands that once lined the Duwamish River have been destroyed by development.

Time was when wetlands were considered swamps with monsters lurking in the eelgrass, but now wetlands are recognized as vital to the ecology. In the Seattle area, you can see wetlands at the following locations:

- Arboretum waterfront, Seattle
- Camelot Park, Federal Way
- Cougar Mountain Park, Issaquah
- Discovery Park, Seattle
- Flaming Geyser State Park, south of Black Diamond

- Jenkins Creek Park, Kent
- Juanita Bay City Park, Kirkland
- Lake Wilderness Park, Renton
- Licton Springs City Park (once used by Native Americans as a health spa), N 97th and Ashworth, Seattle
- Marymoor Park, Redmond
- Mercer Slough, Bellefields Nature Park, Bellevue
- Seattle Aquarium Wetlands Exhibit
- Twin Ponds County Park, First Avenue NE and N 155th Street
- Wallace Swamp Creek Park, NE 175th and 73rd Avenue NE

THE OIL TRUTH

The chances of an oil spill in Puget Sound are greater than you might think. It's true that tankers can't come this far down into the Sound, but oil barges bunker fuel in and out of the port daily. Tankers have spilled oil at Anacortes, Grays Harbor, and Port Angeles. To report a spill, contact the Coast Guard, 217-6232.

You can't help with actual cleanup unless you go through Specialized Ocean Training, a 45-hour course that costs $1,000. But you can volunteer to help with bird and wildlife cleanup by calling the Department of Wildlife, 774-8812, or by contacting the oil company responsible for the spill.

TAKING CARE OF WATER

Adopt-A-Beach Program
P.O. Box 21486
Seattle, WA 98111-3486
624-6013
Contact: Chrys Bertolotto

Adopt-A-Park Program
684-4557

Adopt-A-Stream Program
(206) 388-3487
Contact: Tom Murdoch

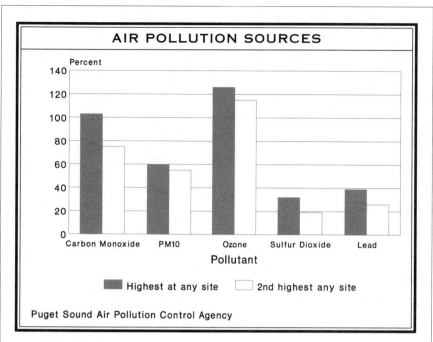

AIR POLLUTION SOURCES

Percent

Legend: ■ Highest at any site □ 2nd highest any site

Puget Sound Air Pollution Control Agency

Causes adverse health effects. Period.

So where do we stand? Seattle is not demonstrably better or worse in terms of air pollution than other cities of its size. In fact, the last year we had any "Unhealthful" days was in 1988, when there were five. And 1986 was the last time we had a "Very Unhealthful" day.

Since the 1970s carbon monoxide pollution in the downtown area has

An informal survey of clean air experts reveals areas they would not want to live in because of poor air quality—places downwind of Seattle, such as Issaquah or Kent. "There is a definite pollution plume. And Boeing is the culprit." Toward the west, things improve a bit.

Green Lake Information
684-4075

Seattle Drainage and Wastewater Utility
Dexter Horton Bldg., Rm. 660
710 Second Ave.
Seattle, WA 98104
684-7774

Seattle Solid Waste Utility
684-7600

Seattle Water Department
710 Second Ave., 10th floor
Seattle, WA 98104
Conservation: 684-5879

EVERY BREATH YOU TAKE

The Puget Sound Air Pollution Control Agency (PSAPCA) ranks the air in Seattle in four classes: Good, Moderate, Unhealthful, and Very Unhealthful.

Good: Little or no health risk at all.
Moderate: Toxins building up in the air, excessive amounts of carbon monoxide in downtown areas. Haze starts obscuring the outline of the city.
Unhealthful: Carbon monoxide levels

downtown rise past federal safety standards. Unhealthful air causes adverse health effects in people in the highest health risk categories (the very young, the very old, pregnant women, those with heart or lung ailments) and respiratory irritation in normally healthy people. You know this is happening when the city outline begins to disappear.
Very Unhealthful: Cough, cough.

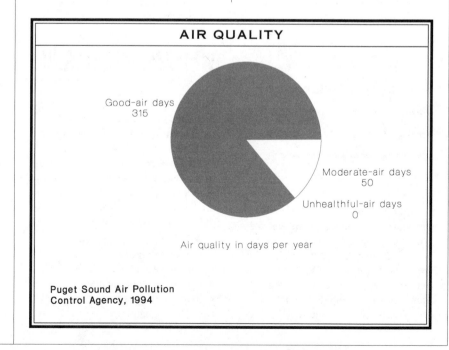

AIR QUALITY

Good-air days
315

Moderate-air days
50

Unhealthful-air days
0

Air quality in days per year

Puget Sound Air Pollution
Control Agency, 1994

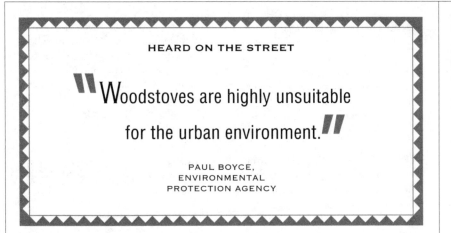

been reduced by more than 90%, mainly as a result of requiring pollution abatement equipment on automobiles and clean-air scrubbers on industrial smokestacks.

That's the good news. It turns out that two problems are still lurking: wood smoke and car exhaust. A federal report says that 500 people in the Seattle area die prematurely every year because of tiny particles in the air from these sources. New standards are in the works, and soon local pollution-control authorities may crack down more than they currently do on woodstove use. Also, our weather does not always disperse pollutants, resulting in a declaration of an "air pollution episode" a few times each year. The "episode" usually lasts only 24 hours. Burn bans are a result of "impaired air quality," and the city usually has about four of them a year.
Source: PSAPCA

THE OZONE PROBLEM

High-level ozone is good; low-level ozone is bad. Up high, the ozone protects the earth from ultraviolet rays. Low-level ozone produced by a photochemical reaction of volatile fumes (from gasoline, paint, and solvents) mixed with oxides of nitrogen (from industry, auto exhaust, and wood smoke) is a killer. This reaction requires sunlight, which we don't have much of, so it shouldn't be a

problem, right? Wrong. Though we might not have as many days of sun as other places, when we do, we often have what PSAPCA calls "bad ozone."

How can you tell? When your eyes feel irritated, there's too much ozone in the air. You're inhaling a potent oxidant into your lungs that, over the long term, can cause respiratory problems, especially in children.

THE BAD NEWS — BARELY HOLDING THE LINE

With a staff of 47 and an annual budget of just $600,000, the state Air Pollution Control Board is worried. The *2010 Report*, produced by the Washington Air Quality Coalition, cites air pollution as the #1 health risk in the state if we keep on doing what we're doing now. In Washington, 800,000 people are at risk, 600,000 of those in King County. They are primarily young children, the elderly, pregnant women, and those with heart ailments, asthma, and emphysema.
Source: Washington Air Quality Coalition

WHEN TO STAY INSIDE

The absolute worst conditions for pollution are:
In winter: During cold, clear weather when there is little wind and therefore no vertical mixing and no horizontal movement. With woodstove

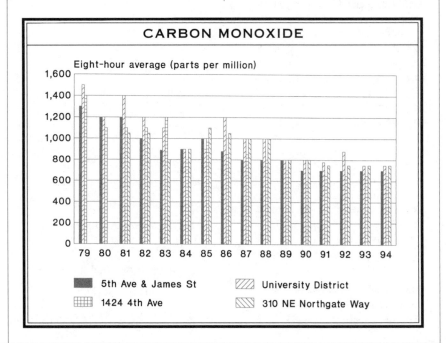

CARBON MONOXIDE

Eight-hour average (parts per million)

Legend:
- 5th Ave & James St
- 1424 4th Ave
- University District
- 310 NE Northgate Way

use, this leads to higher levels of carbon monoxide buildup.

In summer: When we get extended sunny weather and air movement tends to move off land toward water because of high pressure.

When can you breathe easiest? During the rain. Rainy weather is best for air quality because it cleans the air. So next time it rains on your parade, just smile and breathe deeply.

THE HAZARDOUS HEARTH

Statewide 1.12 million households burn wood, half with fireplace only. In some residential areas, it's estimated that wood burning accounts for as much as 85% of air pollution.

In 1981 the city began requiring that all woodstoves have a permit. The permit costs about $80, and although the ordinance is virtually unenforceable, most major home insurers are making sure homeowners have a permit for their stoves. After you pay the fee, a building inspector comes to your home to inspect the stove and its installation and, for newer stoves, you must show a certificate guaranteeing that your stove meets emission standards.

As smog from woodstoves has settled over the city in recent years, air emission regulations have been tightened; opacity (smoke density) restrictions are stricter than ever, and state-trained smoke readers wander the city looking for violations. They use "a visual observation technique" (in other words, they look at the smoke coming from your chimney) and can fine you if your smoke is too dense. (Too dense is anything over 20% opacity—the extent to which an object viewed through the smoke is obscured.)

Usually, dense smoke means you are using wet or green wood, or that your fire needs more air.

Department of Construction and Land Use
Woodstove permits: 684-8464

BANNING BURNING

In Seattle, burning is banned about eight days a year, usually in December and January. Ban announcements are made on radio and TV, or you can call the Puget Sound Air Pollution Control Agency for ban information, (800) 595-4341. The burn-ban season is October–March; April–September you're usually welcome to burn. If wood burning is your only source of heat, you can burn even when a ban is in effect.

The truth is, there are only two smoke cops to enforce burn bans in the city—the Puget Sound Air Pollution Control Agency doesn't have enough money to hire more. So you could probably get away with burning on a ban day, but should you? NO.

Wood smoke is a real and growing problem during winter months, when temperature inversions trap air in the Puget Sound lowlands. Wood-

All this talk of recycling and the mailbox is full of junk mail, made from paper that began life as trees. To stop junk mail, or at least reduce it by 75%, write to the central clearinghouse for mailing lists: Mail Preference Service, Direct Marketing Association, 6 E 43rd Street, New York, NY 10017-4610. Tell them to remove your name from their list. Or write directly to companies that send you unwanted mail—using their prepaid envelope.

stoves and fireplaces contribute respirable particulates into the air. That means that when you say, "Ah, that wood-smoke smell!" and inhale deeply, the smoke particulates enter your lungs unfiltered, to the deepest (and most sensitive) areas of your respiratory tract.

BREATHING RESOURCES

American Lung Association
2625 Third Ave.
Seattle, WA 98121
441-5100

Environmental Protection Agency
1200 Sixth Ave.
Seattle, WA 98101
553-1200

Puget Sound Air Pollution Control Agency
110 Union St., Suite 500
Seattle, WA 98101
343-8800
Provides air quality index and burn-ban information.

ALL EYES ON OUR GARBAGE

Seattle virtually bursts its buttons when bragging about its nationally celebrated recycling programs. So New York has barges of garbage looking for a home? Ha—Seattle's got it all figured out: Don't dump that garbage, reuse it.

Seattle has always been recycling-minded: 24% of the city's waste stream was diverted from landfills because of recycling in 1987 before the official curbside collection program began in 1988. With that new program, things took off.

- The recycling rate for single households (not apartments) has grown from 18% in 1987 to a whopping 90% plus in 1996.

- Multi-family households signed up for curbside recycling is not quite as high: 52%.
- Average monthly recycling weight per household for 1995 was 63 pounds.
- The program is responsible for taking 40% fewer tons of residential garbage to area landfills annually. The city's goal is 60% by 1998.
- To sign up, call 684-7600 for single households, 684-7665 for apartments.
- The program has won awards and been considered state-of-the-art by other cities for a couple of reasons, including its rate structure.

Source: Seattle Solid Waste Utility

WHY THE RATE STRUCTURE IS SUCH A BIG DEAL

Most parts of the country charge for garbage service through property taxes or fixed fees for unlimited garbage service. But Seattle uses a volume-based rate structure— the rate goes up for each additional can of garbage as a kind of penalty for not recycling. (It's gently referred to by the Solid Waste Utility as an incentive to recycle instead of a penalty.)

Seattle Solid Waste Utility
710 Second Ave.
Seattle, WA 98104
684-7600 or 684-8877
684-HELP (message phone for missed collections)
Collection, complaints, and billing info.

BECOMING A RECYCLER

The curb/alley recycling collection program accepts glass, tin, or aluminum; PET plastic soda pop and liquor bottles; milk and juice jugs; soap and detergent bottles; shampoo and lotion bottles. Also accepted are newspaper and mixed wastepaper (magazines, advertising mail, cardboard, etc.).

To get free recycling containers, just call the city at 684-7600. Listen to a long menu of instructions about which number to punch next, and hold on; eventually you'll get a Real Person on the phone.

You are eligible for recycling

Trying to get someone at the Solid Waste Utility? The main number— 684-7600—can be a black hole. Instead, try the Solid Waste Utility switchboard, 684-7666. A REAL person answers.

pickup if you live in a single-family home or a multifamily dwelling with up to four units.

If you live north of the Ship Canal, three plastic bins will be delivered to your home and then will be emptied once a week. If you live south of the Ship Canal, a 60- or 90-gallon cart on wheels will be delivered to your home and emptied once a month.

If your garbage or recycling containers haven't been picked up when they were supposed to be, call 684-HELP and leave a message. The message line is on 24 hours a day, seven days a week. Either your problem will be solved or someone will return your call.

APARTMENT PRESSURE

Apartments are eligible to sign up for the recycling program, but there's a catch: notices go out only to building owners. It's up to the residents to apply pressure so owners will sign up. For info on apartment recycling, call the Solid Waste Utility at 684-7665.

YARDS OF YARD WASTE

The city also offers recycling services to benefit your yard.

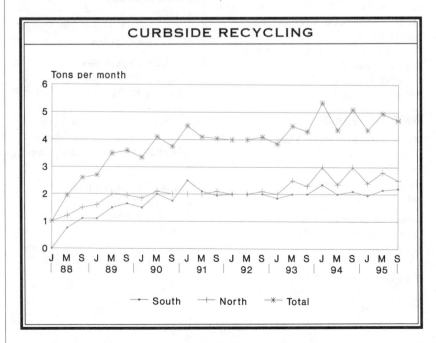

CURBSIDE RECYCLING

Tons per month

— South   — North   —*— Total

Hauled away

For $4.25 a month, the city will pick up grass, leaves, small branches, weeds, sod, brush, or twigs.

The city won't pick up hazardous waste, or large rocks and branches over 4 inches in diameter.

Put your yard waste in an old garbage can, a cardboard box, or a tied bundle and leave it at the curb or alley by 7am on your assigned day, and voilà! It disappears. North of Yesler Way, pickup is weekly on the same day as your garbage collection (during the winter, it's monthly). South of Yesler Way it's every other week from March to October, and once a month November to February.

Sixty-five percent of all city residents have signed up for the yard waste program.

Home-grown compost

The city contracts with Seattle Tilth Association for its Master Composter program, which offers brochures on composting, a fact sheet on mulching, compost bin designs, and more. Tilth operates a Compost Hotline 30 hours a week: operators answer questions and take orders for free home compost bins. You'll get a complimentary composting consultation along with your bin. You can also be trained to be a Master Composter.

Seattle Tilth Association
Compost Hotline: 633-0224

RECYCLABLE METAMORPHOSES

Ever wonder what happens to your discards?

- Rabanco Recycling Company hauls your yard waste to its landfill in Roosevelt, Washington, where it is ground up twice, sifted through a screen, and laid out in windrows. Eventually it will be sold for compost.
- Some plastics are used to make such things as carpet fiber, drainpipes, distributor caps, egg cartons, and polyester fiberfill for ski jackets.
- Paint that ends up at the hazardous waste site is bulked and made into new paint. It's available at Parker Paints, 5500 14th NW, 783-8418.
- Private companies pick up old mattresses and lawn mowers from the transfer sites and refurbish them.

FINAL DESTINATIONS

If something's got to go, here are some places to take it. Any King County resident can use the following transfer stations at no charge. But be creative; the dump's not the only destination in town. Recycle, donate, reuse.

Household hazardous wastes (liquids, tires, hazardous wastes, asbestos) must go to specified sites during limited hours. The Hazardous Waste Hotline, 296-4692, can tell you about hours and wastes accepted or give you referrals for removal of asbestos and radon. Call the same number for the schedule and locations of King County's Wastemobile, which is stationed at various sites outside the city limits where people can take their hazardous wastes.

You can take motor oil and car batteries to either the North or South Transfer Station, but any other hazardous wastes (old paint, unidentified chemicals, etc.) must go to the South Transfer Station. Old tires can be taken to the South Transfer Station as well (limit four).

Where to take it

Aurora Hazardous Waste Shed
125th and Aurora
296-4692
By appointment only,
Sun.–Tues., 10am–4pm.

Cedar Hills Landfill
16925 Cedar Falls Rd. SE
North Bend
296-4490
Hazardous wastes; call ahead.

North Transfer Station
1350 N 34th
(N 34th St. and Carr Place N)
Mon.–Fri., 8am–5:30pm; Sat., 8am–7pm; Sun., 9am–6pm. Hazardous waste, Thurs.–Sat., 10–4 only.

South Transfer Station
78800 Second Ave. S
(Second Ave. S and S Kenyon St.)
Mon.–Fri., 7am–7pm; Sat., 8am–8pm; Sun., 9am–6pm. Hazardous waste, Sun.–Tues., 10–4 by appointment.

Donating household items

Here are some organizations that accept usable castoffs. Call for pickup or drop-box locations.

Community Services for the Blind
633-0160

Goodwill Industries
329-1000

NW Center for the Retarded
285-5441

St. Vincent de Paul
767-3835

Salvation Army
624-0200

Other resources

Friends of Recycling
684-4685
Volunteers who help their neighbors become super recyclers.

Seattle Solid Waste Utility
710 Second Ave., Room 505
Seattle, WA 98104
684-7600
Offers free 50-page "Use It Again, Seattle!" guide listing repair shops, rental outlets, and secondhand stores in Seattle.

Washington Toxics Coalition
4516 University Way NE
Seattle, WA 98105
632-1545
Offers a free guide on how to dispose of hazardous household products.

WHITHER THE WEATHER

Seattle isn't always the Emerald City. Sometimes it's politically correct to have brown lawns (and politically incorrect to be listed among the "Top 10 Water Users" in a local paper). When drought threatens, as it did in the early '90s, Seattleites begin to joke

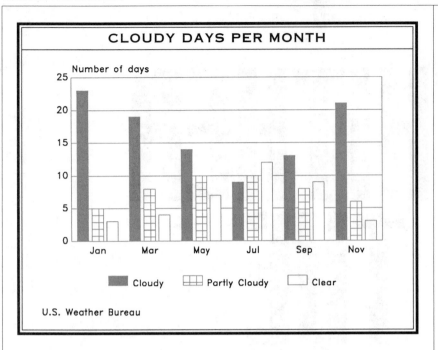

CLOUDY DAYS PER MONTH

Number of days

Cloudy · Partly Cloudy · Clear

U.S. Weather Bureau

on local weather. Lately, they've identified a variability in Seattle's weather, but no real trend toward warming or cooling is apparent. The "cloud people" do report that the snowpack has been below normal since the mid-'70s. Part of the difficulty in spotting trends is that the weather records are relatively recent compared to long-term weather cycles.

A QUICK REPORT

- Average number of cloudy days: 201
- Average number of partially cloudy days: 93
- How much of the maximum available sunshine Seattle gets each day: 45%
- Average yearly rainfall, inner city: 34.1 inches
- Average yearly rainfall, King County: 39 inches
- Average accumulation of snow and sleet, inner city: 8.1 inches
- Average accumulation of snow and sleet, King County: 15 inches
- Average date of first freeze: December 1

about having to change Seattle's nickname and convince visitors that brown lawns are intentional—to match the latte culture.

But we needn't have worried. Rain reigns after all, and the drought threat is all but forgotten—until next time. The culprit in this weather teeter-totter is El Niño, a warming of the Pacific Ocean off South America that occasionally affects the weather here and causes drought conditions. When it sneaks in, the snowpack in the mountains decreases and everyone becomes aware that that's where we get our water.

More common, however, is an accursed condition of drizzle that has Seattleites wondering in May and June if we'll ever see the summer sun.

SEATTLE'S "CLOUD PEOPLE"

Weather watchers have been tracking Seattle's weather for 100 years— a short time when you consider how long weather has been around. But things haven't changed that

much: The first entry in the United States Weather Bureau (Seattle) log reads, "May 1, 1893: Cloudy but pleasant with light to fresh southerly winds."

The University of Washington has a group referred to as "the cloud people." They are really part of the Department of Atmospheric Sciences, and they usually have an eye

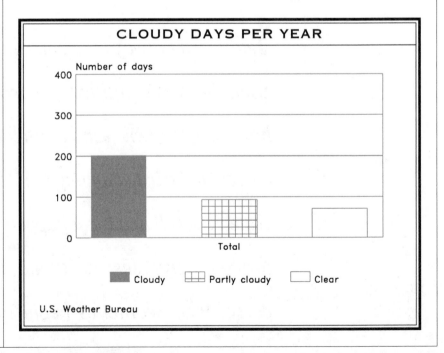

CLOUDY DAYS PER YEAR

Number of days

Total

Cloudy · Partly cloudy · Clear

U.S. Weather Bureau

- Average date of last freeze: February 23
- Average freeze-free period: 281 days

Source: U.S. Weather Bureau

WEATHER TO THE MAX

Seattle's greatest snowstorm: January 6, 1880, when 40 inches covered the ground. Hundreds of barns collapsed and transportation was halted, but the snow melted pretty quickly.

Seattle's coldest days: January 31, 1893—a low of 3°F with 24 inches of snow in downtown Seattle. Green Lake was frozen to a depth of 10 inches near the shore, 8½ inches in the center. And then on the same day 57 years later (January 31, 1950), it was even colder: 0°F. That week the temperature reached only as high as 8°F.

Seattle's hottest day: July 16, 1941—100°F. The same temperature was reached again on June 9, 1955. In 1945 the weather station was moved to Seattle-Tacoma International Airport. August 9, 1981, when the temperature reached 99°F, became the hottest day on record there, until July 23, 1991, when that record was matched, causing some to wonder if this represented a 10-year cycle.

TORNADOES, HEAT ISLANDS, AND MORE

Of course, where we are has a lot to do with who we are. At 47° 36′ N and 122° 20′ W, Seattle is on roughly the same latitude as Munich, Salzburg, Paris, and Qiqihar, Mongolia.

The Seattle area is sheltered from coastal storms by the Olympic Mountains to the west and from inland cold waves and heat waves by the Cascade Range to the east. Downtown

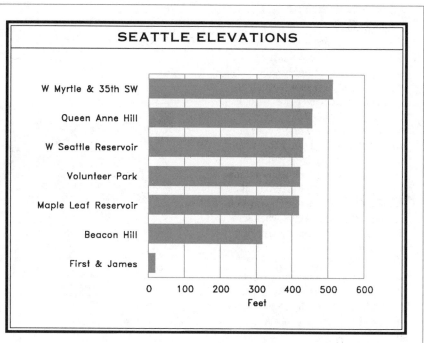

SEATTLE ELEVATIONS

Seattle is transformed into a "heat island" by buildings, steam pipes, pavement, autos, and sewers, which retain heat, raising the temperature 1° to 3° F higher than it is in the surrounding countryside.

The area's warmish winters come from the ever-present rain and clouds that trap the heat energy of condensation and hold it near the ground. An influx of cold, dry, dense continental polar air can cause a drop in Seattle temperatures, but the Cascades block most of this air. Usually the area is blessed with maritime weather: Sea breezes flow toward the land from Puget Sound (and even from Lake Washington) during the day; land breezes flow back toward the water at night.

Trees help keep the environment temperate, but clear-cutting causes hotspots, which become coldspots in winter. Trees also thrust air upward on the windward side of mountains, and that phenomenon can account for as much as 6% of local rainfall.

Chicken Little, if she were a Seattleite, would be right: The city sky *does* fall—in the form of 257,090,863.98 *tons* of rain each year.

Seattle has less thunder and lightning than many parts of the United States, averaging only six thunderstorms a year. The city also has less risk of damage from hail, since most of the hail here is small, ⅛ to ¼ inch in diameter, and most falls in late winter and early spring before new

Prevailing winds

	MPH	Direction	Windchill factor
Jan.	11	SE	16°
Feb.	11	SW	20°
Mar.	12	SW	23°
Apr.	11	SW	27°
May	11	SW	—
June	10	SW	—
July	10	SW	—
Aug.	9	SW	—
Sept.	9	N	—
Oct.	10	S	—
Nov.	10	S	26°
Dec.	11	SSW	20°

Explanation: For instance, on an average day in January, the wind blows 11 mph from the southeast. The outside temperature feels like 16° F.
Source: U.S. Weather Bureau

plant growth.

Seattle also has "graupel," which looks like a cross between snow and hail, but is really crumbly snow pellets the size of buckshot to small peas. But no local ever says, "Look, it's graupeling outside!"

One of Seattle's worst winter hazards is invisible, but you know it when you hit it, whether you're on foot or in the car. Black ice is a transparent film of frozen water that takes on the color of the material on which it forms. Black ice occurs when temperatures hover around the freezing and melting points, as they often do during a Seattle winter. Typically, moisture freezes on a freeway overpass, melts, and then quickly freezes again. Unbeknownst to a traveler, the roadway has become treacherously slick.

Winds are usually mild, but few will forget the Inaugural Day blast of 1993, when winds gusted up to 88 mph in the city and 94 mph at Hood Canal. Trees fell like toothpicks and signs flew like something out of Kansas. It wasn't the area's worst windstorm, though. On February 13, 1979, winds reached 80 mph, with gusts up to 110 mph, blowing apart the Hood Canal Bridge. And during the famous Columbus Day storm on

October 12, 1962, the West Point lighthouse recorded 83 mph winds.

Tornadoes are rare, but one did occur at View Ridge/Sand Point on September 28, 1962, and another in south King County on December 12, 1969.

Seattle has fewer bugs than other cities because most bugs need intense heat to thrive. And, though we're Way Out West, we don't have tumbleweed or sagebrush.

Spring fever? It's not just our imagination. Weather affects the circulatory system of human beings, and our bodies respond to changes in temperature. The listlessness brought on by balmy spring weather is real, as is the extra pep we feel when it's windy or rainy. The rainy-day pep that brings shoppers out to crowd the malls is the reason malls were created in Seattle in the first place. Northgate, the first covered mall in the United States, opened in 1950.

DEBUNK THAT MYTH

It's Japanese currency and not the Japanese Current, as many people think, that is affecting the area. According to the National Weather Service, the Japanese Current is very weak near our coastline. The California Current is warmer and stronger. The prevailing westerly air currents cross vast reaches of ocean, acquiring water vapor and a temperature near that of the sea. This effect is from the general currents of the ocean, not from the Japanese Current.

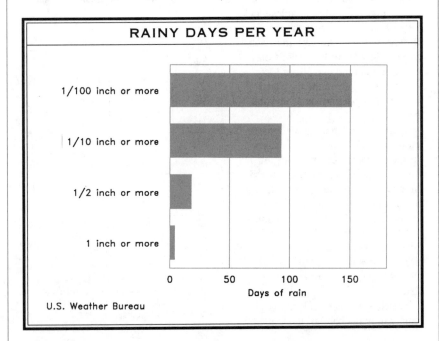

RAINY DAYS PER YEAR

U.S. Weather Bureau

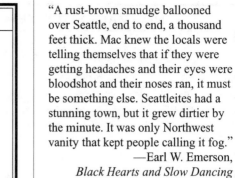

SEATTLE'S MONTHLY PRECIPITATION

Inches

10 inches of snow equals 1 inch of rain

Monthly total   Snow/sleet

U.S. Weather Bureau

"A rust-brown smudge ballooned over Seattle, end to end, a thousand feet thick. Mac knew the locals were telling themselves that if they were getting headaches and their eyes were bloodshot and their noses ran, it must be something else. Seattleites had a stunning town, but it grew dirtier by the minute. It was only Northwest vanity that kept people calling it fog."
—Earl W. Emerson, *Black Hearts and Slow Dancing*

"Summers in Seattle are like that—hot one day and chilly the next. What visitors don't understand is that too many days without rain, too many hours of uninterrupted sunshine, cause Seattleites to get crabby."
—J. A. Jance, *Improbable Cause*

"If Mount Rainier is visible in the afternoon, it is a sure sign of good weather for the next 24 hours."
—Anonymous

WEATHER LORE (TRUE STUFF)

- Heavy rainfall occurs about 30 days after a meteor shower.
- Raindrops are not always round or teardrop shaped. According to a study by General Electric scientists, raindrops can change their form as often as 50 times per second. They can look like jellybeans, pancakes, gourds, peanuts, hot dogs, ducks, footballs, and even human feet.
- When rain is due, ants go into hiding, spiders tighten their webs, and a halo forms around the sun or moon.
- "Big snow, little snow—little snow, big snow" is an Indian saying that refers to the size of snowflakes versus the quantity of snow.
- On a spring or summer day, good weather is likely if dew is on the grass before sunrise.
- Early morning ground fog means the day's weather will be good.
- Waterbirds fly higher in good weather than in bad.

LOCAL WEATHER OBSERVATIONS

"Their land has a blurry beauty (as if the Creator started to erase it but had second thoughts)."   —Tom Robbins, *Another Roadside Attraction*

SEATTLE CEMENT?

Yes, our snow really is wetter than elsewhere. Because Seattle's temper-

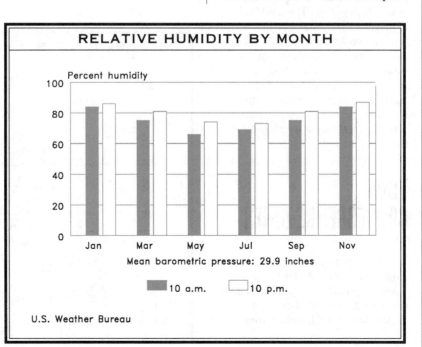

RELATIVE HUMIDITY BY MONTH

Percent humidity

Mean barometric pressure: 29.9 inches

10 a.m.   10 p.m.

U.S. Weather Bureau

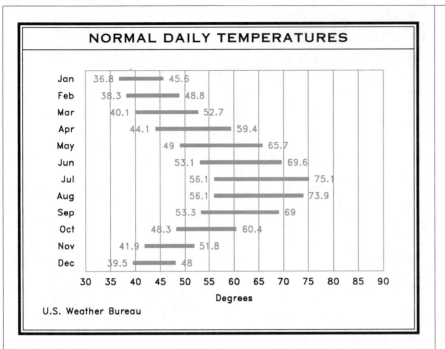

NORMAL DAILY TEMPERATURES

Month	Low	High
Jan	36.8	45.5
Feb	38.3	48.8
Mar	40.1	52.7
Apr	44.1	59.4
May	49	65.7
Jun	53.1	69.6
Jul	56.1	75.1
Aug	56.1	73.9
Sep	53.3	69
Oct	48.3	60.4
Nov	41.9	51.8
Dec	39.5	48

Degrees

U.S. Weather Bureau

atures hover around the freezing point of 32°F, our snow is warmer and actually contains more moisture per snowflake. Wet snow occurs at temperatures high enough to bond crystals into large snowflakes and is typical of the maritime borders of continental land masses lying between latitudes 40° and 60°.

One inch of rain near the freezing point is equivalent to about 10 inches of wet, heavy snow. The same inch of rain at temperatures well below freezing would produce 12 inches or more of drier, fluffier snow with very solid crystals. Unlike Seattle snow, this snow is very cold, very light, and is not bonded together. Seattle's wet snow, because it compacts more easily, is ideal for snowballs (though it makes for tough skiing!).

YOUR CONVERGENCE ZONES

Seattle has plenty of mini-climates, mostly due to rain shadows, wind channeling, and convergence zones where cold air from inland masses combines with mild, wet air from the Sound.

The largest rain shadow is created by the Olympic Mountains to the advantage of places like Sequim, on the Olympic Peninsula, where half as much rain falls as in Seattle, which is far enough outside the shadow to get dumped on.

Within the city, on average 386 feet above sea level, the tops of hills are likely to be rainier or snowier than the flats. So yes, it really does

snow more on Queen Anne Hill, which is both high and in a convergence zone. Northwest Seattle lies close to the Sound, and the weather there tends to be worse due to several convergence zones.

Tall downtown buildings cast shadows at ground level but generate heat at the same time, and so act as both mini-convergence zones and wind channels. The Columbia Seafirst Center at Fifth and Spring is challenging Fourth and Union's longtime title as Seattle's windiest corner. The curved shape and extreme height of this building (954 feet) generate twisterlike winds that can keep city debris whirling in the air.

The base of the east side of the Safeco Building (308 feet) in the University District is suspected of being windier than anywhere else in the U District.

THE SHAKING EARTH

Is there such a thing as earthquake weather? Probably not, though longtime *P-I* weatherman Walt Rue once wrote that it's conceivable air pressure might have a contributing effect if all other conditions were right.

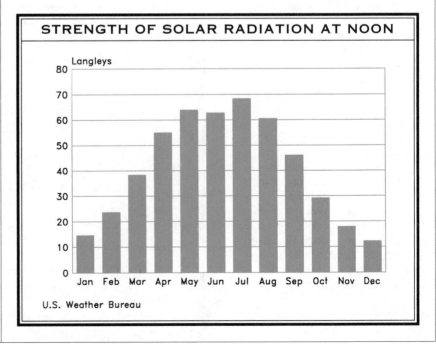

STRENGTH OF SOLAR RADIATION AT NOON

Langleys

U.S. Weather Bureau

Most scientists disagree, however. We do know that animals are sensitive to earthquakes and birds have been known to leave an earthquake area prior to the event. Perhaps the unusual stillness prompts people to notice something different in the air and call it earthquake weather.

Seattle's two greatest quakes occurred under the following conditions:

April 13, 1949

Barometric pressure 30.26 inches
Sky overcast
Temperature 50°F
Wind 4 mph from the north

April 29, 1965

Barometric pressure 30.14 inches
Sky clear
Temperature 47°F
Wind 4 mph from the east-southeast

HIDDEN FAULTS AND UPFRONT ERUPTIONS

Ever since the 1989 San Francisco earthquake, there has been intense interest in knowing when the "big one" will hit Seattle. The truth is that not a great deal is known about earthquakes here, except that we have small quakes daily, that we have had major ones, and that we can continue to expect small quakes every day and a major one "someday."

The reason it's so difficult to predict even major earthquakes in this area is that, according to the UW Seismology Lab, Seattle and the rest of Western Washington are covered by deep silt and glacial deposits that cover faults until a quake occurs. There might be lots of faults around— but they're hidden.

Another thing that's hidden is the state of the soil. In the event of a quake, liquefaction is a big fear for Seattle, with its filled tidelands in the downtown area. (Liquefaction means the soil is transformed from a solid state to a liquefied state.) Those liquefaction areas run, in addition to other places, along Alaskan Way. Remember what's there? Right, the

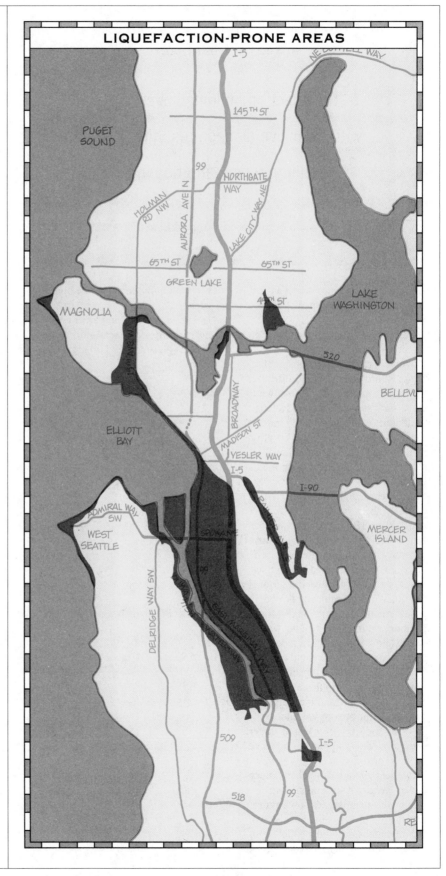

LIQUEFACTION-PRONE AREAS

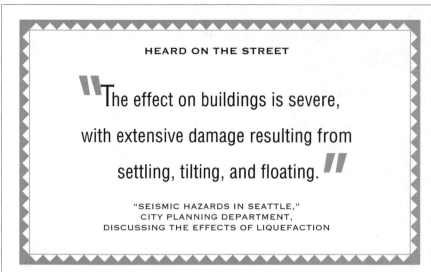

HEARD ON THE STREET

"The effect on buildings is severe, with extensive damage resulting from settling, tilting, and floating."

"SEISMIC HAZARDS IN SEATTLE,"
CITY PLANNING DEPARTMENT,
DISCUSSING THE EFFECTS OF LIQUEFACTION

Alaskan Way Viaduct, someday to be renamed the Alaskan Way Floating Bridge.

Most seismic activity here is the direct result of major earth plate movement rather than slippage of faults within a plate as in California. Still, some major faults are known to exist, such as the Mount St. Helens fault zone, which is about 65 miles long. The Mount St. Helens eruptions in 1980 may have eased pressure along the fault lines and postponed a huge quake.

As if earthquakes weren't enough to worry about, what about volcanoes? Mount Rainier had major rockfalls in 1963 and 1985, though this probably doesn't indicate increased volcanic activity. Instead, scientists say it is a function of rock deterioration thanks to volcanically heated gases. An ancient eruption of Mount Rainier sent mudflows all the way to what is now Burien, and a federal report warns a mudflow could easily happen again without a major eruption. Mount Baker to the north is also an active volcano, and typically fault lines lie in the area of volcanoes.

If Mount Rainier or Mount Baker were threatening to blow or let some of their rock give in to gravity, you'd be warned about it through the emergency broadcast system on your radio. But scientists are now saying that the mudflows could burst down the mountainsides like a bullet train, without announcing their arrival. And we thought mountains were our friends.

For earthquake preparedness, instruction, and general information, the UW Seismology Lab highly rec-

What to do when the storm hits:

- Call 911 in a real emergency.
- For shelter, call the Red Cross, 323-2345.
- Stay inside—blowing debris is dangerous.
- Do what lots of the 750,000 City Light and Puget Power customers without power did during the 1993 Inaugural Day storm: Take the kids to a hotel—one with power. In fact, during that storm one Bellevue family discovered that everyone in the hotel hot tub was from their neighborhood.

ommends Information Circular 85, *Washington Earthquakes*, published by Washington Department of Natural Resources Publications Dept., Division of Geology, TY-12, Olympia, WA 98504.

WEATHER SURVIVAL, INDOORS AND OUT

Our weather doesn't seem extreme compared to other areas of the country, but it is unpredictable. You can leave home in the morning with wool sweaters, gloves, and L.L. Bean duck boots and be roasting by noon. Dressing to be warm and dry, but not too warm and not too encumbered, can be tricky.

Clothing trends

Seattle has changed. Used to be that Seattleites dressed in what some called the Seattle tux:
- Cotton turtleneck T-shirt
- Chamois shirt
- Ragg wool sweater
- Khaki pants
- Gore-Tex hooded jacket with zippers, pockets, and drawstrings

Sure, turtlenecks are still "in," but REI's managers report heavy sales in the '90s for:
- Teva sandals (the ones with the Velcro fasteners)
- Short-sleeve button-up cotton floral shirts
- Synthetic fleece pullovers
- Glacier glasses (sunglasses for climbing)
- In-line skates

What's out?
- Walking shoes. Instead people are buying cross-trainers, shoes they can wear for biking, hiking, etc.

BUMBERSHOOT COUTURE

If layered dressing is a matter of survival, so apparently is an umbrella. This is a change from the old days when true Seattleites looked down their wet noses at anyone carrying a bumbershoot. It's a rare downtown office that doesn't have a "department umbrella" for those surprise squalls someone wasn't ready for. But some of us still would not be caught dead under one.

The Bon Marché alone estimates it sells over 13,000 umbrellas per year. Add to this the numbers sold by Nordstrom, Fred Meyer, Lamonts, J.C. Penney, PayLess, Kmart, and every drugstore, supermarket, and convenience store in the city—and that's a lot of umbrellas. How many? We called ShedRain in Portland, third-largest umbrella company in the world and largest supplier of umbrellas to the West Coast. They were too busy making umbrellas to count how many they sell, but they did say they restock most large Seattle stores four times a year, in contrast to other areas of the country, which order once or twice each year.

RUMORS, RUMORS

Seattle's iffy weather has given rise to two odd rumors, both of which we would like to confirm are true (or mostly true).

Rumor 1. It never rains on the Bellevue Arts and Crafts Fair.

According to Nancy Fisher of the Bellevue Arts and Crafts Fair, never in its 50-year history has the event been canceled or postponed due to rain. It's held the last full weekend in July, and though Fisher would not go so far as to say no stray raindrops have ever fallen, she does say that the Fair is annually besieged by callers wanting to know the coming year's dates; they then schedule weddings, picnics, barbecues, and other outdoor events the same weekend.

The attending hearsay that the "no rain" condition is insured by Lloyd's of London is not true, but only because the Fair has never called Lloyd's. According to a local Lloyd's representative, Lloyd's will insure virtually anything for a price.

Rumor 2. More sunglasses are sold each year in Seattle than anywhere else in the nation.

David McDonald, local sunglass representative, says Seattle is always in the top 5% of shades-selling centers. Top sales months are January through July or August. Why does Seattle, with its scarcity of sun, sell so many sunglasses? Simple, says McDonald. "It's not like LA, where you have to wear your sunglasses every day and you know where they are. People here use their sunglasses so seldom they lose 'em, sit on 'em, don't have 'em when they need 'em. Then they have to buy another pair."

WEATHER INFO

Have pencil and paper handy when calling these phone numbers. You'll get masses of menu numbers, alternate phone numbers, temperatures, wind speeds, and more thrown at you. If you hang up and call back after going for a pencil, you may have to wait through several busy signals as the recording you just hung up on wends its way to the end and rewinds. Ain't technology wonderful?

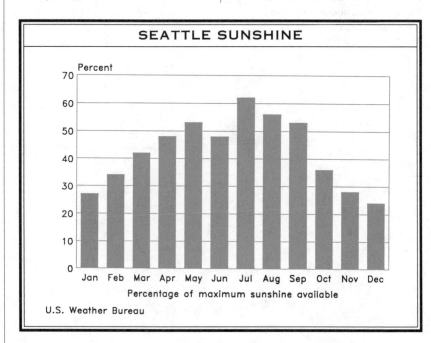

SEATTLE SUNSHINE

Percentage of maximum sunshine available

U.S. Weather Bureau

Forecasts

National Weather Service Forecast
526-6087

Pilot One-Call Briefing
767-2726
Menu numbers for local weather conditions and route forecasts for many routes from "Seattle to. . . ."

Seattle Times Infoline
464-2000
Menu numbers: Inland Waters, 9910; Straits and Coast, 9911

Best days for a picnic: For people who don't like surprises, such as rain during a summer barbecue, there are days to bet on. Odds favor scheduling an event during the "Dog Days," a period beginning July 26 and lasting four to six weeks, when Sirius the Dog Star rises with the sun. According to ancient astrologers, this is a time of plagues, madness, and drought. Four of Seattle's eight typically driest days occur during this stretch. July 26 is consistently one of Seattle's driest days—a good time to go on a picnic—although July 19, historically Seattle's driest day, might be better if you want to avoid the plagues and madness that start the following week.

Special reports

Air Pollution Control
296-5100
Air-quality index and burn ban info.

Marine Weather Radio Broadcasts
VHF Weather 1 or Weather 2
NOAA KHB60, 162.55 Megaherz
Or purchase a weather radio. Cost?
About $185.

Washington State Highway District
649-4366
Mountain-pass highway condition reports, October 1 through March 31.

Boating info

Coast Guard
Emergencies: 217-6000

Harbor Patrol Unit
684-4071

Ski reports

Cascade Ski Report
634-0200

Northwest Ski Report
634-2754

Seattle Times Infoline
464-2000
Cascade Ski Report: Menu #9011

Conservation Information Hotline
684-3800
For info on conservation for electrically heated homes and rental properties, cash discounts on weatherization.

Storm damage

To report power outages:

Puget Power
(800) 321-4123

Seattle City Light
Outage hotline: 625-3000
To report outages, problems with power, trees on the line. If your outage is not mentioned in the recording, stay on the line to report it.

To report flooding:

Seattle Drainage and Wastewater Utility
For street and yard flooding, 684-7508 north of Denny Way, 386-1218 south of Denny Way and citywide nights and weekends. For sewer odors and backup: 684-7506 north of Denny Way; 386-1230 south of Denny Way and citywide nights and weekends.

To report downed trees, road damage:

Seattle Engineering Department
386-1218

INDEX

N

T

ABOUT THE AUTHOR

Theresa Morrow is the quintessential Seattle native. Not only was she born in Seattle, she was raised in a classic box house on Capitol Hill, learned to roller-skate in an alley, swam at Denny Blaine Park, and ate burgers at Dick's. She was kissed by a Seafair pirate when she was 15, attended Holy Names Academy, Seattle University, and the UW, and worked as a reporter for *The Seattle Times*. She has also worked for a maritime industry publication and for a local multimedia company (hasn't everyone?).

Her father was one of the founders of Group Health Cooperative and her brother is retired from Boeing.

Theresa still wears a Gore-Tex jacket, but now has a polar fleece vest too. Sometimes she wears them both to her second office at the Cloud Room. (And she admits, when pressed, that she once lived on the Eastside—Mercer Island to be exact—in what later became a "tear-down.")

SEATTLE SURVIVAL GUIDE REPORT FORM

Got a tip. . . a find. . . a fact. . . or other useful information that we missed?
Give us your feedback below (including names and phone numbers of
agencies and organizations), and help us make the next edition of the
Seattle Survival Guide even better!

_____

_____

_____

_____

Your Name _____

Address _____

City, State, Zip Code _____

Phone _____

Send to:
  Seattle Survival Guide
  Sasquatch Books
  615 Second Avenue, Ste. 260
  Seattle, Washington 98104